W9-AUM-996

Special Edition
Using
Visual
Basic®
.NET

Brian Siler and Jeff Spotts

201 W. 103rd Street
Indianapolis, Indiana 46290

CONTENTS AT A GLANCE

SPECIAL EDITION USING VISUAL BASIC® .NET

Copyright © 2002 by Que

All rights reserved. No part of this book shall be reproduced, stored in a retrieval system, or transmitted by any means, electronic, mechanical, photocopying, recording, or otherwise, without written permission from the publisher. No patent liability is assumed with respect to the use of the information contained herein. Although every precaution has been taken in the preparation of this book, the publisher and authors assume no responsibility for errors or omissions. Nor is any liability assumed for damages resulting from the use of the information contained herein.

International Standard Book Number: 0-7897-2572-x

Library of Congress Catalog Card Number: 20-01090466

Printed in the United States of America

First Printing: December 2001

05 04 03 02   4 3 2 1

Trademarks

All terms mentioned in this book that are known to be trademarks or service marks have been appropriately capitalized. Que cannot attest to the accuracy of this information. Use of a term in this book should not be regarded as affecting the validity of any trademark or service mark.

Warning and Disclaimer

Every effort has been made to make this book as complete and as accurate as possible, but no warranty or fitness is implied. The information provided is on an "as is" basis. The author(s) and the publisher shall have neither liability nor responsibility to any person or entity with respect to any loss or damages arising from the information contained in this book or from the use of the CD or programs accompanying it.

Associate Publisher
Dean Miller

Acquisitions Editor
Michelle Newcomb

Development Editors
Marla Reece-Hall
Sarah Robbins
Maureen McDaniel
Katie Pendergast

Managing Editor
Thomas F. Hayes

Project Editor
Tricia S. Liebig

Copy Editor
Sossity Smith

Indexer
Chris Barrick

Proofreader
Paula Lowell

Team Coordinator
Cindy Teeters

Interior Designer
Ruth Harvey

Cover Designer
Ann Jones

Page Layout
Gloria Schurick

CONTENTS

ABOUT THE AUTHORS

Brian Siler has been developing Visual Basic applications since 1994. He received his bachelor of science degree in computer science from the University of Memphis in 1995. In addition to his day job as lead systems analyst for a major hotel corporation, Brian occasionally develops custom VB applications for other individuals. He has created many types of computer programs, including client/server, Active Server Pages, and "n-tier" Web applications. Brian is familiar with a variety of databases, including Microsoft SQL Server, Sybase, and Microsoft Access. Additional information about some of Brian's VB projects as well as sample source code is available on the Web at www.vbinsider.com. He has coauthored two previous Visual Basic books. Brian may be contacted via e-mail at bsiler@vbinsider.com.

Jeff Spotts is a financial systems advisor for Federal Express Corporation. A 1980 graduate of the University of Memphis, he also teaches programming classes at Southwest Tennessee Community College in Memphis. In addition, he develops custom applications for individuals and businesses and has a growing portfolio of Visual Basic database applications plus a variety of Web-based systems using VBScript and Active Server Pages. Jeff is a Microsoft Certified Professional (MCP), has been involved with computer hardware and software since the late 1970s, and has been programming with Visual Basic since just after its introduction. Jeff is a coauthor (with Brian Siler) of Que's *Special Edition Using Visual Basic 6* and has contributed to several other titles. He may be contacted via e-mail at jspotts@vbinsider.com.

DEDICATIONS

To my family, for your continued support of my writing, and my girlfriend Carrie, for your patience and understanding during the writing process.

—Brian Siler

To Tina and Lauren, and the newest member of our family, Shadow. I appreciate your love and support throughout the process of writing this book, and in everything else I do. You are the reason for my success.

In memory of John H. Thomas, who was promoted to Heaven this year. "Dop," we miss you every day!

—Jeff Spotts

ACKNOWLEDGMENTS

The authors wish to take the time to acknowledge all the teachers in the world; both those who are teachers by profession and those friends and co-workers who continue to offer us their valued advice and support.

TELL US WHAT YOU THINK!

As the reader of this book, *you* are our most important critic and commentator. We value your opinion and want to know what we're doing right, what we could do better, what areas you'd like to see us publish in, and any other words of wisdom you're willing to pass our way.

As an associate publisher for Que, I welcome your comments. You can fax, e-mail, or write me directly to let me know what you did or didn't like about this book—as well as what we can do to make our books stronger.

Please note that I cannot help you with technical problems related to the topic of this book, and that due to the high volume of mail I receive, I might not be able to reply to every message.

When you write, please be sure to include this book's title and authors as well as your name and phone or fax number. I will carefully review your comments and share them with the authors and editors who worked on the book.

Fax: 317-581-4666

E-mail: feedback@quepublishing.com

Mail: Associate Publisher
Que
201 West 103rd Street
Indianapolis, IN 46290 USA

INTRODUCTION

Congratulations! You have decided to embark on learning Visual Basic .NET.

This is an exciting time for Visual Basic programmers. Visual Basic .NET is a different animal from its predecessors. Even if you have been programming with Visual Basic for years, there is suddenly a lot of new stuff to learn. From a totally redesigned user interface to new language features and architectural changes, Visual Basic .NET represents an evolutionary step forward. Visual Basic has always made it easy to develop Windows programs, and Visual Basic .NET continues that tradition. However, the .NET framework was created clearly with Internet application development in mind. With the latest version of VB, you can create Web applications using the Visual Basic forms programming model and deploy them, all from within the Visual Studio .NET environment.

The Visual Basic language has been improved as well. Not only does it support new programming features (such as inheritance), but the language itself also shares a common foundation with other Visual Studio .NET languages. This fact, along with the wealth of new programming functionality provided by the .NET framework, really levels the playing field between the capabilities of Visual Basic and C++.

Okay, so now you are excited about learning Visual Basic. Your next question is, "What will this book do for me?"

WHO SHOULD READ THIS BOOK

We feel that this book has something to offer for all skill levels. If you have never used Visual Basic before, the initial chapters provide the necessary step-by-step instructions to get you used to the Visual Studio programming environment. Users of previous versions of Visual Basic (experienced or not) will appreciate extensive, detailed coverage of the new features available in VB .NET and explanations of the changes from previous versions. Readers who are new to computer programming in general should note that technical details are sprinkled with "words of wisdom" and real-world examples to help you understand new concepts. We make very few assumptions about our readers, other than the following:

- Readers should already be familiar with the Microsoft Windows operating system. Although the examples in this book were developed using Windows 2000, any recent Windows operating system will do.

- Readers should know how to start applications on the system, browse the Web, as well as copy and download files. In other words, they are "power users" of their computer.

- Readers should have a general idea of some of the different categories of computer programs commonly available; that is, a word processing program or spreadsheet.

- Finally, readers should have an open mind and be eager to learn!

HOW THIS BOOK IS ORGANIZED

Computer programming books can serve different audiences. Some readers may need a reference to find information about a particular topic quickly. Other readers might want to follow the book in tutorial style by reading each chapter start to finish. Readers of *Special Edition Using Visual Basic .NET* should be able do either. Each topic is explained in a narrative fashion, with lists, pictures, and sample code to allow the reader to quickly absorb the technical details. For those seeking instant gratification, many chapters include exercises that provide step-by-step instructions to try out a particular topic on your own. *Special Edition Using Visual Basic .NET* is divided into six parts and a section of appendices.

PART I: GETTING STARTED WITH VISUAL BASIC .NET

If you're enthusiastic about learning how to program, one of the best ways to remain so is to see results quickly. That's why we've targeted the first section of this book at the new-to-.NET developer. If you have never used Visual Basic before, the introductory chapters will provide real experiences you can keep in mind to better understand other topics. If you are already an experienced user of a previous version of Visual Basic, this section should give you a good feel for what has changed in the .NET world.

Chapter 1, "Introduction to Visual Basic .NET," discusses some general programming concepts and high-level design strategies. As you will learn, design is very important in creating a successful application.

In Chapter 2, "Creating Your First Windows Application," you work step-by-step through the process of building a fully functional application in Visual Basic.

Chapter 3, "Creating Your First Web Application," walks you through setting up an interactive Web site using Visual Basic .NET.

Chapter 4, "Understanding the Development Environment," gives you a tour of the new development environment and points out some of its useful features.

In Chapter 5, "Visual Basic Building Blocks," you learn the fundamentals about the Visual Basic language and how you use that language to write programs.

Each of these chapters in the first part of the book is designed to quickly make you comfortable with creating applications in the Visual Studio .NET development environment.

PART II: VISUAL BASIC PROGRAMMING FUNDAMENTALS

The second section of the book explores the Visual Basic language in more detail. This section is designed to explain language concepts that are critical to creating Visual Basic applications.

In Chapter 6, "Storing Information in Variables," you are led into the world of variables and data types. You learn how to create and use variables, and how to perform math and string operations.

Chapter 7, "Controlling the Flow of Your Program," discusses loops and decision structures. In this chapter you will learn how to control what your program does, based on the input given to it.

Chapter 8, "Managing Program Tasks with Procedures," takes a look at how to create custom program functions and subroutines. By learning about these concepts, you can become a more efficient programmer.

Object-oriented programming is covered in Chapter 9, "Creating Code Components." Not only does this chapter take a look at how to create and use custom classes, but we also describe how to access these classes as part of a multi-tier Web application.

PART III: BUILDING WINDOWS APPLICATIONS

Part III, "Building Windows Applications," expands the fundamental knowledge that you have gained so far by exploring various types of components you can use in Windows-based applications.

Chapter 10, "Understanding Windows Forms," introduces you to the techniques used when designing and interacting with a Windows form.

Chapters 11 and 12 provide a useful reference to some of the built-in components Visual Basic provides for you to use when you build your programs. These components, or controls, can be used for a variety of application tasks, such as displaying text or initiating actions within a program. Chapter 11, "Fundamental Controls," explores some of the more commonly used controls, while Chapter 12, "Advanced Controls," discusses some additional, more specialized controls.

Chapter 13, "Using Dialog Boxes," takes an in-depth look at a familiar user-interface component, the dialog box.

In Chapter 14, "Designing an Effective User Interface," you learn about some user interface design principles that can make your application more appealing to the end user. In addition, we introduce you to adding graphics and pictures to your programs.

Chapter 15, "Multiple Document Interface (MDI) Applications" explores a special type of user interface in more detail. As you will learn, an MDI application provides a framework by which you can easily organize multiple forms in a visually pleasing manner.

You learned a lot about the built-in Windows controls in Chapters 11 and 12. Chapter 16, "Creating Your Own Windows Controls," walks you through the process of creating, and then enhancing, your own Windows controls.

PART IV: WORKING WITH THE WEB

The fourth section in the book is devoted to building Internet applications.

Chapter 17, "Using Active Server Pages.NET," takes a tour of creating dynamic Web content through the use of Visual Basic code.

Chapter 18, "Web Applications and Services," shows you how to program within the Webforms model, using Visual Studio to create versatile Web-based programs.

Chapter 19, "Web Controls," introduces you to some of the built-in components that you can use in a .NET Web application.

PART V: VISUAL BASIC AND DATABASES

Database programs make up a large percentage of all programs in use in the business world today. These programs range in complexity from simple programs for managing mailing lists to complex programs handling reservations and billing for major corporations. Part V, "Visual Basic and Databases" takes you through the process of building database applications to meet a variety of needs.

Chapter 20, "Database Basics," discusses the Structured Query Language (SQL) and shows you how to use SQL to create and manipulate data.

Chapter 21, "ActiveX Data Objects (ADO)," shows you how to use the ADO programming model to access your data from within Visual Basic code.

In Chapter 22, "Using ADO.NET," we discuss Microsoft's latest model for working with databases, ADO.NET. ADO.NET, which is part of the .NET framework, brings some new structures and concepts to the Visual Basic world.

Finally, Chapter 23, "Creating and Using Reports," shows you how to output data from your database applications to a printed report using Crystal Reports and other techniques.

PART VI: ADVANCED PROGRAMMING TOPICS

In Part VI, "Advanced Programming Topics," you are exposed to some additional material that is useful for any application developer.

Chapter 24, "Working with Files," discusses how your programs can use different types of files for information storage and retrieval purposes.

Chapter 25, "Interacting with Other Applications," shows you how to have your programs interact with other Windows applications, such as your word processor or e-mail system. In doing so, you can add features of these applications to your own program.

In Chapter 26, "Debugging and Performance Tuning," you learn how to make your programs faster and more efficient, as well as how to identify and report errors.

Chapter 27, "Writing a Pocket PC Application," takes a look at an exciting emerging technology and describes how you can use a Pocket PC application to capture data.

ADDITIONAL REFERENCES

You can use the Appendices as a guide to some of the things you'll need to know as you develop your Visual Basic .NET applications.

Appendix A, "Packaging Your Applications," shows you how to prepare the Visual Basic programs that you write for distribution.

Appendix B, "Tips on Conversion from VB6," is for users of previous versions of Visual Basic. We discuss some ways to get the most out of VB .NET when converting an existing application.

SOURCE CODE AND PROGRAMS USED IN THIS BOOK

All the source code from the listings and programs included in this book is available via download from the Que—Macmillan Computer Publishing Web site. You can download the listings code to save typing time and errors as you follow examples in the book. You also can obtain all the programs built in the book and additional sample programs we've included.

To access this material, follow these steps:

1. Point your browser to the following URL:

   `www.quepublishing.com`

2. Enter the book's ISBN as directed:

   0-7897-2572-X

3. Follow the instructions to access and download the specific code or program you are looking for.

CONVENTIONS AND SPECIAL ELEMENTS USED IN THIS BOOK

This book includes various conventions and special elements to highlight specific things and make using the book easier. Familiarize yourself with these conventions and elements, and allow them to enhance your reading experience.

CONVENTIONS

The following list details conventions used in the book:

- *Italic type* is used to emphasize the author's points or to introduce new terms. You may also see italics used in code samples to indicate a placeholder for additional code.

- Screen messages, code listings, and command samples appear in `monospace type`.

- URLs, newsgroups, Internet addresses, and anything you are asked to type also appears in `monospace type`.

- Occasionally, a code sample or listing will show a portion of program code with certain lines set in **bold** type. In such cases, the bold type signifies code you are to add to existing code. This approach enables you to see what you are supposed to add or change in context.

- Because of the space limitations of this book's pages, a few code lines in this book's examples cannot be printed exactly as you must enter them. In cases where breaking such a line is necessary to fit within the book's margins, the Visual Basic continuation character (_) will be used at the end of the line that is broken. You can leave these characters out and enter the code on a single line, or just enter the characters as they appear. Visual Basic will understand the code either way. If you download the code from the Web site, you will not have to worry about adding this character.

SPECIAL ELEMENTS

Certain types of information are set off in special book elements. The following explanations and examples indicate the kinds of elements you will encounter in the book.

At the end of each chapter you may find a "From Here . . . " section, a Q&A, or a Troubleshooting section to wrap up the chapter. These sections refer you to other chapters that cover related material or extend the topic you just read about. They are designed to help you synthesize the information or troubleshoot problems.

→ See cross-references within each chapter for directions to more information on a particular topic.

Tip

Tips present short advice on a quick or often overlooked procedure.

Note

Notes provide additional information that might help you avoid problems, or offer advice that relates to the topic.

Caution

Cautions warn you about potential problems that a procedure might cause, unexpected results, and mistakes to avoid.

Sidebar

Longer discussions not integral to the flow of the chapter are set aside as sidebars. Look for these sidebars to find out even more information.

SYSTEM SUGGESTIONS FOR VISUAL BASIC .NET

As with most types of software, a more powerful computer will make Visual Studio .NET perform faster. Usually the "minimum system requirements" printed on the box are just that, bare minimum requirements that may not always be useful in the real world. In writing this book, we found that while Visual Studio .NET worked acceptably on a variety of computers, you will more likely enjoy the experience if you use a fast computer with plenty of memory. The author's test computers generally met or exceeded the following specifications:

- 733 megahertz Pentium III class processor
- 512 megabytes of RAM.
- A large hard drive with several gigabytes of free disk space
- A fast hard drive (for example, ultra-DMA)
- A fast video card.
- An Internet connection

These are, of course, personal recommendations based on my own experience and should be taken with a grain of salt. Even if your computer falls below these baseline requirements, you may still be able to use it. For example, although VB .NET ran noticeably slower on a Pentium II-450 megahertz computer with 256 megabytes of RAM, it was still very usable. In general, increasing a computer's RAM memory seemed to make the most difference in overall performance.

We also found that for developing Web applications (which include communication between two computers) a home network was very handy. Networked PCs allow you test distributed applications in a realistic setting, by splitting parts of your program across multiple computers. In addition, if you have an "always on" Internet connection such as a cable modem or DSL service, I suggest purchasing a network router. This inexpensive device allows you to share your Internet connection with all PCs on your home network.

Getting Started with Visual Basic .NET

CHAPTER 1

INTRODUCTION TO VISUAL BASIC .NET

In this chapter

Thank you for deciding to make this book part of your library. We hope that it will serve as your guide to the exciting new world of Microsoft Visual Basic .NET.

UNDERSTANDING PROGRAMMING AND VISUAL BASIC'S ROLE

Before we jump into the technical details of Visual Basic .NET, we would like to answer some common questions about computer programming in general, and how Visual Basic fits into the overall picture. We also want to get you thinking about some important concepts that apply to computer programming in any language.

WHAT IS A COMPUTER PROGRAM?

A computer program (also known as an application) is a series of instructions that enables a computer to perform a specific task. A programming language such as Visual Basic is used to translate instructions, as we humans understand them, into the steps that the computer can comprehend and follow. A computer program can be designed to perform a single, basic task, such as calculating conversions between different units of measure or keeping track of your grocery list. Other computer programs may be far more complex and perform very specialized tasks, such as tracking the satellites orbiting Earth at any given moment.

Traditionally, computer programs have fallen into two very broad categories—packaged and custom.

Packaged programs are those that you can purchase in a software store, via mail order, direct from a manufacturer, and so on. Packaged programs (sometimes known as *canned* programs) are predesigned to accomplish one or more specific tasks. For example, you may purchase Microsoft Word to meet your word processing needs, Symantec's WinFax Pro to enable your computer to send and receive faxes, or McAfee's VirusScan to help prevent viruses from attacking your system. You also may be interested in game programs such as Maxis' The Sims or Microsoft's Flight Simulator. All these programs are among the thousands upon thousands of software packages that are available for Windows-based personal computers (PCs).

Custom programs (also known as *proprietary* programs) are usually designed for a specific purpose within a particular organization. For example, a company may need an application that tracks product orders from the time they are placed until they are actually shipped. If there is no packaged program available that meets the company's specific needs, a custom program could be developed. One advantage of a custom program in this case is that the program can be continually modified as the company's needs change—packaged programs generally can't be modified by the user.

Over the past few years, as use of the Internet has exploded, a new category of software is emerging. This new category of software, known as *distributed applications*, utilizes the Internet (or other large-scale connectivity, such as a local intranet) to allow several different layers of an application to run at different locations. Application Service Providers (ASPs) allow companies to access programs and store data on their servers. Thanks to the Internet, these services are accessible to nearly everyone. Visual Basic .NET, as part of the larger Visual Studio .NET infrastructure, is Microsoft's attempt to bring these types of applications within the domain of the VB programmer. For example, you can create a Web service with Visual Basic .NET and provide an enormous amount of functionality to distributed applications.

Many distributed applications are known as multi-tier, or n-tier, applications. This term relates to the distribution of the processing power required to execute the program. A multi-tier application involves several "layers" of computers, each of which is responsible for providing a specific portion of the processing that creates or responds to the end user's experience. For example, a user may access a Web-based e-commerce application such as eBay or Amazon.com through his Web browser; in this case, his computer provides the front-end interface. In turn, his Web browser connects to other computers that generate catalog pages, perform product searches, and manage order entry and credit card processing. Typically, in addition to the client's PC, one or more Web servers, database servers, and other applications may be involved. In a case such as this, several layers (tiers) of processing provide the overall experience to the user.

A BRIEF PROGRAMMING LANGUAGE PRIMER

When you get down to a computer's most basic level, the microprocessor that is at the core of the computer's functionality doesn't understand anything other than numeric instructions. To make matters worse, the only instructions that the processor can understand are incredibly simplistic commands, most of which have to do with moving numbers around between memory locations. These commands that the processor understands are known as *machine language*, or the most basic language that the machine (the PC) can use.

Machine language is known as a *low-level* language, because it's all the way down at the processor's level of understanding. As you might imagine, writing programs in machine language is an incredibly daunting task. Fortunately, you don't have to get down to that level to create computer programs. Several higher-level programming languages have been developed to enable us to write programs. These programming languages enable programmers to write instructions in something resembling English; the instructions are then converted into a program containing machine-language instructions that the processor can understand.

Some examples of programming languages that have developed over the years include ForTRAN and COBOL, which are generally used with mainframe computers, as well as BASIC, Pascal, C, and C++, which are commonly used to write programs at the personal computer level.

THE EVOLUTION OF VISUAL BASIC

Visual Basic is a descendant of BASIC, which has been around for several decades. BASIC (an acronym for *Beginners' All-Purpose Symbolic Instruction Code*) was originally developed at Dartmouth University in 1964 as a language for beginning programmers. BASIC was often the first language that programmers learned to become familiar with programming basics before moving on to more powerful languages.

However, Visual Basic is much more significant than just an upgrade to BASIC. To understand why, you only need to understand the changes that Windows brought to the computing world. Most readers are familiar with the Windows operating system, which is what made Bill Gates rich and famous. The core idea (which was not invented by Gates but by Xerox) is a graphical operating system using metaphors for computer concepts that the average person can understand. For example, computer files are represented as graphical icons stored in file folders on a desktop the user can view. Each open window has certain expected behavior, such as the ability to scroll or change positions. Although we pretty much take it for granted today, Windows made computers much more intuitive to use and helped bring personal computing to the masses.

As easy as it was to use Windows, writing programs for it in a traditional language could be a major headache. One common test of a programming language is to print the text "Hello World" on the screen. Prior to Windows, this could be accomplished in most languages with just one or two lines of code. However, an early Windows programming book (for the C language) described several screens of code (more than 80 lines) just to create a "Hello World" window. This extra code was required to create a window that interacted and behaved appropriately with the operating system.

Visual Basic, which has evolved into an extremely powerful application development tool, takes a lot of complexity out of programming for the Windows environment. Rather than write code to draw a window or process operating system events, you can graphically design windows using the mouse. Since its introduction, Visual Basic has gradually left its reputation as a beginners' language far behind and become one of the most popular—and powerful—Windows programming languages. The latest version of Visual Basic, Visual Basic .NET, taps into the world of distributed Web applications and represents perhaps Visual Basic's most ambitious leap forward.

One very nice feature of Visual Basic is that you can use it to create a solid application very quickly. As you'll see throughout this book, Visual Basic makes short work of what would normally be very time-consuming programming tasks. This frees up the programmer to spend his time developing the application's functionality, rather than spending time on mundane, repetitive programming tasks. Visual Basic is often referred to as a Rapid Application Development (RAD) tool.

THE IMPORTANCE OF APPLICATION DESIGN

A college English professor of mine was once describing different types of novelists: "A traditionalist author usually orders his story beginning-middle-end, a modernist might reverse that order, and a post-modernist would only include two of the three parts."

Unfortunately, authors of computer programs don't (usually) have the luxury of such flexibility. Although it is true that with a visual programming system such as Visual Basic it is easy to just sit down and start hacking out code, with most computer programs this is not a good idea! Like anything in life, a program that is built on a shaky foundation can be plagued with problems. Your program's purpose is to solve a specific problem, and the design determines how it will solve that problem. It is very important to spend time on design *before* you start coding. Investing a significant amount of time in program design will benefit both you and the users of your programs.

HOW DESIGN FITS INTO THE PROGRAMMING PROCESS

The life of a computer program generally begins when an end user asks someone to create it. From the end user's requirements, the programmer must determine how the program will accomplish the intended goal. Although the purpose of this book is to teach you the technical aspects of creating programs with Visual Basic, we would be remiss if we did not mention another important step: the design of the program.

Regardless of the programming language used, the following types of questions must be addressed when designing your programs:

- What are the specific tasks the program needs to perform?
- Who are the users of this program?
- What will the user interface (screens) look like?
- What type of architecture should I use (Web-based, client-server)?
- What will the databases look like?

The ideas presented in this section are by no means all-inclusive, but rather one set of general guidelines. Your technique, of course, may be totally different.

TIPS FOR A GOOD DESIGN

How do I come up with a good design and how do I know it is good? There is no magic series of steps that will guarantee a successful application. Following I have listed some tips from personal experience that will hopefully get you started thinking about how you currently design programs and how you can improve.

TIP 1: UNDERSTAND THE REQUIREMENTS IN DETAIL

Obviously, you have to know what problem the application is supposed to solve before you can write the application. The person for which you will be writing the application, or end user, will know non-technical business requirements such as "I need to track customer orders" and hopefully even have some detailed specifications or processes in mind. As the designer of an application, it is your responsibility to expand the level of detail in the end user requirements enough so that an appropriate software system can be developed.

Bridging the gap between the end user's business knowledge and your technical knowledge is very important. Keep in mind, end users don't know programming or understand the significance of making different types of changes. For instance, a typical user might not dare to ask you to change a field caption (which is an easy change in Visual Basic), but on the other hand they might involuntarily omit a critical requirement of the system, which totally invalidates your design! The symptom of this problem is after delivery of your program the end user has a lot of questions that begin with "But what about . . . ?"

The way to avoid these problems is to spend a lot of time planning and discussing the requirements of the program with the end user to make sure that both of you understand them completely. Altering a design during the planning stages of a project is a lot cheaper and faster than altering it after the project is finished. A good rule of thumb is to ask questions until you are tired of it, then keep on going! Even though you may not understand all aspects of the user's business, and they will certainly not understand all the technical aspects of programming, it is important to keep an open line of communication.

One design tool that may help everyone understand the application is the use of a *prototype*. A prototype is a partially functional or nonfunctional version of the application to give the user an idea of what the final product will look like. This is easy to do in Visual Basic and can be useful in extracting more requirements from the user.

TIP 2: MAKE YOUR DESIGN FLEXIBLE

Flexibility refers to the ability of your programs to adapt to a changing environment. End users will often come up with new requirements as the problem or process the software supports changes over time. A flexible program is able to accommodate minor changes in requirements with minimal or no code changes. For example, suppose you are writing a database application that needs to store when a customer order is placed and shipped. You could store these dates in the following database table:

```
Order#   OrderDate   ShipDate
12345    1/1/99      1/2/99
```

Suppose in the future, the users of the program want to add a delivery date. With the previous table design, you will have to add a new column to the database, altering the table design. However, suppose you had originally created the table as follows:

```
Order#   DateType   AssociatedDate
12345    ORDER      1/1/99
12345    SHIP       1/2/99
12345    DELIVERY   1/3/99
```

With this more generic table design, the additional requirement of a delivery date is accomplished by simply adding another record to the database. (Of course you may still need to modify the user interface, but these modifications will be easier because it is based on the same underlying database.)

→ Please **see** Chapter 20, "Database Basics," for more information on database design.

Although the second design is more flexible, the first one has the potential to be faster, because everything about an order is stored on one database record instead of three. The key is to understand the requirements well enough to achieve the appropriate balance of flexibility and speed.

TIP 3: KEEP CODE MAINTAINABILITY IN MIND

When you write Visual Basic code, you should try to make it as clear as possible so that yourself and others can maintain it in the future. This means it is important to have documentation at all levels, from comments in the code itself to pictures, flowcharts, and user instructions.

Although coding style itself is not necessarily a design issue, making decisions during the design process to use standard coding practices and naming conventions will have a direct impact on a program's maintainability. This is especially important if you work on a development team where more than one person will be working on the same program.

Consider, for example, the following section of code:

```
Public Sub ChangeCount(ID as String, NewValue As Integer)
    Dim OldValue As Integer
    OldValue = GetCurrentCounter(ID)
    If OldValue < NewValue then Call UpdateCurrentCounter(ID,NewValue)
End Sub
```

This code in the previous function is very simple; it accepts an ID and a new value, and calls some other functions to update a counter if the new value is greater than the old value. However, the purpose behind the function is not very clear. Now, read the following version of the function, which has been rewritten in a clearer style:

```
Public Sub ChangeCount(astrUserID As String, aintNumLogins AS Integer)

    'This function updates the login counter for the given user

    Dim lintCurrentLogins AS Integer

    lintCurrentLogins = GetCurrentCounter(astrUserID)

    'Only update if passed value is greater than current value
    If lintCurrentLogins < aintNumLogins Then
        Call UpdateCurrentCounter(astrUserID, aintNumLogins)
    End If
End Sub
```

→ For more information on declaring variables, **see** "Declaring and Naming Variables," **p. 140**

Notice that there are comments to explain both the general purpose of the function and any sections that may not be already clear to the reader. The variables have been declared with a prefix to indicate the scope (*l* for local, *a* for argument) and data type (*int* for Integer, *str* for string). The use of indentation, blank lines, and a multi-line If statement makes the code visually easier to comprehend. By deciding on techniques such as these you can create code that people can understand quicker.

TIP 4: DESIGN FOR REUSE

Another tip that applies to group application development is reuse. If you write a lot of the same types of programs, you do not want to "reinvent the wheel" each time. For example, if you write a function that connects to a database and returns a recordset, you should be able to use it on all your database projects. If you keep the modules of your program well separated by functional requirements and avoid hard-coding values where appropriate, you can create code that you can use again and again.

TIP 5: TEST YOUR DESIGN

After you write a program but before it is technically finished, there is usually a testing process to find bugs in the program. The primary goal of testing is, of course, to validate that the program successfully performs the desired tasks. Another goal of an application tester is to attempt to break your application through the use of borderline and invalid input.

The same types of "testing to break it" techniques can apply to the design of your program. This is especially applicable in database design because you can often look at the table layouts and joins to see limitations. If you can get the end users to agree to as many absolute facts as possible ("No, there will never be two active management types at the same time") then you can verify that your database design will accommodate their needs. Discussing your plan with other competent developers and trying to shoot as many holes in it as possible also can be a useful activity.

BIG CHANGES IN VISUAL BASIC .NET

Visual Basic .NET includes a large number of major enhancements since the previous version, Visual Basic 6.0. We will discuss these enhancements throughout this book. Some of these enhancements, which are part of the complete overhaul of Visual Studio (Visual Basic's parent product), include the following:

- *Web Forms*—allow you to build Web pages to run in client browsers
- *Web Services*—run on Web servers to be invoked across the Internet or an intranet
- *Server Explorer*—provides an easy-to-use interface to server-based components
- *Visual Component Designer*—assists in creating server-side components

In addition, Visual Basic itself has received a number of much-needed improvements, including

- *Inheritance*—allows classes to be inherited and reused
- *Multithreading*—allows you to build free-threaded applications
- *Initializers*—allow you to set the initial values of variables as they are defined
- *Structured Exception Handling*—centralizes the handling of program errors

In addition, Visual Studio .NET makes extensive use of eXtensible Markup Language (XML), a markup language that provides a format for describing structured data. Visual Studio .NET also utilizes a standardized Integrated Development Environment (IDE), which is the interface in which you build your applications. This will greatly simplify the porting of your skills from one Visual Studio .NET language to another.

FROM HERE . . .

This chapter has given you an overview of the application development process, the history of Visual Basic .NET, and some handy programming tips. The remainder of this book will serve as a guide as you begin to develop your own applications.

- The next chapter, "Creating Your First Windows Application," will walk you step-by-step through the process of developing a fully functional application that will run on a Windows-based PC.

- Chapter 3, "Creating Your First Web Application," shows you how to use Visual Basic .NET to develop programs that can be accessed across the Internet or an intranet via a Web browser.

- You will receive a thorough introduction to Visual Basic .NET and the Visual Studio .NET development environment in Chapter 5, "Visual Basic Building Blocks."

CHAPTER

2

CREATING YOUR FIRST WINDOWS APPLICATION

In this chapter

You have probably read programming books that walk you step-by-step through the process of creating your first program. Typically, you create some form of the classic "Hello, World!" application. In this extremely simple example, the user is asked to initiate some action such as clicking a button or pressing a key, and the computer responds with a message such as "Hello, World!" A slightly more advanced variation asks for the user's name and responds with a customized greeting like "Hello, Lauren!"

Although examples like this might be sufficient for demonstrating that you can indeed use a programming language to create a program, the resulting application isn't very useful. Our approach is to begin with a sample program that not only demonstrates the fundamentals of creating a Visual Basic .NET application, but also can be used in the real world.

In this chapter, you'll create a Windows-based Loan Calculator program that calculates the periodic payment needed to repay a loan, based on various factors such as the loan term and interest rate. Your users will be able to input and modify values for these and other variable factors, perform the calculation, and view the results. In addition, they will be able to view an amortization schedule for the entire life of the loan.

Note

The application you'll be creating was adapted from a shareware program I wrote named "My Amortizer." With proper planning and design, Visual Basic .NET can be used to create commercial-quality software applications.

Before you begin, take a look at what the final product will look like. Figure 2.1 shows the Loan Calculator's main screen as it's being used.

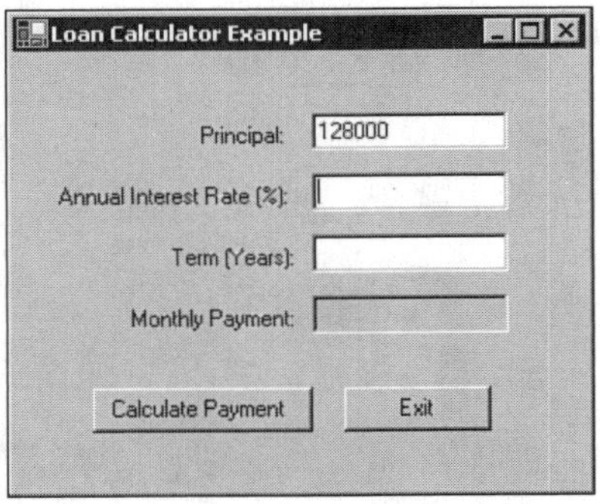

Figure 2.1
The Loan Calculator program offers the user a variety of options.

SETTING UP A NEW WINDOWS PROJECT

To develop a Visual Basic .NET application, you must first enter the Visual Basic .NET development environment, then set up a project. In Visual Basic terminology, a *project* acts as a repository for all the files needed to create an application.

STARTING VISUAL BASIC .NET

Begin by starting the Visual Basic .NET Integrated Development Environment (IDE). When Visual Basic .NET's IDE opens, you will normally see the Get Started pane of the Visual Studio Start Page, shown in Figure 2.2.

Figure 2.2
A new Visual Basic .NET session displays the Visual Studio Start Page.

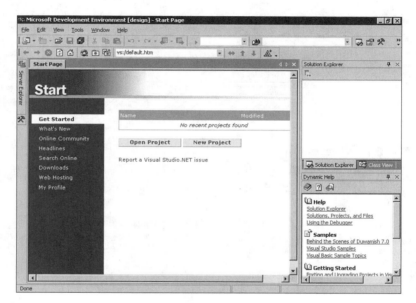

> **Note**
>
> If this is the first time you have ever started Visual Basic .NET, you may see the My Profile pane of the Visual Studio Home Page instead of the Get Started pane (see Figure 2.3). If this is the case, simply click the Get Started link on the left side of the page.

Figure 2.3
If you have never started Visual Basic .NET before, you may see a different part of the Visual Studio Start Page.

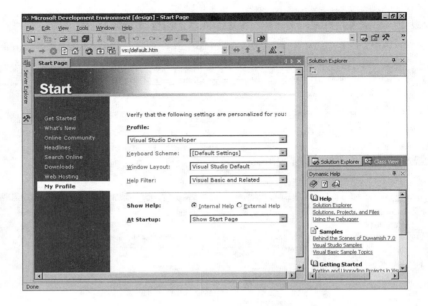

CREATING A NEW PROJECT

Click the Create New Project button to start a new Visual Basic .NET project. You will be presented with the New Project dialog box, as illustrated in Figure 2.4.

Figure 2.4
The New Project dialog box assists you in the setup of a new project.

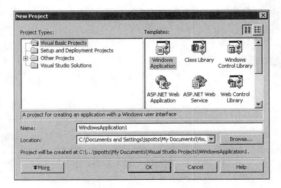

As you will learn in the course of reading this book, Visual Basic .NET allows you to create a number of different types of projects. For our example, we will be creating a standard Windows application that can run on the Microsoft Windows platform.

Process the New Project dialog box as follows:

- In the Project Types box, make sure Visual Basic Projects is selected.
- In the Templates box, click Windows Application.

- In the Name text box, type the name by which you want your project to be known. For this example, we'll use the name `Loan Calculator`.

- Make sure the Location box contains the path to the folder where you want to store your Visual Studio projects. When Visual Studio .NET is first installed, the default project location is the Visual Studio Projects subfolder of your My Documents folder; however, you can change this location by clicking the Browse button (or by typing a valid path). A subfolder for this new project will be created in that location, as reported just below the Location box ("Project will be created at...").

After you have completed filling out the New Project dialog box, click OK. Visual Basic .NET will create the files needed for your new project, create the appropriate subfolder, and save the project files in that subfolder. You will then see the main Visual Basic .NET design screen, as shown in Figure 2.5.

Figure 2.5
Visual Basic .NET's design screen is where you build your application's user interface.

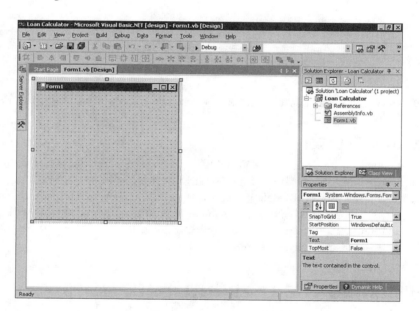

Notice Visual Basic .NET's title bar; specifically, the word *[design]* after Microsoft Visual Basic .NET. This means that you are in d*esign mode* (also known as *design time*), a name for the time you spend designing your program. Later, when you run your program, Visual Basic .NET will be in *run mode*.

As in previous versions of Visual Basic, a new Windows Application project consists of one *form*, or window, which will typically serve as your program's main user interface. Visual Basic applications are comprised of one or more components, such as forms, code modules, and classes, along with controls and other components.

Look at the *Solution Explorer* in the upper-right area of the screen in Figure 2.5 and shown in Figure 2.6. It consists of a list of the contents of the current project. Because you've just begun this project, it contains only a single form named Form1.vb. A project can grow to include many components; the Solution Explorer helps keep them organized. The last part of the text in Visual Basic .NET's title bar—*(Form1.vb [Design])*—tells you that Form1 is the current form active in the development environment, and that it, too, is in design mode.

Figure 2.6
The Solution Explorer lists the components that make up a project.

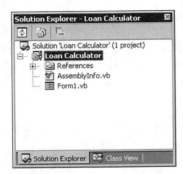

→ To learn all about Visual Basic .NET's development environment **see** "Understanding the Development Environment," **p. 75**

SAVING YOUR WORK

Unlike previous versions of Visual Basic, and much to the delight of VB programmers, Visual Basic .NET names and saves the files that comprise a project *before* you begin working on the project. By default, Visual Basic .NET is set to automatically save your project files whenever you build and/or run a program. You can change this setting in the Projects and Solutions section of the Environment folder in the Options dialog box, which can be accessed by clicking Tools, Options in the menu system.

DESIGNING THE USER INTERFACE

Now that you have set up your working environment, it's time to design the user interface, which is the visual part of the program that your user sees and interacts with. Typically, when developing Windows applications, you design the user interface first and then write the code that makes the program come alive.

GETTING INFORMATION FROM THE USER

Most computer programs are interactive—they need to receive information from the user as well as provide information back to the user. A Windows-based Visual Basic program interacts with its user through controls that are placed on the program's form(s). A *control* is an object that interacts with the user or the program. Many of Visual Basic's controls can be used to obtain input from the user.

The user interface for the Loan Calculator program will be responsible for accepting input, displaying output, and initiating the loan calculations. You will utilize three of Visual Basic .NET's most commonly used controls:

- **TextBox controls**—accept textual information needed from the user, and display certain information back to the user.

- **Label controls**—act as captions, displaying information to the user. Labels are similar to text boxes, except that the user can't edit the information presented in them.

- **Button controls**—the user can click these to initiate program actions. Users of previous versions of Visual Basic should note that Button controls were previously called CommandButton controls.

All these controls are part of the basic set of controls found in Visual Basic .NET's Toolbox (see Figure 2.7).

Figure 2.7
Visual Basic .NET's Toolbox contains the controls needed to build applications.

ADDING A TEXTBOX CONTROL

The TextBox control, also known simply as a *text box*, is (as its name implies) a *box* that displays and accepts *text*. In a way, it's similar to a text box you might find on a survey or application form, which is designed to accept input (from a pen or pencil) as well as display information. The TextBox control is one example of how far programming languages have advanced. Earlier programming environments required a lot of work to exchange information with the user. One of the fundamental concepts of Visual Basic has always been that it works in conjunction with Windows to take care of the mundane details of where text is positioned on the screen, how it's retrieved from the user, and so on. Your Visual Basic program simply needs to be concerned with the text in the text box; the control itself takes care of the rest.

ADDING A CONTROL TO A FORM

For a Visual Basic program to use a control, that control must be placed on a form. For your Loan Calculator program, begin by placing a TextBox control on the main form:

1. By default, the Toolbox automatically hides itself. To make the Toolbox appear, hover your mouse pointer over the vertically oriented Toolbox tab on the left edge of the screen. The Toolbox will "fly in," as shown in Figure 2.8.

Figure 2.8
The Toolbox appears when you hover near the left edge of the screen.

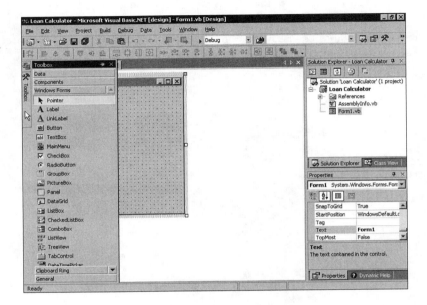

2. Click the tool for the TextBox control in the Toolbox.
3. Move the mouse pointer to the Form1 form, which will probably be partially obscured by the Toolbox window. Note that the pointer changes to a crosshair with a tiny image of a text box attached to it, indicating that you're about to draw a TextBox control.
4. Click anywhere in a blank area of Form1. This will cause a default-sized (100 pixels wide by 20 pixels high) TextBox control to appear on Form1 at the point where you clicked (see Figure 2.9).

Figure 2.9
The new text box appears on the form and is selected (notice the sizing handles).

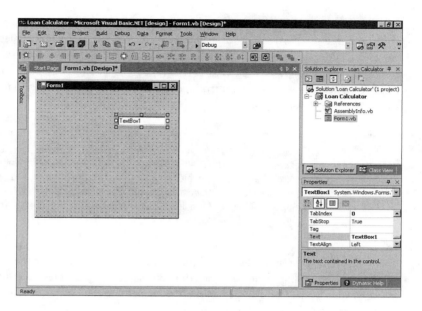

> **Tip**
>
> You also can add a control to a form by double-clicking the control's Toolbox icon. This places a control directly on the form. You can then move and resize the control as desired with the sizing handles, as described in the upcoming section, "Moving and Resizing a Control."

The procedures used to add a TextBox control to a form are the same as those for drawing most controls on a form.

SETTING A CONTROL'S PROPERTIES

After you have added a control to a form, you will usually want to set one or more of the control's properties. *Properties* are settings that control the appearance and behavior of an object. For the text box you just added, you want to set the Name and Text properties.

The Name property is very important. It is used in program code to identify the control. Because a program will likely have many controls of the same type, you can use the control's Name property to identify the particular control for which a particular code statement is written.

Every control must have a name, which is represented by the value of its Name property. In addition, every control on a particular form must have a *unique* name, unless it's part of a control array. (*Control arrays* are covered in detail in Chapter 10, "Understanding Windows Forms"; for now, just make sure all your controls on a given form have unique names.)

Visual Basic assigns a default name to every control placed on a form. Because this is the first text box you've placed on this form, its default name is TextBox1. Subsequently placed text boxes would be named TextBox2, TextBox3, and so on. It's very good programming practice to change the default control names to be more descriptive. Assume, for example, you have three text boxes on a form that are used to accept a customer's last name, first name, and address. If you change the default names of TextBox1, TextBox2, and TextBox3 to something more descriptive, such as txtLName, txtFName, and txtAddress, it will be much easier to remember what each control's purpose is when you (inevitably) must modify your program's code at some future date.

Tip

Note that the control names I suggested begin with the prefix txt. It's common to begin a control's name with a three-character lowercase prefix denoting the type of control, the rest of the name describing the control's purpose. Thus, when debugging program code, it is immediately clear that txtLName refers to a TextBox control that contains last name information. Other commonly used prefixes include lbl for Label controls and btn for Button controls.

To change the name of the first text box you placed on the form for the Loan Calculator project, you must first make sure the control is selected. The selected control is the one for which properties will be changed in the Properties window, which is found in the lower-right portion of the development environment. As you'll see a little later, multiple controls can be selected at the same time. You can tell whether a control is selected if it has a series of eight sizing handles around its borders. The selected control's name also appears in the Properties window's Object box, which is the drop-down list just below the Properties window's title bar. If the desired control isn't selected, simply click it one time to select it.

Now that the control is selected, take a look at the Properties window, which is a list of properties that apply to the selected object at design time and the current values of those properties. The left side lists the names of the properties that apply to the selected object and that can be changed at design time; each property's current value is denoted in the right side of the Properties window.

Note

By default, the properties listed in the Properties window are categorized according to their function. Until you are more familiar with the properties that apply to the various types of controls, I recommend that you switch the Properties window to its other display option, which arranges the properties alphabetically by name. To do so, click the Alphabetic icon just below the Properties window's Object box. Even if you do this, however, the Name property will appear at the top of the window due to its importance.

Click the Name property. If you have sorted the Properties window alphabetically, the Name property is located near the very top of the list (due to its importance). If your Properties window is in Categorized view, you'll find the Name property in the Design category. Clicking the Name property makes it the current property (note that the property name is highlighted). Note the default value—TextBox1—of the Name property on the right side. At this point, you can simply type a new value for the Name property, or edit the existing value.

Change the value of your TextBox control's Name property by typing a more descriptive name—let's use txtPrincipal, because the user will enter a principal amount here—and pressing Enter. Figure 2.10 shows the Properties window after making this change.

Figure 2.10
Use the Properties window to set values for your controls' properties.

A TextBox control's Text property represents the text that's entered in the box—that is, what is displayed inside the box on the screen. As the user types in a text box while a program is running, Visual Basic constantly modifies the text box's Text property to reflect the current contents of the box. By default, a new text box contains its own name; your new text box contains TextBox1 in its Text property (recall that TextBox1 was the control's name when it was created). For the Loan Calculator program, you don't want anything in the Text property when the program starts; in other words, you want the box to start off empty. To accomplish this, locate the TextBox control's Text property in the Properties window. Select the current value (TextBox1), and press the Delete key.

> **Tip**
>
> Property values appearing in boldface type in the Properties window are an indication that those specific properties' values have been changed from their default (original) values.

ADDING THE REMAINING TEXT BOXES

Now that you've added one TextBox control to the form, it should be a simple matter to add the other text boxes that you need for your Loan Calculator program. Add three more text boxes to the form; name them txtIntRate, txtTerm, and txtPayment. Clear their Text properties as well.

The last text box you added, txtPayment, will be used to display the calculated payment to the user. Therefore, the user should not be able to type in that box. A text box's ReadOnly property is designed to prevent the user from being able to change text in a text box at run-time. Locate the ReadOnly property for txtPayment. Note that its default value is False, which allows the user to modify the control's contents. Use the drop-down arrow to change the ReadOnly property to True. Notice that the TextBox control on the form has now become grayed-out. This is a visual clue to the user that he cannot enter that text box.

When you're done, your form should look similar to the one shown in Figure 2.11.

Figure 2.11
The interface of the Loan Calculator program has four text boxes.

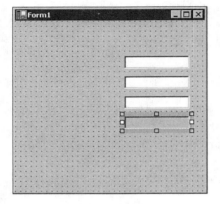

If your form doesn't look exactly like the one in Figure 2.11, don't worry. One nice thing about a visual design environment is that you can change the appearance of objects quite easily.

> **Tip**
>
> To draw multiple controls of the same type, hold down the Ctrl key when you select the control's tool in the Toolbox. That tool will remain selected in the Toolbox even after you've finished drawing a control. You can keep drawing multiple instances of that control without having to reselect the tool. When you're through drawing that control, select the Toolbox's pointer tool to return the mouse pointer to its normal state.

MOVING AND RESIZING A CONTROL

If you don't like where a control is positioned, simply use the mouse to drag it to a new location.

If you want to change the size of a control, you must first select it, which causes the sizing handles to appear. You can then use the mouse to change the control's size by dragging the sizing handles. The handles on the control's top and bottom edges change its height. The handles on the control's left and right edges change its width. The handles on the control's corners change its height and width simultaneously.

> **Note**
>
> By default, some controls (including the TextBox control that we are working with right now) have only two of the eight sizing handles activated; the others are grayed-out. That's because the TextBox control's AutoSize property is set to True by default. The AutoSize property automatically controls the height of a TextBox control based upon the size of the font used for the text that will be displayed by the control. Therefore, the sizing handles that affect the control's height are not available.

You also can change the size and position of objects by modifying their Size and Location properties, respectively, in the Properties window:

■ An object's Size property consists of a pair of two numbers that reflect the object's height and width, respectively (in pixels). Clicking the plus sign next to the name of the Size property in the Properties window will allow you to enter Width and Height properties individually.

■ An object's Location property consists of a pair of two numbers that reflect the object's x-position (distance from the left edge of its container to the left edge of the object) and y-position (distance from the top edge of its container to the top of the object), respectively (in pixels). Clicking the plus sign next to the name of the Location property in the Properties window will allow you to enter X and Y properties individually.

MOVING A GROUP OF CONTROLS

Now that you have created text boxes for the user's input, you should label them so that the user knows what to enter in each box. This will involve adding Label controls to the form. Depending upon where you drew the TextBox controls, you may need to move them to the right to ensure that there is enough room for the labels on the left. You could drag each text box individually; however, it is quicker to move them all together at the same time. You can easily select them all and move the entire group. To do this, click one of the text boxes to select it, and then hold down Ctrl while you click each of the others. Notice that each text box that you select in this manner gets its own set of sizing handles. After you have them all selected, begin dragging one of them. As you drag, the entire group is dragged at once. Drop the controls on the right side of the form; as you are dragging them, you will see outlines of the selected controls being moved, as depicted in Figure 2.12.

Figure 2.12
Selecting multiple controls enables you to move them together as a group.

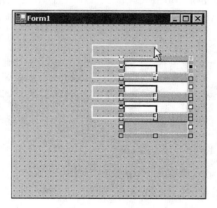

> **Tip**
>
> Instead of Ctrl+clicking multiple controls, you can select a group of controls by drawing a rectangle around them. Click and hold down the left mouse button in an empty area of the form. Note that a "rubber-band" box stretches as you move the mouse. Draw the box around all the controls you want to select.

LABELING YOUR PROGRAM'S CONTROLS

Obviously, the user needs to know which values are to be entered into each of the text boxes. The easiest way to do this is to add a Label control next to each text box. The label will then act as a caption for the text box, containing a brief description of what data is to be entered there.

Although the user perceives Label controls and TextBox controls to be quite different, they are very similar from a programmer's perspective. They can both contain the same types of text, although the text in a Label control can't be modified by the user. However, by setting various properties of a Label control, the *appearance* of the text contained in it can be altered in many ways. Figure 2.13 illustrates several Label controls demonstrating a variety of looks.

Figure 2.13
Labels can take on many different sizes and appearances.

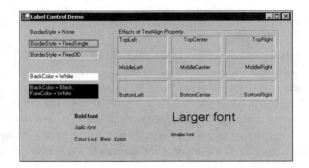

To continue our earlier analogy of a survey form, Label controls are like the words that are preprinted on the form to identify the purpose of the text boxes. The key difference between a Label control and a TextBox control is that a Label control contains text that the user cannot change. As with a TextBox control, the text contained in a Label control is stored in its `Text` property.

Note

In previous versions of Visual Basic, the text displayed in a Label control was contained in a property called `Caption`. Effective with Visual Basic .NET, Label controls have a `Text` property instead.

To add a Label control to a form, follow these steps:

1. Hover over or click the Toolbox tab so the Toolbox is displayed.
2. Select the Label control's tool in the Toolbox.
3. Click a blank area of the form to place a Label control on it.
4. In the Properties window, change the Label control's `Name` property to `lblPrincipal`.
5. Change the Label control's `Text` property to `Principal`.

6. Change the Label control's TextAlign property to MiddleRight, using the drop-down arrow next to the property setting (see Figure 2.14). This makes the label align its caption along the middle of the right side, next to its corresponding text box, as is common with caption labels.

Figure 2.14
Clicking the drop-down arrow for the TextAlign property allows you to visually specify the alignment of the label's text.

7. Resize and reposition the label so it is fairly well lined up with the first text box.

You should now be able to see how the Label control will aid the user in determining what to type in the first text box. Create three more Label controls, one for each of the remaining text boxes. Use the recommended values for the Name and Text properties outlined in Table 2.1 (don't forget to set the TextAlign property as well). When you're finished, your form should look like the one shown in Figure 2.15.

TABLE 2.1   NAME AND TEXT PROPERTIES FOR THE LOAN CALCULATOR PROGRAM'S LABEL CONTROLS

Name Property	Text Property
lblPrincipal	Principal:
lblIntRate	Annual Interest Rate (%):
lblTerm	Term (Years):
lblPayment	Monthly Payment:

Note

Because lblIntRate has a longer caption in its Text property, you may need to resize the label to make it wider so all the text will fit on one line.

Figure 2.15
The Loan Calculator program's labels show the user what to enter in the text boxes.

CHANGING A FORM'S PROPERTIES

Just as you define a control's appearance and behavior by setting its properties, you also can set the properties of a form to govern its appearance and behavior.

Just like controls, forms have a Name property. The default name for a project's first form is Form1; subsequently added forms are named Form2, Form3, and so on. Because there is only one form in this project, we will leave its name as the default Form1.

The form's Text property governs what is displayed in the form's title bar. Change the form's title bar for our sample application by setting the Text property to something more descriptive, like Loan Calculator Example.

If you need to change the size of your Loan Calculator form to accommodate the controls you added, you can do so using the techniques for resizing objects described earlier in this chapter.

ADDING COMMAND BUTTONS

So far, your sample application's form has a set of text boxes to accept the user's input and a set of labels to identify those text boxes. You also need some way for the user to initiate actions—this is the purpose of Button controls. A user can click a Button control, also commonly known as a *command button* (or simply a *button*), to cause something to happen. You can add a button to a form just like you add other controls—by using the mouse to draw it.

Like text boxes and labels, command buttons have a Text property that enables you to specify the text that will appear on the button's face, so the user will know what the button does.

 To complete the interface of the Loan Calculator program, use the Toolbox's Button control tool to add two buttons near the bottom of the form. Set their Name and Text properties according to Table 2.2. Figure 2.16 shows the completed Loan Calculator interface.

TABLE 2.2   Name AND Text PROPERTIES FOR THE LOAN CALCULATOR PROGRAM'S BUTTON
CONTROLS

Name Property	Text Property
btnCalculate	Calculate Payment
btnExit	Exit

Figure 2.16
After you have added
the Button controls,
the Loan Calculator's
interface is complete.

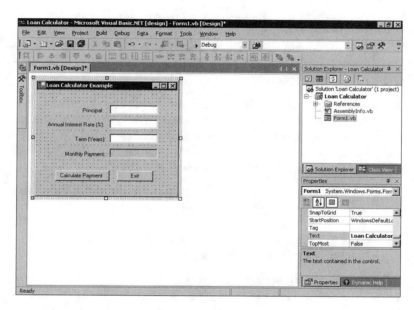

Note

As with lblIntRate, you may need to widen btnCalculate to accommodate its
wider caption.

KEEPING YOUR PROJECT SAFE

Now that you've completed designing the Loan Calculator's interface, this would be an
excellent time to save your work so far. Because Visual Basic .NET automatically saved your
files when the project was created, resaving it is very easy—and highly recommended. In
fact, it makes sense to save your work regularly throughout the development process. You
never know when you'll have problems; a quick save only takes a few seconds, and could
save you a lot of work when those problems do happen.

To resave your project, choose File, Save All from the menu system, or simply click the Save All
button on the toolbar. Because you've already told Visual Basic .NET where to save the files
that make up your project, they're automatically saved in the same location, using the same filenames. If you have added new components (forms, modules, and so on) since the last save, you
will be prompted for a filename and location for each of the newly added components.

CODING YOUR PROGRAM'S ACTIONS

As mentioned earlier, the user interface of the Loan Calculator program is now complete. However, it doesn't actually do anything at this point. For your program to become functional, you need to write some code. The term *code*—as it is used in this book—refers to one or more lines of programming commands, written in a particular programming language (Visual Basic, in our case).

RESPONDING TO EVENTS

Visual Basic is an object-oriented, event-driven language. This means that a program's interface is comprised of *objects* (controls, forms, and so forth); the program is taught what actions to perform when *events* happen to those objects.

An event is usually initiated by the user. By anticipating the possible events that can (and should) occur to the various objects in your program, you can write code to respond to those events appropriately. For example, in the case of a Button control labeled Exit, your code should respond to that button's Click event by ending the program. This code should execute whenever the Exit button's Click event occurs.

You cause a program to respond to events by placing code in *event handlers*. An event handler is a *sub procedure*, or standalone block of code, that is executed when a particular event occurs to a particular object. In the case of a user clicking an Exit button, you need to add code to the Exit button's Click event handler. Let's illustrate this by writing code for the Click event handler of your Loan Calculator program's Exit button.

Double-click the Exit button (btnExit) that you placed on the sample application's form. You'll see a new window called a *Code window* (see Figure 2.17). You can open a separate Code window for each form (or other kind of module) in your project, and this is where you place code that relates to that form and the objects contained in it. Notice that the Code window already contains a small amount of code. This prewritten code has to do with how Windows manages Windows forms.

Because you double-clicked on the Exit button to enter the Code window, your cursor should be automatically placed in the event handler for the Exit button's Click event. Specifically, you should find your cursor in the middle of a sub procedure, beginning with the words Private Sub and ending with the words End Sub. A *sub procedure* (also known simply as a *procedure*) is a discrete sequence of code statements that has a name and is executed as a unit.

Figure 2.17
The Code window is a full-featured editor for the code that relates to your program's objects.

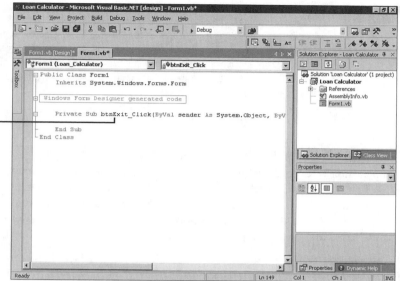

Sub procedure name

The part after the words `Private Sub` denotes the sub procedure's name. This particular sub procedure is named `btnExit_Click`, a predefined name that denotes that it is the `Click` event handler for the control named `btnExit`. (There is also some more information after the procedure name; don't be concerned with this right now.) Visual Basic .NET will execute any code located within this sub procedure whenever the `Click` event occurs to this Button control.

Note

Most objects can react to one of several different events. Each type of object has a default event, which is the event that usually occurs to that type of object most often. For example, the `Click` event is the one that occurs most often to a Button control. The default event is the one that is opened in the Code window when you double-click an object that doesn't already have any code associated with it.

To cause the program to end when the user clicks the Exit button, you simply need to add one line of code—Visual Basic's `End` statement—to the `btnExit_Click` procedure. Your cursor should already be on the blank line between the `Private Sub btnExit_Click()` and `End Sub` statements; if it's not, simply click there. Press Tab twice to indent the code (that makes it easier to read), then type the word `End`. Press Enter to insert a new blank line into the procedure (this isn't necessary, but the extra blank line improves readability). When you're done, your complete sub procedure should look like this code:

```
Private Sub btnExit_Click(ByVal sender As System.Object, _
    ByVal e As System.EventArgs) Handles btnExit.Click
    End

End Sub
```

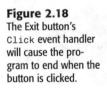

Note

Due to printing requirements, the first line of code (`Private Sub btnExit...`), which will appear as a single line of code in your Code window, appears as two separate lines as printed earlier. We have broken the single line into two by using the underscore (_), which Visual Basic recognizes as the code continuation character. Visual Basic treats two (or more) lines joined by an underscore as a single line of code.

Congratulations! You just wrote your first Visual Basic code.

SPECIFYING EVENT HANDLERS

Look at the two drop-down list boxes near the top of the Code window, as shown in Figure 2.18. The *Class Name box* (the one on the left) lists all the objects that have been placed on the current form, as well as two special sections named Base Class Events (which represents the form itself) and Overrides. The options available in the *Method Name box* (on the right) change based upon which object is currently selected in the Class Name box.

You should see `Form1 (Loan_Calculator)` selected in the Class Name box; this indicates that the current code window relates to the `Form1` object in the `Loan Calculator` project. The Method Name box should display `btnExit_Click`, indicating that you are currently editing that event handler.

Using these two drop-down list boxes enables you to navigate to any portion of the Code window. Think of the code for a particular form as one long text file; the Code window is a navigation tool that helps you quickly display a specific object/event combination.

Figure 2.18
The Exit button's `Click` event handler will cause the program to end when the button is clicked.

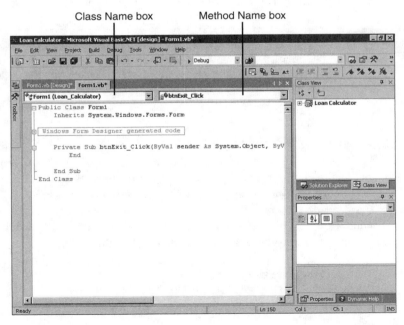

When you double-click a control at design time, the Code window automatically opens to the procedure that serves as the event handler for the default event of the control you clicked, unless some event other than the default already has code in its event handler. In that case, the event handler that contains code is selected, in case you want to edit that code. Of course, you can use the Class Name and Method Name boxes at any time to quickly locate the desired object/event combination.

Tip

In addition to double-clicking an object, you can also open the Code window by pressing F7, by clicking the View Code button in the Solution Explorer window, or by selecting View, Code from the Main menu.

PART
I
CH
2

Now that you've properly coded the Exit button to end the application, all that remains is to code the Calculate Payment button (btnCalculate). Its function is to calculate the monthly payment amount based on the information that the user has supplied. This code will be written as the Click event handler for the Button control btnCalculate. You could display the btnCalculate button's Click event handler by bringing the form designer to the front and double-clicking btnCalculate; however, because the Code window is already open, you might find it more efficient to drop down the Code window's Class Name box and select btnCalculate, then use the Method Name box to select the Click event. This displays the btnCalculate_Click event handler in the Code window.

WRITING PROGRAM CODE

The procedure that calculates the loan payment will be more complex than the Exit procedure. Obviously, the code that performs the payment calculation needs to be more involved than a simple End statement. Also, you must do some additional housekeeping in this procedure, as you will be using variables.

A *variable* is a temporary storage location for information. Very often, your programs will need to remember information—such as calculation results, the user's name, order totals, and so on—as the program is running. Think of a variable like a white board that the program can use to remember information. Within certain guidelines, the program can write information on the white board, modify that information, even erase it completely. One important consideration is that when the program finishes, the white board is *always* erased completely.

→ For more information about variables, **see** Chapter 6, "Storing Information in Variables," **p. 139**

VARIABLE DECLARATIONS

The first part of the Calculate sub procedure will be used to declare the variables you'll need. That means that you will tell Visual Basic the *names* of the variables that the procedure will be using, as well as what *type* of information each variable may contain. By default, Visual Basic .NET requires you to declare your variables. A program will not run if you have used variables that you did not declare. You can turn this option off, but it's always good practice to force yourself to declare your variables before using them. This helps reduce the need for debugging problems caused by misspelled variable names.

Your Calculate procedure uses four variables—one each to hold the principal amount, the interest rate, the loan term, and the calculated monthly payment. Make sure the cursor is on the blank line between `Private Sub btnCalculate_Click()` and `End Sub`. Press Tab to indent the code, then type the following line:

```
Dim decPrincipal As Decimal
```

Notice that when you press Enter after typing this code, the cursor doesn't go back to the left margin of the code window. The code editor assumes that you want to indent the next line of code to the same level as the preceding line. This aids in your code's readability. You can increase the level of indent by pressing Tab; Shift+Tab or Backspace will decrease the indent level.

As you can tell from this code, the general format for declaring variables is the word `Dim`, followed by a variable name, the word `As`, and the variable's type. As with object names, you should follow a naming standard. Throughout this book, we'll use a very common variable naming standard that uses the first three (lowercase) characters of the variable name as a prefix designating its type; the remaining portion of the variable's name (usually beginning with an uppercase character) describes its purpose. The variable named `decPrincipal`, for example, is a Decimal type variable that will store the principal amount. Some variable types and their common prefixes are outlined in Table 2.3.

Tip

You may have noticed that when you typed the space after the word `As`, a list of different types appeared on the screen. This feature helps you select an applicable keyword as you are entering code. When you typed the `d` that begins the word `decimal`, the list automatically moved to the keywords beginning with `d`. When the desired keyword has been selected, you can simply press Enter (or click the keyword with the mouse), and the desired word is completed for you.

TABLE 2.3 PREFIXES USED IN A COMMON VARIABLE NAMING CONVENTION

Prefix	Variable Type
str	String
int	Integer
lng	Long Integer
sng	Single-precision Floating Point
dbl	Double-precision Floating Point
dec	Decimal (often used for money data)
bln	Boolean (True/False)
var	Variant

Add the following line of code for the next declaration:

```
Dim decIntRate As Decimal
```

This would be a good time to point out that multiple variables can be declared on the same line of code. Add the following line of code to declare two more variables:

```
Dim intTerm As Integer, dblPayment As Double
```

> **Tip**
>
> In previous versions of Visual Basic, each variable listed in a single-line declaration had to have its own type specifically stated; otherwise, its type would have defaulted to Variant. In Visual Basic .NET, however, you can declare multiple variables of the same type on a single line. For instance, the line
>
> ```
> Dim intTest1, intTest2 as Integer
> ```
>
> will declare both `intTest1` and `intTest2` as Integer types.

PROCEDURE CODE

The procedure code is the remaining part of the procedure that does the actual work. In your Loan Calculator program, this part of the procedure will be responsible for retrieving the input values from the first three text boxes, calculating the monthly payment, and displaying the payment in the fourth text box.

Enter the following two lines into the Code window (after the variable declaration statements):

```
'Store the principal in the variable decPrincipal
decPrincipal = txtPrincipal.Text
```

The first line is a comment explaining what's going on. A comment is denoted by a single quotation mark ('), usually at the beginning of a line. When Visual Basic encounters a single quote on a line, the remainder of the line is ignored. Visual Basic then looks to the next line for the next instruction.

The second line of this code retrieves the information that the user entered into the `txtPrincipal` text box, placing the value into the variable `decPrincipal`. This is done with an assignment statement, much like an assignment statement in algebra—a variable appears on the left side of the equal sign, and the value to be placed in that variable appears on the right side.

To retrieve the information that the user entered into the `txtPrincipal` text box, we access the text box's `Text` property. Recall how we set the `Text` property of our program's text boxes to an empty string at design time. We also can access the `Text` property of a text box using code at *runtime* (while the programming is running) to capture what the user has entered into the text box.

Note

> Even though a TextBox control contains textual information and our `decPrincipal` variable expects a numeric value, Visual Basic takes care of the data type conversion implicitly.

Tip

> As you enter the remaining code, you'll notice several more comments within the code statements. Again, a *comment* is a line of code that isn't executed; rather, it's used to explain the purpose or functionality of the executable portions of the code. Comments, which are a form of documentation, help a programmer to quickly understand the purpose of a section of code when he or she must edit it at some point in the future. It's usually a very good idea to include a lot of comments in your code. You may think you'll remember why you solved a problem a certain way, but when you look at code that you (or someone else) wrote weeks, months, or even years earlier, comments will make the code's purpose much clearer.

Enter the remaining code presented in Listing 2.1 in the Code window, between what you have already entered and the End Sub statement. The comments should help you understand how the code works. Figure 2.19 shows the completed sub procedure in the Code window.

LISTING 2.1   CODE TO CALCULATE THE MONTHLY PAYMENT

```
'Convert interest rate to its decimal equivalent
'   i.e. 12.75 becomes 0.1275
decIntRate = txtIntRate.Text / 100

'Convert annual interest rate to monthly
'   by dividing by 12 (months in a year)
decIntRate = decIntRate / 12

'Convert number of years to number of months
'   by multiplying by 12 (months in a year)
intTerm = txtTerm.Text * 12
'Calculate and display the monthly payment.
'   If the interest rate is zero, the payment is
'     the principal divided by # of periods.
'   The Format function makes the displayed number look good.
If decIntRate = 0 Then
    dblPayment = decPrincipal / intTerm
Else
    dblPayment = decPrincipal * _
        (decIntRate / (1 - (1 + decIntRate) ^ -intTerm))
End If
txtPayment.Text = Format(dblPayment, "$#,##0.00")
```

Figure 2.19
Entering the code to calculate the monthly payment completes the `Click` event handler for `btnCalculate`.

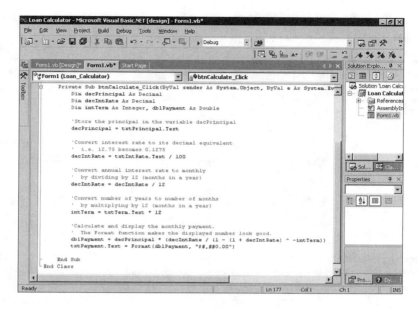

RUNNING YOUR PROGRAM

I'll bet you're anxious to see your program in action! Before running it, however, make sure you save your work so far. To run the program, you need to execute Visual Basic's Start command using any of these methods:

- Click the Start button on the Visual Basic toolbar.
- Choose Debug, Start from the menu system.
- Press F5.

When you execute the Start command, Visual Basic compiles your program to check for certain types of errors; if your Output window is visible, you will see the results as it builds the application. If no errors are found, the program will begin executing and you'll see your user interface. Notice in Visual Basic's title bar that you've gone from Design mode to Run mode, meaning that the program is actually running. Because the application is object-oriented and event-driven, it's waiting for you (the user) to cause an event to occur to an object, such as typing in a text box or clicking a button.

Test your program by entering values for the principal, term, and interest rate. Use these values for your first test:

Principal	128000
Interest Rate	9.75
Term	30

After entering these values, click the Calculate Payment button. The monthly payment displayed should be $1,099.72 (see Figure 2.20).

Figure 2.20
The Loan Calculator program is now fully functional and can calculate loan payments.

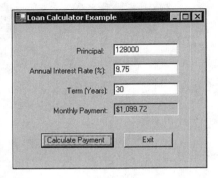

> **Note**
>
> Because this program is a demonstration of basic programming techniques, its interface is quite simple, and very little effort has gone into making it error-proof. Numbers must be typed without thousands separators or dollar signs for the calculations to work properly. As you develop your programming skills later in the book, you'll see how to overcome these types of limitations.

Test the program with other combinations of numbers. When you're through, end the program by clicking your application's Exit button. This will return you to the design environment.

FROM HERE...

The Loan Calculator program has enabled us to dive right in to writing a Visual Basic program from scratch. In this chapter, you learned how to do the following:

- Start Visual Basic
- Begin a new project
- Add controls to a form
- Set properties of your project's objects
- Write code to bring the program to life

Believe it or not, these steps comprise the core of Visual Basic .NET programming for the Windows environment. You've seen simple examples of all these steps, but most Visual Basic programming involves repetition of these steps over and over until the desired results are obtained.

As you start working with more complex applications, you'll see many ways to practice and enhance these fundamental Visual Basic programming skills. Refer to the following chapters for additional related information:

- To see how to build an application much like this one for Web-based deployment, see Chapter 3, "Creating Your First Web Application."

- To see how to use Visual Basic's fundamental components to create your own applications, see Chapter 4, "Understanding the Development Environment."

- To learn more about the components that you use to build Visual Basic applications, see Chapter 5, "Visual Basic Building Blocks."

CREATING YOUR FIRST WEB APPLICATION

In this chapter

It is rare these days to find someone interested in computers who is not also familiar with using the World Wide Web. The World Wide Web, the most popular application on the global Internet, has leaped into the public consciousness so thoroughly that "dot-com" ads for Web sites now appear in virtually all forms of visual media. As a result, the ability to develop Web sites is a valuable skill for any computer programmer to learn. In this chapter, we will get you started with Web development by creating a simple Web Application project in Visual Studio .NET. A Web Application project allows you to apply your existing knowledge of Windows application development in Visual Basic. As an interesting parallel, we will show you how to create the same application from the previous chapter, but on a Web page. After you have mastered the basics in this chapter, the second part of the book provides additional detail on how you can use your VB knowledge on the Web.

> **Note**
>
> Web page design (making pages pretty) and Web application development (making pages functional) are two distinct areas of Web development. In this book, we cover both, but primarily are concerned with the latter activity.

GETTING STARTED WITH WEB APPLICATIONS

When you request a Web page with your Internet browser, the end result is a document that appears on your screen. A document by itself is not much of an application in the traditional sense. However, when you include the activities going on behind the scenes that generate a Web page, the term Web application makes more sense. For example, when you click the Buy button at your favorite online store, a program may execute to validate your credit card number and other information in a customer database.

The major difference between a Web application, such as the online store, and a traditional Windows application is that most of the code resides on a *Web server* instead of your local PC. The Web server does all the hard work, and then serves the resulting Web page back to your browser. There are two major advantages to this centralized architecture:

- Your code only exists in one place, so it can be updated easily.
- Installation of your application by end users is not required. This is because the Web application can send standard Web syntax, such as the Hypertext Markup Language (HTML), which the user's browser already understands.

UNDERSTANDING WEB APPLICATION PROJECTS

There are a lot of different ways you can use Visual Basic in a Web site. Some of the most common are as follows:

- **ASP.NET**—You can create Active Server Pages, which contain Visual Basic code that executes on the server.

- **Visual Basic Classes**—Classes that have been compiled into a DLL file can be installed on your Web server. These classes, which contain business logic and database functions, can be called from ASP.NET pages or exposed as Web services.
- **Client-Side Scripting**—VBScript, a subset of the Visual Basic language, can be used to execute code inside of the user's browser after the Web page has been delivered. This allows you to create a richer UI experience than can be achieved with standard HTML.

Each of the previous methods can be used independently (and, incidentally, without Visual Studio .NET) to create a functional Web application. However, a Visual Studio .NET Web Application project combines the previous elements together transparently.

> **Note**
>
> In addition to the methods listed here, you also can use WinForms on the Web, by using the Web as your data transfer backbone. For more information on this, see Chapter 17, "Using Active Server Pages.NET."

→ For more details on using classes and ASP.NET, **see** Chapter 17, "Using Active Server Pages.NET," **p. 443**

CONNECTING TO YOUR WEB SERVER

As we mentioned earlier, the content and programs of a Web application are stored on a Web server. Therefore, in order to develop Web applications, you will need to identify a Web server on your network. For the purposes of development and testing, this Web server can be the same computer on which you have installed Visual Studio.

Before creating a Web Application, you need to verify that a Web server is active and you know its address (or URL). The easiest way to see whether a Web server exists is to try to connect to it with Internet Explorer. Start Internet Explorer, type **http://*servername*** in the address box, and press Enter. If your Web server is up and running, some type of Web page should be displayed, as shown in Figure 3.1.

> **Note**
>
> If you want to use your current PC as the Web server, `http://localhost` is often defined as a valid Web address.

If you get a non-error response from your Web server, then you have identified a working address. If you get an error message, or are unable to determine the address, please consult the troubleshooting section at the end of this chapter.

Figure 3.1
If you have not published any Web pages or changed the default configuration of your Web server, you may see a page similar to the one pictured here, which is a default page for Internet Information Server 5.0.

Note

If you are using a separate Web server machine, it must have the Microsoft .NET Framework installed, which is included with Visual Studio. Please see the troubleshooting section at the end of this chapter for more details.

CREATING A WEB APPLICATION PROJECT

Now that you have identified a Web server and verified it is running, we can begin the creation of the sample application. The first step is to start Visual Studio .NET and create a new Web Application project. To do this, first click the Create New Project link. Next, single-click the ASP.NET Web Application icon. You should see the dialog box pictured in Figure 3.2.

Figure 3.2
When you create a new ASP.NET Web Application project, Visual Studio will immediately connect to the *Web* server and copy several project files there.

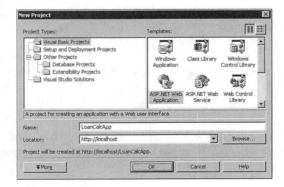

In the name box, type **LoanCalcApp**, which is the name of our sample project. In the Location box, type your Web server's address.

Note

The Web server address plus the project name is the virtual directory where your Web application files will be stored on the Web server.

Next, click OK to create your new project. Visual Studio will connect to the Web server and create the new Web application. Your project will then be opened in Visual Studio for you to work with, as pictured in Figure 3.3.

Figure 3.3
Note that a Web form has no visible borders, as with a windows form.

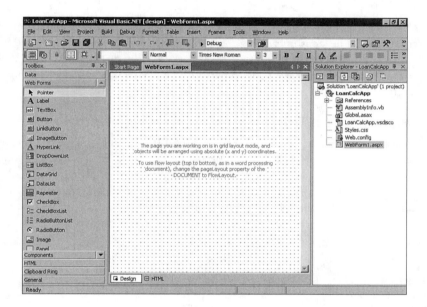

Note

If the project does not open, but you get an error message, you may need to perform additional Web server configuration. Please see the section, "Troubleshooting Web Applications," at the end of this chapter for more information.

SETTING THE pageLayout PROPERTY

If you have followed the example in Chapter 2, "Creating Your First Windows Application," or designed forms in previous versions of Visual Basic, you know that you design the interface of an application by drawing and arranging objects on a form. When the form is presented to the user, the objects appear as you designed them, because their arrangement (or layout) is saved with the form.

Web forms work a little differently; they are presented to the user based on the Web browser's interpretation of instructions received from the Web server.

PART

I

CH

3

In support of the Web architecture, Visual Studio provides two different ways to specify the layout of Web forms: linear and grid-based. (The message in the middle of the Web form in Figure 3.3 indicates grid mode is selected.) Each layout mode has significant impact on the way the browser displays the Web form; this will be discussed later. For the sample project, we will use the default grid layout mode, which more closely parallels windows form design.

→ For more information on the pageLayout property, **see** Chapter 18, "Web Applications and Services," **p. 475**

CREATING THE SAMPLE WEB APPLICATION

Now we are ready to begin the process of designing our sample application, a loan payment calculator. The steps in creating this project are very similar to those used in the previous chapter. First, we will design the user input screen by placing fields on a Web form. Next, we will write Visual Basic code to perform the payment calculation and present the results to the user. Finally, we will run and test the program.

DESIGNING THE WEB FORM

As you learned in the previous chapter, Visual Basic comes with many predefined objects called *controls*. Each has a specific purpose and can be used as needed in your applications. The first step in adding a control to your application is displaying the Toolbox window. You do this by choosing Toolbox from the View menu, or clicking the word Toolbox on the left of the screen. Figure 3.4 shows the Toolbox window.

Figure 3.4
The controls available for use in Web Applications are in a section of the Toolbox labeled "Web Forms."

For the loan calculator project, we will be using the following controls:

■ **TextBox**—This control allows the user to input text or numeric values. In this project we will be using four text boxes.

- **Label**—A label control is used for displaying text. The Loan Calculator will use four label controls to identify the text boxes.

- **LinkButton**—This control allows the user to initiate a program action. We will use one LinkButton so the user can process the payment calculation.

As you may have noticed, the Web Forms controls are very similar to their Windows counterparts. As you work with Web applications, you will find some subtle differences.

ADDING THE FIRST TEXTBOX

To add the first TextBox control to the project, draw it on the Web form by following these steps:

1. Display the Toolbox window.
2. Single-click the TextBox control.
3. Position the mouse over a blank area on the Web form designer. The mouse pointer will change to a crosshair.
4. Click and hold the mouse button. Drag the mouse to draw a rectangular box.
5. Release the mouse button. A TextBox control should now appear on the Web form.

PART

I

CH

3

Note

Freehand drawing and movement of controls on a Web form is only possible in the grid layout mode. If you are using linear layout mode, you need to double-click the control or drag it from the toolbox to the form.

Now that we have drawn the TextBox control, we need to set some key properties. As you may recall from Chapter 2, every control has a unique name, which you use to manipulate the control with Visual Basic code. By default, Visual Studio assigns sequentially numbered names such as TextBox1, TextBox2, and so on. However, you should always change the names of your text boxes to something more meaningful.

To change the name of the text box you just created, you will need to set its ID property by performing these steps:

1. To select the text box, single-click it with the mouse. A series of dots around the border will appear.
2. Press the F4 key to display the Properties window.
3. Find the ID property in the list, shown in Figure 3.5.
4. Set the value of the ID property to txtPrincipal. This designates the text box for the principal loan amount.

Figure 3.5
The **ID** property of a
Web text box corre-
sponds to the **Name**
property of a windows
text box.

ADDING THE FIRST LABEL

A text box appears as a rectangular box with space for the user to type information. For the user to know the purpose of a text box on the screen, we need to label it. A similar control, the Label control, is typically used to label text boxes. To label the txtPrincipal text box perform the following steps:

1. Display the Toolbox window.
2. Single-click the Label control.
3. Position the mouse over a blank area on the Web form designer. The mouse pointer will change to a crosshair.
4. Click and hold the mouse button. Drag the mouse to draw a rectangular box.
5. Release the mouse button. The new Label control should now appear on the Web form.

Using the mouse, drag the controls around on the screen so that the Label control is positioned to the left of the text box, as shown in Figure 3.6.

As with the text box, we will need to set the ID property of the label to something more meaningful than the default value. Go ahead and change it to lblPrincipal. Also you need to set the Text property of the label. The Text property determines what the label displays on the screen when the program is running. By default a label displays the word Label. Using the Properties window, change this property to the word Principal. Your screen should look similar to Figure 3.6.

Figure 3.6
In Visual Studio .NET, the `Caption` property of a label has been replaced by the `Text` property.

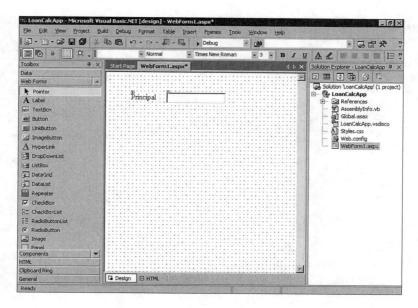

ADDING THE REMAINING LABELS AND TEXT BOXES

To draw the three additional text boxes and labels, you could simply display the Toolbox window and repeat the previous steps. However, it is a little quicker to use the copy and paste method. Copying and pasting controls is just like copying and pasting text in a word processor. First, select the object(s) you want to copy and press Ctrl+C. Then, press Ctrl+V to create a new copy. You will still have to set the individual properties of each new control, but the copy and paste method saves the time of drawing the control and keeps the size of controls consistent.

Using the copy and paste method, create three additional Label and TextBox controls. Set the property values as listed in Tables 3.1 and 3.2. After creating all the text boxes and labels, arrange the controls so that your form looks similar to Figure 3.7.

TABLE 3.1 ADDITIONAL LABEL CONTROLS

Name (ID Property)	Text (Text Property)
lblIntRate	Annual Interest Rate (%)
lblTerm	Term (Years)
lblPayment	Monthly Payment

Figure 3.7
Arrange the labels to the left of the text boxes, so that each label indicates to the user what information is in the associated text box.

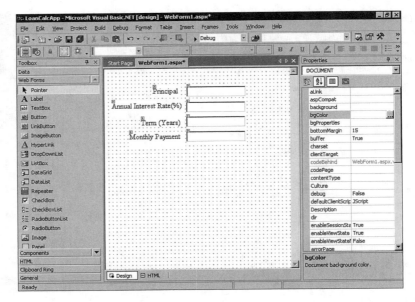

TABLE 3.2   ADDITIONAL TEXTBOX CONTROLS

Name (ID Property)

txtIntRate
txtTerm
txtPayment

With the addition of all the text boxes and labels, we have provided a means for the program to accept input from the user (the principal, interest rate, and term) as well as display a result (the monthly payment).

Note

We could have used a Label control for the monthly payment amount, because it is used for displaying data only. However, it was easier to use a text box for visual consistency.

ADDING A LINK BUTTON

In the previous chapter we added a Button control so that the user could tell the program to process the calculation. In the case of the Web, we will use a control called the LinkButton, which works like a regular button but looks like a Web hyperlink.

Note

There is another control, called the Hyperlink, not to be confused with the LinkButton control, which we will be using to execute VB code on the Web server.

To add the link button, perform these steps:

1. Display the ToolBox window.
2. Single-click the LinkButton control.
3. Move the mouse pointer to a blank area of the Web form designer. The mouse pointer will change to a crosshair.
4. Hold down the mouse button and draw a LinkButton control.
5. Position the LinkButton control so that it is centered below the text boxes and Label control.
6. Change the ID property of the link button to cmdCalculate. (The cmd prefix is my personal naming convention for buttons; it stands for command.)
7. Change the Text property of the link button to Calculate Payment.

Congratulations—you have just finished designing your first Web form. Next, you will write the code to make the program work.

WRITING THE VISUAL BASIC CODE

Now that we have designed the user interface for the Web form, we need to add Visual Basic code to make the program do something useful. The event that will trigger the loan calculation is the user clicking the cmdCalculate link. Therefore, we will add code that executes every time the click event occurs.

To display the Code window associated with your Web form, right-click the WebForm1.aspx file in the Solution Explorer and choose View Code. The code editor will display the file WebForm1.aspx.vb, which contains the server-side code associated with your Web form.

Note

In this chapter the application code resides in a file with a .vb extension on the Web server. There is also a second code component to a Web form that resides on the client and contains the HTML and script code. We will cover this later in the book.

Using the leftmost drop-down box at the top of the code editor window, select the cmdCalculate object. Open the rightmost drop-down box and select the Click procedure. You should see the following lines of code added to the window, which represent the beginning and end of the Click procedure.

```
Public Sub cmdCalculate_Click(ByVal sender As Object,_ByVal e As System.EventArgs)
Handles cmdCalculate.Click

End Sub
```

Enter the following code so that the cmdCalculate_Click method appears as shown in
Listing 3.1.

LISTING 3.1   cmdCalculate.zip—LOAN PAYMENT CALCULATOR

```
Public Sub cmdCalculate_Click(ByVal sender As Object,_
ByVal e As System.EventArgs) Handles cmdCalculate.Click
        Dim decPrincipal, decIntRate As Decimal
        Dim intTerm As Integer
        Dim dblPayment As Double

        'Store the principal in the variable cPrincipal
        decPrincipal = txtPrincipal.Text.ToDecimal

        'Convert interest rate to its decimal equivalent
        '  i.e. 12.75 becomes 0.1275
        decIntRate = txtIntRate.Text.ToDecimal / 100

        'Convert annual interest rate to monthly
        '  by dividing by 12 (months in a year)
        decIntRate = decIntRate / 12

        'Convert number of years to number of months
        '  by multiplying by 12 (months in a year)
        intTerm = txtTerm.Text.ToInt16 * 12

        'Calculate and display the monthly payment.
        '  The Format function makes the displayed number look good.
        dblPayment = decPrincipal *_
(decIntrate / (1 - (1 + decIntrate) ^ -intTerm))
        txtPayment.Text = Format(dblPayment, "#.00")
End Sub
```

Note

The loan payment calculator uses the same code as the previous chapter. Please read
the section "Writing Program Code" for an explanation of how the code works.

TESTING YOUR WEB APPLICATION

Click the start button to compile the program. The Internet Explorer browser should
appear and display your Web form, as pictured in Figure 3.8. Enter some sample numeric
values in the text boxes and click the link to calculate the loan payment. Note that the
Web version of the Loan Calculator works just like its Windows counterpart from
Chapter 2. One advantage of the Web version is that you should now be able to go to any
other machine on your network—even a PC without Visual Studio installed—and run the
application from your Internet browser.

Note

If Visual Studio gives you an error about not being able to attach to a debug session, you may need to install the remote debugging feature on the Web server. See the troubleshooting section at the end of this chapter for more details. However, you can still run the Web application manually by opening Internet Explorer and accessing the address `http://servername/LoanCalcApp/WebForm1.aspx`.

Figure 3.8
Web applications allow you to create applications that can run in a browser, eliminating the need for complex client installations.

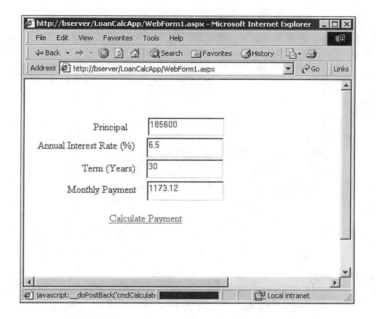

Users of previous versions of Visual Basic will especially appreciate the fact that Visual Studio allows you to create a functional Web site using the same techniques you would for any other VB program! As we will see later in the book, many of the other VB features you are familiar with, such as interactive debugging, can be used on the Web.

ENHANCING YOUR WEB APPLICATION

The sample loan payment calculator application displays the monthly payment in a text box control. However, it would be even more useful if it displayed the portion of interest and principal that make up each month's payment. This type of loan analysis is known as an *amortization schedule*. In this section, we will add an amortization schedule to the Loan Calculator program. By doing so, you will learn how to add Web forms to a project as well as display information in a tabular format.

ADDING A SECOND WEB FORM

As you may recall from Chapter 2, a new Windows Application project includes a single windows form, called Form1.vb. Similarly, a new Web Application includes a single Web form named WebForm1.aspx. To add a new Web form, right-click on the project name (LoanCalcApp) in the Solution Explorer. Choose Add WebForm from the pop-up menu and you will see the dialog box shown in Figure 3.9.

Figure 3.9
You can add new forms to a project from the Project menu, the Solution Explorer, or by pressing Ctrl+Shift+A for the New Project Item dialog box.

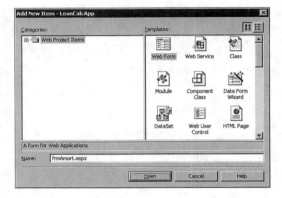

Change the name of the new Web form item in the Name box to frmAmort.aspx and press OK. The new Web form will be added to the Solution Explorer window.

> **Note**
>
> Attentive readers may be wondering why we left the name of the original as the default, WebForm1.aspx. You cannot change the name of a form when it is open, and Visual Studio .NET starts new projects with the form designer already open. The authors felt opening and closing forms would confuse beginners and detract from the more important concepts. However, when you have mastered the basics of working with forms, you should definitely start using descriptive form names for *all* your forms.

NAVIGATING TO A NEW WEB FORM

Now our sample Web application contains two forms. We need to provide a way for the user to switch from the first form to the second. To accomplish this, we will modify the original form we created in the last section (WebForm1.aspx). We will add a button to this form that causes the browser to display the new Web form (frmAmort.aspx). However, we do not want this button to be available until after the user has already determined the monthly payment, because the amounts from the first form are necessary for the amortization calculations. To add the button, follow these steps:

1. Right-click WebForm1.aspx and choose View Designer.
2. Display the Toolbox. Single-click the Button control.

3. Draw a Button control on the Web form and place it below the Calculate Payment link.

4. Press the F4 key to display the properties of the Button control.

5. Change the ID property of the button to cmdShowDetail.

6. Set the Visible property to False.

7. Change the Text property to Amortization Schedule.

When you have finished drawing the button, your Web form should look similar to Figure 3.10.

Figure 3.10
The Button and LinkButton controls appear differently but serve essentially the same purpose.

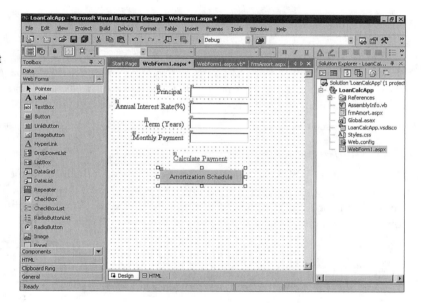

Now let's add some code. Right-click WebForm1.aspx and choose View Code. Find the code for the cmdCalculate_Click procedure you entered earlier. Add the following additional line of code just before the End Sub statement:

```
cmdShowDetail.Visible = True
```

The previous line of code simply makes the button visible to the user. The reason we added it to the end of the cmdCalculate_Click procedure is to make sure the user does not click the Button control until he has already clicked the LinkButton control to populate the data in the Payment text box.

Now, using the class and method drop-down boxes in the code editor, find the Click procedure for the cmdShowDetail button. Add the code in Listing 3.2.

LISTING 3.2 cmdShowDetail.zip—DISPLAYING THE DETAIL FORM

```
Public Sub cmdShowDetail_Click(ByVal sender As Object,_
ByVal e As System.EventArgs) Handles cmdShowDetail.Click

        'Store text box values in session variables
        Session.Add("Principal", txtPrincipal.Text)
        Session.Add("IntRate", txtIntRate.Text)
        Session.Add("Term", txtTerm.Text)
        Session.Add("Payment", txtPayment.Text)

        'Display the amortization form

        Response.Redirect("frmAmort.aspx")

End Sub
```

The code in Listing 3.2 stores the values of the text boxes as *session variables*. (Session variables are a way to store information on the server that needs to be shared between Web pages.) The final line of code uses the `Response.Redirect` method to display `frmAmort.aspx`.

→ For more information on session variables, **see** Chapter 17, "Using Active Server Pages.NET," **p. 443**

DESIGNING THE AMORTIZATION FORM

The amortization Web form contains a lot more data than the loan payment form. To display this data in a neatly organized manner, we will use the Table control. The Table control appears in the browser as a familiar HTML table. To add a Table control to the amortization form, do the following:

1. Right-click `frmAmort.aspx` in the Solution Explorer and choose View Designer.
2. Display the Toolbox and single-click the Table control.
3. Drag the Table control from the Toolbox window to the Web form.
4. Press F4 to display the Properties window.
5. Change the `ID` property of the table to `tblAmortize`.
6. Change the `GridLines` property of the table to `Both`.

After adding a Table control, your screen should look similar to Figure 3.11.

Like the other controls on a form, the table is an object with properties and methods. The table has a collection of row objects, and each row object contains a collection of cell objects. The cells in a table can contain text or even other controls. Although you can set up rows and cells at design time, in the sample application we will do everything dynamically using Visual Basic code.

→ For more information on the Table control, **see** Chapter 19, "Web Controls," **p. 501**

Right-click `frmAmort.aspx` in the Solution Explorer and choose View Code. Find the `Page_Load` method of the `frmAmort` object in the code editor and enter the code from Listing 3.3.

Figure 3.11
An empty Table
control appears as
a placeholder in
design mode.

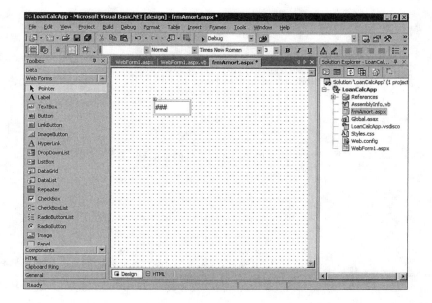

LISTING 3.3   frmDetailLoad.zip

```vb
Private Sub Page_Load(ByVal sender As System.Object,_
ByVal e As System.EventArgs) Handles MyBase.Load
        Dim intTerm As Integer              'Term, in years
        Dim decPrincipal As Decimal         'Principal amount $
        Dim decIntRate As Decimal           'Interest rate %
        Dim dblPaymnent As Double           'Monthly payment $

        Dim decMonthInterest As Decimal     'Interest part of monthly payment
        Dim decTotalInterest As Decimal = 0 'Total interest paid
        Dim decMonthPrincipal As Decimal    'Principal part of monthly payment
        Dim decTotalPrincipal As Decimal = 0 'Remaining principal

        Dim intMonth As Integer             'Current month
        Dim intNumPayments As Integer       'Number of monthly payments
        Dim i As Integer                    'Temporary loop counter
        Dim rowTemp As TableRow             'Temporary row object
        Dim celTemp As TableCell            'Temporary cell object


        If Not IsPostBack Then   ' Evals true first time browser hits the page

            'SET UP THE TABLE HEADER ROW
            rowTemp = New TableRow()
            For i = 0 To 4
                celTemp = New TableCell()
                rowTemp.Cells.Add(celTemp)
                celTemp = Nothing
            Next
            rowTemp.Cells(0).Text = "Payment"
            rowTemp.Cells(1).Text = "Interest"
```

LISTING 3.3 CONTINUED

```
        rowTemp.Cells(2).Text = "Principal"
        rowTemp.Cells(3).Text = "Total Int."
        rowTemp.Cells(4).Text = "Balance"
        rowTemp.Font.Bold = True
        tblAmortize.Rows.Add(rowTemp)

        'PULL VALUES FROM SESSION VARIABLES

        intTerm = Convert.ToInt32(Session("Term"))
        decPrincipal = Convert.ToDecimal(Session("Principal"))
        decIntRate = Convert.ToDecimal(Session("IntRate"))
        dblPaymnent = Convert.ToDouble(Session("Payment"))

        'CALCULATE AMORTIZATION SCHEDULE
        intNumPayments = intTerm * 12
        decTotalPrincipal = decPrincipal
        For intMonth = 1 To intNumPayments
            'Determine Values for the Current Row
            decMonthInterest = (decIntRate / 100) / 12 * decTotalPrincipal
            decTotalInterest = decTotalInterest + decMonthInterest
            decMonthPrincipal = Convert.ToDecimal(dblPaymnent)_
- decMonthInterest
            If decMonthPrincipal > decPrincipal Then
                decMonthPrincipal = decPrincipal
            End If
            decTotalPrincipal = decTotalPrincipal - decMonthPrincipal

            'Add the values to the table
            rowTemp = New TableRow()
            For i = 0 To 4
                celTemp = New TableCell()
                rowTemp.Cells.Add(celTemp)
                celTemp = Nothing
            Next i
            rowTemp.Cells(0).Text = intMonth.ToString
            rowTemp.Cells(1).Text = Format(decMonthInterest, "$###0.00")
            rowTemp.Cells(2).Text = Format(decMonthPrincipal, "$###0.00")
            rowTemp.Cells(3).Text = Format(decTotalInterest, "$###0.00")
            rowTemp.Cells(4).Text = Format(decTotalPrincipal, "$###0.00")
            tblAmortize.Rows.Add(rowTemp)
            rowTemp = Nothing
        Next intMonth

    End If

End Sub
```

The code in Listing 3.3 may seem like a lot to take in at first, but it is actually very simple. First, we create the header row of the table by creating individual TableCell objects and appending them to a TableRow object. The temporary variables rowTemp and celTemp are used to set up the table. Next, several variables are assigned values from session variables, which were provided by the previous Web form. Finally, we enter a loop that uses variable values and mathematics to calculate each month's payments. After determining the values, a new row is added to the table.

One interesting thing to note about this code is that it all takes place in the `frmDetail_Load` procedure, which is executed when the Web page is loaded. The `If` statement checks the `NotPostBack` property so that the code is only executed the first time this page is requested.

TESTING THE PROGRAM

To test your program, click the Start button on the toolbar or press the F5 key. Internet Explorer will start and you will see the loan payment form, as shown in Figure 3.10. Enter the following values:

> Principal: `175000`
>
> Term: `30`
>
> Interest Rate: `7.5`

Click the `Calculate Payment` link. The Payment text box should be populated with the value `1223.63` and the Amortization Schedule button should appear. Click the button and you should see the Amortization schedule pictured in Figure 3.12.

Figure 3.12
A Table control provides an easy way to format data in a grid-like fashion.

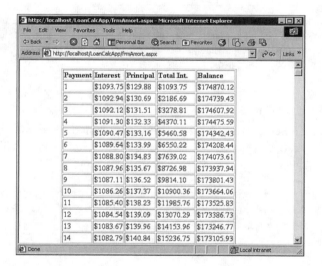

If you understand how the Loan Calculator application works, then you have learned some important fundamental concepts of Web applications. However, in these few pages we have only scratched the surface of a vast new area in Visual Basic .NET. Check out the topics of interest in this area:

- Working with styles, client-side script, and HTML is covered in Chapter 18, "Web Applications and Services."

- More in-depth coverage of the controls you use with Web forms is discussed in Chapter 19, "Web Controls."

- Debugging your Visual Basic code is discussed in Chapter 26, "Debugging and Performance Tuning."

- More on Active Server Pages can be found in Chapter 17, "Using Active Server Pages.NET."

TROUBLESHOOTING WEB APPLICATIONS

Web applications involve communication between multiple computer programs, specifically the Web browser and the Web server. Usually these programs reside on separate machines connected to a network. As you might imagine, problems can arise if your Web server or network is not configured correctly. In this section we will discuss some basic troubleshooting steps that may help you with common problems.

For terminology purposes, we will refer to the PC on which you have installed Visual Studio .NET as the *development machine* and the PC or server running Microsoft Internet Information Services as the *Web server*. These may or may not refer to the same physical computer. The term *browser* refers to the Microsoft Internet Explorer Web browser.

Note
It is acceptable to run a Web server on your development machine for testing, especially if you are uncomfortable with making configuration changes. However, for serious team development efforts or when publishing the final product, you will need to have a separate, dedicated Web server.

VALIDATING IIS INSTALLATION

Internet Information Server (IIS) is the Web server program created by Microsoft. It is bundled with many operating systems, such as Windows 2000 and Windows NT, and available as an add-on for others.

Note
The troubleshooting steps in this section are based on Windows 2000, but can be used as a general guide.

The first step in making sure that IIS is installed and running is displaying the home page in your browser. This was described in the earlier section, "Connecting to Your Web Server."

Note
An "Under Construction" page does not mean anything is wrong with the Web server, just that there are no Web pages published. This is actually a good sign; if you can display an under construction page from your development machine, the Web server is working.

If you cannot access the Web server from a browser on your development machine, it may indicate one of the following problems:

- Internet Information Services has not been installed.

■ There is a network connectivity problem between the development machine and the Web server, or you are using an incorrect Web server address.

INSTALLING IIS

To determine whether IIS is installed, go to the Web server and display the control panel. Find the Services icon (located under Administrative Tools in Windows 2000). In the list of services, look for the World Wide Web Publishing Service and make sure the status is Started, as pictured in Figure 3.13.

Figure 3.13
The World Wide Web Publishing service is not installed by default on Windows 2000 Professional, but can be easily added from the installation CD.

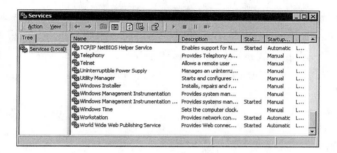

If you do not see the World Wide Web Publishing Service listed, you will need to install IIS or use another computer as the Web server. The following steps describe how to add Internet Information Services to a computer that is running the Windows 2000 Professional operating system.

1. Click the Start button, Settings menu, and the Control Panel icon.
2. Double-click the Add/Remove Programs icon.
3. Click the Add/Remove Windows Components icon.
4. In the list of components, find Internet Information Services. If the check box beside it is not selected, click it. If the check box is already selected, click the Details button and make sure all of the sub-components are selected.
5. Click Next and continue following the onscreen instructions. You may be prompted to insert the Windows installation CD.

When the World Wide Web publishing service is running in the services list as shown in Figure 3.13, you should first try to open Internet Explorer *on the server itself* and display the http://localhost address. If the browser test is successful from the Web server, try it from the development machine.

CHECKING NETWORK CONNECTIVITY

If you still cannot connect to the Web server from the development machine, this may indicate a network problem between the two machines. To troubleshoot most networking problems, you will need two key pieces of information: the computer's unique name and numeric network address (known as the IP address). If you are running Windows 2000, perform the following steps to determine this information:

1. Right-click the My Computer icon, select Properties, and click the Network Identification tab to determine the computer's name.

2. Open a Command Prompt window (under the Accessories menu), type IPCONFIG and press Enter to display the computer's IP address.

Although troubleshooting network connectivity problems in detail is beyond the scope of this book, the simple PING test described next may help. The PING command is often used as a test of network connectivity between two machines. It works by sending a signal to the specified machine and informing the sender if a reply is received and how fast.

1. From the development machine, open a Command Prompt window.

2. Type **PING** followed by a space and the Web server name. Press Enter and note the response.

3. Type **PING** followed by a space and the Web server IP address. Press Enter and note the response.

The results of a successful ping test are displayed in Figure 3.14.

If PING tests fail for both the name and address, contact your network administrator for help. If you have a home network, consult the documentation included with your network equipment.

If both PING tests are successful, you should be able to connect to the Web server.

If the PING by number is successful but the PING by name is not, you can try either of the following options:

1. Use the numeric address to access your Web server, as in http://192.168.0.1.

2. Locate the HOSTS. file on your machine. Contained within this file are instructions for adding the IP address so that you can access the machine by name.

The World cannot Wide Web has a lot of information about setting up and configuring networks. For example, the Web site http://www.howstuffworks.com/home-network.htm contains some useful information about setting up a network in your home.

INSTALLING THE .NET FRAMEWORK

The Microsoft .NET framework includes the Common Language Runtime and other important files needed by .NET applications. The .NET framework must be installed on the Web server. If you are using the same physical machine for development and Web services, you already installed it with Visual Studio .NET.

If you are using a separate computer than your development machine as a Web server, you may need to install the .NET framework. The .NET framework is a major Microsoft initiative and will probably be included in future operating systems and service packs for the current ones. However, at the time of this writing, it had to be installed as an add-on in the form of the Microsoft .NET Software Development Kit (SDK).

To install the .NET framework on a separate Web server, please see the readme.htm file that accompanies Visual Studio .NET. The section "Configuring the Server Computer" contains instructions for configuring a remote Web server for use with Visual Studio .NET.

At the time of this writing, we were able to prepare a computer for use as a remote Web server by performing the following steps:

1. Install Windows 2000 Professional.

2. Add IIS components as described in the previous section, "Validating IIS Installation."

3. Begin the installation of Visual Studio .NET. Install the Windows Component Update (Part 1).

4. When the Windows Component Update has finished installing, click Server Setup, located in the lower corner of the Visual Studio .NET Setup screen. After clicking this link, you should see the Server Setup screen. Scroll down the list of server components until you see the Web Development section, pictured in Figure 3.15.

5. Click the Install button to configure the Web Development components.

6. Run Visual Studio .NET setup and install the Remote Debugger.

7. Restart the computer.

Figure 3.15
In order to debug Web Applications on a remote Web server, you may need to install the Web Development Server Components of Visual Studio .NET.

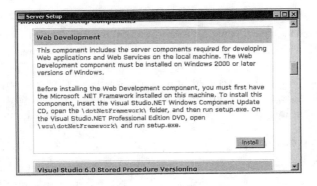

Note

At the time of this writing, we could run Web Applications successfully on a remote machine by just installing the .NET SDK from Microsoft's Web site. However, for remote debugging to work we had to perform the steps described previously.

WEB ACCESS MODES

As you learned earlier in this chapter, the files that make up your Web application reside on a Web server. Visual Studio .NET updates these files on the server when you create or run your Web Applications. There are actually two *Web access modes* Visual Studio .NET uses to communicate with a Web server:

- **FrontPage Extensions**—These extensions are an add-on to IIS that allows Visual Studio .NET to access files on the Web server using only the Web server address.
- **File Share Access**—Requires a network drive connection to the hard drive of the Web server where the application files are stored.

If you followed the instructions in the earlier section entitled "Validating IIS Installation" or those in the Visual Studio .NET readme.htm file, you installed the FrontPage Extensions. By default, Visual Studio .NET will attempt to connect using file share access over the \\machinename\wwwroot$\application share. If Visual Studio cannot connect to your Web server, you may see a message similar to Figure 3.16.

Figure 3.16
Visual Studio .NET can publish Web applications via the FrontPage extensions or network file shares.

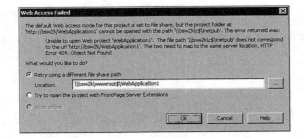

Some users or Web server administrators may not want to install the FrontPage extensions on their Web server. This may be due to (unfounded or not) fears of hackers or excessive use of server resources. (However, FrontPage extensions should be safe to install on a development Web server. They are not required for the application to run in production.) For more details on the advantages and disadvantages of each Web access method, see the "Web Access Methods" topic in the Help files.

> **Note**
>
> Even if you have FrontPage extensions installed, you may run into problems if they are not configured correctly. In addition to the message shown in Figure 3.16, Visual Studio may ask you to configure or check server extensions. To find these options, perform the following steps:
>
> 1. Right-click the My Computer icon and choose Manage.
> 2. Under Services and Applications, find Internet Information Services and expand the menu tree.
> 3. Right-click the Default Web site in your IIS manager.
>
> The All Tasks submenu contains these options.

If you want to access a Web application without using FrontPage extensions, you can use file share access. To do this you must provide a path to get to the Web application directory via the file system. For example, if you are using your local drive, `C:\Inetpub\WWWRoot\LoanCalcApp` might be the path. If the Web server is a separate machine from the development machine, you will have to provide a path using a mapped network drive or UNC path.

CHAPTER 4

UNDERSTANDING THE DEVELOPMENT ENVIRONMENT

In this chapter

GETTING STARTED

The easiest way to learn is by doing; that is why we began the book with chapters that included the step-by-step creation of sample applications. However, the user interface changes in Visual Studio .NET are so far reaching that an in-depth exploration of them may be helpful as well. During this chapter we will explain many different aspects and new features of Visual Studio .NET. Please follow along where applicable, and feel free to refer to this chapter while reading the rest of the book.

THE VISUAL STUDIO START PAGE

Just about every recent update to a Microsoft product has included a Web browser interface somewhere. Visual Studio .NET is no exception to this trend. As you can see from Figure 4.1, starting the latest version of Visual Studio displays the Visual Studio Start Page, which is a Web page containing links to recent projects and other items of interest.

Figure 4.1
One result of Visual Studio's cosmetic overhaul is the addition of the Visual Studio Start Page.

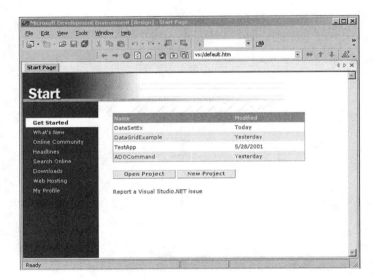

The Start Page lists the names of recently opened Visual Studio projects, plus includes hyperlinks to create a new project or open a project file from disk. You can, of course, accomplish these same tasks from the File menu, although because the Web page requires only a single mouse click, you may find it to be a bit quicker.

Note

The Start Page is really a Web page; the files associated with it are stored in Visual Studio's \common\ide\html directory. An adventurous user might want to try customizing these files to make the Start Page even more useful.

The Start Page also includes sections that link you to Web resources and customizes certain settings within the development environment, which we will discuss at the end of the chapter.

CREATING AND OPENING PROJECTS

As with previous versions, one basic unit of work in Visual Basic is a project. When you use Visual Basic .NET, you are generally working with one or more open projects. Projects are organizers for related components (screens, code, and so forth) of an application. Solutions, which will be discussed in the following section, are containers for one or more projects. To start a new project, click the Create a New Project link on the Start Page to display the New Project dialog box (see Figure 4.2).

Figure 4.2
Visual Studio .NET's New Project dialog box includes not only Visual Basic projects, but also those for other programming languages in the Visual Studio family.

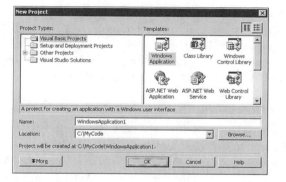

PART

I

CH

4

There are many different types of VB projects; the one you select depends on the type of application you want to create. There are projects to create user interfaces for both Windows and the Web, as well as projects to create services and business-layer components used by these applications. The following list summarizes the different types of projects you can create using Visual Basic .NET:

 Windows Application—Creates an application with a Windows user interface, similar to the Standard EXE application in previous versions of Visual Basic.

 Class Library—Creates a DLL containing one or more classes, which can be accessed from other applications. This type of application is where you create your business objects for use in a client-server or multi-tier application. (Similar to VB6's ActiveX DLL project.)

 Windows Control Library—Creates a Windows custom control. (Similar to an ActiveX control in previous versions of VB.)

 Web Application—Creates a Web application on a Web server. Although you can design Web applications in Visual Studio much like Windows applications, the output is a Web site instead of a Windows executable. This allows others to access your application over a network using their Web browsers.

Web Service—Creates a project on a Web server, which provides services to other applications over the Web.

 Web Control Library—Creates a custom control using Web forms.

 Console Application—A Windows application without forms, this application does all of its input/output in a command prompt window.

 Windows Service—A service accessible over a Windows network.

 Empty Project—A blank Visual Studio project.

 Empty Web Project—A blank Visual Studio Web project.

 New Project in Existing Folder—Creates an empty project associated with a specified folder.

Many of these different project types are covered in more detail throughout the book. As you may have noticed, two main categories stand out—Web projects and Windows projects. This book contains two major sections, each dealing with a specific area—Part III, "Working with Windows," and Part IV, "Working with the Web."

WORKING WITH PROJECT FILES

Let's try a simple exercise in creating a new project. From the Visual Studio home page, click the link titled Create a New Project and you will see the New Project dialog box. Under the list of project types, select the Visual Basic folder. Select the Windows Application project type by single-clicking the Windows Application icon. Next, enter `MyWinApp` in the Name box. Also, make a mental note of the directory listed in the Location box. Finally, click the OK button and Visual Studio will set up your new project. The new project contains a single Windows form called `Form1.vb`. (This should be familiar to users of previous versions of Visual Basic, because the Standard EXE project also by default includes a single form.)

Next, let's look at some of the files that have been created behind the scenes, even before you have written the first line of Visual Basic code. Minimize your Visual Studio window so that you can see your Windows desktop. Right-click the My Computer icon and choose Explore from the menu to launch the Windows Explorer. Now, navigate to the directory that was listed in the Location box when you created the project. (For example, my directory is `C:\Documents and Settings\Administrator\My Documents\Visual Studio Projects\MyWinApp`.) Notice that several files have been created by Visual Studio .NET in this directory. The following files are most important in the context of our discussion of projects and solutions:

- `Form1.vb` and `Form1.resx`—These files contain the VB code and design of your form. They replace the .frm and .frx files from previous versions of Visual Basic.

- `MyWinApp.vbproj`—This file is the project file, equivalent to the .vbp and .mak files from previous versions of Visual Basic.

- **Assemblyinfo.vb**—Compiled components in the .NET world are known as assemblies. This file contains general information about your assembly, such as the product version number.

- **MyWinApp.sln**—This is the solution file. As we will learn in the next section, a solution organizes a group of one or more projects.

In addition to the previously mentioned files, Visual Studio creates some additional files and directories that contain user settings and intermediate files used during the compile process. We will discuss some of these later in the book. It is important to note that the files listed previously are the only ones necessary to move your project code to another VB developer's computer. (The solution file isn't strictly necessary because it can be recreated, but is especially helpful if your solution contains multiple projects.) The `bin` and `obj` directories contain compiler output files and will be automatically re-created if they are deleted or missing.

Tip

By default, Visual Studio stores projects in the `My Documents\Visual Studio Projects` folder. You may find it more convenient to create a shorter folder name in which to save your projects, especially if you like using the command prompt. I usually use place my Visual Basic projects in their own folders underneath a `Projects` or `VBCode` folder, which is located only one level deep on the hard drive. The default directory For projects can be changed in the Visual Studio Environment settings, as described at the end of this chapter.

→ For more information on distributing your finished programs, **see** Appendix A, "Packaging Your Applications" **p. 761**

It is also interesting to note that that most files in Visual Studio are text-based and use the XML format. This means they can be viewed (and edited) using any text editor such as Notepad. Taken a step further, you can actually create an entire VB program using a text editor and then compile it using the command-line compiler. This means it is possible to create Visual Basic applications without even using Visual Studio .NET Of course, for large projects, using a text editor may be somewhat impractical, and we think that Visual Studio provides enough value to warrant its existence as a development tool!

Tip

Placing a shortcut to notepad.exe (or another text editor) in your `SendTo` directory is invaluable because it allows you to right-click any file and view it. Your `SendTo` directory is either located under the `Documents And Settings` folder for your user ID, or the `Windows` directory.

When you created the sample `MyWinApp` project, all the files were saved to disk immediately. This is possible because Visual Basic .NET requires you to set a project Name and Location *before* you start working on the project. The location is the home directory for your project, which contains associated project files. This is a welcome departure from the old approach, which requires manual creation of a project directory and then saving each file in a project individually. In Visual Basic .NET, the project directory is created by default using the project name, and new forms and code files you create in Visual Studio are saved in that directory.

UNDERSTANDING SOLUTIONS

The term *project* has been around since the beginning of Visual Basic. However, starting with Visual Studio .NET, a new organizational term has been introduced—the *solution*. Users of Visual Studio .NET should understand the difference between a project and a solution. Projects, as you already know, contain the component pieces of your application, such as forms or modules of code. Each of these pieces is stored in a separate file on the disk.

Solutions represent the Visual Studio workspace. Therefore, they may encompass multiple projects. (Solutions are roughly similar to Visual Basic project groups from previous versions, with the exception that you are always working in a solution, even if it only contains a single project.)

Note

A project can be thought of as a file that points to a bunch of other files. For example, if you have created a VB application with 10 forms, the project file is what knows these 10 forms are part of the same project. Similarly, the solution file knows which projects go together, and represents a snapshot of a group of open projects.

To further clarify, there are two solution-related options available when creating a new project:

- **Add to Solution**—Adds the project to whatever projects you already have open. For example, when you create a Class Library project, you will want to create another type of project (such as a Windows Application) to test your class. In this case, the solution would contain two projects.

- **Close Solution**—Closes whatever solution you were working on previously, and creates the new project in its own solution.

Note

Another interesting new feature in Visual Basic .NET is the ability to add items to your solution that are not necessarily related to your Visual Basic code. For example, you can associate text files, SQL queries, Word documents, or pictures with projects and solutions and launch them from within Visual Studio .NET.

To display these options, click the More button on the New Project dialog box, as pictured in Figure 4.2

UNDERSTANDING THE SOLUTION EXPLORER

One of the most important parts of Visual Studio .NET is the Solution Explorer, as shown in Figure 4.3. The Solution Explorer displays the names of all the different items in your project in a hierarchical list. At the top of the hierarchy is the name of the current solution; beneath the solution name each project is listed with sections for files and references. After the projects other non-project items and files are listed.

Figure 4.3
The Solution Explorer can be displayed from the View menu.

ADDING ITEMS TO A PROJECT

Let's continue with our sample project from the previous section, MyWinApp, to demonstrate adding items to the project using the Solution Explorer. (If you have already closed the sample application, just click on the appropriate link on the Visual Studio Home Page to re-open it.)

Figure 4.3 shows the Solution Explorer as we left it from the last section. Note there is one form in our project, aptly named Form1.vb. Let's add an additional form to the project. To do this, right-click the project name (second line from the top) and expand the Add menu. Choose the Add New Item option and you will see the dialog box pictured in Figure 4.4.

Figure 4.4
There are many different types of items you can add to your Visual Basic projects.

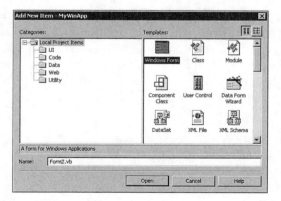

PART

I

CH

4

As you can see from the figure, these available project items are divided into categories. Expand the Local Project Items folder and then single-click the UI folder underneath it. This will filter the list of item templates on the right side of the screen to include only the user-interface items. For this example, we want to add a new Windows Form to our project, so single-click Windows Form in the template list. Finally, notice the default name of `form2.vb` is suggested. Normally good programming practice would dictate that we change such a non-descriptive name, but for the purposes of this UI discussion, just click the Open button to accept the default name. The new form should be added to the project. Your Solution Explorer should now look similar to Figure 4.5.

Note

Users of previous versions of Visual Basic may be wondering about the new Inherited Form option, which allows adding a new form that mimics another form's visual characteristics. For more on Inherited forms, see Chapter 10, "Understanding Windows Forms."

Figure 4.5
The Solution Explorer after adding an additional form to the sample project.

NAVIGATING WITH THE SOLUTION EXPLORER

Now that we have seen how you can add items to a project with the Solution Explorer, let's look further at its main purpose: project navigation. Much like using the Windows Explorer to manipulate files on your hard drive, you use the Solution Explorer to access components within your Visual Studio projects and solutions. Previous versions of Visual Basic had something called the Project Explorer, and the Solution Explorer works very much the same way with respect to navigating between forms. You can jump to either the code window or the designer window for a form by right-clicking the object and selecting the appropriate menu option, or using the toolbar.

To demonstrate, right-click the Form1.vb object in the Solution Explorer window. A menu will appear. Click View Designer and you will see the visual component of the form, which appears as a gray square. Right-click the form again and choose View Code. You will see the VB code stored in the form object. These options are also toolbar buttons on the Solution Explorer. A third button, the Properties button, allows you to view the file properties of the selected object.

Note

The *file properties* of a form in the Solution Explorer are different from the *object properties* that can be accessed by right-clicking the object in the designer.

ADDING ADDITIONAL PROJECTS

Our sample solution currently only contains one project. Let's make things more interesting by adding an additional project to see how it affects the Solution Explorer. Right-click the solution name, `MyWinApp`, which is listed on the topmost line of the Solution Explorer. Choose Add, then New Project and you will again see the New Project dialog box pictured in Figure 4.2. This time select the Class Library project template and click the OK button. Visual Studio will create a new Class Library project in the current solution and cause the Solution Explorer to look similar to Figure 4.6.

Figure 4.6
The Solution Explorer with multiple projects open.

PART

I

CH

4

Note

When multiple projects are open, the project shown in boldface is the *startup project*. The startup project usually represents the UI portion of your solution and is the project that will be started when you click the Run button.

The solution shown in Figure 4.7 is fairly typical in that it includes a class that (presumably) contains business logic along with a UI project to use it. However, a solution is just an organizational structure for projects. Before a project can use functionality from another project, you will need to add a *reference*.

ADDING REFERENCES TO A PROJECT

As you may have already noticed, each project in the Solution Explorer contains a References folder. By *referencing* a library of functions that is external to a project, you can make those functions available to the project. Often these functions are located in a DLL file on your hard drive. One example might be a DLL that interacts with video camera hardware and provides functions to control the camera from Visual Basic. (DLL stands for

Dynamic Link Library and is just a type of file that can be installed on your system. In Visual Studio .NET, Microsoft's documentation calls these groups of external functions *assemblies* and points out that they may be contained in a variety of files.)

Note

The fact that project references are displayed in this manner is a change new to this version of Visual Basic. In previous versions, references were only accessible from a menu.

Expand the References folder and you will see several entries, most of which begin with `System`. These references contain functionality provided by the .NET framework that is included in new projects by default. For example, `System.Windows.Forms` is necessary for drawing a form.

When you add a reference, it does not necessarily have to be an externally compiled program or group of system functions. Often during VB development you will reference other VB projects. Consider our sample solution, which contains a Class Library project, `ClassLibrary1`. If you want to use this class's methods from the `MyWinApp` project, you might create an instance of the class by placing the following lines of code somewhere in `form1.vb`:

```
Dim objTemp As ClassLibrary1.Class1
objTemp = New ClassLibrary1.Class1
```

→ For more information on creating your own classes, **see** Chapter 9, "Creating Code Components," **p. 223**

However, without adding a reference, the VB compiler will find errors in the code because it does not know the class name. To make the classes in the `ClassLibrary1` project known to the `MyWinApp` project, you have to add a reference. Just because two projects are loaded in the same solution does not mean that their code components are meant to interact.

Let's continue our example by adding a reference. Right-click the word *References* under the `MyWinApp` project and choose Add Reference from the menu. The References dialog box shown in Figure 4.7 will appear.

Figure 4.7
The References dialog box is organized according to components from the .NET framework, COM components, and Projects.

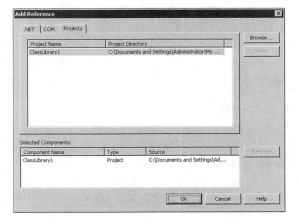

Click the Projects tab, and you will see the class library project. Click the Select button and OK, and ClassLibrary1 will be added to the references list of the MyWinApp project.

If you do not feel you have a firm enough grasp on references, do not worry! This section was intended to introduce them from the point of view of the Project Explorer, rather than explore their relationship to VB code.

→ To learn more about assemblies, references, and namespaces, **see** Chapter 5, "Visual Basic Building Blocks," **p. 113**

THE VISUAL STUDIO .NET WORK AREA

As you can see in Figure 4.8, there are a lot of windows open during a typical Visual Studio .NET session. Each window has a different purpose related to the design or execution of your project. In the very early days of VB, each of these windows was a top-level window within the operating system and could be stacked or moved independently. Recent versions of Visual Basic have used a more structured, Multiple Document Interface (MDI) environment in which child windows are docked within the boundaries of a parent window. VB.NET continues to take the organized approach but, like its predecessors, can be adjusted to suit individual tastes. This section explores the different windows you will encounter within Visual Studio.

PART

I

CH

4

UNDERSTANDING WINDOW BEHAVIOR

Figure 4.8 shows examples of the different window styles available in Visual Studio .NET. Each type of window has a different behavior in relation to other open windows. For example, some windows obscure parts of other windows when visible, instead of merging with the parent window. As you work with windows in the Visual Studio environment, you may want to try different window settings to find the window arrangement with which you are most comfortable.

AUTO-HIDE WINDOWS

Auto-hide windows are new to VB .NET. They appear as flat buttons on the outer edge of the screen (for example, the Server Explorer and Toolbox in Figure 4.8). Hovering over the icon causes the window to slide out and display its contents. When an auto-hide window loses focus, it slides off the screen automatically. The title of the most recently displayed auto-hide window is displayed adjacent to the icon. Only the Server Explorer and Toolbox are set to auto-hide mode by default.

Tip

Auto-hide windows seem like they will be great for tasks that are mouse-oriented, such as drawing controls on a form. Because the Toolbox window is used during design only, more screen real estate is available for code and other windows to display debugging information.

Figure 4.8
Visual Basic .NET
has several styles of
windows. To change
the appearance of a
window, right-click its
title bar to display the
context menu.

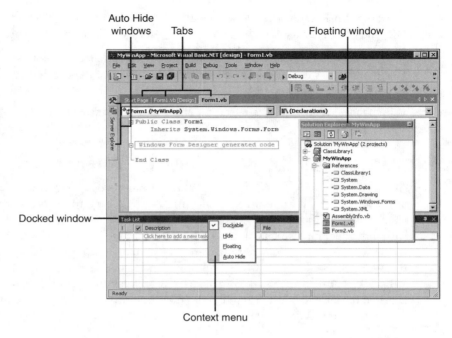

Auto Hide windows   Tabs   Floating window

Docked window

Context menu

> **Note**
>
> Click the thumbtack icon to make an auto-hide window remain visible on the screen.

DOCKABLE WINDOWS

Dockable windows are resizable windows that can be anchored in a fixed position within the development environment. When docked windows are resized, other docked windows take up the unused space. The advantage of a docked window is that it can be positioned to remain visible at the same time as other docked windows.

In order to free a dockable window, right-click the title bar and choose Floating from the menu. (If you do not select floating, then the window will jump to the tab box.)

To dock a window within the development environment, first make sure Dockable is selected. Next, drag the window to the title bar of another window to dock it. As with previous versions of VB, docking can be a bit tricky; it may require practice before you get comfortable with it.

FLOATING WINDOWS

You can position floating windows on top of other windows within the development environment. The advantage of a floating window is that it can be displayed quickly without a lot of resizing. One example is using the Properties window during form design. If the Properties window is docked, you may have to resize it to read all of the text. By using floating mode, you can display it by pressing its shortcut key (function key F4), set the properties, and then close the window.

Note

A floating window can be especially useful when you have memorized the shortcut key to display it. For example, pressing Ctrl+Alt+L (or Ctrl+R, depending on your profile settings) displays the Solution Explorer, which can be used as a starting point to navigate to any other window in your project.

TABBED DOCUMENT AREA

You may notice in Figure 4.8 that the code windows are organized using tabs, much like the tabs on a file folder. This is a new feature in Visual Studio .NET, which allows you to quickly access the documents in your project, such as Web pages, code, and forms. To select a tab, just single-click the tab's title and the corresponding window is displayed.

Note

You can use Ctrl+F6 to quickly cycle through the tab windows, or Ctrl+F4 to close the current window. (These have been standard Windows keystrokes for a long time. In addition, Alt+F4 will close an active top-level window.)

If you look closely at the tabbed section in Figure 4.8, you will notice three small buttons on the far right of the tabs. If you have opened so many documents that all of their tabs will not fit on the screen, you can use the arrow buttons to scroll the tabs left or right. The third button closes the current window.

You can customize the look of your tabbed documents by re-ordering the tabs and creating additional tab groups. To create a new tab group, right-click on the title of a window you want to include in the new group and a context menu will appear. You may choose to create a new tab group with either horizontal or vertical orientation. Figure 4.9 shows a screen with two horizontal tab groups.

PART

I

CH

4

Figure 4.9
Visual Studio allows you to organize code and design windows using multiple tab groups.

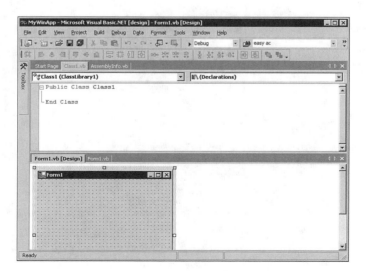

By dragging tabs with your mouse, you can re-order documents within a tab group or move a document window to another tab group. To remove a tab group, either drag all documents out of it or repeatedly click the close button until all tabs have disappeared. Note that while you can have multiple tab groups, they all must have the same orientation; that is, you can have horizontal or vertical groups but not both.

Note
An asterisk (*) next to the title of a document tab indicates changes have been made but not yet saved to disk.

MAKING THE MOST OF AVAILABLE SCREEN SPACE

Power users of the Visual Studio .NET environment will want to have a lot of windows open at once. For example, as you type in the code window, the dynamic help and task list continuously update themselves with pertinent information. You may also want to display immediate or watch windows while simultaneously viewing code. To use all of the information effectively, we suggest that you increase desktop video resolution to 1,024 × 768 or higher. (For readability purposes, photos in this book are taken at a resolution of 800 pixels × 600 pixels.)

Right-click the background of your Windows desktop and choose Properties from the context menu. Select the Settings tab, as pictured in Figure 4.10, and change your screen area to a size with which you are comfortable. Some developers even go so far as to use Windows' multiple monitor support, which allows you to create a desktop that spans more than one monitor!

Figure 4.10
For the best possible development experience, set your desktop area to a high resolution.

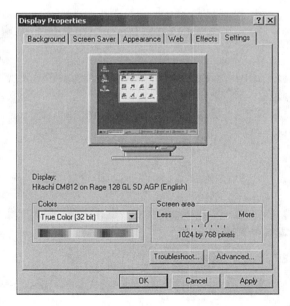

DESIGNING VISUAL COMPONENTS

One special type of window in the Visual Studio work area is a Designer window. Designer windows are where you draw the look of your Visual Studio .NET applications, just as an artist paints on a canvas. Designing the look of your program is often the most fun part of using Visual Basic. Unlike the code, which is hidden from the user, the design allows the programmer to show off his or her creativity.

Note

If you have been paying attention, you probably realize by now that many objects in your applications have both a visual component as well as a code component. These two components may be part of the same object, such as a Windows form. A Windows form designer is indicated by the word [Design] next to the document title.

If you read the introductory chapter, then you already know the basic process of adding controls to a form. In this section, we will discuss some of the finer points, such as working with groups of controls.

→ If you are not familiar with the basics of drawing controls, **see** Chapter 2, "Creating Your First Windows Application," **p. 21**

To perform the exercises in this section, you will need to set up a sample project. Using knowledge you have acquired from Chapter 2, "Creating Your First Windows Application," and earlier in this chapter, perform the following tasks:

1. Start Visual Studio and create a new Windows Application project.
2. Place three TextBox controls on the form.
3. Place a Label control on the form beside each text box.
4. Place a Button control on the form.

Finally, align the various controls so they look similar to Figure 4.11. Creating this example will allow you to easily follow along with the concepts described in the text.

MOVING AND SIZING CONTROLS

To arrange controls on a form, you must move and resize them. These activities are almost second nature to a Visual Basic programmer, but worth mentioning because of some changes in Visual Studio .NET.

To demonstrate, single-click the topmost textbox on the sample form. Notice the dashed line that appears at the outer edge of the textbox, indicating that it is the selected control. After you have selected the control, try pressing the arrow keys on your keyboard while holding down the Ctrl key. Notice that the control moves around on the screen, providing a more precise control of movement than the mouse. This is a new feature in Visual Studio .NET. (You can also move controls in the traditional manner as we did in Chapter 2 by clicking and dragging with the mouse.)

PART

I

CH

4

Figure 4.11
Making controls line up is easy thanks to the grid of dots in the background of the form.

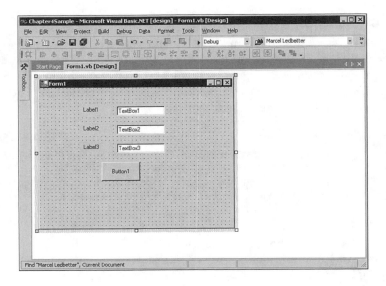

When you move a control with the mouse, its default behavior is to align itself with the grid of dots displayed on the background of the form. (This grid is not displayed when your program is running, but instead is merely a design aid.) Often developers will want to position objects with more or less more precision than that provided by the default grid settings. Even in previous versions of Visual Basic, developers have been able to change the size of the grid or disable the grid to allow free-form control alignment. However, a great new addition to this version of Visual Studio is the ability to set these options on a per-form basis! This is accomplished through the Form Properties window.

To change the grid settings, first select the form by single-clicking in an area that is on the form but outside a control. Next, press F4 to display the Properties window and find the GridSize property. The default setting of 8 pixels between dots provides a lot of precision, but the setting can be changed as low as 2×2 if desired. Another property, SnaptoGrid, determines whether or not the controls automatically align themselves with the grid.

Note

The Windows Forms Designer options folder (under the Tools, Options menu) lets you set the grid size for new forms. Even though the grid size can be set on a per-form basis, you may want to set this option to specify a default size for new forms.

In addition to changing a control's position, you will usually end up changing either its height or width to make it look the way you want. You can resize controls using the keyboard arrows in combination with the Ctrl and Shift keys, or by dragging the mouse. To demonstrate keyboard resizing, first single-click any text box on our sample form. Next, press either the right or left arrow key while simultaneously holding down the Shift and Ctrl keys to change the width of the text box.

Before we leave the topic of resizing controls, let's take a closer look at what happens when you select a control. Figure 4.12 shows our sample form with the TextBox1 control selected.

Note that some of the boxes around the edge of the text box are white in the center while others are gray. This is a new feature in Visual Studio .NET that indicates whether or not to resizing is allowed in a particular dimension. When you position the mouse over an active sizing box, the pointer will change to arrows pointing in just two directions. Hold the mouse button down and drag the mouse to resize the object in those directions.

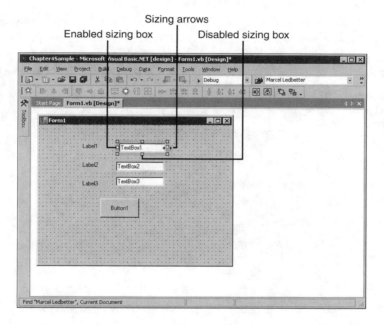

Figure 4.12
When sizing objects in a Designer window, the color of the sizing boxes indicates the directions in which they can be resized.

In the case of our text box, the MultiLine property is set to False so the TextBox control can only be resized in the horizontal direction. To demonstrate how the sizing boxes are affected by this property, press F4 to display the Properties window. Find the MultiLine property in the list and change its value to True. Notice that the sizing boxes now all appear white, and positioning the mouse over them changes the mouse cursor to the appropriate resize arrows.

WORKING WITH MULTIPLE CONTROLS

As you already know, before you can change something about a control, you have to select the control. Thus far we have selected controls on a form by single-clicking the desired control with the mouse.

However, there are times when you will need to make changes to a group of controls at once and therefore need to select a group of controls. Selecting multiple controls requires a

PART

I

CH

4

little more dexterity, but is still accomplished very easily within the Visual Studio environ-ment. There are two basic methods of doing this:

- Hold down the Shift or Control key and single-click each control with the mouse that you want to include in the control group. To remove a control from your group, simply click it again.

- Using the mouse pointer, draw a box that touches all the controls you want to include in the group. To do this, click an empty area of the form and drag the mouse. A box with dashed edges will appear. When you release the mouse button, any controls within the box's boundaries will be included in your control group.

Go ahead and create a control group that includes all of the textboxes on our sample form. Notice that selection boxes appear around all of the controls, as pictured in Figure 4.13.

Figure 4.13
When selecting a group of controls, the primary control in the group has sizing boxes of a different color.

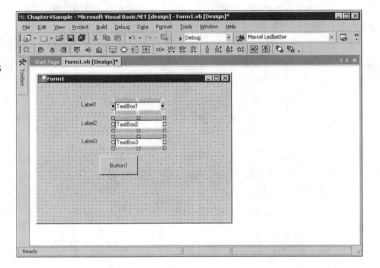

After you have selected a group of controls, you can move or resize them at the same time. However, even more useful is the ability to set common control properties. In the case of TextBox controls, developers frequently want them to appear empty at program startup. Let's clear the text from our textboxes by clearing the text in the Text property. First, press the F4 button to display the Properties window. Note that when displaying the Properties window for a group, no control name is shown and some of the properties are missing. Find the Text property in the list and place the cursor in the value column. Press the Spacebar and then the Enter key. The contents of all three textboxes will be cleared.

USING THE FORMAT MENU

If you have a lot of controls on a form that are haphazardly arranged, your form will look messy. To arrange your controls you could just move and size them with the mouse so that they visually look similar. However, Visual Studio provides the Format menu to make this process easier. Before using most functions on the Format menu, you first have to select a group of controls. Let's call one of the controls in a group the *primary* control. By using the options on the Format menu, you can make the other controls in the group change to look like the primary control.

> **Note**
>
> The primary control in a group of controls can be selected by single-clicking the desired control after selecting the rest of the group.

The format menu provides the following options for working with groups of controls:

- **Align**—Use these options to make all the selected controls have the same relative positions on the grid.
- **Make Same Size**—Causes every control in the group to take on the same height, width, or both.
- **Spacing**—Changes the amount of empty form space between each control in a group, or removes it all together.
- **Center in Form**—Centers the selected controls on the form.

The final two options on the Format menu apply to individual controls, as well as control groups. *Order* refers to the layering of controls. In other words, if you have two controls drawn on top of each other, use the options in this submenu to determine which one shows up on top.

The *Lock Controls* option can be used to prevent you from accidentally moving or sizing controls on a form. By selecting a control and choosing this option, the sizing/movement indicator will change and you will be unable to move the control until you have unlocked by clicking the option again.

→ In this section we have discussed arranging controls during form design. To learn more about control alignment during program execution, please **see** Chapter 14, "Designing an Effective User Interface," **p. 357**

WORKING WITH INVISIBLE CONTROLS

We have seen how controls such as textboxes can be arranged on a form. However, there are some controls that the developer cannot position, such as the Timer control. The Timer control has been included in many previous versions of Visual Basic. Like other controls, it provides a piece of preprogrammed functionality you can use in your applications. However, it has no user interface when a program is running and is therefore invisible to the user. No matter where you try to draw them, invisible controls will be placed at the bottom of the Designer window, as shown in Figure 4.14.

→ For more information about the use of the timer control, **see** Chapter 12, "Advanced Controls," **p. 309**

PART

I

CH

4

Figure 4.14
Staring with Visual Studio .NET, Windows controls that are only visible at design time are not drawn on the form itself.

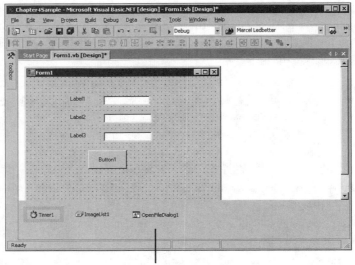

Invisible controls area

SPECIAL CONSIDERATIONS FOR THE WEB

Throughout this section, all of our examples have been using Windows applications. However, Visual Studio .NET also allows you to design Web applications in much the same manner. Instead of using a Windows form designer window, you use a Web form designer window to place and arrange controls.

Many of the features and principles we have discussed in this section also apply to Web forms, but often in a more limited or slightly different fashion.

The main reason for these limitations is simply the nature of the Web itself. Windows applications are ultimately compiled into executable code and all the user interface elements the operating system has to offer; but Web applications are restricted to a standard group of HTML elements that must be rendered by a remote user's Internet browser. The degree of control available to the developer is just not the same. Because of this, we have devoted an entire chapter to building Web applications.

Note

The Web designer allows you to select a group of controls, but you must surround them with the selection box rather than just touch them.

→ To learn more about designing Web applications, **see** Chapter 18, "Web Applications and Services," **p. 475**

In addition to creating a snazzy user interface, you have to make your program actually do something by adding Visual Basic code. For example, in Chapter 2, you wrote code that took values from textboxes and used them to make a sample loan calculator program work.

In the example, you typed Visual Basic code into Visual Studio's Code Editor. The Code Editor works much like a word processing program in that you just type text into it. However, instead of checking your spelling and grammar, the Visual Basic Code Editor checks to make sure you have entered syntactically correct code statements. In this section, we will discuss some special features you will find useful when entering code.

→ To review the loan calculator sample application, please **see** Chapter 2, "Creating Your First Windows Application," **p. 21**

To provide an example that we can refer to from the text, you will need to create a sample application. Using knowledge you have acquired from Chapter 2 and earlier in this chapter, perform the following tasks:

1. Start Visual Studio and create a new Windows Application project.
2. Place a Button control on the form.
3. Double-click the Button control to display the code window for the form.
4. In the `Click` event for `Button1`, enter the following two lines of code exactly:

```
'The following is a silly sample program!
MessageBox.Show("The current date and time is " & Now)
```

Your screen should look similar to the one shown in Figure 4.15.

PART

I

CH

4

Figure 4.15
The Visual Basic .NET Code Editor not only gives you access to your own code, but also the code generated by the form designer used to create your forms and controls.

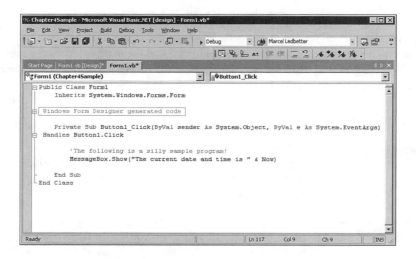

> **Note**
>
> One of the ways the Code Editor helps make the coding task easier is by providing a feature called *Intellisense*. As you type your code, you will be presented with lists of function parameters and object properties so you won't have to remember them. By pressing Ctrl+Space you can have Visual Studio attempt to guess a partial word you have typed.

NAVIGATING TO SPECIFIC FUNCTIONS

The code behind a form is really just one big file. To open it without any specific point in mind, you can right-click the form in the Solution Explorer and choose View Code. However, many times you will want to navigate to a specific point inside the Code Editor.

To create the sample Click event procedure shown in Figure 4.15, you used one of the most common ways to navigate inside the Code Editor window—double-clicking a control. Double-clicking a Button control takes you to the Button's Click event procedure. Similarly, double-clicking another type of control will take you to one of its many events. If an event procedure does not exist, a stub procedure is created so you can enter new code.

However, this method is not always efficient because you may want to access some of the other events associated with a control, or add subroutines that aren't associated with any control.

To navigate to the code associated with specific objects on your form, you use the two drop-down boxes at the top of the Code Editor window. Use the drop-down box on the left to pick the *class name* and the box on the right to pick the *method name*.

To further understand how these drop-down boxes work, look again at Figure 4.15. The selected class is Form1 and the selected method is Button1_Click. As you can see from the way the code is arranged in the Code Editor window, the Button1_Click subroutine procedure is completely contained within the declaration of the form, which begins with Public Class Form1 and ends with the End Class statement.

The hierarchical nature of the code in Visual Basic .NET forms may cause some initial confusion for existing VB programmers. However, these code navigation boxes operate in much the same way they always have. Simply pick the object you want to work with on the left, and the event you want to work with on the right. Visual Basic .NET's more object-oriented approach to code layout actually makes sense when you think about it; your forms are classes that contain other classes, such as textboxes and buttons.

> **Note**
>
> To see the list of all events for the form, including those for which you have not written code, select (Base Class Events) from the class name box.

> **Note**
>
> During informal discussions it is accepted practice to use the terms *object* and *class* interchangeably. However, it is important to understand the distinction. A class is like a template. Objects are created based on a class and objects of the same class behave the same way. To learn more about objects and classes, please see Chapter 5, "Visual Basic Building Blocks."

To access other classes contained within the Form1 class, such as controls you have placed on the form, expand the class drop-down box and select the appropriate class name. For example, go ahead and select the Button1 class.

Note

The icons in the class drop-down box indicate the accessibility of the class. For example, the icon for private classes includes a padlock.

Whenever a class is selected, you can expand the Method drop-down box to display available methods for the selected object. The Method box in Figure 4.16 shows some of the methods associated with the Button class.

Figure 4.16
In a method listing, a boldface method name indicates that code has been written for that method.

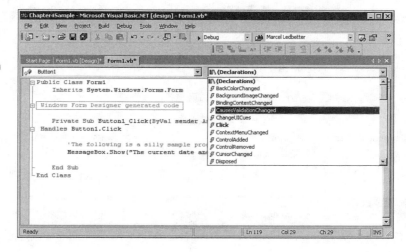

Notice that Visual Studio .NET also includes an icon next to the name of the method. The lightning bolt icons indicate the method is an event procedure.

SEARCHING FOR CODE

If you have used a Web site search engine, you are familiar with the concept of searching for information by entering a search word. Similarly, if you are looking for a specific variable or function name in your Visual Basic code, there are several ways to get to it. Visual Basic's Edit menu, located under the Find and Replace submenu, contains commands for doing just that. However, serious Visual Basic programmers will want to commit the most important search-related shortcut keys to memory (see Table 4.1).

TABLE 4.1   SHORTCUT KEYS FOR FINDING CODE

Keystroke	Purpose
Ctrl+F	Initiate a search
F3	Repeat a search
Ctrl+H	Find and replace

Pressing Ctrl+F will display the Find dialog box, which is pictured in Figure 4.17.

PART

I

CH

4

Figure 4.17
In Visual Studio .NET, regular expressions and wildcard characters can be used when searching your code.

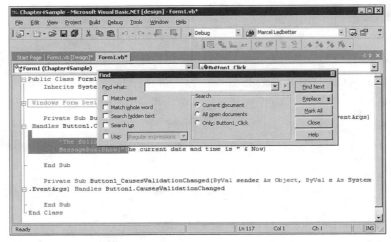

Basic searching for a specific word in your code is easy; just type the word in the Find What box and press Enter. To repeatedly search for the same text, press the F3 key. If the text is found, it will be selected in the Code Editor window.

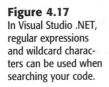

Note A drop-down box on the main toolbar also keeps track of your recent searches and can be accessed without displaying the Find dialog box.

This type of searching capability should be familiar to users of previous editions of Visual Basic. However, Visual Studio .NET adds several new powerful capabilities. One of these new features is the addition of *wildcards* and *regular expressions*, which allow you to search for a pattern of characters, not just a specific character. To tell Visual Basic the desired pattern, you create an expression by combining normal letters, numbers, and special characters.

To demonstrate, let's perform wildcard and regular expression searches on our sample project. Press Ctrl+F to display the Find dialog box, and enter the following text:

```
Button?_Click
```

Next, click the Use check box and select Wildcards from the drop-down list. (This instructs the search engine to evaluate expressions rather than searching for just the literal text.) Click the Find Next button, and notice that the text Button1_Click is highlighted in your code. This is because the 1 matched the question mark in the wildcard expression. As you might have guessed, the question mark (?) is used to represent any single character in an expression. If your code contained a Click event for Button2, the previous search would have found that code as well. (Note that Button10 would not be found by the preceding wildcard expression, because the question mark is used to indicate only a *single* character. To find one or more characters with a wildcard, use an asterisk [*] instead.)

> **Note**
> A printable list of regular expressions and wildcards, with examples of their use, can be found in the help files.

Regular expressions work like wildcards but are a lot more powerful. Visual Studio .NET supports a large number of regular expression characters that can be used to build complex patterns. For demonstration purposes, suppose we want to find code where the letters s or l occur together, but only when followed by an a or o.

First, press Ctrl+F to display the Find dialog box, and enter the following characters in the Find What box:

```
[l|s]^2[a|o]
```

Click the Use check box and choose Regular Expressions from the drop-down list. Then, click the Find Next button repeatedly. Notice that the search finds only the llo in follow-ing and the ssa in MessageBox.

Starting from right to left, the sample regular expression has three main parts. The first part, enclosed by brackets, indicates a group of letters to find, either an l or an s. The second part, ^2, means only match when the previous expression occurs two times. The rightmost part of the expression is another bracketed letter group that includes the letters a and o. Because the last part includes only these two letters, the search does not find the lly in silly.

> **Note**
> Regular expressions have been a mainstay of the UNIX community for years. Tutorials and examples to help you understand them can be found on the Internet.

MARKING CODE WITH BOOKMARKS

Another button you may have noticed on the Find dialog is the Mark All button, which is used to create *bookmarks* in your code. Bookmarks in the Code Editor can be used to mark text that you want to refer to at a later time, similar to bookmarks in real life.

> **Note**
> Bookmarks are different than breakpoints, which have meaning during the debugging process and are discussed in a later chapter.

When you perform a search and click the Mark All button, a bookmark is placed on each line of code that matches the search. Bookmarks are represented by small blue squares in the margin of the Code Editor. Figure 4.18 shows the results of adding bookmarks to all lines of code with the word End in them.

Figure 4.18
Bookmark navigation commands can be found in the Bookmarks submenu under the Edit menu or on the Bookmarks toolbar.

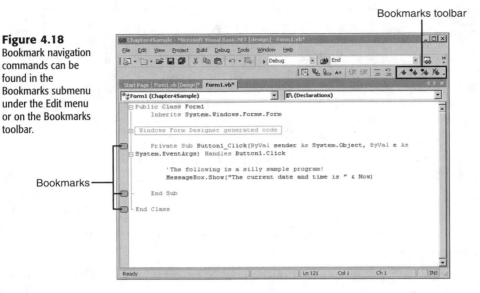

Bookmarks toolbar

Bookmarks

The easiest way to jump from bookmark to bookmark is by using the Bookmarks toolbar, also pictured in Figure 4.18.

Note

The Find command is not the only way to add bookmarks. You can add them manually with the toolbar, or add a task list shortcut as described later in this chapter.

COPYING AND PASTING CODE

There are some shortcut keys that every Windows developer should know (see Table 4.2). Although some might argue the most important of these is the key used to undo mistakes, the Cut, Copy, and Paste keys are equally important.

TABLE 4.2   KEYS TO MEMORIZE

Keystroke	Purpose
Ctrl+X	Cut selected text
Ctrl+C	Copy selected text
Ctrl+V	Paste selected text
Ctrl+Z	Undo a mistake

These keystrokes are probably already second nature to you because they are shared across a variety of Windows applications. However, Visual Studio .NET adds a new concept to the cut and paste world you know and love: the *Clipboard Ring*.

Traditional copy and paste operations allow for a single item in the buffer. However, Visual Studio .NET keeps track of each piece of text you copy in an area of the Toolbox called the Clipboard Ring, pictured in Figure 4.19.

Figure 4.19
You can drag code snippets from the Toolbox to the Code Editor with the mouse.

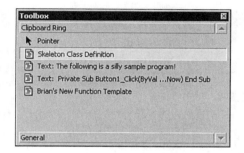

The easiest way to use the Clipboard Ring is to press the Shift key when you paste text. By repeatedly pressing Ctrl+Shift+V instead of the familiar Ctrl+V, you can cycle through text that you have recently copied to the clipboard. By default, text displayed in the Clipboard Ring is just displayed as with the word *Text* followed by a few characters of the actual text. By right-clicking one of these items, you can name it. For example, the clipboard item called Brian's New Function Template might contain a standard function template that I can use repeatedly by dragging it to the Code Editor with the mouse.

Note The Clipboard Ring is temporary; items will disappear from it when you exit Visual Studio.

PART
I

CH
4

USING THE TASK LIST

One of the exciting new Visual Studio .NET features is the addition of the Task List window. The Task List window simplifies coding by consolidating errors and other programming tasks into a centralized list. In previous versions of Visual Basic, typing errors in your code triggered nasty message boxes that interrupted the flow of coding, sometimes even after you realized the error and were trying to correct it. Visual Studio .NET's syntax error checking is much less intrusive and operates in the background, very similarly to the automatic spell check feature of Microsoft Word. Although these errors are indicated in your code with wavy lines, they are also placed on the Task List. Clicking on an error in the Task List automatically opens the appropriate code window and jumps to the associated line of code. In addition to tracking your errors, the Task List can also track important sections of code that represent future to-do items or other important project notes.

VIEWING THE TASK LIST

To view the Task List window, choose Show Tasks from the View menu and select one of the options. Each option in the menu represents a different view of the project's current tasks. For example, errors are added automatically to the task list by Visual Basic, but you may also add manual comments. Depending on what you are working on, you might want to temporarily hide some of the tasks. Table 4.3 describes the options in the Task List menu and how they affect the subset of tasks that is displayed.

TABLE 4.3 TASK LIST OPTIONS

Option	Tasks Displayed
All	All types of open tasks
Comment	Tasks generated from program comments
Build Errors	Errors reported from the compiler
User	Tasks you have manually entered
Shortcut	Shortcuts to lines of code

Additional filters can be applied in combination with the preceding ones, such as the following:

- **Current File**—Restricts tasks to current code file only
- **Checked**—If user tasks are shown, includes checked tasks only
- **Unchecked**—If user tasks are shown, includes unchecked tasks only

Note

The word *filtered* will appear in the Task List window caption if you are not displaying all tasks.

The Task List, as shown in Figure 4.20, displays several columns of information. By clicking on the gray column headers you can sort the Task List as desired. From left to right, these columns are as follows:

- **Priority**—You can set this to high, medium, or low, and an appropriate icon will be displayed.
- **Type**—A type icon indicates the type of task: a user task, a program error, a shortcut, or a comment.
- **Checked**—You can check user tasks to provide a visual indicator that they have been completed.
- **Description**—Provides a brief description of the task.
- **File**—The path to the file pertaining to the task, if applicable.
- **Line**—The line of code pertaining to the task, if applicable.

Figure 4.20
The Task List provides centralized management of your errors, to-do items, and bookmarks.

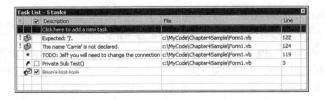

UNDERSTANDING THE DIFFERENT TYPES OF TASKS

 Errors are added and removed from the Task List by Visual Basic. Seasoned VB users will appreciate the fact that they can hurriedly type lines of code without being interrupted by an in-your-face message box with every typo. A quick glance at the Task List allows you to jump to and correct any errors on your own schedule.

 Comment tasks are tasks that Visual Basic generates after scanning the comments in your program. If your comments contain certain key words such as TODO or HACK, the comment is added to the Task List. When you send code to someone else, adding a TODO comment is a good way to inform him of any changes he needs to make to get the code to work on his PC. Removing the TODO from the comment will remove it from the Task List.

Note

If you want to store different types of comment-related tasks in the Task List, you can change the key words by choosing Options from the Tools menu and selecting Task List from the Environment folder.

 User tasks are a type of task that you manually enter. An example of such a task might be "Send a new copy of this executable to Marge" or a task that does not have a line of code associated with it. To enter a new task, just single-click the words "Click here to add a new task" and type a description. You can also set a priority, or click in the check mark column to indicate that the task has been completed. To delete user tasks from the list, single-click the task and press the Delete key on your keyboard.

 Shortcut tasks are exactly what they sound like: shortcuts to a specific line of code. For example, if you are working with a particularly large project over a period of several days, you can mark a section of code you want to revisit. Just choose the Edit menu, the Bookmarks submenu, and click Add Task List Shortcut (You can also get to this menu by right-clicking in the Code Editor.) When you select this option, the line of code will be added to the Task List.

USING DYNAMIC HELP

Help in Visual Basic has always been just a click away, provided you have the help files installed or accessible on CD. The easiest way to access help is to click what you need help with and press the F1 key to ask the system for help. You can click objects, windows, or even words in the Code Editor. Pressing F1 causes a list of appropriate topics to be displayed. In addition, all the search capabilities of the MSDN library (Microsoft Developer's Network) have been integrated into Visual Studio. Several different types of help windows can be displayed in Visual Studio such as Contents, Search, and Index. By using the mouse and docking techniques described earlier, you can position each of these windows as desired. These Help windows can also be separated by tabs within a single window for easy access, as shown in Figure 4.21.

Figure 4.21
All of the Help windows pictured here are accessible from the Help menu or via shortcut keys and can be arranged any way you like.

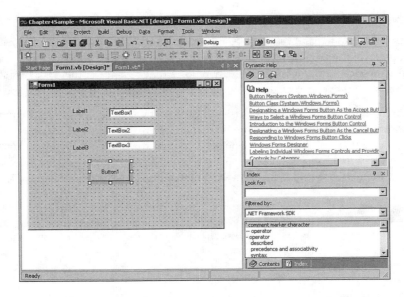

Although readers are probably familiar with searching a help index or reading a table of contents, Visual Studio .NET's new *Dynamic Help* feature merits additional explanation. Dynamic Help works silently in the background (much like the Task List) to provide the developer with continuous assistance. In the example shown in Figure 4.21, the developer has drawn a Button control on a Windows form. The Dynamic Help window automatically updated itself with information pertaining to buttons, control creation, and other related topics. Clicking on one of these links opens the selected article within the Help files.

Tip

The Help files will often include sample code, which you can easily copy and paste back into your own projects.

If you are new a new user of Visual Studio .NET, I suggest keeping the Dynamic Help window visible while you work. If you see a topic that interests you, simply click on the hyperlink to read more about it.

OTHER USEFUL WINDOWS IN THE IDE

In this chapter we have described some of the most important windows that you will be using as you develop applications with Visual Basic .NET. However, there are many additional windows available that you will encounter as you develop applications. Because these windows are generally more specialized and require knowledge of coding practices, they are covered later in the book. However, the following is a quick review, along with reference to chapters where they are covered in more detail:

- The *Object Browser* is used to explore the properties and methods of objects. It can be accessed by pressing F2. For more detailed information, see Chapter 5.

- *Internet-related windows* such as Internet Explorer and the Favorites window should be familiar to users of the Internet.

- *Debug-related windows* such as the Immediate window, Watch window, and Command window are used to trace and troubleshoot your programs.

CUSTOMIZING THE DEVELOPMENT ENVIRONMENT

Customizing the development environment means making changes to the default behavior of Visual Studio to better suit an individual developer's needs. Visual Studio .NET has many new customization features available never seen before in the Visual Studio family of products. In addition to an enormous amount of user settings, Visual Studio allows the use of macros like other Microsoft products such as Excel. In this section we will describe some of the customization options you can use to make your programming experience more personalized.

CHANGING YOUR ENVIRONMENTAL POLICY

You can control the look and feel of Visual Studio by setting some of the many available options. To access the Options dialog box, shown in Figure 4.22, click the Tools menu and choose Options.

Figure 4.22
Environment options allow developers to customize Visual Studio to suit their tastes.

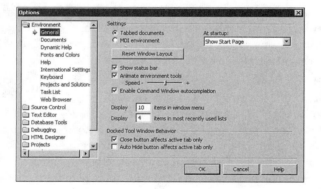

Notice that the options are organized by category using a series of folders. Because all languages in Visual Studio share the same user interface, some of the options do not apply to Visual Basic .NET. There are, in fact, so many options that discussing them all in detail would be beyond the scope of this chapter. Please feel free to experiment with the other options, but keep in mind that most exercises in this book assume the reader is using the default settings.

Because the options in the Environment folder generally relate to the other topics already discussed in this chapter, the following are some highlights:

- **General**—The General settings, shown in Figure 4.22, are pretty much self-explanatory. By adjusting window styles and fine-tuning animation speed, you can make the windows in your development environment behave the way you want.

PART
I

CH
4

- **Documents**—This section controls how Visual Studio opens and displays documents. Developers will probably find the options relating to the Find box the most useful items on this screen. As with previous versions of Visual Basic, searching for text in the Code Editor (using Ctrl+F and F3) displays a message box when you transverse the entire scope of the search. By clearing the Show Message Boxes check box, you can just keep cycling through your searches continuously. The message box will not interrupt you, and the status bar will inform you when you have reached the end of your search.

- **Dynamic Help**—The Dynamic Help options allow you to determine the type and order of articles displayed in the Dynamic Help window. For example, if you learn by example rather than instruction, you may want to move the Samples item to the top of the list. In this case, just single-click it and click the Move Up button.

- **Fonts and Colors**—Elements in the Visual Studio environment have certain default colors—text is black on a white background, comments are green, and so on. Use the options in this section to change the color scheme to your liking.

- **Help**—Lets you choose to display the help windows inside or outside of the Visual Studio environment, as well as select from any of the help libraries installed on your system.

- **International Settings**—Changes the language you are using.

- **Keyboard**—During this chapter we have mentioned several shortcut keys; for example, F4 displays the Properties window. Using the Keyboard options here, you can change this key setting and many others. Your group of custom keyboard shortcuts can then be saved as a keyboard template. Several templates are already defined, such as those that mimic keyboard shortcuts from earlier versions of Visual Basic. (Note that this book uses the keyboard settings from either the Visual Basic or Default Settings group.)

- **Projects and Solutions**—This section contains some useful options related to opening and saving projects. First, you can set your default project directory to something shorter than "My Documents," which may be useful for command-line users. You can also choose to display the Output and Task List windows automatically when a program is compiled. The Output window is frequently used for printing debug information during program execution, and the Task List as you know lists program errors. Selecting these two options means you do not have to worry about opening these windows before starting your program. The other option on this screen controls Visual Studio's behavior when saving projects. I recommend leaving it on the Save changes setting, so if your computer crashes during program execution you will not lose your changes.

- **Task List**—You can add additional words, also known as tokens, that will be placed on the Task List when encountered in your program's comments.

- **Web Browser**—Controls the address of the Visual Studio Home Page, the Internet Search Page, and other browsing options.

USING MACROS

No one likes to get stuck in a rut performing the same task over and over again. Macros can help this problem by automating a group of frequently used keystrokes. For example, if you know you are always going to put a certain group of statements or comments at the beginning of every subroutine, you can create a macro to type them for you.

Macros are like a tape recording of words you have typed and certain actions you performed within the development environment. Playing back the recording causes these actions to be repeated again. In this section we'll create a simple Visual Studio macro and show how to edit the code contained in the macro. To start, make sure Visual Studio is open to a new Windows application.

RECORDING A SIMPLE MACRO

Begin by placing a Button control on the form. Double-click the Button control to open the code window for the button. Place the cursor in the Click event for the button.

The macro-related commands in Visual Studio are located on the Tools menu, under the Macros submenu. To begin recording a macro, click the Record Temporary Macro option now. You will see a new floating toolbar pop up—the Recorder (see Figure 4.23).

Figure 4.23
When recording a macro, note the cassette icon in the status bar and the appearance of the Recorder toolbar.

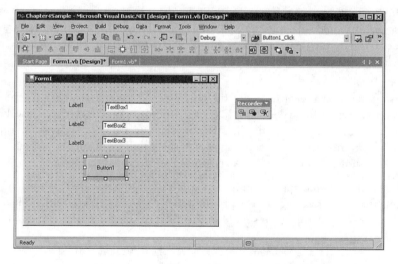

The Recorder allows you to stop and pause the recording of a macro, much like you stop or break a program during execution. To record your macro, you simply perform the activity as you would normally and the recorder will remember your keystrokes.

Type the following line of code in the editor and press Enter:

```
MessageBox.Show("Hello, World!")
```

Next, click the Stop Recording button on the Recorder toolbar to stop recording the macro. You have now successfully recorded a macro.

EXECUTING YOUR MACRO

Visual Studio has a special window used to manage macros, the Macro Explorer, which is shown in Figure 4.24. Go ahead and display the window now by selecting the Tools menu, Macros, Macro Explorer. You should see TemporaryMacro, which is the name of the macro you just created.

Figure 4.24
The Macro Explorer window can be displayed by pressing Alt+F8.

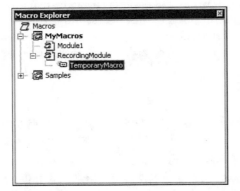

Double-click TemporaryMacro. This will run the macro you just created, and another MessageBox statement should appear in the code window. Although this macro is not very complicated, it does illustrate the basic purpose of a macro: to cut down on the amount of typing.

EDITING MACRO CODE

Using the macro recorder is not the only way to create or change a macro. Macros are stored as Visual Basic code, just like your other programs, so you can easily modify the code itself. To demonstrate, right-click the TemporaryMacro in the Macro Explorer and choose Edit from the menu. A new instance of Visual Studio will appear on your screen. This screen, shown in Figure 4.25, is known as the Macros IDE.

This screen should appear familiar to you. In fact, macros are really just Visual Studio projects that take advantage of the programmable aspects of Visual Studio itself. Notice the code for our macro, which should look similar to the following:

```
Sub TemporaryMacro()
    DTE.ActiveDocument.Selection.Text = "MessageBox.Show(""Hello"", World!"")"
    DTE.ActiveDocument.Selection.NewLine()
End Sub
```

The previous code is actually very easy to follow. The DTE object, which stands for Development Tools Environment, exposes methods and properties that allow you to manipulate the Visual Studio environment with regular Visual Basic code. The first statement instructs Visual Studio to enter some text in the active document; in this case, the result is to type a MessageBox statement into our code window. The second line of code inserts a new line.

Figure 4.25
A default macro project called `MyMacros` is automatically loaded with Visual Studio.

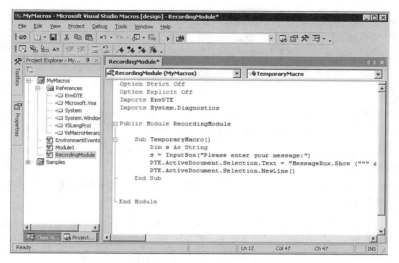

Let's modify the code and see how the results affect our macro. Change the code in the macro so it looks like the following:

```
Sub TemporaryMacro()
    Dim s As String
    s = InputBox("Please enter your message:")
    DTE.ActiveDocument.Selection.Text = "MessageBox.Show (""" & s & """)"
    DTE.ActiveDocument.Selection.NewLine()
End Sub
```

Now, close the Macros IDE and return to your Visual Studio project. Double-click the macro name (`TemporaryMacro`) in the Macro Explorer. An input box will appear asking you to type in a message. Enter some text and a `MessageBox` statement will be generated that includes the text.

PART
I
CH
4

> **Tip**
>
> In addition to aiding in coding tasks, the DTE object can be useful in managing projects and files. To learn more, view the code for the many sample macros included with Visual Studio .NET.

ORGANIZING YOUR MACROS

The macro we created in the previous section was called `TemporaryMacro`. As you might imagine, the next time you choose the Record Temporary Macro option from the menu the previous macro will be erased. To prevent this, you can rename the macro using the Macro Explorer. To complete our sample exercise, go ahead and rename your new macro. Right-click the word `TemporaryMacro` and choose Rename from the menu. Change the name of the macro to `NewMessageBox`. Now, when you create a new temporary macro, this macro will not be overwritten.

As you saw in the previous section, the code for macros is stored in a project. This is a special type of project, known as a Macro Project. As you can see from Figure 4.25, the name of the default the Macro project is MyMacros. You can load or create other Macro projects in the Macro Explorer by right-clicking the word Macros in the Macro Explorer. In addition, right-clicking a code module within a macro project allows you to add and delete macros from the module.

CUSTOMIZING THE VISUAL STUDIO TOOLBARS

The toolbars and buttons in Visual Studio behave similarly to those found in other Microsoft products. They can be dragged and positioned to your liking on any side of the screen. This section shows how to create your own toolbar and add a button to it that will execute the sample macro we created in the previous section.

To begin creating a custom toolbar, first display the Customize dialog box by clicking the View menu, Toolbars, and Customize. The Customize dialog box is shown in Figure 4.26.

Next, press the New button and enter a name for the new toolbar, such as My Toolbar. Your toolbar will be added to the list of available toolbars and appear on the screen as a floating gray window, also pictured in Figure 4.26.

Figure 4.26
Visible toolbars are indicated in the Customize dialog box by a check mark next to their name.

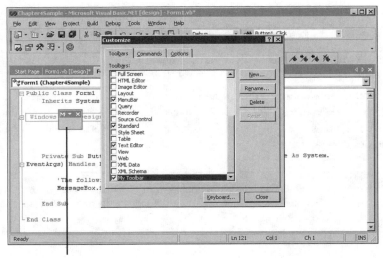

New toolbar

In order to make your toolbar useful, you need to add a command to it. Click the Commands tab at the top of the Customize dialog box. You will see all of the available Visual Studio commands grouped by categories. Scroll through the category list until you find the Macros category, and then select it. Your macros should appear on the right side of the dialog box. If you followed the sample from the previous section, you should have a macro called NewMessageBox available.

Using the mouse, drag the NewMessageBox command from the Customize dialog box to the new toolbar. Notice that the macro appears on the toolbar as text. However, it is traditional for toolbar buttons to contain images. To assign an image to your macro, right-click the macro name on the toolbar, and you should see the menu shown in Figure 4.27. Select Change Button Image, and pick one of the available images. The new image will appear on the toolbar next to the macro name. Finally, right-click again and choose Default Style to hide the macro name and show only the button image.

Note

You can also draw custom toolbar images by clicking the Edit Button Image menu option.

Note

You can drag macros and other commands to existing Visual Basic toolbars, as well as custom toolbars.

Figure 4.27
Toolbar buttons can appear as images, text, or both.

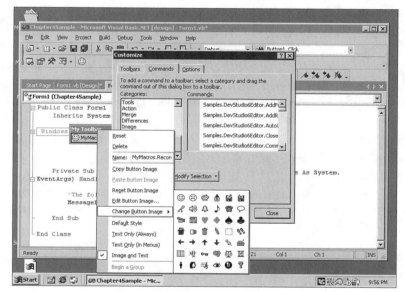

PART

I

CH

4

Tip

Although the macro name is included by default, you can change the button name from the menu shown in figure 4.27. Because the button will appear as a tooltip, you may want to change it to something more descriptive.

Now that you have created a new custom toolbar, close the Customize dialog box by clicking the close button. To complete our exercise, drag your new toolbar to the top of the screen so that it docks with the other toolbars. To test the toolbar, open a code window and click the button. Your macro should be executed.

TROUBLESHOOTING

Help, I have lost a window! How can I get it back?

The View menu contains several window commands. Some are located in the Other Windows submenu. Debug windows can be displayed under the Windows submenu of the Debug menu. Help-related windows are accessible from the Help menu.

While trying to customize one of Visual Studio's toolbars, I accidentally made a mess of it. How do I restore the original buttons?

By using the Reset button, you can restore the original toolbar configuration. Just display the Customize dialog box described earlier in this chapter, highlight the toolbar name, and click Reset.

I am trying to open a project from Windows Explorer. Which project file do I need to double-click?

You can double-click either the solution file, which has a sln extension, or the project file, which has a vbproj extension. (To see extensions, you may need to set the appropriate file option in Windows Explorer). Note that if you click on the project file, the associated solution will be opened if it exists. If a solution file is unavailable, Visual Studio will create a new solution for your project.

When I exit Visual Studio .NET, I am not always prompted to save my project. How can I be sure my work is saved to disk?

Visual Studio .NET automatically saves your work when you run your program. If you open Visual Studio and change your code but do not recompile, you will be prompted to save your work when exiting. If you do not like the automatic-save behavior, it can be disabled in the Environment Options dialog box.

VISUAL BASIC BUILDING BLOCKS

In this chapter

If you have read the first few chapters of the book, you should be familiar with the steps involved in creating a simple application in the Visual Studio environment. However, to become a competent VB programmer, you need to understand some terms and ideas that are central to the VB language. Designing the visual parts of your program is a fairly intuitive process. However, there are some subtleties to the terminology and syntax that every VB programmer needs to know. By understanding these foundation concepts, you will be able to more quickly master advanced topics.

TERMINOLOGY YOU MUST KNOW

As a programmer, you will be writing lots of code. After reading Chapter 2, "Creating Your First Windows Application," you should be familiar with some basic terms used to describe parts of the code: variables, events, properties, and so on. In this section, we will attempt to familiarize you with several terms frequently used to describe and categorize Visual Basic code structures.

UNDERSTANDING OBJECTS AND CLASSES

To understand Visual Studio .NET, you must understand the concept of an *object*. In the real world, an object is a thing such as the car you drove to work this morning, or the DVD movie you watched last night. Objects with similar characteristics (such as all cars or all DVDs) can be grouped together into a *class*. For example, the following statement describes the DVD class:

DVDs contain a movie title and are 5 inches in diameter. They can be played in a video disc player or a computer.

Suppose you go to the video store and rent several DVD movies. All the movies are a member of the same class, but each movie is a separate object. In a lot of books, the terms *class* and *object* are used interchangeably. This is fine for discussion purposes, but as a developer you should be aware that there *is* a difference.

> **Note**
>
> A class is a template that describes objects belonging to the class. An object is an *instance* of a class. For example, "Brian's truck" is an instance of the truck class.

So how do we apply the concept of objects to Visual Basic programming? Just as there are objects in real life, there are objects in program code. You can use objects and classes (both of your own design and those provided by others) in your programs to help solve a problem. This is known as *object-oriented programming* (OOP). The strict definition of OOP and creating your own objects is discussed in Chapter 9, "Creating Code Components."

→ For more on creating your own classes, **see** Chapter 9, "Creating Code Components," **p. 223**

UNDERSTANDING MEMBERS

An object has has attributes that make it unique, such as the name of the movie contained on a DVD. Objects can also perform tasks. In the case of a car, accelerate or honk horn are things you can do with a car object.

In Chapter 2, we described the controls we placed on a form as objects. A Button control has *properties* (such as length, width, text) as well as *events*, which allow the object to trigger an action. We also called some *methods* contained within objects, such as the ToString method used to convert an object's value to a character string.

In Visual Basic, the definition of a class may include properties, methods, and events. Collectively these parts of an object are known as its *members*. Consider the following sample class definition for a car shown in Figure 5.1 (some of the code listings have been collapsed).

Method box

Figure 5.1
As you add methods to a class, they will appear in the Method drop-down box in the upper-right corner of the code editor.

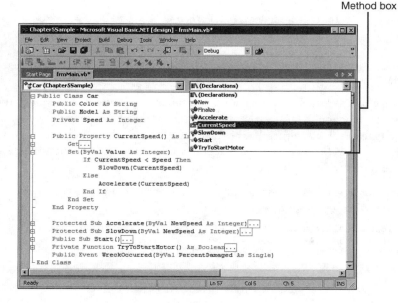

PART

I

CH

5

As you can see from Figure 5.1, the Car class contains properties, methods, and events declared with VB code. The modifiers (such as Public and Private) that precede the member definition are used to control the access to the member. For example, Private members cannot be accessed from VB code outside the class definition, but Public members can. In our sample, users of the Car class cannot access the private Speed variable directly; they must use the CurrentSpeed property. All the different types of access and their meanings will be discussed in Chapter 8, "Program Tasks with Functions and Procedures."

→ For more on access to members, **see** Chapter 8, "Managing Program Tasks with Functions and Procedures," **p. 201**

UNDERSTANDING METHOD TYPES

Of all the different types of members, the term *method* bears some clarification. Methods are units of code within a class that perform a task, but they come in several different forms. The following are all statements you might read or hear that indicate execution of a method:

- Invoke a method
- Call a function
- Execute a procedure (or subroutine)
- Fire an event

Each of these statements is a variation on the same thing but has a specific connotation. Let's look at the two most common types of methods, *functions* and *subroutines*. The following function gets the current system time:

```
Private Function GetCurrentTime(Optional ByVal IncludeSeconds As Boolean = True)
As String
        If IncludeSeconds = False Then
           Return Format(Now, "hh:mm")
        Else
           Return Format(Now, "hh:mm:ss")
        End If
End Function
```

The previous sample code is known as a function because it has a value, much like a mathematical function. The As String declaration at the end of the function declaration indicates the type of value returned by the function. Like a mathematical function, a function in VB also may have input *parameters* that control the return value. The IncludeSeconds parameter determines whether the function returns the seconds.

Another type of method is the subroutine, or procedure. The GetCurrentTime function rewritten as a procedure would look like this:

```
Private Sub GetCurrentTime(ByRef CurrentTime As String, Optional ByVal
IncludeSeconds As Boolean = True)
        If IncludeSeconds = False Then
           CurrentTime = Format(Now, "hh:mm")
        Else
           CurrentTime = Format(Now, "hh:mm:ss")
        End If
End Sub
```

Unlike the function, the subroutine itself does not have a value. However, it can still send values back to the caller using output parameters. In the previous example the ByRef parameter CurrentTime contains the desired result.

→ For more on parameters, **see** Chapter 8, "Managing Program Tasks with Functions and Procedures," **p. 201**

The previous examples demonstrate two ways of accomplishing the same task, but with slightly different syntax. The following lines of code show how to call the function and subroutine. In each case, the output value of the GetCurrentTime method is assigned to a string variable, ReturnValue.

```
ReturnValue = GetCurrentTime(False) 'Calls the function
GetCurrentTime(ReturnValue,False)   'Calls the sub
```

As you can see from the example, the return value of a function can be assigned to a variable using the equals (=) assignment operator. The parameters to a method call are enclosed in parentheses.

Note

> The procedure call syntax has changed slightly in this version of Visual Basic. In Visual Basic 6.0, you had to use the `Call` keyword when calling a procedure with parentheses around the parameters, or omit the parentheses. In Visual Basic .NET the `Call` keyword is optional and parentheses are always used.

UNDERSTANDING EVENTS

The concept of events and *event-driven programming* is essential to developing applications for the Windows environment. With a text-based user interface (such as DOS) that is running a single program at a time, control over program execution is straightforward. However, Windows applications are inherently event-driven, meaning that the flow of program execution is controlled by the events that occur as the program is running. The user or system can initiate events in any order. For example the user may click a button, scroll a list box, or close a window. This seemingly un-ordered execution of code is often a stumbling block for programmers used to mainframe environments attempting to learn Visual Basic.

Note

> As one astute reader pointed out, event-driven programs have actually been around for a long time. For example, the program that drives air-traffic control radar reacts to an external event (the presence of a plane) and updates the screen.

SELECTING AN EVENT HANDLER

A special type of method, the event handler, allows you to write code to respond to events. In Chapter 2 and Chapter 3, "Creating Your First Web Application," you added code to the procedure that handled a Button control's `Click` event. An event is something external to your program. When an event *fires* it executes the procedure that handles the event. When the user clicks a button he is causing an event within the program, so there is an associated method that handles that event.

Recall from Chapter 2 that you use the drop-down boxes at the top of the Code Editor window to select an event procedure. The object is selected in the Code window's upper-left drop-down list box (the *Class* box); the appropriate event procedure is selected in the upper-right drop-down list box (the *Method* box). When that object/event combination occurs at runtime, if code has been written for that combination, Visual Basic executes the code. If no code has been written for the combination, Visual Basic ignores the event. Figure 5.2 shows an example of an event procedure written for a specific control and event.

Figure 5.2
Visual Basic responds to an event only if you write code for the event.

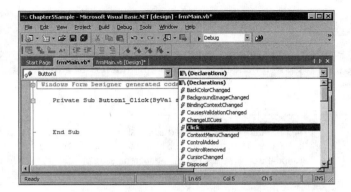

Users of previous versions of Visual Basic will note that events are treated more like methods in Visual Basic .NET. While events in Visual Basic 6.0 had specialized parameters, event procedures in Visual Basic .NET have more generic arguments and are treated similarly to other types of methods. As you can see in Figure 5.2, a lightning bolt icon is displayed next to the names of the events during the process of selecting an event procedure. However, after selecting an event, the icon changes to a method icon, because the event procedure is really just a method within a class that handles the event.

Tip

If you enter a Code window by double-clicking an object, the Code window automatically selects that object's most commonly used event procedure. For example, if you double-click a command button at design time, the Code window is opened to that command button's Click event procedure.

WRITING AN EVENT PROCEDURE

To understand how events occur continuously throughout your program, follow these steps to write a simple example:

1. Start a new Windows Application project.
2. Double-click the form in the designer window to open the Code window. By default, if no other code exists for the form, you are placed in the form's Click event procedure.
3. From the Class selection box, select the Base Class Events. (Note this will be the last item in the list of objects.)
4. From the Method box, select the MouseMove event.

Note

Notice that when you make a selection, Visual Basic automatically sets up the skeleton of a procedure with the procedure's name and the End Sub statement (which denotes the end of the procedure).

The procedure name for an event procedure contains the name of the object and the name of the event. In this example, Form1 is the object and MouseMove is the event. Notice that the MouseMove event procedure also has some parameters; The sender parameter contains information about the caller, and the e parameter contains arguments specific to this event, in this case the coordinates of the mouse.

5. At this point, you can write program statements to take whatever action(s) should happen in response to an occurrence of the event. Add the following line of code to the event procedure:

```
Me.Text = "The mouse coordinates are " & e.X & "," & e.y
```

Your event procedure should now look like this:

```
Private Sub Form1_MouseMove(ByVal sender As Object, ByVal e As
System.Windows.Forms.MouseEventArgs) Handles MyBase.MouseMove
        Me.Text = "The mouse coordinates are " & e.X & "," & e.Y
End Sub
```

The preceding code displays the values of the X and Y parameters in the form's title bar by setting the Text property of the form. Click Visual Basic's Start button, or press F5, and move the mouse pointer over the form. You should see the form's title change as the mouse pointer moves.

Most of these events you encounter in Visual Basic are the direct result of actions initiated by the users; however, other objects, including those of your own creation, invoke some events. To learn more about creating and raising your own events, please see Chapter 9.

UNDERSTANDING NAMESPACES

One of the main advantages of object-oriented programming is code reuse; classes can be shared among programs. By using already-written classes you can save yourself a lot of work. An organizational unit containing shared code components is known as a *namespace*. One of the most exciting things about Visual Basic .NET is the amount of functionality available from classes built into the .NET framework. Table 5.1 lists a few examples of some namespaces provided by the .NET framework for use in your programs.

TABLE 5.1   EXAMPLES OF NAMESPACES

Name	Purpose
System.Math	Mathematical functions
System.Drawing.Graphics	Drawing lines, and so on
System.Windows.Forms	Windows Forms
System.Diagnostics	Diagnostics, error log
Microsoft.VisualBasic	VB .NET functions
System.Net.Sockets	TCP Sockets

Tip

To see a complete list of namespaces (several pages long) search for *namespaces* in the Help Index. Throughout this book we will be describing many of these namespaces in detail.

Above the namespace main level is another organizational unit known as an *assembly*. Quoting the help file, an assembly is " . . . a reusable, versionable, and self-describing building block of a Common Language Runtime application." (For users of previous versions of Visual Basic, an assembly is like a DLL you can reference in a project.) To access namespaces in an assembly within your project, you add a reference to the assembly containing the namespace. When you start a new project, the `System` and `Microsoft.VisualBasic` namespaces are automatically available to you.

→ For more on adding a reference, **see** Chapter 4, "Understanding the Development Environment," **p. 75**

USING THE IMPORTS STATEMENT

As long as you have the namespace available via an assembly reference, you can use its components in your Visual Basic program by typing the fully qualified name. For example, suppose you want to declare a `Socket` object. The `Socket` object is part of the `System.Net.Sockets` namespace and can be referenced with the following line of code:

```
Dim skListen As System.Net.Sockets.Socket
```

Notice namespaces are organized hierarchically using dot notation, and can contain namespaces within themselves. Every time you type a period, you will see the list of available members at the current level.

To cut down on the amount of typing to access `Socket`, place an `Imports` statement followed by the namespace name at the top of your code module. Assuming we added the line `Imports System.Net.Sockets` to the top of the code module, the preceding assignment statement could be rewritten as follows:

```
Dim skListen As Socket
```

You can always use the long name, but if you want to omit the namespace name you must use an `Imports` statement so the compiler knows to which namespace you refer.

Note

If you are using namespaces with identically named members, you may need to use fully qualified names to differentiate them.

When you start a new project, Visual Studio .NET imports several namespaces by default. These are shown in Figure 5.3.

Figure 5.3
The Imports in the Project Property pages can be accessed by right-clicking the project name in the Solution Explorer and choosing Properties.

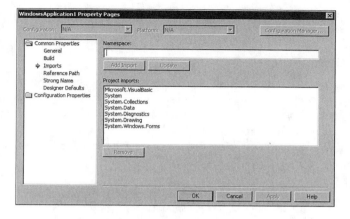

There are two ways to add Imports to your project:

1. The Project Property pages, shown in Figure 5.3. Any imports added here will be available to all forms and modules in your project.

2. Type an Imports statement at the top of your code module. This will only affect the current code module.

EXERCISE: USING THE System.NET NAMESPACE

We have already discussed the theory behind using namespaces, references, and the Imports statement. In this section, we create a sample function to determine your computer's IP address. One practical use for this program might be for owners of cable modems, whose IP address changes often. A friend of mine uses a similar program that e-mails him the IP address of his home PC so he can always connect to it from work. During the process you'll learn how to use Visual Studio tools such as the Object Browser, Intellisense, and the help files to effectively use namespaces. To begin, start Visual Studio .NET and create a new Windows Application.

Our task at hand involves the network. From reading the help files, we know that a System.NET namespace exists that contains network-related functions. Because the System namespace is a part of a new Windows application by default, you do not need to go through the process of adding a new reference. However, an Imports statement will make it easier to access components within the namespace. Follow these steps to add a new Imports statement to your form code:

1. From the Solution Explorer, right-click Form1.vb and choose View Code.

2. Scroll to the very top of the form code, where you see the other Imports statements.

3. Add the following new line of code after the last Imports statement:

```
Imports System.Net
```

Now you are ready to directly access the classes and other components within the `System.Net` namespace from your code.

USING THE OBJECT BROWSER

The help files provide a lot of detail about how to use the namespaces included with the .NET framework. However, at certain times you may want to explore the objects on your own to learn about their methods, properties, and events. The Object Browser window allows you to browse and search classes. To display the Object Browser, select the View menu, Other Windows, then Object Browser. You will see a window similar to the one pictured in Figure 5.4.

Figure 5.4
The Object Browser window can be displayed from the View menu or by pressing Ctrl+Alt+J.

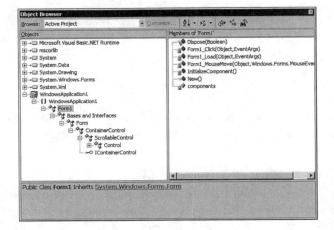

You can, of course, explore the classes listed on the left side of the Object Browser by navigating through the tree list. However, in this exercise we are looking for something specific, so we will use the Object Browser's Find Symbol button. Click the Find Symbol button, which appears on the toolbar as a binoculars icon. You will see the Find Symbol dialog box, shown in Figure 5.5.

Figure 5.5
The Find Symbol dialog box allows you to search namespaces loaded in the active project, or namespaces you select through the References dialog box.

For our sample exercise, we are looking for things related to IP address, so we'll be searching for the symbol IP. However, we will need to narrow our search so that we do not find unrelated words that contain the string IP, such as Description. A reasonable guess is that the class we want begins with the letters IP, so go ahead and select the Find Prefix option. This will constrain the search to symbols that begin with IP. To begin the search, perform the following steps:

1. Type IP in the Find What box.
2. Choose Active Project in the Look In box.
3. Click the Find button.

After you have clicked the Find button, you should see the results window pictured in Figure 5.6.

Figure 5.6
To browse symbols returned as the result of a search, right-click the name and choose Browse Definition.

As you can see from the results, there are several promising looking classes, especially IPAddress and IPHostEntry. After looking at their definitions in the Object Browser (and the help files), you will find that the IPAddress class stores an IP address and the IPHostEntry stores a list of IP addresses for a specific host (or computer). So, to solve our problem you will need to figure out a way to discover a computer's host name. By performing another search for Host with the Object Browser, you will discover a function called GetHostName within the System.Net.DNS namespace which accomplishes just that.

WRITING THE SAMPLE CODE

Now that we have the information we need, you can start writing the code. Place a command button on the form and enter the following code in the Click event:

```
Dim MyHostName As String = DNS.GetHostName()
Dim MyHostEntry As IPHostEntry
Dim MyIPAddr As IPAddress
```

PART
I

CH
5

```
MyHostEntry = DNS.GetHostByName(MyHostName)

For Each MyIPAddr In MyHostEntry.AddressList
        MessageBox.Show("Your ip address = " & MyIPAddr.ToString)
Next

MyHostEntry = Nothing
MyIPAddr = Nothing
```

When you run the program and click the button, your IP address will be displayed in a message box. As you can see, the code is fairly simple and does not require any API calls or custom controls as it might have in previous versions of Visual Basic.

ERROR HANDLING

Computers really aren't that smart. They do *exactly* what you tell them to, so if you make a mistake and tell them to do something completely wrong, they will try to do it anyway. An *error* is something that isn't supposed to happen in your program. There are many different types of errors that may occur in a computer program, such as syntax errors, logic errors, and runtime errors. Syntax errors are generally caught while you are typing the code and can be fixed easily because Visual Studio tells you it doesn't understand what you typed. Logic errors can usually be identified by incorrect operation of the program, and are fixed by examining and then correcting an erroneously designed section of code.

However, errors that occur at runtime are especially disastrous, because they can happen unexpectedly and in front of the end user. Consider, for example, the following two simple lines of Visual Basic code:

```
File.Copy ("myfile.doc","newfile.doc")
MessageBox.Show ("The file has been copied.")
```

During normal operation, the lines of code execute in order. The first line makes a copy of a file, and the second line displays a message telling the user the file has been copied. Both lines are syntactically and logically correct, and they will not cause an error when building your program. However, there is still a potential for runtime errors. For example, what happens if a user runs your program and the file myfile.doc is missing? Or the destination file already exists? These types of runtime errors must be *handled* by program code, otherwise the computer won't know what to do. Attempting to run the previous code on a computer where the source file does not exist will produce the message shown in Figure 5.7.

Note

As you will see in Chapter 24, "Working with Files," there is a function used to determine whether or not a file exists. However, this is just one easy example; there are many other situations that can cause runtime errors.

Figure 5.7
Avoid cryptic messages and ungraceful exits by adding error-handling code to your programs.

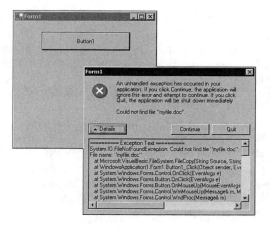

As you can see, the default runtime error message is meant for a programmer, not an end user. The user is left with a couple of choices: Click Quit and the program ends, or click Continue and the program attempts to keep running. As a programmer, you really don't want the user to do either, especially if the other parts of the program depend on the missing file!

STRUCTURED ERROR HANDLING WITH EXCEPTIONS

These types of errors are *exceptions* to the normal process and order of code execution. The purpose of the `File.Copy` function is to copy files, so when it could not find the source file, it threw an exception back to the function that called it. You can write code to catch the exception and then handle the error appropriately.

It may sound a lot like baseball, but that is exactly how structured error handling works in Visual Studio .NET: by throwing and catching exceptions. When an error happens during the execution of a method, the method throws it back to the caller. If the program code does not catch the exception, it gets thrown all the way back to the users and they see the message shown in Figure 5.7.

Now, let's add some error-handling code to our example:

```
Try
        File.Copy("myfile.txt", "yourfile.txt")
        MessageBox.Show("The file has been copied")

Catch FileMissingError As FileNotFoundException
        Dim strMessage As String
        strMessage = FileMissingError.Message
        strMessage = strMessage & "Please make sure this file exists and try
again."
        strMessage = strMessage & "The program will now exit."
        MessageBox.Show(strMessage, "Error has occurred",
_MessageBoxButtons.OK, MessageBoxIcon.Error)
        Application.Exit()
End Try
```

The additional code includes some new keywords, Try and Catch. When you are writing code to catch exceptions, you enclose both the code that may cause the exception and the code to handle it in a Try . . . End Try block. Within this block you can use one or more Catch statements to check for exceptions. When our sample code executes normally, then only the File.Copy and the first MessageBox statement will be executed. However, if an exception of type FileNotFoundException is thrown, the code beneath the Catch statement will be executed to handle the exception.

Let's examine the exception-handling code a little closer. The code is very simple in that it just displays a message to the user and exits the program. However, notice that we declared an object variable, FileMissingError, which stores the returned exception. We then use the Message property of the exception object when creating our message to the user. This is where Visual Basic's object-oriented nature comes in very handy. Because an exception is an object, there may be specific properties and methods that you can use to better handle the exception in your code. In the previous sample, we know that the Message property contained the file path of the missing file, so we displayed it for the user.

Note The help files contain specific exception types associated with the included classes.

The File.Copy method can throw other types of exceptions besides a FileNotFound exception. You can code for as many specific exceptions as you want using multiple Catch statements, or just use the generic System.Exception class to handle any other exceptions generically:

```
Try
     File.Copy("myfile.txt", "yourfile.txt")
     MessageBox.Show("The file has been copied")

Catch FileMissingError As FileNotFoundException
     Dim strMessage As String
     strMessage = FileMissingError.Message
     strMessage = strMessage & "Please make sure this file exists and try again."
     strMessage = strMessage & "The program will now exit."
     MessageBox.Show(strMessage, "Error has occurred",_
MessageBoxButtons.OK, MessageBoxIcon.Error)
     Application.Exit()

Catch BadErr As System.Exception
     MessageBox.Show(BadErr.ToString, "Error has occurred",_
MessageBoxButtons.OK, MessageBoxIcon.Error)
     Application.Exit()

End Try
```

In the examples we have looked at so far, our only action in the case of an exception has been to terminate the program. For an unknown exception this may be okay, but in the case of a missing file it may be a little drastic. By careful placement of the `Try` statement, we can provide the users with an error message that gives them the ability to fix the error:

```
Dim Answer As DialogResult
Dim bKeepTrying As Boolean = True

While bKeepTrying

    Try

        File.Copy("c:\myfile.txt", "c:\yourfile.txt")
        MessageBox.Show("The file has been copied")
        bKeepTrying = False

    Catch FileMissingError As FileNotFoundException
        Dim strMessage As String
        strMessage = FileMissingError.Message
        strMessage = strMessage & "Make sure this file exists and try again."
        strMessage = strMessage & "Fix the problem and press RETRY or CANCEL."
        Answer = MessageBox.Show(strMessage, "Error has occurred",_
        MessageBoxButtons.RetryCancel, MessageBoxIcon.Stop)
        If Answer = DialogResult.Cancel Then
            bKeepTrying = False
        End If

    End Try

End While

If Answer = DialogResult.Cancel Then
    Application.Exit()
End If
```

The previous example uses a `While` loop to allow the user to retry the file copy operation as many times as he wants.

In this section, we have described the basics of catching exceptions. However, there is a lot more to know in the area of error handling. An additional statement can be added to the `Try` block, the `Finally` statement, to add code that must always run whether there is an exception or not. The code typically placed here is used to close resources and clean up after the function executes. We will cover other exception-related topics, such as logging errors to the event log and throwing your own exceptions, in Chapter 9.

→ To learn more about user-defined errors, **see** Chapter 9, "Creating Code Components," **p. 223**

UNSTRUCTURED ERROR HANDLING WITH `On Error Goto`

Structured error handling with the `Try`, `Catch`, `Finally` statements is new to Visual Basic .NET. If you have been programming in VB for a while you also may be familiar with the `On Error Goto` statement, also known as unstructured error handling. Our file copy example rewritten using the older syntax might look like the following:

```
Dim Answer As DialogResult = DialogResult.Retry

On Error Goto FileCopyError
```

```
RetryHere:
        File.Copy("myfile.txt", "yourfile.txt")
        MessageBox.Show("The file has been copied")
        Answer = DialogResult.OK
        Exit Sub

FileCopyError:
        Dim strMessage As String
        If err.Number = 53 Then
            strMessage = "Missing file: " & err.Description
        Else
            strMessage = "Error " & err.number & ": " & err.Description
        End If
        Answer = Messagebox.Show(strMessage, "Error has occurred",_
            messagebox.IconStop + messagebox.retrycancel)
        If answer = winforms.dialogresult.Retry Then
            Resume RetryHere
        Else
            Application.Exit()
        End If

End Sub
```

To initiate unstructured error handling, you add an On Error Goto statement and provide a *label* for the program to branch to in case of an error. You can label lines of code by placing text followed by a colon (:) on a line. In the previous example, RetryHere and FileCopyError are labels. If an error occurs, the program jumps to the code labeled FileCopyError.

When an error has occurred, you use one of several statements to control the flow of the program:

- Exit the subroutine after informing the user of the error, with the Exit Sub statement.
- Use a Resume *label* statement to jump to another portion of code
- Use a Resume Next statement to continue executing on the line following the error.

Although this style of error handling is still supported in Visual Basic .NET, it is based on the infamous Goto statement, which may make the order of code execution harder to follow. Another disadvantage is the Error object passed back to the program is not as detailed as the specific exceptions-type objects you can use with Catch. In our example, we use the Number and Description properties of the Error object.

INTRODUCTION TO DEBUGGING

As we mentioned earlier, logic errors are problems with your program's logic. They are often hard to track because the program doesn't stop working, it just produces incorrect results. To help track down these bugs in your program, Visual Basic provides several tools:

- *Breakpoints* allow you to have VB stop on a certain line of code. You can then trace the code forward from the breakpoint a line at a time.
- *The Immediate window* provides a way to execute statements (such as changing a variable's value or calling methods) while your program is in debug mode.

- *The Output window* provides a way to dump debug information to the screen, such as variable values.

- *Watches* provide a way to keep track of the values of objects or variables during a program's execution.

In this chapter we will look at the basics of debugging your programs. To learn even more, see Chapter 26, "Debugging and Performance Tuning."

→ For more on debugging, **see** Chapter 26, "Debugging and Performance Tuning," **p. 717**

STOPPING PROGRAM EXECUTION WITH A BREAKPOINT

An example of a serious bug is accidentally creating an infinite loop. As a test, suppose that you want to use a `While` loop to print the numbers from 1 to 100 in the Immediate window. Start a new Windows Application project, place a button on the form, and enter the following code in the `Click` event procedure:

```
Dim i As Integer
i=1
While i <= 100
        Debug.WriteLine("Count=" & i)
        Application.DoEvents()
Wend
```

Run the program. Before clicking the button, display the Output window (select the View menu, Other Windows, and Output window or press Ctrl+Alt+O). Click the button and you should immediately spot the bug, which causes the same value to be printed over and over again. As a matter of fact, the erroneous `While` loop will never stop.

When you are working in Visual Basic's IDE, you know that you can click the Stop button to end the program, fix the code, and then restart the application. However, to solve a lot of problems, you might want to debug your programs while they are executing. In the case of our sample program, we have created a tight loop, so you may have to right-click on the form in the task bar and choose Close. Go ahead and stop the sample program now.

Place the mouse cursor on the line of code at the top of the procedure (`i=1`) statement and press F9. A red dot should appear in the margin of the code editor, indicating a *breakpoint*. The next time you run the program, it will stop when it encounters the breakpoint.

Run the program again and click the button. Notice that code execution stops (the numbers in the Output window are not printing), but your program is not completely stopped. The forms are still loaded, and the variables still contain their contents. Visual Basic highlights the next statement and places a yellow arrow indicator in the margin of the Code window.

This paused state of execution is known as *break mode*. Breakpoints are lines of code designated to put Visual Basic in break mode before they execute. By using breakpoints, you can run the program normally and then stop execution and begin debugging your code at the desired location. While you are in break mode, you can view or change variable values in the Immediate window. In some cases, you can even modify the code and continue execution.

> **Note**
>
> You also can enter break mode by using the Break button on Visual Basic's Debug toolbar, or pressing Ctrl+Break.

> **Tip**
>
> The easiest way to know whether you are in break mode is to look at Visual Basic's caption, which will have the word [break] in it. You also can look at the buttons on the toolbar, or try to type in the Immediate window.

> **Note**
>
> Correcting errors like this one *before* compiling the program is best. Because users are running outside the Visual Basic IDE, they have no way of pausing or ending an infinite loop other than killing the task from the Windows Task Manager.

In the example, you obviously forgot a statement to increment the counter variable i. Because the value of i never changes, the While condition will never become False. To fix this error, stop the program and modify the code as follows to include the missing line:

```
Dim i As Integer
i=1
While i <= 100
        Debug.WriteLine("Count=" & i)
        Application.DoEvents()
        i = i + 1
Wend
```

Next, press F5 or click the VB Start button after adding the statement. The program should now count up to 100 and then stop.

STEPPING THROUGH YOUR CODE

When you are in mode, you have more options besides restarting execution. You can step through code line by line or skip statements entirely. Visual Basic has three methods of stepping through code, each of which can be performed from the Debug toolbar or a shortcut key:

- **Step Over**—steps through lines in the current procedure but not through lines in any called procedures (the shortcut key is F10).
- **Step Into**—steps through lines in the current procedure and into any called procedures (Shortcut key: F11)
- **Step Out**—runs until the end of the current procedure (the shortcut key is Shift+F11).

Note

If your profile is set to "Visual Basic Developer," step shortcut keys will be F8 and Shift+F8. To change your profile settings, choose "My Profile" from the Visual Studio Start Page.

To demonstrate stepping through code, run the sample project again and click the button. Because the breakpoint is still in place, the program should go into break mode. Press F10 several times. Notice that the program executes a line every time you press the function key. It also highlights the next statement in the Code Editor window, as shown in Figure 5.8.

Figure 5.8
Breakpoints allow you execute a program up to a certain line; you can then examine a variable's value and continue running to the next breakpoint.

Breakpoint

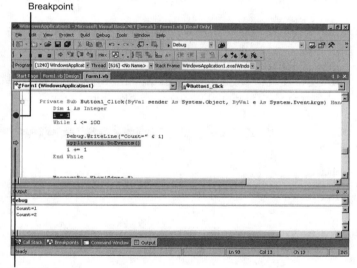

Next statement indicator

If you want to skip statements or execute them again, you can use the Set Next Statement feature. Simply put the cursor on the statement you want, and then press Ctrl+Shift+F10 or choose Debug, Set Next Statement. You also can drag the arrow in the left margin so that it points to the next statement you want to execute.

Try it now: Step through the sample program until the arrow is pointing to the line of code that increments the variable i. Next, drag the arrow back to the previous Debug.WriteLine statement, and step through it again by pressing F10. Notice that you have caused the same value of i to be printed twice.

SENDING TEXT TO THE OUTPUT WINDOW

We have already demonstrated you can use the `Debug.WriteLine` statement to send debug text to the Output window.

Note

> In previous versions of Visual Basic, there was no Output window; the `Debug.Print` statement sent debug information to the Immediate window. This functionality has been replaced by `Debug.Write` and `Debug.WriteLine`.

Some other examples of information you might send to the Output window are statements that indicate a section of the program is finished, or how long it took to complete.

WORKING WITH THE IMMEDIATE WINDOW

The Immediate window provides a way for you to enter code statements while a program is in break mode. To display the window, make sure that the program is in break mode, and press Ctrl+Alt+I or select Immediate window from the Debug Windows menu. Some examples of statements you might enter using the Immediate window are shown in Figure 5.9.

Figure 5.9
You can copy and paste statements from the Code window to the Immediate window to execute them manually.

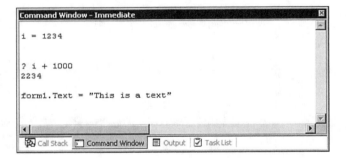

Figure 5.9 demonstrates assigning a variable to a value, printing the variable's value in a mathematical calculation, and setting a form property.

WATCHING VARIABLE VALUES

While you are in break mode, printing out variable values in the Immediate window is common practice. However, Visual Basic includes other special features for keeping track of variables during program execution. One of them is simple; just hover the mouse pointer over the variable name, and the value appears in a ToolTip. The other, more advanced method is to use the Watch window, as shown in Figure 5.10.

Figure 5.10
In the Watch window, you can view and change variable values.

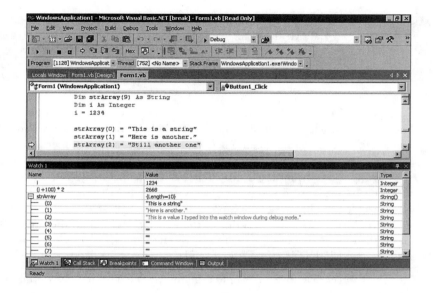

To monitor a variable in the Watch window, simply right-click the variable name while in break mode and choose Add Watch from the context menu. Try it now: Start a new Windows Application project. Place a button on the form and enter the following code in the Click event:

```
Private Sub Form_Load()

Dim strArray(10) As String
Dim i As Integer

i = 1234

strArray(0) = "Here is a string"
strArray(1) = "Here is another"
strArray(2) = "Still another one"

End Sub
```

While you are still in Design mode, place a breakpoint on the first assignment statement. Start the program, and click the button. When the breakpoint halts execution, right-click on strArray and choose Add Watch from the Context menu.

Note

If the Watch window is not visible, press Ctrl+Alt+W or select it from the Windows submenu of the Debug menu.

PART

I

CH

5

> **Note**
>
> The Watch window supports drag-and-drop. For example, you can highlight a variable in your code with the mouse and drag it to the Watch window to automatically add a new watch.

Next, press F10 to step through the lines of code; notice the changes in the Watch window. The values for each element of strArray should be displayed in the window. You can even double-click a variable and enter a new value (which is just like entering an assignment statement in the Immediate window). Also note that variables with multiple dimensions (such as arrays or objects) are displayed in a tree-like hierarchy. This feature can be handy when you are dealing with complex objects such as an ADO recordset. You can also use the Watch window to display simple expressions based on a variable value. The Watch window in Figure 5.10 shows both the value of the variable i as well as the value of i with 100 added, then multiplied by 2. To watch a custom formula, simply click in the Name column of the Watch window and enter the formula.

Because the strArray variable is only valid during the button's Click event, if you are debugging another area of the program, the watch entry for strArray will read "Unable to evaluate this expression." If you want to remove an entry from the Watch window, highlight it and press the Delete key.

Watches and breakpoints are saved with a Visual Studio solution, so the next time you open it, the watches will return. However, if you just want to temporarily use a Watch window to peek at a variable's contents, you can use the Quickwatch window. To display the Quickwatch window, follow the same steps as you would with the Watch window, but choose "Add Quickwatch." The Quickwatch window is shown in Figure 5.11.

In this section we have described how to manually add a watch. However, Visual Studio .NET also contains several automatic views of the Watch window:

- **Autos**—Automatically picks variables to watch.
- **Locals**—Watches local variables only.
- **Me**—Members of the current object.

Figure 5.11
The Quickwatch window provides the same view of a variable's contents as the Watch window, but cannot be continuously displayed on the screen.

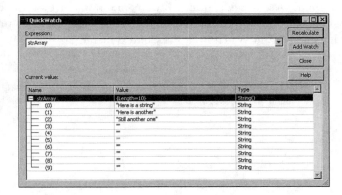

All these windows can be displayed from the Windows submenu of the Debug menu. They are in some ways more useful than a manually added watch because they are automatically updated as you enter a different section of code.

FROM HERE . . .

This chapter was called "Visual Basic Building Blocks" because it covers a wide variety of topics you need to know about to become an effective VB developer. As you learn more about the Visual Basic language, you may want to learn more about these topics in the following chapters:

- To learn more about the Visual Basic language itself and organizing your code using procedures, read Chapter 8.

- For additional information about objects and object-oriented programming, see Chapter 9.

- To find out how more about the events associated with forms and controls, see Chapter 10, "Understanding Windows Forms."

VISUAL BASIC PROGRAMMING FUNDAMENTALS

CHAPTER **6**

STORING INFORMATION IN VARIABLES

In this chapter

In this chapter we will discuss *variables*. Variables are used to store information in the computer's memory while your programs are running. Three components define a variable:

- The variable's name (which correlates to its location in memory)
- The type of information being stored
- The actual information itself

Suppose you are given this assignment: "Go count all the cars in the parking lot." As you count each car, you are storing information in a variable. Your location in memory is either a notepad or your brain. The type of information being stored is a number. And the actual information you are storing is the current number of cars.

As the name *variable* suggests, the information stored in a variable can change (vary) over time. In the example of counting cars, the count will be increased periodically. With any variable, there are two basic functions you can perform: storing information (writing on the notepad) and retrieving information (reading what is written on the notepad).

An *assignment statement* is used to store information in a variable, as in the following example:

```
Dim LoneliestNumber As Integer
LoneliestNumber = 1
```

In the example, the variable name is *LoneliestNumber*, the type of the variable is `Integer`, and the value being stored is the number 1.

Note

Many of the code samples in this chapter will be simple one- or two-line examples. To try any of these code samples, perform the following steps:

1. Create a new Windows Application Project.
2. Place a button on the form.
3. Put the sample lines of code in the button's `Click` event.
4. Use either the `Debug.WriteLine` function or the `MessageBox.Show` function to display the result.

You can use the same sample application for all the code samples in this chapter. The code for the major examples can be downloaded from the Web.

DECLARING AND NAMING VARIABLES

The first line of code is a `Dim`, or *Dimension*, statement, used for *dimensioning* (or *declaring*) variables. When your program declares a variable, it is, in essence, telling Visual Basic, "Set aside a memory location that will be used to store variable information; I will reference it by this name." The last two words in the `Dim` statement tell Visual Basic what type of information you plan to store—in this case, integer numbers. This information helps determine how much memory is to be set aside for the variable.

Note

Variables also can be declared with other keywords besides `Dim`, such as `Public` and `Private`. For more details, see the section in Chapter 8, "Managing Your Program Tasks with Functions and Procedures," called "Understanding Scope and Accessibility."

NAMING CONVENTIONS

In naming a variable, you have a tremendous amount of flexibility. Variable names can be simple, or they can be descriptive of the information they contain. The example at the beginning of the chapter uses a classic rock song reference, which is a syntactically legal name but not very descriptive of the variable's actual purpose! As a general rule, you should make your variable names descriptive enough to make your code easy to read, but also keep the names as short as possible to make the code easy to type. For example, if we are using a variable to store the number of seats remaining, the following two variable declarations describe that fact clearly:

```
Dim NumberOfSeats As Integer
Dim SeatsRemaining As Integer
```

Although you are allowed great latitude in naming variables, you must adhere to a few restrictions:

- The name must start with a letter, not a number or other character.
- The remainder of the name can contain letters, numbers, and/or underscore characters. No spaces, periods, or other punctuation characters are allowed.
- The name must be unique within the variable's scope. (Scope refers to the context in which the variable is defined, as you will learn in Chapter 8.)
- The name cannot be one of Visual Basic's reserved words.

Tip

After you have declared a variable and are referencing it in code, such as an assignment statement, the Ctrl+Space shortcut key can be used to complete the variable name after typing only a few characters. By making your variable names unique as possible within a small number of characters, you can type the variable names very quickly using Ctrl+Space.

To make sure variable names make sense to a programmer reading the code, an organization may want to establish a *naming convention*. A naming convention is just an agreed-upon way of assigning variable names so you can tell more about them. Table 6.1 lists a sample naming convention that uses a variation of the Hungarian style naming convention. This type of naming convention adds a lowercase prefix to the variable name, to indicate its type.

TABLE 6.1   SAMPLE VARIABLE NAMING PREFIXES

Variable Type	Prefix	Example
String	str	strFirstName
Integer	int	intAge
Long Integer	lng	lngPopulation
Double	dbl	dblThrustRatio
Boolean	b	bTaxable

Frequently programmers also use additional prefix letters to indicate the scope of the variable, as in the following examples:

```
Dim lstrUserID As String   'l indicates local variable
Dim astrUserID As String   'a indicates function argument
Dim mstrUserID AS String   'm indicates module-level
```

Starting with Visual Studio .NET, Microsoft seems to be getting away from prefix-oriented naming conventions. Many of the classes simply use descriptive names with uppercase at the beginning of each word. Hovering the mouse over a variable in code displays the variable's declaration statement in a tooltip, making it easy to immediately know the variable's data type. The samples listed here are just samples; a good guideline is to be consistent within your development group.

CHANGES TO THE DIM STATEMENT

Visual Basic .NET introduces some changes to the way variables can be declared. Multiple declarations of the same type are now easier, as in the following example:

```
Dim x, y As Integer
```

In the previous line of code, x and y are both Integer variables. In Visual Basic 6.0, declaring two Integer variables in the same Dim statement required specifying the type after each variable, as follows:

```
Dim x As Integer, y As Integer
```

Starting in Visual Basic .NET, both of the previous two code statements will create Integer variables x and y.

Another new feature is the ability to *initialize* a variable within the Dim statement. Initializing a variable simply means assigning it a starting value, and is frequently performed with an assignment statement immediately after the declaration, as in the following example:

```
Dim BottlesOfBeer As Integer
BottlesOfBeer = 99
```

Starting with Visual Basic .NET, you can replace the previous two lines of code with a single declaration and initialization statement:

```
Dim BottlesOfBeer As Integer = 99
```

It should be noted that initialization only works for one-variable `Dim` statements.

Note

> Although there is a default value for new variables (0 for numbers), it is good programming practice to initialize your variables rather than depending on this default value.

UNDERSTANDING DATA TYPES

Okay, you know what a variable does and how to name it. But what can you store in a variable? The simple answer is: *almost anything*. A variable can hold a numeric value; a string of text; or a reference to an object, such as a form, control, or database. This chapter looks specifically at using variables to store numbers, strings, and dates. Table 6.2 lists Visual Basic's data types:

TABLE 6.2   VISUAL BASIC DATA TYPES

Visual Basic .NET Data Type	Values Stored	Example	Memory Requirements
Boolean	True/False	True	2 bytes
Byte	0–255	122	1 byte
Char	Single Character	A	2 bytes
Date	Dates and Times	12/21/1970 02:00 PM	8 bytes
Decimal	Decimal or Whole	19.95D	16 bytes
Double	Decimal Numbers	1.23E-10	8 bytes
Integer	Whole Numbers	8675309	4 bytes
Long	Whole Numbers	19-digit number	8 bytes
Object	A *reference* to an object of any type		4 bytes
Short	Whole Numbers	32,123	2 bytes
Single	Decimal Numbers	.0000123	4 bytes
String	Characters	HELLO	Depends on length

PART

II

CH

6

Note

> The little Integer from VB 6.0 has finally grown up! A Visual Basic .NET `Integer` variable can store the entire range of values of a Visual Basic 6.0 `Long` variable. (This brings a welcome level of consistency to those programmers who work with the `int` type in SQL databases.) A new type, the `Short` type, takes the place of the VB6 `Integer` with a range of -32,768 to +32,767.

> **Note**
>
> The `Currency` data type from earlier versions of Visual Basic has been eliminated. The help files suggest using the new `Decimal` data type as a replacement.

> **Note**
>
> The `Variant` data type, capable of storing any other variable type, has been eliminated. Because all of the base data types derive from the `Object` class, Microsoft has named `Object` as the new universal data type.

In Visual Basic .NET, even the most basic data types act like objects, with their own properties and methods. When you type a variable name in the Code Editor and press the period key, you will see all the associated methods and properties.

WORKING WITH NUMERIC DATA TYPES

There are a variety of types used for storing numeric data. In math, numbers can either be *whole* or *fractional*. Whole numbers, such as years or ages, can be stored in variables of type `Short`, `Integer`, or `Long`. Numbers with decimal places, such as monetary values or scientific measurements, can be stored in `Decimal`, `Single`, or `Double` variables. The following lines of code demonstrate assigning numbers to the various numeric data types:

```
Dim SelectedYear As Short = 1999
Dim USPopulation As Integer = 283727132
Dim WorldPopulation As Long = 6132426512
Dim ShoeSize As Single = 1234.5E-2
Dim Temperature As Double = 98.6
Dim CostOfDoingBusiness As Decimal = 59.95D
Dim SerialNumber As Decimal = 90125
```

Notice we included two examples of assigning a value to a `Decimal` variable. The `Decimal` type can store decimals or whole numbers. However, Visual Basic by default assumes numbers typed with decimal places are single or double, so we added the `D` character to indicate the value `59.95` is a decimal value. The `D` is an example of a *literal type character*, which helps Visual Basic determine what type of value a literal number in your code represents. The other type characters are listed next:

Character	Data Type
F	`Single`(Floating point)
D	`Decimal`
I	`Integer`
L	`Long`
R	`Double`
S	`Short`

These literal type characters are necessary only when you type numbers directly in your program and Visual Basic does not choose the correct data type. As you will see in upcoming sections, numeric variables are also used to store the result of a mathematical calculation or the contents of another variable.

Bits, Bytes, and Storage Space

The memory required for a given data type varies with the range of numbers it can store. As you saw in Table 6.2, memory requirements for data storage are measured in bytes, which is itself a data type. To be as efficient as possible, do not choose a data type that is too large for what you intend to store. At their most basic level, computers work with *bits*, which are 1's and 0's that represent the on-or-off status of an electronic circuit. 8 bits together make up a *byte*. For example, the following binary bit pattern represents the number 171:

```
10101011
```

Starting from right and moving left, each bit represents a power of 2: 2 raised to the 0 power, 2 raised to the 1st power, and so on. To convert the binary number above, I added up the following values:

```
(128 * 1) + (64 * 0) + (32 * 1) + (16 * 0) + (8 * 1) + (4 * 0) + (2 * 1) + (1 * 1)
= 171
```

By setting all of the bits to 1, you would get a value of 255, which is the maximum value of the Byte data type.

Just think of all the data you can store in a small amount of space by using a bitmap—not the visual kind, but a string of bits where each on-off value represents something specific to your application. Consider this: If you need to store an on/off flag in your application and you use a character, it will take up two entire bytes of memory—just to store the same type of on/off value as a bit! Just imagine how many bytes are wasted in an XML file, which contains hundreds of characters just to specify the format of the file.

The point is not to suggest that you try this—one purpose for using a high-level language such as Visual Basic is to not have to worry about such low-level details—but rather to give some perspective on storage space. Memory and disk space are cheap today, but you can easily appreciate the hard work of the early computer programmers and other bitheads who today continue to work with bit-level operations.

CONVERTING NUMBERS BETWEEN DATA TYPES

Visual Basic performs conversions implicitly and explicitly. *Implicit conversions* are automatic. For example, you could declare a variable of type Integer and assign the value 1.5 to it, which is not a valid integer value. Visual Basic would automatically convert the number using rounding and store 2 in the Integer variable. *Explicit conversions* are performed by calling conversion functions. As you will see throughout this chapter, the System.Convert class contains many static methods you can use to explicitly convert from one data type to another. Explicit conversion provides a higher degree of control over the conversion process and less chance for unexpected loss of data. You can force the use of only explicit conversions by setting the compiler's Option Strict setting to On. To do this, right-click your project's name in the Solution Explorer and choose Properties. Under the Build settings section, you set the Option Strict setting to On, as pictured in Figure 6.1.

Even when you set the Option Strict setting to On, certain types of conversions are still performed automatically, without having to call a conversion function.

PART

II

CH

6

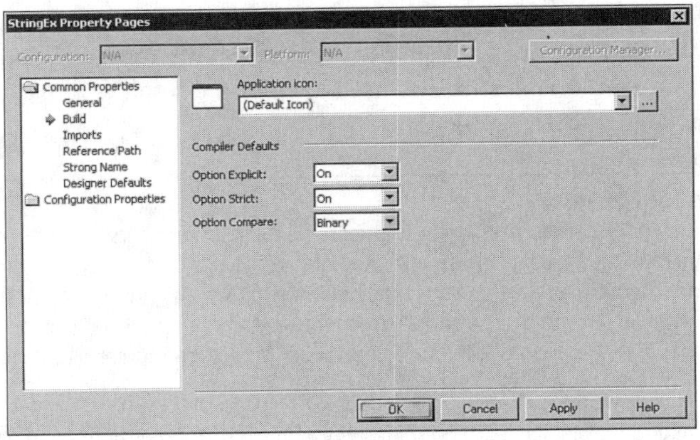

Figure 6.1
Set Option Strict
to On to enforce
explicit conversions
in your program.

Although every rule has exceptions, the general rule for automatic conversion of numbers is as follows:

If the data conversion does not result in a loss of data, the conversion is allowed. Otherwise, an error occurs.

To help explain conversions, Microsoft uses the terms *widening and narrowing*. Widening conversions are allowed, which means values can generally be moved from one type of variable to a wider type automatically, but not the reverse. In our previous example, you could store the Integer value of the USPopulation variable in the WorldPopulation variable using an assignment statement, but not the other way around. Conversions also are necessary when performing certain mathematical operations, because the result of a calculation may be of a wider type than the inputs.

The easiest way to convert numbers is by using the conversion methods provided by the Convert class. Figure 6.2 shows how the conversion methods are displayed in a pop-up menu if you type the variable name followed by a period.

The following lines of code convert a decimal number to an integer and then back to a decimal:

```
DecimalPrice = 19.95D
IntegerPrice = Convert.ToInt32(DecimalPrice)
DecimalPrice = IntegerPrice
```

The previous code sample uses the ToInt32 function when converting the wider Decimal value to a value of type Integer. Note that the process of converting a decimal value to an integer value rounds off the fractional part of the number. Because the Integer data type cannot store the part to the right of the decimal point, that information is lost, even after converting the value back to a Decimal type. After the previous lines of code are executed, both the Integer and Decimal variables will contain the value 20.

Figure 6.2
Microsoft's Intellisense technology provides a list of methods in the `Convert` class, which can be used to convert variables from one type to another.

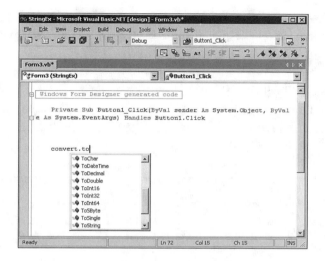

Note

Visual Basic's `Integer` type is the equivalent of the .NET framework's `Int32` type. Similarly, `Short` is `Int16` and `Long` is `Int64`.

FORMATTING NUMBERS FOR DISPLAY

To convert a number to a string for displaying it on the screen, you can simply use the `ToString` method, as in the following line of code:

```
TextBox1.Text = SalesTotal.ToString
```

However, when writing down a number in real life, people often *format* the number to suit their needs. For example, adding commas, currency symbols, and other notations make the number more readable for others. Similarly, when you need to display a number on the screen or print a report, you need to make it as easy for others to visually comprehend.

Note

The `ToString` method of numeric data types will accept formatting codes, as in the following example:

```
Messagebox.Show(DecimalPrice.ToString("C"))
```

PART

II

CH

6

The `Format` function is a single function that can handle formatting of dates, numbers, and strings. It accepts a value and a control string, which can represent either a user-defined or named (system-defined) format. The following examples show how the format function can be used to format a monetary amount:

```
Debug.WriteLine(Format(DecimalPrice, "C"))
Debug.WriteLine(Format(DecimalPrice, "$#,###.00"))
```

The first line of the previous code uses a named format, C, which stands for Currency. Format specifiers are enclosed in double quotation marks. Table 6.3 shows some examples of the predefined formats for numbers.

TABLE 6.3 NAMED FORMATS TO MAKE DISPLAYING NUMBERS EASY

Format Description	Format String	Sample Input	Output
Currency—Prints the number with a thousands separator and two digits after the decimal point.	C	1234.56	$1,234.56
Percent—Multiples the number by 100 anddisplays the number followed by the percent sign.	P	0.0123	1.23%
Fixed—Prints at least 1 digit to the left of the decimal and two digits to the right of the decimal.	F	1.55555	1.56
General—No special formatting.	G	.567	0.567
Hexi—Works with whole numbers only.	X	1234	4D2
Scientific—Displays the number in scientific notation.	E	0.0123	1.230000E-002
Standard—Prints the number with the thousands separator, and prints at least one digit to the left and two digits to the right of the decimal point.	N	1234	1,234.00

Note

For a complete list of available number formats, see the help topic "Predefined Numeric Formats."

If the named formats in Visual Basic don't meet your needs, you can define your own formats. You specify a format by indicating where the digits of the number should be placed, if thousands and decimal separators are used, and by listing any special characters that you want printed. For example, the following line of code displays a number with four decimal places and a thousands separator:

```
MessageBox.Show(TotalDistance, "##,##0.0000")
```

The codes you can use in specifying the format are defined in Table 6.4.

TABLE 6.4   CODES FOR DEFINING NUMERIC FORMATS

Symbol	Purpose	Meaning
0	Digit placeholder	Displays the digit or displays 0 if no digit appears in that location.
#	Digit placeholder	Displays the digit or displays nothing if no digit appears in that location. This causes leading and trailing zeros to be omitted.
.	Decimal separator	Indicates where the decimal point is displayed.
,	Thousands separator	Indicates where the separators are displayed.
%	Percentage indicator	Indicates where a percent sign is displayed. Also causes the number to be multiplied by 100.
E-, E+, e-, e+	Scientific Notation	Using E- or e- displays a minus sign next to negative exponents but displays no sign for positive exponents. Using E+ or e+ displays a sign for any exponent.

You should be aware that the named formats, as well as the ToString conversion methods, are *culture-aware*. This means they will be affected by the regional and culture settings of the system on which the program is running. For more information on regional formatting, see the later section entitled "Understanding Regional Settings."

USING MATH OPERATIONS

Processing numerical data is one of the key activities of many computer programs. Mathematical operations determine customer bills, interest due on savings or credit card balances, average scores for class tests, and many other bits of information. Visual Basic supports a number of different math operators that you can use in program statements. These operations and the Visual Basic symbol for each operation are summarized in Table 6.5. The operations are then described in detail in the following sections.

TABLE 6.5   MATH OPERATIONS AND THE CORRESPONDING VISUAL BASIC SYMBOL

Operation	Operator
Addition	+
Subtraction	-
Multiplication	*
Division	/
Integer division	\
Modulus	Mod
Exponentiation	^

PART
II

CH
6

In Visual Basic, you use mathematical operations to create equations. These equations can include multiple operators, variables, and expressions, as in the following example:

```
Result = (115 + Val(TextBox1.Text)) / 69 * 1.0825
```

The preceding line of code assigns the result of the mathematical expression to a variable named Result, which itself may be used in another calculation or displayed on the screen.

ADDITION AND SUBTRACTION

The two simplest math operations are addition and subtraction. If you have ever used a calculator to do addition and subtraction, you already have a good idea how these operations are performed in a line of computer code.

A computer program, however, gives you greater flexibility in the operations you can perform than a calculator does. Your programs are not limited to working with literal numbers (for example, 1, 15, 37.63, –105.2). Your program can add or subtract two or more literal numbers, numeric variables, or any functions that return a numeric value. Also, as with a calculator, you can perform addition and subtraction operations in any combination. Now take a look at exactly how you perform these operations in your program.

USING THE ADDITION OPERATOR

The operator for addition in Visual Basic is the plus sign (+). The general use of this operator is shown in the following syntax line:

```
result = number1 + number2 [+ number3]
```

result is a variable that contains the sum of the numbers. The equal sign indicates the assignment of a value to the variable. number1, number2, and number3 are the literal numbers, numeric variables, or functions that are to be added together. You can add as many numbers together as you like, but each number pair must be separated by a plus sign.

Note

When assigning the results of an equation to a string, such as a text box, you can enclose the equation in parentheses and use the ToString method to avoid declaring another variable:

```
TextBox2.Text = (1 + 2 + 3).ToString
```

USING THE SUBTRACTION OPERATOR

The operator for subtraction is the minus sign (-). The syntax is basically the same as for addition:

```
result = number1 - number2 [- number3]
```

Although the order does not matter in addition, in subtraction, the number to the right of the minus sign is subtracted from the number to the left of the sign. If you have multiple numbers, the second number is subtracted from the first, then the third number is subtracted from that result, and so on, moving from left to right. For example, consider the following equation:

```
result = 15 - 6 - 3
```

The computer first subtracts 6 from 15 to yield 9. It then subtracts 3 from 9 to yield 6, which is the final answer stored in the variable result.

Tip

You can control the order of operations by using parentheses. For example, the following line of code assigns 12 to the variable result:

```
result = 15 - (6 - 3)
```

You can create assignment statements that consist solely of addition operators or solely of subtraction operators. You can also use the operators in combination with one another or other math operators. The following code lines show a few valid math operations:

```
val1 = 1.25 + 3.17
val2 = 3.21 - 1
val3 = val2 + val1
val4 = val3 + 3.75 - 2.1 + 12 - 3
```

Note in the previous lines of code we are adding fractional numbers together, so the variables are assumed to be type Double. (By placing a D after the numbers, you could store the result in a Decimal or Double type.) Addition and subtraction can also be combined with other operations, as we'll see in the next section.

MULTIPLICATION AND DIVISION

Two other major mathematical operations with which you should be familiar are multiplication and division. Like addition and subtraction, these operations are used frequently in everyday life.

USING THE MULTIPLICATION OPERATOR

Multiplication in Visual Basic is straightforward, just like addition and subtraction. You simply use the multiplication operator—the asterisk (*) operator—to multiply two or more numbers. The syntax of a multiplication statement, which follows, is almost identical to the ones for addition and subtraction:

```
result = number1 * number2 [* number3]
```

As before, result is the name of a variable used to contain the product of the numbers being multiplied, and number1, number2, and number3 are the literal numbers, numeric variables, or functions.

USING THE DIVISION OPERATORS

Division in Visual Basic is a little more complicated than multiplication. In Listing 6.1, you see how one type of division is used. This division is what you are most familiar with and what you will find on your calculator. This type of division returns a number with its decimal portion, if one is present.

However, this type is only one of three different types of division supported by Visual Basic. They are known as *floating-point division* (the normal type of division, with which you are familiar); *integer division*; and *modulus*, or *remainder*, *division*.

Floating-point division is the typical division that you learned in school. You divide one number by another, and the result is a decimal number. The floating-point division operator is the forward slash (/):

```
result = number1 / number2 [/ number3]

'The following line returns 1.333333
Debug.WriteLine(4 / 3)
```

Integer division divides one number into another and then returns only the integer portion of the result. The operator for integer division is the backward slash (\):

```
result = number1 \ number2 [\ number3]

'The following line returns 1
Debug.WriteLine(4 \ 3)
```

Modulus, or remainder, division divides one number into another and returns what is left over after you have obtained the largest integer quotient possible. The modulus operator is the word mod:

```
result = number1 mod number2 [mod number3]

'The following line returns 2, the remainder when dividing 20 by 3
Debug.WriteLine(20 Mod 3)
```

As with the case of addition, subtraction, and multiplication, if you divide more than two numbers, each number pair must be separated by a division operator. Also, like the other operations, multiple operators are handled by reading the equation from left to right.

Figure 6.3 shows a simple form that is used to illustrate the differences between the various division operators. The code for the command button of the form is shown as follows:

```
Dim FirstNumber, SecondNumber As Integer

FirstNumber = TextBox1.Text.ToInt32
SecondNumber = TextBox2.Text.ToInt32

TextBox3.Text = (FirstNumber / SecondNumber).ToString
TextBox4.Text = (FirstNumber \ SecondNumber).tostring
TextBox5.Text = (FirstNumber Mod SecondNumber).ToString
```

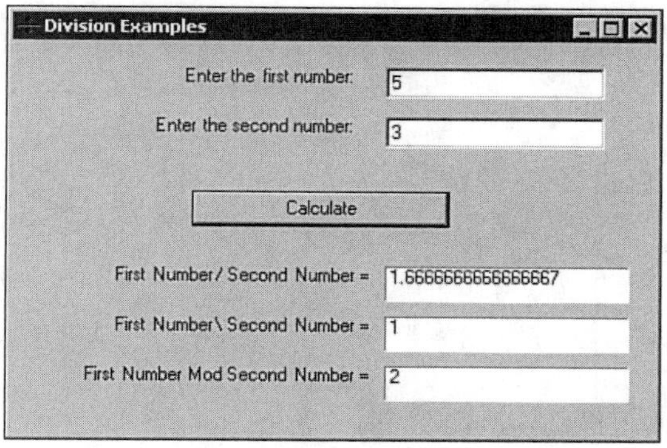

Figure 6.3
This program demonstrates the difference between Visual Basic's three types of division operators.

After you set up the form, run the program, enter **5** in the first text box and **3** in the second text box, and then click the command button. Notice that different numbers appear in each of the text boxes used to display the results. You can try this example with other number combinations as well.

USING MULTIPLICATION AND DIVISION IN A PROGRAM

As a demonstration of how multiplication and division might be used in a program, consider the example of a program to determine the amount of paint needed to paint a room. Such a program can contain a form that allows the painter to enter the length and width of the room, the height of the ceiling, and the coverage and cost of a single can of paint. Your program can then calculate the number of gallons of paint required and the cost of the paint. An example of the form for such a program is shown in Figure 6.4. The actual code to perform the calculations is shown in Listing 6.1.

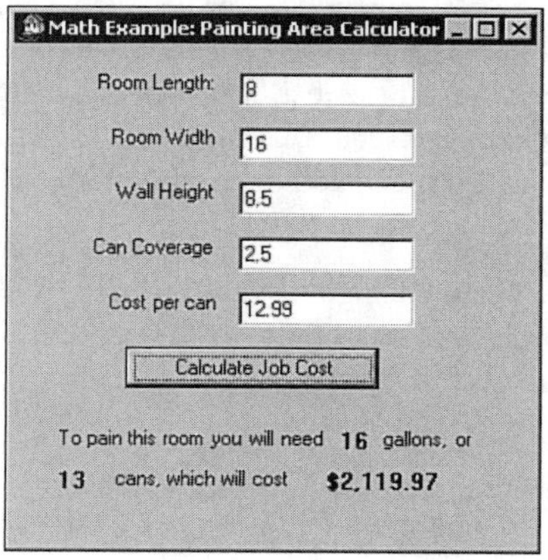

Figure 6.4
Multiplication and division are used to determine the amount of paint needed for a room.

PART

II

CH

6

LISTING 6.1   MATHEX.ZIP—PAINTING COST ESTIMATE USING MULTIPLICATION AND DIVISION OPERATORS

```
Dim RoomLength As Double
Dim RoomWidth As Double
Dim RoomHeight As Double
Dim CanCoverage As Double
Dim CanCost As Decimal
Dim GalsPerCan As Double
Dim RoomPerimeter As Double
Dim WallArea As Double
Dim NumCans As Double
Dim ProjCost As Decimal

'GET INFORMATION FROM TEXT BOXES
RoomLength = Val(txtRoomLength.Text)
RoomWidth = Val(txtRoomWidth.Text)
RoomHeight = Val(txtWallHeight.Text)
CanCoverage = Val(txtCoverage.Text)
CanCost = Convert.ToDecimal(txtCanCost.Text)
GalsPerCan = Val(txtGallons.Text)

'CALCULATE NUMBER OF CANS (ROUND UP)
RoomPerimeter = 2 * RoomLength + 2 * RoomWidth
WallArea = RoomPerimeter * RoomHeight
NumCans = WallArea / CanCoverage
lblCansNeeded.Text = Math.Ceiling(NumCans).ToString

'CALCULATE NUMBER OF GALLONS AND COST
lblGallonsNeeded.Text = GalsPerCan * NumCans
ProjCost = Convert.ToDecimal(Math.Ceiling(NumCans) * CanCost)
lblCost.Text = Format(ProjCost, "C")
```

Notice the code in Listing 6.1 introduces the Val function, which converts a string value to a Double. To test this code, start by creating a new EXE project in Visual Basic. Add six text boxes to the form; set their Name properties to txtRoomLength, txtRoomWidth, txtWallHeight, txtGallons, txtCoverage, and txtCanCost. These text boxes are to accept information from the user; use three labels called lblGallonsNeeded, lblCansNeeded, and lb lblCost to report information back to the user. You might want to add descriptive Label controls beside each text box, as in the figure.

Next, add a command button to the form. Change its Name property to btnCalculate. Enter the lines of code in Listing 6.1 into the command button's Click event procedure. Save and run the program to see it in action.

EXPONENTIATION

Exponents are also known as *powers* of a number. For example, 2 raised to the third power (2^3) is equivalent to 2×2×2, or 8. Exponents are used quite a lot in computer operations, where many things are represented as powers of two. Exponents are also used extensively in scientific and engineering work, where mathematical terms are often represented as powers of 10 or as natural logarithms. Simpler exponents are used in statistics, where many calculations depend on the squares and the square roots of numbers.

To raise a number to a power, you use the *exponential operator*, which is a caret (^). Exponents greater than one indicate a number raised to a power. Fractional exponents indicate a root, and negative exponents indicate a fraction. The following is the syntax for using the exponential operator:

```
answer = number1 ^ exponent
```

The equations in the following table show several common uses of exponents. The operation performed by each equation is also indicated.

Sample Exponent	Function Performed
3 ^ 2 = 9	This is the square of the number.
9 ^ 0.5 = 3	This is the square root of the number.
2 ^ -2 = 0.25	A fraction is obtained by using a negative exponent.

Note

You can also use the `Math.Pow` and `Math.Sqrt` functions to calculate powers and square roots.

INCREMENTING THE VALUE OF A VARIABLE

One frequent use of variables is a counter, where you update the same variable with the result of an equation:

```
RocketCountdown = RocketCountdown - 1
```

If you are not familiar with computer programming, seeing the same variable name appear both on the right and left of the equal sign might look a little strange to you. It tells the program to take the current value of a variable (`RocketCoundown`), add another number to it, and then store the resulting value back in the same variable.

Starting with Visual Basic .NET, new operators have been added to make incrementing and decrementing a variable's value easier. The following lines of code demonstrate how you can save a little typing by using the decrement and assign (`-=`) operator:

```
RocketCountdown -= 1
```

Other new operators are available for the other mathematical operations (`*=`, `+=`, and so on) which work the same way.

OPERATOR PRECEDENCE

Many expressions contain some combination of the operators just discussed. In such cases, knowing in what order Visual Basic processes the various types of operators is important. For example, what's the value of the expression 4 * 3 + 6 / 2? You might think that the calculations would be performed from left to right. In this case, 4 * 3 is 12; 12 + 6 is 18; 18 / 2 is 9. However, Visual Basic doesn't necessarily process expressions straight through from left to right. It follows a distinct order of processing known as *operator precedence*.

Simply put, Visual Basic performs subsets of a complex expression according to the operators involved, in this order:

- Exponentiation (^)
- Negation (-)
- Multiplication and division (*, /)
- Integer division (\)
- Modulus arithmetic (Mod)
- Addition and subtraction (+, -)

Within a subset of an expression, the components are processed from left to right. When all subset groups have been calculated, the remainder of the expression is calculated from left to right.

In the previous example (4 * 3 + 6 / 2), the multiplication and division portions (4 * 3, which is 12, and 6 / 2, which is 3) would be calculated first, leaving a simpler expression of 12 + 3, for a total of 15.

An important note is that you can override normal operator precedence by using parentheses to group subexpressions that you want to be evaluated first. You can use multiple nested levels of parentheses. Visual Basic calculates subexpressions within parentheses first, innermost set to outermost set, and then applies the normal operator precedence.

BUILT-IN MATH FUNCTIONS

In addition to the basic mathematical operations already discussed, Visual Basic .NET includes a class devoted entirely to Math, aptly named the Math class. This class is included in the System namespace, so your Visual Basic .NET programs automatically have access to a wide variety of functions, such as the following:

- *Rounding functions* such as Round, Ceiling, and Floor allow you to round double or decimal numbers up or down to the next whole number.
- The *comparison methods* Max and Min compare two numbers or numeric variables and return the greater or lesser value.
- The *sign-related functions* Abs and Sign allow you to determine the absolute value of a number, as well as whether it is positive or negative.
- *Trigonometry* functions such as Sin, Cos, and Tan allow you to work with geometric angles.

Note that all the functions in the Math class are static, shared methods. This means you do not need to declare an object variable to use them:

```
Dim x As Double = 6.5444
Debug.WriteLine(Math.Floor(x))      'Returns 6
```

The math namespace also includes two shared fields, E and PI, which work like constant values. For example, all the trigonometry functions work in radians but you can use PI to convert the value to degrees:

```
Dim AnswerRadians As Double = Math.Asin(0.5)
Dim AnswerDegrees As Double = AnswerRadians * (180 / Math.PI)
Debug.WriteLine(AnswerDegrees)   'Returns 30 degrees
```

If you didn't fall asleep in math class, you should be able to apply many of the built-in functions to solving equations you already know. For more information on all of the math functions, see the Help file topic *Math Members*.

USING DATE AND TIME VALUES

Visual Basic .NET provides the versatile Date data type to store date and time values. The following lines of code are examples of using date variables:

```
Dim dtWWII As Date = #12/7/1941#
Dim dtKing As Date = Convert.ToDateTime("Aug 16, 1977 4:00 PM")
Dim dtJFK As Date = Convert.ToDateTime("November 23, 1963")
Dim dtMoon As New Date(1969, 7, 20)
```

The first line of the previous code uses the pound (#) symbol to assign a date value directly to a variable of type date. The next two examples use methods to convert strings containing date and time expressions to the Date type. The final line of code shows how the constructor method can be used to initialize a date by supplying parameters for the year, month, and day.

Depending on how you need to use dates in your program, you may use any of the preceding methods. Listed next are a couple of points to keep in mind when working with the Date data type:

1. The Date data type always stores a date *and* a time value to the millisecond, whether or not you need both parts. As we will see, there are methods and properties to extract only the parts you need for display or calculation purposes.

2. Visual Basic's Date data type is based on the .NET DateTime data type, so some of the functions (such as Convert.ToDateTime) will reference the .NET spelling. When declaring variables you may use either.

In this section, we will explore some of the functions used to manipulate date and time values.

DETERMINING THE CURRENT DATE AND TIME

It is often useful to determine the current system date and time in a Visual Basic program. Some possible uses for the system date and time are:

- Logging when program actions occur.
- Running a job or performing some action periodically.
- Measuring the speed of your application.

There are a couple of different functions, Now and Today, that return a Date value containing the current system time. Now returns the current date and time; Today returns the current date with the time set to midnight. For example, these two lines of code produce different output:

```
Debug.WriteLine(Date.Now)
Debug.WriteLine(Date.Today)
```

If today were February 27, 2001 at 6:45 P.M. the following values would be returned:

```
2/27/2001 06:45:00 PM
2/27/2001 12:00:00 AM
```

Note the output of Today does not include the current time, which is useful when doing date-range comparisons.

DATE AND TIME FORMATS

The previous sample lines show the default date/time format when a Date value is converted to a string. However, when displaying dates on a report or in a text box you may want to use a more readable format. As with numbers, you can create a format string to determine which parts of the date are displayed. By placing characters in the format string that represent the desired parts of the date, you can build your own custom date format. Table 6.6 lists some examples of format strings and the outputs they produce for August 16, 1945, 1:15 P.M.

TABLE 6.6   EXAMPLES OF DATE AND TIME FORMAT STRINGS

Format String	Output String
M/d/yy	8/16/45
MM/dd/yyyy	08/16/1945
MM/dd hh:mm:ss tt	08/16 01:15:00 PM
MMMM d, yyyy H:mm	August 16, 1945 13:15
dddd, MMM d, yyyy	Thursday, Aug 16, 1945

Note

Date and time format strings are case-sensitive. For example, M refers to the month and m refers to the minute. A complete list of the characters you can use to build a format string is included in the help files under the topic *User-Defined Date/Time Formats*.

To change the format of a date, pass the format string as a parameter to the Format function or the ToString method of a date object. The following sample lines of code show how to use date formatting:

```
Dim TheDate As Date = Now
Dim OutputString1, OutputString2 As String
OutputString1 = Format(TheDate, "M/d/yy")
OutputString2 = TheDate.ToString("M/d/yy")
```

As you can see, the `Format` function works the same way it does for numbers. If you do not specify a format and simply convert your date value to a string, the output may be affected by settings in your Windows Control Panel. (We will discuss this more in the upcoming section called "Understanding Regional Settings.")

> **Note**
>
> The output of the Format method/function is a string. To convert a string back to a date, you can use the `Convert.ToDateTime` method, as shown in an earlier example. However, make sure that the string is a valid date or an exception will occur.

EXTRACTING PARTS OF A DATE

If you need to work with dates in an automated fashion, you might want to extract just part of a date. Suppose, for example, you need to schedule a process to back up files every Saturday. As you saw in the last section, you can use the `Format` function to get a string containing just the parts of a date you want, including the day of the week. However, a date object also contains several properties that can be used to more easily extract a specific portion of a date. In our example, the `DayOfWeek` property could be used to check the current day of the week:

```
If Now.DayOfWeek = 6 Then BackUpFiles()
```

In the previous line of code, we used the `DayOfWeek` property to determine the current day of the week, but `DayOfWeek` can be used with any date object. It returns an Integer value directly, and is more efficient than comparing strings using the `Format` method. A complete list of properties used to extract date parts are listed in Table 6.7

TABLE 6.7   PROPERTIES USED TO OBTAIN SPECIFIC PARTS OF A DATE

Property Name	Information Returned	Type Returned
Date	Date Only	Date
TimeofDay	Time Only	TimeSpan
Month	Month (1–12)	Integer
Day	Day of the Month (1–31)	Integer
Year	Year	Integer
Hour	Hour (0–23)	Integer
Minute	Minute (0–59)	Integer
Second	Second (0–59)	Integer
Millisecond	Millisecond (0–999)	Integer
DayOfWeek	Weekday Number (0–6)	Integer
DayOfYear	Day of Year (1–366)	Integer
Ticks	Ticks since 1/1/0000	Long

Note

When extracting parts of a date, users of previous versions of Visual Basic may also be familiar with functions such as DatePart, Year, Month, and Day. These functions are still supported in Visual Basic .NET. However, the authors feel the new properties described here are a better fit with object-oriented coding practices.

Most of the properties listed in Table 6.7 are fairly self-explanatory. However, a new type (TimeSpan) and a new time format (Tick) are introduced. These will be discussed in the upcoming section "Working with Time Intervals."

WORKING WITH DATE INTERVALS

One advantage of using a Date variable to store dates and times (rather than an integer or string) is that it provides a large amount of built-in functionality to manipulate the date. As we have already seen, date values can be formatted and parsed into parts very easily. Even more useful is the ability to add, subtract, and compare date values just as you would numbers. For example, suppose you are managing the construction of thousands of hotels. Thirty days prior to the opening date of the hotel, you need to send a form letter to the owner reminding him of the upcoming opening. The following sample function uses the AddDays method of the Date class to determine whether the letter needs to be sent:

```
Private Function NeedToSendLetter(ByVal OpeningDate As Date) As Boolean

    Dim ThirtyDaysAgo As Date

    'Subtract 30 days from system date
    ThirtyDaysAgo = Date.Today.AddDays(-30)

    'Check if opening date is within 30 day range
    If OpeningDate >= ThirtyDaysAgo And OpeningDate <= Date.Today Then
        Return True
    Else
        Return False
    End If

End Function
```

As you can see from the sample code, the AddDays method of a Date object returns a date value. This date value is determined by adding the number of days passed as a parameter to the date stored in a Date object. This function also demonstrates that dates can be compared using the same operators used with numeric values, such as greater than or equal to (>=).

Note

There are functions built into the date class to add all types of intervals, such as AddHours, AddMinutes, and AddMilliseconds. When you type a period after the name of a date object in the Code Editor, the automatic statement completion function will show you a list of these methods.

We have just seen how to add a specified number of intervals to a date. However, if you want to determine the number of intervals between two dates, use the `DateDiff` function. The `DateDiff` function accepts a constant representing the type of interval, and the dates you want to compare. It returns a double value representing the number of intervals between the two dates. If we go back to our example of tracking opening dates of hotels, we could easily use the `DateDiff` function to determine the number of days between the opening date and today:

```
Private Function DaysUntilOpening(ByVal OpenDate As Date) As Long

Return DateDiff(DateInterval.Day, Date.Today, OpenDate)

End Function
```

The sample function `DaysUntilOpening` returns the number of days between the opening date and today. Note that the `DateDiff` function will return a negative number if the second date parameter is less than the first, or zero if the two dates are on the same day. In our example, the caller of the `DaysUntilOpening` would know that the hotel is already open if the value returned was less than or equal to zero.

Working with Time Intervals

Another special type, `TimeSpan`, contains members for working with periods of time. As you saw in Table 6.7, the `TimeOfDay` method of a date object returns a `TimeSpan` that represents the period of time since midnight. However, time spans represent time intervals independent of a date. The following code demonstrates some methods of the `TimeSpan` class:

```
Dim MyInterval As TimeSpan

MyInterval = TimeSpan.FromMinutes(12345)

Debug.WriteLine("Number of Days: " & MyInterval.Days)
Debug.WriteLine("Number of Hours: " & MyInterval.Hours)
Debug.WriteLine("Number of Ticks: " & MyInterval.Ticks)
```

In the sample code, we created a `TimeSpan` variable called `MyInterval` that represents a period of time of 12,345 minutes. We then used methods of the `TimeSpan` class to display other types of intervals within the time period. The output from the previous lines of code is

```
Number of Days: 8
Number of Hours: 13
Number of Ticks: 7407000000000
```

Notice that the output for the `Timespan.Ticks` property is a huge number. A *tick* is the most precise measure of time in Visual Basic. It represents a time interval of 100 nanoseconds and can be stored in a variable of type `Long`. The `Ticks` property of any date value contains the number of ticks since 1/1/0000. One use for ticks is measuring the performance of your application.

→ For more on measuring performance, **see** Chapter 26, "Debugging and Performance Tuning," **p. 717**

HANDLING TWO-DIGIT YEAR INPUT

Historians will no doubt look back in amusement at late 1999. As you may recall, the looming "Year 2000 problem" was on everyone's mind at the time. Doomsayers predicted that our technologically over-dependent society would plunge into chaos as computers worldwide failed to correctly recognize the year 2000. The local Memphis paper even ran an article on a man who was stockpiling toilet paper and raising live chickens—just in case. As it turns out, the Y2K problem failed to produce even a decent disaster *movie*, let alone the societal meltdown some people had anticipated.

However, the Y2K problem did bring to the public's mind the way two-digit years are handled by computers. Writing the year with only two digits will probably always be an accepted form of date notation. As a VB programmer, you should be aware of how to handle two-digit years. Consider, for example, the following representations of dates:

```
7/12/43
```

```
430712
```

When a user enters one of the preceding strings in a text box, how do you know what year they really mean? If your program deals with birthdays, obviously they mean 1943. However, if you are writing a program that processes bank loans or other future dates the user may mean 2043. As you already know, variables of type `Date` contain the year, which can be retrieved using the `Year` property or `DatePart` function. However, date values can also be stored in other types, such as an integer or string. The date conversion routine `Convert.ToDateTime` would convert the aforementioned year to 1943. (The default behavior is years from 00-30 are converted to the 2000s, 30-99 are converted to the 1900s. As we will see in a moment, this range can be changed using the Windows Control Panel.) Of course, if you represent the year using four digits then you can specify any year you want.

Another consideration is what happens if the user omits the year altogether. Visual Basic's built-in date conversion routines add the current year if a year is not specified:

```
'The variable dtChristmas will contain the current year
Dim dtChristmas As Date = Convert.ToDateTime("12/25")
Debug.WriteLine(Format(dtChristmas, "MM/dd/yyyy"))
```

However, this may not always be appropriate to your application. Microsoft Money, for example, is smart enough to know that at the end of the year I may be entering checks for the new or old year, so it does not automatically assume the current year.

There is a nice touch you can add to your program's user interface that will help eliminate confusion over what date is actually entered. Simply add code to format the date when a user exits the field, adding slashes and the appropriate number of year digits. Listing 6.2 shows an example of this function.

LISTING 6.2   CHECKDATE.ZIP—CONVERTING STRINGS TO DATES

```
Private Function CheckValidDateString(ByRef DateString As String) As Boolean

   'If the user did not type slashes, make a guess based on the length
   If InStr(DateString, "-") = 0 And InStr(DateString, "/") = 0 _
      And InStr(DateString, "\") = 0 Then

      If DateString.Length = 4 Then
         DateString = DateString.Substring(0, 2) & "/" & DateString.Substring(2)
      ElseIf (DateString.Length = 6 Or DateString.Length = 8) Then
         DateString = DateString.Substring(0, 2) & "/" & _
         DateString.Substring(2, 2) & "/" & DateString.Substring(4)
      End If

   End If

   'If you can convert the string to a date and format it, it is valid
   Try
      DateString = Format(Convert.ToDateTime(DateString), "MM/dd/yyyy")
      Return True

   Catch e As Exception
      Return False

   End Try

End Function
```

To test the previous function, place it in your form class. Next, draw several text boxes on the form, and in their Leave events place lines of code similar to the following:

```
Dim s As String = TextBox1.Text
If CheckValidDateString(s) Then TextBox1.Text = s
```

Run the program, and enter some dates using two-digit years, dashes instead of slashes, or just numbers with no slashes. As you tab from one text box to the next the date will be reformatted appropriately, providing a nice visual confirmation.

WORKING WITH STRINGS

Look at the keys of your computer keyboard and you will see a lot of examples of characters, such as numbers, letters, and symbols. Visual Basic .NET provides two data types for working with character data. A Char type variable can store a single character value. The more commonly used String variable stores a group of these characters, usually a piece of text such as a word. As you have already seen in numerous examples, to identify a literal string in Visual Basic code, you use double-quotation marks (") as delimiters:

```
Dim MyName As String = "Brian"
```

The quotation marks around a string value allow the compiler to separate it from other words, such as variable names. Quotes used to delimit a string are not actually stored with the string. However, a string variable can contain double-quotes:

```
MyName = "George ""Machine Gun"" Kelly"
```

As you can see from the sample previous line of code, to include a double quote within a string, you simply use double-quotation marks. You also can use the Chr function, which returns a character based on a numeric code:

```
MyName = "George " & Chr(34) & "Machine Gun" & Chr(34) & "Kelly"
```

The number 34 represents the numeric code for the quote character. Whatever method you use to add quotes to your string, the result is the same. If you were to print or display the example string MyName you would see the following value:

```
George "Machine Gun" Kelly
```

As you develop your applications, you use strings for many purposes. The better you manipulate the strings that you use, the more professional your programs appear. Visual Basic allows you to be quite flexible as you work with the strings in your programs. In this section, we will review the many functions you can use to manipulate character strings.

STRING CONCATENATION

One operation you will frequently perform on a string is *concatenation*. The concatenation operator, which is the ampersand symbol (&), combines two or more strings of text, similar to the way the addition operator combines two or more numbers. When you combine two strings with the concatenation operator, the second string is appended directly to the end of the first string. The result is a longer string containing the full contents of both source strings. The following lines of code show examples of string concatenation:

```
Dim s1 As String = "Ebony"
Dim s2 As String = "Ivory"

s1 = s1 & s2
s1 = s1 & "123"
s1 &= "Hello" & 456 & "7"
s1 &= (2 * 4)
Messagebox.Show(s1)
```

As you can see from the examples, you can use the concatenation operator to combine any number of strings or numeric expressions. After the previous lines of code are executed, the string stored in the variable s1 would be the following:

```
EbonyIvory123Hello45678
```

Two concatenation features new in VB .NET are the &= operator and the String.Concat method. The &= operator, demonstrated above, provides a shorthand approach for assigning the result of concatenation operation back to the to the original variable. Concat is a static method in the String class which provides the same functionality as the & operator:

```
strFullName = String.Concat(strFirstName, " ", strLastName)
```

The Concat method returns a string that represents the concatenation of all of its parameters. The previous line of code uses the static method, which does not require an instance of a string variable. However, Concat by itself (even as a method of a string object) does not alter the value of a string variable unless it is used in an assignment statement.

Note

> The standard concatenation operators will suffice for most applications. However, the .NET Framework also provides the StringBuilder class, for extra high-performance. For more information, see the help topic "StringBuilder Class."

DETERMINING THE LENGTH OF THE STRING

For many operations, you may need to know how many characters are in a string. You might need this information to know whether the string with which you are working will fit in a fixed-length database field. Or, if you are working with individual characters of a string, you may want to make sure that the character number you are referencing is valid. In any case, to determine the length of any string, you use the Length property of the string, as illustrated in the following code sample:

```
Dim strName As String = "John Doe"
Dim intNameLength As Integer

'The length of the sample string is 8
intNameLength = strName.Length
```

Note that the Length property returns the total count of characters in the string, including white spaces.

WORKING WITH PARTS OF A STRING

You will find many situations in which you need to work with only part of a string. For example, your company may use internal identification numbers in which characters or groups of characters mean something by themselves. Another example would be taking a string containing someone's complete name and parsing it into separate first and last name fields. You can easily accomplish these tasks by using the Substring method of the String class, which returns characters starting from a specified position in a string.

To use the Substring method, simply pass the starting index of the string and the number of characters you want to extract. If you omit the second argument, Substring will return all characters in the string starting from the specified index.

Note

> You may already be familiar with Left, Right, and Mid from previous versions of Visual Basic. The SubString method provides the same functionality in a more object-oriented fashion.

PART

II

CH

6

Remember, indexes in VB .NET are zero-based, so to extract characters from the leftmost part of a string, you would need to pass zero as the starting index. The following statement retrieves the first three characters of a string:

```
strAreaCode = strPhone.SubString(0,3)
```

To retrieve characters from the middle of a string, pass the index of the starting position. (As you will see in a moment, the `Instr` function provides a way to search a string and return the starting index.)

```
strPhone = "901-555-1212"
strPrefix = strPhone.SubString(4,3)      'Returns 555
strLocalNumber = strPhone.SubString(4)   'Returns 555-1212
```

Notice that if we omit the second parameter to substring, it returns all of the characters in the string from the index to the end.

To retrieve a specified number of characters from the right side of a string, you will need to subtract from the length of the string to find the starting index:

```
strSuffix = strPhone.SubString(strPhone.Length - 4)
```

The previous line of code returns the rightmost four characters in the string `strPhone`. However, if the length of the string happens to be less than 4, such as a blank phone number, an exception will occur. Valid indexes in a string are positive and the subtraction from any length less than 4 would result in a negative index being passed to the `Substring` function. You can safeguard against this exception by making sure your calculated starting index is zero or greater:

```
strSuffix = strPhone.SubString(Math.Max(0,strPhone.Length - 4))
```

`Max` is a function available in the `Math` class we discussed earlier in this chapter.

CHANGING THE CASE OF A STRING

Strings are frequently used to store alphabetic characters, such as names. The String class provides a few useful methods used to change the case (or capitalization) of a string. The easiest ones to use are `ToUpper` and `ToLower`, which convert the characters in a string to upper- and lowercase, respectively:

```
Dim TestString As String = "Easy As 123"
Messagebox.Show(TestString.ToUpper)    'Returns EASY AS 123
Messagebox.Show(TestString.ToLower)    'Returns easy as 123
```

Note that white spaces and numbers in the string are not affected, only the characters whose case can be changed.

Although these functions may appear to be somewhat trivial, they actually are quite useful for checking user input against a predefined value or a range of values. If you convert the user's input to uppercase, you can compare it to an uppercase test string, as in the following example:

```
Select Case txtOperation.Text.ToUpper
```

```
      Case "WASH"
         ' Do Something
      Case "RINSE"
         ' Do Something Else
      Case "SPIN"
         ' Do Something Else Yet
      Case Else
         MessageBox.Show("Invalid Input!!")

   End Select
```

Note

The string methods return values, but they do not modify the input. Consider the following example with the `ToUpper` method:

```
Dim s1 As String
Dim s2 As String
s1 = "which case am i"
s2 = s1.ToUpper
```

After this code is executed, the variable `s2` appears in all uppercase letters, whereas `s1` remains unchanged, unless you put `s1` on both sides of the assignment statement, like this:

```
s1 = s1.ToUpper
```

In the preceding code, if the `ToUpper` method had not been applied to the value of the text box, the user would receive the invalid input message even if he or she had entered a correct choice in lowercase or mixed case (`Rinse`, for example).

Another Visual Basic function, `StrConv`, performs special conversions of strings. `StrConv` can convert a string to *proper case*, in which the first letter of each word is capitalized. The following code sample demonstrates this technique:

```
StrConv("DR. STIRLING P. WILLIAMS", VbStrConv.ProperCase)
```

The constant passed as the second parameter to `StrConv` indicates the type of conversion to perform. Most of the additional conversions are either redundant (converting to all uppercase or all lowercase, for example) or beyond the scope of this book (converting between different types of Japanese characters). The result of the preceding call to `StrConv` would return a string like the following:

```
Dr. Stirling P. Williams
```

The proper case conversion handles most names, but suffixes like `III` would be incorrectly converted to `Iii`.

SEARCHING A STRING

For many string-related tasks, the first programming requirement is to determine whether a word, phrase, or other group of characters exists in a string and, if so, where. The capability to find one string within another enables you to perform word searches within text. You can

PART

II

CH

6

do these searches to perform a global replacement of a string, such as replacing the word *catastrophe* with the words *opportunity for improvement* throughout a word processing document.

Another, more common, reason for searching within a string is *parsing* the string. For example, suppose you have an input string that contains a person's name in this format: "Bobby Lee Schwartz." If you have a file of a hundred such strings, putting this information into a database with separate first and last name fields would be a little difficult. However, you can use a string search function along with a little program logic to parse the string into smaller pieces.

A new function in Visual Basic .NET than be used to search a string for a character or string is the IndexOf method. The IndexOf method has several overloaded parameter lists, but in its simplest form it accepts the search string and returns the index where it starts:

```
Dim strSentence As String
Dim intFoundPosition As Integer

strSentence = "I'll see you next Tuesday"
intFoundPosition = strSentence.IndexOf("you")
```

If the IndexOf method cannot find the string, it returns the value –1. You can check the return value of IndexOf with an If statement to determine whether the search was successful:

```
If intFoundPosition < 0 Then
      Debug.WriteLine("I couldn't find you!")
Else
      Debug.WriteLine("I found you at position " & intFoundPosition)
End If
```

In our example, the IndexOf method should return a value of 9, which is the index of the *y* in the word *you*. The index value returned from a search can be used with the other sting functions mentioned in this section to manipulate or change specific characters.

Note

String searches are case-sensitive.

Note

At the time of this writing, the traditional Visual Basic string search function, Instr, was still supported. However, it still uses a 1-based index for string characters. To avoid confusion of string indexes when working with other string functions, the authors recommend using the newer IndexOf method instead.

Another common type of search uses a parameter to tell the IndexOf function the index from which to start the search. For example, the function call

```
Debug.WriteLine ("Pride cometh before a fall".IndexOf("e",6))
```

returns the value of 9, even though the first *e* in the string is at position 4, because the search starts from position 6. You also can specify an ending range for the search by providing an ending index:

```
Debug.WriteLine ("Pride cometh before a fall".IndexOf("a",0,10))
```

The extra parameters in the previous line of code instruct the IndexOf function to start the search at index 0 and end the search at index 10, so a search for an *a* in this range would be unsuccessful. When you use parameters to specify a search range, they must be positive integers within the valid index ranges for the string, or the function will throw an exception.

Before we leave the subject of searching strings, we should mention another function new to .NET, the EndsWith method. It simply returns True or False depending on whether a string ends with a particular set of characters:

```
If FilePathName.ToUpper.EndsWith("JPG") Then
    FileDescription = "Picture file"
ElseIf filepathname.EndsWith("MP3") Then
    FileDescription = "Music File"
End If
```

As with the IndexOf method, searches using EndsWith are case sensitive.

GETTING RID OF EXTRA SPACES

It is normal for some strings contain to spaces in the middle of the string, which are necessary for proper spacing of words, paragraphs, and so on. However, you also may end up with spaces at the beginning or end of your strings, which often are unwanted spaces. These spaces typically occur when the user accidentally types a space at the beginning or end of a text field, and can interfere with comparisons:

```
Dim s1 As String = "Hello        "
Dim s2 As String = " Hello "
Dim s3 As String = "     Hello"
```

Although they contain the same word, the extra spaces in the strings cause them to be non-equivalent, and the Length property of each contains a different value. This difference is especially crucial with text box input; a user could inadvertently type three characters of text and then a bunch of spaces in a text box. If you need to concatenate the input with another string or use it in an If statement, the extra spaces are included. However, Visual Basic provides some string-trimming functions to eliminate the trailing spaces.

To get rid of the spaces at the end of a string, you can use the Trim or TrimEnd methods. The Trim method works with both ends of a string, but TrimEnd only removes spaces from the right:

```
"  Test String  ".Trim            'Removes spaces from left and right
"  Test String  ".TrimEnd(Nothing) 'Removes spaces from right only
"x Test String x".Trim            'Does not remove any spaces
```

Note

Both `Trim` and `TrimEnd` also have the ability to remove characters other than spaces. For example, the following code trims the string *rac* from both ends of the word *racecar*, which leaves only an *e*:

```
MessageBox.Show("racecar".Trim("rac".ToCharArray))
```

`Trim` and `TrimEnd` work with leading and trailing characters. In other words, if there is a character between the end of the string and the search character, these functions will not trim the character. However, Visual Basic .NET provides two other methods that can be used for removing or substituting characters anywhere in the string: `Remove` and `Replace`.

```
"Extraordinary".Remove(0,4)     'Returns "ordinary"
"Pop".replace("o"c, "a"c)  'Returns "Pap"
```

`Remove` accepts a start and ending index and returns a string with all characters in the index range removed. `Replace` replaces each occurrence of a character with another character.

ADDING CHARACTERS TO THE ENDS OF A STRING

Just as there are times when you don't need any extra spaces in your strings, there are sometimes reasons to pad a string with extra characters. For example, my company bought new Accounts Payable software that required the conversion of vendor identification numbers from a 9-character string with no extra digits to a 10-digit format with leading zeroes. By using the `PadLeft` and `PadRight` methods of the String class, this can easily be accomplished:

```
strNewVendorNumber = strOldVendorNumber.PadLeft(10, "0"c)
```

The first parameter to the `PadLeft` function is the desired total string length, including padding. The second parameter is the character to pad in order to meet the desired length. Leaving the second parameter off will pad the string with spaces.

`PadLeft` and `PadRight` add a single character a repeated number of times to the end of the string. However, there are times when you way want to add a set of characters to the middle of the string. You can accomplish this with the `Substring` method and concatenation operators, but Visual Basic provides a shortcut: the `Insert` method. The `Insert` method inserts a string into another string at the specified index.

USING ARRAYS

All the variables discussed so far have been single-instance variables. Often, however, you may find it very useful to work with *arrays*. An array is a group of variables of the same type, sharing the same name. In this way, processing groups of related areas is easy. For example, you might want to have a group of variables that tracks the sales in each of your company's four regions. You can declare a decimal variable for each region, plus one for the total sales across all regions, like this:

```
Dim Reg1Sales, Reg2Sales As Decimal
Dim RegSales3, Reg4Sales As Decimal
Dim TotalSales As Decimal
```

Then, if you want to calculate the total sales for all regions, you might use this code:

```
TotalSales = Reg1Sales + Reg2Sales + Reg3Sales + Reg4Sales
```

This approach isn't all that cumbersome. However, what if you have 20 regions? Or several hundred? You can see how working with large numbers of related variables could get messy very quickly.

You can greatly simplify this example by using an array. The following line of code creates an array to contain the 20 regional sales figures:

```
Dim RegionalSales(19) As Decimal
```

Note the array declaration looks similar to a regular variable declaration, with the addition of the number 19 in parentheses. Each element in an array is accessed using an *index*, which starts at zero. This is important to consider, because it means 19 is the maximum index value. So the RegionalSales array contains 20 decimal values, numbered 0 to 19.

> **Note**
>
> Starting in Visual Basic .NET, array indexes start at 0 and the older syntax of specifying boundaries with the To keyword is no longer supported.

Values in an array (also known as *array elements*) work in assignment statements just like regular variables:

```
RegionalSales(15) = 2000.00
TextBox1.Text = RegionalSales(3).ToString
```

Array indexes themselves can also be variables, as in the following example, which adds all of the regional sales figures:

```
Dim CurrentRegion As Integer

For CurrentRegion = 0 to 19
    TotalSales = TotalSales + RegionalSales(CurrentRegion)
Next
```

Note this example's use of a *loop*. The block of code beginning with the For instruction and ending with the Next instruction defines a group of program statements that will be repeated a certain number of times (in this case 20). Using loops makes short work of processing variable arrays. Loops are discussed in Chapter 7, "Controlling the Flow of Your Program."

DYNAMIC ARRAYS

In the previous example, when we declared the variable array RegionalSales we specified the maximum index number, 19. Because arrays are zero-based, specifying a maximum index value of 19 creates an array with 20 elements. However, at certain times you may need to declare an array variable without knowing in advance how many elements are contained within it. One example might be if the user is typing in an unknown number of values or you are reading them from a file. To change the size of an array, you can use the ReDim or

ReDim Preserve statements. (The word Preserve means you want to preserve the data in the array, ReDim by itself causes the data to be lost each time array is re-dimensioned.) As an example, the following code reads a list of strings from a file, adding each string to an array.

```
Dim TestFile As StreamReader = File.OpenText("inputfile.txt")
Dim NumElements As Integer = 0
Dim BunchOfStrings() As String

While TestFile.Peek <> -1
     NumElements = NumElements + 1
     ReDim Preserve BunchOfStrings(NumElements - 1)
     BunchOfStrings(NumElements - 1) = TestFile.ReadLine()
End While

TestFile.Close()

Messagebox.Show("Number of elements in the array=" & NumElements)
Messagebox.Show("Last index number in the array=" & UBound(BunchOfStrings))
```

In the sample code, notice that no size for the BunchOfStrings array is provided, although the parentheses are still used to indicate it is a variable array. The ReDim Preserve statement within the While loop causes the array to grow as the counter variable NumElements is increased. Note that because array indexes start at zero, the count of elements in the array is always 1 greater than the maximum index value. To determine the maximum index value, you can use the Ubound function, which returns the upper boundary of an array.

INITIALIZING AN ARRAY

In our examples up to this point, we have used the assignment statement to put values in an array. However, a new feature in Visual Basic .NET is the ability to initialize an array in the Dim statement by placing the array values in curly braces ({ }). The following example shows how an array of integers can be initialized:

```
Dim PowersofTwo() As Integer = {1, 2, 4, 8, 16, 32, 64, 128}
```

Initialization with curly braces can only be used when you do *not* specify the array boundaries explicitly. Instead, the number of array elements is set to the number of elements contained within the braces. (You can still expand or shrink the array in code using ReDim.) In the previous line of code, the resulting array PowersOfTwo contains eight elements. The element in index 0 is 1, index 1 is 2, and so on.

SORTING AND SEARCHING AN ARRAY

All variable arrays are based on the .NET Framework's built-in Array class, which means they all inherit certain functions from it. Two of the most useful of these functions are the ability to sort and search an array.

SORTING AN ARRAY

You can use the Sort function of an array to sort an array of strings or numbers. The following code sample prints the contents of an array, sorts it, and prints the array again:

```
Dim strNames() As String = {"Betty", "Alphonse", "Xavier", "Susie"}
Dim CurIndex As Integer

For CurIndex = 0 To Ubound(strNames)
    Debug.WriteLine(strNames(CurIndex))
Next

'The following line of code does the sorting
Array.Sort(strNames)

For CurIndex = 0 To Ubound(strNames)
    Debug.WriteLine(strNames(CurIndex))
Next
```

The Sort method actually moves the contents of an array, changing the elements to be indexed alphabetically. After running the sample code, Alphonse would be at index 0 and Xavier at index 3.

Note

If you want to sort in descending order, use the Sort method followed by the Reverse method.

SEARCHING A SORTED ARRAY

The Array class also provides the ability to search an array for an element, but the array you are searching must be sorted. The BinarySearch method simply returns the index of the element if it finds it, or a negative number if it does not.

```
Dim FoundPosition As Integer
Dim SearchStudent As String = "Susie"
Array.Sort(strNames)
FoundPosition = Array.BinarySearch(strNames, SearchStudent)
```

If we use the sample array data from the previous section, FoundPosition would contain the array value 2.

ARRAYS WITH MULTIPLE DIMENSIONS

We have seen how an array can store a value associated with an index, but what if you need to store more than one value per index? For example, earlier we stored a sales figure for each region. Suppose we needed to store more than one number for each region, such as sales for each quarter. The following statement declares a *two-dimensional* array:

```
Dim RegionalSales(19, 3) As Decimal
```

PART

II

CH

6

To add extra dimensions to an array, you simply specify the size of the new dimension in parentheses, separated by a comma. In the `RegionalSales` array, the first dimension contains 20 elements and the second dimension contains four. The following code shows how to access each element in the array:

```
Dim CurrentRegion As Integer
Dim CurrentQuarter As Integer
For CurrentRegion = 0 To RegionalSales.GetUpperBound(0)
    For CurrentQuarter = 0 To RegionalSales.GetUpperBound(1)
        Debug.WriteLine("Sales for Region " & CurrentRegion & " Quarter " & _
        CurrentQuarter & " are " & RegionalSales(CurrentRegion, CurrentQuarter))
    Next
Next
```

Notice in the preceding sample code we used the `GetUpperBound` method to determine the maximum array index for each dimension.

Note

The `GetUpperBound` function is zero-based, unlike the `UBound` function mentioned earlier. Both can be used to determine the maximum array index for a given dimension. In other words, the following statements are equivalent:

```
UBound(RegionalSales,2)
RegionalSales.GetUpperBound(1)
```

UNDERSTANDING REGIONAL SETTINGS

In the age of the Internet, you may find your programs running in multiple countries. Each country may use a different notation for numbers and dates. For example, some countries use the pound (£) instead of the dollar ($) symbol to indicate currency. The Windows operating system allows the user to set up numeric, date, time, and currency formats specific to their *locale*. Figure 6.5 shows the Control Panel screen from Windows 2000, which determines the default numeric formats.

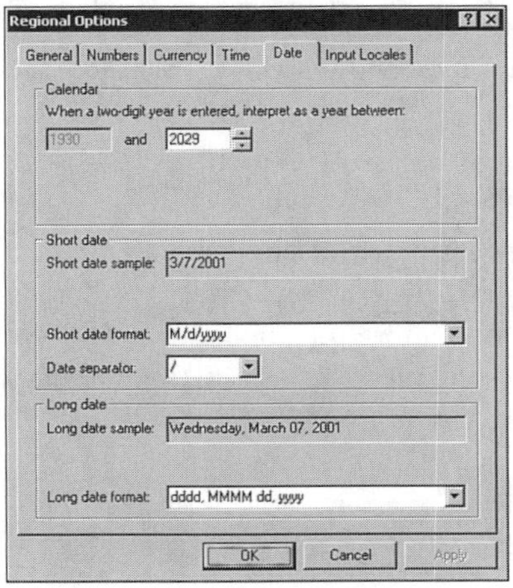

Figure 6.5
To change the default format for dates and other numbers, use the Regional Options icon in the Windows Control Panel.

What does this mean to the Visual Basic programmer? There are a couple of ways you can use region (or culture) information:

- *Predefined format strings* allow your program to automatically display data in the correct regional format.
- The *System.Globalization* namespace provides capabilities to determine information about the formats in a culture.

USING NAMED FORMATS

In earlier sections, we showed how to format dates and numbers using custom strings containing characters representing the desired format of the number. However, it is worth noting that the predefined formats for dates and numbers change depending on the format set in the control panel, as in the following examples:

```
Dim MyDate As Date = #12/10/1972#
Debug.WriteLine(Format(MyDate, "d"))
Debug.WriteLine(Format(MyDate, "D"))
```

The d and D predefined date formats correspond to the short and long date formats shown in Figure 6.5. If you modify these settings and restart your program, the output format of the preceding lines of code will change.

Note

The .ToString conversion function for numbers uses the current culture.

USING FORMATS FROM OTHER CULTURES

The System.Globalization namespace contains information about various cultures and the formats they use. Up to this point, we have demonstrated formatting by using the Format function, which always uses the current culture. However, the ToString method of the numeric and date data types can be used with any culture installed on your machine. You simply pass the format string and an instance of the CultureInfo class and the number is formatted appropriately, as in the following example:

```
Dim TestNumber As Integer = 123456
Dim strMessage As String
Dim RegInfo As CultureInfo

For Each RegInfo In CultureInfo.GetCultures(CultureTypes.InstalledWin32Cultures)
    strMessage = "The " & RegInfo.NativeName & " number format is"
    strMessage &= TestNumber.ToString("n", RegInfo.NumberFormat)
    ListBox1.Items.Add(strMessage)
Next
```

The code sample demonstrates using the standard predefined number format (n) of each culture. Figure 6.6 shows the different formats displayed by the previous code.

PART

II

CH

6

Figure 6.6
The `CultureInfo` class for a culture contains formatting information for the country or region.

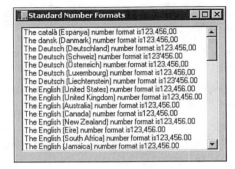

> **Note**
>
> The `Application.CurrentCulture` property contains information about the current culture settings.

If you do not specify a format provider, the `ToString` method uses the current culture settings.

EXERCISE: PARSING STRINGS

In this chapter, you have learned about several functions to manipulate strings. You have also seen how arrays can be used to store multiple variables together. In this section we will combine your knowledge of arrays and strings and introduce two useful methods, `Split` and `Join`. The `Split` function parses a string into array elements, and the `Join` function combines array elements into a string. To begin this exercise, start a new Windows application project in Visual Studio .NET.

USING `Split` TO SEPARATE A STRING

If you are exchanging data with another company, you may be receiving a file delimited by commas, spaces, or tabs. For example, I use a program to pull stock information off a Web site and store it in a database. The stock information returned includes the symbol, price, and change in a comma-separated format as follows:

```
"XYZ",1.23,-4.5
```

You can, of course, use the search functions described earlier to find the commas and extract individual values with the `Substring` function. However, the `Split` function of the string class automatically separates the string into pieces. To demonstrate, you will need to set up a form:

1. Add two text boxes to the form. Set the `Name` properties to `txtInput` and `txtSeparator`. Using labels, label these controls "Input String" and "Separator Character," respectively.

2. Add a button named `btnSplit`. Change the caption to `Split String`.

3. Add a list box to the form named `lstOutput`.

4. Enter the code in Listing 6.3 in the button's `Click` event.

LISTING 6.3   STRINGEX.ZIP—PARSING A STRING WITH THE Split METHOD

```
Dim TempArray() As String
Dim CurIndex As Integer

lstOutput.Items.Clear()
If txtInput.Text.Length > 0 And txtSeparator.Text.Length > 0 Then
    TempArray = txtInput.Text.Split(txtSeparator.Text.ToCharArray)
    For CurIndex = 0 To TempArray.GetUpperBound(0)
        lstOutput.Items.Add(TempArray(CurIndex))
    Next
End If
```

Run the program by pressing the F5 key. Type a sentence in the input box and a space in the separator box. Click the button and you should see results similar to those shown in Figure 6.7.

Figure 6.7
With one line of code, the split function can break an string into pieces, each of which has its own array index.

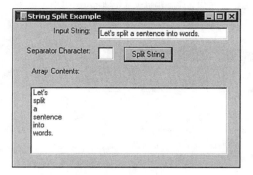

CREATING A STRING FROM AN ARRAY

The Join function works just the opposite of the Split function; it combines the elements in an array into a string, adding a delimiter. For the sample exercise with Join, set up another Windows Application project. Design the form as follows:

1. Add a text box to the form. Set the Name property to txtArraySize and label it "Random numbers to generate:"

2. Add a button beside the text box named btnJoin. Change the caption to Join Array Elements.

3. Add another text box to the form. Because it may contain multiple lines of text, set its Multiline property to True and size it large enough to contain several lines of text. Set the Name property to txtOutput.

4. Enter the code in Listing 6.4 in the button's Click event.

PART

II

CH

6

LISTING 6.4   STRINGEX.ZIP—CREATING A STRING FROM AN ARRAY

```
Dim TempArray() As String
Dim RandomInteger As New System.Random()
Dim CurIndex As Integer
```

LISTING 6.4   CONTINUED

```
Dim NumElements As Integer = val(txtArraySize.Text).ToInt32

'Generate random numbers, put in TempArray
If NumElements > 0 Then
    ReDim TempArray(NumElements)
    For CurIndex = 0 To NumElements - 1
        TempArray(CurIndex) = RandomInteger.Next(1000).tostring
    Next
End If

'Join array elements into a comma-separated string
txtOutput.text = String.Join(",", temparray)
```

Run the program and enter a number in the text box. The `For` loop generates a string array of the specified size containing random numbers. The result of the `Join` function is shown in Figure 6.8.

Figure 6.8
An example use of
`Join` might be to
combine database
fields for an external
program that requires
a comma-separated
text file.

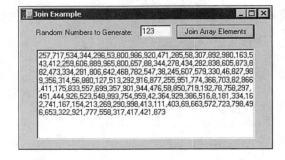

CHAPTER 7

CONTROLLING THE FLOW OF YOUR PROGRAM

In this chapter

Two of the fundamental strengths of computers are their capabilities to execute instructions quickly and to make decisions precisely. In this chapter, you will learn how to take advantage of these capabilities in two very important ways: through the use of decision-making techniques and the use of loops, which allow portions of code to run a controlled number of times.

In the last chapter, you learned about a class of code statements known as assignment statements, which are used to set and modify the values of variables. Another group of statements is important for handling more complex tasks. These statements are known collectively as *control statements*. Without control statements, your program would start at the first line of code and proceed line by line until the last line was reached, at which point the program would stop.

One type of control statement is the *decision statement*. This statement is used to control the execution of parts of your program, based on conditions that exist at the time the statement is encountered. The two basic types of decision statements are `If` statements and `Select Case` statements. The other major type of control statement is the *loop*. You use loops to perform repetitive tasks in your program. Three main types of loops are supported by Visual Basic: counter loops, conditional loops, and enumerator loops.

UNDERSTANDING If STATEMENTS

For many decisions, you may want to execute a statement (or group of statements) only if a particular condition is `True`. Two forms of the `If` statement handle `True` conditions: the *single-line* `If` statement and the *multiple-line* `If` statement. Each uses the `If` statement to check a condition. If the condition is `True`, the program runs the commands associated with the `If` statement. For example, the following two `If` statements perform the same function:

```
'Single-Line IF
If x > 5 then x = 0

'Multiple-Line IF
If x > 5 Then
    x = 0
End If
```

In the code sample, the condition is the value of the variable x being greater than 5. If this condition is `True` the statement x=0 will be executed. If the condition is `False` (in the preceding example, if x is *not* greater than 5), the commands on the `If` line (single-line `If`) or between the `If` and `End If` statements (multiple-line `If`) are skipped, and the next line of code is executed.

THE SINGLE-LINE If STATEMENT

You use the single-line `If` statement to perform a single task when the condition in the statement is `True`. The task can be a single command, or you can perform multiple commands by calling a procedure. The following is the syntax of the single-line `If` statement:

```
If condition Then command
```

The argument *condition* represents any type of logical condition, which can be any of the following:

- Comparison of a variable to a literal, another variable, or a function
- A variable or database field that contains a `True` or `False` value
- Any function or expression that returns a `True` or `False` value

The argument *command* represents the task to be performed if the condition is `True`. This task can be any valid Visual Basic statement, including a procedure call. The following code shows how an `If` statement is used to display a message only if the statement is executed before the noon hour:

```
If Date.Now.Hour < 12 Then Messagebox.Show("Good morning!")
```

USING MULTIPLE COMMANDS WITH AN If BLOCK

If you need to execute more than one command in response to a condition, you can use the multiple-line form of the `If` statement. It also is known as a *block* `If` statement. This construct bounds a range of statements between the `If` statement and an `End If` statement. If the condition in the `If` statement is `True`, all the commands between the `If` and `End If` statements are executed. If the condition is `False`, the program skips to the first line after the `End If` statement. The following example shows how a block `If` statement is used in processing a market exhibitor's payments. If the exhibitor has a deposit on file, the deposit amount is moved to the total amount paid, and a procedure that processes a reservation is called.

```
If DepositAmt > 0 Then
    TotalPaid = TotalPaid + DepositAmt
    DepositAmt = 0
    UpdateReservation(ExhibitorID)
End If
```

Note that indenting lines of code in a multiple-line `If` statement is a customary formatting practice that makes the code more readable. As you type a multi-line `If` statement in the code editor, Visual Basic .NET automatically indents the code contained in an `If` block and adds the `End If` when you type the word `Then` and press Enter. This feature can be disabled under the "Visual Basic Specific Options" section in the Text Editor Folder of the Options dialog box.

> **Note**
>
> Many programmers never use the single-line format of the `If` statement, preferring the readability and structure of the block `If`.

WORKING WITH THE False CONDITION

Of course, if a condition can be `True`, it also can be `False`; and sometimes you might want code to execute only on a `False` condition. Other times, you might want to take one action if a condition is `True` and another action if the condition is `False`. The following sections look at handling the `False` side of a condition.

USING THE Not OPERATOR

One way to execute a statement, or group of statements, for a False condition is to use the Not operator. The Not operator inverts the actual condition that follows it. If the condition is True, the Not operator makes the overall expression False, and vice versa. The following code uses the Not operator to invert the value of the Boolean variable Taxable, which reports an exhibitor's sales and use tax status. Taxable is True if the exhibitor is to pay taxes, and False if he or she is not. The code tests for the condition Not Taxable; if this condition evaluates to True, the exhibitor is not taxable.

```
If Not Taxable Then
    SalesTax = 0
    UseTax = 0
End If
```

HANDLING True AND False CONDITIONS WITH Else

The other way of handling False conditions allows you to process different sets of instructions for the True or False condition. You can handle this "fork in the road" in Visual Basic with the Else part of the If statement block.

To handle both the True and False conditions, you start with the block If statement and add the Else statement, as follows:

```
If condition Then
    statements to process when condition is True
Else
    statements to process when condition is False
End If
```

The If and End If statements of this block are the same as before. The condition is still any logical expression or variable that yields a True or False value. The key element of this set of statements is the Else statement. This statement is placed after the last statement to be executed if the condition is True, and before the first statement to be executed if the condition is False. For a True condition, the program processes the statements up to the Else statement and then skips to the first statement after the End If. If the condition is False, the program skips the statements prior to the Else statement and starts processing with the first statement after the Else.

Note

If you want to execute code for only the False portion of the statement, you can just place code statements between the Else and End If statements. You are not required to place any statements between the If and Else statements.

If you have several commands between the If and End If statements, you might want to repeat the condition as a comment in the End If statement, as in this example:

```
If TotalSales > ProjectedSales Then
        '
        ' A bunch of lines of code
        '
Else
        '
        ' Another bunch of lines of code
        '
End If  'TotalSales > ProjectedSales
```

Adding this comment makes your code easier to read.

WORKING WITH MULTIPLE If STATEMENTS

In the preceding sections, you saw the simple block If statements, which evaluate one condition and can execute commands for either a True or a False condition. You also can evaluate multiple conditions with an additional statement in the block If. The ElseIf statement enables you to specify another condition to evaluate when the first condition is False. Using the ElseIf statement, you can evaluate any number of conditions with one If statement block. The following lines of code demonstrate how you can use ElseIf to test for three possibilities—whether the contents of the variable TestValue are negative, zero, or positive:

```
If TestValue < 0 Then
        lblResult.Text = "Negative"
    ElseIf TestValue = 0 Then
        lblResult.Text = "Zero"
    Else
        lblResult.Text = "Positive"
    End If
```

The preceding code works by first evaluating the condition in the If statement. If the condition is True, the statement (or statements) immediately following the If statement is executed; then the program skips to the first statement after the End If statement.

If the first condition is False, the program skips to the first ElseIf statement and evaluates its condition. If this condition is True, the statements following the ElseIf are executed, and control again passes to the statement after the End If. This process continues for as many ElseIf statements as are in the block.

If all the conditions are False, the program skips to the Else statement and processes the commands between the Else and the End If statements. The Else statement is not required.

USING BOOLEAN LOGIC IN If CONDITIONS

Often you will use the standard If..Then..Else syntax, which is easy to understand because it reads like a sentence from a book. However, there are a couple of special situations that you may encounter when using the If construct that are worth mentioning:

- *Logical operators* can cause problems if not used correctly.
- *Short-circuiting* works with Boolean conditions to eliminate extra work.

The result of the evaluation of an If condition is a True or False value. As you may have noticed in previous examples, Boolean operators such as And, Or, and Not can be used to build more complex expressions from smaller ones:

```
If (WeeklyHrs > 30 And HireDate < Date.Now.AddYears(-1)) Or Status = "FullTime"
Then
    EligibleForBenefits = True
Else
    EligibleForBenefits = False
End If
```

The previous If statement could be stated as follows in plain English:

"In order to be eligible for benefits, you must either be a full-time employee or work more than 30 hours a week and have been hired for over a year."

Note the use of parentheses to group logical conditions, such that the result of the And comparison is evaluated and that result is used in the Or condition. The logical operators used with True/False conditions are as follows:

- **And**—Expressions on both sides of the And must evaluate True for the result to be True. If one or more expressions in the And comparison is False, the result is False.
- **Or**—If either side of an Or comparison is True, or both sides are True, then the result is True. The result of an Or is False only if both expressions are False.
- **Xor**—This stands for *exclusive or*. This operator is similar to Or but False if both sides are True. It can be read in English as "one or the other but not both."
- **Not**—Negates the result of an expression, Not True is False and Not False is True.

A common mistake is to use Or when you really mean And. For example, if a computer dating service is looking for single females over 21, this could cause quite a problem:

```
'Probably not what the programmer intended!
If Age >= 21 Or Sex = "F" Or Married = False Then
```

In the previous expression, if any one of the above expressions is True, the statements in the If will be executed. For example, a married 20-year-old lady or a two-year-old baby boy would cause the Or condition to evaluate to True. When you want multiple conditions to be required, And is usually the correct choice.

Another interesting aspect of Boolean expressions is the fact that you can often determine the result without looking at the whole expression. For example, with an And condition both sides must be `True` for the expression to be `True`; therefore if the left side of an `And` evaluates to `False`, you can assume the entire statement is `False`. This concept is known as *short-circuiting*, because you do not have to evaluate the whole expression. Short-circuiting was not supported in Visual Basic 6.0, but is supported in Visual Basic .NET. Every programmer should be aware of this concept, which is used to avoid unnecessary processing when using Boolean expressions:

```
If Process1BillionRecords() And Process1BillionMore() Then
```

Because of short-circuiting, if the `Process1BillionRecords` function returns `False`, the second function call would never be executed. Usually, you would not want to process an extra billion records (which we assume will take some time) because the expression is already known to be `False`. Most of the time short-circuiting works in your favor, but if you actually count on a function being executed in an `If` statement no matter what its return value, you may want to store the result of each call in a Boolean variable and then use `And` to compare the variables.

USING Select Case

Another way to handle decisions in a program is to use the `Select Case` statement. It allows you to conditionally execute any of a series of statement groups based on the value of a test expression, which can be a single variable or a complex expression. The `Select Case` statement is divided into two parts: test expression to be evaluated and a series of `Case` statements listing the possible values.

HOW Select Case WORKS

The `Select Case` structure is similar to a series of `If/Then/ElseIf` statements. The following lines of code show the syntax of the `Select Case` block:

```
Select Case testvalue
   Case value1
      statement group 1
   Case value2
      statement group 2
End Select
```

The first statement of the `Select Case` block is the `Select Case` statement itself. This statement identifies the value to be tested against possible results. This value, represented by the *testvalue* argument, can be any valid numeric or string expression, including literals, variables, or functions.

Each conditional group of commands (those that are run if the condition is met) is started by a `Case` statement. The `Case` statement identifies the expression to which the *testvalue* is compared. If the *testvalue* is equal to the expression, the commands after the `Case` statement are run. The program runs the commands between the current `Case` statement and the next `Case` statement or the `End Select` statement. If the *testvalue* is not equal to the value expression, the program proceeds to compare the expression against the next `Case` statement.

The End Select statement identifies the end of the Select Case block.

> **Note**
> Only one case in the Select Case block is executed for a given value of *testvalue*.

> **Caution**
> The *testvalue* and *value* expressions should represent the same data type. For example, if the *testvalue* is a number, the values tested in the Case statements also must be numbers.

Case statements within a Select Case structure also can handle *lists*, *ranges*, and *comparisons* of values in addition to discrete values. Note the use of Case Is < 0, Case 1 to 9, and Case Is > 50 in this example:

```
Select Case QuantityOrdered

    Case Is < 0  'note use of comparison
        MessageBox.Show("Order quantity cannot be negative!")

    Case 1, 2, 3 'note use of value list
        DiscountAmount = 0

    Case 4 To 9  'note use of range
        DiscountAmount = 0.03

    Case 10 To 49
        DiscountAmount = 0.08

    Case Is > 50
        DiscountAmount = 0.1

End Select
```

In the same Select Case statement, an integer quantity is compared against several values. Depending on the quantity value, a different discount amount is set.

HANDLING OTHER VALUES

The preceding example works fine if your test variable matches one of the conditions in a Case statement. But how do you handle other values that are outside the ones for which you tested? You can have your code do something for all other possible values of the test expression by adding a Case Else statement to your program. The Case Else statement follows the last command of the last Case statement in the block. You then place the commands that you want executed between the Case Else and the End Select statements.

You can use the Case Else statement to perform calculations for values not specifically called out in the Case statements. Alternatively, you can use the Case Else statement to let users know that they entered an invalid value.

Consider a simple form used to enter three test scores for a student into three text boxes. A Calculate button computes the average of the test scores and uses a Select Case block to determine the student's letter grade based on the average test score. Listing 7.1 shows the code behind the Calculate button's Click event.

LISTING 7.1   SELCASE.ZIP—USING Select Case TO DETERMINE A STUDENT'S LETTER GRADE

```
Private Sub btnCalc_Click(ByVal sender As System.Object,_
        ByVal e As System.EventArgs) Handles btnCalc.Click
        Dim SumOfGrades As Integer
        Dim NumericAverage As Double

        SumOfGrades = Convert.ToInt32((Val(txtTest1.Text) +_
                        Val(txtTest2.Text) + Val(txtTest3.Text)))

        NumericAverage = (SumOfGrades / 3)
        txtAverage.Text = Format(NumericAverage, "n")

        Select Case Convert.ToInt32(NumericAverage)
            Case Is = 100
                txtLetterGrade.Text = "A+"
            Case 93 To 99
                txtLetterGrade.Text = "A"
            Case 83 To 92
                txtLetterGrade.Text = "B"
            Case 73 To 82
                txtLetterGrade.Text = "C"
            Case 63 To 72
                txtLetterGrade.Text = "D"
            Case Is < 63
                txtLetterGrade.Text = "F"
        End Select

    End Sub
```

To test this code, follow these steps:

1. Add five text boxes named txtTest1, txtTest2, txtTest3, txtAverage, and txtLetterGrade to a form.

2. Add a command button named btnCalc.

3. As with any form, you should add Label controls as appropriate to identify the text boxes.

4. Enter the code from Listing 7.1 into the Click event procedure of btnCalc.

5. Click the VB Start button.

If you enter some grades into the input text boxes and click the button, the numeric and letter average will be displayed, as shown in Figure 7.1.

PART

II

CH

7

Figure 7.1
To determine the
letter grade, we
convert the numeric
average to an integer,
which rounds it up,
as shown here.

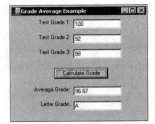

STRUCTURING YOUR CODE LOGICALLY

Before we leave the subject of control-flow statements, we need to mention something about the influence of programming style on your code. You have an enormous amount of freedom when writing VB code, but you should not let that freedom cause you to write messy code. As an example, let's look at test grades again. We have already covered how to do averaging and number-to-letter conversion using a Select Case statement. However, suppose someone enters an invalid numeric grade in one of the text boxes, such as 789 or −1234? Validating the data entered in the text boxes will require adding some If statements before you attempt to average the grades. If any of the grades entered is not a valid numeric grade, you should not average them but instead report this to the user.

Suppose we have a function called ValidGrade() that returns True or False depending on whether the text box value is a number between 0–100. Each programmer may come up a different way of arranging the input validation code. For example, you could type the If statements in a nested manner as follows:

```
If ValidGrade(txtTest1.Text) Then
      If ValidGrade(txtTest2.Text) Then
            If ValidGrade(txtTest3.Text) Then

                  ' INSERT LISTING 7.1 HERE

            End If
      End If

Else
      MessageBox.Show ("Invalid grade entered!")
End If
```

You also can use an And operator and put all the grade validation calls in the same If condition:

```
If ValidGrade(txtTest1.Text) And ValidGrade(txtTest2.Text)
   And ValidGrade(txtTest3.Text) Then

      ' INSERT LISTING 7.1 HERE

Else
      MessageBox.Show("Invalid grade entered!")
End if
```

Finally, you could just do all the input validation up front and exit the subroutine early if there are any problems:

```
If Not ValidGrade(txtTest1.Text) Then
    MessageBox("Invalid grade entered!")
    Exit sub
End if

If Not ValidGrade(txtTest2.Text) Then
    MessageBox("Invalid grade entered!")
    Exit sub
End if

If Not ValidGrade(txtTest3.Text) Then
    MessageBox("Invalid grade entered!")
    Exit sub
End if
' INSERT LISTING 7.1 HERE
```

As you can see, there are at least three different ways of validating the text box values by different arrangement of the If statements. Let's look at the structure of each in more detail:

- *Nested If statements* are probably the most correct in an academic sense, because there is essentially only one path through the function. One If statement is executed, which happens to contain another If, and so on. The drawback is that if you have a lot of nested Ifs and many lines of code, it may be difficult to keep all the nested conditions straight when reading the code.

- *Boolean operators* such as And allow you to include multiple conditions on the same line. This method is about as logical as the nested If, but may be less cluttered and easier to read on the screen. However, when using And you need to be aware of *short-circuiting*, as described earlier, to avoid unnecessary execution of the ValidGrade function.

- *Exiting the function early* is an entirely different approach to solving the problem. I have seen VB programmers use this method because it separates the input validation and task at hand entirely. However, when showing another developer this code, he said "that type of coding would get you fired where I used to work." I asked why and his answer was that having multiple exit points in a function makes the logic too hard to follow. So, to keep the code truly logical, you should move the validation code to a separate function:

```
If CheckTextBoxes() Then
    ' INSERT LISTING 7.1 HERE
Else
    MessageBox.Show("Invalid grade entered!")
End If
```

As you can see, even programming style can influence the flow of your program code. As you gain more experience programming, you will be able to write code that is logically easier to follow. Another good way to learn more about these types of issues is to study computer science in school. One result of a good computer science education is that you will learn about good programming practices you can use with any computer language.

WORKING WITH LOOPS

The other major type of control statement is the *loop*. You use loops to perform repetitive tasks in your program. Each time the task repeats, the loop is said to have completed an *iteration*. The three main types of loops are supported by Visual Basic: counter loops, conditional loops, and enumerator loops. Counter, or For, loops perform a task a set number of times. Conditional, or Do, loops perform a task while a specified condition exists or until a specified condition exists. Enumerator loops are used to perform an action on each item in a group of objects. Each of these types of loops is discussed in the following sections.

For LOOPS

A counter loop also is known as a For loop, or a For/Next loop, because the ends of the loop are defined by the For statement and the Next statement. At the beginning of a For loop, you define a counter variable, as well as the beginning and end points of the variable's value, and optionally the Step value, or the amount it is to be increased or decreased after each pass through the loop. The first time the loop is run, the counter variable is set to the value of the beginning point. Then, after each time the program runs through the loop, the value of the counter is incremented by the Step value and checked against the value of the endpoint. If the counter is larger than the end point, the program skips to the first statement following the loop's Next statement.

> **Caution**
>
> Although you can use any numeric variable for the counter, you need to be aware of the limits of variable types. For example, trying to run a loop 40,000 times using a Short variable causes an error during execution because a Short variable has a maximum value of 32,767.

The following code illustrates using a simple For/Next loop to print the numbers 1 through 10 and their squares in the Output window:

```
Dim i As Integer, sOutput As String

For i = 1 To 10
    sOutput = i & " squared is " & (i * i)
    Debug.WriteLine(sOutput)
Next i
```

The sample For loop illustrates some interesting points. First, notice that you are free to use the counter variable (i) in other statements such as mathematical equations. Second, notice the For block ends with the counter variable i after the Next keyword. This is entirely optional; you may just use the word Next by itself and the For loop will execute the same way. Including the variable name in the Next statement makes your program easier to read, especially when you are working with nested loops.

Note

If you have not been programming for a while, you may be wondering why people and books use the variable names i and j as loop counters. The answer is that these variables were traditionally used for this purpose and taught to programmers.

You also should be aware that each time the Next statement is executed, the counter variable is incremented regardless of whether the loop is to be executed again. In the previous sample, the loop executes 10 times and only 10 values are printed. However, if you check the value of i after the loop is finished it will be set to 11.

USING For LOOPS WITH ARRAYS

The next example shows the use of a For/Next loop to reset the elements of three variable arrays to zero. Iterative processing allows these few lines of code to take the place of many. Using For/Next loops in conjunction with arrays in this manner is quite common:

```
For CurIndex = 0 To 9
    MonthSales(CurIndex) = 0
    MonthExpenses(CurIndex) = 0
    MonthProfit(CurIndex) = 0
Next
```

As you can see in this example and in others in the book, arrays and For loops are often used together. A For loop provides an easy way of looking at or processing each element of an array because the counter variable can be used as the array index.

Note

In VB .NET, all array indexes start as zero. It is important to be conscious of this fact when processing arrays in a loop. For example, if your array has 10 elements, their index values will be 0 to 9. Array indexes are discussed in Chapter 6, "Storing Information in Variables."

Caution

It is not good programming practice to reset the value of the counter variable inside a For loop. Doing so can cause an infinite loop.

EXITING A For LOOP EARLY

Typically, you will want a For loop to run through all the values of the counter variable. However, sometimes you might want the loop to terminate early. To do so, simply place an Exit For statement at the point in your loop where you want the loop to stop. The Exit For statement is typically associated with an If statement that determines whether the loop needs to be exited. In the following sample code from a trivia game, the player's score is examined after each question. If the score dips below zero, no more questions are asked.

```
For intQuestion = 1 To intMaxQuestions

    bCorrect = AskAQuestion()

  If bCorrect Then
      intScore = intScore + 1
  Else
      intScore = intScore - 1
  End If

    If nScore <= 0 Then Exit For
Next intQuestion
```

When the loop terminates (either because all questions have been asked or the score drops below zero), program execution will continue at the statement following the Next statement.

CHANGING THE Step VALUE

By default, a For loop increments the counter by 1 and counts up. However, you can include the optional Step keyword to specify how the counter is incremented. The code is the first example from this section, rewritten to count down instead of up:

```
Dim i As Integer, sOutput As String

For i = 10 To 1 Step -1
    sOutput = i & " squared is " & (i * i)
    Debug.WriteLine(sOutput)
Next i
```

The only differences between this example and the earlier one are the reversed start and end values and the addition of the Step value. Normally, if the beginning value of the loop is greater than the ending value, the loop does not execute at all. However, the Step statement makes the loop count backward, so the loop executes until the counter variable is less than the end point.

Do LOOPS

The key feature of a conditional loop is, of course, the *condition*. The condition is any expression that can return either a True or a False value. It can be a user-defined function, such as ValidGrade; the value of a property, such as the Checked property of a radio button; or an expression, such as ArrayIndex < 15. The two basic types of conditional loops are the Do While loop, which repeats *while* the condition is True, and a Do Until loop, which repeats *until* the condition is True.

USING Do While STATEMENTS

The keyword While in the Do While statement tells the program that the loop will be repeated while the condition expression is True. When the condition in a Do While loop becomes false, the program moves on to the next statement after the Loop statement.

You can use two forms of the Do While loop. The difference between the two is the placement of the condition. You can place the condition either at the beginning of the loop or at the end.

The first form of the Do While loop places the condition at the beginning of the loop, as shown in the following example.

```
Do While CurrentSpeed <= SpeedLimit
    CurrentSpeed = IncreaseSpeed(1)
Loop
```

This code repeatedly calls the IncreaseSpeed function while the condition CurrentSpeed <= SpeedLimit is true. By placing the While condition clause in the Do statement, you tell the program that you want to evaluate the condition *before* you run any statements inside the loop. If the condition is True, the repetitive statements between the Do statement and the Loop statement are run. Then the program returns to the Do statement to evaluate the condition again. As soon as the condition is False, the program moves to the statement following the Loop statement. Both the Do and the Loop statements must be present to use a DO While loop.

With this form of the loop, the statements inside the loop might never be run. If the condition is False before the loop is run the first time, that is, the car is already traveling at or above the speed limit, the program just proceeds to the statements after the loop. However, there may be times when you always want to execute the statements within the loop at least once, regardless of the condition.

To run the Do While loop at least once, you must use the second form of the Do While loop. This form of the loop places the condition in the Loop statement. This placement tells the program that you want the loop to run at least once and then evaluate the condition to determine whether to repeat the loop:

```
' This will execute 10 times
Dim Counter AS Integer = 0

Do
      Counter += 1

Loop While Counter < 10
```

Be careful when using the loop in such a manner because statements between the Do and Loop statements will be executed without first checking the loop condition. For example, it might be incorrect to assume that there is data in a file or data set. In cases like this, the other form of the Do Loop statement is more appropriate.

Caution

Do not put the While condition clause in both the Do and the Loop statements because doing so causes an error when you try to run your program.

Note

> If you are working on code that was developed by someone else, you might find a loop that starts with a `While` statement and ends with a `Wend` statement (`Wend` stands for "While-End," or the `End` of the `While` loop). This type of loop, left over from earlier versions of BASIC, works the same as a `Do While` loop with the `While` clause in the `Do` statement. Starting with Visual Basic .NET, the `Wend` statement has been replaced with the more descriptive `End While` statement. However, the `Do While` type of loop is more flexible.

USING A `Do Until` STATEMENT

The `Do Until` loop is basically the same as the `Do While` loop except that the statements inside a `Do Until` loop are run only as long as the condition is `False`. When the condition becomes `True`, the loop terminates:

```
Dim CarStarted As Boolean
Do
  CarStarted = ActivateStarter()
Loop Until CarStarted
```

As with the `Do While` loop, the `Do Until` loop has two forms: one with the condition in the `Do` statement and one with the condition in the `Loop` statement. If you place the condition in the `Do` statement, it is evaluated before the statements in the loop are executed. The following lines of code illustrate a frequent use of the `Do Until` statement: reading and processing database records.

```
Dim cn As New
SqlConnection("server=bserver\NetSDK;uid=sa;pwd=;database=GrocerToGo")
Dim cmd As New SQLCommand("select name from sysobjects", cn)
Dim rdr As SQLDataReader

cmd.Connection.Open()
rdr = cmd.ExecuteReader()
Do Until Not rdr.Read
    Debug.WriteLine(rdr.GetString(0))
Loop
cn.Close()
```

The sample loop does not execute at all if the `Read` function of the `SQLDataReader` object returns `False`. Otherwise, if no records were available to read, the `GetString` method would throw an exception. This is an advantage of testing the condition at the beginning of the loop.

→ For more on databases, **see** Chapter 22, "Using ADO .NET," **p. 599**

If you place the condition in the `Loop` statement, the code within the loop will always execute at least once. Consider the following example:

```
Dim Sum As Integer = 0
Dim NewInput As Integer = 0

Do
  NewInput = Convert.ToInt32(InputBox("Current Sum=" & Sum & " Enter 0 to exit."))
  Sum = Sum + NewInput
Loop Until NewInput = 0
```

Even though the variable `NewInput` is initialized to the value 0, the loop executes before the `Until` condition is encountered. Executing this example causes the input box to be displayed repeatedly until the user enters 0.

ENUMERATION LOOPS

Another type of loop supported by Visual Basic is the `For Each` loop. The `For Each` loop is considered to be an enumeration loop, because it is used for processing (or enumerating) each member of a set of objects in an array or collection.

One example of a collection is the `DataRows` collection, which contains the rows in a database table. The following code uses nested `For Each` loops to print the fields and values of each table row:

```
' Assumes Dataset has been filled
Dim CurrentRow As DataRow
Dim CurrentCol As DataColumn

For Each CurrentRow In DS.Tables(0).Rows
    For Each CurrentCol In DS.Tables(0).Columns
        debug.Write(CurrentRow(CurrentCol).ToString() & " ")
    Next
    debug.writeline("")
Next
```

The variables `CurrentRow` and `CurrentCol` act similar to the counter variable in a `For..Next` loop in that it contains the current item being processed.

The `For Each` loop can also be used with an array, as in the following example:

```
Dim MyNumber As Integer
Dim MyArray() As Integer = {5, 7, 9, 3, 1, 6, 8}

For Each MyNumber In MyArray
    If MyNumber > 5 Then Debug.WriteLine(MyNumber)
Next MyNumber
```

The code first creates a variant array containing seven integers and then uses the enumeration loop to list each integer with a value greater than 5.

EXERCISE: THE POP-UP ELIMINATOR

As a concluding exercise for this chapter, we will develop a *pop-up eliminator* application. If you have used the World Wide Web, you probably are already familiar with pop-ups, as shown in Figure 7.2. These additional windows display ads or other information in a separate Internet Explorer window, which must be closed to avoid cluttering up the screen. To help eliminate this nuisance, we will write a sample program that will automatically close these windows for you. In doing so, we will use several types of decision and control statements, including the `If` statement and several types of loops.

PART

II

CH

7

Figure 7.2
Secondary windows such as "pop-up" advertisements can be really annoying when you are trying to browse the Internet.

CREATING THE SAMPLE FORM

To create the sample application, perform the following steps:

1. Create a new Windows Application Project.
2. Add a list box to the form and set its `Name` property to `lstStatus`.
3. Add two button controls to the form. Set their names to `btnStart` and `btnStop` and their `Text` properties to `Start` and `Stop`, respectively.
4. Drag a `Timer` control to the form. It will appear at the bottom. Change its `Name` property to `tmrCheck`.
5. Set the `Enabled` property of `tmrCheck` to `True`.
6. Set the `Interval` property of `tmrCheck` to `2000`.

Your form is now designed and should look similar to the one in Figure 7.3.

→ For more on the Timer control, **see** Chapter 12, "Advanced Controls" **p. 309**

ADDING THE CODE

Open the code window for the form and find a section within the form class after the code generated by the form designer. Enter the code in Listing 7.2.

Figure 7.3
A Timer control will be used to repeatedly update the list box with a list of Internet Explorer windows.

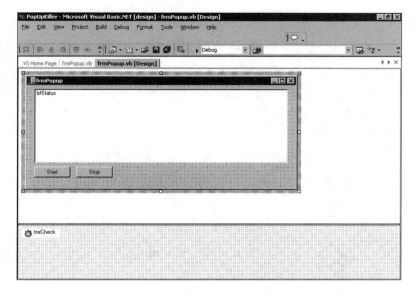

LISTING 7.2   POPUP.ZIP—CUSTOM FUNCTIONS USED BY THE SAMPLE APPLICATION

```
'API Declarations
Private Declare Function FindWindow Lib "user32" Alias "FindWindowA"_
(ByVal ClassName As String, ByVal lpWindowName As String) As Integer
Private Declare Function GetClassName Lib "user32" Alias "GetClassNameA"_
(ByVal hwnd As Integer, ByVal lpClassName As String,_
ByVal intMaxCount As Integer) As Integer
Private Declare Function GetWindowText Lib "user32" Alias "GetWindowTextA"_
(ByVal hwnd As Integer, ByVal lpWindowText As String,_
ByVal cch As Integer) As Integer
Private Declare Function GetWindow Lib "user32"_
(ByVal hwnd As Integer, ByVal wCmd As Integer) As Integer
Private Const GW_HWNDNEXT As Integer = 2
Private Declare Function SendWin32Message Lib "user32" Alias "SendMessageA"_
(ByVal hwnd As Integer, ByVal wMsg As Integer, ByVal wParam As Integer,_
ByVal lParam As Integer) As Integer
Private Const WM_CLOSE As Integer = &H10
Private Const WM_COMMAND As Integer = &H111

'Array of Windows we do NOT want to close
Private IEWindowsToKeep() As Integer

Private Sub GetIEWindowList(ByRef WindowHandleList() As Integer)
    Dim hwndCurrent As Integer                'Current window handle
    Dim sClassName, sWindowCaption As String  'Class and window names
```

PART

II

CH

7

LISTING 7.2 CONTINUED

```
    Dim intClassLen, intCaptionLen As Integer    'Length of class and window names
    Dim sDisplayInfo As String
    Dim intWindowCount As Integer = 0

    'Some Windows API calls require pre-filled strings
    Const Max_Chars As Integer = 50
    sClassName = Space(Max_Chars + 1)
    sWindowCaption = space(Max_Chars + 1)

    'Add window information to the list box and array
    lstStatus.Items.Clear()
    hwndCurrent = FindWindow("IEFrame", Nothing)
    Do While hwndCurrent <> 0
        intClassLen = GetClassName(hwndCurrent, sClassName, Max_Chars)
        intCaptionLen = GetWindowText(hwndCurrent, sWindowCaption, Max_Chars)
        If intCaptionLen > 0 And intClassLen > 1 Then
          If sClassName.Substring(0, 2) = "IE" Then
            sDisplayInfo = "Class:" & sClassName.Substring(0, intClassLen) & chr(9)
            sDisplayInfo &= "Caption:" & sWindowCaption.Substring(0, intCaptionLen)
            sDisplayInfo &= "Handle: " & hwndCurrent
            lstStatus.Items.Add(sDisplayInfo)
            intWindowCount += 1
            ReDim Preserve WindowHandleList(intWindowCount)
            WindowHandleList(intWindowCount - 1) = hwndCurrent
          End If
        End If
        hwndCurrent = GetWindow(hwndCurrent, GW_HWNDNEXT)
    Loop
End Sub

Private Sub CloseExtraIEWindows(ByRef WindowList() As Integer)
  Dim i As Integer
  For i = 0 To Ubound(WindowList)
      If array.BinarySearch(IEWindowsToKeep, windowlist(i)) < 0 Then
          'Send messages to close the window
          lstStatus.Items.Add("Closing window " & windowlist(i))
          SendWin32Message(windowlist(i), WM_COMMAND, &HA021, 0)
          SendWin32Message(windowlist(i), WM_CLOSE, 0, 0)
      End If
  Next
End Sub
```

The code in Listing 7.2 contains several *Windows API declarations*. API declarations are native Windows functions that are not part of the .NET framework and therefore must be declared in order to be accessed from within Visual Basic .NET. In this program they are used to work with the windows on your system. Each window has a *handle*, which is a unique number that identifies it. The GetIEWindowList custom function uses API calls to retrieve the handles for all of the open Internet Explorer windows and stores them in an integer array. This array, along with a second, class-level integer array (IEWindowsToKeep) is used by another custom function, CloseExtraIEWindows. This function closes any Internet Explorer Windows that are not in the IEWindowsToKeep array.

→ For more on the Windows API, **see** Chapter 25, "Interacting with Other Applications," **p. 699**

For the program to function, we'll need to add code to three event procedures:

- The Tick event of tmrCheck initiates the checking process. The Timer control will fire this event about every two seconds.
- The Click event of btnStart fills the IEWindowsToKeep array.
- The Click event of btnStop stops the process so you can open additional Internet Explorer windows.

The code for each of these event procedures is in Listing 7.3.

LISTING 7.3 POPUP.ZIP—EVENT PROCEDURES CODE FOR THE SAMPLE APP

```
Private Sub tmrCheck_Tick(ByVal sender As Object,_
   ByVal e As System.EventArgs) Handles tmrCheck.Tick
   Dim ListOfIEWindows() As Integer
   tmrCheck.Enabled = False
   GetIEWindowList(ListOfIEWindows)
   If Not ListOfIEWindows Is Nothing Then
      If Not IEWindowsToKeep Is Nothing Then
         CloseExtraIEWindows(ListOfIEWindows)
      End If
   End If
   tmrCheck.Enabled = True
End Sub

Private Sub btnStart_Click(ByVal sender As Object,_
   ByVal e As System.EventArgs) Handles btnStart.Click
      Dim ListOfIEWindows() As Integer
   tmrCheck.Enabled = False

   GetIEWindowList(ListOfIEWindows)

   If Not ListOfIEWindows Is Nothing Then
      IEWindowsToKeep = ListOfIEWindows
      Array.Sort(IEWindowsToKeep)
      MessageBox.Show("Any new IE Windows will be closed.")
   Else
      MessageBox.Show("Please open some IE windows first")
   End If

   tmrCheck.Enabled = True

End Sub

Private Sub btnStop_Click(ByVal sender As Object,_
   ByVal e As System.EventArgs) Handles btnStop.Click   IEWindowsToKeep = Nothing
   Messagebox.Show("Stopped closing windows.")
End Sub
```

TESTING THE PROGRAM

To test your program, perform the following steps:

1. Run the program.
2. Open as many Internet Explorer windows as you would like to use.
3. Click the Start button.
4. Begin browsing the Web. Any new windows that pop up should be quickly closed. You can test this by clicking Ctrl+N (open new window) in Internet Explorer.

As the program is running, you will see a list of Internet Explorer windows displayed in the list box, as shown in Figure 7.4.

Figure 7.4

The sample application displays a list of open Internet Explorer windows and indicates which ones it has closed.

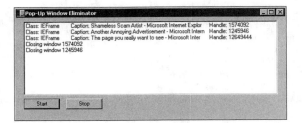

FROM HERE . . .

In this chapter, we have introduced you to the basics of loops and decision control statements. To learn more about what you can accomplish using the Visual Basic language, please see the following chapters:

- To learn how to create your own custom functions, read Chapter 8, "Program Tasks with Functions and Procedures."
- For information on object-oriented programming techniques, see Chapter 9, "Creating Code Components."
- To learn how to interact with a database using Visual Basic code, read Chapter 22, "Using ADO .NET."

MANAGING PROGRAM TASKS WITH PROCEDURES

In this chapter

In the preceding two chapters, you began to learn about writing code to make your programs accomplish various tasks. You saw how you can manipulate data and how control statements allow you to execute repetitive tasks and to execute statements selectively. However, creating a good, maintainable program involves more planning than just writing code.

One of the tasks you should learn to do is to create reusable pieces of code and reusable program pieces so that you are not constantly reinventing the wheel (or the program, in this case). Another important skill is the ability to manage those various pieces of code effectively. This chapter deals with both of these aspects of project management. First, you learn how you can use *procedures* to eliminate repetitive code in your programs. Then you learn how those procedures and other program components are added to your project.

PROCEDURES DEFINED

As you create more and larger programs, you will often find yourself using the same block of code over and over in several places throughout your program (and in multiple programs). Surely, there must be a better way to handle repetitive code than to just place it in multiple locations in your program, right? Of course there is. The solution is to use *procedures*. Procedures are segments of code that perform a particular task and then return processing to the area of the code from which they were called. This means that a single procedure can be called from multiple places in your code and, if managed properly, can be used with multiple programs.

You have already been exposed to working with procedures even if you didn't know it. Each time you entered code to be executed by a Button control (or another type of control) in response to an event, you were building a type of procedure known as an *event handler*. Event handlers are procedures that are automatically called by a program when an event is triggered. As you might already know, you can also create your own procedures and call them when you need them. The procedures that you build are often referred to as *user-defined sub procedures* (or subroutines). Although the code in earlier examples was entirely contained in event handler procedures, a "real" program might contain a large amount of code in standalone user-defined sub procedures.

TYPES OF PROCEDURES

When writing code for your Visual Basic .NET applications, there are four types of procedures you can create:

- *Sub Procedures* perform a specific task. You will learn about sub procedures throughout this chapter. Sub procedures are often known simply as "procedures," and are denoted by the keyword Sub at the beginning of the procedure.

- *Function Procedures* return a value to the code that called them. Function procedures are discussed later in this chapter. They are denoted by the keyword Function at the beginning of the procedure.

- *Event-Handling Procedures*, or "event handlers," are invoked in response to an event having occurred to an object. Events can be triggered by the user or by the program. You have already worked with event-handling procedures, and will continue to do so throughout this book. Event handlers are normally identified by the name of the object followed by an underscore and the name of the event that invokes the procedure. For example, btnExit_Click denotes the Click event handler for the Button control named btnExit. Regardless of the procedure's name, however, the Handles keyword at the end of the procedure's definition (Handles btnExit_Click would have been at the end of the preceding example) declares which object/event combination is handled by the procedure.

- *Property Procedures* are used when assigning values to the properties of user-created objects, and when retrieving the values of those properties. Property procedure definitions include the keyword Property. They are covered in Chapter 16, "Creating Your Own Windows Controls."

All these types of procedures are similar at their most basic level; that is, they are all procedures. The concepts discussed throughout the remainder of this chapter apply to each type.

WORKING WITH SUB PROCEDURES

The key idea behind working with any type of procedure is to break down your program into a series of smaller tasks. Each of these tasks can then be encapsulated in a procedure, function, or possibly a class. (Classes are discussed in Chapter 9, "Creating Code Components.") Programming in this manner presents several advantages:

- You can test each task individually. The smaller amount of code in a procedure makes debugging easier and makes working on the same project with other developers easier.

- You can eliminate redundant code by calling a procedure each time a task needs to be performed instead of repeating the program code.

- You can create a library of procedures that can be used in more than one program, saving yourself development time in new projects.

- Program maintenance is easier for a couple of reasons. First, because code is not repeated, any edits to a block of code must be performed only once. In addition, separating key components (for example, the user interface and the database functions) allows you to make major changes in one part of the program without recoding the whole thing.

Tip

To make your code reusable, use comments often. This extra detail allows another programmer (or yourself after a long period of time) to quickly see the purpose of each procedure and how it accomplishes its task.

Note

The techniques discussed in the following sections, while specifically targeted toward sub procedures, can be applied to function procedures as well.

PROCEDURE LOCATION

Procedures are created by typing the procedure code into the Code editor. Most often your procedure will be a method contained within a class, such as a Windows form class. In this case, you would enter the procedure within the form's class declaration (analogous to its Code window). You can display the form's class declaration by right-clicking the form in the Solution Explorer and choosing View Code. Procedures can also be declared within other types of classes, or in a *module*. A module is simply a file that contains Visual Basic code, but which is not associated with a particular form. If you want to add a module to your project, choose Add Module from Visual Basic .NET's Project menu, give the module an appropriate filename in the Add New Item dialog box, then click Open.

Note

The *location* of a procedure's code within your project is different from its *accessibility*, which will be discussed later.

CREATING A SUB PROCEDURE

As with your program as a whole, the process of creating a procedure starts with design. You need to determine the task to be performed, what information will be needed by the procedure, and what information will be returned by the procedure. After you complete this task, you can start the actual coding of the procedure. To start building a procedure in Visual Basic .NET, you simply begin typing the procedure in a code window.

Note

Whether you create your procedure in the Code window of a form or in a module, you must ensure that the procedure's code is placed within the correct portion of the Code window. If your procedure is in a form's Code window, it must be placed somewhere between the `Public Class` *formname* and `End Class` statements. In a module, the procedure must be between the `Module` *modulename* and `End Module` statements.

To create a sub procedure, you place your cursor in the Code window in a location that is not within a currently defined function or procedure. For example, you might place the cursor after the `End Sub` statement of a procedure, before the `Sub` statement of another procedure, or at the top of the Code window (below the code that is automatically generated by Visual Basic .NET). Figure 8.1 shows examples of where you might start.

Figure 8.1
Start a procedure in the Code window by using a Sub statement.

Start code at the beginning of the form

Start code between two other procedures

Start code after all other procedures

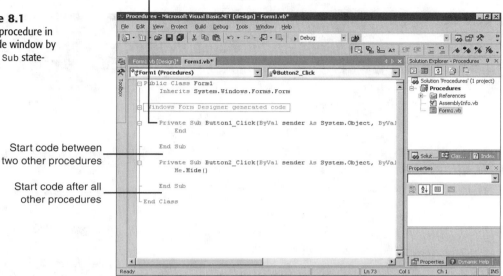

Tip

Placing your procedures in alphabetical order makes finding them easier when you page through the Code window. However, regardless of the order in which they were entered, they will always be listed in alphabetical order in the Code window's Method Name drop-down box.

Let's walk through the steps involved in creating a sample procedure named FirstProc:

1. Begin with a new Windows Application project. Open the Code window for Form1 by clicking the View Code button in the Solution Explorer.
2. Place the cursor just above the End Class line near the bottom of the Code window.
3. Press the Tab key, then type the keyword Sub followed by a space.
4. Type the name of your new procedure (FirstProc).
5. Press the Enter key to create the procedure.

When you press Enter, three things happen: A set of parentheses is added at the end of the Sub statement, an End Sub statement is placed in the Code window, and the current object in the Method Name drop-down list of the Code window becomes your new procedure name. Figure 8.2 shows these changes for your FirstProc procedure.

The Method Name drop-down list changes to the new procedure name

Figure 8.2
The End Sub statement is automatically added when you define a new procedure.

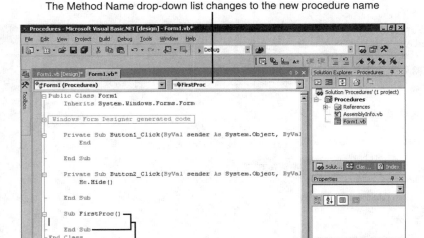

Parentheses and End Sub are added automatically

You are now ready to enter any commands that you want to be executed when the procedure is called. For this example, let's include a simple MessageBox command that alerts the user (you) that the FirstProc sub procedure has been invoked.

1. Make sure the cursor is between the Sub FirstProc and End Sub lines in the Code window.

2. Type the following line of code, then press Enter:

```
MessageBox.Show("FirstProc has been invoked!")
```

EXECUTING THE PROCEDURE

After you develop a procedure, you need a way to execute it as necessary from other parts of your program. To execute a procedure, you use the Call statement with the name of the procedure (*procname* refers to the name of the procedure):

```
Call procname([arguments])
```

However, the Call keyword is optional, so you can invoke a procedure by simply typing its name:

```
procname([arguments])
```

With either method, you simply specify the procedure name and any arguments that may be required by the procedure. (You will learn about arguments a little later in this chapter.)

Let's complete our example by adding a Button control that will invoke the FirstProc sub procedure when clicked:

1. Enter Form1's Design mode by clicking the "Form1.vb [Design]" tab at the top of the Code window.

2. Add a Button control to the form.

3. Change the Button control's Name property to cmdTest, and change its Caption property to Click Me.

4. Double-click cmdTest so you can create its Click event procedure (which is automatically named cmdTest_Click).

5. Type Call FirstProc and press Enter.

6. Add a second Button control to the form. Set its Name property to cmdTest2 and its Caption property to Me Too.

7. Add the code Call FirstProc to cmdTest2's Click event procedure as well.

> **Note**
> Remember, the Call keyword is optional. We're using it explicitly here for clarity.

You can now test your FirstProc sub procedure by running the program and clicking the Click Me and Me Too buttons. Each time you click either button, you should be presented with a message box reporting that FirstProc has been invoked. Note that the same block of code (FirstProc) is being executed from multiple locations (the Click event procedures of the two buttons).

PASSING DATA TO A PROCEDURE WITH ARGUMENTS

The procedure in the previous example did not require any data to do its job. It simply displayed a message box reporting that the procedure had been invoked. Often, your procedures will need to receive some data from the calling part of your program to perform their intended tasks. You can accomplish this by passing *arguments* to your procedures.

Arguments (also known as *parameters*) are pieces of information passed to procedures. To use arguments in a procedure, you first code the procedure so it is expecting an argument. You must then make sure you supply values for the arguments when you call the procedure.

Let's illustrate this concept with an example of a procedure that uses an argument. Suppose your program needs to log various operations and errors to a text file. A procedure that handles writing messages to the log file, along with the date and time that the message was written, could be very useful.

CREATING A PROCEDURE THAT ACCEPTS ARGUMENTS

In this example, we will create a sub procedure named LogPrint. It will receive one argument, which represents the message that we want to write to the log file. This will also be a good opportunity to demonstrate placing procedures in a separate module, rather than putting them in a form's Code window.

To begin creating the `LogPrint` sub procedure, perform the following:

1. Start with a new Windows Application project, or continue working with an existing one.

2. Select Project, Add New Item from Visual Basic .NET's menu system.

3. In the Add New Item - Procedures dialog box, make sure Module is selected in the Templates area on the right, give it an appropriate filename (the default, `Module1.vb`, is fine for our example), and click Open.

4. You should be taken to `Module1`'s Code window. If not, right-click `Module1.vb` in the Solution Explorer, and choose View Code.

5. Position the cursor between the `Module Module1` and `End Module` delimiters.

6. Type `Public Sub LogPrint(strMessage As String)` and press Enter.

Let's pause here to discuss the line of code you just typed. As you already know, `LogPrint` is the name of the sub procedure, and the `Public` keyword declares that it can be called from anywhere in the application. The remainder of the line—the part in parentheses—is the *argument list* for the procedure. The argument list consists of a series (in this case, only one) of argument names and types. This example tells us that the procedure expects to be passed one argument of type String. `strMessage` is the name that will be used to represent that argument within the procedure, just as if it were a variable.

Note

You may have noticed that when you pressed Enter after typing the `Public Sub` statement, Visual Basic .NET added the keyword `ByVal` before your `strMessage` argument. This specifies that when the procedure is invoked, the value sent from the calling code for the `strMessage` argument will be passed by value as opposed to being passed by reference. Don't worry about this for now; you will learn about passing arguments by value and by reference later in this chapter.

This procedure will utilize file input/output operations that are exposed through the `System.IO` namespace. Therefore, we need to reference the namespace in this module. To do so, place the cursor at the top of the module—at the beginning of the `Module Module1` line—and press Enter. Move the cursor up to the blank line that was created (above `Module Module1`), then type the following:

```
Imports System.IO
```

→ For more on namespaces, **see** "Understanding Namespaces," **p. 119**

To continue coding the procedure, place the cursor back in the body of the `LogPrint` procedure (between `Public Sub LogPrint` and `End Sub`) and type the following lines of code:

```
Dim filLogFile As TextWriter, strFullMsg As String
filLogFile = File.AppendText("c:\eventlog.txt")
strFullMsg = Now & " - " & strMessage
filLogFile.WriteLine(strFullMsg)
filLogFile.Close()
```

Let's examine this code line-by-line. The first line, `Dim filLogFile As TextWriter, strFullMsg As String`, declares that this procedure will have two local variables. The first variable, `filLogFile`, will be a variable of the `TextWriter` class, which is inherited from the `System.IO` namespace and provides character output functionality. Recall that we referenced `System.IO` at the beginning of the module. We will utilize `filLogFile` in this procedure to handle the work of writing to our log file. The second variable, `strFullMsg`, is a String that will be used to construct the full message line to be written to the log file.

Line two, `filLogFile = File.AppendText("c:\eventlog.txt")`, invokes the `AppendText` method of the File class to create a TextWriter variable (`filLogFile`) that appends text to a file named `c:\eventlog.txt`. If this file does not exist, it will be created; otherwise, it will be appended to.

The third line, `strFullMsg = Now & " - " & strMessage`, uses the argument that will be passed into the procedure. Note how the argument, `strMessage`, is treated just like any other variable within the procedure. We use the `Now` function, which reports the current system date and time, to combine with a hyphen and the input argument `strMessage` to create the complete line that will be written to the log file.

The next line, `filLogFile.WriteLine(strFullMsg)`, invokes the `WriteLine` method of the `filLogFile` object to actually write the text contained in `strFullMsg` to the log file.

Finally, the last line (`strmOutput.Close()`) closes the TextWriter and releases the system resources that it uses.

PASSING ARGUMENTS TO THE PROCEDURE

When calling a procedure that expects arguments, you supply values for the arguments by listing them in the `Call` statement, in parentheses after the procedure name. Each value supplied can be in the form of a variable, a literal string or number, or some combination of the two. Any of the following would be valid calls to the `LogPrint` procedure:

```
Call LogPrint("Program started normally.")

strTemp = "User logged on."
Call LogPrint(strTemp)

Call LogPrint("Error opening file " & strUserFile)
```

You can test your `LogPrint` procedure by adding a Button control to your project's main form, then using some form of the `Call` statement to invoke `LogPrint` with a test message. After you have done this a few times, use Windows Explorer to locate the file `c:\eventlog.txt`. Double-click it to view its contents in Notepad.

Remember, you can omit the `Call` keyword when invoking a procedure:

```
LogPrint("Program started normally.")
```

The `LogPrint` procedure is simple, yet it saves a lot of time in the long run. It makes the calling code shorter and more readable. In addition, if you ever want to change the format of the output file or change the destination of the log information from a text file to a database, printer, or pager, you have to modify only the `LogPrint` function itself.

OPTIONAL ARGUMENTS

Typically, you must include the same number of arguments in the calling statement as are present in the definition of the procedure. Occasionally, however, you may need to create a procedure that has one or more optional arguments. You can accomplish this by using the Optional keyword before one or more of the arguments in the argument list portion of the Sub statement.

Consider an enhancement to the LogPrint procedure whereby under certain circumstances you want to display information to the user via a message box in addition to writing a line to the log file. You can modify the declaration of the LogPrint procedure to include an optional second argument that represents text to be displayed in a message box as follows:

```
Public Sub LogPrint(ByVal strMessage As String, _
  Optional ByVal strDisplayMsg As String = "")
```

Notice the keyword Optional in the preceding declaration. Arguments marked as optional can be left out when calling a procedure. In a procedure's declaration, an optional argument can be given a default value to be utilized if the calling code does not use the argument. In the previous example, if the calling program does not explicitly specify a value for the strDisplayMsg argument, the default value (an empty string, which was specified via the code = "" at the end of the optional argument declaration) is passed to the procedure. If your procedure needs to know whether a value was passed, you can use an If statement to compare the value of the argument to the default.

> **Note**
>
> When declaring optional arguments in a procedure's argument list, you must specify a default value. This ensures that the argument is populated whether or not it was included in the call to the procedure.

> **Tip**
>
> If you are calling a procedure that asks for multiple arguments, and you want to specify some of the arguments while leaving out one or more optional ones, you can use commas to skip over the optional arguments that you are leaving out. As an example, consider the procedure MyProc, which asks for four arguments, of which the second and third are optional. If you want to include the first, third, and fourth arguments but leave out the (optional) second argument, you could utilize the following calling code:
>
> ```
>     Call MyProc(155, , 2.87, 37000)
> ```
>
> This would have the effect of passing the value 155 for MyProc's first argument, using the default value for its optional second argument, passing 2.87 for the third argument, and 37000 for the fourth argument.

After you have allowed for the possibility of one or more optional arguments, you can include code in your procedure to utilize the arguments. In the case of LogPrint, we will check to see whether the optional argument, strDisplayMsg, contains some value other than an empty string. We can assume that if it does contain an empty string, either the calling code did not pass a value for the argument, or an empty string was actually passed, indicating that no message is to be displayed to the user. If strDisplayMsg contains something other than an empty string, its contents will be displayed to the user via a message box.

Here is the code for the revised LogPrint:

```
Public Sub LogPrint(ByVal strMessage As String, _
  Optional ByVal strDisplayMsg As String = "")
    Dim filLogFile As TextWriter, strFullMsg As String
    Dim intTemp As Integer
    If strDisplayMsg > "" Then
        intTemp = MessageBox.Show(strDisplayMsg, "System Message")
    End If
    filLogFile = File.AppendText("c:\eventlog.txt")
    strFullMsg = Now & " - " & strMessage
    filLogFile.WriteLine(strFullMsg)
    filLogFile.Close()
End Sub
```

To call your modified LogPrint procedure with only one argument, use code just as if it only required a single argument:

```
Call LogPrint("Program started normally.")
```

If you want to provide the second argument, simply add it to the argument list of the calling code, as follows:

```
strTemp1 = "Invalid logon attempt by SNEWSOM."
strTemp2 = "An invalid logon attempt has been detected and logged."
Call LogPrint(strTemp1, strTemp2)
```

> **Caution**
>
> Be sure that the values supplied by the calling statement match the data types expected by the procedure. Violating this condition results in an error when you run your program.

ARGUMENT PASSING OPTIONS

When declaring arguments in your procedures, you can specify how they will be passed to the procedure by the calling program. Depending on the option you select, the arguments used by a procedure can provide two-way communication between the procedure and the calling program. The arguments passing options are as follows:

- ByVal, which stands for *by value*, means the value of the argument is passed to the procedure from the calling program. This is the default argument-passing mechanism and is generally used with input-only arguments.

- ByRef, which stands for *by reference*, means that the calling program passes a memory reference to the procedure. This method of argument declaration can not only be used to send information into a procedure, but also to return information to the calling program.

For example, the following procedure gets the height and width of a rectangle from the arguments list and then calculates the area and perimeter of the rectangle. These values are returned through the arguments list:

```
Sub CalcRectangle(ByVal nWidth as Integer, ByVal nHeight as Integer, _
    ByRef nArea as Integer, ByRef nPerimeter as Integer)
    nArea = nWidth * nHeight
    nPerimeter = 2 * (nWidth + nHeight)
End Sub
```

The procedure's first two arguments, nWidth and nHeight, are passed using the ByVal (by value) keyword, indicating that the actual value of the parameter is passed into the procedure. The other two arguments, nArea and nPerimeter, are passed ByRef (by reference) Using ByRef causes the calling code to pass a reference to the *memory location* used by a variable as the parameter (instead of the actual values of the variables). This allows the procedure to modify the variables, which in turn can be read by the calling code to determine the results of the calculations performed by the procedure.

The procedure can be called by using variables for both the input and output arguments, as follows:

```
nWid = 5
nHgt = 5
nArea = 0
nPerm = 0
CalcRectangle (nWid, nHgt, nArea, nPerm)
```

It can also be called by using literal values for the input arguments and variables for the output arguments:

```
nArea = 0
nPerm = 0
CalcRectangle 4, 10, nArea, nPerm
```

In either case, after the call to CalcRectangle, the values of nArea and nPerm can be referenced by the calling code in order to determine the results of the calculations:

```
MessageBox.Show("The area of the rectangle is " & nArea)
```

Note

If you use literal values for the ByRef arguments, obviously you cannot access the return values.

To further clarify this difference, think back to our discussion of variables in Chapter 6, "Storing Information in Variables." A variable points to a storage location in the computer's memory. Using the ByRef keyword forces the calling program's variable and the parameter to share a memory location. Because both variable names point to the same memory location, changes made within the procedure will be available to the calling program, as in the following example function:

```
Sub ChangeString(ByRef AnyString As String)
    AnyString = "After"
End Sub

Dim sSampleString As String
sSampleString = "Before"
ChangeString sSampleString
```

Changing the value of AnyString within the procedure causes the value of sSampleString to be changed as well. This capability enables the procedure to modify the value that is then passed back to the calling code. On the other hand, using the ByVal keyword makes the calling program's variable and the parameter use separate memory locations. This approach causes the procedure to use a copy of the information that was passed to it, which prevents the procedure code from modifying the value used by the calling program. However, you can still modify the variable within the scope of the procedure.

EXITING A PROCEDURE EARLY

As your programs, and therefore your procedures, grow in complexity, sometimes you might not need to execute all the commands in the procedure. If you need to exit the procedure before all the commands have been executed, you can use the Exit Sub statement.

One way that I often use the Exit Sub statement is in the beginning of the procedure in a routine that checks parameters for proper values. If any of the parameters passed to a procedure are the wrong type or have values that could cause a problem for the procedure, I use Exit Sub to terminate the procedure before the error occurs. Using the statement this way is a type of *data validation*. The following code modifies the previous area calculation code to perform this check:

```
Sub CalcRectangle(ByVal nWidth as Integer, ByVal nHeight as Integer, _
    ByRef nArea as Integer, ByRef nPerimeter as Integer)
    If nWidth <= 0 Or nHeight <= 0 Then
        nArea = 0
        nPerimeter = 0
        Exit Sub
    End If
    nArea = nWidth * nHeight
    nPerimeter = 2 * (nWidth + nHeight)
End Sub
```

Depending upon the coding conventions employed by your organization (or by yourself), having multiple exit points within a procedure may be frowned upon. If so, the preceding procedure could be rewritten as follows:

```
Sub CalcRectangle(ByVal nWidth as Integer, ByVal nHeight as Integer, _
    ByRef nArea as Integer, ByRef nPerimeter as Integer)
    If nWidth > 0 And nHeight > 0 Then
        nArea = nWidth * nHeight
        nPerimeter = 2 * (nWidth + nHeight)
    Else
        nArea = 0
        nPerimeter = 0
    End If
End Sub
```

WORKING WITH FUNCTION PROCEDURES

Function procedures are similar to sub procedures, with one key difference: They return a value. This means that somewhere in the body of the function procedure, a value will be calculated, retrieved, or otherwise created and set to be the function's return value. This value can subsequently be used by the calling code; typically, it is assigned to a variable or used in expressions. Visual Basic offers a number of built-in functions that you can use, such as Val, which returns the numeric representation of a string, or Left, which returns a specified number of characters from the left end of a string. Function procedures let you build your own custom functions as well.

BUILDING A FUNCTION

To build a function, select the place in a Code window where you want the function to appear and then enter the keyword Function followed by the name of the function and a list of its expected arguments. Before pressing Enter, however, you should specify the data type of the value that will be returned by the function, just as if you were declaring a variable.

We will demonstrate this with an example. Suppose you want to build a function that will calculate the area of a triangle. Thinking back to your Geometry years, you remember that the area of a triangle is equal to one-half of its base times its height. You can create a function that performs this complex calculation for you. Begin by placing the cursor in an appropriate area of a Code window (such as the module from the previous example), then type the following line of code:

```
Function TriangleArea(sngBase As Single, sngHeight As Single) As Single
```

Let's examine this function declaration. It begins with the word Function, telling Visual Basic that you are defining a function procedure (as opposed to a sub procedure). Next follows the argument list, which declares that this function will expect two arguments, sngBase and sngHeight, each of the Single data type. The last part of the declaration, a final As Single, declares that the return value of the function itself will be of the Single data type.

> **Note**
>
> If you are using Option Strict, you must always declare a type for the return values of your functions. This is good practice, even if you do not use Option Strict.

When you press Enter, the closing line of the function, End Function, will be added for you, and the keyword ByVal will be added to each argument, because passing by value is the default behavior unless you specify otherwise.

Complete coding the TriangleArea function by adding the following lines of code in the body of the procedure:

```
Dim sngTemp As Single
sngTemp = sngBase * sngHeight / 2
TriangleArea = sngTemp
```

The first line declares a local variable named sngTemp to be used in the calculation. The second line, sngTemp = sngBase * sngHeight / 2, uses the two arguments (which were declared in the function's declaration) to perform the calculation, temporarily storing the result in the sngTemp variable. Finally, the last line, TriangleArea = sngTemp, actually sets the function's return value to the result of the calculation.

Tip

You can use the Return statement to return a function's value instead of setting the function's name to the desired return value. In this example, Return sngTemp would serve the same purpose as TriangleArea = sngTemp.

Note

This particular function could have been coded with a single line of code, TriangleArea = sngBase * sngHeight / 2. We used a longer version here to aid in the explanation.

INVOKING A FUNCTION

Your calling code can utilize the return value just like the result of a built-in function. To test the TriangleArea function, do the following:

1. Add two TextBox controls to your sample project's Form1. Name them txtBase and txtHeight and clear their Text properties.

2. Place Label controls next to the text boxes to identify them. Set their Text properties to Triangle Base: and Triangle Height:.

3. Add another Label control that will be used to report the calculated area of the triangle. Name it lblArea. You might want to label it with yet another Label control whose Text property is set to Area:.

4. Add a Button control named btnCalculate. Set its Text property to Calculate Area.

5. Add the following code to the Click event handler for btnCalculate:

```
Dim sngB As Single, sngH As Single
sngB = txtBase.Text
sngH = txtHeight.Text
lblArea.Text = TriangleArea(sngB, sngH)
```

After declaring two local temporary variables, this code populates the Single variables sngB and sngH with the Text properties of the text boxes txtBase and txtHeight, respectively. It then calls the TriangleArea function, using the return value to set the Text property of lblArea.

Note

Although your function code can assign a value to the function multiple times, only the last value assigned before the end (or exit) of the function is returned.

Note

If for some reason you want to call a function but have no need for the return value, you can simply use the `Call` statement to invoke the function just as if it were a sub procedure. This technique will, in effect, discard the function's return value.

There are a number of functions built and demonstrated in the `FunctionDemo.zip` project, which you can download from www.quepublishing.com.

UNDERSTANDING SCOPE AND ACCESSIBILITY

When you create a procedure, you might want to limit where it can be called from, where its variables can be accessed from, and how resources are allocated to make its code available to other parts of your program. The *scope* of a variable or procedure refers to its availability to be used by other parts of your code, and is determined by the context in which it is declared. Scope is also known as *visibility*.

Another term you will become familiar with is *accessibility*. A procedure's accessibility refers to its availability to other components (such as programs and link libraries) outside of the project in which it is defined that comprise your total solution.

In this section, you will learn about how to determine the scope and accessibility of your applications' variables and procedures.

SCOPE OF VARIABLES

A variable's scope is determined by where and how it is declared. There are four levels of variable scope, each of which is discussed next in ascending order of broadness of scope.

BLOCK-LEVEL VARIABLES

A block-level variable is only available within the block of code in which it is declared. A block of code is defined as a group of statements that ends with an `End`, `Next`, or `Loop` statement, such as an `If ... End If` block, a `For ... Next` block, or a `Do ... Loop` block. The following code would generate an error when the `MsgBox` statement is reached, because `strTemp` is a block-level variable that is only available inside the `If ... End If` block:

```
If 3 > 4 Then   'This condition will always fail
    Dim strTemp As String
    strTemp = "This is a temporary string."
End If
MessageBox.Show(strTemp) 'This line causes an error!
```

PROCEDURE-LEVEL VARIABLES

A procedure-level variable is available throughout the procedure in which it is declared, but not to any other code. For example, if you were to declare a variable named `strTemp` in a procedure named `Proc1`, it would be available for use throughout `Proc1`. However, a procedure named `Proc2` could not use the `strTemp` variable.

In the following code example, `strTemp` represents a typical procedure-level variable declaration:

```
Sub Proc1()
    Dim strTemp As String 'strTemp is available throughout this procedure
    strTemp = "This is the string's contents"
    MessageBox.Show(strTemp)
End Sub
```

MODULE-LEVEL VARIABLES

Variables declared using either the `Dim` or `Private` keyword at module level (class level); that is, within the definition of a module but not inside any specific procedure, are available to any procedure in that module.

PROJECT-LEVEL VARIABLES

A project-level variable is one declared at module (class) level using either the `Public` or `Friend` keyword. As the term implies, project-level variables are available throughout your project.

SAME-NAMED VARIABLES

One thing that may seem to override the variable scope rules discussed previously would be if your project had multiple variables with the same name declared in different places. In such a case, the variable with the most restrictive active scope would be available. For example, in the following sample code the instance of `strTemp` defined as a procedure-level variable, which contains the value `Narrow`, would be displayed as a result of the `MsgBox` statement:

```
Module Module1
    Dim strTemp As String = "Wide"
    Sub Proc1()
        Dim strTemp As String
        strTemp = "Narrow"
        MessageBox.Show(strTemp) 'Displays "Narrow"
    End Sub
End Module
```

SELECTING A SCOPE

Generally speaking, when declaring your variables you should use the narrowest scope possible. Block-level and procedure-level variables only utilize system resources as long as a procedure is active, whereas module-level and project-level variables utilize system resources as long as the application is running. However, if you need to share data throughout an application, you must use project-level scope.

PRESERVING VARIABLES BETWEEN PROCEDURE CALLS

Typically, when a procedure is executed, the variables it uses are created, used in the procedure, and then destroyed when the procedure is terminated. However, sometimes you might want to preserve the values of the variables for future calls to the procedure. You can handle this task by using the Static keyword when declaring variables within a procedure whose values you want to be retained even after the procedure has finished executing.

When Static is used in a variable declaration, only the variables included in the Static statement are preserved. Each time the following example is invoked, the (retained) value of the static variable intCounter is incremented, and the new value is displayed via a message box:

```
Private Sub StaticTest()
    Static intCounter As Integer
    intCounter = intCounter + 1
    MessageBox.Show("Value=" & intCounter)
End Sub
```

SCOPE OF PROCEDURES

Like variables, a procedure's scope is determined by *how* it is defined. Where a procedure is defined is irrelevant, because all procedures are defined at class (module) level. A procedure's scope can be either project-level or class-level, as discussed next.

PROJECT-LEVEL PROCEDURES

If you want to have your procedure or function available throughout your program, use the Public keyword when you define the procedure, as in the following example:

```
Public Sub Proc1()
    'code statements go here...
End Sub
```

Using the Public keyword allows a procedure defined in one class to be called from any other class within a project. However, you have to be careful with the names of public procedures because each public procedure must have a name that is unique throughout the current scope.

If you omit the keywords Public and Private from the Sub statement, the procedure is set up by default as a project-level procedure.

CLASS-LEVEL PROCEDURES

Using the Private keyword in the Sub or Function statement allows a procedure to be accessed only from the class in which it is defined. This makes it a class-level (also known as module-level) procedure. Code in one class (or module) cannot invoke class-level procedures defined in another class. The following illustrates the definition of a class-level procedure:

```
Private Sub Proc1()
    'code statements go here...
End Sub
```

This approach, of course, poses advantages and disadvantages. One advantage is that a class-level procedure is resident in memory only while the class in which it is stored is loaded, conserving system resources. A disadvantage is that the procedure is not accessible from other classes.

Tip

For efficiency's sake, it's important to place your procedures in the appropriate scope. Giving a procedure a scope that is too broad (for example, making a procedure project-level when it only needs to be class-level) wastes valuable system resources. If you create a project-level procedure, your program must allocate appropriate resources to make it available to all parts of your program. Using the `Static` keyword in variable declarations to force a procedure to "remember" its local variables causes an extra allocation of resources as well. In general, you should make procedures class-level if possible, and avoid the use of static variables as well. If you use this approach, your program can manage memory more efficiently because it is free to unload the various sections of code as needed.

Note

When working with event procedures in other chapters, you might have noticed that they are, by default, protected class-level procedures. This is because, typically, controls are not accessed outside the form on which they reside. This is an example of *information hiding*, or *encapsulation*, a technique used in object-oriented programming. If you are sharing a module with a team of developers, you could define the functions they call as project-level, while the internal procedures they don't need to know about can remain at class level.

ACCESSIBILITY OF PROCEDURES AND VARIABLES

Accessibility refers to how parts of your program are visible to other programs that utilize your program's components. The accessibility of a procedure or variable is determined by which keyword is used in the declaration statement. The accessibility of a variable or procedure can be one of five levels—Public, Private, Friend, Protected, or Protected Friend—each of which is discussed in this section.

PUBLIC ACCESSIBILITY

A procedure or variable declared using the `Public` keyword can be used from any part of your project, but not from other projects.

PRIVATE ACCESSIBILITY

Use of the `Private` keyword in a procedure or variable declaration limits the accessibility of the procedure or variable to the class (module) in which it is defined. For variables, this only holds true if the variable is declared at module level. Variables declared inside a procedure are always private.

FRIEND ACCESSIBILITY

The `Friend` keyword declares a procedure or variable to be available across your entire assembly. The term *assembly* refers to a project or group of projects that is compiled, or assembled, together as one executable solution. Friend variables and procedures can be accessed by any code in any portion of the assembly.

PROTECTED ACCESSIBILITY

Protected variables and procedures, defined using the keyword Protected, are similar to private variables in that they are normally only available inside the class in which they are declared. However, if you derive a new class from an existing class that contains protected variables or procedures, the derived class can also access them.

You will learn about derived classes in Chapter 9, "Creating Code Components."

PROTECTED FRIEND ACCESSIBILITY

Finally, the Protected and Friend accessibilities can be combining by using the keyword combination Protected Friend. This expands the accessibility of a variable or procedure to both the entire assembly and derived classes.

REUSING FUNCTIONS AND PROCEDURES

As you have seen in the examples in this chapter, you can create a procedure in either of two places: a form or a module. Where you place the procedure depends on where you need to use it and what its purpose is. If the procedure is specific to a form or modifies the properties of the form or its associated controls, you should probably place the procedure in the form itself.

If, on the other hand, you are using the procedure with multiple forms in your program or have a generic procedure used by multiple programs, you should place it in a module. The storage location of your procedure is determined by where you create it. If you want, you can move a procedure from a form to a module or vice versa using cut-and-paste editing or even drag-and-drop editing.

STORING A PROCEDURE IN A FORM FILE

> **Note**
>
> In Visual Basic .NET, form files and modules are both types of classes.

To create a procedure in a form file, you just need to choose the form from the Solution Explorer window and then access the code for the form. You do so either by double-clicking the form itself (or any control) or choosing the View Code button in the Solution Explorer window. After the Code window appears, you create a procedure as described in the earlier section "Creating a Sub Procedure."

USING A MODULE FILE FOR PROCEDURES

A module file contains only code—no form elements or events. If you already have a module file in your project, you can create a new procedure by selecting the file, opening the Code window, and then using the steps listed earlier to build the procedure.

Tip

Double-clicking the module name in the Solution Explorer window automatically opens the Code window for the module.

If you don't have a module file in your project, or if you want to use a new module, you can create a module by selecting Project, Add Module. You can also create a new module by clicking the arrow on the Add New Item button in the toolbar and then choosing Add Module from the drop-down menu. Either way, you are presented with the Add Module dialog box; select the Module icon, give it a filename, and click Open. A new module is created, and the Code window appears for you to begin editing.

Note

The toolbar button for adding new forms and modules is a drop-down button, which means clicking on the arrow gives you a list of items. After an item has been selected, the icon on the button changes.

Tip

If you have a library of common functions, such as printing routines, keep them in a separate module file so that you can easily add the library to different projects.

FROM HERE...

In this chapter, you have learned about the following:

- The general definition of procedures
- How to create and use procedures
- Passing parameters to procedures
- Function procedures, which return a value
- The scope and accessibility of procedures
- Reusing procedures

Procedures are but one of many different concepts that you will use as you learn to write code. The following chapters can provide more information to you as you develop your coding skills:

- For an introduction to writing a Visual Basic application, see Chapter 2, "Creating Your First Windows Application."
- For a thorough discussion of the pieces that make up a well-rounded application, see Chapter 5, "Visual Basic Building Blocks."
- To learn more about how to use variables in your applications, see Chapter 6, "Storing Information in Variables."
- To learn how to cause your code to make decisions and execute repetitively, see Chapter 7, "Controlling the Flow Of Your Program."

CHAPTER 9

CREATING CODE COMPONENTS

In this chapter

As you develop more (and better) applications, you will find many opportunities to reuse code that you have already written. You may be tempted to copy code from old projects and paste it into your new projects. You would quickly learn, however, that doing so has several drawbacks. One of the chief drawbacks of this technique is the need to manage multiple copies of the same code. If you have developed a procedure that solves a certain problem, and you copy and paste that procedure into multiple projects, what happens if you discover a bug in the procedure? You must locate each project that uses that procedure, make the appropriate changes, and recompile each application.

A much better way is to create a *code component*, which is essentially a custom class that contains procedures and functions that can be used by multiple applications. This approach allows you to incorporate object-oriented programming (OOP) techniques into your applications, making them reusable and portable.

Note

Technically, there is a difference between a *code component* and a simple class. A code component starts out as a class; it becomes a component when it conforms to a standard for component interaction, which is provided by the IComponent interface. This interface ensures that components utilize .NET's Common Language Specification (CLS), which is the backbone for components authored in any of the .NET languages and includes basic language features needed by many applications. In essence, you can create components using any of the .NET languages and incorporate them into the .NET framework; in turn, they can be used by any other .NET language, regardless of their origin.

Object-oriented programming techniques are useful because they allow you to reuse your code efficiently. This chapter discusses how to create classes in Visual Basic .NET. Classes allow you to create objects and take advantage of object-oriented programming techniques in Visual Basic. When working on a large project, for example, each team member can create a specific class and make it available for others to use.

UNDERSTANDING CLASSES

Having used controls and forms in Visual Basic .NET applications, you have already used classes and objects. For example, when you draw a text box on a form, you are actually creating a specific *instance* of the TextBox class. For example, if you draw five text boxes on your form, you have created five instances of the TextBox class. Even though each instance is a distinct entity, they were all created from the same template. A form itself is an instance of the Form class.

Instances of a class are known as *objects*. Each different class is a template from which a specific type of object is created. In this example, the TextBox class defines that a text box has a Text property. However, the class definition itself does not contain information about the *contents* of the properties. Instead, an object you create from the class, for example, txtLastName, actually contains that information.

OBJECT-ORIENTED PROGRAMMING

You probably have heard the term *object-oriented programming (OOP)* or read about it in programming books and magazines. A key element of OOP is its use of reusable objects to build programs.

OOP begins in the design stage, when you determine the objects needed for an application. For example, suppose you have to write a system to manage paychecks for employees. A traditional design plan would be to determine each program function, such as "Adding an employee to the database" or "Printing an employee paycheck." An object-oriented design would instead try to separate programming tasks along the lines of the objects in the program (employees, database, paycheck, and so on). For a design to be considered object-oriented, several facts must be true about the objects. These fundamental concepts of OOP are summarized in the following list:

- **Encapsulation.** Encapsulation, or information hiding, refers to the fact that objects hide the details of how they work. For example, when you set the Text property of a text box, you do not know (or care) how the text box internally repaints the characters. Information hiding allows the programmer of an object to change how an object works without affecting the users of the object.

- **Inheritance.** A new object can be defined based on an existing object, and it can contain all the same properties and methods. For example, you can create a new object that contains all the standard properties and methods of an existing object, plus a few of your own. You can just add your own extra properties and "inherit" the existing ones.

- **Polymorphism.** Although many objects can have methods bearing the same name, the method can perform differently for each of the objects. Through polymorphism, the program runs the method appropriate for the current object. For example, the + operator can be used with both strings and integers. Even though the same symbol is used for both data types, Visual Basic knows to perform different operations.

An important consequence of an OOP approach is reusable code. Part of what makes an object reusable is its interface, or the methods and properties the object uses to communicate with the outside world. If you build objects with well-defined interfaces, it is easy to change the object internally or even add new interfaces without affecting programs that use the object.

CLASSES IN VISUAL BASIC

You can create your own classes in Visual Basic .NET by adding a Class template to an existing project, or by building a class library consisting of one or more classes. Classes can contain several types of elements:

- **Properties.** These elements are used to assign and retrieve values from the class.
- **Methods.** These are public functions or subroutines that are defined in the class.
- **Events.** Just as a control can raise events in the form that contains it, an object created from your class can also raise events in its containing object.

Class modules also contain two special events of their own: `New` and `Finalize`. The `New` event is triggered when a new instance of the class is created, and the `Finalize` event occurs when the object is destroyed.

Object definitions are created in a class module. A class module is like a standard code module in that it contains only variable declarations and procedure code. There is no user interface component of a class module. However, a class can take action using a form that is in the program, just like a normal code module. Class modules can be used in several ways, such as the following:

- In a Visual Basic .NET project, a class module provides a way to create multiple instances of objects anywhere in your program, without using global variables.

- You can create Class Library objects and compile them into a DLL that other programmers can use in their code. For example, you can put all your business financial rules in a class and compile it as a DLL. Other programmers can reference the DLL and use the financial rules in their applications.

- You can build an add-in to Visual Basic, to enhance the functions of the Visual Basic IDE.

BUILDING A CLASS

The easiest way to learn is by doing, so let's create a sample class. This sample class module will define a new type whose purpose is to contain employee information. After setting up the class itself, you will learn how to expose properties, methods, and events to its user.

STARTING A NEW CLASS LIBRARY PROJECT

Begin by creating a new project in Visual Basic .NET. Select Class Library from the list of templates available, and name the project `MyClasses`. Click OK to create a class library project named `MyClasses`. Notice that the Solution Explorer window contains a file named `Class1.vb`; this file will contain the code that defines your new class.

Note

You can include multiple classes in a Class Library project by choosing Project, Add Class from the menu system. For simplicity's sake, our sample program will only include a single class.

After the new class has been created, you should give it a unique and descriptive name. The name of a class module is much more significant than the name of a standard code module because you actually use the class name within program code. Many developers like to use the letter `c` or `cls` to indicate a class name. This simple class example will be an employee class, so name the class module `clsEmployee`.

To rename it, go to the Code window for `Class1` and change the class definition `Public Class Class1` to `Public Class clsEmployee`. Next click `Class1.vb` in the Solution Explorer window and change its `File Name` property in the Properties window to `clsEmployee.vb`.

Now that the infrastructure is complete, this would be a good time to save your project.

The complete `MyClasses` sample project is available for download on the Internet at `www.quepublishing.com`.

ADDING PROPERTIES TO THE CLASS

After the class module has been created, you can add your own properties. Properties in your own classes are used in the same way as those of controls, for storing and retrieving information. You can add properties to your class in two ways: by using public variables and property procedures.

PUBLIC VARIABLES

Using public variables is the easiest way to create properties. For the sample `clsEmployee`, you can add a few simple properties with the following code. Type these lines in the Code window just below the `Public Class clsEmployee` line:

```
Public FirstName As String
Public LastName As String
Public DateHired As Date
```

> **Note**
>
> Your classes will also usually have several private variables, but only the public variables will be visible to the rest of your application when the object is created.

After you create an object from your class (you will see how shortly), you can use these properties just like those in a custom control:

```
MyObject.FirstName = "June"
MyObject.LastName = "Thomas"
MyObject.DateHired = #2/18/1991#
lblEmployeeInfo.Text =  MyObject.FirstName & " " & MyObject.LastName
```

One drawback of using public variables for object properties is that no validation is performed on them. In the example, you can assign any values to the `FirstName`, `LastName`, and `DateHired` properties, as long as the value is of the correct type. In addition, public variables return an unprocessed value; you do not have a chance to manipulate the information before returning it.

PROPERTY PROCEDURES

Property procedures are more flexible than public variables because they offer the advantage of being able to execute code when someone accesses a property. Property procedures are written like functions; but to users of an object, they behave just like properties. Property procedures provide a way for your users to both retrieve (`Get`) and assign (`Set`) the value of a property, and are discussed in detail in Chapter 16, "Creating Your Own Windows Controls."

→ **See** "Adding a New Property to Your Control," **420**

As we mentioned earlier, you can use Public variables to act as simple properties, but no data validation can be done on them. Consider the case of a `Salary` property. If we were to expose a `Salary` property as a simple Public variable, we would run into problems if the user attempted to set the value of the `Salary` property to an unacceptable value, such as a negative number. It would make sense to expose the `Salary` property as a Property procedure to give us the opportunity to perform some simple data validation.

Let's illustrate by creating the `Salary` property for our Employee class. The class will contain a private variable named `dSalary`, in which the employee's salary is stored internally to the class. Users of the class cannot see the `dSalary` variable directly; instead, it is exposed through the `Salary` property. The `Salary` property will consist of a Property procedure with two parts: the `Get` portion of the procedure contains code that retrieves the value of `dSalary` and passes it along to the user; the `Set` portion contains code that accepts the user's input and, *if valid*, assigns it to the internal `dSalary` variable.

Set up the internal `dSalary` variable for the property value by entering the following line of code into the Code window for the `clsEmployee` class, just below the public variable declarations you entered earlier:

```
Private Shared dSalary As Decimal
```

To create the Property procedure for the `Salary` property, type the following line of code into the Code window:

```
Public Property Salary() As Decimal
```

When you press Enter, a complete Property procedure shell for the `Salary` property is created, as illustrated in Figure 9.1.

Figure 9.1
Visual Basic .NET creates Property procedure shells automatically.

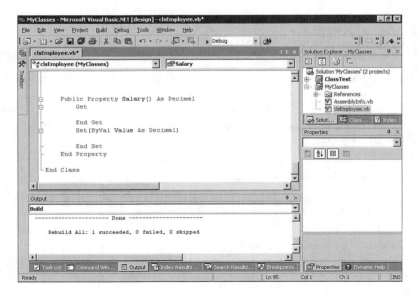

When creating this procedure shell, Visual Basic .NET adds the framework for the Get and Set portions of the procedure, which will be executed when the user attempts to retrieve or assign, respectively, the value of the property.

When users access the Salary property, the appropriate portion of the property procedure is executed. When the user attempts to retrieve the value of the property, the Get portion of the property procedure reads the value from the internal nSalary private variable and returns it to the user (via the Return keyword). When the user attempts to assign the value of the property, the Set portion of the Property procedure examines the value provided by the user, which is passed into the procedure via the Value parameter, and sets the internal nSalary variable appropriately.

PART

II

CH

9

CREATING THE Salary PROPERTY PROCEDURE

The following illustrates the complete Property procedure for the Salary property. Go ahead and enter the code now:

```
Public Property Salary() As Decimal
    Get
        Return dSalary
    End Get
    Set(ByVal Value As Decimal)
        If Value >= 0 Then
            dSalary = Value
        Else
            RaiseEvent DataError("Salary cannot be negative.")
        End If
    End Set
End Property
```

ADDING A FullName PROPERTY

Adding another property that returns the full name of the employee gives us a chance to demonstrate how some basic code can create a value-added property. Simply put, the FullName property will concatenate the first and last names of the employee (along with a space in the middle) and return the assembled string. Add the FullName Property procedure shown next to the Code window, just below the Salary property:

```
ReadOnly Property FullName() As String
    Get
        Return Trim(FirstName & " " & LastName)
    End Get
End Property
```

Note that the FullName property is ReadOnly, meaning that the user can retrieve it but not set it. Because of this, there is no need for a Set portion of the Property procedure.

ADDING A Department PROPERTY

Next, let's add a Department property to the class. Users will be able to set the Department property to a string specifying an employee's department; however, the value will be stored internally as an Integer. The Department property procedure will be responsible for converting between the internal property value and the external representation seen by the user of the class. Set up the internal variable for the property value, which we'll call nDeptNum, by entering the following line of code into the Code window for the clsEmployee class, just below the public variable declarations you entered earlier:

```
Private Shared nDeptNum As Integer
```

CREATING THE Department PROPERTY PROCEDURE

The following illustrates the complete Property procedure for the Department property. Go ahead and enter the code now:

```
Public Property Department() As String
    Get
        Select Case nDeptNum
            Case 1
                Return "Marketing"
            Case 2
                Return "Accounting"
            Case Else
                Return ""
        End Select
    End Get
    Set(ByVal Value As String)
        Select Case Trim(UCase(Value))
            Case "MARKETING"
                nDeptNum = 1
            Case "ACCOUNTING"
                nDeptNum = 2
            Case Else
                nDeptNum = 0
        End Select
    End Set
End Property
```

In the preceding code, the Property procedure actually stores the value representing the employee's department in a private integer variable (nDeptNum). However, users of the object always assign and retrieve a string. In a real-world program, this procedure would probably be more complex, doing things like storing a series of predefined department names in a database and allowing the user to specify a new department name to be added to the database.

ADDING A Supervisor PROPERTY

We will add one more property that is slightly more interesting. One of the main reasons for creating a class in the first place is to be able to create multiple instances of that class. Consider our Employee class. A program that uses it might need to create an instance for each member of a department. One nice feature would be to add a Supervisor property. Because the supervisor is (presumably) an employee as well, then he or she should be represented by an instance of the Employee class. The Supervisor property will accept another instance of the Employee class as its value. In other words, you don't set the Supervisor property to a String or an Integer; you set it to an Employee class type.

The Supervisor property will be stored internally through a Private variable of the Employee type, much like the Salary property is stored internally in the Private dSalary variable. Add the following declaration in the same area of clsEmployee's Code window as the other declarations:

```
Private objSupervisor As clsEmployee
```

The Supervisor Property procedure is pretty straightforward. Go ahead and enter it into the Code window now:

```
Property Supervisor() As clsEmployee
    Get
        Return objSupervisor
    End Get
    Set(ByVal Value As clsEmployee)
        objSupervisor = Value
    End Set
End Property
```

> **Note**
>
> If you try to access the Supervisor property for an instance of clsEmployee whose Supervisor property has not been set, you will get an error. You can get around this by using code like
>
> `If objEmp.Supervisor Is Nothing Then code Else code.`

ADDING A METHOD TO THE CLASS

As you know, objects perform actions via methods, such as the Add method of a ListBox control or the Focus method of a Button control. You can create methods in your own classes by adding public procedures or functions to the class module. Public procedures and functions work just like regular procedures and functions, but the Public keyword indicates that they will be visible to users of your object.

To demonstrate the use of a method in our sample Employee class, we will create a ChangeSalary method. This method will accept a single argument, representing the percentage—positive or negative—by which we want to change an employee's salary.

Enter the following code in the Code window for the Employee class:

```
Public Function ChangeSalary(ByVal sngAmt As Decimal)
    If (sngAmt > 1) Or (sngAmt < -1) Then
        sngAmt = sngAmt / 100
    End If
    Salary = Salary * (1 + sngAmt)
End Function
```

This example gives us the opportunity to demonstrate some rudimentary data validation. Note how the code examines the value of the input argument, sngAmount, to see whether it is in the range -1 to 1. If the value does not fall within that range, which represents -100% to 100%, we assume that the user entered the desired salary change as a percentage number, rather than the decimal equivalent of a percentage. In this case, we will divide the input argument by 100 to convert it to a true decimal amount. In other words, if the user enters

25 with the intention of granting a 25% raise, the argument will be converted to the decimal equivalent of `0.25` to complete the calculation.

ADDING AN EVENT TO A CLASS

You have already learned that objects raise events, like when a Button control raises the `Click` event (in response to a user having clicked the button). Events provide a way for an object to execute code written by the user of the object. The object triggers the event by way of an *event handler*. You already know how to place code in event handlers. To create an event in your own class, you need to do two things:

1. Declare the event in the class.
2. Use the `RaiseEvent` statement to trigger the event when appropriate.

Let's illustrate this concept by adding a sample `DataError` event to the `Employee` class. This event will be available to tell the user that some type of data error has occurred.

Suppose you want to return an error if a user attempts to set the value of the `Salary` property to a negative number. Simply adding a `RaiseEvent` statement to the right place in the `Salary` Property procedure will cause an error to be raised when necessary.

DECLARING THE EVENT

Before you can raise an event, you must declare that the event can exist. You do so by using an `Event` statement, which tells a class the name of an event that might be raised at some point. Type the following line of code near the top of `clsEmployee`'s Code window, just below the variable declarations:

```
Public Event DataError(ByVal sErrorMsg As String)
```

RAISING THE EVENT

Now that you have taught the class that an event *may* happen, you need to add code to raise the event when appropriate. You will do so by adding an `Else` clause to the `If` statement that decided whether the user-supplied value for the `Salary` property was positive. Modify the `Salary` property procedure so it looks like this:

```
Public Property Salary() As Decimal
    Get
        Return dSalary
    End Get
    Set(ByVal Value As Decimal)
        If Value >= 0 Then
            dSalary = Value
        Else
            RaiseEvent DataError("Salary cannot be negative.")
        End If
    End Set
End Property
```

> **Note**
>
> A single event can be raised from multiple locations within the class. For example, you might want to replace the Public variable that handles the DateHired property with a true Property procedure, which could check to see whether the date supplied was reasonable (for example, dates in the future may not be acceptable). When an invalid date is detected, you could use code such as `RaiseEvent DataError("Invalid Date Hired")`.

THE LIFE CYCLE OF YOUR CLASS

When working with custom classes, you might need to be concerned about what happens when instances of the class are created, and what happens when they are no longer needed. These can be handled by working with the class' *constructors* and *finalizers*.

CONSTRUCTORS

The term *constructor* refers to the procedure that executes when an instance of a class is created. You can write code in the constructor procedure to control what happens. For example, you may want to keep track of how many instances of a class are currently active. Although this is not particularly useful for the `Employee` class, we will demonstrate how to accomplish this.

Add the following declarations after the other declaration statements near the top of the Code window:

```
Public Shared ClassInstanceCount As Long = 0
Private Shared NextInstanceID As Integer = 1
Public ReadOnly InstanceID As Integer
```

This sets up the following three variables:

VARIABLE	PURPOSE
ClassInstanceCount	Keeps track of how many instances of `clsEmployee` are alive. As a Shared variable, it exists only at the class level; therefore, each instance of `clsEmployee` sees the same copy of `ClassInstanceCount`. As a Public variable, it will serve as a quasi-property reporting how many instances of `clsEmployee` are alive.
NextInstanceID	A Private variable used internally to hold the value to be assigned to the `InstanceID` variable for the next instance to be created.
InstanceID	A Public variable acting as a property, `InstanceID` reports the ID of the current instance of `clsEmployee`.

The default constructor for the `clsEmployee` class is the `Sub New` procedure, which executes each time an instance of `clsEmployee` is created, and does not yet exist in our sample application. To create and display the shell of the `Sub New` procedure, select New from the Method Name box in the Code window. Add the following code to `Sub New`:

```
Public Sub New()
    InstanceID = NextInstanceID
    NextInstanceID += 1
    ClassInstanceCount += 1
End Sub
```

As you can see, this code sets the value of the `InstanceID` property to the next available value (as determined by the value of `NextInstanceID`), then increments `NextInstanceID`, and finally increments the `ClassInstanceCount` counter, which keeps track of how many copies of the class are alive.

You can place in the `Sub New` constructor any other code that you need to execute when a new instance of your class is created. For example, you might want to set some internal values, such as the date the instance was created; write information to a database; or ensure that any dependent classes are loaded.

FINALIZERS

A class' *finalizer*, which is code executed by the `Finalize` event handler, is invoked just before an instance of that class is destroyed. This gives you a chance to do any housekeeping necessary to clean up.

To access the `Finalize` event handler of your class, choose Finalize from the Method Name box in the Code window. Note that one line of code (`MyBase.Finalize`) is placed in the procedure already. After that line, add the following:

```
ClassInstanceCount -= 1
```

This decrements the counter that keeps track of how many copies of the class are alive.

THE COMPLETE CODE

Listing 9.1 shows the complete code for the `clsEmployee` class.

LISTING 9.1   MYCLASSES.ZIP—THE COMPLETE CODE LISTING FOR THE `clsEmployees` CLASS

```
Public Class clsEmployee
    Public FirstName As String
    Public LastName As String
    Public DateHired As Date
    Private dSalary As Decimal
    Private nDeptNum As Integer
    Private objSupervisor As clsEmployee

    Public Shared ClassInstanceCount As Long = 0
    Private Shared NextInstanceID As Integer = 1
    Public ReadOnly InstanceID As Integer

    Public Event DataError(ByVal sErrorMsg As String)

    Public Property Salary() As Decimal
        Get
```

```
            Return dSalary
        End Get
        Set(ByVal Value As Decimal)
            If Value >= 0 Then
                dSalary = Value
            Else
                RaiseEvent DataError("Salary cannot be negative.")
            End If
        End Set
    End Property

    ReadOnly Property FullName() As String
        Get
            Return Trim(FirstName & " " & LastName)
        End Get
    End Property

    Public Property Department() As String
        Get
            Select Case nDeptNum
                Case 1
                    Return "Marketing"
                Case 2
                    Return "Accounting"
                Case Else
                    Return ""
            End Select
        End Get
        Set(ByVal Value As String)
            Select Case Trim(UCase(Value))
                Case "MARKETING"
                    nDeptNum = 1
                Case "ACCOUNTING"
                    nDeptNum = 2
                Case Else
                    nDeptNum = 0
            End Select
        End Set
    End Property

    Property Supervisor() As clsEmployee
        Get
            Return objSupervisor
        End Get
        Set(ByVal Value As clsEmployee)
            objSupervisor = Value
        End Set
    End Property

    Public Function ChangeSalary(ByVal sngAmt As Decimal)
        If (sngAmt > 1) Or (sngAmt < -1) Then
            sngAmt = sngAmt / 100
        End If
        Salary = Salary * (1 + sngAmt)

    End Function
```

LISTING 9.1   CONTINUED

```
    Public Sub New()
        InstanceID = NextInstanceID
        NextInstanceID += 1
        ClassInstanceCount += 1
    End Sub

    Protected Overrides Sub Finalize()
        MyBase.Finalize()
        ClassInstanceCount -= 1
    End Sub
End Class
```

USING A NEW CLASS IN AN APPLICATION

Of course, a new custom class does no good if you do not use it in an application. To use your new class in an application, you must create a reference from the project in which you want to use the class to the project that contains the class. We'll illustrate this point by adding a new test project to our sample class project.

SOLUTIONS

When you created the Class Library project earlier in this chapter, Visual Basic .NET automatically created a solution to contain that project. Simply put, a *solution* is a container for the projects that together comprise an application. Notice that the Solution Explorer window contains a solution named MyClasses, which was created as a container for (and named for) the MyClasses project that you created.

ADDING A PROJECT TO A SOLUTION

To add a new project to the current solution, choose File, Add Project, New Project from the menu system. In the Add New Project dialog box, choose the Windows Application template, give the project an appropriate name (let's use ClassTest for this example), and click OK. Note that the Solution Explorer window now includes a second project, ClassTest.

The complete ClassTest test project is available for download on the Internet at www.quepublishing.com.

SETTING THE STARTUP PROJECT

Notice that MyClasses is displayed in bold font in the Solution Explorer window, whereas ClassTest is not. This indicates that MyClasses is the Startup Project for the current solution. A solution's Startup Project is the project that will be executed when the application is run (either from the design environment or as a compiled program). Because a class cannot be run as a standalone application, we need to make ClassTest the Startup Project. To do so, simply right-click ClassTest in the Solution Explorer window, then choose "Set as StartUp Project" from the shortcut menu. Note that ClassTest is now bold, and MyClasses is not.

ADDING A REFERENCE

Even though the new ClassTest project is part of the same solution as MyClasses, you still need to add a reference before ClassTest can use the classes that make up the MyClasses class library. Add a reference as follows:

1. In the Solution Explorer window, right-click the References folder under the ClassTest project, then choose Add Reference from the shortcut menu.

2. In the Add Reference dialog box, click the Projects tab.

3. Click the MyClasses class library project, then click the Select button to put MyClasses in the Selected Components area of the dialog box.

4. Click OK. Notice that the References folder for ClassTest in the Solution Explorer window now contains a reference to MyClasses.

DECLARING AND USING OBJECTS

To use a class that you have defined, you need to create *instances* of that class in your applications. To do so, you will declare object type variables, using the new class as the variable's type, with a syntax similar to the following:

```
Dim objEmp As New clsEmployee
```

The New keyword actually causes an instance of the class clsEmployee to be created and stored in the object variable objEmp. However, sometimes you may want to delay the actual creation of the instance until later in the program, even though the variables are declared initially. In this case, use the New keyword when you are ready:

```
Dim objEmp As clsEmployee
'
'Later...
Set objEmp = New clsEmployee
```

In the preceding code, the actual object instance is not created until the Set statement is executed. In the first example, the object instance is created the first time a property or method of the object is referenced.

DESTROYING OBJECTS

Assigning Nothing to an object variable frees up resources associated with the object and causes the code in the class module's Terminate to be executed. You accomplish this feat by setting the object variable equal to the keyword Nothing:

```
objTemp = Nothing
```

Tip

Even though the contents of objects are no longer available when a form or module containing them is destroyed, it is good programming practice to set objects equal to Nothing when you are finished with them. This ensures that all memory resources are freed and the object is destroyed.

In the following section, you will set up the sample program to use your new `clsEmployee` class.

USING THE EMPLOYEE CLASS IN THE SAMPLE PROGRAM

The first thing you need to do to use the `clsEmployee` class in the sample program is to declare one or more instances of that class. Follow these steps to get started:

1. In the Solution Explorer window, right-click `Form1.vb` in the `ClassTest` project, then choose View Code from the shortcut menu.

2. You will see the Code window for `Form1.vb` of the `ClassTest` project. Type the following declaration in the Code window, just below the "Windows Form Designer generated code" area:

```
Dim WithEvents objEmp1 As New MyClasses.clsEmployee
```

> **Note**
>
> The `WithEvents` keyword in the `Dim` statement is necessary to allow the object to utilize the custom events that were created for it.

IMPORTING THE CLASS LIBRARY

While entering that declaration, you might have expected `clsEmployees` to be available from the editor's Auto List Members feature when you typed the spacebar after `Dim objEmp as New`. Instead, you had to specify the name of the class library, `MyClasses`; when you typed the period after the name of the class library, then you had access to the `clsEmployee` class contained in it. You can make members of the `MyClasses` library available throughout the current class (`Form1.vb`) by using an `Imports` statement. Place the following line of code at the very top of the Code window for `Form1.vb`, even above the `Public Class Form1` line:

```
Imports MyClasses
```

Now, go back and delete the `objEmp1` declaration you typed previously, then start typing it again. This time, when you press the spacebar after `Dim objEmp1 as New`, you will be able to choose `clsEmployee` from the Auto List Members feature. You have eliminated the need to type the `MyClasses.` qualifier before members of that library.

→ **See** "Using the Imports Statement," **p. 120**

After reentering the declaration for `objEmp1`, add two more declarations as shown here:

```
Dim WithEvents objEmp2 As New clsEmployee
Dim WithEvents objEmp3 As New clsEmployee
```

PLANNING FOR EVENTS

Because we declared our two object variables using the `WithEvents` keyword, we can reasonably expect that one or more events might occur. We can write code to handle those events just like any normal event handler. In the Code window for `Form1.vb`, drop down the Class Name box and choose `clsEmp1`; then drop down the Method Name box. Notice that the

DataError event we defined is available. Click it, and a shell DataError event handler is created. Add one line of code so the event handler looks like this:

```
Private Sub objEmp1_DataError(ByVal sErrorMsg As String) Handles objEmp1.DataError
    MessageBox.Show(sErrorMsg, "Error!", MessageBoxButtons.OK, _
        MessageBoxIcon.Warning)
End Sub
```

This code, which executes if something triggers the DataError event you coded for clsEmployee, will simply show the user a message box containing the error message that was reported by the DataError event. Add the following error handlers for the other two instances of clsEmployee:

```
Private Sub objEmp2_DataError(ByVal sErrorMsg As String) Handles objEmp2.DataError
    MessageBox.Show(sErrorMsg, "Error!", MessageBoxButtons.OK, _
        MessageBoxIcon.Warning)
End Sub

Private Sub objEmp3_DataError(ByVal sErrorMsg As String) Handles objEmp3.DataError
    MessageBox.Show(sErrorMsg, "Error!", MessageBoxButtons.OK, _
        MessageBoxIcon.Warning)
End Sub
```

SETTING PROPERTIES FOR THE EMPLOYEE OBJECTS

Here's where it all comes together. The following code sets various properties of the three clsEmployee objects we declared as the test project's main form loads. Add it to the end of Public Sub New in Form1.vb's Code window (you will have to click the plus sign next to "Windows Form Designer generated code" to see Sub New):

```
objEmp1.LastName = "Mertz"
objEmp1.FirstName = "Fred"
objEmp1.DateHired = #9/20/1928#
objEmp1.Salary = 57000
objEmp1.Department = "Marketing"

objEmp2.LastName = "Ricardo"
objEmp2.FirstName = "Ricky"
objEmp2.DateHired = #10/15/1951#
objEmp2.Salary = 71500
objEmp2.Department = "Marketing"

objEmp3.LastName = "Nelson"
objEmp3.FirstName = "Frank"
objEmp3.DateHired = #12/4/1927#
objEmp3.Salary = 99124
objEmp3.Department = "Accounting"

objEmp1.Supervisor = objEmp2
objEmp2.Supervisor = objEmp3
```

Of particular interest are the last two lines, objEmp1.Supervisor = objEmp2 and objEmp2.Supervisor = objEmp3, which sets the Supervisor property of objEmp1 and objEmp2 to two other instances of clsEmployee, objEmp2 and objEmp3, respectively.

TESTING THE PROPERTIES

Let's see whether the properties are working as expected. Try the following:

1. Add a Button control to `Form1.vb`. Change its `Name` property to `cmdShowInfo1` and its `Text` property to `Show Emp1 Info`.

2. Add the following code to `cmdShowInfo1`'s `Click` event handler:

```
Private Sub cmdShowInfo1_Click(ByVal sender As System.Object,_
    ByVal e As System.EventArgs) Handles cmdShowInfo.Click
    Dim sTemp As String
    sTemp = "Employee: " & objEmp1.FullName & vbCrLf
    sTemp += "Salary: " & FormatCurrency(objEmp1.Salary) & vbCrLf
    sTemp += "Department: " & objEmp1.Department & vbCrLf
    sTemp += "Supervisor: " & objEmp1.Supervisor.FullName & vbCrLf
    sTemp += "Instance: " & objEmp1.InstanceID
    sTemp += " of " & objEmp1.ClassInstanceCount
    MessageBox.Show(sTemp, "objEmp1 Info")
End Sub
```

3. Add a second Button control to `Form1.vb`. Change its `Name` property to `cmdShowInfo2` and its `Text` property to `Show Emp2 Info`.

4. Add the following code to `cmdShowInfo2`'s `Click` event handler:

```
Private Sub cmdShowInfo2_Click(ByVal sender As Object, ByVal e As_
    System.EventArgs) Handles cmdShowInfo2.Click
    Dim sTemp As String
    sTemp = "Employee: " & objEmp2.FullName & vbCrLf
    sTemp += "Salary: " & FormatCurrency(objEmp2.Salary) & vbCrLf
    sTemp += "Department: " & objEmp2.Department & vbCrLf
    sTemp += "Supervisor: " & objEmp2.Supervisor.FullName & vbCrLf
    sTemp += "Instance: " & objEmp2.InstanceID
    sTemp += " of " & objEmp2.ClassInstanceCount
    MessageBox.Show(sTemp, "objEmp2 Info")
End Sub
```

5. Add a TextBox control to `Form1.vb`. Change its `Name` property to `txtSalPct` and clear its `Text` property.

6. Add a Label control to the left of the `txtSalPct` text box. Set its `Text` property to `Enter Salary Change Percent:`.

7. Add a Button control near the label and text box you just added. Change its `Name` property to `cmdChangeSalary`, and set its `Text` property to `Change Emp1 Salary`.

8. Add the following line of code to the Event handler for `cmdChangeSalary`:

```
objEmp1.ChangeSalary(txtSalPct.Text)
```

Save and run your program. When you click the "Show Emp1 Info" button, you should see a message box containing all the properties you set for `objEmp1`, as depicted in Figure 9.2. Notice that the `FullName` and `Supervisor` properties did their job.

Figure 9.2
The first instance of the Employee class is displayed.

Click the "Show Emp2 Info" button and see the properties for objEmp2, as shown in Figure 9.3.

Figure 9.3
Different instances of the Employee class have different property values.

Next, enter a number into the text box, click the "Change Emp1 Salary" button, then click the "Show Emp1 Info" button again. You should see that the first employee's salary has been modified by the percentage you entered into the text box, as shown in Figure 9.4.

Figure 9.4
The Salary property for the first instance of the Employee class has been increased 5% by the ChangeSalary method.

Finally, test the DataError event by modifying the code that initially sets properties for the three instances of clsEmployee so that at least one of them attempts to set the salary to a negative number. When you run the program again, an error message like the one shown in Figure 9.5 should be displayed.

Figure 9.5
Because the program attempted to set the Salary property to an invalid number, the DataError event displays an error message.

USING REMOTING TO WORK WITH DISTRIBUTED OBJECTS

As you build and create custom classes, often you will need use these classes in a distributed manner. A typical scenario is when a program on an end user's computer creates a remote instance of an object containing business logic on another computer. A local network or even the Internet might connect these computers. If you were to try to create this type of architecture on your own, you would need to handle a lot of complex administrative tasks: network communications, associating object instances with clients, and so on. Fortunately, the .NET framework provides *Remoting*, which makes interprocess communication much easier. Remoting abstracts the process of creating objects and using their method calls across network boundaries.

UNDERSTANDING REMOTING CONCEPTS

Although .NET Remoting makes network communication between classes easier, working with remote objects is different enough that you still have to learn a few new concepts.

- In designing a class that you want to make remotable, you must inherit Remoting functionality from another class.

- You must be aware that remote objects can be created and destroyed in a manner that is different from local objects.

- You can make decisions regarding Remoting communications that affect the performance and reach of your remote objects.

After you have mastered these architectural concerns, you will find that the bulk of your code (method calls using an object variable) works the same whether the object is local or remote.

CREATING A REMOTE-CAPABLE CLASS

When you create an instance of an object locally, the object is stored in local memory until you are through with it, then the garbage collection process releases the associated memory. However, when you create an object remotely, the object is stored in the remote computer's memory, so using its methods involves a lot of communication back and forth across the network. The process of moving an object across the network is known as *marshalling* the object. All you have to do to make your own class support this process is inherit from the MarshalByRef class, as in the following example:

```
Public Class MyBusinessObject

    Inherits MarshalByRefObject

    Public Sub TestSub(ByVal sInput As String, ByRef sOutput As String)
        sOutput = sInput.ToUpper
    End Sub

End Class
```

The previous code sample uses inheritance to create a class called MyBusinessObject based on the MarshalByRefObject class. The MarshalByRefObject class provides the means by which the object definition and parameters can be transmitted across the network. By adding this single line of code, your class can be activated remotely if desired.

WORKING WITH STATEFUL AND STATELESS OBJECTS

Remote objects can be created as *stateful* or *stateless*. One easy way to understand these concepts is to consider them from the calling program's point of view. For example, consider the following lines of code, which create an instance of a fictional calculator class and then call methods to perform addition:

```
Dim MyCalculator As CalcObject
Dim Result As Integer

MyCalculator = New CalcObject()
MyCalculator.Operation = Addition
MyCalculator.EnterNumber(2)
MyCalculator.EnterNumber(3)
Result = MyCalculator.Calculate()
```

The preceding code sample first sets the Operation property, then calls the EnterNumber method a couple of times, and finally executes the Calculate function. It seems simple enough, but in order for this code to work, the MyCalculator object must be a stateful object. In other words, it must maintain internal state between each subsequent method call, keeping track of the numbers entered and other properties set by the client. A lot of the objects in Visual Basic work in this same manner, such as the text boxes on your form or variables in your functions. A stateless object, on the other hand, is created only for the time that it takes to execute the current method call and then is immediately destroyed. As a result, its methods are usually written to be processed like transactions:

```
Dim MyCalculator As AnotherCalcObject
Dim Result As Integer

MyCalculator = New AnotherCalcObject()
Result = MyCalculator.Calculate(Addition,2,3)
Result = MyCalculator.Calculate(Subtraction,10,5)
```

In the second code sample, a stateless version of the Calculator object is called. This code performs the same task, but in a different manner. Instead of executing methods that rely on internal object values, all the information needed for the addition calculation is passed to the object in a single method call. This is because with a stateless remote object, the calling program cannot assume that each time it accesses an object variable, the variable will refer to the same instance of the class. You might think that this is a disadvantage, but actually in some ways it is an advantage! If you are able to write your methods in such a way that each method call is an independent transaction, your client doesn't care which object instance it calls, so the object is free to service other clients, thus making your application more scalable. (And you can always store state on the client using variables or in a back-end database accessed by the stateless object.)

In the .NET Remoting world, the server creates stateless objects in *single call* mode. For stateful objects, the server can create one single object instance to handle all incoming requests (this is known as *singleton* mode), or the client can control object instantiation (this is known as *client activation*). In this section we will focus on stateless objects, because they can be used in more scalable applications. For more information on the other types, see the Help topic "Remoting."

UNDERSTANDING CHANNELS

Although .NET Remoting hides many of the low-level networking details from the programmer, you still need to be aware of different types of communication *channels*. A channel is simply a path over the network between two computers. The process of converting an object into a format suitable for transmission across a channel is known as *serialization*. The two basic types of channels, which use different means of serialization, are listed next:

- *TCP Channels* use the TCP/IP protocol to transmit objects as binary data. As with any TCP/IP connection, a machine name (or numeric address) plus a port number is necessary to uniquely identify a channel.

- *HTTP Channels* are built on top of TCP/IP, but use text-based data formats such as XML and text-based protocols like SOAP. HTTP channels are a little slower than TCP channels, but are generally more firewall-friendly.

As you might imagine, TCP channels are suited for high-performance intranet communication, while HTTP channels are better for use over the Internet. In this section, we'll focus on TCP channels. Later in the book we will discuss Web Services, which use the HTTP protocol to access remote objects on a Web server.

→ For more on Web Services, **see** Chapter 18, "Web Applications and Services," **p. 475**

USING A REMOTE OBJECT

Now that you are familiar with the basic concepts, we will build a sample distributed application that uses a remote object. This application will be divided into three parts:

- The *business object* is a Windows Class Library project that contains the functionality you want to offer remotely. So that you may learn about the Remoting architecture and apply it to your own programs, the functionality of our example will be a simple temperature conversion class.

- The *host application* is a Windows Application project that runs on the server where the business object is located. Its purpose is to set up the communication channel and register the business object with the Remoting framework.

- The *client application* is a Windows Application project that runs on the client. It uses the functionality of the remote business object.

Setting Up the Sample Application

To create the sample application, you'll need to perform the following steps:

1. Start Visual Studio.NET and create a new Windows Class library called `TempConverter`.
2. Right-click the solution name and choose to add a new project. Add a Windows Application project called **HostApp**.
3. Right-click the solution name and choose to add a new project. Add a Windows Application project called **ClientApp**.
4. Right-click the solution name and choose Properties.
5. From the Properties dialog box, select the option for Multiple Startup Projects.
6. Set the Action for `TempConverter` to `None`. Set the Action for `ClientApp` and `HostApp` to `Start`. This will make both projects start when you begin a debug session in Visual Studio.

PART
II
CH
9

Now that you have set up the framework for this example, we will proceed with writing code for each of the three projects in your solution.

Creating the Business Object

First, we'll create the class that contains the heart of the program: the business object. The name business object, incidentally, describes the layer of a multi-tier application that contains logic related to business functionality, rather than database access or the user interface.

➔ For a picture of a multi-tier application, **see** Chapter 22, "Using ADO.NET," **p. 599**

To create the example business object, right-click the Class1.vb file in the Solution Explorer and display the Code window. Enter the code from Listing 9.2 to create the `clsTemperature` class.

LISTING 9.2   REMOTING.ZIP—Coding the Business Object

```
Public Class clsTemperature
    Inherits MarshalByRefObject

    Public Function CtoF(ByVal CelsuisTemp As Single) As Single
        'Converts Celsius temperature to Fahrenheit
        Return CelsuisTemp * 9 / 5 + 32

    End Function

    Public Function FtoC(ByVal FahrenheitTemp As Single) As Single
        'Converts Fahrenheit temperature to Celsius
        Return (FahrenheitTemp - 32) * 5 / 9

    End Function

End Class
```

The class definition in Listing 9.2 is just like any other class we have discussed in this chapter, only it inherits from the `MarshalByRefObject` class. As we mentioned earlier, to create a class that is remotable, all you need to do is add this single line of code. Before continuing with the example, choose Build TempConverter from the Build menu to verify that you do not have any syntax errors.

IMPORTING THE REMOTING NAMESPACES

Setting up a remotable business object is really easy. As a matter of fact, the business object class is not really aware of Remoting. However, the other parts of the distributed application that host or call remote objects have to be aware of Remoting and network channels. Therefore, you'll need to add references to .NET Remoting classes in both the `ClientApp` and `HostApp` projects:

1. Using the Solution Explorer, right-click the References folder in each project and add a new reference to `System.Runtime.Remoting`.

2. Add the following `Imports` statements to the `Form1` class in each project:

```
Imports System.Runtime.Remoting
Imports System.Runtime.Remoting.Channels
Imports System.Runtime.Remoting.Channels.Tcp
```

After you have added these necessary references, the code in these projects will be able to call methods in .NET Remoting classes.

SETTING UP THE HOST PROGRAM

As we mentioned earlier, the class library project itself is not aware of Remoting, so a host program is used to fill in the gaps. The host program opens a communication channel by which a client can request an instance of the business object, and registers the business object type with the Remoting framework. After performing these initial steps, the Remoting framework takes over and handles client requests.

Note

Classes can also be hosted in IIS and exposed as Web Services, eliminating the need to write a custom host program. For more details, see Chapter 18, "Web Applications and Services."

Because the host program will be responsible for registering the class with the Remoting framework, it needs to be aware of the class definition. As you may recall from Chapter 4, "Understanding the Development Environment," to make one project aware of another project in the same solution, you need to add a reference. To add a reference, perform the following steps:

1. Right-click on References in the `HostApp` project and choose Add Reference.

2. From the Add Reference dialog box, select the Projects tab.

3. Highlight the `TempConverter` class and click the Select button. Click OK to add the reference.

Next, add two Command buttons to your form. Set their `Name` properties to `btnStart` and `btnStop`. Set their `Text` properties to `Start Service` and `Stop Service`, respectively. Finally, enter the code for the host program, shown in Listing 9.3.

LISTING 9.3   REMOTING.ZIP—SETTING UP THE HOST PROGRAM

```
Private Sub btnStart_Click(ByVal sender As System.Object, ByVal e As
System.EventArgs) Handles btnStart.Click
    Dim MyChannel As TcpChannel
    Dim MyPort As Integer = 12345
    Dim MyEndPoint As String = "TempConverter"
    Dim MyObjType As System.Type

    'Register a TCP Channel
    MyChannel = New TcpChannel(MyPort)
    ChannelServices.RegisterChannel(MyChannel)

    'Register the class
    MyObjType = GetType(TempConverter.clsTemperature)
    RemotingConfiguration.RegisterWellKnownServiceType _
      (MyObjType, MyEndPoint, WellKnownObjectMode.SingleCall)

    MessageBox.Show("Server Started!")
End Sub

Private Sub btnStop_Click(ByVal sender As System.Object, ByVal e As
System.EventArgs) Handles btnStop.Click

    Application.Exit()

End Sub
```

The code for the `btnStart` event in Listing 9.3 performs two basic tasks: creating a communication channel and registering the object with the Remoting framework. First, the `RegisterChannel` method is called to set up a new TCP channel on port `12345`.

Note
> When choosing a port number for a custom application, try to avoid numbers that are established standards (such as 80 for Web browsing or 21 for FTP).

Next, the `RegisterWellKnownServiceType` method is invoked, which actually makes the object available for remote access. This call has three parameters:

- The type definition of your business object class.
- The endpoint string, which is part of the URI (or Uniform Resource Identifier) used to locate a remote object.
- The object mode, which is set to `SingleCall` to indicate stateless activation.

Note that the act of creating the channel and registering the object are independent in the code. The channel is just a means of connecting to the Remoting framework. Through the use of the URI string, the Remoting framework can create multiple types of objects using the same channel.

> **Note**
>
> When the host program exits, any Remoting services or channels it created will be destroyed.

CREATING THE CLIENT PROGRAM

The final part of our distributed application is the client process. The client will create a remote instance of the clsTemperature class and call a method to perform the temperature conversion. Before entering the client application code, you will need to add a reference to the TempConverter project, just as we did for the host application. Observant readers may be wondering why this client reference is needed, because the entire purpose of using an object remotely is to *not* have to install it on the client machine! The answer is that while the client does not require direct access to the object, it still needs to know type information about the object. This type of information, also known as *metadata*, specifies the method names and parameters of the remote object.

To create the client program, add two text boxes to your form, named txtTempC and txtTempF. Add buttons beside each, named btnConverttoF and btnConvertToC. Finally, enter the code from Listing 9.4.

LISTING 9.4   REMOTING.ZIP—SETTING UP THE CLIENT

```
Private Function PerformConversion(ByVal ConversionType As String, _
    ByVal InputTemp As Single) As Single


    'Build URI string
    Dim MyPort As Integer = 12345
    Dim MyMachine As String = "brianpc1"
    Dim MyEndPoint As String = "TempConverter"
    Dim URIString As String
    URIString = "tcp://" & MyMachine & ":" & MyPort & "/" & MyEndPoint

    'Create the remote object instance
    Dim MyRemoteObject As TempConverter.clsTemperature
    Dim MyObjType As System.Type = GetType(TempConverter.clsTemperature)
    MyRemoteObject = CType(Activator.GetObject(MyObjType, URIString),
TempConverter.clsTemperature)

    'Call a method on the remote object
    If MyRemoteObject Is Nothing Then
        MessageBox.Show("Error!")
    Else
        If ConversionType.ToUpper = "CTOF" Then
            Return MyRemoteObject.CtoF(InputTemp)
        Else
```

```
                        Return MyRemoteObject.FtoC(InputTemp)
             End If
         End If

     End Function

     Private Sub btnConvertToC_Click(ByVal sender As System.Object, _
         ByVal e As System.EventArgs) Handles btnConvertToC.Click
         txtTempC.Text = PerformConversion("FTOC", Convert.ToSingle(txtTempF.Text))
     End Sub

     Private Sub btnConvertToF_Click(ByVal sender As Object, _
         ByVal e As System.EventArgs) Handles btnConvertToF.Click
         txtTempF.Text = PerformConversion("CTOF", Convert.ToSingle(txtTempC.Text))

     End Sub
```

Note that in Listing 9.4, a URI string is used that enables the client to find the remote object. A URI, which stands for Uniform Resource Indicator, includes the machine name, channel and port, and endpoint. The URI string from Listing 9.4 looks like this:

```
tcp://brianpc1:12345/TempConverter
```

The GetObject method of the Activator class is one means of creating a remote object instance. However, this returns the object as a generic value of type Object, so the Ctype function is included to convert the remote reference to the locally defined type clsTemperature.

TESTING THE EXAMPLE

Now that you have created the three parts of the distributed application, click the Visual Studio Start button. The two forms from the client and host applications should appear. Click the Start Server button on the host application and wait for the confirmation message box. Next, test the remote functions by converting various temperature values in the client app.

If you have another PC on your network with the .NET Framework installed, move the files ClientApp.exe and TempConverter.dll from your project's bin directory to this machine. As long as the host application is running on the first PC, you should be able to run the client from the second PC. You can run the command NETSTAT from a Command Prompt window to verify a connection between the PCs using port 12345.

In our simple example, we used a reference to TempConverter.dll to provide metadata information to the client application, which means that this DLL would need to be distributed with the client application. However, referencing the class directly during development is just one way to provide this information to the client. Microsoft also recommends the following approaches:

- Create an interface DLL file that clients use to obtain metadata information. The remote object on the server can implement this interface.

- Use the SOAPSUDS.EXE tool, which can read a class and build a DLL you can reference from the client application.

Our example is very simple and just scratches the surface of the features of .NET Remoting. For more information on Remoting, please read the very extensive documentation included with the .NET Framework SDK.

FROM HERE...

In this chapter, you learned how to create your own custom classes. The following chapters will help you work with similar concepts:

- To see how to use class programming concepts to create a custom control that you can use on Windows forms, see Chapter 16, "Creating Your Own Windows Controls."
- To learn more about writing code that you can include in your custom classes, see Chapter 7, "Controlling the Flow of Your Program," and Chapter 8, "Managing Program Tasks with Procedures."

BUILDING WINDOWS APPLICATIONS

UNDERSTANDING WINDOWS FORMS

In this chapter

This is the first chapter in a section on developing applications for Windows, and so we'll be discussing all things related to the canvas of your programs—the Windows form. In this chapter, we will discuss how to create different form styles, how to add menus to a form, and how to manage multiple forms within your Visual Basic code. After you are comfortable with forms, the next few chapters will explore the controls you can use on those forms.

CHANGING THE LOOK OF YOUR FORMS

When you add a new form to your project, you are presented with a plain gray square box. As you add controls to your form, you change its appearance. However, there are a lot of changes you can make to the form itself to make it more interesting and useable. To understand some of these changes, let's quickly review the different parts of a form, as indicated in Figure 10.1.

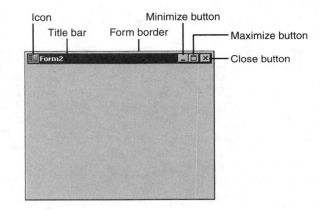

Figure 10.1
To give your application a more professional appearance, change the form caption by setting the Text property.

Setting form properties can control each of the elements pictured in Figure 10.1. You may have already learned some of the basic properties of a form, such as the Text property, which controls the text that is displayed in the title bar, or the Icon property, which controls the image that is displayed both in the title bar and in the task bar when the form is minimized. In this section, we will discuss properties of a form that can be used to control how the form looks and behaves when the user interacts with it.

CHANGING THE BORDER STYLE OF A FORM

If you work with a lot of Windows applications, you know that forms take on different styles depending on their use in an application. For example, Microsoft Word allows you to resize a document to fit the entire screen if necessary. On the other hand, the settings for your screen saver appear in a fixed window that cannot be resized or minimized.

The FormBorderStyle property of a Windows form determines what title bar elements are displayed on the form, and whether the user can control the form's size and position. By default, the FormBorderStyle property of a form is set to Sizable, which means the user has total freedom over resizing the form at runtime.

The seven possible settings that control the FormBorderStyle property are listed in Table 10.1. Several examples of different FormBorderStyle settings are shown in Figure 10.2.

TABLE 10.1   FormBorderStyle **PROPERTY SETTINGS**

Setting	Effect
None	No border, title bar, or control buttons are displayed for the form. The user cannot move or resize the form.
FixedSingle	The title bar and control buttons are displayed for the form. The user cannot resize the form.
Sizable	The title bar and control buttons are displayed. The user can resize the form by clicking and dragging the border. This setting is the default.
Fixed3D	The title bar and control buttons are displayed. A three-dimensional border is displayed, which makes the form look inset. The user cannot resize the form.
FixedDialog	Visually similar to the FixedSingle form.
FixedToolWindow	The form has a single-line border and displays only the title bar and Close button. They are shown in a reduced font size.
SizableToolWindow	This is the same as the Fixed ToolWindow, except that the form has a sizable border.

PART
III
CH
10

Figure 10.2
Changing the FormBorderStyle property can give a form many different appearances.

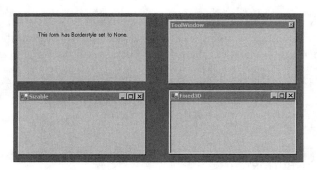

Note

Setting the FormBorderStyle property to prevent resizing does not affect the form's appearance in the design environment; it does so only at runtime.

UNDERSTANDING TITLE BAR BUTTONS

In Table 10.1, several of the FormBorderStyle definitions indicate that a control box and the Close, Minimize, and Maximize buttons would be displayed in the title bar of the form. This behavior is the default. But even with these border styles, you can individually control whether these elements are enabled on the form.

HIDING THE MINIMIZE AND MAXIMIZE BUTTONS

The MaximizeBox and MinimizeBox properties each have a True or False setting that determines whether the particular element is clickable by the end user. The default setting for each of these properties on a sizable form is True. (Tool window forms do not have these buttons.) If you set a property to False, the corresponding element is displayed in a grayed-out mode to indicate it is disabled on the form, as pictured in Figure 10.3. If you set both the MinimizeBox and MaximizeBox properties to False, the buttons will disappear from the title bar.

Control Box menu

Figure 10.3
The control box of a Windows form is the icon in the upper-left corner, which will display a menu containing resize options when clicked. The shortcut key for this menu is Alt+Space.

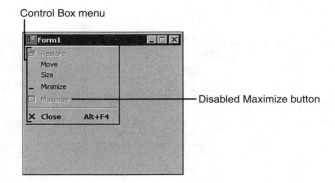

Disabled Maximize button

The Control Box menu pictured in Figure 10.3 automatically displays the menu options in the state that corresponds to the state of the associated title bar button. If you set a form's ControlBox property to False, *all* of the title bar buttons will disappear completely.

Note

You can use the WindowState property to minimize or maximize a form with code, regardless of the state of the title bar buttons.

DISPLAYING A HELP BUTTON

Another button available for use in the title bar is the help button. A help button allows the user to ask your program for help on a particular section of the form. A help button works differently from most buttons, in that using it is a two-step process. First, the user clicks the help button, which changes the mouse cursor to a question mark. Next, the user clicks a control on your form, such as the text box with which she needs assistance. Clicking a control after clicking the form's help button causes its HelpRequested event to fire. In this event, you can write code to display relevant information. However, enabling this button is a little tricky. Not only do you have to set the `HelpButton` property to `True`, but you also have to set the `MinimizeButton` and `MaximizeButton` properties to False. Although this may seem like a strange restriction at first, it makes sense when you consider the help box is designed for use with dialog boxes; as you will see in an upcoming section, for other types of forms, it is common to provide a Help menu for program documentation.

→ For more on dialog boxes, **see** Chapter 13, "Using Dialog Boxes," **p. 335**

WORKING WITH SIZE AND POSITION

Forms and controls have a size, which is represented by the `Size` property, and a position, which is represented by the `Location` property. Because a computer screen is a two-dimensional object, each of these properties is itself an object with properties for each dimension. A form's size is made up of a height and a width component; its location is made up of x and y coordinates in relation to the screen. These components and their relationships are shown in Figure 10.4.

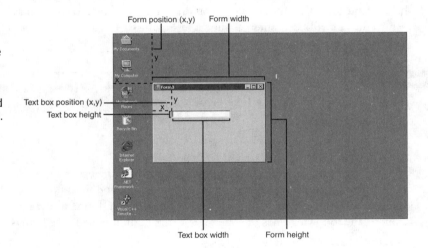

Figure 10.4
The location and size properties of a text box are measured relative to the form; the form is measured relative to the screen.

FORM SIZING PROPERTIES

As you've seen, you can modify an object's size by selecting it and dragging a sizing handle at design time. You also can change the values of its `Height`, `Width`, or `Size` properties at runtime. The following lines of code double a form's size when executed:

```
Me.Height *= 2
Me.Width *= 2
```

Notice the use of the keyword `Me`, which refers to the current instance of an object. Using `Me` allows you to specify the current form object from within the form class, without naming it explicitly.

Notice in the previous lines of code that Height and Width are separate, top-level properties. The Size class allows you to specify the height and width of a form at the same time:

```
Dim ExtraLarge As New Size(123,456)
Me.Size = ExtraLarge
```

The Size class is used to represent a rectangular area of pixels. If you resize an object at design time or runtime with the mouse, you will see a corresponding change in the Height, Width, and Size properties.

UNDERSTANDING THE Location PROPERTY

In addition to controlling an object's *size*, you can also control its *position* on the screen with the Left, Top, and Location properties. As with the size properties, you can set each coordinate of the location individually using the Left or Top properties, or all at once by declaring an object of type Position. The Left property specifies the distance of the left side of an object from the left side of the object's container. The Top property specifies the distance of the top edge of an object from the top edge of its container. In the case of a standard form, the container is the entire screen. If you draw a control on a form, such as a text box, the form is the control's container, as shown in Figure 10.4. The text box's Height and Width properties relate to the form that contains it.

Note

The ToString method of the Size and Position objects formats their values in coordinate style format, with parentheses.

SETTING BOUNDARY SIZES

Even if your FormBorderStyle property is set to allow the user to resize the form, you can control the range of sizes allowed by setting minimum and maximum sizes. You can do this at design time or runtime by setting the MaximumSize and MinimumSize properties. As an example, the following lines of code set a form's minimum and maximum size:

```
Me.MinimumSize = New Size(100,100)

Dim NewSize AS Size
NewSize = Screen.GetWorkingArea(Me).Size
NewSize.Height \= 2
NewSize.Width \= 2
Me.MaximumSize = NewSize
```

The first line of code sets the minimum size of the form to 100 × 100 pixels. The next few lines of code determine the screen's size and set the maximum form size to half of that area. In other words, if your screen is 1,024 × 768, then the code statements would make the maximum form size 512 × 384 pixels. Notice that we use the GetWorkingArea method of the Screen class to determine the size of the working area of the current form. To test this code, place it in a button's Click event. Experiment with resizing the form, then click the button and notice that resizing becomes restricted.

> **Note**
>
> The MinimumSize and MaximumSize properties affect both code statements and user-initiated resizing. For example, if you set a form's size to a size larger than the allowed maximum size, the form size will change to the maximum size.

If you set size restrictions but then later want to remove them, set the MinimumSize and MaximumSize properties to (0,0).

ADDING AUTOMATIC SCROLLBARS

Visual Basic .NET forms include an interesting new feature called AutoScroll, which automatically creates scrollbars for your form, as shown in Figure 10.5.

Figure 10.5
AutoScroll creates scrollbars when the form dimensions are too small to display all the controls. Background images are not affected.

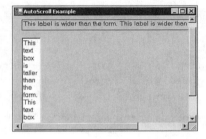

To use AutoScroll, just set a form's AutoScroll property to True, either at design time or runtime. Setting the AutoScroll property to True provides a visual indication to the user that controls exist outside the viewable area. A summary of the AutoScroll-related form properties is next:

- **AutoScroll**—Controls automatic scrollbars. If you allow the user to manually resize a form, the scrollbars will appear and disappear as needed.

- **AutoScrollMargin**—Allows you to pad the controls with a margin so that the scrollbars appear when the form's borders fall within the margin. By default, this property is set to a Size of (0,0).

- **AutoScrollMinSize**—The minimum size that will make the scrollbars appear, regardless of whether there are controls outside the form's visible area.

- **AutoScrollPosition**—Gets or sets a Position containing the scrollbar settings. For example, if the scrollbars are at their topmost and leftmost positions, this property will contain the position (0,0).

SETTING FORM STARTUP OPTIONS

Your form position can change while your program is running, either when the user moves it or you set a new value for the Position property. However, you can set the StartPosition property to tell Visual Basic where you want the form to be initially displayed. You can pick one of the following options for the StartPosition property:

- **CenterParent**—The form appears centered within the border of its parent form. For example, if Form1 calls the ShowDialog method of Form2 and the StartPosition property of Form2 is set to CenterParent, then Form2 will be centered in relation to Form1.

- **CenterScreen**—Centers the form in relation to the entire screen.

- **Manual**—The form will appear at the coordinates specified in the Location property, which defaults to (0,0)—the upper-left corner screen.

- **WindowsDefaultLocation**—Allows Windows to determine the starting position, based on the other open windows.

- **WindowsDefaultBounds**—Allows Windows to determine the starting position and size of the form.

VISUAL EFFECTS

As we will see in a future chapter, you can use classes from the System.Drawing namespace to draw objects and print text directly on a form or control. However, there are a few properties of a form that can be used to create some interesting visual effects.

→ For more on Drawing and Graphics, **see** Chapter 14, "Designing an Effective User Interface," **p. 357**

CHANGING FORM COLORS

The BackColor property can be used to set the color of the background area of the form, which appears behind the controls. Instead of a plain gray form, you can set the background to the color of your choice:

```
Me.BackColor = Color.Honeydew
Me.BackColor = Color.FromKnownColor(KnownColor.Desktop)
Me.ForeColor = Color.FromName("Yellow")
```

Note

For a list of system-defined colors available in Visual Basic, see the help topic "Color Members."

The first line of the previous code sets the background color to one of the built-in color constants, Color.Honeydew (yes, Honeydew!). The next line of code uses a *system color*, which means the actual color of the form will be affected by the user's color scheme in the Windows control panel. In the example, the form background is set to the same color as the Windows desktop. The final line of code uses the FromName method to specify a color by name. You also can set color values to custom colors, such as those returned by a ColorDialog control.

→ For more on the Color dialog box, **see** Chapter 12, "Advanced Controls," **p. 309**

The ForeColor and BackColor properties of a form affect controls that are placed on the form, such as labels and buttons. For example, if you add a label control to a form, the label's ForeColor and BackColor colors will match the form. If you do not explicitly set the label's colors, they will remain linked to those of the form and change when the form colors are changed. This is true both at runtime and in design mode.

ADDING A BACKGROUND IMAGE

Another nice effect you can add to a form is a background image. Controls can be placed on top of the image, as shown in Figure 10.6.

Figure 10.6
A background image can be used to create a custom login screen or About box.

The easiest way to set the background image for a form is to use the Properties window at design time. However, if you need to load images from disk after your program is running, you can set the property to any valid Image object, as in the following example:

```
Dim imgTemp As Image
imgTemp = Image.FromFile(Application.StartupPath & "Horse.jpg")
Me.BackgroundImage = imgTemp
```

→ For more on graphics formats, **see** Chapter 14, "Designing an Effective User Interface," **p. 357**

The preceding lines of code create an instance of the Image class using an image file, horse.jpg, and assign it to the BackgroundImage property of the form. The code assumes the image file is located in the same folder as the application executable, which is the bin directory when you are debugging in Visual Studio. If the image dimensions are less than the form size, the image is tiled repeatedly on the form background.

Note

Set the background color of a control to Color.Transparent to allow the user to view the form's background image through the control.

CREATING TRANSPARENT FORMS

Two new properties, TransparencyKey and Opacity, allow you to create transparent forms, meaning you can see other forms or the Windows desktop behind your application. To use the Opacity property, assign a double value between 0–1 to represent the desired percentage of opaqueness. For example, the following line of code sets a form's Opacity to 50%:

```
Form1.Opacity = 0.5
```

To see the Opacity property in action, using a scrollbar perform the following steps:

1. Add a Horizontal scrollbar control to your form. Set its Name property to scrOpacity.

2. The Min and Max properties of the scrollbar should already be set to 0 and 100, respectively. Set the Value property of the scrollbar to 100.

3. Add a Label control to your form. Set the Name property to lblOpacity.

4. Add the following two lines of code to the scrollbar's Scroll event:

```
Me.Opacity = scrOpacity.Value / 100
lblOpacity.Text = Me.Opacity.ToString
```

Now run the sample program. As you move the scrollbar, the form should appear to fade in and out, as shown in Figure 10.7.

Figure 10.7
The Opacity property can use to create fade-ins and other ghostly form effects.

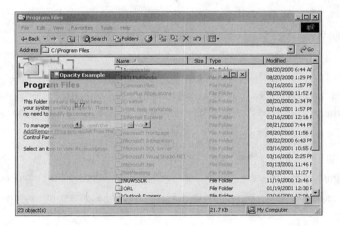

The TransparencyKey property is similar to the Opacity property in that it allows you to see through the form, but with two important differences:

- The transparent parts of the form do not accept events such as the mouse click; in other words you can still access the controls on an opaque form even if you can't see it, but a transparent area of a form allows you to click through it.

- Form transparency is either total or not based on a color; opacity is a percent value that applies to all colors.

To demonstrate a transparent form, add a Label control to your form and set the `BackgroundColor` property of the label to blue. Set the `TransparencyKey` property of the form to the same color as the label background. When you run the program, your form will appear to have a hole in it—clicking in the transparent area will activate the window behind the form.

Note

The `Opacity` property is not supported at 256-color resolution. Make sure you have at least 16-bit color selected to use this property.

ADDING MENUS TO YOUR FORMS

One of the most important aspects in designing any program is providing the users with easy access to all the program's functions. Users are accustomed to accessing most functions with a mouse click or two. In addition, they want all the functions located conveniently in one place. To help facilitate this strategy, most commercial Windows programs provide a menu bar across the top of the screen. Although today's users may be more accustomed to using hyperlinks, a menu system is still a convenient way to provide access to your program's functions, especially if screen space is limited. In this section we will show you how to create a menu bar on a form. We will also describe how to create a *context menu*, which is a menu that pops up when the user clicks a form or control.

GETTING STARTED

The first step in creating a menu is determining what program commands need to be on the menu and how these commands should be organized. For example, look at Visual Basic's own main menu. As you can see, the commands are organized into functional groups (File, Edit, View, and so forth).

When you create your program's menu, you should group similar items. In fact, if possible, you should use groups with which your users are already familiar. This way, users have some idea where to find particular menu items, even if they've never used your program. The following list describes some standard menus you will find on many menu bars:

- **File**—This menu contains any functions related to files used by your program. Some of the typical menu items are New, Open, Close, Save, Save As, and Print. If your program works extensively with different files, you also might want to include a quick access list of the most recently used files. If you include a File menu, the program's Exit command is usually located near the bottom of this menu.

- **Edit**—The Edit menu contains the functions related to editing of text and using the Windows Clipboard. Some typical Edit menu items are Undo, Cut, Copy, Paste, Clear, Find, and Replace.

- **View**—The View menu might be included if your program supports different looks for the same document. A word processor, for example, might include a normal view for editing text and a page-layout view for positioning document elements, as well as a variety of zoom options. Another use of the View menu is to allow the users to display special forms in your program, such as the Visual Basic View, Toolbox option.

- **Tools**—This menu is a catchall for your program's utilities or helper functions. For example, a spelling checker, grammar checker, or other less-frequently used options.

- **Window**—This menu typically is included if your program uses a Multiple Document Interface (MDI), which will be discussed in a later chapter. MDI programs, like Microsoft Word, support the simultaneous editing of different documents, databases, or files. The Window menu lets users arrange open documents or switch rapidly between them.

- **Help**—The Help menu contains access to your program's Help system. Typically, it includes menu items for a Help Index (a table of contents for help), a Search option (to let the users quickly find a particular topic), and an About option (providing summary, authoring, and copyright information regarding your program).

You can use these six standard menus as a basis for creating your own menu system. The items in the previous list are examples of *top-level* menu items, because they are at the top of the menu hierarchy, always visible on the screen, and very general in nature. Beneath the top-level are *submenu* items, which represent more specific menu choices. For example, the File menu item does not do anything by itself, but the items beneath it all perform specific file-related functions.

> **Note**
>
> Occasionally, the text of a menu item ends with an ellipsis (. . .). The ellipsis is an accepted menu standard that indicates more information is required to execute the command. One example is Visual Basic's own Print menu item, which displays a dialog box for the user to enter additional information.

> **Note**
>
> The top-level/submenu organization is just an accepted convention; from the programming point of view each item in the menu is treated the same. Although it would seem odd to a user, there is nothing to prevent you from initiating program actions from a top-level item.

USING THE MENU EDITOR

The .NET framework provides menu functionality via classes, and like any other classes they can be created entirely in code by instantiating objects. However, it is much easier to add menus using the Menu Editor provided by Visual Studio, which generates the code for you. To work with the Menu Editor, you place one of the following controls on the form:

1. `MainMenu`—This control is typically used to create a menu that will appear at the top of your form. You can add more than one `MainMenu` control to a form and switch between them programmatically.

2. `ContextMenu`—This is used to provide pop-up functionality. It can be tied to a control or form via the `ContextMenu` property, as we will see in a moment.

When you drag either type of menu control to your form, it will appear in the bottom area of the form for invisible controls, as shown in Figure 10.8. To edit a menu, you select it by single-clicking its icon, then the Menu Editor will appear beneath the form's title bar.

Figure 10.8
Starting with Visual Studio .NET, the Menu Editor is integrated into the form and no longer appears as a separate dialog box.

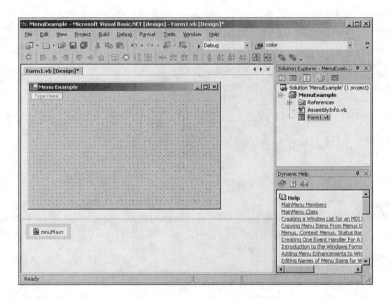

CREATING THE FIRST MENU ITEM

A menu is a collection of menu items. All the menu item objects are basically treated the same, although their appearance and organization can be altered. Each menu item contains text (usually only a word or two), which the user can click with the mouse to select an option.

To see how the Menu Editor works, we will walk through creating a simple menu. Perform the following steps to create a sample menu.

1. Start a new Windows Application project.

2. Display the toolbox and drag a `MainMenu` control to the form.

3. Single-click the `ManuMenu1` control. Using the Properties window, change the name of the control to `mnuMain`.

4. When you select the menu, notice the words *Type Here* appear at the top of the form, as shown in Figure 10.8. This is the location of the first menu item.

5. Type **File** in the Type Here box and press Enter.

You have just created a new menu item. As you type the text for each menu item, you will notice that additional Type Here boxes appear, as shown in Figure 10.9. As you might imagine, typing in one of those boxes will create an additional menu item.

ADDING ADDITIONAL MENU ITEMS

By creating menu items in the appropriate Type Here box, you can create new top-level menus or submenus. Notice that a black arrow indicates a menu item that contains a submenu.

Figure 10.9
Type below the current menu item to continue adding items to the same menu list; to create a submenu, type in the box to the right of the current item.

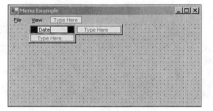

Note

You can use Tab, Enter, down arrow to quickly enter several menu items without lifting the mouse.

You can add new menu items from left-to-right, top to bottom, very quickly. However, if you need to go back and insert a new menu item before an existing one, just right-click the menu item and choose Insert. If you accidentally add an empty menu item or need to delete an extra menu item, right-click the unwanted item and choose delete. After you have keyed in your menu items, you can immediately see how the menu will look in Design mode by using the mouse to navigate it.

To continue creating our sample menu, perform the following steps.

1. Beneath the File menu, create new menu items for Open and Exit.

2. Create an additional top-level menu item, View.

3. Beneath the View menu item create two submenu items, Date and Time.

ADDING CODE TO RESPOND TO MENU EVENTS

As you can see, it is very easy to add items to a menu. If you run the sample program, you will see the menu bar displayed in your form. However, just designing the menu is not enough to make it useful. You also have to write VB code and associate it with the menu items, usually in the `Click` event.

SETTING MENU ITEM NAMES

Each item in your menu is like a control, and as you know, controls have properties. When you created the sample menu, you were actually setting the values of the menu items' `Text` properties. The `Text` property determines what text is displayed in the menu. One of the most important of these properties is the `Name` property, which you use to identify the menu item in your code. You also can enter these using the Menu Editor. To learn how to do this, right-click any of the sample menu items you just created and choose `Edit Names` from the menu. You should see the menu names displayed in the Menu Editor, as shown in Figure 10.10.

PART
III
CH
10

Figure 10.10
You can edit both
the control name or
display text of a
menu item using
the Menu Editor.

I typically use a hierarchical structure to assign the `Name` property of my menu items. Each menu item's name begins with the prefix `mnu`, followed by words that describe the portion of the menu in which the item is located. For example, `mnuFileSendToFax` is used to represent the menu item with the caption `Fax Recipient`; I can tell from the name that this item is in the `Send To` submenu of the `File` menu. As with any object you create in VB .NET, providing a readable variable name that follows a known naming convention will make it easier to understand your code.

→ For more on naming conventions, **see** Chapter 6, "Storing Information in Variables," **p. 139**

Note

You can display the Properties window of a menu item just like any other control, and use it to set both the `Name` and `Text` properties.

Following along with our sample application, use the Menu Editor to rename the menu items as follows:

Text	Name
File	mnuFile
Open	mnuFileOpen
Exit	mnuFileExit
View	mnuView
Date	mnuViewDate
Time	mnuViewTime

CODING THE Click EVENT

Menu items generally work like button controls in that you click them and something happens. To demonstrate, perform the following modifications to the sample program:

1. From the form designer, double-click the Open menu item. The Code Editor will be opened to the Click event for mnuFileOpen. Enter the following lines of code:

   ```
   Dim dlgFile As New OpenFileDialog()
   dlgFile.ShowDialog()
   ```

2. Enter the following line of code in the Click event for mnuFileExit:

   ```
   Application.Exit()
   ```

Now press F5 to run the sample program. Click the Open menu item and a File Open dialog box will appear. Click the Exit option and the program will end.

CHANGING MENU BEHAVIOR AND APPEARANCE

You now know how to create a standard menu item that acts like a button control. However, there are times when you may need a menu item that is used to turn an option on or off rather than initiating an action. Also, you may want to separate menu items so they appear more organized to the user. To get an idea of the many different ways you can customize your menu, look at Figure 10.11.

ADDING CHECK MARKS

By default, menu items are created to initiate an action. However, some menu items can be used to indicate the status of an option or select from a group of options. Check marks can be used with menu items to indicate selected options and are controlled by two key properties:

- **Checked**—If this property is set to True, a check mark is displayed to the left of the menu item. Generally the Checked property is controlled with VB code, although you also can use the Properties window or by clicking in the margin when using the Menu Editor.

- **RadioCheck**—Determines whether the check marks appear as a check or a round radio button.

Checked menu item

Separator bar   Shortcut key

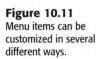

Figure 10.11
Menu items can be
customized in several
different ways.

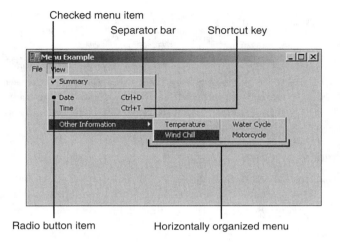

Radio button item   Horizontally organized menu

Note

Check marks are not available on items that contain submenus.

Keep in mind that these properties only control visual aspects of a menu item; the events
and function of the menu item is no different than any other. In our sample program,
perform the following steps to make the View menu work:

1. Add a text box to the form. Set its Name property to txtInfo.

2. Place the following lines of code in the Click event of mnuViewDate:

```
If mnuViewDate().Checked <> True Then
    mnuViewDate().Checked = True
    mnuViewTime().Checked = False
    txtInfo().Text = Format(Date.Now, "MM/dd/yyyy")
End If
```

3. Place the following lines of code in the Click event of mnuViewTime:

```
If mnuViewTime().Checked <> True Then
    mnuViewTime().Checked = True
    mnuViewDate().Checked = False
    txtInfo().Text = Format(Date.Now, "hh:mm:ss")
End If
```

Run the program and try clicking on the menu items in the View menu. The code in the
Click event not only updates the text box with the appropriate information, but also displays
a check mark beside the appropriate item.

Note

If you want to use a check mark to indicate an on/off setting, you can use the `Not` operator, as in the following example:

```
mnuShowDetail.Checked = Not(mnuShowDetail.Checked)
```

The line of code will toggle the check mark each time the menu item is selected. You can then use an `If` statement to take appropriate action based upon the value of the `Checked` property.

USING KEYSTROKES IN A MENU

Using keystroke combinations instead of a mouse is a quicker way to access program functions that is available in many Windows programs. You can let users access your menu items in the same way. Two types of key combinations can be used: *access keys* and *shortcut keys*.

If a menu item has an access key defined, the access key is indicated by an underscore beneath the letter in the item's caption (for example, the *x* in E<u>x</u>it). You create an access key by placing an ampersand (&) in front of the appropriate letter in the `Text` property of a menu item. (To display an & character in your menu, simply type two ampersands.) For the File menu, the `Text` property would be `&File`. To use a top-level access key, press `Alt` and the access key. For example, in Visual Basic press Alt+F to open the File menu, then release the Alt key and press the letter x to exit the program.

Note

Visual Basic provides automatic access keys for top-level menu items such as File, View, and so on, using the first letter of the menu. You can override the default by defining another access key. The access key indicators for top-level menus are not displayed until you press the `Alt` key. (Pressing and releasing the `Alt` key by itself will activate the menu bar and allow you to use the arrow keys to move from item to item.)

Another way to use the keyboard to access the menu is to add a shortcut key. A shortcut key can be used to instantly execute the `Click` event of a menu item without any menu navigation. To create a shortcut key, display the Properties window for a menu item and assign a value to the `Shortcut` property, shown in Figure 10.12.

The `ShowShortcut` property determines whether the menu displays the shortcut key, so the user can learn it. If this is set to `True`, the shortcut appears to the right of the menu item text.

ORGANIZING YOUR MENU

As you saw earlier in this section, you can create new menu items to the right of a submenu item. This multi-level approach to organizing your menu allows you to group related items. In addition to using menu levels to organize the items in your menu, you might want to further separate items in a particular level. Placing *separator bars* in the menu breaks up a long list of items and further groups the items, without your having to create a separate level. To place a separator bar in your menu, right-click a menu item in the Menu Editor and choose Insert Separator. A horizontal line will be displayed before the current menu item. As an example, the Exit option is usually separated from the other options in your File menu.

Figure 10.12
Shortcut keys allow you to quickly execute menu commands.

Another way of organizing your menu is to use the `BarBreak` property to create a new column. If your submenu has a lot of items, setting the `BarBreak` property of a menu item to `True` will cause the item and subsequent items to be placed in separate columns, as shown in Figure 10.11.

ENABLING AND DISABLING MENUS

A menu item's `Visible` and `Enabled` properties work just like they do with any other object. When the `Visible` property is set to `True`, the menu item is visible to the users. If the `Visible` property is set to `False`, the item (and any associated submenus) are hidden from the users. You have probably seen the `Enabled` and `Visible` properties used in a word processing program (though you might not have been aware of how it was accomplished), where only the File and Help menus are visible until a document is selected for editing. After a document is open, the other menu items are shown.

Changing the setting of the `Visible` property allows you to control what menu items are available to the users at a given point in your program. Controlling the menu this way lets you restrict the users' access to menu items that might cause errors if certain conditions are not met. (You wouldn't want the users to access edit functions if no document was open to edit, right?)

The `Enabled` property serves a function similar to that of the `Visible` property. The key difference is that when the `Enabled` property is set to `False`, the menu item is *grayed out*. This means that the menu item still can be seen by the users but cannot be accessed. For example, the standard Edit, Cut and Edit, Copy functions should not be available if no text or object is selected, but nothing is wrong with letting the users see that these functions exist.

USING CONTEXT MENUS

So far, the discussion of menus has looked at the menu bar that appears along the top of the form. Visual Basic also supports *pop-up menus* in your programs. A pop-up menu, also known as a *context menu*, is a small menu that appears somewhere on your form in response to a program event.

Pop-up menus often are used to handle operations or options related to a specific area of the form (see Figure 10.13)—for example, a format pop-up menu for a text field that lets you change the font or font attributes of the field. You can find such context-sensitive in Visual Basic itself, for example, when you right-click an object in the Solution Explorer, a context menu allows you to view the code or designer associated with that object.

DESIGNING THE MENU

You can create a pop-up menu in the same way that you created the main menu for your program—with the Menu Editor. Just drag a ContextMenu control to the form and edit the menu items as you did with the MainMenu control. To add a context menu to our sample program, perform the following steps:

1. Add a new ContextMenu control to the form. Set its Name property to mnuPopUp.
2. Using the Menu Editor, add one menu item to the context menu. Set its Text property to Clear and its Name property to mnuClear.

Your context menu in design mode should look similar to Figure 10.13.

Figure 10.13
Because a context menu is not displayed in the menu bar, it does not have a top-level menu item, only submenus.

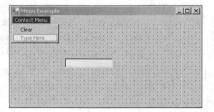

ASSOCIATING A CONTEXT MENU WITH A CONTROL

After you have designed your menu, you need to set the ContextMenu property of a control or form to make the menu display. Go ahead and set the ContextMenu property of txtInfo to mnuPopUp and run the program. When you right-click the text box, you will see the Clear option appear.

> **Note**
>
> Text box controls have a default context menu that includes copy and paste commands. By associating your context menu with the text box control, you replace the default menu.

CHANGING MENU ITEMS WITH CODE

As you might imagine, writing VB code for items in a context menu is very similar to writing code for a main menu. In our sample context menu, you could add the following line of code to the Click event of mnuClear, which would clear the text box:

```
txtInfo.Text = ""
```

However, this code works for a specific text box. What if you want to associate the same context menu with every text box on your form? Fortunately, you can:

```
Private Sub Form1_Load(ByVal sender As System.Object,_
 ByVal e As System.EventArgs) Handles MyBase.Load

'During startup, we add a custom MouseDown event handler to all the text boxes
Dim ctlTemp As Control
For Each ctlTemp In Me.Controls
  If TypeOf ctlTemp Is TextBox Then
      AddHandler ctlTemp.MouseDown, AddressOf MyMouseDownEvent
  End If
Next

End Sub


Private Sub MyMouseDownEvent(ByVal sender As Object, ByVal e As MouseEventArgs)
'The custom event handler creates a context menu dynamically
'for the text box that called it.

Dim CurrentTextBox As TextBox = CType(sender, TextBox)
If e.Button = MouseButtons().Right Then
  Dim PopUpMenu As New ContextMenu()
  Dim MyMenuItem As New MenuItem("Clear " & CurrentTextBox.Text)
  AddHandler MyMenuItem.Click, AddressOf ClearTextBox
  PopUpMenu.MenuItems.Add(MyMenuItem)
  CurrentTextBox.ContextMenu = PopUpMenu
End If
End Sub


Private Sub ClearTextBox(ByVal sender As Object, ByVal e As System.EventArgs)
'A menu item fires this event, so we have to create several objects to
'work our way back to the source text box.

Dim pmTemp As MenuItem = CType(sender, MenuItem)
Dim cmTemp As ContextMenu = CType(pmTemp.Parent, ContextMenu)
Dim CurrentTextBox As TextBox = CType(cmTemp.SourceControl, TextBox)
CurrentTextBox.Text = ""

End Sub
```

As you can see, doing everything with code requires a lot more work than using the Menu Editor. (Keep in mind this can be simplified a bit by creating the menu controls in Design mode and manipulating them in code.) However, the advantage of the previous code is that it will work with any number of text boxes, and is able to use characteristics of the text box itself in the menu. For example, the menu item displays "Clear" followed by the text in the text box. Because this menu is created every time the user right-clicks the text box, the menu item will always be up to date.

WORKING WITH MULTIPLE FORMS

By default, a Windows Application project includes a single form. However, you can add additional forms as needed, to represent the dialog boxes and other screens in your application. In an event-driven environment like Windows, each form can accept events independently; you can allow the user to have complete freedom in moving, resizing, and switching between the forms of your application. In this section, we'll discuss managing multiple forms in your Visual Basic projects.

ADDING ADDITIONAL FORMS TO A PROJECT

The easiest way to add an additional form to your project is to right-click the project name and display the context menu. Choose "Add Windows Form" to add a new form to the project. You can also add an existing form from a disk file by choosing Add Existing Item.

SETTING A FORM'S NAME

Windows forms have a *filename* and a *class name*. The class name works like the name of any other class in VB .NET; you use it in code to create new instances of the form class. The filename is just the name of the operating system file in which the code for the class is stored. It is generally a good idea to keep these two names the same to avoid confusion. By default, new forms are assigned generic names similar to the way Visual Basic assigns control names (for example Form2, and so on). However, it is good programming practice to name your forms more appropriately. If you specify a form's filename when adding it to your project, the class name will automatically be set to the same name, without the .vb extension. To change the name of a form already in your project, you need to set both its class name and filename. You can specify a form's filename by renaming it in the Solution Explorer. To set the class name, you can simply modify the form class in the Code Editor, as shown in Figure 10.14.

Note You can also set the class name of a form in design mode by right-clicking it and displaying the Properties window.

When you rename a form class you may need to change the startup object for your project, as we will see in a moment.

Form class name   Form filename

Figure 10.14
The first line of the
code for a form con-
tains its class name.
Code within the form
class can use Me to
reference it.

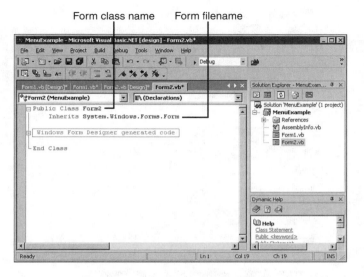

ADDING INHERITED WINDOWS FORMS

Every form you create is a class based on the Windows Form class provided by the .NET framework. In Figure 10.14, you can actually see that the new form class (Form2) is defined using an Inherits statement. In addition to inheriting from the .NET classes, you can also add forms that inherit the characteristics of forms you have previously created. One reason you might want to do this is to copy the looks and controls of a form instead of creating them again.

Let's construct a quick example to show how you can use inheritance to save time when designing forms:

1. Start Visual Studio .NET and create a Windows Application project.

2. Rename the default form's class name to frmBase. This form will be the base form from which other forms can inherit characteristics.

3. Drag two text box controls to the form. Display the Properties window for TextBox1 and set its Modifiers property to Public, as shown in Figure 10.15.

4. In order to use Inherited forms, you must first build your project. Choose Build from the Build menu.

5. Right-click the project name in the Solution Explorer to display the context menu. Choose "Add Inherited Form . . . " from the context menu.

6. In the Add New Item dialog box, enter **frmInhertied.vb** for the filename and press Open. The Inheritance Picker dialog box will appear, as shown in Figure 10.16.

7. Select frmBase and click OK. Your new form should be added to the project. Notice that it already contains the two text boxes from the base form, and also has inherited other properties, such as the size and title bar text.

Figure 10.15
The `Modifiers` property determines whether inherited forms can modify control properties.

Figure 10.16
The Inheritance Picker allows you to create a form based on an existing form, copying its properties and controls.

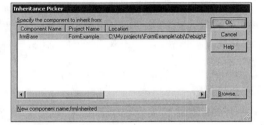

8. Open the form designer for `frmInherited`. Set the `Text` property of the form to `Inherited Form`.

9. Add a new textbox to `frmInherited`. You should now have three text boxes on the form. Notice that the two inherited text boxes have an icon in the upper-left corner to indicate they are inherited controls, as shown in Figure 10.17.

10. Display the Properties window for each of the inherited text boxes. Notice that you can only change the one marked as `Public`; the private text box is locked and cannot even be moved around on the form.

11. As a final test, display the designer for `frmBase` again, change the `Text` properties of its text boxes, and move them around. You should notice that the changes are propagated down to the inherited form.

As we have seen from the example, Visual Basic allows you to design a form once and reuse its visual characteristics via inheritance, just as you would with inherit any other object in object-oriented programming.

Figure 10.17
Hovering over an inherited text box will display a ToolTip indicating it is an inherited object.

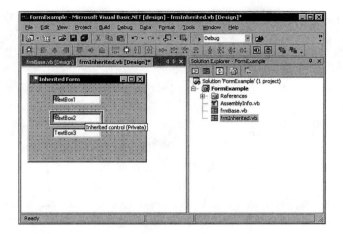

SHOWING AND HIDING FORMS WITH CODE

Each Windows Application project has a *startup object*, which is set to Form1 by default. Using the Project Property Pages dialog box, as shown in Figure 10.18, you can set the startup object to any of the forms in your project, or to the Main procedure of a form or module.

Figure 10.18
When you run your program, Visual Basic will create an instance of the startup form and display it on the screen. You must write code statements to display additional forms.

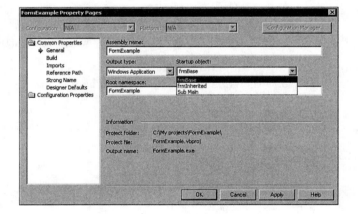

Because forms are classes, to show a new form you simply create an instance of the form class and call its Show method:

```
Dim MyForm as New frmTemp
MyForm.Show()
```

It is very easy to create forms based on a class. In fact, you could enclose the previous statements in a loop and create as many instances of `frmTemp` as you want using the `MyForm` variable. (Of course, if you need to manipulate the form after you show it, you will need to keep the reference to it.)

If you have a reference to another form, you can access its public properties, methods, and controls:

```
MyForm.Text = Now.ToString
MyForm.txtInfo.Text = "This is some text"
MyForm.Hide()
```

The first line of code sets the `Text` property of the form to the current time. The second line sets the `Text` property of a text box on the form. (In this example, the `Modifiers` property of `txtInfo` is assumed not to be `Private`, as described in the previous section.) The third line of code uses the `Hide` method to make the form invisible.

USING MODAL FORMS

If you show a form with the `Show` method as described in the previous section, the form acts totally independent. However, there are times when you might want to have more strict control over the order in which the user processes the forms. For example, you may want to display a secondary form so that the user must view it before returning to the main form. You can achieve this effect by displaying the second form *modally*. Modal forms appear on top of a parent form, and the user cannot access the parent form until the modal form has been closed or hidden. To show a modal form, you use the `ShowDialog` method.

As a demonstration of modal forms, we will look at how a form can be shown modally to aid in data entry. Figure 10.19 shows the sample project with both forms.

Figure 10.19
Modal forms can be used to display helper dialog boxes, such as the list of valid hotel code selections.

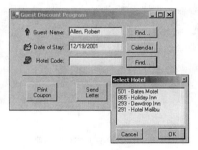

Figure 10.19 is a fictional application that collects information about a hotel guest and prints a discount coupon. The form in the background is the main data entry form. If the user knows all the information (name, date, and hotel code number), he can quickly key it in using a single form. If he does not know all the information, he can display helper forms with the buttons to the right of the text boxes. In the figure, the user did not know the hotel code, so he clicked the Find button to display a list of valid hotel codes. The user can then

select a hotel code from the secondary form. When the user clicks OK to close the secondary form, the text box is populated with the selected hotel.

Now, let's look at how the code works. The hotel search form itself is very simple, it just has a list box and two buttons. There are two public properties on the helper form used to pass the information back to the main form:

```
Public SomethingSelected As Boolean
Public SelectedHotel As String
```

The first property, SomethingSelected, holds a true or false value indicating whether the user actually selected a hotel or just clicked the Cancel button. The second property, SelectedHotel, stores the selected hotel code from the list box. (For the purposes of this discussion, assume the helper form also contains internal methods that load the hotel list from a database.)

Note

An alternative to using properties would be to make the controls on a secondary form public, and access their properties directly from the main form. However, this would not be a very good programming practice. Using properties or other interfaces allows you to change the design of the helper form independent from the other parts of the application.

The code for the OK and Cancel buttons simply sets the properties appropriately and closes the form:

```
Private Sub btnOK_Click(ByVal sender As System.Object,_
   ByVal e As System.EventArgs) Handles btnOK.Click

If Not (lstHotels.SelectedItem Is Nothing) Then
   SomethingSelected = True
   SelectedHotel = lstHotels.SelectedItem.ToString
   Me.Close()
End If

End Sub

Private Sub btnCancel_Click(ByVal sender As System.Object,_
   ByVal e As System.EventArgs) Handles btnCancel.Click
   SomethingSelected = False
   Me.Close()
End Sub
```

The code that initiates the display of the helper form is in the Click event of a button on the main form:

```
Private Sub btnSelectHotel_Click(ByVal sender As System.Object,_
   ByVal e As System.EventArgs) Handles btnSelectHotel.Click

   Dim frmSelect As HotelSelectForm
   frmSelect = New HotelSelectForm()
   frmSelect.ShowDialog()
```

```
      If frmSelect.SomethingSelected Then
          txtHotelCode.Text = frmSelect.SelectedHotel
      End If

      frmSelect = Nothing

End Sub
```

The first three lines of code create a new instance of the form and display it using its
ShowDialog method. Next, the If statement pulls information out of the helper form and
populates the text box. Finally, the reference to the helper form is set to Nothing because we
no longer need it. As you look at the previous code, you should keep in mind a very important property of modal forms:

Code execution in the parent form stops until the modal form is closed.

In other words, the previous If statement is not executed until frmSelect is closed. This is
the main difference between the ShowDialog and Show methods. If you used the Show method
in the preceding code, the If statement would be executed immediately, which is not the
intended effect.

CLOSING FORMS AND ENDING THE APPLICATION

As you saw in Chapter 5, you can use the Application.Exit method to end your application.
This will close all open forms. However, you also can end your application by closing the
startup object. For example, suppose you have a startup form, Form1, which uses the Show
method to display Form2. Whenever the user closes the startup form (Form1), the other forms
will disappear and the application will end. This behavior is different from previous versions
of Visual Basic, where as long as there was a form loaded the program would continue running. The reason for the change can be found in VB .NET's more object-oriented nature; in
our example Form2 was created within the context of Form1, so it makes sense that it should
be closed if Form1 is closed.

FROM HERE . . .

This chapter covered some of the important properties you need to set when adding forms
to your project, and how to control the display of multiple forms. In order to find out even
more about forms and form design, please read the following chapters:

- To learn how to use multiple forms in a parent-child relationship, read Chapter 15,
  "Multiple Document Interface (MDI) Applications."

- For information on proper control placement and form design, see Chapter 14,
  "Designing an Effective User Interface."

- To find out about a special type of form, the dialog box, see Chapter 13, "Using
  Dialog Boxes."

- To explore the many controls you can use on your windows, see Chapter 11,
  "Fundamental Controls," and Chapter 12, "Advanced Controls."

CHAPTER 11

FUNDAMENTAL CONTROLS

In this chapter

In Chapter 2, "Creating Your First Windows Application," you were introduced to the use of controls. As you have seen by now, working with controls is a major part of the design and coding of a Visual Basic application.

Visual Basic .NET includes a large number of controls that enable you to easily develop applications with many of the same features as programs from Microsoft and other vendors. In this and subsequent chapters, you will learn about many of the controls included with Visual Basic .NET.

The controls discussed in this chapter are loosely grouped according to function. Space does not permit us to demonstrate building a sample application around each control. Instead, we discuss how to use each control, including suggestions for use in your own programs. I suggest that you create a "test" project that you can use to explore the use of the controls in which you are interested as you read about them.

Each control is accompanied by a picture of its Toolbox icon, as well as a table listing commonly used properties that apply to that control.

 You can download a sample project demonstrating the use of all the controls discussed in this and subsequent chapters from http://www.vbinsider.com. The sample project includes comments in its code to explain how it works. Look for the file named ControlDemo.ZIP.

INTRODUCTION TO CONTROLS

As you have learned, a *control* is an object that interacts with the user or the program. The Visual Basic .NET help system's definition of controls states that "components that provide visible parts of the user interface are called *controls*." Technically, however, a control does not have to be visible in the user interface. The Timer control, for example, is *never* visible to the user.

You have also learned how to set some of the properties that govern a control's appearance and behavior. Table 11.1 describes common properties that apply to virtually all controls.

TABLE 11.1 PROPERTIES COMMON TO CONTROLS

Property	Description
Name	The name utilized by program code when referring to the control. Visual Basic assigns default names that end with sequential numbers (TextBox1, TextBox2, and so on); however, it is good practice to change the names of controls that will need to be referenced in code at some point.

Property	Description
Size	An ordered pair of numbers that specifies the width and height, respectively, of the control (in pixels). For example, a control whose `Size` property is set to `64, 24` would be drawn to be 64 pixels wide and 24 pixels high. A control's size may also be expressed as individual `Width` and `Height` properties in lieu of the ordered pair. Clicking the plus sign to the left of the `Size` property in the Properties window reveals the `Width` and `Height` properties. The `Size` property, as well as the `Width` and `Height` properties, can be modified at design time by dragging a selected control's sizing handles or by typing new values into the Properties window. The `Width` and `Height` properties can also be changed for most controls at runtime with code like `cmdTest.Height = 300`.
Location	An ordered pair of numbers that specifies the horizontal and vertical position of the upper-left corner of the control (in pixels) respective to the left and top edges of its container. For example, a control (drawn on a form) whose `Location` property is set to `120, 270` would be drawn so that its upper-left corner is 120 pixels from the left edge of the form and 270 pixels from the top edge of the form. A control's location may also be expressed as individual `X` and `Y` properties in lieu of the ordered pair, where `X` represents the distance from the left edge and `Y` represents the distance from the top edge of the control's container. Clicking the plus sign to the left of the `Location` property in the Properties window reveals the `X` and `Y` properties. The `Location` property, as well as the `X` and `Y` properties, can be modified at design time by dragging a control to a new location on the form or by typing new values into the Properties window. The `X` and `Y` properties can also be changed for most controls at runtime with code like `cmdTest.X = 50`.
Enabled	Set to `True` or `False` to specify whether the control is enabled; that is, whether the user may interact with the control. For example, a `Button` control whose `Enabled` property is set to `False`, while visible to the user, cannot be clicked. Typically a control whose `Enabled` property is set to `False` has a "grayed-out" appearance.
Visible	Set to `True` or `False` to specify whether the control can be seen by the user at runtime.
Locked	A control whose `Locked` property is set to `True` cannot be moved or resized at design time. Typically, once you have arranged the controls on a form the way you want them, you will set the `Locked` property of each control to `True` to avoid accidentally moving or resizing it. You can set the `Locked` property of all of a form's controls at one time by right-clicking the form, and then selecting Lock Controls from the pop-up menu.
BackColor	The background color of the control, specified by clicking the drop-down arrow in the Properties window and selecting the desired color.
ForeColor	The color used to display text on the control, specified by clicking the drop-down arrow in the Properties window and selecting the desired color.
TabStop	The `TabStop` property determines whether the user can move the focus to the control by pressing the Tab key. A control whose `TabStop` property is set to `False` is bypassed as the user tabs from control to control.

PART

III

CH

11

TABLE 11.1 CONTINUED

Property	Description
TabIndex	If the control's TabStop property is set to True, the TabIndex property determines the order in which controls receive the focus. Each control on a form has a unique TabIndex property; by default, the TabIndex property is assigned in ascending order as controls are added to the form at design time. The first control placed on a form receives a TabIndex property of 0, the second control receives 1, and so forth. You can change the order in which the controls on a form are "tabbed to" by manually modifying the TabIndex properties of the controls. Alternately, Visual Basic .NET has a nice tool that lets you click the controls on a form in the order in which you want them to be accessed. You can use this tool by clicking View, Tab Order in Visual Basic .NET's Main menu while the desired form is displayed in Design mode.
Font	For controls that display text (including caption-like text, like on a Button control), the Font property determines the font used to render that text. Clicking the ellipsis in the Properties window presents you with a dialog box in which you can select a font. The Font property has individual subproperties (Name, Size, Unit, Bold, Italic, Strikeout, and Underline) that can be accessed by clicking the plus sign to the left of the Font property in the Properties window. To set these subproperties in code, use a statement like txtName.Font.Bold = True.
Cursor	Determines which pointer appears when the user passes the mouse over the control. Clicking the drop-down arrow in the Properties window presents a number of possible mouse pointers. For example, you may want the mouse pointer to change to a hand when the control is passed over, indicating that the control may be clicked.

BASIC CONTROLS

We will begin our discussion of controls by revisiting three controls—the TextBox, Label, and Button controls—that you have already worked with in earlier chapters. They are probably the controls that are used most often by Visual Basic developers. Figure 11.1 illustrates a typical data entry form utilizing each of these controls.

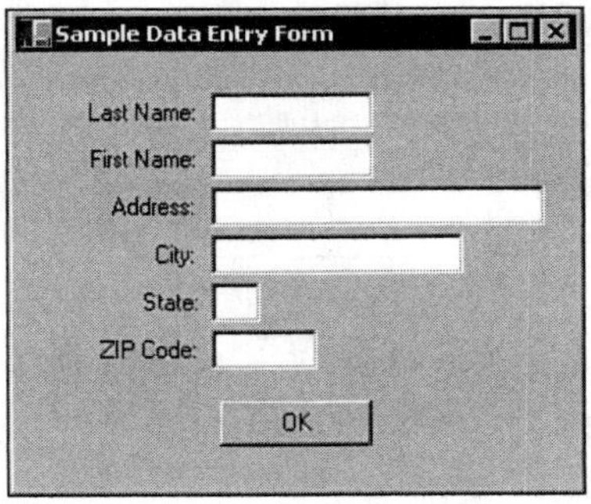

Figure 11.1
Text boxes, labels, and buttons are frequently used controls.

Note

The basic controls presented here are discussed in more detail in Chapter 2. See the sections "Adding a TextBox Control," "Labeling Your Program's Controls," and "Adding Command Buttons" in that chapter.

THE TEXTBOX CONTROL

Because much of what programs do is to retrieve, process, and display information in the form of text, you might guess (and you would be correct) that the major workhorse of many programs is the TextBox control. The text box allows you to display text; more importantly, however, it also provides an easy way for your users to enter and edit text and for your program to retrieve the information that was entered.

A TextBox control presents your program's user with an area in which he can enter or modify text. That text can be accessed by your program through the TextBox control's Text property.

Tip

When your user is in the process of entering or editing text in a TextBox control, he can use standard Windows techniques to assist him. For example, he can select a portion of the text and press Ctrl+C to copy the text to the clipboard, Ctrl+X to cut the text, or Ctrl+V to paste text from the clipboard into the TextBox control. Alternatively, he can right-click inside the text box and select Cut, Copy, Paste, or Delete from the context menu that appears.

PART

III

CH

11

HANDLING MULTIPLE LINES OF TEXT

Normally, you use the text box to handle a single piece of information, such as a name or an address. If needed, however, the text box can handle thousands of characters of text.

By default, the text box accepts a single line of text. This is adequate for many purposes, but occasionally your program needs to handle a larger amount of text. The TextBox control has two properties that are useful for handling larger amounts of text: the MultiLine and ScrollBars properties.

The MultiLine property determines whether the information in a text box is displayed on a single line or wraps and scrolls to multiple lines. If the MultiLine property is set to True, information is displayed on multiple lines, and word wrapping is handled automatically. Users can press Enter while typing to force a new line. The ScrollBars property determines whether scrollbars are displayed in a text box, and if so, what types of scrollbars (Horizontal, Vertical, or Both). The default value of None causes no scrollbars to be displayed, although the user can still use the mouse or arrow keys to navigate to text that he can't see. The scrollbars are useful if more text is stored in the Text property than fits in the text box. The ScrollBars property has an effect on the text box only if its MultiLine property is set to True. Figure 11.2 shows several text boxes that illustrate the effects of the MultiLine and ScrollBars properties.

Figure 11.2
You can use a text box to enter single lines of text or entire paragraphs.

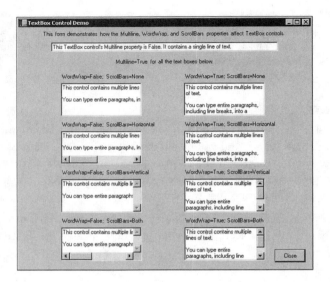

VALIDATING INPUT

When accepting freeform text input from a user, you often need to perform some data validation before proceeding. For example, if you have a text box for the quantity of an item ordered, you may want to see if the user entered a value other than a number into the text box.

You can use a TextBox control's Validating event to validate the user's input. This event handler can contain code that validates the information in the associated control. It is triggered by another control whose CausesValidation property is set to True. The following is a typical Validating event handler that uses the IsNumeric function to ensure that the data entered into a text box is numeric:

```
Private Sub txtQuantity_Validating(ByVal sender As Object, _
    ByVal e As System.ComponentModel.CancelEventArgs) _
    Handles txtQuantity.Validating
    If Not IsNumeric(txtQuantity.Text) Then
        MessageBox.Show("You must enter a number in the Quantity field.")
        txtQuantity.Focus()
    End If
End Sub
```

Table 11.2 lists the properties that you will use with TextBox controls most often.

TABLE 11.2	COMMON TEXTBOX CONTROL PROPERTIES
Property	**Description**
Text	The text contained in the control. You can set the Text property either at design time using the Properties window or at runtime using program code such as txtManager.Text = "Chris Cawein". Your user can change the Text property at runtime by simply typing in the text box.

Property	Description
Multiline	Determines whether the text in the control can extend to more than one line. The default value is False.
ScrollBars	For multiline text boxes, this property determines whether horizontal and vertical scrollbars are displayed to help the user navigate the text area. The default value is None. Other possible values are Horizontal, Vertical, and Both.
AutoSize	When set to True (the default), the control's height will be automatically maintained based on the control's font size. AutoSize does not apply if the control's Multiline property is set to True. Notice that when AutoSize is True, any sizing handle that would normally modify the control's height is disabled at design time.
AcceptsReturn	If Multiline is set to True, this property determines whether a Return character (the Enter key) is accepted as input in the text box. The default value is False.
AcceptsTab	If Multiline is set to True, this property determines whether a Tab character is accepted as input in the text box. The default value is False.
BorderStyle	Set to Fixed3D (the default), FixedSingle, or None to determine the appearance of the border surrounding the text box.
CharacterCasing	Text entered into the text box can be automatically converted into either all uppercase or all lowercase characters by setting the CharacterCasing property to Upper or Lower, respectively. The default value is Normal.
MaxLength	Sets the maximum number of characters that may be entered into the text box. The default value is 0, which specifies that there is no maximum.
PasswordChar	Specifying a character for the PasswordChar property causes that character to be displayed instead of the text contained in the control. Typically, an asterisk is used to prevent the display of a password as it is being entered. This property is only functional if the TextBox control's Multiline property is set to False.
ReadOnly	When set to True, the text in the control cannot be changed by the user. The default value is False.
SelectionLength	The number of characters in the TextBox control's Text property that are selected (highlighted). Used in conjunction with the SelectionStart property.
SelectionStart	The position of the first character in the TextBox control's Text property that is selected (highlighted). Used in conjunction with the SelectionLength property.
TextAlign	Determines how text is aligned within the control. The possible values are Left (the default), Right, and Center.
WordWrap	If Multiline is True for this control, WordWrap determines whether content that is too wide for the control is automatically wrapped to the next line. The default is True.

THE LABEL CONTROL

You use a Label control to display information that the user cannot change. Typically, Label controls are used to identify ("label") input areas or other information that is displayed on a form. A Label control's Text property determines what text is displayed in it.

Tip

When assigning a label's Text property, you can force a new line by including a carriage return and line feed combination. This technique, as well as its nomenclature, is a throwback to the ancient days of manual typewriters. When a manual typewriter user reached the end of a line, she had to move the paper up manually to the next line (a line feed) and return the carriage to the beginning of that line (a carriage return). In Visual Basic .NET, you can insert a carriage return/line feed combination by inserting ASCII characters 13 and 10 into the caption at the point where the line should break. Visual Basic supplies a predefined constant, vbCrLf, to help you accomplish this task:

```
Label1.Text = "First Line" & vbCrLf & "Second Line"
```

Table 11.3 shows you properties that are commonly used for Label controls.

TABLE 11.3   COMMON LABEL CONTROL PROPERTIES

Property	Description
Text	The text displayed in the label. As with TextBox controls, you can set the Text property either at design time using the Properties window or at runtime using program code such as lblDirectorName.Text = "Jerry Williams". However, your user cannot change the Text property of a Label control.
AutoSize	When set to True, the label's size will be automatically maintained based on its contents and font size. The default value is False.
BorderStyle	Set to None (the default), FixedSingle, or Fixed3D to determine the appearance of the border surrounding the label.
Image	Specifies an image that is to be displayed on the label.
ImageAlign	Specifies where on the label the image specified by the Image property will be aligned. There are nine possible locations—any of the four edges, any of the four corners, and MiddleCenter (the default). Click the drop-down arrow to specify the location.
UseMnemonic	If set to True (the default), an ampersand (&) in the label's Text property will designate the next letter as an access key for a control whose TabIndex property is one higher than the label's TabIndex property. For example, if a Label control whose TabIndex property is 11 has UseMnemonic set to True, and its Text property contains A&ddress, pressing Alt+D at runtime would shift the focus to a TextBox control whose TabIndex property is 12.

Figure 11.3 shows how some of these properties affect the appearance of Label controls.

Figure 11.3
Label controls can exhibit a wide range of appearances.

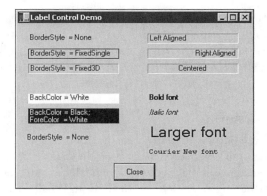

Note

If you use an ampersand (&) in a control's Text property to assign an access key, you should be aware that Windows 2000's default settings do not cause a visible underscore to be displayed under the access key until the user presses Alt.

THE BUTTON CONTROL

A control important to practically every application that you will develop is the Button control. This control lets users initiate actions by using the mouse to click a button. You set up a Button control by drawing the button on a form and then setting its Text property to the text that you want displayed on the button's face. Some typical Button controls are illustrated in Figure 11.4.

Figure 11.4
Button controls are one way a user can dictate program actions.

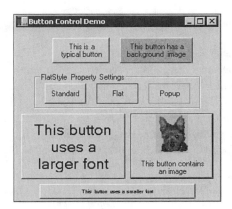

WRITING CODE FOR A BUTTON

As you have seen in several examples now, the main purpose of a Button control is to execute program code when the button is clicked. To activate this functionality, you write a Click event handler that Visual Basic automatically invokes each time the button is clicked. Double-click a Button control at design time to create or modify the button's Click event handler in the Code window. The following is a typical `Click` event handler for a button named `btnExit`:

```
Private Sub btnExit_Click(ByVal sender As System.Object, _
    ByVal e As System.EventArgs) Handles btnExit.Click
    ActiveForm.Close()
End Sub
```

USING THE KEYBOARD WITH A BUTTON

Although users most often use buttons by clicking them with the mouse, some users prefer accessing commands through the keyboard. This is often the case for data-entry programs. To accommodate these users, you can make your program trigger buttons when certain keys are pressed. You do so by assigning an *access key* to the button. When an access key is defined, the user can hold down Alt and press the access key to trigger the Button control's `Click` event.

You assign an access key when you set the Button control's `Text` property. Simply place an ampersand (&) in front of the letter of the key you want to use. For example, if you want the users to be able to press Alt+P to invoke a Print button, you set the `Text` property to `&Print`. The ampersand does not show up on the button, but the letter for the access key is underlined. The caption `Print` then appears on the button.

Tip

If for some reason you need to display an ampersand on the face of a button, simply use two of them in a row in the `Text` property; for example, `Save && Exit` produces the caption `Save & Exit`.

CREATING AN ACCEPT BUTTON

One button on a form can be designated as that form's *Accept button*. When this is the case, the user can simply press Enter while the focus is on any control (except another command button or a text box) whose `MultiLine` property is to trigger the default button. This action invokes the default button's `Click` event handler, just as if the users had clicked it with the mouse, and is commonly used for data entry forms. To set up a button as the Accept button, set the `AcceptButton` property of the form (not of the button itself) to the name of the button that should act as the Accept button. Only one button on a form can be the Accept button.

CREATING A CANCEL BUTTON

You can also designate one button on a form as the *Cancel button*, which is similar to the Accept button but works with the Esc key. If the user presses Esc while working with the form, the Cancel button's `Click` event handler will be invoked. To make a button into a Cancel button, set the `CancelButton` property of the form (not of the button itself) to the name of the button that should act as the Cancel button. As with Accept buttons, only one button on a form can be a Cancel button.

Table 11.4 presents commonly used Button control properties.

TABLE 11.4   COMMON BUTTON CONTROL PROPERTIES

Property	Description
Text	The text displayed on the face of the button. You can set the `Text` property either at design time using the Properties window or at runtime using program code such as `txtLastName.Text = "Cawein"`. Including an ampersand (&) before one letter of the `Text` property will define that letter to be the button's Access key. This means that the user can initiate the button's `Click` event by pressing Alt plus the Access key. For example, if a button's `Text` property contains `&Calculate`, pressing Alt+C at runtime will invoke the button's `Click` event handler, just as if the button had been clicked with the mouse.
FlatStyle	Determines the appearance of the button and how it changes when the user moves the mouse over the button. The `Standard` setting (which is the default) causes the button to be displayed like a typical Windows button. A setting of `Flat` causes the button to appear flat against the form at all times. (The text displayed on the button changes color when hovered over.) A setting of `Popup` makes the button appear flat until it is hovered over, at which time it changes to look like a standard button.
Image	Specifies an image that is to be displayed on the button.
ImageAlign	Specifies where on the button the image specified by the `Image` property will be aligned. There are nine possible locations—any of the four edges, any of the four corners, and `MiddleCenter` (the default). Click the drop-down arrow to specify the location.
TextAlign	Determines how text is aligned on the button. Like the `ImageAlign` property, there are nine possible values; `MiddleCenter` is the default.

CONTROLS FOR MAKING CHOICES

You have already learned how to acquire input from users through the use of a TextBox control. This approach works well for a number of data-gathering needs, but what if you just want a simple piece of information, such as "Do you own a car?" or "What is your marital status?" In these cases, the choice of answers you want to provide is limited to two or, at most, a few fixed choices. If you set up a text box to handle only the words *yes* and *no*, your program will have a problem if users type Maybe or Yeah, or if they misspell a word.

You can eliminate this problem, however, and make your programs easier to use by employing controls to display and accept choices. In the following sections, you will examine several controls used for making choices. You can offer these choices through the use of check boxes, option buttons, lists, and combo boxes:

- **Check box**—Switches one or more options on or off
- **Option buttons**—Selects a single choice from a group
- **List box**—Displays a list of predefined choices
- **Combo box**—Like a list box, but also allows the user to specify a choice other than the predefined ones

■ **Checked list box**—A list box that displays a check box by each item in the list, allowing the user to easily select multiple list items

In addition, you will learn about the GroupBox control, which assists you in grouping other controls.

THE CHECKBOX CONTROL

You use the CheckBox control to get an answer of either "yes" or "no" from the user. This control works like a light switch. It is either on (checked) or off (unchecked); normally, there is no in between. When a check box is on, a check mark is displayed in the box. It indicates that the answer to the check box's corresponding question is "yes." When the check box is off, or unchecked, the box is empty, indicating an answer of "no."

The Checked property of a CheckBox control is set to either True or False depending on whether the user has checked or unchecked the box. You can set the Checked property in code (chkTest.Checked = True) to modify the check box as your program is running.

In addition to being checked or unchecked, a CheckBox control may possibly have a third state in which a check mark appears, but the background of the check box is gray. This is known as an *indeterminate* state and usually indicates that a partial choice (some, but not all, of a number of subchoices) has been made. For example, you may have a check box that designates whether a group of users has access to a particular application. Perhaps some, but not all, of the members of that user group are to be granted access. In that case, you could have a check box for the overall group; that check box would contain a grayed check, and there might be a Details or Members button that leads to a form where there are individual check boxes for each user. The Checked property does not report an indeterminate check box. Instead, you can utilize the CheckBox control's CheckState property, whose value may be Unchecked, Checked, or Indeterminate. Normally, your user cannot set a check box to the indeterminate state by clicking it; typically, you do so in program code by determining whether none, all, or some of the subchoices have been selected. If you do want to give the user the ability to directly select the indeterminate state, you can set the CheckBox control's ThreeState property to True. This allows the user to cycle between all three possible check box states, rather than the normal two (Unchecked and Checked).

> **Note**
>
> If the ThreeState property is set to True, the Checked property will return True if CheckState is either Checked or Indeterminate.

Table 11.5 discusses commonly used properties that apply to CheckBox controls.

TABLE 11.5   COMMON CHECKBOX CONTROL PROPERTIES

Property	Description
Appearance	If set to `Button`, the control looks like a Button control whose appearance toggles between pressed and unpressed. The default setting is `Normal`, which causes it to look like a normal check box.
AutoCheck	If for some reason you do not want your user to be able to check or uncheck the box by clicking on it, set `AutoCheck` to `False`. The default value of `True` causes the control's state to change whenever the user clicks it.
CheckAlign	Specifies where the check box is located within the boundaries of the control. There are nine possible locations—any of the four edges, any of the four corners, and `MiddleCenter`. The default is `MiddleLeft`. Click the drop-down arrow to specify the location.
Checked	Indicates `True` or `False`, depending on whether the box is checked or unchecked. When a CheckBox control is first added to a form, the `Checked` property is set to `False` by default.
CheckState	Indicates the "check state" of the check box. Possible values are `Unchecked`, `Checked`, and `Indeterminate` (grayed).
FlatStyle	Determines the appearance of the check box and how it changes when the user moves the mouse over the button. The `Standard` setting (which is the default) causes it to be displayed like a typical check box. Other possible settings are `Flat` and `Popup`.
Image	Specifies an image to be displayed on or in the control.
ImageAlign	Specifies where within the control the image specified by the `Image` property will be aligned. There are nine possible locations—any of the four edges, any of the four corners, and `MiddleCenter` (the default). Click the drop-down arrow to specify the location.
Text	The text that is displayed as the radio button's caption.
TextAlign	Specifies where the text specified by the `Text` property is aligned within the boundaries of the control. There are nine possible locations—any of the four edges, any of the four corners, and `MiddleCenter`. The default is `MiddleLeft`. Click the drop-down arrow to specify the location.
ThreeState	When set to `True`, the user can cycle through all three possible `CheckState` values (`Unchecked`, `Checked`, and `Indeterminate`) by clicking the check box. When set to the default value of `False`, the user can only toggle between `Unchecked` and `Checked`; she cannot set the `CheckState` property to `Indeterminate`.

PART
III
CH
11

Figure 11.5 shows various types of check boxes.

Figure 11.5
A check box can indicate a "yes" or "no" response to a question.

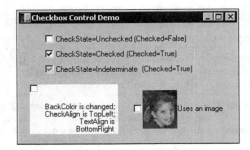

THE RADIOBUTTON CONTROL

Radio buttons are like the buttons that select stations on a car radio; they exist in a group, and only one of them can be selected at a time. They are useful for presenting a fixed list of *mutually exclusive* choices. Only one of a group of radio buttons may be selected at any given time. As with CheckBox controls, RadioButton controls have a Checked property that indicates via True or False values whether the control is selected or not.

Try it yourself: Draw several RadioButton controls on a form, and then run the program. Initially, each radio button's Checked property has the default value of False. However, notice that if you click any one of them to select it, and then subsequently select a different button in the group, the one that was selected will automatically become unselected. Figure 11.6 illustrates a group of RadioButton controls, only one of which is selected.

Figure 11.6
Only one radio button in a group can be selected.

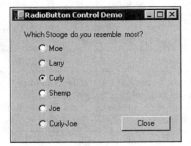

One major difference between RadioButton controls and CheckBox controls is that only one of the RadioButton controls in a group can be selected at any given time, whereas the selection state of CheckBox controls is independent of all other controls. How, then, do you define a group of radio buttons? The simplest type of group includes all the RadioButton controls that are placed directly on a form. However, a special type of control called a GroupBox control is available to assist in grouping radio buttons. You will learn about the GroupBox control in the next section.

PART

III

CH

11

Note

> RadioButton and GroupBox controls are equivalent to the OptionButton and Frame controls, respectively, provided in previous versions of Visual Basic.

To utilize RadioButton controls in your code, you typically write statements that examine the Checked property of the applicable radio buttons as needed. For example, suppose you have created a form that asks the user to enter registration information. You might have a group of three radio buttons, rbRepublican, rbDemocrat, and rbIndependent, to allow the user to specify his or her political preferences. Your procedure that processes the form could include code like the following:

```
If rbRepublican.Checked Then
    Call ProcessConservative()
ElseIf rbDemocrat.Checked Then
    Call ProcessLiberal()
ElseIf rbIndependent.Checked Then
    Call ProcessMiddleOfRoad()
Else
    Call ProcessNoPref()
End If
```

Alternatively, you may want to add code to the Click event handlers of each of your radio buttons if you want to perform some action as soon as the button is clicked. For example, you may be coding a trivia game that presents your users with a question and a number of multiple-choice answers. You could write code to score the question in the Click event handlers of each of the possible answers (represented by RadioButton controls). Of course, using this approach does not allow your user to change his mind once he has clicked one of the choices.

Tip

> A common misconception about RadioButton controls is that there is a property that reports which one of a group of buttons is selected. While such a property might be handy, this isn't the case. One technique I use to emulate this functionality is to create a form-level variable to let me know which button is selected; the Click event handler of each individual button sets the value of the variable. For example, if I have a group of radio buttons to allow the user to tell me his favorite baseball team, each button's Click event handler could set the variable strFavoriteTeam to a different value.

Table 11.6 shows properties that are commonly used in relation to RadioButton controls.

TABLE 11.6   COMMON RADIOBUTTON CONTROL PROPERTIES

Property	Description
Appearance	If set to Button, the control looks like a Button control whose appearance toggles between pressed and unpressed. The default setting is Normal, which causes it to look like a standard radio button.

TABLE 11.6   CONTINUED

Property	Description
AutoCheck	If for some reason you do not want your user to be able to select the radio button by clicking it, set AutoCheck to False. The default value of True causes the control to be selected when the user clicks it.
CheckAlign	Specifies where the button itself is located within the boundaries of the control. There are nine possible locations—any of the four edges, any of the four corners, or MiddleCenter. The default is MiddleLeft. Click the drop-down arrow to specify the location.
Checked	Contains True or False, depending on whether the control is selected or not. When a RadioButton control is first added to a form, the Checked property is set to False by default. You can determine a default choice by setting the Checked property of one button to True. Remember, no more than one radio button in a group can have a Checked property of True at any given time.
FlatStyle	Determines the appearance of the radio button and how it changes when the user moves the mouse over it. The Standard setting (which is the default) causes it to be displayed like a typical radio button. Other possible settings include Flat and Popup.
Image	Specifies an image that is to be displayed on or in the control.
ImageAlign	Specifies where within the control the image specified by the Image property will be aligned. There are nine possible locations—any of the four edges, any of the four corners, and MiddleCenter (the default). Click the drop-down arrow to specify the location.
Text	The text that is displayed as the radio button's caption.
TextAlign	Specifies where the text specified by the Text property is aligned within the boundaries of the control. There are nine possible locations—any of the four edges, any of the four corners, and MiddleCenter. The default is MiddleLeft. Click the drop-down arrow to specify the location.

THE GROUPBOX CONTROL

The GroupBox control, mentioned in the previous section, allows you to group controls such as radio buttons and check boxes. Think of a GroupBox control as a container for other controls. It is a rectangular box into which you can place any number of controls. All the RadioButton controls placed in a particular GroupBox control are treated as a group; that is, only one of the radio buttons *in that group* may be selected at a given time. However, radio buttons in other GroupBox controls (or placed directly on the form) may be selected as well, within the constraints of their own group(s).

In addition to delineating groups of radio buttons, GroupBox controls are handy for creating visual groups of other types of controls as well. Figure 11.7 shows GroupBox controls that contain RadioButton and CheckBox controls. Note that within a group box any combination of check boxes, but only one radio button, may be selected.

Figure 11.7
The GroupBox control lets you place controls in logical groups.

One property of note that applies to the GroupBox control is the `Text` property, which contains the text that appears as a caption at the top of the control's surrounding border.

THE LISTBOX CONTROL

As its name implies, you can use the ListBox control to present a list of choices. Figure 11.8 shows a simple list box used to pick a state abbreviation for use on a mailing label. This figure shows all the components that make up the list box.

Figure 11.8
A simple list box contains a series of choices for the user.

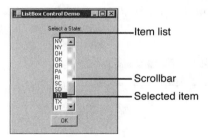

The key parts of the list box are the following:

- **Item list**—This is the list of items from which the users can select. These items are added to the list in the design environment or by your program as it is running.
- **Selected item**—This is the item that has been chosen by the user. Depending on the style of list you choose, a selected item is indicated by a highlight bar or by a check in the box next to the item.
- **Scrollbar**—This part indicates that more items are available on the list than will fit in the box and provides the users with an easy way to view the additional items.

To the user, using a list box is similar to choosing channels on a TV. The cable company decides which channels to put on the selection list. The customer then can pick any of these channels but can't add one to the list if she doesn't like any of the choices provided. With a list box, the choices are set up by you, the programmer; the user can select only from the items you decide should be available.

When you first draw a list box on the form, it shows only the border of the box and the text ListBox1 (the default name of the first list box). No scrollbar is present and, of course, no list items are available. A vertical scrollbar is added to the list box automatically when you list more items than fit in the box. If the items in your list box are wider than the control displays, you can add a horizontal scrollbar by setting the HorizontalScrollbar property to True.

ADDING ITEMS TO A LIST BOX

Obviously, for a list box to be functional, you need to add items to its list. There are several ways to accomplish this, either at design time or at runtime. You may want to create a sample Windows Application project and add a ListBox control to Form1.vb in order to test each method.

ADDING ITEMS AT DESIGN TIME To add items to a list box at design time, make sure the ListBox control on the form is selected; then look for the Items property in the Properties window. Actually, Items is a collection to which members can be added. If you click the ellipsis (...) next to the Items property, you will be presented with the String Collection Editor window, as shown in Figure 11.9. You can use the String Collection Editor to enter the items that you want to be displayed in your list box. Put each item on a separate line. Click the OK button to close the editor; you can now see the items you added to the list box at both design time and runtime.

Figure 11.9
The String Collection Editor allows you to enter items into a list box at design time.

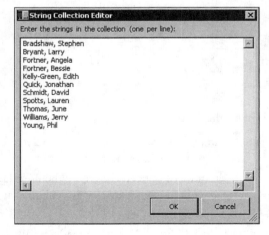

ADDING ITEMS AT RUNTIME WITH THE Add **METHOD**   If you want to add items to your list box at runtime, you can do so by invoking the Add method of the ListBox control's Items collection at runtime. Typically, you place such initialization code after the InitializeComponent call in your form's predefined New procedure, which is executed when an instance of your form is created. The following code illustrates a form's Sub New, which has been modified to add six employee names to a ListBox control named lstAribanistas in this manner:

```
Public Sub New()
    MyBase.New

    Form1 = Me
    'This call is required by the Win Form Designer.
    InitializeComponent()

    'TODO: Add any initialization after the InitializeComponent() call
    lstAribanistas.Items.Add("Newsom, Steve")
    lstAribanistas.Items.Add("Morrison, Robert")
    lstAribanistas.Items.Add("James, Bob")
    lstAribanistas.Items.Add("Watson, Mike")
    lstAribanistas.Items.Add("Brown, Zondra")
    lstAribanistas.Items.Add("Johnson, Cathy")
    lstAribanistas.Items.Add("Burton, Eric")
    lstAribanistas.Items.Add("Wright, Mamon")
    lstAribanistas.Items.Add("Phillips, Jerry")
End Sub
```

Figure 11.10 shows this list box at runtime.

Figure 11.10
A list box can show a
number of choices.

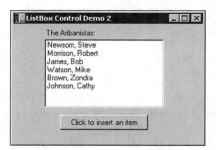

INSERTING ITEMS AT RUNTIME WITH THE Insert **METHOD**   If you want to add an item to a specific position in an existing ListBox control's list, you can use the Insert method of the ListBox control's Items collection. The Insert method allows you to specify the specific position within the list as well as the text to insert. Note that when specifying the position, numbering begins with zero (0); the first item in the list is position 0, the second is position 1, and so forth. The following code shows how to add a new item in position 3 (the fourth position) of a list box:

```
lstAribanistas.Items.Insert(3, "Phillips, Jerry")
```

You can see the results of this new addition to the list box in Figure 11.11.

Figure 11.11
A new item has been added to the list box.

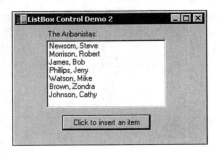

ASSIGNING AN ARRAY TO A LIST BOX You can also assign an entire array of variables to the All property of the Items collection of a list box. This will cause the list box to be populated with the members of the array. The following code demonstrates this technique:

```
Dim strDays() As String = {"Sunday", "Monday", "Tuesday", "Wednesday", _
                           "Thursday", "Friday", "Saturday"}
lstWeekDays.Items.All = strDays
```

Figure 11.12 shows this list box that has been populated from an array.

Figure 11.12
You can use an array to populate a list box all at once.

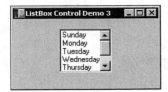

REMOVING ITEMS FROM A LIST BOX

There may be times when you want to remove individual items, or even the entire list of items, from a list box. Visual Basic provides methods for each task, as discussed next.

REMOVING INDIVIDUAL ITEMS WITH THE Remove METHOD The ListBox control's Items collection has a Remove method whose purpose is to delete a specific item from the list box. You do so by specifying the desired item's position in the list box, specifying the text of the item, or indicating that you want the currently selected item removed (using the SelectedItem property, which contains the index of the item that is currently highlighted). The following code demonstrates all three methods:

```
'Remove the third item (index 2):
lstTest.Items.Remove(2)
'Remove the item whose text is "Nashville"
lstTest.Items.Remove("Nashville")
```

```
'Remove the currently selected item:
lstTest.Items.Remove(lstTest.SelectedItem)
```

Note that either of the first two methods will generate an error if you attempt to remove an item that does not exist. The third method will generate an error if no item is selected.

The following illustrates a sample KeyDown procedure that can be used to delete an item from a list box when the user presses the Delete key while a particular item is selected. Note that the KeyCode property of the KeyEventArgs class specifies which key the user pressed and is compared to the Delete member of the Keys enumeration. This tells the procedure whether the Delete key was pressed; if so, the Remove method is invoked to delete the selected item:

```
Private Sub lstTest_KeyDown(ByVal sender As Object, _
    ByVal e As System.Windows.Forms.KeyEventArgs) _
    Handles lstTest.KeyDown
    If e.KeyCode = keys.Delete Then
        lstTest.Items.Remove(lsttest.SelectedIndex)
    End If
End Sub
```

REMOVING ALL ITEMS WITH THE Clear METHOD You can remove all the items in a list box's Items collection by invoking the Clear method, as follows:

```
lstTest.Items.Clear
```

ACCESSING MEMBERS OF THE Items COLLECTION

In addition to providing methods to allow you to add and remove list box items, the Items collection gives you access to the contents of the list. You can access the members of the Items collection using an index, much as you access the elements of a variable array. When utilizing the index, remember that the first item in the list box has an index of 0. Therefore, the first item of a ListBox control named lstTest would be accessible through lstTest.Items(0), the second item through lstTest.Items(1), and so on.

If you do not know how many items are in the list, the Count property of the Items collection will provide this information.

The following code uses a message box to display, one by one, the items in a ListBox control's list:

```
Dim i As Integer
For i = 0 To lstTest.Items.Count - 1
    'Remember that the index begins with 0 for the first item,
    ' so the counter variable must start at 0 and go up to
    ' one less than the Count property.
    MsgBox(lstTest.Items(i))
Next i
```

ACCESSING THE CURRENTLY SELECTED ITEM

If the user has selected an item in the list, the ListBox control provides you with two properties that allow you to access the selected item. The `SelectedIndex` property tells you the index of the selected item, whereas the `SelectedItem` property contains the actual item that has been selected. To illustrate, assume that you have a list box that contains city names. `Memphis` is in the second position (index 1) and has been selected by the user. The code `MsgBox lstTest.SelectedIndex` would return a value of 1, telling you that the second item in the list has been selected. `MsgBox lstTest.SelectedItem` would provide you with the actual contents of that position, `Memphis`.

> **Note**
>
> `SelectedIndex` returns a value of -1 if no item is selected.

Another way to retrieve the value of the list box item selected by the user is to check the list box's `Text` property. The `Text` property contains the item from whichever line of the list box has been selected. If no list box item has been selected, the `Text` property contains an empty string (`""`).

DETERMINING THE INITIAL SELECTION

Depending on your application, you might want to set the initial item for a list box. For example, you can set the choice in a program that needs to know your citizenship. You can provide a list of choices but set the initial value to `United States` because that would be the selection of most people in this country.

You set the initial value by using the `SelectedIndex` property of the `Items` collection. For example, if `United States` is the fourth entry in the list, you can use the following code to cause that item to be preselected (recall that `SelectedIndex` begins its counting with zero):

```
lstCitizenship.Items.SelectedIndex = 3
```

This statement causes the fourth item in the list (with an index of 3) to be displayed when the list box is first shown. You can set the initial choice in this manner for a list box, a checked list box, or a combo box. You also can set the initial selection of a list box by setting its `Text` property to the value of the desired list item, as follows:

```
lstCitizenship.Text = "United States"
```

SORTING LIST BOX ITEMS

You have seen how to modify a list by adding and removing items. But what do you do if you want your entire list sorted in alphabetic order?

Fortunately, this task is simple. To sort the list, you simply set the ListBox control's `Sorted` property to `True`. Then, no matter in which order you enter your items, they appear in alphabetic order to the users. The indexes of the list items are adjusted as they are added so that they remain in order.

> Because the `Sorted` property causes list items to be placed in alphabetical order, numeric items may not appear to sort properly. For example, a list containing the numbers 1, 2, 3, 11, 23, 100, and 200 would be sorted in the order 1, 100, 11, 2, 200, 23, 3, which is correct if the values are treated as text instead of numbers. This may be confusing to your users.

WORKING WITH MULTIPLE SELECTIONS

Sometimes you need to let the users select more than one item from a list. The list box supports this capability with the `SelectionMode` property. This property has four possible settings: `One`, `None`, `MultiSimple`, and `MultiExtended`:

- The default setting, `One`, means that multiple selections are not permitted, and the list box can accept only one selection at a time. If one item is selected and the user clicks a second item, the first item is automatically deselected.

- A setting of `None` specifies that the user cannot select items in the list at all.

- With a setting of `MultiSimple`, a user can use the mouse to select and deselect multiple items. If one item is selected and he clicks another item, that second item will be selected in addition to the first item.

- The other setting of the `MultiSelect` property, `MultiExtended`, is more complex. In this mode, users can use standard Windows techniques to select multiple items. They can select a range of items by clicking the first item in the range and then, while holding down the Shift key, clicking the last item in the range; all items between the first and last item are selected. To add or delete a single item to or from the selection, users hold down the Ctrl key while clicking the item.

Getting the selections from a multiple-selection list box is a little different from getting them for a single selection. Because the `SelectedItem` and `SelectedIndex` properties work only for a single selection, you can't use them. Instead, the ListBox control provides two other collections, `SelectedItems` and `SelectedIndices`, which provide an array of item values and indices, respectively, containing only the items that have been selected. Each supports a `Count` property so you can know how many items have been selected.

To illustrate this, the following code uses the `SelectedItems` collection to display all selected items in message boxes:

```
Dim i As Integer
For i = 0 To lstTest.SelectedItems.Count - 1
    MessageBox.Show(lstTest.SelectedItems(i))
Next i
```

Table 11.7 is a listing of commonly used properties that apply to ListBox and CheckedListBox controls.

TABLE 11.7   COMMON LISTBOX AND CHECKEDLISTBOX CONTROL PROPERTIES

Property	Description
BorderStyle	How the border is drawn around the control. The default setting, Fixed3D, shows a three-dimensional border. BorderStyle can also be set to FixedSingle, which gives it a flatter appearance.
MultiColumn	When set to True, displays the list items in multiple columns. The default value is False.
ColumnWidth	Determines how wide each column is (in pixels) when MultiColumn is set to True.
HorizontalScrollbars	Determines if the ListBox control will display a horizontal scrollbar if its contents are wider than the control. The default value is False.
HorizontalExtent	If HorizontalScrollbars is True, this property sets the width (in pixels) by which the list box can be scrolled horizontally.
Items	The actual items contained in the list. See the text for a description of the Items collection.
ScrollAlwaysVisible	When set to False (the default), the vertical scrollbar appears only when needed (that is, when the list contains more items than will fit in its height). A setting of True causes the vertical scrollbar to be shown regardless of the size of the list.
SelectionMode	Determines if and how the control allows more than one item to be selected at the same time. See the text for a full description.

Tip

You can add code to a list box control's Click or DoubleClick event handler to cause an action to occur when a user clicks or double-clicks an item in the list. This causes the list box to act like a mini-menu. In the event handler code, you can examine the value of the ListBox control's SelectedIndex or Text property to see which item the user clicked. This technique is often used to allow the user to double-click an item in a list to view some details about the item.

THE CHECKEDLISTBOX CONTROL

The CheckedListBox control is almost identical to the ListBox control, except in the way its list items are presented. In a CheckedListBox control, each item in the list has a check box to the left of the item's text. The user can check or uncheck individual items in the list. One thing to keep in mind is that a *checked* item is different from a *selected* item. The CheckedListBox control does not support the Multi- settings of the SelectionMode property (although they may appear in the Properties window), so your user cannot select multiple items (although she can check multiple items). Figure 11.13 illustrates a typical CheckedListBox control.

Figure 11.13
A checked list box lets the user mark entries to select them.

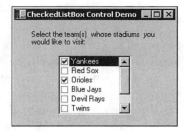

DETERMINING CHECKED ITEMS

To figure out which items in a CheckedListBox control have been checked, you need to use the GetItemChecked method for each item in the control's list. The following code will display message boxes containing each checked item in the CheckedListBox control clbTest:

```
Dim i As Integer
For i = 0 To clbTest.Items.Count - 1
    If clbTest.GetItemChecked(i) = True Then
        msgbox(clbTest.Items(i))
    End If
Next i
```

The properties presented in Table 11.8 are noteworthy for the CheckedListBox control in addition to the ListBox properties you saw in Table 11.7.

PART
III
CH
11

TABLE 11.8 COMMON CHECKEDLISTBOX CONTROL PROPERTIES

Property	Description
CheckOnClick	When set to True, when the user clicks an unselected item, the item is selected and its check box is checked (or unchecked if it was already checked). The default value is False; in this case, the user must click an item once to select it, and then click it again to check it. This technique is confusing, so you should consider setting this property to True.
ThreeDCheckBox	Determines whether the check box displayed by each list item has a 3D appearance. A setting of False (the default) displays flat check boxes.

THE COMBOBOX CONTROL

As its name implies, the ComboBox control combines the functionality of two other controls—list boxes and text boxes. The ComboBox control functions much like a list box. However, in addition to being able to select from predefined choices, the user can enter freeform text as well (depending on how the ComboBox control is configured).

The ComboBox control supports three distinct styles, each of which provides slightly different functionality for the user. The style displayed by a ComboBox control is determined by its Style property. Each of the styles is discussed in the following sections.

THE DROP-DOWN COMBO BOX

The default configuration, of a ComboBox control is the drop-down combo box, which is specified by setting the control's Style property to DropDown. This type of combo box presents the user with what appears to be a normal text box combined with a drop-down list (see Figure 11.14). The user can either type an entry into the text box portion of the control or click the drop-down arrow to select an item from the list portion of the control. In either case, the item she typs or selects is stored in the control's Text property.

Figure 11.14
The drop-down combo box lets the user click to reveal and select from the list or type an alternative item in the text box.

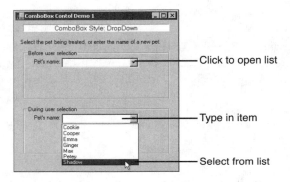

THE SIMPLE COMBO BOX

Setting a ComboBox ,control's Style property to Simple causes the control to look like a text box on top of a list box (see Figure 11.15). As with the drop-down style, the user can either type information into the text box or select an item from the list portion. If he selects an item from the list, that item is put into the text box portion. Again, in either case, the item is stored in the control's Text property.

Figure 11.15
The simple combo box displays a text area and a list at the same time.

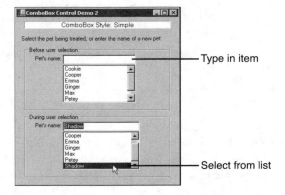

THE DROP-DOWN LIST COMBO BOX

This final combo box ,style, which is specified by setting the Style property to DropDownList, displays a drop-down list *without* a text box for the user to supply a freeform entry (see Figure 11.16). He can only select an item from the predefined list. In essence, this style works just like a list box. It saves screen space, however, as the control itself only displays one line. The list is contained in the drop-down portion, which is only visible when activated.

Figure 11.16
The drop-down list style of combo box works like a list box but saves screen space.

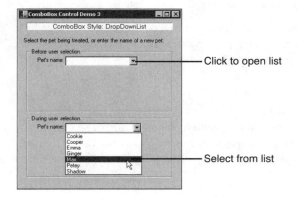

Click to open list

Select from list

PART
III

CH
11

> **Note**
>
> You can only change the Height property for a ComboBox control if its Style property is Simple. The height of combo ,boxes of the other two styles—DropDown and DropDownList—will be automatically configured, since the list portion is not normally visible.

MANAGING COMBO BOX ITEMS

The combo box ,has much in common with the list box. Both use the Add, Remove, and Clear methods of the Items collection to modify the contents of the list. Both can present a sorted or an unsorted list. The techniques used to manage members of the list portion of a combo box are identical to those used for a list box, as discussed earlier in this chapter.

> **Caution**
>
> The initial value of a combo box's Text property is the name of the combo box. If you do not want this name to appear in your combo box on startup, set a default selection using the techniques described earlier in this chapter, or set the Text property in code. Alternatively, you can simply delete the contents of the Text property while you are in the design environment.

WORKING WITH CHOICES NOT ON THE LIST

The real power ,of the combo box is its ability to allow users to enter choices other than those on the list. This capability is available with two styles of combo boxes—the simple combo box and the drop-down combo box. Both styles provide a list of items from which you can select, and both allow you to enter other values. The difference between the two styles is the way in which you access items already in the list.

With a simple combo box, your users can access the items in the list using the mouse or the arrow keys. If the users don't find what they want on the list, they can type new choices.

The drop-down combo box works like a combination of the drop-down list and the simple combo box. You select an item from the list the same way you would for a drop-down list, but you also can enter a value that is not on the list.

In any case, ,the value your user enters into a combo box—whether he enters it by clicking a predefined option or by typing a new value into the text box—can be accessed through the ComboBox control's Text property.

FROM HERE...

In this chapter you learned about some of the fundamental controls that you will use regularly as you build Windows applications using Visual Basic .NET. Chapter 12, "Advanced Controls," continues this discussion by presenting some of the more advanced controls that are available for you to use.

CHAPTER **12**

ADVANCED CONTROLS

In this chapter

In Chapter 11, "Fundamental Controls," you learned how to work with some of the controls that are used most commonly in Visual Basic .NET applications. This chapter introduces you to some of the controls that you may not use as often, but which provide some very handy specialized functionality.

As in Chapter 11, the controls presented in this chapter are loosely grouped according to function. We will discuss the fundamental usage of each control; feel free to experiment with them in test applications as you read through each control's description.

You may want to refer to the section "Introduction to Controls" in Chapter 11 for an overview of basic control functionality, as well as a summary of properties that are common to most controls.

You can download a sample project demonstrating the use of all the controls discussed in this chapter from www.quepublishing.com. The sample project includes comments in its code to explain how it works. Look for the file named ControlDemo.ZIP.

AUTOMATICALLY CONTROLLING A CONTROL'S SIZE AND POSITION

Before starting our discussion of specific controls, we will examine two properties that assist with managing the position and sizing of controls on forms. These properties apply to a large number of controls, including the basic controls discussed in Chapter 11.

The Anchor and Dock properties manage the position and sizing of controls as the user changes the size of a form. These two properties are examined in the following sections.

ANCHORING CONTROLS

When you place a control on a form, its position on the form is specified by setting its Location property, which defines the distance from the left edge of the form to the left edge of the control (the X subproperty) and the distance from the top edge of the form to the top edge of the control (the Y subproperty). The control's size is determined by its Size property, which defines the width and height of the control, specified by its Width and Height subproperties. If the user resizes the form, the size of the control remains constant, as does its position relative to the upper-left edge of the form.

> **Note**
>
> Technically, a control's Location property contains a Point object, which in turn contains X and Y subproperties. In code, this might look like Button1.Location = New Point (25, 275), defining the X subproperty as 25 and the Y subproperty as 275. This would cause Button1 to appear 25 pixels from the left edge of the form and 275 pixels from the top edge of the form. Similarly, the Size property contains a Size structure, which specifies the size of a rectangular region by using Width and Height properties.

Depending on your application, you may want a control to be resized or repositioned as the user resizes the form. Visual Basic .NET now provides an Anchor property, which allows you to specify any (or all) of the four edges of a form to which you want a control to be anchored. Normally, a control's Anchor property is set to Top, Left, which means that the control's distance from the top and left edges of the form will remain constant, no matter how the form is resized. Changing the Anchor property to some other combination of edges, such as Top, Bottom, Left, will cause the control's distance from those edges to remain constant as the form is resized. The control's Location and Size properties are adjusted as necessary to accomplish this.

To change a control's Anchor property, you click the drop-down arrow next to the property in the Properties window. You will see a box, shown in Figure 12.1, where you can click pointers to the four edges of the form. The top and left pointers will already be selected, representing the default Top, Left value of the property.

Figure 12.1
When setting the Anchor property, you can visually select any combination of the form's edges to which a control will be anchored.

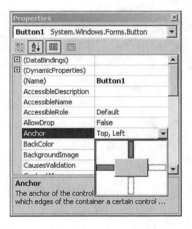

PART

III

CH

12

Note
If the combination of edges specified by the Anchor property includes a pair of opposite edges (Left and Right, or Top and Bottom), the control must be resized for the respective distance to those edges to remain constant.

One use of the Anchor property is to keep the size of an image constant relative to the size of the form containing it. Figure 12.2 shows a form containing a PictureBox control whose Anchor property has been set to all four edges (Top, Bottom, Left, Right). The PictureBox control's SizeMode property has been set to StretchImage, which causes the image displayed in the control to be resized to match the size of the control. In Figure 12.3, the form has been resized to be larger; note how the Image control has been resized to maintain its anchoring to all four corners.

Figure 12.2
This form contains an
Image control whose
Anchor property
binds it to all four
corners.

Figure 12.3
The form has been
made larger; the
Image control has
resized itself so that
the distance from it to
all four edges of the
form remains con-
stant.

Figures 12.4 and 12.5 illustrate another nice use for the Anchor property—keeping a button located near the lower-right edge of a form. Figure 12.4 shows a form with an Exit button near the lower-right corner of the form. The Button control's Anchor property has been changed from the default value of Top, Left to Bottom, Right. Figure 12.5 shows the same form after having been resized. The Exit button remains in the same relative lower-right position.

Figure 12.4
This form has an Exit
button near its lower-
right corner.

Figure 12.5
Because the Exit button's Anchor property is set to Bottom, Right, the button appears in the same lower-right corner even when the form is enlarged.

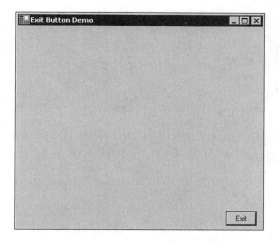

DOCKING CONTROLS

In certain situations, you may want to have a control "docked" to one edge of a form. You can use the control's Dock property to enable this capability. You set the Dock property to one of the four edges of the form—Top, Bottom, Left, or Right—to dock it to that edge. A docked control will always be positioned flush against the respective edge of its container form. Its "opposite" size dimension will be modified to take up the entire width or height of the form. In other words, if you set a control's Dock property to Left, that control will always be positioned flush against the left edge of the form, and its Height property will be automatically adjusted so that the control takes up the entire height of the form.

One special value of the Dock property, Fill, causes all four edges of the control to be docked to all four edges of the form. A control whose Dock property is set to Fill will always take up the entire inner area of the form. You can see an example of the Fill value of the Dock property in the sample application developed in Chapter 15, "Multiple Document Interface Applications." In that program, a TextBox control's Dock property is set to Fill in order for the text box to always fill the form that contains it.

One potential use of the Dock property is to have a Label control displaying status information always positioned along the bottom edge of the form and taking up the form's entire width, as illustrated in Figure 12.6.

PART

III

CH

12

Figure 12.6
The status label shown here is docked to the lower edge of the form.

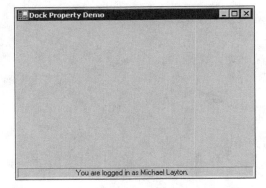

> **Note**
>
> The Anchor and Dock properties cannot be used at the same time for the same control. If, for example, you set the Anchor property of a control to something other than its default value, and set its Dock property to Bottom, Left, for instance, the control's Anchor property reverts to its default value of Top, Left.
>
> When you want a control to remain positioned along one (or more) of the form's edges, use the Dock property. If you want a control's position inside the form (not docked to an edge) to remain constant, use the Anchor property.

SPECIALIZED DATE INPUT CONTROLS

Visual Basic .NET includes two controls that allow your programs to accept date (and possibly time) information as input. These two controls are discussed in this section.

THE DATETIMEPICKER CONTROL

When you want to allow your users to enter date and time information directly, the DateTimePicker control is a flexible and user-friendly entry tool. Its basic interface allows the user to enter a date in one of two predefined formats, a time in a predefined format, or a date and/or time in a customizable format. Depending on how you set its properties (see Table 12.1), the DateTimePicker offers the user either a dynamic drop-down calendar from which to select a date or a formatted text box in which he can manually enter a date or time, with spinners (small up and down arrows) to assist him. A typical DateTimePicker control is illustrated in Figure 12.7.

Figure 12.7
The DateTimePicker control makes it easy for the user to enter date information.

Tip

When the user is selecting a date from the calendar-like interface, if he clicks the year at the top of the control, he will be given up and down buttons that he can use to quickly move the calendar a year at a time. In addition, clicking the month name causes a list of all 12 months to appear; he can click the name of a month to go quickly to that month.

Once the user has selected a date or time in a DateTimePicker control, that information is available to your program via the control's Value property, which returns a DateTime value. You can then use one of several methods of the DateTime structure to retrieve the information in the control in a String format that you can use. For example, the ToShortDateString method would retrieve the date contained in the DateTimePicker control and return it as a short-formatted date, as follows:

```
lblBirthDate = DateTimePicker1.Value.ToShortDateString
```

Table 12.1 shows examples of some of the formats in which you can retrieve the date and time information contained in the Value property of a DateTimePicker control by using various methods of the DateTime structure.

PART

III

CH

12

TABLE 12.1   METHODS FOR RETRIEVING DATA FROM THE DATETIMEPICKER CONTROL

Method	Type	Example
ToShortDate	Date	02/18/2002
ToLongDate	Date	Monday, February 18, 2002
ToShortTime	Time	23:55
ToLongTime	Time	23:55:37

The DateTimePicker control is customized using the properties described in Table 12.2.

TABLE 12.2   COMMON DATETIMEPICKER CONTROL PROPERTIES

Property	Description
Format	Specifies the format of the information being requested from the user. The default value is Long, which accepts and displays dates in the format "day-of-week, month, day, year;" for example, Monday, November 12, 2001. Another possible value for this property is Short, which displays a shorter date format (11/12/2001). Setting the property to Time accepts time information (10:42:35 PM). The fourth value, Custom, is used in conjunction with the CustomFormat property to utilize a special format.
CustomFormat	This property is set to a string value to specify how a customized date or time format is to be displayed and accepted in the control. For example, a CustomFormat of dddd M/d/yyyy HH:mm would display the day of the week, the month/day/year, and the time in 24-hour format (Friday, April 27, 2001 23:11).
ShowUpDown	When set to False (the default), the control will display a drop-down arrow that the user can click to view a navigable pop-up calendar. When he clicks a date in the calendar, that date is used to populate the date in the control. Setting this property to True replaces the drop-down arrow with up and down spinners. He can then select any of the date or time fields (year, for example) and use the spinners to automatically move the selected portion of the date or time up or down.
MaxDate	The latest possible date that may be entered or selected in the control. The default value is 12/31/9998.
MinDate	The earliest possible date that may be entered or selected in the control. The default value is 1/1/1753.
CalendarFont	The font used to display the pop-up calendar. The CalendarFont property supports the subproperties Name, Size, Unit, Bold, Italic, Strikeout, and Underline.
Value	The Value property contains the date and time currently displayed in the control. You can set the Value property using code like DateTimePicker1.Value = #11/12/1962# (note that literal dates are enclosed in pound signs instead of quotes). You can retrieve the Value property in a similar manner (lblBirthdate.Text = DateTimePicker1.Value.ToString).

Note

See the Help system topic for the CustomFormat property for a complete list of acceptable characters and their meanings.

THE MONTHCALENDAR CONTROL

When you need to let your application's users select a date, the MonthCalendar control (shown in Figure 12.8) provides an easily navigable, graphical calendar to make this task easy. Unlike the DateTimePicker control, the MonthCalendar control does not have an input area into which the user can type a date; its date entry and display is done entirely through the calendar-like interface. Also, while the DateTimePicker control allows your user to specify a single date, the MonthCalendar control supports the selection of a series of dates.

Figure 12.8
The MonthCalendar control gives your program's users an easy way to select a range of dates.

The MonthCalendar control's `SelectionRange` property contains a `SelectionRange` class value, representing the starting and ending dates that are currently selected in the control's interface. You can access the `Start` and `End` subproperties of the `SelectionRange` property to determine the date range that the user has specified in the control. The following sample code will populate two `Label` controls, `lblStartDate` and `lblEndDate`, with the beginning and ending dates specified in a MonthCalendar control (by using the `ToString` method of the `Start` and `End` subproperties of the `SelectionRange` property):

```
lblStartDate.Text = MonthCalendar1.SelectionRange.Start.ToString
lblEndDate.Text = MonthCalendar1.SelectionRange.End.ToString
```

You can use the properties described in Table 12.3 to customize and utilize the MonthCalendar control.

PART
III

CH
12

TABLE 12.3   COMMON MONTHCALENDAR CONTROL PROPERTIES

Property	Description
AnnuallyBoldedDates	An array of `DateTime` values that are to be shown in boldface type on the calendar each year.
BoldedDates	An array of nonrecurring `DateTime` values that are to be shown in boldface type on the calendar.
CalendarDimensions	Sets the number of months to be displayed in a MonthCalendar control at one time. The `CalendarDimensions` property is set to a pair of values representing the width and height of the "grid" of calendar months. `CalendarDimensions.Width` and `CalendarDimensions.Height` are directly accessible as subproperties as well. The default `CalendarDimensions` setting is 1, 1, which displays a single month.
FirstDayOfWeek	Specifies the first day to be displayed in each week of a calendar.

TABLE 12.3   CONTINUED

Property	Description
MaxDate	Specifies the latest date that the calendar will accept. The default value is 12/31/9998.
MinDate	Specifies the earliest date that the calendar will accept. The default value is 1/1/1753.
MonthlyBoldedDates	An array of DateTime values that are to be shown in boldface type on the calendar each month.
ScrollChange	The number of months that the calendar will be moved when the user clicks one of the arrow controls that are used to navigate the calendar. The default value is the number of months displayed (as determined by the CalendarDimensions property); the maximum value is 20000.
SelectionStart	The beginning date of the selected range of dates.
SelectionEnd	The ending date of the selected range of dates.
SelectionRange	The entire range of selected dates (see the previous text).
ShowToday	When set to True (the default), the current date (as specified by the TodayDate property) is displayed at the bottom of the calendar.
ShowTodayCircle	When set to True (the default), the current date (as specified by the TodayDate property) is circled in the appropriate month of the calendar.
ShowWeekNumbers	When set to True, the week number of each week is displayed along its left side. The default value is False.
TitleBackColor	Specifies the color to be used as the background of the control's title area, which displays month and year information.
TitleForeColor	Specifies the color to be used for the text in the control's title area, which displays month and year information.
TodayDate	Specifies the date that the calendar displays as the current date. The default value is the current system date.

OTHER SPECIALIZED CONTROLS

Visual Basic .NET includes a number of controls that perform specific functions. Some of these controls are discussed in the following sections.

THE LINKLABEL CONTROL

The LinkLabel control is a welcome enhancement to the standard Label control. As you may have gathered from its name, the LinkLabel control is much like a normal Label control, but it allows the user to click one or more Web-like hyperlinks to perform some action, such as opening a new form or visiting a Web page. The hyperlink analogy will be familiar to Web-savvy users.

As you will see, you can designate all or part of the text that makes up a LinkLabel control's Text property to be a hyperlink. When the user clicks the hyperlink text in the control, the LinkClicked event is fired, and code that you have placed in the control's LinkClicked event handler initiates the desired action.

SPECIFYING A SINGLE HYPERLINK

If you want a LinkLabel control to contain a single hyperlink, you simply set the control's LinkArea property to a LinkArea object, which at its most basic specifies the first character of the text that is to be a hyperlink, along with the number of characters that make up the length of the hyperlink. As with most properties, this can be done at design time in the Properties window or by using code at runtime.

SETTING THE LinkArea PROPERTY AT DESIGN TIME   After setting the Text property of a LinkLabel control to the desired caption, you can designate the part of the text that you want to act as a hyperlink by setting the LinkArea property in the Properties window. If you click the plus sign next to the LinkArea property, it will expand to reveal the property's two subcomponents—Start and Length. Start specifies the first character of the control's Text property that is to act as a hyperlink. Character counting is zero-based; that is, the first character is position 0, the second character is position 1, and so on. Length specifies how many characters are to be used as the hyperlink. You can type individual values for the Start and Length components in their respective boxes in the Properties window, or you can type both values separated by a comma (12, 4, for example) next to the LinkArea property itself. Figure 12.9 illustrates a LinkLabel control whose LinkArea property is set to 4, 17. Notice that the mouse pointer has changed to the pointing-hand icon that is typically displayed when hovering over a hyperlink.

Figure 12.9
You can use the LinkArea property to designate all or part of a LinkLabel control's caption as a hyperlink.

Note

By default, the LinkArea property includes all characters in the current Text property and continues to do so—even when the Text property changes—until you specifically change it.

Tip

If you click the ellipsis (...) next to the LinkArea property in the Properties window, the LinkArea Editor dialog box displays the current contents of the control's Text property; you can easily select the desired link text here, and the LinkArea property will be set for you. You can even change the control's Text property from this dialog box.

PART
III
CH
12

SETTING THE LinkArea PROPERTY AT RUNTIME   You can set the value of a LinkLabel control's LinkArea property dynamically at runtime as well. You do so by setting the property's value to a LinkArea object that you can create on-the-fly, using code like the following:

```
LinkLabel1.LinkArea = New LinkArea(12, 9)
```

SPECIFYING MULTIPLE HYPERLINKS IN A SINGLE LINKLABEL CONTROL

It is not at all unusual for a single LinkLabel control to contain more than one hyperlink. For example, consider the label shown in Figure 12.9. Its Text property contains The Memphis Grizzlies, who moved from Vancouver in 2001, are the NBA's newest team. You may want the words "Memphis Grizzlies" to link to that team's Web site, while the word "NBA" links to the National Basketball Association's Web site. To create multiple links within a single LinkLabel control, you utilize the control's Links property, which exposes the control's LinkCollection class, using code at runtime.

When a LinkLabel control will have multiple links, it makes sense to use the Links property to add *all* desired links to the LinkCollection at runtime. Keep in mind, however, that by default a LinkLabel control's full text is treated as a hyperlink. You will need to clear this default full-text hyperlink before adding new hyperlinks; otherwise, you will have overlapping hyperlinks, which will lead to a runtime error.

When using the Links property to add a new link to the control's LinkCollection, you must specify the link's starting position, its length, and (optionally) a value for the Link object's LinkData property. The LinkData property contains information that will be useful when the link is clicked to help identify *which* of a control's links was clicked because all the control's links share the same event handler. In this case, we will use the LinkData property to specify the URL that applies to each of the control's links.

The following initialization code, placed in the New procedure of the form containing the LinkLabel control, will use the Clear method of the Links property to clear all hyperlinks from the control, and then add two hyperlinks as suggested previously:

```
LinkLabel1.Links.Clear()
LinkLabel1.Links.Add(4, 17, "http://www.grizzlies.com")
LinkLabel1.Links.Add(65, 3, "http://www.nba.com")
```

The resulting LinkLabel control is shown in Figure 12.10.

Figure 12.10
A LinkLabel control can contain multiple hyperlinks.

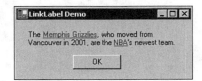

REACTING TO THE SELECTION OF A HYPERLINK

Of course, the whole point of a LinkLabel control is for some action to occur when the user clicks the hyperlink. When the user clicks one of a LinkLabel control's hyperlinks, the control's LinkClicked event handler is invoked. If the LinkLabel control contains only one hyperlink, writing code for the LinkClicked event handler to initiate the appropriate action is a simple matter. Typically, you will want to open another form or use a browser to open a Web page. The following code will cause an instance of frmDestination to be loaded when LinkLabel1's link is clicked:

```
Dim f as New frmDestination()
f.Show()
```

Reacting to the user having clicked a link in a LinkLabel control that contains more than one link is a little trickier. Fortunately, the LinkData property of the Link object allows us to specify information related to that specific link. The LinkData property of the active link is provided to the LinkClicked event handler via the argument e, which is of type LinkLabelLinkClickedEventArgs. In the example demonstrated in the previous section, each new member added to the LinkCollection (via the Links property) was assigned a URL for its LinkData property. Making use of this information, the following LinkClicked event handler for LinkLabel1 will cause the user's default Web browser to open and display the appropriate URL when any of LinkLabel1's links are clicked:

```
Private Sub LinkLabel1_LinkClicked(ByVal sender As System.Object, _
    ByVal e As System.Windows.Forms.LinkLabelLinkClickedEventArgs) _
    Handles LinkLabel1.LinkClicked
    System.Diagnostics.Process.Start(e.Link.LinkData)
End Sub
```

Tip

When writing code to react to the user having clicked a link in a LinkLabel control, be sure to put the code in the control's LinkClicked event handler, not the Click event handler. The Click event occurs when the user clicks any part of the label, even if the part he clicks is not a hyperlink.

PART

III

CH

12

CHANGING THE APPEARANCE OF LINKS

The LinkLabel control supports several properties that govern how the links appear and behave. These properties are discussed in the following sections.

THE LinkBehavior PROPERTY   The LinkBehavior property specifies how and when the link(s) contained in a LinkLabel control is underlined to indicate that it is a link. The possible values for the LinkBehavior property, supplied via the LinkBehavior enumeration, are summarized in Table 12.4.

TABLE 12.4 VALUES FOR THE `LinkBehavior` PROPERTY

`LinkBehavior` Member	Description
`AlwaysUnderline`	The link is always underlined to indicate that it is a link.
`HoverUnderline`	The link is underlined only when the mouse pointer passes over the link.
`NeverUnderline`	The link is never underlined.
`SystemDefault`	The link is displayed using the system's default link behavior, specified by the user. This is the default value of the `LinkBehavior` property.

THE `LinkColor` PROPERTY   The `LinkColor` property is used to specify the color that is initially displayed for the link(s) contained in a LinkLabel control. You use a `Color` object to specify the value of this property. The default value of the `LinkColor` property is `Color.Blue`, causing links to initially appear in blue text. You can change the `LinkColor` property in the Properties window at design time or at runtime by using code like `LinkLabel1.LinkColor = Color.Aquamarine`.

THE `ActiveLinkColor` PROPERTY   The `ActiveLinkColor` propert is used to specify the color in which a link is displayed while it is being clicked. The default value of the `ActiveLinkColor` property is `Color.Red`.

THE `VisitedLinkColor` PROPERTY   After the user has clicked a link, you may want the link to appear in a different color from unvisited links (which is typical Web hyperlink behavior). The `VisitedLinkColor` property allows you to specify the color to be used for links that have been visited (as determined by the `LinkVisited` property described in the next section). The default value of the `VisitedLinkColor` property is `Color.Purple`.

THE `LinkVisited` AND `Visited` PROPERTIES   Even though you can specify a color in which visited links are to be displayed, the fact that a link has been visited is not maintained automatically. For a link to be displayed in the color designated by its `VisitedLinkColor` property, you must set the LinkLabel control's `LinkVisited` property to `True`. However, the `LinkVisited` property only applies to the first link contained in a LinkLabel control. If a LinkLabel control contains multiple links, you must set the `Visited` property of the appropriate `Link` object in the LinkLabel control's `LinkClicked` event handler, as illustrated here:

```
Private Sub LinkLabel1_LinkClicked(ByVal sender As System.Object, _
    ByVal e As System.Windows.Forms.LinkLabelLinkClickedEventArgs) _
    Handles LinkLabel1.LinkClicked
    e.Link.Visited = True
    System.Diagnostics.Process.Start(e.Link.LinkData)
End Sub
```

THE TIMER COMPONENT

Sometimes you will want to write code that runs at specific time intervals or after a certain amount of time has elapsed. The Timer component provides this functionality by executing code at set time increments. Some possible uses for the Timer component include the following:

- Provide status updates during a lengthy operation
- Close a form (such as a splash screen) after a certain period of time has elapsed
- Provide simple animation

The Timer component works by firing the `Tick` event (and, in turn, invoking the `Tick` event handler) at specific time intervals. You control the length of time between `Tick` events by setting the timer's `Interval` property to the number of milliseconds that should elapse between `Tick` events. (A millisecond is a thousandth of a second; therefore, 1,000 milliseconds equal one second.) Once the timer has been activated (either by invoking its `Start` method or by setting its `Enabled` property to `True`), code that you place in the `Tick` event handler is executed each time the number of milliseconds specified by the `Interval` property elapses.

Let's demonstrate how to use the Timer component by creating a simple stopwatch program. This program will use the Timer component to continually update a Label control containing the elapsed time since the stopwatch's Start button is clicked.

SETTING UP THE STOPWATCH APPLICATION

Follow these steps to set up the stopwatch application:

1. Start a new Windows Application project. Name it `Stopwatch`.
2. Set the `Text` property of the application's single form (`Form1`) to Stopwatch Demo.
3. Add a Label control named `lblElapsedTime` to `Form1`. Enter `00:00:00`, representing no elapsed time, as its `Text` property. Set its `Font` property to Courier New, 36 point. Set its `TextAlign` property to `TopCenter`. Size and position the label so that its entire contents are visible.
4. Drag a Button control to `Form1`; give it the name `cmdStart`. Set its `Text` property to `Start`.
5. Add a second Button control to `Form1`; give it the name `cmdStop`. Set its `Text` property to `Stop`. Also, set its `Enabled` property to `False`; the user should not be able to click the Stop button until the stopwatch has been started.
6. Drag a Timer from the Toolbox to `Form1`. Note that the new Timer (`Timer1`) does not appear on the form itself, but in the tray area below the form. The Timer component is not visible to the user at runtime.
7. To calculate the stopwatch's elapsed time, the application will need a form-level variable to remember when the user clicked the Start button. Open the Code window for `Form1` and type `Dim dStart As DateTime` just above the `End Class` line.

An example of the completed form is shown in Figure 12.11.

PART

III

CH

12

Figure 12.11
The stopwatch application has a simple user interface.

CODING THE START BUTTON

When the user clicks the Start button, the following things need to happen:

- The dStart variable should be set to remember when the user started the stopwatch.
- The Timer component should be activated.
- The Start button should be disabled because the user should not be able to click it after the stopwatch has already started.
- The Stop button should be enabled.

Enter the Click event handler in Listing 12.1 for cmdStart, which will accomplish the desired tasks.

LISTING 12.1   STARTING THE TIMER COMPONENT

```
Private Sub cmdStart_Click(ByVal sender As System.Object, _
    ByVal e As System.EventArgs) Handles cmdStart.Click
    dStart = Now
    Timer1.Start()
    cmdStart.Enabled = False
    cmdStop.Enabled = True
End Sub
```

CODING THE STOP BUTTON

The Stop button should accomplish the following:

- The Timer component should be deactivated.
- The Start button should be enabled.
- The Stop button should be disabled.

To handle these actions, enter the following Click event handler for cmdStop:

```
Private Sub cmdStop_Click(ByVal sender As System.Object, _
    ByVal e As System.EventArgs) Handles cmdStop.Click
    Timer1.Stop()
    cmdStart.Enabled = True
    cmdStop.Enabled = False
End Sub
```

CODING THE TIMER COMPONENT

Of course, the mostimportant job in this application belongs to the Timer component. Once the timer's `Start` method is invoked, the default value of its `Interval` property, 100 milliseconds, will cause the timer's `Tick` event to fire every tenth of a second, which is fine for this application. The timer's `Tick` event handler, which is executed with each `Tick` event, needs to calculate the elapsed time (in seconds) between the start time (which has been stored in the `dStart` variable) and the current time (represented by the `Now` method of the `System.DateTime` structure). The difference is converted to a string representing hours, minutes, and seconds and then displayed in the `lblElapsedTime` label. To enter the `Tick` event handler for `Timer1`, perform these steps:

1. Make sure you are in the Code window for `Form1`.
2. Click the Code window's Class Name drop-down box and select Timer1.
3. After Timer1 is selected in the Class Name drop-down box, select Tick from the Method Name box.
4. Enter the following code as the `Tick` event handler for `Timer1`:

```
Private Sub Timer1_Tick(ByVal sender As Object, _
    ByVal e As System.EventArgs) Handles Timer1.Tick
    Dim lHrs As Long, lMins As Long, lSecs As Long
    lSecs = DateDiff(DateInterval.Second, dStart, DateTime.Now)
    lHrs = Int(lSecs / 3600)
    lSecs -= (lHrs * 3600)
    lMins = Int(lSecs / 60)
    lSecs -= (lMins * 60)
    lblElapsedTime.Text = Format(lHrs, "00") & ":" & _
        Format(lMins, "00") & ":" & Format(lSecs, "00")
End Sub
```

Listing 12.2 shows the complete code for the Stopwatch application to this point. Later in this section, you will see how to add more functionality to the application.

PART
III
CH
12

LISTING 12.2   CODING THE STOPWATCH APPLICATION

```
Dim dStart As DateTime

Private Sub cmdStart_Click(ByVal sender As System.Object, _
    ByVal e As System.EventArgs) Handles cmdStart.Click
    dStart = DateTime.Now
    Timer1.Start()
    cmdStart.Enabled = False
    cmdStop.Enabled = True
End Sub

Private Sub Timer1_Tick(ByVal sender As Object, _
    ByVal e As System.EventArgs) Handles Timer1.Tick
    Dim lHrs As Long, lMins As Long, lSecs As Long
    lSecs = DateDiff(DateInterval.Second, dStart, DateTime.Now)
    lHrs = Int(lSecs / 3600)
    lSecs -= (lHrs * 3600)
    lMins = Int(lSecs / 60)
```

LISTING 12.2   CONTINUED

```
    lSecs -= (lMins * 60)
    lblElapsedTime.Text = Format(lHrs, "00") & ":" & _
        Format(lMins, "00") & ":" & Format(lSecs, "00")
End Sub

Private Sub cmdStop_Click(ByVal sender As System.Object, _
    ByVal e As System.EventArgs) Handles cmdStop.Click
    Timer1.Stop()
    cmdStart.Enabled = True
    cmdStop.Enabled = False
End Sub
```

TESTING THE STOPWATCH APPLICATION

Save and run the application. When you click the Start button, the Timer's Start method is invoked, enabling the timer. The Label control is continually updated with the number of hours, minutes, and seconds since the Start button was clicked. The Stop button causes the stopwatch to stop. A running version of the Stopwatch application is pictured in Figure 12.12.

Figure 12.12
The Stopwatch application uses the Timer component to update a Label control with elapsed time information.

THE NOTIFYICON CONTROL

The NotifyIcon control provides some nice functionality for which Visual Basic developers have been clamoring for some time; namely, the ability to place a "live" icon in the system tray.

Four important properties of the NotifyIcon control define its appearance and behavior:

- The Icon property specifies the icon that is to appear in the system tray.
- The Visible property determines whether the control is visible in the system tray.
- The Text property defines the ToolTip text that is displayed when the user hovers the mouse pointer over the tray icon.
- The ContextMenu property specifies a ContextMenu control that is popped up when the user right-clicks the NotifyIcon control.

In addition, the Click, DoubleClick, and MouseMove events give you the opportunity to write code to react to your users' interaction with a NotifyIcon control.

To illustrate the NotifyIcon control, we will enhance the Stopwatch application that was created in the preceding section. This time, we will add a tray icon indicating that the

Stopwatch application is running, even if the user minimizes the form. We will write code to cause the form to become hidden if the user minimizes it. A context menu will allow the user to restore the main form or exit the application from the tray icon. Furthermore, if the user hovers over the tray icon, a ToolTip will display the current value of the stopwatch.

MODIFYING THE STOPWATCH APPLICATION

The following steps will take you through the process of enhancing the Stopwatch application to utilize a NotifyIcon control in the system tray:

1. Begin with the Stopwatch application that we created in the preceding section.
2. Drag a ContextMenu control to Form1. Add the following menu items to the ContextMenu control:

Menu Item Name	Text Property
mnuRestore	&Restore
mnuExit	E&xit

3. Drag a NotifyIcon control to Form1.
4. Set the NotifyIcon control's Icon property to an appropriate icon. I used the icon timer01.ico, which by default is installed with Visual Studio .NET in the C:\Program Files\Microsoft Visual Studio.NET\Common7\Graphics\icons\Misc folder.
5. Set the NotifyIcon control's ContextMenu property to ContextMenu1, which you created in step 2. When you select the ContextMenu property in the Properties window, notice that you are presented with a drop-down list box listing any ContextMenu controls that exist on Form1.
6. Set the NotifyIcon's Text property to Stopwatch is Stopped, which will be the initial value of the icon's ToolTip until the stopwatch is started.
7. To cause the form to be hidden if the user minimizes it, enter the following as the form's Resize event handler (which is executed whenever the user resizes the form, including minimizing it). The code checks to see if the current value of the form's WindowState property indicates that it is minimized; if so, the form is hidden:

```
Private Sub Form1_Resize(ByVal sender As Object, _
    ByVal e As System.EventArgs) Handles MyBase.Resize
    If Me.WindowState = FormWindowState.Minimized Then
        Me.Visible = False
    End If
End Sub
```

8. Add the following code as the Click event handler for the mnuRestore menu item. This code causes the form to return to visibility and un-minimize itself:

```
Private Sub mnuRestore_Click(ByVal sender As Object, _
    ByVal e As System.EventArgs) Handles mnuRestore.Click
    Me.Visible = True
    Me.WindowState = FormWindowState.Normal
End Sub
```

PART

III

CH

12

9. Add the following code as the `Click` event handler for the `mnuExit` menu item:

```
Private Sub mnuExit_Click(ByVal sender As Object, _
    ByVal e As System.EventArgs) Handles mnuExit.Click
    Me.Close()
End Sub
```

10. Add the code `NotifyIcon1.Text = "Elapsed Time: " & lblElapsedTime.Text` to the end of the existing `Timer1_Tick` event handler. This code sets the value of the NotifyIcon control's `Text` property, which updates its ToolTip each time the `Tick` event fires. The complete `Timer1_Tick` event handler is as follows:

```
Private Sub Timer1_Tick(ByVal sender As Object, _
    ByVal e As System.EventArgs) Handles Timer1.Tick
    Dim lHrs As Long, lMins As Long, lSecs As Long
    lSecs = DateDiff(DateInterval.Second, dStart, DateTime.Now)
    lHrs = Int(lSecs / 3600)
    lSecs -= (lHrs * 3600)
    lMins = Int(lSecs / 60)
    lSecs -= (lMins * 60)
    lblElapsedTime.Text = Format(lHrs, "00") & ":" & _
        Format(lMins, "00") & ":" & Format(lSecs, "00")
    NotifyIcon1.Text = "Elapsed Time: " & lblElapsedTime.Text
End Sub
```

Listing 12.3 shows the newly enhanced Stopwatch application.

LISTING 12.3   **ENHANCING THE STOPWATCH APPLICATION**

```
Dim dStart As DateTime

Private Sub cmdStart_Click(ByVal sender As System.Object, _
    ByVal e As System.EventArgs) Handles cmdStart.Click
    dStart = DateTime.Now
    Timer1.Start()
    cmdStart.Enabled = False
    cmdStop.Enabled = True
End Sub

Private Sub Timer1_Tick(ByVal sender As Object, _
    ByVal e As System.EventArgs) Handles Timer1.Tick
    Dim lHrs As Long, lMins As Long, lSecs As Long
    lSecs = DateDiff(DateInterval.Second, dStart, DateTime.Now)
    lHrs = Int(lSecs / 3600)
    lSecs -= (lHrs * 3600)
    lMins = Int(lSecs / 60)
    lSecs -= (lMins * 60)
    lblElapsedTime.Text = Format(lHrs, "00") & ":" & _
        Format(lMins, "00") & ":" & Format(lSecs, "00")
    NotifyIcon1.Text = "Elapsed Time: " & lblElapsedTime.Text
End Sub

Private Sub cmdStop_Click(ByVal sender As System.Object, _
    ByVal e As System.EventArgs) Handles cmdStop.Click
    Timer1.Stop()
    cmdStart.Enabled = True
    cmdStop.Enabled = False
```

```
End Sub

Private Sub mnuRestore_Click(ByVal sender As System.Object, _
    ByVal e As System.EventArgs) Handles mnuRestore.Click
    Me.Visible = True
    Me.WindowState = FormWindowState.Normal
End Sub

Private Sub mnuExit_Click(ByVal sender As System.Object, _
    ByVal e As System.EventArgs) Handles mnuExit.Click
    Me.Close()
End Sub

Private Sub Form1_Resize(ByVal sender As Object, _
    ByVal e As System.EventArgs) Handles MyBase.Resize
    If Me.WindowState = FormWindowState.Minimized Then
        Me.Visible = False
    End If
End Sub
```

TESTING THE MODIFIED STOPWATCH APPLICATION

You have now enhanced the Stopwatch application to include a system tray icon. Save and run the modified application. Notice that a tray icon appears. Start the stopwatch and hover the mouse pointer over the tray icon, noticing that the ToolTip contains the current value displayed by the stopwatch. Minimize the stopwatch form; notice that the form disappears, but the tray icon is still visible and still displays the stopwatch value when hovered over. Right-click the tray icon to see the context menu. Click Restore to make the form reappear.

THE PROGRESSBAR CONTROL

A progress bar, shown in Figure 12.13, is commonly used to give the user a visual indication of how long an operation has taken and how much of the operation is remaining. Typically, a progress bar is used to display how much of a file remains to be downloaded, how many records of a database have been processed, and so on. The progress bar starts with an empty panel, which a bar expands to fill as the operation progresses. Visual Basic .NET provides the ProgressBar control to let you add this capability to your programs.

Figure 12.13
The ProgressBar control is used to show the user how much of an operation is remaining.

To use the ProgressBar control, draw one on a form and set its properties appropriately. The main properties that control the progress bar are Minimum, Maximum, and Value. The Minimum and Maximum properties define the range that the bar will cover, and the Value property dictates the current position of the bar. In other words, if Minimum is set to 0 and Maximum is set to 100, a Value property setting of 50 would cause the bar to fill about half of the control's available area.

A typical use of the ProgressBar control is to display the status of a database operation while it is in progress. You can set the Maximum property to the number of records being processed; each time a record is processed, you can increment the Value property by one.

As is normal, it's easier to learn about a control by using it. Follow these steps to see a ProgressBar control in action:

1. Start a new Windows Application project.
2. Drag a ProgressBar control to the application's main form (Form1). Set its Minimum property to 0 and its Maximum property to 10.
3. Drag a Button control to Form1.
4. Enter the code from Listing 12.2 as the Click event handler for the Button control:

```
Private Sub Button1_Click(ByVal sender As System.Object, _
    ByVal e As System.EventArgs) Handles Button1.Click
    Dim lThen As Long
    ProgressBar1.Value = 0
    Do While ProgressBar1.Value < ProgressBar1.Maximum
        ProgressBar1.Value += 1
        lThen = Timer
        Do While Timer < (lThen + 1)
            '(Wait for 1 second)
        Loop
    Loop
End Sub
```

This code begins by setting the ProgressBar control's Value property to 0; therefore, it will start off with an empty bar. The first Do loop increments the progress bar's Value property by one until it reaches its maximum value (10). So that the progress bar doesn't move so fast that you can't see it, the internal Do loop causes the program to pause for one second each time through the external loop.

When you save and run the application, click the Button control. You will see the ProgressBar control's bar expand to fill the control's area over the course of about 10 seconds.

SCROLLBARS

Windows users are familiar with the concept of scrollbars, which provide a graphical way to perform tasks such as controlling the current position within a document or making adjustments to the volume of a media clip.

Scrollbars work just like the real-world volume control on your stereo system, which can be set to any point between certain maximum and minimum values. From the programmer's point of view, the Visual Basic scrollbar controls return a numeric value; it is the programmer's responsibility to use this value appropriately in an application.

Visual Basic .NET provides two types of scrollbars for entering numerical data: the HScrollBar (horizontal scrollbar) control and the VScrollBar (vertical scrollbar) control. These two controls are shown in Figure 12.14.

Figure 12.14
The HScrollBar and
VScrollBar controls
can be used to enter
and display a numeric
value graphically.

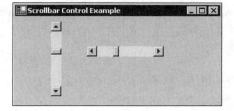

The only difference between the two controls is the orientation of the bar on the form. The following section examines the HScrollBar control, but it applies equally to the VScrollBar control.

SETTING UP THE SCROLLBAR

To use a scrollbar, you simply use properties to set and retrieve the range of acceptable values that the user may enter, as well as the actual current value. The three most important properties, available at both design time and runtime, are as follow:

- `Value`—Retrieves or sets the current numeric value
- `Minimum`—Controls the minimum value of the `Value` property
- `Maximum`—Controls the maximum value of the `Value` property

To use these properties, set the `Minimum` and `Maximum` properties to values representing the range you want and then access the `Value` property to find the result. One typical range is from 0 to 100, where the users would enter a number as a percentage.

> **Note**
>
> The scrollbars can accept Int32 type numbers (32-bit integers), which can be anywhere in the range of -2,147,483,647 to 2,147,483,647. However, valid values for the `Value` property depend on the values of the `Minimum` and `Maximum` properties. Remember this point when you are setting a scrollbar value from code because a value outside the current range causes an error.

PART
III
CH
12

The `Scroll` event of the scrollbar fires whenever the bar is scrolled; the `Scroll` event handler is a good place to put code that utilizes the control's `Value` property. To test a scrollbar, start a new Windows Application project. Place a horizontal scrollbar and a TextBox control on the form. Then enter the following code in the initialization area of the form's `New` procedure:

```
HScroll1.Minimum = 0
HScroll1.Maximum = Me.Width
TextBox1.Left = 0

Private Sub HScroll1_Change()
    TextBox1.Left = HScroll1.Value
End Sub
```

Run the program and set the scrollbar to different values by dragging; clicking; and using the arrow, Home, and End keys. The text box should change positions on the form to match the current setting of the scrollbar.

CONTROLLING THE SIZE OF THE VALUE CHANGES

If you have used ascrollbar in a word processor or other program, you know that clicking the arrow at either end of the bar moves you a short distance, and clicking between an arrow and the position button moves you a larger distance. The scrollbar controls work the same way, and you get to set how much the numbers change with each kind of move. The scrollbar's Value property changes every time you click the scrollbar or drag the position button, as indicated in Figure 12.15.

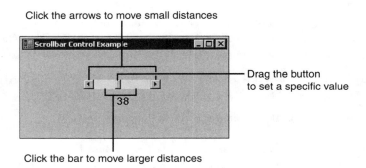

Click the arrows to move small distances

Figure 12.15
Clicking various parts of the scrollbar changes its value by different amounts.

Drag the button to set a specific value

Click the bar to move larger distances

The amount that the Value property increases or decreases when an arrow is clicked is controlled by the SmallChange property (unless such a change would exceed the bounds of the Minimum and Maximum properties). This property gives you very fine control over the numbers being entered. Its default value is 1, which is probably a good number to use for most purposes.

When you click between the arrow and the position button, the Value property can change by a larger amount than if you click an arrow. The amount of this change is set by the LargeChange property. The default setting of the LargeChange property is 10. The setting you use depends on your application.

Tip

A good rule of thumb is to set the LargeChange property to a number about 5%–10% of the total range (for example, a value of 50 for a 0–1000 range).

DISPLAYING THE SCROLLBAR'S POSITION NUMERICALLY

Although the visual representation provided by a scrollbar is nice, users cannot tell what the range is or the exact numeric value. Sometimes you may need to write code to provide more detailed feedback. For example, suppose you are using a scrollbar to select a fiscal year for a report. The scrollbar's Maximum property can be set to the current fiscal year, and its Minimum property can be set to the earliest year for which data exists. As users move the scrollbar, you can display the value they are scrolling through and then, when they release the mouse, invoke the code that actually generates the report.

Code such as the following, placed in a scrollbar's Scroll event handler, will display the current contents of the Value property in a Label control's Text property:

```
Label1.Text = HScrollBar1.Value
```

Tip

Be sure to display an initial value in the Label control, either by setting its Text property at design time or by using code in the form's New procedure at runtime.

FROM HERE...

This chapter has introduced you to more of the great variety of controls that are available to use in your applications. The following chapters contain more information about other controls that you may find useful:

- Chapter 13, "Using Dialog Boxes," teaches you about techniques for displaying dialog boxes to ask the user for information, including the DialogBox controls that are built into Visual Basic .NET.

- To learn more about controls that help enhance your applications' user interfaces, see Chapter 14, "Designing an Effective User Interface."

- To learn about creating your own customized controls, see Chapter 16, "Creating Your Own Windows Controls."

PART

III

CH

12

CHAPTER 13

USING DIALOG BOXES

In this chapter

A dialog box is a window used to display and/or accept information. Its name comes from the fact that it is, in essence, a *dialog* (or conversation) with the user. A dialog box is usually shown *modally*, which means the user must close it (or "answer the dialog") before continuing with any other part of the program. Visual Basic .NET makes it easier than ever to use dialog boxes in your applications.

In this chapter, you'll look at two dialog boxes built in to Visual Basic .NET: the message box and the input box. Next, you'll learn about several Dialog controls that are provided through the CommonDialog class, which allow you to use different predefined types of standard Windows dialog boxes in your program. Finally, you'll review some guidelines for creating your own customized dialog box by developing a standard Windows form.

As we work through this chapter, we will build a sample project that demonstrates the use of various dialog boxes.

Note   You can download the complete sample project from this book's Web site at www.quepublishing.com. Look for the file named DialogBoxes.ZIP.

Before we get into the details of dialog boxes, go ahead and set up the sample project that we will be using to demonstrate dialog box capabilities throughout this chapter. Perform the following steps:

1. Start a new Windows Application project. Name it DialogBoxes.
2. Click Form1.vb in the Solution Explorer, then change its File Name property in the Properties window to frmDialogBoxes.vb.
3. Click the blank design area of Form1.vb to select it, then change its Name property in the Properties window to frmDialogBoxes.
4. Right-click the DialogBoxes project in the Solution Explorer, then choose Properties from the pop-up menu. In the DialogBoxes Properties Pages dialog box, drop down the Startup object list and make sure frmDialogBoxes is selected as the project's Startup Object, then click OK to close the dialog box.
5. Change the form's Text property to Dialog Box Demo.

Save your work so far as we go on to begin our discussion of dialog boxes.

USING MESSAGE BOXES TO KEEP THE USER INFORMED

A big part of any programming project is providing information to your users about the program's progress and status. Although the forms and controls of your program provide the main interface to the users, they are not necessarily the best vehicles for providing bits of information that require immediate attention, such as warnings or error messages. For providing this type of information, a message box is often the best means of communication.

UNDERSTANDING THE MESSAGE BOX

A *message box* is a simple form that displays a message and at least one command button to the user. The button is used to acknowledge the message and close the form. Because message boxes are built in to the .NET framework, you do not have to worry about creating or showing a form for this purpose.

Although message boxes are quite useful, they do have a few limitations:

- The message box cannot accept text input from the user. It can only display information and handle the selection of a limited number of choices.

- You can use only one of a set of predefined icons and one of several predefined button sets in the message box. You cannot define your own icons or buttons.

- By design, the message box requires a user to respond to a message before any part of the program can continue. This means that the message box cannot be used to provide continuous status monitoring of the program because no other part of the program can be executing while the message box is waiting for the user's response.

A SIMPLE MESSAGE BOX

To use a message box, you call the Show method of the MessageBox class and supply at least one argument. The first argument, *text*, specifies the message that you want to show to the user. To see an example of the simplest form of a message box, follow these steps:

1. Add a Button control to the top left of your sample application's main form. Set its Name property to cmdMsgBox1 and set its Text property to Simple MessageBox.

2. Add the following line of code to the Click event handler for the cmdMsgBox1 button:
   ```
   MessageBox.Show("You clicked me!")
   ```

3. Save and run your sample program. When you click the button you will see a simple message box displayed, as shown in Figure 13.1.

Figure 13.1
A simple message box can be displayed with one line of code.

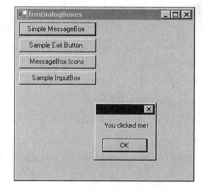

PART

III

CH

13

4. Click OK to close the dialog box, then close the form to end the program.

Note that the message box displays the string that we supplied as the Show method's first (and only) argument.

Note

If the text that you want to display in the message box is long, line breaks will be inserted automatically. You can control where the line breaks will appear by including a carriage return/line feed combination (using the predefined constant vbCrLf) at the appropriate point(s) in your text, as follows:

```
MessageBox.Show("Copyright 2001" & vbCrLf & "Mike Watson
➥Enterprises")
```

ADDING A TITLE

You may have noticed that the title bar of the message box was empty. If you like, you can enhance the message box's Show method to include a caption in the title bar. As you saw in the first example, the *text* argument of the Show method is the actual message to be displayed in the message box. The (optional) second argument, *caption*, is used to specify the caption that will appear in the title bar. To see how this works, modify the Click event handler for cmdMsgBox1 to look like the following:

```
MessageBox.Show("You clicked me!", "My First Message Box")
```

Test the simple message box again, and notice the caption that appears in its title bar, as illustrated in Figure 13.2.

Figure 13.2
You can add a title to your message box by supplying a second argument.

USING MULTIPLE BUTTONS FOR TWO-WAY COMMUNICATION

The simple message box that you have seen so far works well for one-way communication to the user. With a couple of simple changes, you can enhance the message box to allow the user to return information to your program once he has read the message. A classic example of this technique would be asking the user to confirm an action he has requested, such as deleting information or exiting the program.

To use a message box for two-way communication, you need to do two extra things—instruct the message box to display multiple buttons, and capture the value generated by the message box. These techniques are discussed next, then you will incorporate them into an example.

SHOWING MULTIPLE BUTTONS

To cause the message box to display multiple buttons from which the user may choose, you need to use a member of the MessageBoxButtons enumeration as the *buttons* (third) argument of the Show method. You have several choices, as follows:

- **OK.** Displays a single button with the caption OK. This button simply directs the user to acknowledge receipt of the message before continuing.
- **OK, Cancel.** Displays two buttons in the message box, letting the user choose between accepting the message and requesting a cancellation of the operation.
- **Abort, Retry, Ignore.** Displays three buttons, usually along with an error message. The user can choose to abort the operation, retry it, or ignore the error and attempt to continue with program execution.
- **Yes, No, Cancel.** Displays three buttons, typically with a question. The user can answer yes or no to the question, or choose to cancel the operation.
- **Yes, No.** Displays two buttons for a simple yes or no choice.
- **Retry, Cancel.** Displays the two buttons that allow the user to retry the operation or cancel it. A typical use is reporting that the printer is not responding. The user can either retry after fixing the printer or cancel the printout.

You can indicate your choice of button configuration by using one of the following members of the MessageBoxButtons enumeration as the Buttons argument: OK, OKCancel, AbortRetryIgnore, YesNoCancel, YesNo, or RetryCancel.

CAPTURING THE VALUE

Much like a normal function, the MessageBox class returns a value indicating which button the user clicked to close the box. Typically, you will use a variable to store this value; your program can then examine the contents of the variable when processing continues. Visual Basic .NET provides a DialogResult enumeration that contains the possible return values, as follows:

DialogResult **Member**	**Button Clicked**
Abort	The user clicked the Abort button.
Cancel	The user clicked the Cancel button.
Ignore	The user clicked the Ignore button.
No	The user clicked the No button.
OK	The user clicked the OK button.
Retry	The user clicked the Retry button.
Yes	The user clicked the Yes button.

ADDING A TWO-WAY BUTTON TO THE SAMPLE PROGRAM

To add a button demonstrating two-way communication to our project, let's create a button that emulates a typical command to end a program. Follow these steps:

1. Add a second Button control just below the first button on the sample project's frmDialogBoxes.

2. Set the second button's Name property to cmdMsgBox2, and set its Text property to Sample Exit Button.

3. Place the following code in cmdMsgBox2's Click event handler:

```
Dim nTemp As Integer
Dim sMsg As String
sMsg = "Are you sure you want to exit the program?"
nTemp = MessageBox.Show(sMsg, "Confirm Exit", MessageBoxButtons.YesNo)
If nTemp = DialogResult.Yes Then
    Application.Exit()
End If
```

This code uses an Integer variable named nTemp to store the value generated by the message box's Show method when the user clicks a button. It also uses the YesNo member of the MessageBoxButtons enumeration to cause Yes and No buttons to appear in the message box. After the user has closed the dialog box, the code compares the value of nTemp to the Yes member of the DialogResult enumeration. If it matches, then the user has clicked the Yes button to close the dialog box, and the code ends the application.

After adding this code, save and run the program. Click the Sample Exit button, and you will see a dialog box with Yes and No buttons, as shown in Figure 13.3.

Figure 13.3
A message box can include multiple buttons to allow the user to make a choice.

Note

This example also illustrates the use of a String variable (sMsg) to contain the message displayed by the message box. The previous example used a literal string; either is acceptable.

ADDING AN ICON

The message boxes you have seen so far have included a message and a button. You can use the third argument, *icon*, of the Show method to add an icon to your message box. There are eight icons available for you to choose from; the MessageBoxIcon enumeration is provided to assist you in specifying which one you want.

You should choose an icon that helps communicate the situation being reported by the message box. Table 13.1 lists the members of the MessageBoxIcon enumeration and typical uses:

TABLE 13.1   ICONS INDICATE THE TYPE OF MESSAGE BEING SHOWN

Icon	MessageBoxIcon Member	Typical Purpose
 (i)	Asterisk	Informs the user of the status of the program. This message is often used to notify the users of the completion of a task.
 (X)	Error	Indicates that a severe error has occurred. Often a program is shut down after this message.
 (!)	Exclamation	Indicates that a program error has occurred; this error may require user correction or may lead to undesirable results.
 (X)	Hand	Same as the Error icon.
 (i)	Information	Same as the Asterisk icon.
	None	No icon is displayed.
 (?)	Question	Indicates that the program requires additional information from the user before processing can continue.
 (X)	Stop	Same as the Error icon.
 (!)	Warning	Same as the Exclamation icon.

To test the icons, add a third Button control named cmdMsgBox3 to your test program. Set its Text property to MessageBox Icons. Add the following line of code to its Click event handler:

```
MessageBox.Show("I see an icon!", "Icon Test", _
    MessageBoxButtons.OK, MessageBoxIcon.Asterisk)
```

When you run the program and click the MessageBox Icons button, you will see a message box with an Information icon, as illustrated in Figure 13.4.

Figure 13.4
You can add icons to enhance the appearance of your message boxes.

Experiment with different values from the MessageBoxIcon enumeration for the *icon* argument so you can see what the different icons look like.

Note

The possible values for the *icon* argument not only affect the icon that is displayed, but also the sound produced by Windows when a message appears. Your user can set sounds for different message types in the Windows Control Panel.

SETTING THE DEFAULT BUTTON

If you are using more than one button in the message box, you can specify which button is the default. The *default button* is the one that has focus when the message box is displayed. This button is the one that the user is most likely to choose so that he or she can just press the Enter key to select it. For example, if you display a message box to have the user confirm the deletion of a record from a database, you probably should set up the default button so that the No button is the default; therefore, the record would not be deleted if the user just presses Enter. This way, the user must make a conscious choice to delete the record.

To specify which button is the default, you need to specify the fourth argument, *defaultButton*, for the Show argument. The MessageBoxDefaultButton enumeration supplies three values that correspond to the three possible buttons that may be displayed, as follows:

MessageBoxDefaultButton **Member**	**Default Button**
Button1	The first button
Button2	The second button
Button3	The third button

Try experimenting with the *defaultButton* argument on your own.

Note

The MessageBox.Show method supports one more argument, MessageBoxOptions, which allows you to specify some special-purpose functionality of the message box. See the "MessageBoxOptions enumeration" topic in the Help system for more information.

USING INPUT BOXES TO GET INFORMATION FROM THE USER

Many times in a program, you need to get a single piece of information from the user. You might need the user to enter a name, the name of a file, or a number for various purposes. Although the message box lets your user make choices, it does not allow him to enter any information in response to the message. Therefore, you have to use some other means to get the information. Visual Basic provides a built-in dialog box for exactly this purpose: the *input box*.

The input box displays a prompt to tell the user what to enter, a text box where the user can enter the requested information, and two command buttons—OK and Cancel—that can be used to either accept or abort the input data. A typical input box in use is shown in Figure 13.5.

Figure 13.5
An input box lets the user enter a single piece of information in response to a prompt.

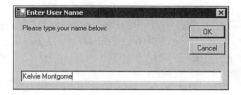

SETTING UP THE InputBox FUNCTION

Programmatically, a call to the InputBox function works much like calling the MessageBox class and utilizing its return value. You can specify a variable to receive the information returned from the input box and then supply the input box's message (prompt) and, optionally, a title and default value.

To see the InputBox in action, perform these steps:

1. Add another Button control on the sample project's frmDialogBoxes.

2. Set this button's Name property to cmdInputBox, and set its Text property to Sample InputBox.

3. Place the following code in cmdInputBox's Click event handler:

```
Dim sMsg As String, sUserName As String
sMsg = "Please type your name below:"
sUserName = InputBox(sMsg, "Enter User Name", "Anonymous")
MessageBox.Show("Hi, " & sUserName & "!")
```

Save and run the sample project, then click the Sample InputBox button. Figure 13.6 shows the input box as initially presented, including the default value in the input area.

Figure 13.6
The InputBox function allows the user to enter information.

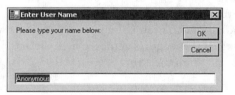

You can see that the user is presented with the prompt that you specified, and he is given a text box in which to type his response. In addition, the text box is populated with the default value (Anonymous).

In this example, the information returned by the InputBox function is stored in the variable sUserName. The first argument, the *Prompt* parameter, represents the message that is displayed to the user to indicate what should be entered in the box. The prompt can display up to approximately 1,024 characters before it is truncated. As with the message box, word wrapping is performed automatically on the text in the prompt so that it fits inside the box. You can insert a carriage return/line feed combination (represented by the predefined constant vbCrLf) to force the prompt to show multiple lines or to separate lines for emphasis.

PART
III

CH
13

After the prompt comes the `Title` argument, which specifies the text in the input box's title bar. The other argument in the preceding example is the `Default` argument. If included, it appears as an initial value in the input box. The user can accept this value, modify it, or erase it and enter a completely new value.

The minimum requirement for the `InputBox` function is simply a prompt parameter, as in this statement:

```
sReturnVal = InputBox("How's the weather?")
```

In addition to the input box's optional parameters to specify a window title and default value, other optional parameters allow you to set its initial screen position. Refer to the complete syntax of the `InputBox` function in Visual Basic's help system.

Note

Unlike the `MsgBox` function, no option in the `InputBox` function specifies any command buttons other than the defaults of OK and Cancel.

VALUES RETURNED BY `InputBox`

When the input box is used, the user can enter text in the input box's entry area, which resembles a text box. If the user types more text than will fit in the displayed entry area, the text he or she has already typed scrolls to the left. After the user is done, he or she can choose the OK or Cancel button. If the user chooses the OK button, the input box returns whatever is in the text box, whether it is new text or the default text. If the user chooses the Cancel button, the input box returns an empty string, regardless of what is in the text box.

To be able to use the information entered by the user, you must determine whether the data meets your needs. First, you probably should make sure that the user actually entered some information and chose the OK button. You can do so by using the `Len` function to determine the length of the returned string. If the length is zero, the user clicked the Cancel button or left the input field blank. If the length of the string is greater than zero, you know that the user entered something.

You might also need to check the returned value to make sure it is of the proper type. If you are expecting a number that will subsequently be compared to another number in an `If` statement, your program should present an error message if the user enters letters. To make sure that you have a numerical value with which to work, you can use the `IsNumeric` function. The `IsNumeric` function's purpose is to indicate whether an expression can be evaluated as a number. If the entire expression is recognized as a number, the function returns `True`; otherwise, it returns `False`.

The following code illustrates additional processing of the returned value of an input box with `IsNumeric` and `Len`:

```
Dim sInputVal As String
sInputVal = InputBox("Enter your age")
If Len(sInputVal) = 0 Then
    MessageBox.Show("No age was entered")
```

```
Else
   If IsNumeric(stInputVal) = 0 Then
      MessageBox.Show("Congratulations for surviving this long!")
   Else
      MessageBox.Show("You entered an invalid age.")
   End If
End If
```

USING THE DIALOG CONTROLS

In earlier sections, you learned what a dialog box is and how to use two simple dialog boxes. Visual Basic .NET provides a series of Dialog controls that let your applications leverage the dialog box functionality built in to Windows. One of the goals of Windows-based programming is to make your applications easy to learn and use. By utilizing the Dialog controls, your users will be able to invoke some of your programs' functionality by using dialog boxes with which they are already familiar.

Although the ease of setup of the Dialog controls is a great benefit, an even bigger bonus is that the resulting dialog boxes are already familiar to the user because they are the same dialog boxes used by Windows itself.

The Dialog controls are exposed through the CommonDialog class, which is used for displaying dialog boxes on the screen. As you will learn in this section, each Dialog control performs a specialized function.

THE FileDialog CONTROLS

The CommonDialog class provides a FileDialog class that, in turn, provides two dialog controls—the OpenFileDialog control and the SaveFileDialog control—that allow your program's users to specify the name and location a file to be opened or saved, respectively. The techniques involved in using these two controls are quite similar.

The OpenFileDialog control and the SaveFileDialog control share the common properties presented in Table 13.2.

TABLE 13.2 COMMON OpenFileDialog CONTROL PROPERTIES

Property	Description
AddExtension	When set to True (the default), the dialog box will automatically add a filename extension if the user types a filename without an extension. The extension added depends upon several factors. If the CheckFileExists property is False (its default), the first extension from the filter specified by the Filter property is used. If, however, CheckFileExists is True, the dialog box will add the first extension from the Filter property that matches an existing file. In either case, if the Filter property is empty, the value of the DefaultExt property is used.
CheckFileExists	When set to True (the default), if the user types the name of a file that does not exist, he is given a warning and the dialog box remains active. When set to False, the user may enter the name of a file that does not exist.

TABLE 13.2   CONTINUED

Property	Description
CheckPathExists	Much like `CheckFileExists`, the default value of `True` causes the dialog box to verify that the path entered by the user is valid. If the user enters a path that does not exist, he is given a warning and the dialog box remains active. When set to `False`, the user may enter the name of a file that does not exist.
DefaultExt	Specifies the default filename extension, which is added to the filename entered by the user if he does not supply an extension.
DereferenceLinks	If the user specifies a shortcut (link) in the dialog box, the `DereferenceLinks` property determines whether the dialog box returns the location and filename of the target of the link, or of the link (`.lnk` file). The default setting of `True` causes the filename and path of the link's target to be returned; a setting of `False` causes the filename and path of the link itself to be returned.
FileName	The full path and filename of the file selected by the user to be opened or saved.
Filter	A String that specifies how the files displayed in the dialog box are filtered. Consists of a series of pairs of filter descriptions and actual filters separated by vertical bar (I) characters. Use of the `Filter` property is discussed in detail a little later in this section.
FilterIndex	Specifies which of the filters provided in the `Filter` property is to be the one displayed first (that is, if the user has not yet dropped down the box containing the possible filters).
InitialDirectory	Specifies the folder displayed when the dialog box is first invoked.
RestoreDirectory	When set to `True`, when the dialog box closes, the current directory is restored to whatever it was before the dialog box was shown. The default value is `False`.
ShowHelp	When set to `True`, a Help button is displayed in the dialog box. You can write code for the dialog box's `HelpRequested` event, which occurs when the user clicks the Help button. The default value is `False`.
Title	Specifies the text to be displayed in the dialog box's Title bar. If nothing is specified for the `Title` property, it defaults to Open for the `OpenFileDialog` control, and Save As for the `SaveFileDialog` control.

The two dialog controls exposed by the `FileDialog` class are discussed in the remainder of this section.

Note

The Open and Save dialog boxes don't actually open or save files; they simply get information from the user as to the names and locations of the files to be opened or saved. Your program must take whatever steps are necessary to complete the operation.

SETTING UP AN OpenFileDialog CONTROL

Let's demonstrate how the FileDialog controls work by adding to this chapter's sample application. First, let's add an OpenFileDialog control:

1. With the sample program's main form displayed, open up the Toolbox and scroll down to the OpenFileDialog control. Double-click this control's tool in the Toolbox to add an instance to frmDialogBoxes.

2. When the Toolbox disappears, you will see something you may not have expected. Instead of the OpenFileDialog control being drawn on frmDialogBoxes, it was actually drawn *below* the form's design area. This area of the Designer window, known as the *tray*, is provided for controls that will not be visible to the user at runtime; therefore, there is no need to display them directly on the form.

3. Add another Button control on the sample project's frmDialogBoxes. Name this button cmdOpenFileDialog and set its Text property to Open File Dialog.

4. Add the following code to cmdOpenFileDialog's Click event handler:

```
Dim sMsg As String
OpenFileDialog1.ShowDialog()
If OpenFileDialog1.FileName > "" Then
    sMsg = "The filename you chose was " & OpenFileDialog1.FileName
Else
    sMsg = "You did not choose a file."
End If
MessageBox.Show(sMsg)
```

Save and run the program, then click the button labeled Open File Dialog. You will be presented with a standard Windows file dialog box, as depicted in Figure 13.7. If you select a file and click Open, a message box shows you the name of the file you selected; if, however, you click the Cancel button or do not select a file before clicking Open, you are told that you did not select a file.

Figure 13.7
The OpenFileDialog control displays a standard Windows dialog box.

This code works by calling the ShowDialog method of the OpenFileDialog control, which displays the dialog box to the user and pauses execution of the program until the user closes the dialog box. The user browses until he finds the file he is looking for, then clicks the Open button; execution of the program then continues. We examine the FileName property of the OpenFileDialog control to determine whether the user picked a file or not; an appropriate message is constructed and displayed in a message box. Notice that the FileName property provides a fully qualified path and filename combination so you know exactly where the file resides.

SETTING UP A SaveFileDialog CONTROL

Using the same techniques you used in the previous section, add a SaveFileDialog control and a button to test it. Name the button cmdSaveFileDialog, and set its Text property to Save File Dialog. Use the following code for cmdSaveFileDialog's Click event handler (you can copy the code from cmdOpenFileDialog and make slight modifications to save some typing):

```
Dim sMsg As String
SaveFileDialog1.ShowDialog()
If SaveFileDialog1.FileName > "" Then
    sMsg = "The filename you chose was " & SaveFileDialog1.FileName
Else
    sMsg = "You did not choose a file."
End If
MessageBox.Show(sMsg)
```

When you run the sample application and click the Save File Dialog button, you are presented with a standard Save As dialog box (shown in Figure 13.8), which is virtually identical to the Open dialog box you saw earlier.

Figure 13.8
The dialog box displayed by the SaveFileDialog control is familiar to your users.

PROCESSING A FileDialogBox'S RETURN VALUE

When you use either an OpenFileDialog control or a SaveFileDialog control, your ultimate goal is to get the name and location of the file that the user wants to open or save. As you have seen, that information is contained in the control's FileName property. It should be noted that the dialog box does nothing more than get a filename from the user and provide that filename to your program. It does not actually open or save a file. The responsibility for that task lies with your program code, based upon the type of file you are working with, what you intend for your program to do with it, and so on.

SPECIFYING FILE TYPES WITH THE Filter PROPERTY

You may have noticed when you tested the FileDialog controls that all files in the current folder were listed. When using the FileDialog controls, you will probably want to specify that only certain file types are listed. If your program reads Microsoft Excel (.XLS) files, for example, you would not want the user to attempt to open batch (.BAT) files. You can restrict (or "filter") the files shown in the dialog box by using the Filter property.

You set the Filter property at design time in the Properties window, or at runtime with an assignment statement in code. The Filter property is a string value that includes a file type description followed by the file extension. It requires a special format, as shown here:

```
cldTest.Filter = "Word Documents (*.doc)|*.doc"
```

The vertical line in the preceding code is known as the *pipe symbol*, and is usually found on a standard keyboard by shifting the Backslash key. This symbol must be present in the filter. Preceding the pipe symbol is a short description of the file type, in this case Word Documents (*.doc). Following the pipe symbol is the actual filter for the files. You typically express the filter as an asterisk followed by a period and the extension of the files that you want to display. Some examples are *.txt, *.doc, and *.*.

If you specify the Filter property with an assignment statement, you must enclose the filter in double quotation marks, as with any string. The quotes are omitted if you specify the filter from the Properties dialog box.

You can specify multiple description|filter pairs within the Filter property. Each pair must be separated from the other pairs by an intermediate pipe symbol, as shown in the following example:

```
controlname.Filter = "Text Files|*.txt|All Files|*.*"
```

To see the Filter property in action, add the following line of code to the OpenFileDialog_Click event handler, just above the call to the ShowDialog method:

```
OpenFileDialog1.Filter = "Text Files (*.txt)|*.txt|All Files (*.*)|*.*"
```

Save and run the program, then click the Open File Dialog button. Note that the common dialog control's Filter property causes only text files to be displayed (as shown in Figure 13.9), unless the user selects another filter by dropping down the Files of type drop-down list.

Figure 13.9
The Filter property limits the files displayed in the dialog box.

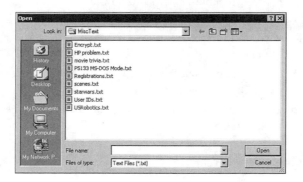

CUSTOMIZING THE FileDialog CONTROLS

You can experiment with the properties presented in Table 13.2 to see how they can customize the FileDialog controls. Here are a few suggestions for you to try:

- Use the InitialDirectory property to control which folder appears when the dialog box is first displayed. By default, the system's current directory is displayed; however, you may want to have the dialog box start up in a specific folder (your application's default data directory, for example).
- The Title property lets you specify the text that appears in the dialog box's title bar.
- The CheckFileExists property is set to True by default; this causes the dialog box to warn the user if he specifies a filenames that does not exist. Try entering nonexistent filenames to see its behavior.

THE FontDialog CONTROL

From time to time, you may want to give your users a way to specify a font to be used for a report, label, and so on. The FontDialog control gives you an easy way to present a Windows-standard font dialog box from which the users may make their selection.

To use a FontDialog control, you simply call its ShowDialog method. After the user makes his selection and clicks OK, the font he chose is stored in the control's Font property. If the user clicks Cancel, then the changes he made to the font displayed in the FontDialog control are discarded.

If you want the FontDialog control to display a specific font on startup, you can set its Font property before calling it. For example, you could use the following line of code to set the FontDialog control's Font property to be the same as the Label control lblTest:

```
FontDialog1.Font = lblTest.Font
```

As with the Save and Open dialog boxes, the Font dialog box doesn't actually change the font. It simply reports—through its Font property—the font that the user has selected.

Let's enhance this chapter's test application to show how the FontDialog control works. Follow these steps:

1. With the sample program's main form displayed, open up the Toolbox and scroll down to the FontDialog control. Double-click its tool in the Toolbox to add an instance to the tray area of frmDialogBoxes.

2. Add another Button control to frmDialogBoxes. Name this button cmdFontDialog and set its Text property to Font Dialog.

3. Add a Label control near the cmdFontDialog button. Set its Name property to lblTest and its Text property to This is sample text.

4. Add the following code to cmdFontDialog's Click event handler:

```
FontDialog1.Font = lblTest.Font
FontDialog1.ShowColor = True
FontDialog1.ShowDialog()
lblTest.Font = FontDialog1.Font
```

This code causes the dialog box's initial font selection to match `lblTest`'s `Font` property. The second line of code specifies that the dialog box should allow the user to choose the font's color as well.

Save and run the test application, then click the Font Dialog button. The Font dialog box appears, as shown in Figure 13.10.

Figure 13.10
The Font dialog box gives your users an easy way to specify a font.

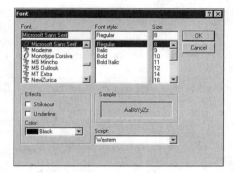

After you select a different font and click OK, the code changes the `Font` property of the Label control to match the font provided via the dialog box. An example of this is depicted in Figure 13.11.

Figure 13.11
The information obtained from the `Font` dialog box can be used to modify the `Font` property of other controls.

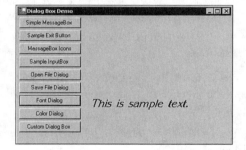

Table 13.3 lists commonly used properties that are specific to the `FontDialog` control.

TABLE 13.3   COMMON `FontDialog` CONTROL PROPERTIES

Property	Description
AllowVectorFonts	The default value of `True` allows vector fonts to be displayed. Setting this property to `False` disallows the display of vector fonts.
AllowVerticalFonts	The default value of `True` causes both horizontally and vertically oriented fonts to be displayed in the dialog box. Setting this property to `False` allows the display of horizontal fonts only.
Color	Specifies the color of the selected font.

TABLE 13.3   CONTINUED

Property	Description
FixedPitchOnly	When set to True, only fixed-pitch fonts are displayed. The default value is False.
FontMustExist	The default value of True does not allow the user to specify a font that does not exist.
MaxSize, MinSize	Specify the maximum and minimum point sizes that a user is allowed to select.
ShowApply	Determines whether an Apply button is shown. The default value is False.
ShowColor	Determines whether a font color selection is available. The default value is False.
ShowHelp	When set to True, a Help button is displayed in the dialog box. You can write code for the dialog box's HelpRequested event, which occurs when the user clicks the Help button. The default value is False.

THE ColorDialog CONTROL

Much like the FontDialog control, the ColorDialog control presents a standard Windows "color picker" dialog box to the user. After he selects a color and clicks OK, the program has access to his chosen color through the control's Color property. The user has the option of choosing one of the standard colors, or creating and selecting a custom color.

Let's get right into an example. Follow these steps to add a ColorDialog control test to our test program:

1. With the sample program's main form displayed, open up the Toolbox and scroll down to the ColorDialog control. Double-click its tool in the Toolbox to add an instance to the tray area of frmDialogBoxes.

2. Add yet another Button control to frmDialogBoxes. Name this button cmdColorDialog and set its Text property to Color Dialog.

3. Add the following code to cmdColorDialog's Click event handler:

```
ColorDialog1.Color = lblTest.BackColor
ColorDialog1.ShowDialog()
lblTest.BackColor = ColorDialog1.Color
```

This code sets the initial value of the ColorDialog control to the background color of lblTest and shows the dialog box. When the user has made his selection and clicked OK, the background color of the lblTest Label control is set to whatever color the user has selected.

Save and run the test application, then click the Color Dialog button. You will see the standard Color dialog box, as shown in Figure 13.12.

Figure 13.12
The user can select a color from the Windows Color dialog box.

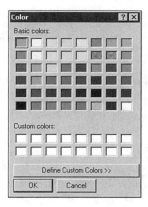

After clicking OK, the background color of the Label control is set to your selection.

Table 13.4 lists commonly used properties that are specific to the `ColorDialog` control.

TABLE 13.4   COMMON ColorDialog CONTROL PROPERTIES

Property	Description
AllowFullOpen	The default value of `True` lets the user define custom colors. Setting this property to `False` disables the Define Custom Colors button.
AnyColor	When set to `True`, the dialog box shows all available basic colors. The default is `False`.
FullOpen	When set to `True`, the custom color controls are visible when the dialog box is first shown. The default value is `False`.
SolidColorOnly	When set to `True`, users can select only solid colors. The default value is `False`.

OTHER CommonDialog CONTROLS

The `CommonDialog` class provides two other dialog boxes—the `PrintDialog` control and the `PageSetupDialog` control. These two controls are discussed in detail in Chapter 23, "Creating and Using Reports."

PART
III

CH
13

CREATING YOUR OWN DIALOG BOXES

Although the `CommonDialog` class provides you with several types of dialog boxes to use in your programs, sometimes you just can't accomplish certain tasks with these built-in tools. For example, if you want to set your own captions for the command buttons in a dialog box, you can't use the message box; nor can the message box handle more than three buttons (not including the Help button). Also, you may need to present a dialog box that asks the user several questions at once. If your program needs dialog box capabilities that the Dialog controls can't offer, you can simply use a standard Windows form to create your own custom dialog box.

VISUAL BASIC'S DIALOG BOX FEATURES

Visual Basic .NET provides several features that make it easy to create custom dialog boxes. They include the following:

- One of the settings for a form's FormBorderStyle property is FixedDialog. This sets up the form so the user cannot resize it.

- You can use a form's ShowDialog method to cause it to be shown as a modal dialog box. The form is shown modally; that is, no code after the call to the ShowDialog method is executed until the dialog box form is closed.

- Forms have a DialogResult property that you can use to report how the user closed (answered) the dialog box. Possible values, provided through the DialogResult enumeration, are OK, Cancel, Abort, Retry, Ignore, Yes, and No. Typically, the Click event handler for each of a dialog box's buttons that can close the box will set the form's DialogResult property; doing so will automatically close the dialog box and return control to the calling form.

- A form that calls a dialog box can examine the dialog box form's DialogResult property to decide how to proceed.

CREATING A CUSTOM DIALOG BOX

The techniques involved in creating a custom dialog box will be easy to demonstrate by adding one to our sample application. We will create a dialog box that will allow the user to change the contents of a variable named sUserName, which will be defined in the main form. Follow these steps:

1. In the Code window for frmDialogBoxes, add the following variable declaration near the top, just below the "Windows Form Designer generated code" designator:

   ```
   Public sUserName As String = "Initial User Name"
   ```

   This creates a String variable named sUserName and sets its initial value to Initial User Name.

2. Choose Project, Add Windows Form from Visual Basic .NET's menu system.

3. In the Add New Item dialog box, make sure the Windows Form template is selected. Enter frmTestDialog.vb as the new form's name and click Open.

4. A new form named frmTestDialog.vb is created and added to the Solution Explorer.

5. If you do not see frmTestDialog's Designer window, right-click its name in the Solution Explorer and choose View Designer from the pop-up menu.

6. Change frmTestDialog's FormBorderStyle property to FixedDialog.

7. Change frmTestDialog's Text property to Custom Dialog Box.

8. Set the form's ControlBox, MaximizeBox, and MinimizeBox properties to False.

9. Add a Label control to the form; set its Text property to New User Name: and set its TextAlign property to MiddleRight.

10. Add a TextBox control to the right of the Label control. Set its `Name` property to `txtUserName` and clear its `Text` property.

11. Add a Button control to the form. Set its `Name` property to `cmdOK` and set its `Text` property to `OK`.

12. Add a second Button control to the form. Set its `Name` property to `cmdCancel` and set its `Text` property to `Cancel`.

13. Set the form's `AcceptButton` property to `cmdOK`. This specifies that if the user presses Enter to close the dialog box, `cmdOK`'s `Click` event handler should be invoked.

14. Set the form's `CancelButton` property to `cmdCancel`. This specifies that if the user presses Esc to close the dialog box, `cmdCancel`'s `Click` event handler should be invoked.

15. Add the following code to `cmdOK`'s `Click` event handler:

    ```
    Me.DialogResult = DialogResult.OK
    ```

    If the user clicks the OK button, this code sets the form's `DialogResult` property to `OK`, and causes the dialog box to close.

16. Add the following code to `cmdCancel`'s `Click` event handler:

    ```
    Me.DialogResult = DialogResult.Cancel
    ```

    If the user clicks the Cancel button, this code sets the form's `DialogResult` property to `Cancel`, and causes the dialog box to close.

17. Open the Designer window for the main form, `frmDialogBoxes`.

18. Add a final Button control to `frmDialogBoxes`. Set its Name property to `cmdCustomDialog` and its Text property to Custom Dialog Box.

19. Add the following code to `cmdCustomDialog`'s `Click` event handler:

    ```
    Dim ThisDlg As New frmTestDialog()
    Dim sMsg As String
    ThisDlg.ShowDialog()
    If ThisDlg.DialogResult = DialogResult.OK Then
        sUserName = ThisDlg.txtUserName.Text
    End If
    sMsg = "The current user name is " & sUserName & "."
    MessageBox.Show(sMsg)
    ```

    This code begins by declaring a variable (`ThisDlg`) to hold an instance of `frmTestDialog`. After invoking the `ShowDialog` method of `ThisDlg`, control will be paused until the user closes the dialog box represented by `ThisDlg`. After he has done so, the code in this procedure continues to check the value of the `DialogResult` property of `ThisDlg` (which was set when the user clicked one of the two buttons). If `DialogResult` is `OK`, then the new user name value entered in the dialog box is used to replace the form-level `sUserName` variable. In any event, the current contents of `sUserName` are shown via a message box so you can see when it was updated.

Save and run your project, then click the Custom Dialog Box button. Click the dialog box's Cancel button and see that `sUserName` still has its initial value. Try going back to the custom dialog box and entering a new name, then clicking OK. `sUserName` is updated with the new name. Experiment with the dialog box to see its behavior.

FROM HERE . . .

In this chapter, you learned how dialog boxes can be used to help the user select files, colors, and fonts in your programs. You also learned how the message box and input box are used to inform the user and to get decisions or single pieces of information. You even saw how to design your own dialog boxes when the built-in ones are insufficient for the task. To learn more about using some of the concepts presented here, take a look at the following chapters:

- To learn more about designing the forms you use in your applications, see Chapter 10, "Understanding Windows Forms."

- For an introduction to writing the code that enables your forms to react to your users' actions, see Chapter 7, "Controlling the Flow of Your Program."

- For a more complete discussion of writing Visual Basic code, see Chapter 8, "Managing Program Tasks with Procedures."

- To see how to use the built-in printer-related dialog boxes, see Chapter 23, "Creating and Using Reports."

CHAPTER 14

DESIGNING AN EFFECTIVE USER INTERFACE

In this chapter

In this chapter, you will learn about the part of the program that everyone sees: the user interface. Some programmers are inclined to leave user interface design as an afterthought, thinking the code is the real "guts" of an application and therefore deserves the most attention. However, user suggestions about fonts, screens, and speed of execution should be taken very seriously. Your users cannot see the code, but the user interface (good or bad) is always right in front of them. Windows offers many opportunities to build an interface that will help get the job done easier. This chapter describes a series of guidelines and examples that will help you make the most of these opportunities; we then discuss some of the elements that you can use to give your programs a professional appearance.

DESIGNING EFFECTIVE FORMS

Forms are the building blocks of your user interface. Although the process of designing a form in Visual Basic is simple, doing it *well* is not very easy. Good form design involves more than just adding controls and writing code. To make a well-designed form, you should understand the form's purpose, how it is going to be used, when it is going to be used, and its relationship with the rest of the program. In addition, within your application, you may have several forms, each of which must be displayed when appropriate. Some users take advantage of the multitasking freedom offered by Windows, whereas others tend to use only one application at a time. Keep this point in mind when you're designing a user interface (UI): You must manage the flexibility that Windows and the .NET framework offer to the programmer so that users with any skill level can effectively use your applications.

KEEP FORMS NEAT AND UNCLUTTERED

The more controls you have on a form, the more important it is to keep them organized. Consider the form shown in Figure 14.1. It looks as though the controls have been placed on the form haphazardly. They are not labeled, lined up, or sized consistently. A better approach is shown in Figure 14.2. Notice that frames, lines, and labels have been added to group related controls. Both illustrations show "working" applications, but the second form has a more visually pleasing appearance, which makes it easier to use.

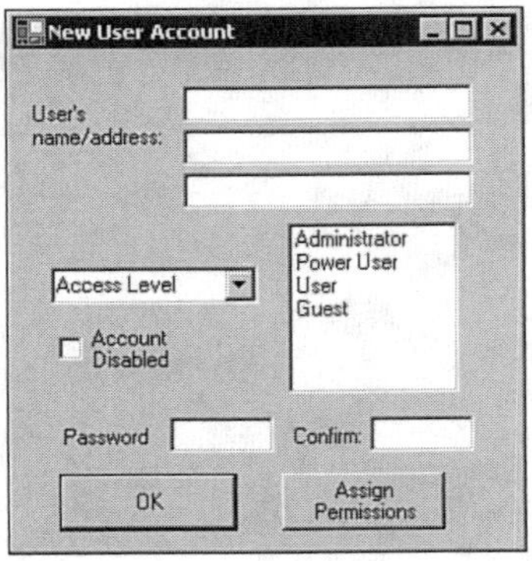

Figure 14.1
A messy form can prevent users from finding the information they need.

Figure 14.2
In a much better design than the form shown in Figure 14.1, frames and labels are used to organize the form.

Visual Basic provides several excellent controls to help you organize a form. One of these controls is the TabControl control, shown in Figure 14.3, which can be used to segregate controls so that only a few of them are displayed at any given time. This way, you can hide infrequently used options from the average users while still making them available if necessary.

Figure 14.3
Use the TabControl control to keep your form a reasonable size.

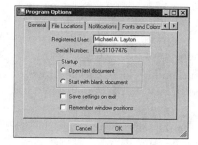

To keep from going overboard with too many controls on a form, you should always keep the form's purpose in mind. Consider the form in Figure 14.3. Everything on the form could fall under the general realm of "Program Options," but each separate category of options is in a different section of the TabControl control. If you do find that you need a separate form, make sure logic dictates which controls you put on it.

In addition, make sure to set the appropriate form properties so that the form acts according to its intended purpose. For example, a form that acts as a dialog box should not have a sizeable border or show up in the Windows taskbar. Dialog boxes are discussed in Chapter 13, "Using Dialog Boxes."

→ For more information on the standard customizable features of dialogs, **see** "Creating Your Own Dialog Boxes," **p. 335**

PART

III

CH

14

PAY SPECIAL ATTENTION TO DATA ENTRY FORMS

Data entry forms are a special breed. They should allow users to work at their own pace, not the programmer's. Common sense is the main rule here: If users have to enter thousands of records into your database, they don't want to answer a yes/no confirmation dialog box for each record.

The preceding section emphasized separating and hiding certain controls. However, a data entry form should maximize the use of form space because showing and hiding forms slows down the process. Speed and ease of use should definitely be among your main goals when designing a data entry form. To make the data entry process faster, follow these guidelines:

- Always provide keyboard shortcuts; never require the use of a mouse. (This is good advice for all forms in your program, not just data entry forms.)

- Keep the layout consistent with the order of the users' tasks. In other words, don't make them jump from one section to another unnecessarily to enter information. If the users are entering information from a paper-based form, the flow of information on your program's interface should match the flow of the paper form as closely as possible.

- Do not require the users to perform unnecessary work. In other words, if fields 2 through 10 require a value only if field 1 has a value, you don't need to make the users always tab through every field. On the other hand, don't make the behavior of your forms too field-dependent; if a form works differently for every possible combination of required fields, you may actually slow down the user.

- Use noticeable but unobtrusive visual and/or audio cues to provide feedback to the users. The way the Visual Basic .NET code editor capitalizes correctly spelled variables and constants is a good example of a visual cue.

- If possible, perform adds and edits on the same form so that the users do not have to learn multiple methods of accessing the same data.

An example of a well-designed data entry form is shown in Figure 14.4. Notice that the form's status bar shows an explanation of each field as it is entered.

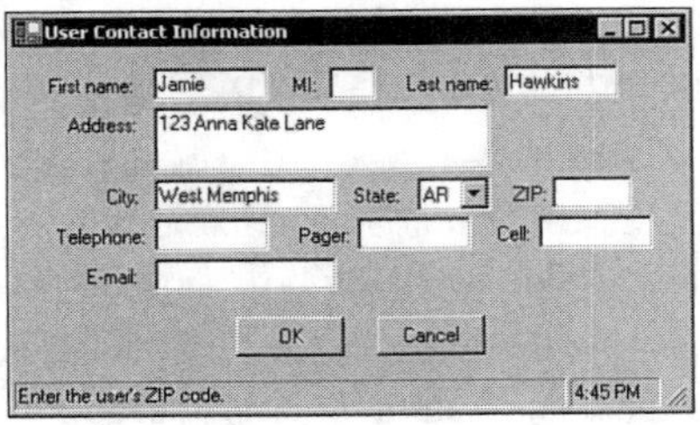

Figure 14.4
In a data entry form, ease of use is of prime importance.

USE THE RIGHT CONTROL FOR THE JOB

Visual Basic provides a number of controls that can be placed on a form. However, keep in mind that some controls work better in certain situations than others. The purpose of the form should help guide you in choosing the appropriate controls. For example, both the `ListBox` and `ComboBox` controls can be used to select from a list of choices. However, the combo box allows you to save form real estate by hiding the list of choices, as illustrated in Figure 14.5.

Figure 14.5
The amount of space available on a form may influence your choice of custom controls.

In Figure 14.5, list boxes could have just as easily been used for the selection criteria. However, using a combo box is more appropriate because it saves space while still accomplishing the intended task.

→ To learn more details for creating a combo box, **see** "The ComboBox Control," **p. 305**

THIRD-PARTY CONTROLS

Third-party controls are useful; however, you should not use them unless doing so is really necessary. Picking a control included with Visual Studio .NET over a third-party control offers several advantages:

- The chances are better that the control will be supported in future versions of Visual Studio.
- Distributing the control to users is easier.
- Many "native" Visual Studio controls provide the users an interface with which they are already familiar.

MULTIPLE FORMS

If your user interface will contain multiple forms, a major decision you have to make is whether to use a single-document interface (SDI) or a multiple-document interface (MDI). Multiple-form programs, discussed in Chapter 15, "Multiple Document Interface Applications," handle multiple forms by enclosing them visually within a "parent" window.

→ To create an app that lets users manage multiple windows, **see** "Overview of MDI Applications," **p. 384**

Forms in an SDI application appear as totally independent windows. Whether you use SDI or MDI, user interaction with forms initiates many program actions through form and control events. If you have multiple forms, you need to code the program so that the users are not allowed to disrupt the intended program flow—for example, show a data form that has not been populated yet.

Figure 14.6 shows an example of what can happen if you do not sufficiently control your user's ability to open windows at will.

Figure 14.6
It is important to control how and when your users may open multiple windows.

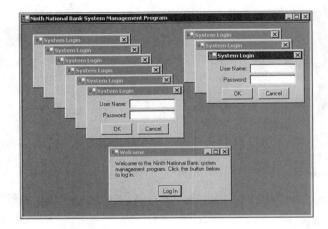

USER PC DIFFERENCES

From a user interface standpoint, extra thought is required when you're writing a program that is designed to run on a PC other than your own. The Windows operating system leaves a lot of room for user customization. One of the most noticeable differences is screen resolution. If you go into the Display applet in Control Panel, you will notice that several options for screen size are available. As a developer and owner of a 21-inch monitor, I like to leave my resolution set to 1,280×1,024 pixels, which allows me to place a lot of things on the screen at once. However, most of your end users are likely to be operating at a lower resolution, say 800×600 or even 640×480. The easiest solution to this problem is to design your forms for a minimum 800×600 resolution. Users at that resolution will see your application fill up the whole screen, while users at higher resolutions will have extra desktop space to open other windows.

USING THE Anchor PROPERTY TO HANDLE FORM SIZE CHANGES

Even if you do plan for a minimum screen resolution, what happens if your user resizes your application's forms? Remember, just because a user's display is set to a particular screen resolution, he can make the window much smaller than that resolution if he desires. Or, if he uses a high screen resolution and makes the window very large, there may be a lot of wasted space. If you do not plan for this situation, users who resize their windows could get unpleasant results, as shown in Figure 14.7.

Figure 14.7
If you do not respond
to users resizing your
form, they may not
see things as planned.

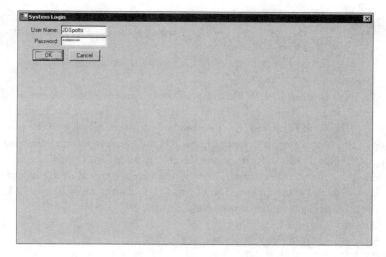

Previously, in order to deal with this situation, you had to write code such as the following in the form's `Resize` event handler to resize and reposition your controls whenever a form was resized:

```
Private Sub Form_Resize()
    If Me.Height <= 1365 Then Exit Sub
    lstMain.Height = Me.Height - 1365
    lstMain.Width = Me.Width - 420
    cmdOK.Top = lstMain.Height + 360
    cmdOK.Left = lstMain.Width - cmdOK.Width
    cmdCancel.Top = cmdOK.Top
    cmdCancel.Left = cmdOK.Left - cmdCancel.Width - 120
End Sub
```

Visual Basic .NET has introduced a nice new feature to make this task much easier. Most controls now support an `Anchor` property, which allows you to specify some combination of the four edges of a control's parent form that it should be bound to.

By default, a control is anchored (bound) to the top and left edges of the form that contains it. If the user resizes the form, the control's position relative to the top and left edges of the form stays constant. As the form is made wider and/or taller, the right and bottom edges of the form get further away from the right and bottom edges of the control.

You can set a control's `Anchor` property to any combination of the four edges of the form—`Top`, `Bottom`, `Left`, and `Right`. When a form is resized, the distance from each edge of the control specified by the `Anchor` property to the respective edge of the form remains constant, even if—and this is the key to how the property works—the control must be resized and/or repositioned in order to maintain these distances. The resizing and repositioning of the control are handled automatically.

PART
III
CH
14

Tip

The Anchor property works best when you use it for a small number of controls on a form.

Figures 14.8, 14.9, and 14.10 illustrate a Button control whose Anchor property has been set to Bottom, Right and a Label control whose Anchor property has been set to Top, Left, Right. As the form is resized, the Exit button's position relative to the bottom and right edges of the form remains constant. This has the effect of making the Exit button stay in the lower-right corner of the form, as the developer intended. In addition, the Label control is resized as the form's size changes, making the text contained in the label react to the form's new size. Figure 14.8 shows the form at its original size, while Figures 14.9 and 14.10 show the form smaller and larger, respectively.

Figure 14.8
This form's Exit button is anchored to the lower-right corner, and its Label control is anchored to three edges of the form.

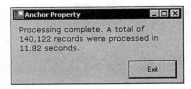

Figure 14.9
As the form gets smaller, the label and the button are repositioned to maintain the distances to their respective anchor edges.

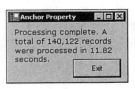

Figure 14.10
Even as the form grows larger, the Exit button's position relative to the lower-right corner is unchanged.

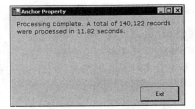

REGIONAL OPTIONS

Another customization that can adversely affect your program is the Regional Options applet in the Control Panel, pictured in Figure 14.11. This dialog box allows users to set their own currency, date, and time formats, among other things. If you use these predefined formats in your program, make sure that your variables, database fields, and calculations can handle them.

Figure 14.11
Make sure your program is prepared to handle changes users make in the Regional Options Control Panel.

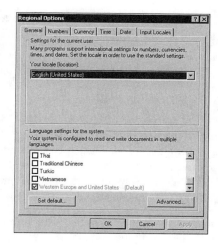

DEALING WITH USER EXPECTATIONS

Users tend to have ideas about how they think Windows applications should behave. Some of these ideas make sense, and some do not. Most likely, these notions are derived from features they have seen in commercial programs. Of course, your users will then expect every simple VB program you write to behave in exactly the same way.

For example, even though your program may have an Exit button, you can count on users to click the Close button in the upper-right corner. If you forget to add code to the `Form_Closed` event to handle this situation, your application could keep running when you don't want it to. The following sections describe several things about which you can count on users having expectations.

EFFECTIVE MENUS

One important part of form design is creating consistent, effective menus. Here are some important guidelines:

- Follow standard Windows layout convention: File, Edit, View, and so on.
- Group menu items logically and concisely.
- Use separator bars to group related items in a drop-down menu.
- Avoid redundant menu entries.
- Avoid top-level menu bar items without drop-down menus.
- Don't forget to use the ellipsis (. . .) to denote menu entries that activate dialog boxes.
- Use standard shortcuts and hotkeys whenever possible.
- Put frequently used menu items in a toolbar.

PART

III

CH

14

The steps involved in using the Menu Editor and in creating a shortcut (context) menu are discussed in Chapter 10, "Understanding Windows Forms."

→ For more details on using the Menu Editor to create context menus, **see** "Adding Menus to Your Forms," **p. 263**

HANDLING MULTIPLE INSTANCES OF YOUR APPLICATION

Most Windows programs are started when users navigate to a shortcut icon using the Start menu, or when they double-click a shortcut icon on the desktop. If users have multiple programs open, they can switch among them by using the taskbar or pressing Alt+Tab. However, many users like to use the program's shortcut icon again, even if the program is already open. Some shortcuts, such as the My Computer icon on the Windows desktop, simply bring up the existing window, whereas others launch a new instance of the program.

If you provide a desktop or Start menu shortcut to your application, users may expect the shortcut to activate an existing instance of the application rather than start a new one. This is especially true if users fill out a form and then minimize it to the taskbar. They may click the shortcut expecting the form to reappear, but if you have not coded for this occurrence, another instance of your application is launched; the user will see an empty form.

For certain applications, allowing multiple instances running at the same time may be desirable. However, if you do not design this capability into your application, errors will surely occur. For example, multiple copies of your application might try to write to the same database at the same time. Fortunately, preventing users from accidentally launching extra copies of your application is fairly easy. Visual Basic .NET's Diagnostics namespace provides a Process class, which gives your program access to processes (programs) running on the computer. The following lines of code, which can be placed in the Form_Load event or Sub Main (depending upon your application's Startup object), will check for the existence of a previous instance of the project, and close the new instance if a previous instance is found:

```
If (UBound(Diagnostics.Process.GetProcessesByName _
    (Diagnostics.Process.GetCurrentProcess.ProcessName)) > 0) Then
    End
End If
```

The preceding lines of code use the current process' ProcessName property to check the list of instances of processes with that name (as reported by the GetProcessesByName method) to end the program if another instance is already running. Although this code prevents conflicts and errors, it does not help the users because they still have to find the previously started application window manually. With a few calls to the Windows API (Applications Programming Interface), you can have your program show the previous application before exiting. Listing 14.1 shows a routine that can be placed in your main (startup) form's Code window to display the previous instance before exiting.

Note

The Windows API is a set of functions and procedures provided by the Windows operating system. Many of them offer functionality not normally provided via the .NET framework. By adding `Declare` statements to your code, as shown next, you can access these functions from within your Visual Basic .NET programs.

LISTING 14.1   PREVINST.ZIP—HANDLING MULTIPLE APPLICATION INSTANCES

```
Private Declare Function FindWindow Lib "user32" _
    Alias "FindWindowA"(ByVal lpClassName As String, _
    ByVal lpWindowName As String) As Integer
Private Declare Function ShowWindow Lib "user32" _
    (ByVal hWnd As Integer, ByVal nCmdShow As Integer) As Integer
Private Declare Function SetForegroundWindow Lib "user32" _
    (ByVal hWnd As Integer) As Integer
Private Const SW_RESTORE As Short = 9

Private Sub Form1_Load(ByVal eventSender As System.Object, _
    ByVal eventArgs As System.EventArgs) Handles MyBase.Load
    Dim sTitle As String
    Dim hWnd As Integer
    Dim lRetVal As Integer
    If (UBound(Diagnostics.Process.GetProcessesByName _
    (Diagnostics.Process.GetCurrentProcess.ProcessName)) > 0) Then
        sTitle = Me.Text
        Me.Text = "newcopy"
        hWnd = FindWindow(Nothing, sTitle)
        If hWnd <> 0 Then
            lRetVal = ShowWindow(hWnd, SW_RESTORE)
            lRetVal = SetForegroundWindow(hWnd)
        End If
        End
    End If
End Sub
```

In the preceding code, you first rename the current application's form caption properties so that the FindWindow API function does not find it. Then you use three API calls to find the window belonging to the previous application, restore it, and move it to the foreground.

PERCEIVED SPEED

Perception is reality. I am referring here to how users' *observations* can influence their like or dislike of your program. Application speed is a prime example. You may have written the fastest code ever, but it matters little if users *think* it runs slowly. VB programmers tend to get defensive when users complain about speed because "the users don't understand how much work the program is doing." However, you can incorporate a few tricks to make your program seem faster.

PART
III

CH

14

The key to a program's perceived speed is that something needs to happen when a user clicks an icon. Users are more willing to wait if they think the computer is working as fast as it can. Booting Windows is a good example; it usually takes quite a long time. However, all the graphics, beeps, and hard drive noise keep you distracted enough to make the wait acceptable. The techniques discussed in this section give you suggestions for creating "faster" applications.

PROGRAM STARTUP TIME

When your program starts, you probably will have some initialization to perform—for example, opening a network database. When set as your application's Startup object, the Sub Main procedure is an excellent place for all the initialization code required at startup time.

However, this technique may cause program startup time to get a bit lengthy, so displaying a *splash screen* during load time is a good idea. A splash screen displays information about the program and its designer, as well as indicating to the user that some action is happening. In Figure 14.12, which illustrates a typical splash screen, notice that the mouse pointer (shown near the bottom-right of the form) has been changed to a combination arrow and hourglass by setting the form's Cursor property to AppStarting. This indicates to the user that the program is actually doing some work while in startup mode.

Figure 14.12
A splash screen gives the user something to look at while program initialization takes place.

INFORM THE USERS OF PROGRESS

When your application looks like it is doing something, users tend to be more forgiving of long wait times. One way to keep them informed is to use a ProgressBar control on your form. If you are updating records in a database, you can use a progress bar to indicate the number of records processed so far. To do so, simply add an extra line of code or two to update the progress bar as you move to the next record.

→ For more information on how to display status, **see** "The ProgressBar Control," **p. 329**

However, sometimes the progress bar is not an option. For example, Visual Basic's FileCopy function might take some time depending on the size of the file. However, FileCopy is a self-contained "black box" function, so you have no place to insert the progress bar update code. In this case, an easy alternative would be to display some type of animation, such as an animated GIF placed in a PictureBox control or an AVI animation file placed in an

Animation control, before starting the file copy. Windows uses this trick when copying files and emptying the Recycle Bin. The users see the animation and think that it is linked to the file copy in progress when, in fact, it is a separate process running by itself.

USING GRAPHICS

A typical user interface for an application consists of a menu, labels, text boxes, buttons, and perhaps a few controls for specific pieces of data. Without graphics, however, an otherwise functional interface can be quite boring and unintuitive. Graphics can be used to enhance the user interface in the following ways:

- Highlighting specific information on the screen
- Providing a different view of information, such as using a graph
- Providing a more intuitive link to the application's functions

The subject of design and use of graphics is large and complex. Obviously, then, this single chapter cannot cover all the bases. However, it will provide you with enough information so that you can begin building a more visually pleasing user interface.

> **Note**
> The Windows API also contains many graphics-related functions.

There are two general ways to enhance your forms with graphics:

- You can add images to controls that accept them, such as `PictureBox` controls, or even to a form.
- You can utilize the graphics methods exposed via .NET's Graphics class, which in turn exposes the GDI+ (Graphics Device Interface) of the operating system, providing a means of displaying graphics on screens and printers.

Each of these techniques, including combinations of both, will be explored in this section.

> **Note**
> Previous versions of Visual Basic provided Line and Shape controls, which were used to place lines and various shapes (rectangles, ovals, and so on) on a form. Visual Basic .NET no longer supports these controls; using the methods provided by the Graphics class is now the preferred way of drawing shapes on a form.

PART
III

CH
14

USING IMAGES IN CONTROLS AND FORMS

Many of Visual Basic .NET's controls, as well as forms themselves, support the inclusion of an image of some type. As you will see in this section, this functionality is provided by two properties that are common to several objects—the `Image` property and the `BackgroundImage` property.

Each of these properties expects to be provided with some type of image file that contains the desired graphic. Some possible sources for these images are drawings you have created in a graphics software package such as Windows Paint or something more robust, pictures taken by a digital camera and saved to graphics files, or actual photographs converted to graphics files by a scanner. The types of graphics files you can display are listed in Table 14.1.

TABLE 14.1   GRAPHICS FILE FORMATS COMPATIBLE WITH VISUAL BASIC .NET

File Extension	Type of File
.BMP	Windows bitmap file
.ICO	Icon
.WMF	Windows metafile
.EMF	Enhanced Windows metafile
.JPG, .JPEG	JPEG images, named after the Joint Photographic Experts Group. Similar to GIF but uses compression to reduce file size; used extensively on Internet Web pages.
.GIF	Graphics Interchange Format. A file format originally developed by CompuServe and used on Internet Web pages.
.PNG	Portable Network Graphics. Designed as the successor to GIF, PNG is gaining acceptance as a good tradeoff between image quality and file size.

USING THE Image PROPERTY

The Image property allows you to specify a graphic to be contained within a control. The Image property is supported by the following controls:

- PictureBox
- Button
- Label
- LinkLabel
- CheckBox
- RadioButton

The Image property is most commonly used in PictureBox controls, whose main purpose is to display a picture. The other controls often use images as an alternate means of conveying the purpose of the control; for example, a Button control whose purpose is to initiate a printing procedure may show a picture of a printer in addition to (or instead of) the word Print.

Figure 14.13 illustrates the use of the Image property for each of the types of controls listed previously.

Figure 14.13
Many controls use the `Image` property to provide visual enhancements that help identify the control's function.

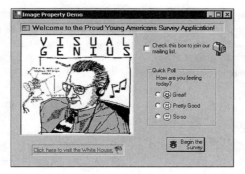

When using the `Image` property for a control, you can also set the control's `ImageAlign` property to specify which of the nine available positions within the control (`TopLeft`, `TopCenter`, `TopRight`, `MiddleLeft`, `MiddleCenter`, `MiddleRight`, `BottomLeft`, `BottomCenter`, or `BottomRight`) you want the image to be aligned to. The default alignment is `MiddleCenter`.

The `Image` property can be set either at design time or runtime, as discussed next.

Image **OBJECTS**   The `Image` property accepts as its value an `Image` object, which is part of a base class that provides functionality for various types of graphics, such as bitmaps, metafiles, and icons. The .NET framework provides a wealth of image manipulation capabilities that you can use in your Visual Basic programs. Once you have loaded a picture into an Image object, you can resize it or convert to another format with just a few lines of code. You can see an example of this technique in Chapter 17, "Using Active Server Pages.NET."

→ **See** "Creating the Picture Viewer Page," **p. 468**

SETTING THE Image **PROPERTY AT DESIGN TIME**   To set the `Image` property of a control at design time, simply select the control in the Designer window, click the ellipsis (. . .) next to the `Image` property in the Properties window, and use the Open dialog box to browse to a file containing a supported graphic. The picture you selected will be displayed in the control both at design time and runtime. Figure 14.14 illustrates a `Button` control that includes a printer icon to give the user a visual clue as to the button's purpose.

Figure 14.14
Adding images to standard controls can help the user understand your program's interface more quickly.

PART

III

CH

14

If you are adding an image to a control that also includes text (a `Button` control, for instance), be sure to manipulate the `TextAlign` and `ImageAlign` properties so that the text is not hard to read. Figure 14.15 shows how the text and image on a control can conflict with each other.

Figure 14.15
Take care when mixing text and graphics that they do not cause confusion.

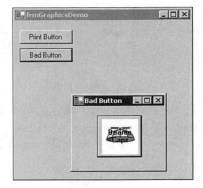

SETTING THE `Image` **PROPERTY AT RUNTIME** To set a control's `Image` property at runtime, you invoke the `FromFile` method of the `Image` class, which creates an image from a specified file and loads it into the control. The following is an example of this technique:

```
PictureBox1.Image = Image.FromFile("c:\images\logo4.gif")
```

CLEARING THE `Image` **PROPERTY** To remove a loaded picture from a control's `Image` property at design time, simply right-click the `Image` property in the Properties window, then click Reset. At runtime, you can use code like the following:

```
PictureBox1.Image = Nothing
```

CONSIDERATIONS OF DESIGN-TIME VERSUS RUNTIME IMAGE LOADING There are some things to consider as you decide whether to place images in your controls at design time or at runtime. When you populate the `Image` property of a control at design time, the image file information is stored as a part of your project (and compiled program); if you load many images in this manner, your program files can get very large. On the other hand, if you load your images dynamically at runtime, your image files are not compiled into your application; in addition, you gain the capability to change images at will. However, if you attempt to load an image file that is corrupt or has been deleted, your program will generate an error that you must deal with.

PictureBox **CONTROL IMAGE CONSIDERATIONS**   As the workhorse for adding images to forms, you will likely use the `PictureBox` control quite often. Because the picture box is a container for an image, you can control the image's position on a form simply by changing the `PictureBox` control's `Location` property. You should also be aware of the `PictureBox` control's `SizeMode` property. This property determines whether and how the control or the image contained in it are resized based upon the relative sizes of the control and the image. The following table lists the four possible values provided through the `PictureBoxSizeMode` enumeration and their effect:

`PictureBoxSizeMode` Member	Button Clicked
Normal	Neither the image nor the control is resized. If the image is larger than the control, it is cropped; if the control is larger than the image, the image is positioned at the upper-left corner of the control.
AutoSize	The control is resized to match the size of the image.
StretchImage	The image is resized to match the size of the control.
CenterImage	If the control is larger than the image, the image is centered inside the control; if the image is larger than the control, the image is placed at the center of the control and the outside edges are cropped.

Figure 14.16 shows the effect the `SizeMode` property has on the `PictureBox` control.

Figure 14.16
The `SizeMode` property changes the way images are displayed in `PictureBox` controls.

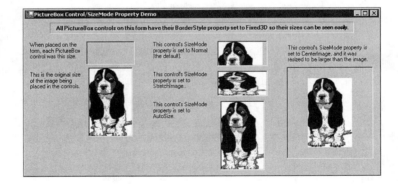

Note
Previous versions of Visual Basic allowed you to set the `Picture` property for a form, which would place a single copy of an image in the upper-left corner of the form, with no tiling or resizing available. If you need to duplicate this functionality, simply place the image in a `PictureBox` control and position the control appropriately.

USING THE BackgroundImage PROPERTY

Several controls, as well as the Form class itself, support a BackgroundImage property. As its name implies, this property specifies an image that is to be used for the background of the object that contains it. Images that are smaller than the object are tiled both vertically and horizontally as necessary to fill it.

Typically, background images are used to enhance the visual appeal of a control or form, as opposed to identifying its functionality (as the Image property does). Figure 14.17 shows a form whose background property is used to enhance the application's appearance; the CheckBox controls' BackColor property is set to Transparent so the background image can show through.

Figure 14.17
Background images change the appearance of forms and controls.

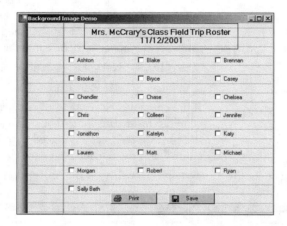

> **Tip**
>
> Using a form's BackgroundImage property is an excellent way to provide a texture behind the rest of the form's objects.

The following controls (as well as the Form class itself) support the BackgroundImage property:

- Button
- CheckBox
- RadioButton
- GroupBox
- PictureBox
- Panel

SETTING AND CLEARING THE BackgroundImage PROPERTY You can set or clear the BackgroundImage property of a form or control at design time or at runtime using the same techniques discussed for the Image property in the previous section.

USING BOTH THE Image **AND** BackgroundImage **PROPERTIES**   Several controls, such as the Button control and the Checkbox control, support both the Image and BackgroundImage properties. In such cases, as you might expect, the image contained in the Image property appears on top of the background image, which is tiled behind the other contents of the control. If you use both the Image property and the BackgroundImage property for the same object, take care that the two images do not look bad together. Figure 14.18 depicts two Button controls exhibiting both the BackgroundImage and Image properties. Notice how the two images complement each other in the first control, while they do not look good together at all in the second control.

Figure 14.18
For some controls, you can have both an image and a background image.

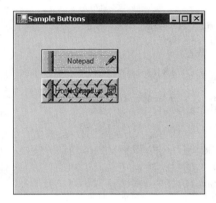

USING GRAPHICS METHODS

Using controls is not the only way to add graphics to your application. The Graphics class, provided via the System.Drawing namespace, also provides several methods that you can use to draw directly on a form. Some of these methods are listed here:

- DrawLine. This method draws a straight line between two points.
- DrawRectangle. This method draws a rectangle or square.
- DrawEllipse. This method draws a circle or oval.
- DrawPolygon. This method draws a closed figure with a number of sides.
- Clear. This method clears the output area of the target object.

The topic of drawing graphics in this manner could easily fill up a book on its own. To get your feet wet, we will demonstrate a simple example of using the graphics methods.

The easiest way to demonstrate the use of the graphics methods is to write code for a form's Paint event. This event occurs when the form is drawn. It is easy to write code that invokes the graphics methods in this event's event handler because it receives an argument of the PaintEventArgs class, which contains data for the Paint event.

PART

III

CH

14

To demonstrate some of the graphics methods, create the `Paint` event handler shown in Listing 14.2 for a form. Comments in the code explain each line. When you run your program, the graphics methods will draw directly on the form. Figure 14.19 shows the form after it has been drawn upon.

LISTING 14.2   DRAWING DIRECTLY ON A FORM WITH THE `Paint` EVENT HANDLER

```
Private Sub frmGraphicsMethods_Paint(ByVal sender As Object, _
    ByVal e As System.Windows.Forms.PaintEventArgs) Handles MyBase.Paint
    'Create an instance of the Graphics class
    '  to provide graphics functionality.
    '  Uses the instance of Graphics provided through
    '  the event arguments.
    Dim g As Graphics = e.Graphics
    'Create two Pen objects to draw in black and red.
    Dim BlackPen As New Pen(Color.Black)
    Dim RedPen As New Pen(Color.Red)
    'Set the Pen objects' width to 2 and 4 pixels.
    BlackPen.Width = 2
    RedPen.Width = 4
    'Invoke the DrawLine method of the Graphics class.
    '  Calls for a Pen object followed by a starting
    '  and ending Point object.
    g.DrawLine(BlackPen, New Point(50, 50), New Point(10, 40))
    g.DrawLine(RedPen, New Point(100, 200), New Point(0, 250))
    'Invoke the DrawArc method.
    g.DrawArc(BlackPen, 175, 22, 100, 150, 45, 180)
    'Invoke the DrawRectangle method.
    '  Calls for a Rectangle object.
    g.DrawRectangle(BlackPen, New Rectangle(100, 50, 66, 33))
    'Invoke the DrawEllipse method.
    '  Calls for a Rectangle object that defines the boundary
    '  of the ellipse.
    g.DrawEllipse(RedPen, New Rectangle(160, 200, 40, 40))
End Sub
```

Figure 14.19
The graphics methods can draw directly on a form.

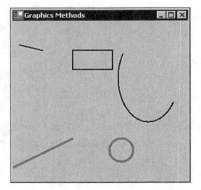

WORKING WITH TEXT AND FONTS

To write almost any program in Visual Basic, you need to know how to work with text. In earlier chapters, you learned something about displaying text in labels and text boxes. You also learned about string functions used to manipulate text in code. This section will expand on that knowledge by showing you how to display text in a way that is most intuitive to the users of your programs.

TEXT BOX BEHAVIOR

In Chapter 5, "Visual Basic Building Blocks," you were introduced to the text box. You already know that the Text property is used to store and retrieve information that the user may change. In addition to the standard properties discussed in that chapter, several other properties make the TextBox control even more versatile:

- ReadOnly. This property prevents the users from entering information in the text box.
- MaxLength. This property limits the number of characters that the text box can accept.
- PasswordChar. This property causes the text box to hide the information typed by the users.
- SelectionLength, SelectionStart, and SelectionText. These properties allow the users to manipulate only the selected (highlighted) part of the text in the text box.

PREVENTING USERS FROM CHANGING TEXT

First, take a look at the ReadOnly property, which allows you to use a text box for display only, taking away the user's ability to change text in that text box. The obvious question is "Why would you want to do that instead of just using a Label control?" One answer is that Windows-savvy users may want to copy text from a TextBox control to the Clipboard to be pasted elsewhere. Although a read-only text box does not allow users to update it, they still can select and copy the text contained in the control, as illustrated in Figure 14.20.

Figure 14.20
Using the ReadOnly property prevents undesired editing of text. In the pop-up menu (automatically implemented by Windows), notice that only the Copy, Paste, and Select All options are available for a locked text box.

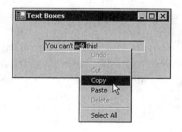

To make a text box read-only, simply set its ReadOnly property to True, as in the following examples:

```
'Sets a single text box to be read-only
txtTest.ReadOnly = True
txtTest.Text = "You can't edit this!"

'Sets every text box on the form to be read-only
Dim objControl As Control
Dim txtTextBox As TextBox
For Each objControl In Me.Controls
    If TypeOf objControl Is TextBox Then
        txtTextBox = objControl
        txtTextBox.ReadOnly = True
    End If
Next objControl
```

Tip

Use of the ReadOnly property can make it easy to design a database access form. The same form can be used for either viewing or editing a record. When you want to allow your user to only view a record, simply set the ReadOnly property of all the text boxes to True, as shown in the last code example shown previously.

Note

Do not confuse the ReadOnly property with the Enabled property. Both properties cause the background of the text box to be grayed out; however, the ReadOnly property does not gray out the text contained in the text box. Additionally, it allows the users to select and copy text from the text box, but the Enabled property does not.

THE MaxLength PROPERTY

When you're designing a data entry form, one of the tasks you must perform is *data validation*. One type of data validation is making sure the data entered will fit in the designated database field. For example, consider a text box whose purpose is to input a seven-digit account number. Although this check can be performed in code with the Len function, you can avoid the extra code by using the TextBox control's MaxLength property. The MaxLength property allows you to specify the maximum number of characters that can be entered in a text box, regardless of its size on the form. If your user attempts to type more characters into the text box than the MaxLength property will allow, the text box will not accept the extra characters, and a system beep will be heard.

Tip

You can programmatically put more text into a TextBox control than its MaxLength property would normally allow. Simply use code to set the Text property to the desired string, as in txtLastName = "Murgatroyd".

THE PasswordChar PROPERTY

If you are using a text box as part of a login form, you will want to be able to hide the password entered by the user. To do so, simply enter a character in the PasswordChar property of the text box. This property changes the text box's display behavior so that the password character is displayed in place of each character in the Text property. You may have seen this effect many times when logging in to applications or in to Windows itself.

Note that the contents of the Text property still reflect what was actually typed by the users, and your code always sees the "real" text. Although you can enter any character, using the asterisk (*) character for hiding text is customary.

EDITING TEXT IN A TEXT BOX

A standard text box allows the user to highlight text either by using the mouse or by using Ctrl or Shift in combination with the cursor keys. Your code can then manipulate the selected text with the SelectionText, SelectionLength, and SelectionStart properties. You can use these properties to work with a selected piece of text in your program. Look at the example in Figure 14.21. In this case, the SelectionText property would contain just the phrase "jumped over the lazy dog." The SelectionLength property would contain the integer value 25, which is the length of that string. And the SelectionStart property would contain the integer value 20, which means the selected phrase starts with the 20th character in the text box.

Figure 14.21
Your users can copy text from one text box and paste it elsewhere.

In addition to determining what has been selected, you can also set the properties from code to alter the selection. First you set the SelectionStart property, then set the SelectionLength property to highlight some characters.

The following code would select the first three characters of the text contained in the TextBox control txtTest when the control gets the focus:

```
Private Sub txtTest_GotFocus(ByVal sender As Object, _
    ByVal e As System.EventArgs) Handles txtTest.GotFocus
    txtTest.SelectionStart = 0
    txtTest.SelectionLength = 3
End Sub
```

The SelectionLength property can be changed multiple times. This causes the selection to increase or decrease in size, automatically updating the SelectionText property. Setting the SelectionText property from code causes the currently selected text to be replaced with a new string—for example:

```
txtTest.SelectionText = "jumped into oncoming traffic."
```

PART

III

CH

14

Note

> One classic use of the properties that govern the selected text in a `TextBox` control has been code like the following, which is placed in the control's `GotFocus` event procedure to cause the entire contents of the text box to be selected when it gets the focus:
>
> ```
> Private Sub txtSelect_GotFocus()
>    txtSelect.SelectionStart = 0
>    txtSelect.SelectionLength = Len(txtSelect.Text)
> End Sub
> ```
>
> Beginning with Visual Basic .NET, however, this functionality is built into the `TextBox` control. All of your text boxes will have their text automatically selected when they get the focus, without your having to write code to accomplish this task.

WORKING WITH FONTS AND COLORS

Although drawings and pictures add a definite visual impact to your applications, the heart and soul of many of your programs will likely be the text fields used for data entry and information display. Often, adding an image to enhance onscreen text is not possible or even useful. Instead, you must make sure that you use appropriate fonts and colors to get your point across.

USING THE FONT OBJECT

If you have used a word processor program, then you are already familiar with fonts. At design time, you assign fonts to controls and forms by using the Properties window. If you change the font of a form from the default setting, any controls subsequently drawn on the form—as well as any existing controls whose `Font` property has not been modified—will use the new font.

You may remember from earlier chapters that the `Font` property of an object is actually an object that has its own properties. The following Font object properties can be used to control the appearance of fonts in your program:

- `Name`. String identifier for one of the fonts installed on your system—for example, `"Arial"` or `"Times New Roman"`.

- `Unit`. Specifies the unit of measurement of the font's size. Used in conjunction with the `Size` property. The default value is `Point`; one point is 1/72 of an inch; therefore, capital letters in a 72-point font are about one inch high. Other possible values include `Pixel`, `Inch`, and `Millimeter`.

- `Size`. Specifies the size of the font, based on the value selected for the `Unit` property. Note that if you change the `Unit` property, the `Size` property is not automatically modified. Therefore, for example, if a Font object's `Unit` property is set to `Point` and its `Size` property is set to `12`, and then you change the `Unit` property to `Inch`, you will end up with 12-inch tall characters!

- Bold. True/False property that controls whether characters are shown in **boldface**. The bold characters appear darker and heavier than non-bold characters.

- Italic. True/False property that determines whether characters are *italicized*.

- Underline. True/False property that controls whether the text is displayed with a thin line under each character.

- Strikeout. True/False property that controls whether a thin horizontal line is drawn through the middle of the text.

ADDING A SPLASH OF COLOR

A form designed with totally battleship-gray components can be dull and plain. However, you can easily assign color to the form and controls on it by using the ForeColor and BackColor properties. To set these properties at design time, you can use one of the colors defined for components of the system (Control, Desktop, Menu, and so on); a member of the Web collection of colors; or a customized color.

To view the possible choices, bring up the Properties window for a control or form, and click on the ForeColor or BackColor property. The color picker window that appears lets you choose between one of the three tabs System, Web, or Custom. The Custom tab is shown in Figure 14.22.

Figure 14.22
You can specify an object's foreground or background color in one of several ways.

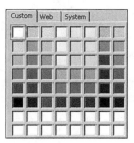

USING FONTS AND COLORS WITH A RichTextBox CONTROL

The text box is great for general use, but the RichTextBox control allows even greater control over how text displayed. The strength of the RichTextBox control, introduced in Chapter 12, "Advanced Controls," is that it can display multiple formats and colors within the same text area.

The standard TextBox control allows you to change the font used to display all the text in the control. The RichTextBox control, however, lets you use multiple fonts and font properties within the same control, as depicted in Figure 14.23.

PART
III

CH
14

Figure 14.23
The `RichTextBox`
control lets you
use many fonts in
one control.

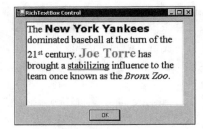

FROM HERE . . .

Although nothing we suggest here can guarantee a successful user interface, a bad user interface will certainly guarantee that no one will use your program. However, with the rapid pace of advances in computing, the definition of what is a "good" interface will surely keep changing. Consider, for example, the process of setting a VCR clock. Early VCR clocks were programmed with buttons and switches, but this method was soon replaced with onscreen displays. Now a broadcast signal makes the whole process automatic in some models. Like the VCR example, your Visual Basic user interfaces will evolve over time, as the industry sets new standards and you learn how to best meet your users' expectations.

CHAPTER 15

MULTIPLE DOCUMENT INTERFACE (MDI) APPLICATIONS

In this chapter

As you begin to write more advanced Visual Basic applications, at some point you will probably want to develop applications that contain a number of forms that need to be organized in a structured manner. If so, you may want to think about creating a Multiple Document Interface (MDI) application. The MDI standard allows your programs to work with multiple forms contained within a parent form. Using the MDI makes your interface cleaner than one that has independent forms scattered about the screen.

The MDI standard can enhance your programs in two ways. First, you can have one container form that acts as the background for your overall application. If a user moves the container form, the child forms contained inside move as well, which helps keep your application's interface organized and self-contained. Second, and perhaps even more powerful, your users can work on multiple documents at one time. MDI applications allow the use of multiple instances of the same form, which can add a great deal of power and flexibility to your programs.

OVERVIEW OF MDI APPLICATIONS

Many of the applications that you create in Visual Basic consist of a series of independent forms, like the ones shown in Figure 15.1. Each of these forms is displayed separately on the screen and is moved, maximized, or minimized separately from any other form. With this type of interface, you cannot easily organize the forms or deal with them as a group. Even with this limitation, this interface is a good one to use for many programs and is probably the most prevalent interface design.

Figure 15.1
This program's user interface consists of two forms that appear to have no visual relationship to each other.

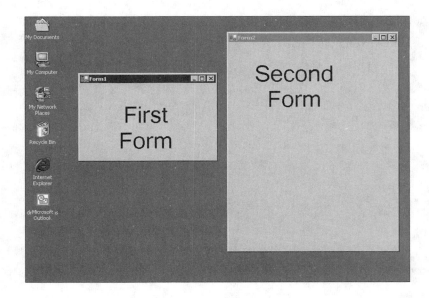

An alternative to this standard interface is the Multiple Document Interface. Forms in an MDI application have a parent/child relationship, which is controlled through form properties. An MDI application has one or more *parent forms* that contain most (or all) of the other forms in the program. Other forms can be *child forms*, which are contained within the parent, or standard forms, which are not. With an MDI application, you can easily organize all the child forms or minimize the entire group of forms just by minimizing the parent form.

Microsoft Excel is a familiar example of an MDI application. If you have worked with Excel, you know that you can open multiple windows in the program, access them easily from the menu, and minimize the whole thing with a single click of the mouse. Figure 15.2 shows three blank workbooks opened simultaneously in Excel as an example of a typical MDI application. The Visual Studio .NET interface itself is another example of the MDI style.

Figure 15.2
MDI applications let you manage multiple document windows with ease.

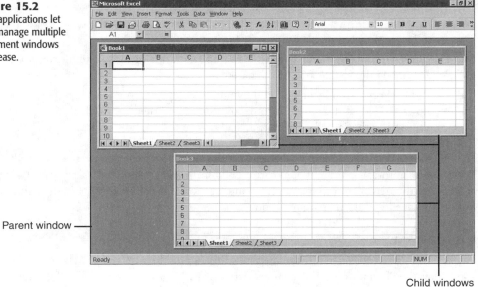

Parent window ⎯

Child windows

Because the easiest way to learn MDI is by example, we will spend the bulk of this chapter creating a sample program as we explain important MDI concepts. The sample program will use a parent form and a template child form to create a simple text editor program similar to Windows Notepad, with one major improvement—the ability to have multiple documents open simultaneously inside the program's interface, rather than having to open multiple instances of the program, as you must do with Notepad.

The multiple-form text editor program you create in this chapter will consist of two forms—an MDI parent form and a template for MDI child forms. The user can create a new text document or open an existing one from a file on disk; in either case, a new instance of the child form template is created to contain each document. The application will also include the ability to save and print a document.

First, though, you need to understand how parent and child windows work.

> **Note**
>
> If you're a Visual Basic 6 veteran, you may be interested to note that MDI parent forms are no longer a separate class. Instead, any standard Windows form can be made into an MDI parent form by setting its MDIParent property to True, as you will see in the following. Also, to create a child form, you now set a standard form's MDIParent property to the form that will serve as its parent; this technique replaces the MDIChild property. This new strategy allows you to have multiple MDIParent forms in one application.

MDI PARENT FORMS

An MDI parent form is a standard Windows form whose properties have been modified slightly. Several characteristics define a typical MDI parent form:

- An MDI parent form acts as a container for child forms; that is, the child forms are drawn inside the confines of the parent forms.
- The parent form automatically provides scrollbars if one or more child forms are positioned outside the visible area of the parent.
- The MDI parent window and all child windows are represented by a single icon on the Windows taskbar. If the parent form is minimized and then restored, all the child forms are returned to the same layout as they had before the application was minimized.

To create an MDI parent form, you simply set the IsMDIContainer property of a standard Windows form to True. When you create a child form (at runtime), you set the MDIParent property of the new form instance to the name of the MDI parent form, and the child form will be displayed within the parent window.

MDI CHILD FORMS

Just as MDI parent forms have characteristics that define their behavior, MDI child forms also behave in a certain way. The characteristics of an MDI child form are as follows:

- Each child form is displayed within the confines of the parent form. A child form cannot be moved outside the boundaries of the MDI parent form.
- When a child window is minimized, its icon is displayed in the parent window, not on the Windows taskbar.
- When a child form is maximized, it fills the entire inner area of the parent form. Also, the parent form's title bar contains the Text properties of both the parent and maximized child forms, with the child form's Text property being enclosed in square brackets after the Text property of the parent; for example, Text of Parent Form - [Text of Child Form].
- When one child form is maximized, all other child forms are maximized as well.

To create an MDI child form, you create an instance of a form at runtime and set that form's MDIParent property to the Name property of an MDI parent form before showing it.

Note

After the `MDIParent` property of a form has been set to make it a child form, that form's `IsMDIChild` property is automatically set to `True`.

CREATING THE PARENT FORM FOR THE SAMPLE APPLICATION

Let's begin working on the sample application by creating an MDI parent form, which will contain the other forms in the application as well as common menu items:

1. Start by creating a new Windows Application project. Name the project `MDIDemo`.

2. Click `Form1.vb` in the Solution Explorer window; then change its `File Name` property in the Properties window to `frmParent.vb`.

3. Right-click the form's Designer window, and then select View Code from the context menu. Rename the form by changing `Public Class Form1` at the top of the Code window to `Public Class frmParent`. (It is possible that the name of the class was changed for you when you changed the `File Name` property in the previous step.)

4. Right-click `MDIDemo` in the Solution Explorer window; then select Properties from the context menu. Change the project's Startup Object to `frmParent`, if it is not already set this way.

5. Change `frmParent`'s `Text` property to `MDI Text Editor`.

6. View `frmParent`'s Designer window, and then set its `IsMDIContainer` property to `True`. The background of the form will then take on a darker appearance, indicating it is a parent form, as shown in Figure 15.3.

Figure 15.3
The MDI parent acts as a container for the child forms.

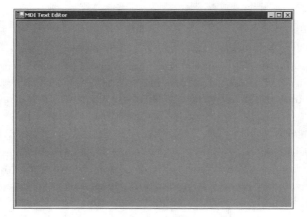

7. Drag an `OpenFileDialog` control to the form. This will be used when the user wants to open an existing file. Change its `Name` property to `dlgOpen`, its `DefaultExt` property to `txt`, and its `Filter` property to `Text Files (*.txt)|*.txt|All Files (*.*)|*.*`.

MENU CONSIDERATIONS

As you learned in Chapter 10, "Understanding Windows Forms," you can add a MainMenu control to a form to provide menu functionality. You may be wondering how menus are displayed in an MDI environment, since MDI parent and child forms can each have their own menu systems. Visual Basic .NET provides a series of properties that govern how menus are displayed when both an active child window and its parent window contain menu controls. These properties, as well as the special MDIList property, are discussed in the following paragraphs.

→ For more information on using the MainMenu control, **see** "Using the Menu Editor," **p. 264**

THE MergeType PROPERTY

Each menu item has a MergeType property that dictates how it behaves when it (or its parent menu) is merged with another menu item. Its possible values, provided through the MenuMerge enumeration, are shown in Table 15.1.

TABLE 15.1 MergeType PROPERTY SETTINGS	
Setting	**Purpose**
Add	The menu item is added to the collection of menu items with which it is being merged. This is the default value.
MergeItems	Submenu items under this menu item are merged with submenu items in the same position in the merged menu's hierarchy.
Remove	This menu item will not be included in the merged menu.
Replace	This menu item replaces a menu item in the same position in the merged menu.

THE MergeOrder PROPERTY

If a menu item is to be merged with or added to another menu, the MergeOrder property specifies which position the item will occupy in the merged menu. This is a zero-based property, so a menu item whose MergeOrder property is set to 0 will appear first in the merged menu, an item with a MergeOrder value of 1 will appear second, and so forth.

THE MDIList PROPERTY

The MDIList property is a special property that specifies that a menu item is to show a list of the Text property for all MDI child forms that are displayed inside the MDI parent form containing this menu item. The list is automatically maintained by Windows and can display up to nine MDI child forms at once. If the user clicks one of the listed child forms at run-time, that child form is automatically brought to the front and given the focus. If more than nine child forms are open, a More Windows menu item, which leads to a dialog box showing all child windows, will be displayed.

CREATING THE PARENT WINDOW'S MENU

Let's continue building the interface of our sample application's parent form by setting up its menu structure:

1. Drag a `MainMenu` control to the form. (Refer to Chapter 10 if you need assistance in working with `MainMenu` controls.) Create two top-level menus, as follows:

Name	Text	Shortcut
mnuFile	File	
mnuWindow	Window	

2. Create four menu items under the File menu, as follows:

Name	Text	Shortcut
mnuFileNew	New	Ctrl+N
mnuFileOpen	Open	Ctrl+O
mnuFileSep	- (hyphen)	
mnuFileExit	Exit	

3. Create four menu items under the Window menu, as follows:

Name	Text	Shortcut
mnuWindowTileH	Tile Horizontal	
mnuWindowTileV	Tile Vertical	
mnuWindowCascade	Cascade	
mnuWindowSep	- (hyphen)	

4. Display the properties window for `mnuWindow` and set its `MDIList` property to `True`. As you will see in a moment, this will automatically create a window list beneath this menu item.

5. Set the `MergeType` property of `mnuFile` to `MergeItems`. This will allow the child's menu items to be combined with those of the parent.

6. Set the `MergeOrder` property for `mnuFileSep` and `mnuFileExit` to `98` and `99`, respectively. This will ensure that the Exit menu item appears at the end of the menu (below a separator bar), which is the Windows standard, even when merged.

CODING THE EXIT MENU

The first bit of code that you will write is to be executed when the user selects Exit from the File menu. You will simply close the parent form with the Close method when the user wants to exit; in turn, any open child windows will be closed before the parent form is closed. This gives each child window the chance to ensure that the data contained in it is saved, as we will see later in this chapter. Code the Exit menu as follows:

1. Right-click frmParent in the Solution Explorer window; then select View Code to open its Code window.

2. In the Code window's Class Name box, select the mnuFileExit menu item; then in the Method Name box, select the Click event. This will create a shell Click event handler for you to fill in with code.

3. Add the following line of code to the mnuFileExit_Click event handler:

```
Me.Close()
```

CREATING THE CHILD FORM TEMPLATE

Now that you have created the parent form, let's continue by creating a template for the child form. In essence, we will be creating a child form *class* at design time; later, at runtime, the application will create instances of the child form class as necessary.

The child form template will contain a single TextBox control whose properties are set to cause it to completely fill the form.

To create the child form template, follow these steps:

1. Select Project, Add Windows Form from the Visual Basic .NET menu system. Name the form frmChild before clicking Open.

2. Drag a MainMenu control to frmChild, and create the File menu and its submenu items as follows:

Name	Text	Shortcut
mnuFile	File	
mnuFileSave	Save	Ctrl+S
mnuFileSaveAs	Save As...	
mnuFileClose	Close	
mnuFileSep	- (hyphen)	
mnuFilePrint	Print	Ctrl+P

3. Set the MergeType property of mnuFile to MergeItems. This will allow the child's menu items to be combined with those of the parent.

4. Drag a TextBox control to the form. Change its Name property to txtMain and clear its Text property.

5. Set txtMain's Font property to a monospaced font, such as Courier New.

6. So that txtMain will fill up the form no matter how the form is sized, set its MultiLine property to True and its Dock property to Fill.

7. Set txtMain's ScrollBars property to Both. This will cause it to automatically display scrollbars if its text takes up more space than is allowed in the control. Also, set its WordWrap property to False so the user can type more text on one line than can be displayed in the control.

8. Drag a SaveFileDialog control to the form, and change its Name property to dlgSave. This control will be used to present a Save dialog box to the user to specify a filename.

9. Drag a PrintDocument control to the form. We will use this control later in the chapter when we add printing capability to the application.

SETTING UP THE CHILD FORM'S PROPERTIES

We want the child form to provide two properties that can be set and retrieved by the parent form that controls it:

- TextSaved, which will be a Public Boolean variable reporting whether the text contained in the child form's text box has been saved. A value of True indicates that the text has been saved and has not changed since it was saved. A value of False indicates either that the text has never been saved, or that it has been modified by the user since the last save.

- FileName, which will will represent the name of the file (and complete path) in which the document represented by this child window is to be saved. If the file has never been saved, the FileName property will contain an empty string ("").

CREATING THE TextSaved PROPERTY

The TextSaved property is a simple Public variable (of Boolean type) that reports whether the document contained in the child form's text box has been saved (or is in need of saving). Because it is a Public variable, its value can be set or retrieved by the parent form, a need that you will discover a little later. To create the TextSaved property, simply type the following line of code at the bottom of the Code window for frmChild, just above the End Class line:

```
Public TextSaved as Boolean
```

CREATING THE FileName PROPERTY

The FileName property is a little more complicated. We will use a Property procedure to handle this property, as a small amount of processing is required when its value is set. The

FileName property will be used to expose a Private String variable named sFileName, so begin by typing the following line of code just after the TextSaved declaration you just entered:

```
Private sFileName as String
```

The following Property procedure will handle the FileName property. The Get portion simply returns the current value of sFileName; however, the Set portion performs a secondary function in addition to modifying sFileName—it sets the Text property of the current instance of frmChild to the current value of the FileName property, using the InStrRev function to locate and remove the path information. If the FileName property is empty, then the form's Text property is set to Untitled. Enter the following FileName property procedure below the two variable declarations you just entered:

```
Public Property FileName() As String
    Get
        Return sFileName
    End Get
    Set(ByVal Value As String)
        sFileName = Value
        If Trim(sFileName) = "" Then
            Me.Text = "Untitled"
        Else
            Me.Text = Mid(sFileName, InStrRev(sFileName, "\") + 1)
        End If
    End Set
End Property
```

Save and run the program. Note that you will see the parent form but no instances of the child form, as illustrated in Figure 15.4. Note also (for future reference) that the application's menu system contains onlythe simple commands we set up for the parent form.

Figure 15.4
The parent form shows a simple menu system but no child forms.

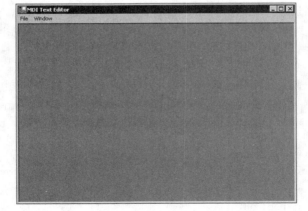

DISPLAYING A NEW CHILD FORM

The next bit of coding we need to deal with involves creating and displaying a new instance of frmChild, the child form. The user might reasonably expect that when the program is first executed, it opens with a blank document window displayed (as Excel does, for example). In addition, there will be a New command on the File menu to allow the user to open new document windows as needed. Because this functionality (opening and displaying a new document window) needs to be invoked from more than one place in the program, it makes sense to code it as a custom procedure.

CREATING THE NewChild PROCEDURE

We will name the custom procedure NewChild, and it is to be coded as a part of the frmParent class. To create the NewChild procedure, right-click frmParent in the Solution Explorer window; then select View Code from the context menu to open frmParent's Code window. Enter the following procedure at the end of the Code window, just above the End Class statement:

```
Private Sub NewChild()
    Dim f As New frmChild()
    f.MdiParent = Me
    f.FileName = ""
    f.TextSaved = True
    f.Show()
End Sub
```

Here is how the NewChild procedure works: It begins by creating a local object variable named f, which creates a new instance of frmChild. It then sets the MDIParent property of the new instance of frmChild to Me (which represents frmParent because that is the class in which this code resides). This causes f (which represents the new frmChild instance) to be a child form contained by frmParent. Next, the FileName property of the new form instance is set to an empty string, which will trigger the FileName property procedure that we created earlier in frmChild's code (in turn setting the new form's Text property to Untitled); then the new child form's TextSaved property is set to True because an empty document does not need to be saved. Finally, the Show method of the new form is invoked to cause the child form to become visible inside the parent.

DISPLAYING A NEW CHILD WHEN THE PROGRAM STARTS

As you have seen, if you were to run the program at this point, the parent window would be displayed with no child windows inside. As we mentioned, the user probably expects a blank document to be open when the program runs. Because we have already created a NewChild procedure to create a new instance of the child form, we simply need to invoke the NewChild procedure at the appropriate place to cause a new child form to be displayed when the program runs. The proper place to create a new child form when the program runs is in the New procedure of frmParent (the application's startup object). You should already have the Code window for frmParent open. Click the plus sign next to the Windows Form Designer generated code region to display all the code that was generated when the frmParent class was created. Add the following line of code at the end of Public Sub New, just above the End Sub line:

```
NewChild
```

After typing this line of code, click the minus sign next to the Windows Form Designer generated code region to hide the generated code again.

TESTING THE CREATION OF A NEW FORM

Save and run your program. The NewChild procedure executes as part of the startup form's initialization. You should see frmParent open as the container for the application and a single instance of frmChild displayed inside frmParent, as illustrated in Figure 15.5. Note that the title bar for frmChild contains the text Untitled (as defined by the FileName property procedure), and the title bar for frmParent contains MDI Text Editor (the Text property you set at design time). You may also notice that the parent form's menu system contains the commands that we set up for both the parent and child forms because the menus' MergeType properties were set to MergeItems. Maximize the child form and note how it expands to fill the entire parent form. Finally, note that when the child form is maximized, the parent's and child's Text properties are merged into the single caption MDI Text Editor - [Untitled], as shown in Figure 15.6.

Figure 15.5
A single new instance of the child form is created when the program begins.

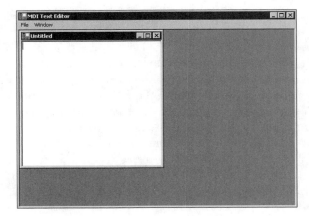

Figure 15.6
Maximizing a child form causes it to fill its parent, and the form's captions merge as well.

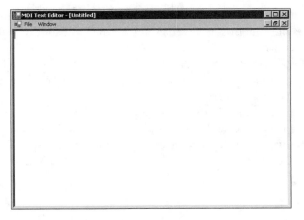

LETTING THE USER CREATE A NEW CHILD FORM

As we discussed earlier, there are two places where we need to create a new instance of the child form. We have already coded the program to create a new child when the application starts. In addition, the user should be able to create a new child form by selecting File, New from the application's menu system. Coding for this is a simple task. In frmParent's Code window, drop down the Class Name list and select the mnuFileNew menu control; then select Click from the Method Name drop-down. You will see a shell Click event handler for the menu control; simply add a call to the NewChild procedure, as follows:

```
Private Sub mnuFileNew_Click(ByVal sender As Object, _
    ByVal e As System.EventArgs) Handles mnuFileNew.Click
    NewChild()
End Sub
```

Save and run the program again. This time you will be able to open multiple child windows by selecting New from the File menu or by pressing the shortcut key for the New menu item (Ctrl+N).

OPENING AN EXISTING DOCUMENT

In addition to being able to open a new blank child window, the user should have the capability of opening an existing text file and placing the contents of the file into a new child document. We will accomplish this functionality via the OpenFileDialog control, dlgOpen, that we placed on the form earlier.

INVOKING THE OPEN FILE DIALOG BOX

The user will expect to be able to open an existing text file by selecting Open from the parent form's File menu. You will accomplish this by adding a single line of code to the Click event handler for the mnuFileOpen menu item:

1. Make sure you are still in the Code window for frmParent.

2. Select mnuFileOpen from the Class Name drop-down; then select Click from the Method Name drop-down.

3. Type the line **dlgOpen.ShowDialog()** so that the Click event handler looks like the following:

```
Private Sub mnuFileOpen_Click(ByVal sender As Object, _
    ByVal e As System.EventArgs) Handles mnuFileOpen.Click
    dlgOpen.ShowDialog()
End Sub
```

OPENING THE FILE AND CREATING A NEW CHILD WINDOW

As you already know if you have used the OpenFileDialog control before, the control itself simply gathers information from the user about a file to be opened; it does not actually open a file. We will accomplish the opening of the file by adding code to the FileOK event handler for dlgOpen, which is invoked when the user has selected a file and clicked OK. Because this code will need to utilize file system I/O functionality provided via the System.IO namespace, you must add an Imports statement referencing that namespace in the frmParent class. Follow these steps:

1. Make sure you are still in the Code window for frmParent.

2. At the very top of the Code window, even above the Public Class frmParent statement, add the code Imports System.IO. This adds I/O functionality to the frmParent class.

3. Select dlgOpen from the Class Name dropdown, then select FileOK from the Method Name dropdown.

4. Type the following code in the FileOK event handler:

```
Private Sub dlgOpen_FileOk(ByVal sender As Object, _
    ByVal e As System.ComponentModel.CancelEventArgs) Handles dlgOpen.FileOk
    Dim f As New frmChild()
    Dim nTemp As Integer = FreeFile()
    Dim MyFile As StreamReader
    f.MdiParent = Me
    MyFile = File.OpenText(dlgOpen.FileName)
    f.txtMain.Text = MyFile.ReadToEnd
    f.txtMain.Select(0, 0)
    MyFile.Close()
    f.FileName = dlgOpen.FileName
    f.TextSaved = True
    f.Show()
End Sub
```

This code begins by creating a new instance of frmChild and setting its MDIParent property to the parent form (represented by Me), much like the NewChild procedure does. In this case, however, it uses the functionality provided by the System.IO namespace to open the text file specified by the user (as determined by dlgOpen's FileName property). The contents of the text file are used to populate the text box txtMain on the new child form, and the text box's Select method is invoked to ensure that the text is not selected when the user first sees it. After closing the text file, the new child form's FileName property is set to the value provided by the OpenFileDialog control's FileName property (which in turn invokes the child form's FileName property procedure). Next, the child form's TextSaved property is set to True because the text is currently unchanged from what is saved on the disk. Finally, the child form's Show method causes it to become visible.

You can learn more about the System.IO namespace in Chapter 24, "Working with Files."

→ For more information on using the System.IO namespace, **see** "Working with File Streams," **p. 681**

CHILD WINDOW MANAGEMENT

Most MDI applications give the user the capability of arranging all open child windows in one of several ways, which are normally accessed through a Window menu. Three common window arrangements are

- **Tiled vertically**—The open child windows are sized as vertical rectangles and arranged side by side.

- **Tiled horizontally**—The open child windows are sized as horizontal rectangles and arranged on top of one another.

- **Cascaded**—The child windows overlap each other in a neat cascading pattern, starting at the upper-left of the parent window.

In any case, when the open child windows are rearranged, they are all resized to the same dimensions (which may vary slightly when the windows are tiled, depending on how many windows are open and how much space is available).

> **Note**
>
> Some applications offer a fourth window arrangement option, *arrange icons*. This arrangement neatly arranges the icons of any minimized documents at the bottom of the parent window.

Visual Basic .NET makes it easy for your applications to supply window-arranging capabilities. Simply invoke the parent form's LayoutMdi method (with the appropriate parameter), and the open child windows are automatically arranged neatly. The LayoutMdi method accepts one of the following four parameters (provided via the MdiLayout enumeration):

- Cascade
- TileHorizontal
- TileVertical
- ArrangeIcons

CASCADING THE OPEN CHILD WINDOWS

To give the user the ability to cascade open child windows, enter the following code in the Click event handler for the mnuWindowCascade menu item:

```
Me.LayoutMdi(MdiLayout.Cascade)
```

Figure 15.7 illustrates a group of child windows that have been cascaded.

Figure 15.7
Cascading causes child windows to be arranged neatly in an overlapping style.

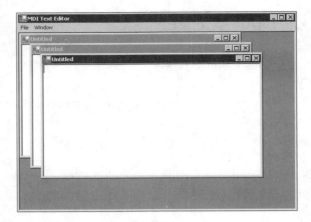

TILING THE OPEN CHILD WINDOWS HORIZONTALLY

To let the user tile the open child windows horizontally, enter the following code in the Click event handler for the mnuWindowTileH menu item:

```
Me.LayoutMdi(MdiLayout.TileHorizontal)
```

Figure 15.8 illustrates a group of child windows that have been tiled horizontally.

Figure 15.8
Tiling child windows horizontally makes them appear on top of each other.

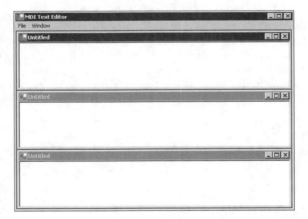

TILING THE OPEN CHILD WINDOWS VERTICALLY

To let the user tile the open child windows vertically, enter the following code in the Click event handler for the mnuWindowTileV menu item:

```
Me.LayoutMdi(MdiLayout.TileVertical)
```

Figure 15.9 illustrates a group of child windows that have been tiled vertically.

Figure 15.9
You can arrange child windows side by side by tiling them vertically.

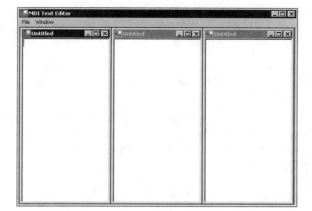

Save and run your program; then test these procedures by creating several new child windows and experimenting with the options under the Window menu.

SWITCHING BETWEEN OPEN WINDOWS

While you still have the program running with multiple child windows open, notice that the Window menu also maintains a list of the Text properties of all open child windows. You can click any of the windows to bring it to the front and give it the focus. This capability is provided automatically via the MDIList property that you set for the mnuWindow menu item.

SAVING FILES

While opening files is a function of the parent form, saving files is a function of the child forms. Typically, applications have both a Save and a Save As command. The Save command simply replaces an existing copy of a named document with a new copy; the Save As command presents a dialog box to let the user change a document's filename before saving it.

Complicating matters slightly, if the user slects the Save command for a document that has never been named or saved, the application should treat it as if the user had selected the Save As command in order to let him select a filename and location.

Before writing the code that will take care of saving and naming the files, let's see how the TextSaved property, which lets us know if a document needs to be saved, is modified by the program as files are changed.

THE TextSaved PROPERTY

When we were setting up the child form template earlier in this chapter, we created a Boolean TextSaved property. Its job is to report whether the text contained in the child form's text box has been saved (or if it is in need of saving). The initial value of TextSaved is True, indicating that the file has not been modified since it was last saved. However, we need to set it to False whenever any text in the text box changes to indicate that the document needs saving. This is a simple matter of adding code to the txtMain text box's TextChanged event handler, which is invoked whenever the text in the text box changes (usually by user interaction):

1. In the Code window for frmChild, select txtMain from the Class Name box; then slect TextChanged from the Method Name box. This will create a shell txtMain_TextChanged event handler.

2. Add the code Me.TextSaved = False to the event handler so it looks like this:

```
Private Sub txtMain_TextChanged(ByVal sender As Object, _
    ByVal e As System.EventArgs) Handles txtMain.TextChanged
    Me.TextSaved = False
End Sub
```

THE SaveFile PROCEDURE

As you will see, the functionality that actually writes a file to disk will need to be called from several locations; therefore, it makes sense to create a standalone SaveFile procedure in the *child* form class. As with the parent form, the child form's Code window needs to include a reference to the System.IO namespace, so enter **Imports System.IO** at the very top of frmChild's Code window, just above the Public Class frmChild. Then, enter the following code at the end in the Code window for the child form, just above the End Class line:

```
Private Sub SaveFile()
    Dim MyFile As StreamWriter
    If sFileName = "" Then
        SaveFileAs()
    End If
    MyFile = File.CreateText(sFileName)
    MyFile.Write(txtMain.Text)
    MyFile.Close()
    Me.TextSaved = True
End Sub
```

If the SaveFile procedure detects that the form's FileName property is empty, it calls the SaveFileAs procedure, which will cause the user to be prompted for a filename and location. Notice that the SaveFile procedure sets the form's TextSaved property to True, indicating, that the text contained in the form's text box has been saved and is unmodified since then.

THE SaveFileAs PROCEDURE

Next, we are going to create a standalone Save As procedure that may seem a little unnecessary at first, but its purpose will become clear soon enough. The Save As procedure will simply invoke the SaveFileDialog control (dlgSave) that we created when we set up the form, using the current contents of the form's FileName property to pre-populate the dialog box's FileName property. Enter the following procedure in the Code window just after the SaveFile procedure:

```
Sub SaveFileAs()
    dlgSave.FileName = Me.FileName
    dlgSave.ShowDialog()
End Sub
```

CODING THE SAVE MENU OPTION

When the user selects Save from the File menu, the program must determine if the user has named the file yet (as determined by examining the value of the internal sFileName variable). If so, then the SaveFile procedure is to be invoked; however, if the document is unnamed, the SaveFileAs procedure must be invoked instead, so that the user will have an opportunity to name the file. Enter the following code into the Click event handler for the mnuFileSave menu item:

```
Private Sub mnuFileSave_Click(ByVal sender As Object, _
    ByVal e As System.EventArgs) Handles mnuFileSave.Click
    If sFileName > "" Then
        SaveFile()
    Else
        SaveFileAs()
    End If
End Sub
```

CODING THE SAVE AS MENU OPTION

When the user selects Save As from the File menu, she is specifically saying that she wants to be presented with the opportunity to specify a new name for the file. The following code, which is to be entered into the Click event handler for the mnuFileSaveAs menu item, will accomplish this by invoking the SaveFileAs procedure we just created (which in turn shows the SaveFileDialog box):

```
Private Sub mnuFileSaveAs_Click(ByVal sender As Object, _
    ByVal e As System.EventArgs) Handles mnuFileSaveAs.Click
    SaveFileAs()
End Sub
```

CODING THE SaveFileDialog CONTROL

When the user is presented with the SaveFileDialog control and clicks OK, he has specified a new filename under which the document is to be saved. The following code, entered into the FileOK event handler of dlgSave, checks the value of the argument that was passed into the procedure, just to make sure the user hasn't cancelled his request or left out the filename. If he has not, the form's FileName property is updated with the dialog box's FileName property, and the SaveFile procedure is invoked to actually save the file:

```
Private Sub dlgSave_FileOk(ByVal sender As Object, _
    ByVal e As System.ComponentModel.CancelEventArgs) Handles dlgSave.FileOk
    If e.Cancel = False Then
        Me.FileName = dlgSave.FileName
        SaveFile()
    End If
End Sub
```

MANAGING DOCUMENTS WHEN WINDOWS ARE CLOSED

When a user closesa child window, the program should check the TextSaved property to see if the document contained in that instance of the child window has been modified since it was last saved. If it has, the user should be given the option of saving the document before the window closes. To do this, we will add code to the child form's `Closing` event handler, which is invoked after the user attempts to close the window, but before the window is actually closed. Follow these steps:

1. In the Code window for frmChild, select (Base Class Events) from the Class Name box; then select Closing from the Method Name box. This will create a shell frmChild_Closing event handler.

2. Enter the following code to complete the frmChild_Closing event handler:

```
Private Sub frmChild_Closing(ByVal sender As Object, _
    ByVal e As System.ComponentModel.CancelEventArgs) Handles MyBase.Closing
    If Me.TextSaved = False Then
        Dim sMsg As String
        Dim nResult As Integer
        sMsg = "Save changes to "
        If Me.FileName = "" Then
            sMsg += "this untitled document"
        Else
            sMsg += Mid(sFileName, InStrRev(sFileName, "\") + 1)
        End If
        sMsg += " before closing it?"
        nResult = MessageBox.Show(sMsg, "System Message", _
            MessageBoxButtons.YesNoCancel)
        Select Case nResult
            Case DialogResult.Cancel
                e.Cancel = True
            Case DialogResult.Yes
                SaveFile()
            Case Else
                'Do nothing; let the window close.
        End Select
    End If
End Sub
```

This code builds a String variable named sMsg to contain a message asking the user if he wants to save the file contained in the child document window. It then displays that message as it invokes a message box, using the Yes/No/Cancel set of buttons. A Select Case statement evaluates the user's response. If he selects Yes, the SaveFile procedure is called (which will, in turn, call SaveFileAs if necessary); if he selects Cancel, the Cancel property of the procedure's arguments is set to True, which aborts the closing of the window; otherwise, the user selects No and the closing of the window can continue.

CODING THE FILE/CLOSE MENU OPTION

When you created the menu system for the child form, you included a Close option under the File menu. This option should serve the same purpose as if the user clicked the window's Close button at the upper-right. The code for this is simple; place it in the Click event handler for the mnuFileClose menu item:

```
Me.Close()
```

TESTING THE FILE FUNCTIONALITY

This would be a good time to save your project and test the file opening and saving functionality. Run the program and create some documents, save them, change their names by using Save As, try to close documents that have not been saved, and so on.

ADDING A PRINT FUNCTION

When you created the child form template, you included a PrintDocument control to allow for printing functionality. Some simple code will activate this feature. You can learn more about the PrintDocument control and printing in general in Chapter 23, "Creating and Using Reports."

CODING THE PRINT MENU COMMAND

Open the Code window for frmChild, and then open the Click event handler for the mnuFilePrint menu item. Add the code **PrintDocument1.Print()** to the procedure; this will cause the PrintDocument control to begin the printing process when mnuFilePrint is clicked. Your event handler should look like the following:

```
Private Sub mnuFilePrint_Click(ByVal sender As Object, _
    ByVal e As System.EventArgs) Handles mnuFilePrint.Click
    PrintDocument1.Print()
End Sub
```

CODING THE PrintDocument CONTROL

A single line of code in the PrintDocument control's PrintPage event handler (which occurs when the control's Print method is invoked) will take care of printing the contents of the txtMain text box to the printer. Enter the following PrintPage event handler for PrintDocument1:

```
Private Sub PrintDocument1_PrintPage(ByVal sender As Object, _
    ByVal e As System.Drawing.Printing.PrintPageEventArgs) _
    Handles PrintDocument1.PrintPage
    e.Graphics.DrawString(txtMain.Text, New Font("Courier New", _
        10, FontStyle.Regular), Brushes.Black, 0, 0)
End Sub
```

SUMMARIZING THE CODE

You have now completed coding the multiple document text editor application. The following sections summarize the code for the two forms that make up the application.

THE PARENT FORM

Listing 15.1 contains all the code for the parent form, frmParent.

LISTING 15.1   MDIDEMO.ZIP—CODE FOR THE PARENT FORM

```
Imports System.IO
Public Class frmParent
    Inherits System.Windows.Forms.Form

#Region " Windows Form Designer generated code "

    Public Sub New()
        MyBase.New()

        'This call is required by the Windows Form Designer.
        InitializeComponent()

        'Add any initialization after the InitializeComponent() call
        NewChild()
    End Sub

    'Form overrides dispose to clean up the component list.
    Protected Overloads Overrides Sub Dispose(ByVal disposing As Boolean)
        If disposing Then
            If Not (components Is Nothing) Then
                components.Dispose()
            End If
        End If
        MyBase.Dispose(disposing)
    End Sub
    Friend WithEvents MainMenu1 As System.Windows.Forms.MainMenu
    Friend WithEvents mnuFile As System.Windows.Forms.MenuItem
    Friend WithEvents mnuFileNew As System.Windows.Forms.MenuItem
    Friend WithEvents mnuFileOpen As System.Windows.Forms.MenuItem
    Friend WithEvents MenuItem4 As System.Windows.Forms.MenuItem
    Friend WithEvents mnuFileExit As System.Windows.Forms.MenuItem
    Friend WithEvents mnuWindow As System.Windows.Forms.MenuItem
    Friend WithEvents mnuWindowTileH As System.Windows.Forms.MenuItem
    Friend WithEvents mnuWindowTileV As System.Windows.Forms.MenuItem
    Friend WithEvents mnuWindowCascade As System.Windows.Forms.MenuItem
    Friend WithEvents MdiClient1 As System.Windows.Forms.MdiClient
    Friend WithEvents dlgOpen As System.Windows.Forms.OpenFileDialog

    'Required by the Windows Form Designer
    Private components As System.ComponentModel.Container

    'NOTE: The following procedure is required by the Windows Form Designer
    'It can be modified using the Windows Form Designer.
    'Do not modify it using the code editor.
    <System.Diagnostics.DebuggerStepThrough()> Private Sub InitializeComponent()
        Me.mnuWindowTileV = New System.Windows.Forms.MenuItem()
        Me.mnuWindowTileH = New System.Windows.Forms.MenuItem()
        Me.mnuFile = New System.Windows.Forms.MenuItem()
        Me.mnuFileNew = New System.Windows.Forms.MenuItem()
        Me.mnuFileOpen = New System.Windows.Forms.MenuItem()
        Me.MenuItem4 = New System.Windows.Forms.MenuItem()
        Me.mnuFileExit = New System.Windows.Forms.MenuItem()
        Me.MdiClient1 = New System.Windows.Forms.MdiClient()
        Me.MainMenu1 = New System.Windows.Forms.MainMenu()
        Me.mnuWindow = New System.Windows.Forms.MenuItem()
```

```
Me.mnuWindowCascade = New System.Windows.Forms.MenuItem()
Me.dlgOpen = New System.Windows.Forms.OpenFileDialog()
Me.SuspendLayout()
'
'mnuWindowTileV
'
Me.mnuWindowTileV.Index = 1
Me.mnuWindowTileV.Text = "Tile Vertical"
'
'mnuWindowTileH
'
Me.mnuWindowTileH.Index = 0
Me.mnuWindowTileH.Text = "Tile Horizontal"
'
'mnuFile
'
Me.mnuFile.Index = 0
Me.mnuFile.MenuItems.AddRange(New System.Windows.Forms.MenuItem() _
    {Me.mnuFileNew, Me.mnuFileOpen, Me.MenuItem4, Me.mnuFileExit})
Me.mnuFile.MergeType = System.Windows.Forms.MenuMerge.MergeItems
Me.mnuFile.Text = "File"
'
'mnuFileNew
'
Me.mnuFileNew.Index = 0
Me.mnuFileNew.Shortcut = System.Windows.Forms.Shortcut.CtrlN
Me.mnuFileNew.Text = "New"
'
'mnuFileOpen
'
Me.mnuFileOpen.Index = 1
Me.mnuFileOpen.Shortcut = System.Windows.Forms.Shortcut.CtrlO
Me.mnuFileOpen.Text = "Open"
'
'MenuItem4
'
Me.MenuItem4.Index = 2
Me.MenuItem4.MergeOrder = 98
Me.MenuItem4.Text = "-"
'
'mnuFileExit
'
Me.mnuFileExit.Index = 3
Me.mnuFileExit.MergeOrder = 99
Me.mnuFileExit.Text = "Exit"
'
'MdiClient1
'
Me.MdiClient1.Dock = System.Windows.Forms.DockStyle.Fill
Me.MdiClient1.Name = "MdiClient1"
Me.MdiClient1.TabIndex = 0
'
'MainMenu1
'
Me.MainMenu1.MenuItems.AddRange(New System.Windows.Forms.MenuItem() _
    {Me.mnuFile, Me.mnuWindow})
'
```

LISTING 15.1   CONTINUED

```vbnet
        'mnuWindow
        '
        Me.mnuWindow.Index = 1
        Me.mnuWindow.MdiList = True
        Me.mnuWindow.MenuItems.AddRange(New System.Windows.Forms.MenuItem() _
            {Me.mnuWindowTileH, Me.mnuWindowTileV, Me.mnuWindowCascade})
        Me.mnuWindow.Text = "Window"
        '
        'mnuWindowCascade
        '
        Me.mnuWindowCascade.Index = 2
        Me.mnuWindowCascade.Text = "Cascade"
        '
        'dlgOpen
        '
        Me.dlgOpen.DefaultExt = "txt"
        Me.dlgOpen.Filter = "Text Files (*.txt)|*.txt|All Files (*.*)|*.*"
        '
        'frmParent
        '
        Me.AutoScaleBaseSize = New System.Drawing.Size(5, 13)
        Me.ClientSize = New System.Drawing.Size(576, 385)
        Me.Controls.AddRange(New System.Windows.Forms.Control() _
            {Me.MdiClient1})
        Me.IsMdiContainer = True
        Me.Menu = Me.MainMenu1
        Me.Name = "frmParent"
        Me.Text = "MDI Text Editor"
        Me.ResumeLayout(False)

    End Sub

#End Region

    Private Sub NewChild()
        Dim f As New frmChild()
        f.MdiParent = Me
        f.FileName = ""
        f.TextSaved = True
        f.Show()
    End Sub

    Private Sub mnuFileNew_Click(ByVal sender As Object, _
        ByVal e As System.EventArgs) Handles mnuFileNew.Click
        NewChild()
    End Sub

    Private Sub mnuFileOpen_Click(ByVal sender As Object, _
        ByVal e As System.EventArgs) Handles mnuFileOpen.Click
        dlgOpen.ShowDialog()
    End Sub

    Private Sub dlgOpen_FileOk(ByVal sender As Object, _
        ByVal e As System.ComponentModel.CancelEventArgs) Handles dlgOpen.FileOk
        Dim f As New frmChild()
```

```
            Dim nTemp As Integer = FreeFile()
            Dim MyFile As StreamReader
            f.MdiParent = Me
            MyFile = File.OpenText(dlgOpen.FileName)
            f.txtMain.Text = MyFile.ReadToEnd
            f.txtMain.Select(0, 0)
            MyFile.Close()
            f.FileName = dlgOpen.FileName
            f.TextSaved = True
            f.Show()
    End Sub

    Private Sub mnuWindowCascade_Click(ByVal sender As Object, _
        ByVal e As System.EventArgs) Handles mnuWindowCascade.Click
        Me.LayoutMdi(MdiLayout.Cascade)
    End Sub

    Private Sub mnuWindowTileH_Click(ByVal sender As Object, _
        ByVal e As System.EventArgs) Handles mnuWindowTileH.Click
        Me.LayoutMdi(MdiLayout.TileHorizontal)
    End Sub

    Private Sub mnuWindowTileV_Click(ByVal sender As Object, _
        ByVal e As System.EventArgs) Handles mnuWindowTileV.Click
        Me.LayoutMdi(MdiLayout.TileVertical)

    End Sub

End Class
```

THE CHILD FORM

Listing 15.2 contains all the code for the child form, frmChild.

LISTING 15.2   MDIDEMO.ZIP—CODE FOR THE CHILD FORM

```
Imports System.IO
Public Class frmChild
    Inherits System.Windows.Forms.Form

#Region " Windows Form Designer generated code "

    Public Sub New()
        MyBase.New()

        'This call is required by the Windows Form Designer.
        InitializeComponent()

        'Add any initialization after the InitializeComponent() call

    End Sub

    'Form overrides dispose to clean up the component list.
    Protected Overloads Overrides Sub Dispose(ByVal disposing As Boolean)
        If disposing Then
            If Not (components Is Nothing) Then
```

LISTING 15.2   CONTINUED

```
            components.Dispose()
        End If
    End If
    MyBase.Dispose(disposing)
End Sub
Friend WithEvents MainMenu1 As System.Windows.Forms.MainMenu
Friend WithEvents txtMain As System.Windows.Forms.TextBox
Friend WithEvents mnuFile As System.Windows.Forms.MenuItem
Friend WithEvents mnuFileSave As System.Windows.Forms.MenuItem
Friend WithEvents mnuFileSaveAs As System.Windows.Forms.MenuItem
Friend WithEvents mnuFileClose As System.Windows.Forms.MenuItem
Friend WithEvents mnuFileSep As System.Windows.Forms.MenuItem
Friend WithEvents mnuFilePrint As System.Windows.Forms.MenuItem
Friend WithEvents dlgSave As System.Windows.Forms.SaveFileDialog
Friend WithEvents PrintDocument1 As System.Drawing.Printing.PrintDocument


'Required by the Windows Form Designer
Private components As System.ComponentModel.Container

'NOTE: The following procedure is required by the Windows Form Designer
'It can be modified using the Windows Form Designer.
'Do not modify it using the code editor.
<System.Diagnostics.DebuggerStepThrough()> _
Private Sub InitializeComponent()
    Me.MainMenu1 = New System.Windows.Forms.MainMenu()
    Me.mnuFile = New System.Windows.Forms.MenuItem()
    Me.mnuFileSave = New System.Windows.Forms.MenuItem()
    Me.mnuFileSaveAs = New System.Windows.Forms.MenuItem()
    Me.mnuFileClose = New System.Windows.Forms.MenuItem()
    Me.mnuFileSep = New System.Windows.Forms.MenuItem()
    Me.mnuFilePrint = New System.Windows.Forms.MenuItem()
    Me.PrintDocument1 = New System.Drawing.Printing.PrintDocument()
    Me.txtMain = New System.Windows.Forms.TextBox()
    Me.dlgSave = New System.Windows.Forms.SaveFileDialog()
    Me.SuspendLayout()
    '
    'MainMenu1
    '
    Me.MainMenu1.MenuItems.AddRange(New System.Windows.Forms.MenuItem() _
        {Me.mnuFile})
    '
    'mnuFile
    '
    Me.mnuFile.Index = 0
    Me.mnuFile.MenuItems.AddRange(New System.Windows.Forms.MenuItem() _
        {Me.mnuFileSave, Me.mnuFileSaveAs, Me.mnuFileClose, _
        Me.mnuFileSep, Me.mnuFilePrint})
    Me.mnuFile.MergeType = System.Windows.Forms.MenuMerge.MergeItems
    Me.mnuFile.Text = "File"
    '
    'mnuFileSave
    '
    Me.mnuFileSave.Index = 0
    Me.mnuFileSave.Shortcut = System.Windows.Forms.Shortcut.CtrlS
    Me.mnuFileSave.Text = "Save"
```

```vb
        '
        'mnuFileSaveAs
        '
        Me.mnuFileSaveAs.Index = 1
        Me.mnuFileSaveAs.Text = "Save As..."
        '
        'mnuFileClose
        '
        Me.mnuFileClose.Index = 2
        Me.mnuFileClose.Text = "Close"
        '
        'mnuFileSep
        '
        Me.mnuFileSep.Index = 3
        Me.mnuFileSep.Text = "-"
        '
        'mnuFilePrint
        '
        Me.mnuFilePrint.Index = 4
        Me.mnuFilePrint.Shortcut = System.Windows.Forms.Shortcut.CtrlP
        Me.mnuFilePrint.Text = "Print"
        '
        'txtMain
        '
        Me.txtMain.Dock = System.Windows.Forms.DockStyle.Fill
        Me.txtMain.Font = New System.Drawing.Font("Courier New", 9.75!, _
            System.Drawing.FontStyle.Regular, _
            System.Drawing.GraphicsUnit.Point, CType(0, Byte))
        Me.txtMain.Multiline = True
        Me.txtMain.Name = "txtMain"
        Me.txtMain.Size = New System.Drawing.Size(292, 273)
        Me.txtMain.TabIndex = 0
        Me.txtMain.Text = ""
        '
        'frmChild
        '
        Me.AutoScaleBaseSize = New System.Drawing.Size(5, 13)
        Me.ClientSize = New System.Drawing.Size(292, 273)
        Me.Controls.AddRange(New System.Windows.Forms.Control() {Me.txtMain})
        Me.Menu = Me.MainMenu1
        Me.Name = "frmChild"
        Me.Text = "frmChild"
        Me.ResumeLayout(False)

    End Sub

#End Region

    Public TextSaved As Boolean
    Private sFileName As String

    Public Property FileName() As String
        Get
            Return sFileName
        End Get
        Set(ByVal Value As String)
            sFileName = Value
```

LISTING 15.2   CONTINUED

```
            If Trim(sFileName) = "" Then
                Me.Text = "Untitled"
            Else
                Me.Text = Mid(sFileName, InStrRev(sFileName, "\") + 1)
            End If
        End Set
    End Property

    Private Sub txtMain_TextChanged(ByVal sender As Object, _
        ByVal e As System.EventArgs) Handles txtMain.TextChanged
        Me.TextSaved = False
    End Sub

    Private Sub SaveFile()
        Dim MyFile As StreamWriter
        If sFileName = "" Then
            SaveFileAs()
        End If
        MyFile = File.CreateText(sFileName)
        MyFile.Write(txtMain.Text)
        MyFile.Close()
        Me.TextSaved = True
    End Sub

    Sub SaveFileAs()
        dlgSave.FileName = Me.FileName
        dlgSave.ShowDialog()
    End Sub

    Private Sub mnuFileSave_Click(ByVal sender As Object, _
        ByVal e As System.EventArgs) Handles mnuFileSave.Click
        If sFileName > "" Then
            SaveFile()
        Else
            SaveFileAs()
        End If
    End Sub

    Private Sub mnuFileSaveAs_Click(ByVal sender As Object, _
        ByVal e As System.EventArgs) Handles mnuFileSaveAs.Click
        SaveFileAs()
    End Sub

    Private Sub dlgSave_FileOk(ByVal sender As Object, ByVal e As
System.ComponentModel.CancelEventArgs) Handles dlgSave.FileOk
        If e.Cancel = False Then
            Me.FileName = dlgSave.FileName
            SaveFile()
        End If
    End Sub

    Private Sub frmChild_Closing(ByVal sender As Object, ByVal e As
System.ComponentModel.CancelEventArgs) Handles MyBase.Closing
        If Me.TextSaved = False Then
            Dim sMsg As String
            Dim nResult As Integer
```

```
                    sMsg = "Save changes to "
                    If Me.FileName = "" Then
                        sMsg += "this untitled document"
                    Else
                        sMsg += Mid(sFileName, InStrRev(sFileName, "\") + 1)
                    End If
                    sMsg += " before closing it?"
                    nResult = MessageBox.Show(sMsg, "System Message", _
                        MessageBoxButtons.YesNoCancel)
                    Select Case nResult
                        Case DialogResult.Cancel
                            e.Cancel = True
                        Case DialogResult.Yes
                            SaveFile()
                        Case Else
                            'Do nothing; let the window close.
                    End Select
                End If
            End Sub

    Private Sub mnuFileClose_Click(ByVal sender As Object, _
        ByVal e As System.EventArgs) Handles mnuFileClose.Click
        Me.Close()
    End Sub

    Private Sub mnuFilePrint_Click(ByVal sender As Object, _
        ByVal e As System.EventArgs) Handles mnuFilePrint.Click
        PrintDocument1.Print()
    End Sub

    Private Sub PrintDocument1_PrintPage(ByVal sender As Object, _
        ByVal e As System.Drawing.Printing.PrintPageEventArgs) _
        Handles PrintDocument1.PrintPage.Graphics.DrawString(txtMain.Text, _
            New Font("Courier New", 10, FontStyle.Regular), Brushes.Black, 0, 0)
    End Sub
End Class
```

FROM HERE...

The sample application developed in this chapter introduces the concepts of creating and managing MDI applications. This is a simple application; you may want to practice your skills by incorporating some of the following suggested enhancements:

■ Assign a unique Text property to each new instance of the child form. As it stands, you may have many child windows open whose captions say Untitled. A more reasonable approach may be to assign consecutively numbered captions (Untitled1, Untitled2, and so on).

■ Show the user a PrintDialog control before printing the document, giving her the option of setting printer options before the actual printing takes place.

■ When the user issues the File, Open menu command to open an existing document, have the blank Untitled document disappear. The user may not want a blank document to remain open if she opens an existing file.

CHAPTER 16

CREATING YOUR OWN WINDOWS CONTROLS

In this chapter

As you have learned, you can use an assortment of the controls included with Visual Basic .NET to build a powerful application quickly. One of the most exciting features of Visual Basic is the ability to create your own controls. These programmer-built Windows controls, known as *custom controls* or *user controls*, can then be used in Visual Basic applications like any other control.

In this chapter, we will take a look at the various approaches you can take and some of the issues that you need to consider when creating user controls.

WINDOWS CONTROL BASICS

You are already familiar with controls such as the TextBox and Label controls. To use these controls, you draw them on a form and direct their behavior through properties, methods, and events. When you create your own Windows control you are creating a similar object, except *you* are determining the properties, methods, and events. After you create your own control, you and others can use it in other Visual Basic projects, just like a TextBox control. You can use your controls in any application or development tool that can use Windows controls, including other .NET projects or Microsoft Internet Explorer. In fact, using custom controls is an ideal way to create a reusable component that can be used both inside a traditional client/server program and on the Internet.

Note
In Visual Basic .NET, custom controls are created in class modules. For simplicity's sake, the sample that you will create in this chapter will contain a single control; however, you can create as many controls as you like within a project by adding multiple custom control class modules.

STEPS INVOLVED IN BUILDING CUSTOM WINDOWS CONTROLS

Creating a custom Windows control in Visual Basic is different from creating a standard Windows Application. Therefore, a brief overview of the steps involved is useful:

1. Create a high-level design to determine what you want your Windows control to do. A Windows control is like a standalone object, so you need to ask yourself: What purpose does the object serve? What appearance do you want it have onscreen? What properties, methods, and events need to be made available to the program using the control?

2. Determine whether you will be using other controls as building blocks for your control. For example, you might want to create a Windows control that includes a third-party grid. When you are using other controls within your control, consider licensing and distribution issues.

3. Start a new Windows Control Library project, and draw the interface for your control.

4. Add code to enable all the properties, methods, and events you want your control to have.

5. A custom Windows control cannot run by itself. Its "runtime" is design time of the host application in which your control is used. You will need to add your custom control to a test project and test it from within Visual Basic. Make sure to use all the properties, methods, and events that you give your control.

6. Compile your control into a DLL file, and perform testing on the compiled version of your control.

7. Deploy your custom control appropriately.

DEVELOPMENT STRATEGIES

Building a User control in Visual Basic can be as easy or difficult as you choose. The level of difficulty depends on whether you use existing controls in your design, how sophisticated the interface will be, and (of course) how much code you have to write to make it work. In any case, there are at least three general reasons why you may want to build a custom control:

- **Combine the functionality of existing controls.**—This approach is also known as building a control from *constituent controls*. It is the easiest way to build a Windows control, because you are just bringing existing controls together. For example, you can package a combo box and a text box together and write minimal code that causes them to interact in the desired manner.

- **Add new functionality to an existing control.**—You can use an existing control as a starting point for your own creative efforts by modifying the control properties. For example, you can take a text box and add a custom property called `TextCaps` that causes the text to always be displayed in capital letters. This approach is a good way to get the exact functionality that you need in a control.

- **Create an entirely new control.**—You can draw the interface yourself with graphics methods, creating a totally original control that does not include any existing controls. Drawing your own control requires a good bit more work than the other two strategies but can be done to provide an original or different user interface. Because of the complexity of this approach, it will not be demonstrated in this chapter. However, you can get an introduction to the types of graphics techniques required to create a control in this manner in Chapter 14, "Designing an Effective User Interface."

CREATING A WINDOWS CONTROL

Assembling a new custom control from existing controls provides many advantages. First, when you add an existing control from the Toolbox to your new custom control, you get the existing control's complete functionality—an important consideration when you think about how many event handlers, methods, and properties are supported by an average control. Second, combining a number of controls into one allows them to be treated as a single unit, which may make things easier from an application architecture standpoint; this approach also allows them to be drawn on the form all at once. An additional advantage is that your users can easily understand a new control made up of controls they already know.

One way to create a custom control is to make it part of a Windows application; the control can then be used only in that application. To do so, choose Project, Add User Control from the menu system, and follow the general guidelines outlined in this section. If you choose to create your control in this manner, a new class module for the control is added to the open project.

More likely, you will prefer to create Windows controls as part of a Windows Control Library project, which initially consists of a single class module in which you will create a control, and which will in turn be compiled into a Dynamic Link Library (DLL) file. (Note that you can include multiple controls in a single Windows Control Library project by adding a new class module for each new control.) Controls created in this manner can be made available to other projects, and even deployed for use on other computers. This is the technique we will use in this example.

The complete MySampleControls sample project that you will create in this section, parts of which are excerpted in code listings, is available for download from www.quepublishing.com. Look for the file named ControlDemo.zip.

STARTING THE NAMETEXT CONTROL PROJECT

Now that you have some background information on Windows controls, you can get started by creating your first custom control. The control that you will build in this section is the NameText control, which will allow the user to his or her name by supplying the various parts—title; first, middle, and last names; and suffix/honorific—individually. The NameText control will be built entirely of existing Label, TextBox, and ComboBox controls. We will build this control as part of a Windows Control Library project so it can be used by other applications.

This example will give you a hands-on understanding of the issues involved in developing custom Windows controls in the Visual Basic .NET environment. First, you will draw the user interface of the control and then add a small amount code to give it functionality.

To build the NameText control, follow these steps:

1. Start Visual Basic .NET, then click the New Project button. (If Visual Basic .NET is already running, choose File, New, Project.)

2. From the New Project dialog box, make sure "Visual Basic Projects" is selected in the Project Types box, and choose Windows Control Library in the Templates box. In the Name box, type **MySampleControls**. When you have entered all the correct information into the New Project dialog box, it should look like Figure 16.1.

3. Click OK. A new project is created containing a User Control object named UserControl1.vb, as shown in Figure 16.2. Note how the User Control object's design area looks like a small form with no borders.

4. Click UserControl1.vb in the Solution Explorer. In the Properties window, change the FileName property of the Control object to NameText.vb.

5. Click the blank design area for the User Control object so the Properties window displays the object's properties. Change the Name property from UserControl1 to NameText.

Figure 16.1
The New Project dialog box is used to create a Windows Control Library project.

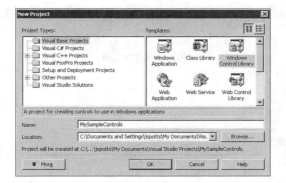

Figure 16.2
A Control object is similar to a small form but has no borders or other standard window elements.

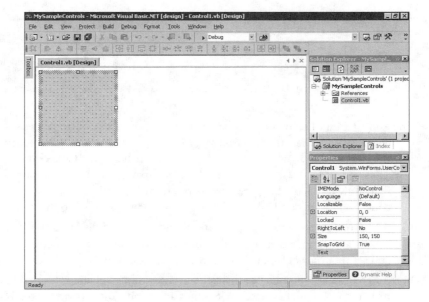

6. Change the GridSize property of the control to 4, 4. I find this grid size makes it much easier to align labels and text boxes with each other.

7. Add five Label controls in a vertical column along the left-hand side of the control's design area. Set their Text properties to Title:, First Name:, Middle Name:, Last Name:, and Suffix:. Set their TextAlign properties to TopRight. Size the labels appropriately; in my sample application, the Size property for all the labels is 80, 16. Arrange the labels so they look like Figure 16.3.

8. Change the Size property of the control itself (not the labels) to 200, 124 to make room for the text boxes that you are about to add, and to remove the extra space at the bottom.

Figure 16.3
Label controls form
the captions for the
NameText control.

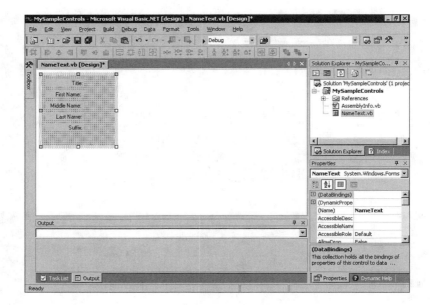

9. Add a ComboBox control to the right of the Title label. Change its Name property to cboTitle and clear its Text property. Make it about 60 pixels wide. Click the ellipsis button next to cboTitle's Items property to invoke the String Collection Editor. Enter the titles Mr., Mrs., Miss, Ms., Dr., and Rev. on separate lines in the String Collection Editor. Click OK to update the Items property; this will add the titles you entered to the Items collection of the combo box, allowing them to be displayed to the user at runtime.

10. Add three TextBox controls, 100 pixels wide, to the right of the First Name, Middle Name, and Last Name labels. Set the values of their Text properties to empty strings, and set their Name properties to txtFirstName, txtMiddleName, and txtLastName.

11. Add another combo box to the right of the Suffix label and clear its Text property. Set its name to cboSuffix. Use the String Collection Editor to add several possible suffixes such as Sr., Jr., III, IV, M.D., Ph.D., and so on.

12. Make sure the TabIndex properties are set so that the controls will be presented to the user in order. CboTitle should have the lowest TabIndex; cboSuffix should have the highest.

13. When you have finished adding controls, your completed NameText control interface should look something like Figure 16.4.

14. As with all projects, saving your work is important. Do so now before continuing.

Figure 16.4
The full set of constituent controls is drawn on the NameText Control object.

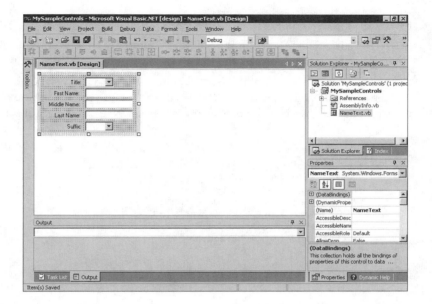

ADDING RESIZE CODE TO THE CONTROL

As you know from using standard controls such as a text box, you can adjust the size of a control in design mode by using the mouse, or by setting its `Size` property or `Width` and `Height` sub-properties. A TextBox control responds appropriately by automatically redrawing itself at the new size. When you are designing your own Windows control, especially one that is made up of existing controls, resizing is an important consideration. As you resize your control, you need to take action to make sure that the constituent controls are not hidden from the user or arranged in a way that prevents useful operation of the control.

To handle this concern, you can add code that responds to the `Resize` event of the NameText control object. This code will be executed whenever someone is drawing or resizing your control in a Visual Basic .NET (or other environment) project, and will ensure that the control does not get sized smaller than its original size. It will also resize the text boxes to fill up most of the available area.

Note

Although the task of having the TextBox control fill out the entire form area could be accomplished with no code by setting its `Dock` property, the technique used here helps to illustrate the process of writing code for your custom controls.

To add the necessary code for the NameText control, take the following steps:

1. Right-click NameText.vb in the Solution Explorer window and choose View Code from the pop-up menu to display the Code window for the NameText control.

2. In the Class Name box of the Code window, select (Base Class Events); then in the Method Name box, select the Resize event. This creates a NameText_Resize event handler, which will be invoked whenever a NameText control is resized in a host application.

3. Add code to the NameText_Resize event handler so it looks like the following:

```
Private Sub NameText_Resize(ByVal sender As Object, _
    ByVal e As System.EventArgs) Handles MyBase.Resize
    If Me.Width < 200 Then Me.Width = 200
    If Me.Height < 124 Then Me.Height = 124
    txtFirstName.Width = Me.Width - 100
    txtMiddleName.Width = Me.Width - 100
    txtLastName.Width = Me.Width - 100
End Sub
```

4. Save the changes to your project.

Note the use of the Me keyword in the program code you added in Step 3. Me refers to the current instance of the class; therefore, Me.Width, for example, refers to the Width property of the current instance of the NameText control.

As the user changes the dimensions of the NameText control, the Resize event handler will be executed. The first two lines in the procedure prevent the user from making the control instance too small. The remaining lines resize the TextBox controls based on the size of the NameText control, so that they will always be 100 pixels narrower than the form. (The 100-pixel figure accounts for the width of each TextBox control's matching Label control, plus a little extra as a margin.)

ADDING A NEW PROPERTY TO YOUR CONTROL

Including multiple controls within a single Windows control groups them visually and allows you to draw the entire set of controls on the form at once. However, for a custom control to be useful, you also need to be able to access its properties, methods, and events as a single control. In other words, if you intend to treat all the constituent controls separately, you really have not gained anything by combining them into one control.

When designing your own controls, you can create properties that can be accessed by the programs that use the controls. Consider how the properties of a standard control work. For example, the Text property of a TextBox control is a commonly used property. When designing an application that uses a TextBox control, you can *set* (assign) the value of the Text property in the design environment (or by using code at runtime). You can *get* (or read) the value of the Text property at design time or at runtime as well.

When creating a property for custom-created Windows controls, you create a Property procedure in the control's Code window. The typical Property procedure has two sections: the

Get section allows users of your control to read the property's value, whereas the Set section allows your users to assign the property's value. The general syntax of a Property procedure is as follows:

```
[Default|ReadOnly|WriteOnly] Property propertyname As type
    Get
        'statements that retrieve the value of the property
    End Get
    Set
        'statements that assign the value of the property
    End Set
End Property
```

If the control's user should only be allowed to read (Get) the value of the property but not assign (Set) it, then you should use the ReadOnly keyword in the procedure declaration, and omit the Set section. Likewise, if the user should be able to assign the property but not retrieve it, you should use the WriteOnly keyword and omit the Get section.

For the NameText control, we will begin by providing a read-only FullName property that assembles the various pieces that the user has entered into the constituent controls into a single value. The FullName property is much like the Text property of a text box. The difference here is that the FullName property returns text from *all* the controls on the form in a single string.

The user has no need to set the FullName property. Later in this chapter, we will create properties for the individual pieces of the full name that the user can set or get.

To set up the FullName property, open the Code window for the NameText control, and add the code in Listing 16.1 at the very bottom (just above the End Class line):

PART

III

CH

16

LISTING 16.1   ROLDEMO.ZIP—CREATING THE FullName PROPERTY

```
ReadOnly Property FullName() As String
    Get
        Dim s As String
        s = ""
        If cboTitle.Text > "" Then
            s &= trim(cboTitle.Text) & " "
        End If
        s &= trim(txtFirstName.Text) & " "
        If trim(txtMiddleName.Text) > "" Then
            s &= trim(txtMiddleName.Text) & " "
        End If
        s &= trim(txtLastName.Text)
        If cboSuffix.Text > "" Then
            s &= " " & trim(cboSuffix.Text)
        End If
        FullName = s
    End Get
End Property
```

Recall that because there is no need for the user to be able to set the value of FullName, the Property procedure is read-only. Consequently, there is only a Get portion, and no need for a Set portion.

The Get portion of the Property procedure code is not complex; it just combines the contents of the constituent controls and returns a single string to the calling application. However, the creation of this custom property illustrates the concept of taking a programming task (combining the address fields into a string) and encapsulating it in an object (the NameText control). The advantage is that other programmers can use this property without having to understand the details of its implementation.

MORE NEW PROPERTIES

Now that you havelearned how to create a read-only property (using the Get portion of a Property procedure), let's enhance the control by adding a few more properties. Specifically, we want to allow a hosting application to be able to read and/or write the values of the individual components of the name. In addition, the code will use the StrConv function to convert the text contained in the constituent controls into proper case values. The five new properties we will create are

- Title
- FirstName
- MiddleName
- LastName
- Suffix

THE TITLE PROPERTY—Get

If the user attempts to retrieve (Get) the value of a NameText control's Title property, our code should create a value for that property by returning the current value of the cboTitle combo box control's Text property. This technique is similar to the process of creating and returning the FullName property we discussed earlier. To code the Get portion of the Title property, begin by typing Property Title As String and pressing Enter (note that because this property will be read/write, you use neither the ReadOnly nor the WriteOnly keyword). Fill in the Get portion of the Property procedure by entering the following line of code between Get and End Get:

```
Title = StrConv(cboTitle.Text, VbStrConv.ProperCase)
```

THE TITLE PROPERTY—Set

If, however, the user attempts to assign (Set) the value of a NameText control's Title property, we must do a little more work. Notice that the Set portion of the Property procedure shell that was created for you includes an argument, ByVal Value As String. The Value argument, whose type must match the overall type of the Property procedure itself, will be populated with the value to which the user is attempting to set the Title property. We can use this value to populate or change the cboTitle control's Title property. Add the following code between Set and End Set:

```
cboTitle.Text = Value
```

Note

The Set portion of the Property procedure gives you an opportunity to validate the user's attempted property value. For example, if your control has a property that should only accept a certain range of values, you can verify that the desired value is acceptable before actually setting the internal property.

THE COMPLETE Title PROPERTY PROCEDURE

The complete code for the Title Property procedure is as follows:

```
Public Property Title() As String
    Get
        Title = StrConv(cboTitle.Text, VbStrConv.ProperCase)
    End Get
    Set(ByVal Value As String)
        cboTitle.Text = Value
    End Set
End Property
```

CODING THE OTHER PROPERTY PROCEDURES

Now that you know how to create a read/write property, the code for the remaining procedures should be fairly easy to understand. The complete code for the remaining four property procedures is listed here in Listing 16.2:

LISTING 16.2   CONTROLDEMO.ZIP—CREATING THE INDIVIDUAL NAME COMPONENT PROPERTIES

```
Public Property FirstName() As String
    Get
        FirstName = StrConv(txtFirstName.Text, VbStrConv.ProperCase)
    End Get
    Set(ByVal Value As String)
        txtFirstName.Text = Value
    End Set
End Property

Public Property MiddleName() As String
    Get
        MiddleName = StrConv(txtMiddleName.Text, VbStrConv.ProperCase)
    End Get
    Set(ByVal Value As String)
        txtMiddleName.Text = Value
    End Set
End Property

Public Property LastName() As String
    Get
        LastName = StrConv(txtLastName.Text, VbStrConv.ProperCase)
    End Get
    Set(ByVal Value As String)
        txtLastName.Text = Value
    End Set
End Property
```

```
Public Property Suffix() As String
    Get
        Suffix = StrConv(cboSuffix.Text, VbStrConv.ProperCase)
    End Get
    Set(ByVal Value As String)
        cboSuffix.Text = Value
    End Set
End Property
```

TESTING THE CONTROL

A custom User control eventually ends up as a part of a DLL (Dynamic Link Library) file. Components contained in a DLL file, when registered on another user's machine, can be added to a Visual Basic project or displayed on a Web page in Internet Explorer. However, during the development process, you need a way to test and debug your Windows controls within the Visual Basic .NET design environment. This process is slightly more complicated than debugging a normal Windows Application project because you have to deal with two separate sets of running code: the new control itself and the project using the new control.

BUILDING THE CONTROL PROJECT

To make the new control available for use by other projects and applications, you must *build* (compile) the `MySampleControls` project, which contains the NameText control. Simply right-click `MySampleControls` in the Solution Explorer window, then choose Build from the pop-up menu.

TESTING WITH A MULTI-PROJECT SOLUTION

The easiest way to test a new component is to use a multi-project solution. Throughout most of the samples in this book, you will open projects one at a time; that is, when you choose New, Project or Open, Project from Visual Basic's File menu, any projects already loaded close. However, the Visual Basic .NET development environment allows you to have multiple projects loaded simultaneously as part of a *solution*, which is a container for projects.

Tip

Each time you create a new project, a solution is created to contain that project, unless you are adding a new project to an existing solution. Notice in the Solution Explorer that a solution named `MySampleControls`—just like the project—was created. This solution is contained in a file named `MySampleControls.sln`.

For the current scenario, where we are creating a new control and want to debug it, a typical solution consists of the project in which we are creating the control itself plus a "throw-away" test project (usually a Windows Application project).

ADDING A TEST PROJECT TO THE SOLUTION

To begin testing the NameText control component, you need to add a Windows Application project to the current `MySampleControls` solution. Just choose File, Add Project, New Project from the menu system, select the Windows Application project template from the Add Project dialog box, and name the project `MyControlTest`. The Solution Explorer window is updated to show both projects, as shown in Figure 16.5.

Figure 16.5
You can add a standard project to your solution to test your new control.

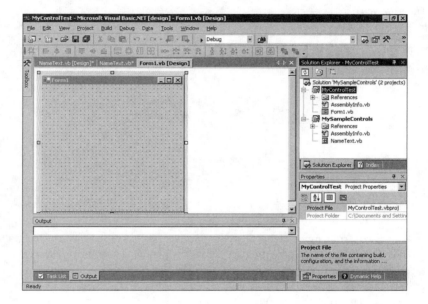

While you're at it, you may want to change the `Text` property of `Form1` to something descriptive, like **NameText Control Test Project**.

REFERRING TO THE NEW CONTROL PROJECT

For our test project (`MyControlTest`) to be able to utilize the new NameText control in the `MySampleControls` project, `MyControlTest` needs to contain a reference to `MySampleControls`. The reference was probably created automatically when you added the test project to the open solution. Check the References folder under the `MyControlTest` project in the Solution Explorer window to see whether there is a reference to the `MySampleControls` project. If there is, you don't need to do anything. Otherwise, you'll need to create the reference manually.

If you do need to add the reference, you can create it as follows: In the Solution Explorer window, right-click the References folder under the `MyControlTest` project, then choose Add Reference from the pop-up menu. You will be presented with the Add Reference window. Click the Projects tab, which will give you a list of all the currently open projects that may be referred to. Click the `MySampleControls` project (which should be the only project listed), then click the Select button to add `MySampleControls` to the Selected Components box. The Add Reference window should then look like Figure 16.6; click the OK button to complete the reference.

Figure 16.6
The Add Reference window allows you to create references from one project to another.

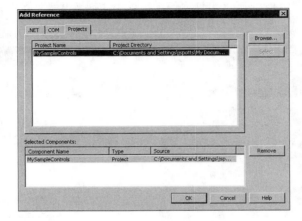

SHUTTING DOWN THE DESIGNER

A user control cannot be used within another project as long as its Designer window is open. If the `NameText.vb [Design]` tab is visible, click it to bring `NameText.vb`'s designer window to the front, then click the X in the upper right to close it.

SETTING UP THE TEST PROJECT

If you cannot see the Designer window for our test project's `Form1.vb`, right-click `Form1.vb` in the Solution Explorer window, then choose View Designer from the pop-up window. Bring up the Toolbox, then scroll down to the bottom of its Windows Forms section. A Toolbox icon for your NameText user control should now be available, as shown in Figure 16.7.

Now your custom Windows control is available. Go ahead and draw an instance on the form, just as you would with any other control. Notice that it appears just as you drew it in its Designer window, but it acts like a single control; all the text boxes within the control move together as you move the control itself; they cannot be selected individually. The control is given a default `Name` property of `NameText1`.

At this point, your NameText control object is loaded and running, so try resizing it on your form. As you change its size with the mouse, the code in its `Resize` event handler keeps the text boxes sized appropriately, as shown in Figure 16.8. If you try to reduce the height of the Address control too much, the control springs back to its minimum size.

Select the `NameText1` control, then check out the Properties window. The custom `FullName` property that we created is listed in the Properties window; however, because it is a read-only property, it is "grayed out" and cannot be modified.

Figure 16.7
The new NameText custom control is now available to use in applications.

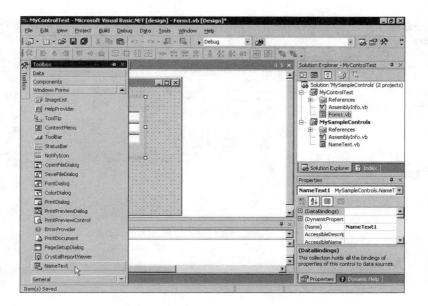

Figure 16.8
As the NameText control is widened, the Resize event code causes the width of the text boxes to increase.

Now, think ahead to when you will be running the test project. How will you know if the NameText control is working properly? We need a way to verify that the NameText control's `FullName` property is being provided properly. We will do so by adding a Button control to the form; when the Button control is clicked, it will display a message box containing the current value of the NameText1 control's `FullName` property.

Add a Button control to the form. Set its `Name` property to `btnDisplay`, and its `Text` property to `Display Full Name`. Enter the following line of code into `btnDisplay`'s `Click` event handler:

```
MessageBox.Show(NameText1.FullName)
```

Notice when you type the dot (.) after `NameText1`, the `FullName` property is available from the Auto Display Members feature of the code editor, as shown in Figure 16.9.

Figure 16.9
The Auto Display
Members feature
lists the custom
`FullName` property
that was created for
the NameText control.

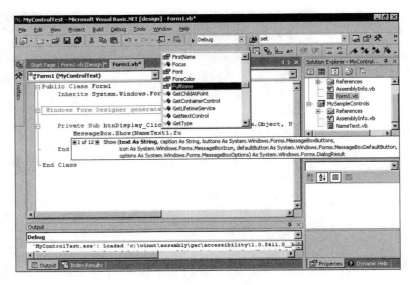

Now when we run the test program and click the button, the current value of the NameText control's `FullName` property will be displayed in a message box.

SETTING THE STARTUP PROJECT

Now that you have drawn an instance of your control on the form, you will want to run the test project. When you are using a multi-project solution, you must specify which project is the *startup project*. Visual Basic .NET gives that project the focus, causing it to be executed when the Start command is given, and starting the other projects automatically as needed. By default, the `MySampleControls` project is set to be the startup project by virtue of having been the first member of the solution. The startup project is indicated by boldface letters in the Solution Explorer window.

Because the NameText control is designed to be used within a project other than the Control Library project in which it was created, you need to set the startup project for the current solution to be the test project, `MyControlTest`. To do so, right-click `MyControlTest` in the Solution Explorer window, and select Set as Startup Project from the context menu that appears, as shown in Figure 16.10. The `MyControlTest` project changes to boldface in the Solution Explorer window to indicate that it is the startup project.

RUNNING THE TEST APPLICATION

Now that you have set up the test program, you are ready to run it to ensure that the NameText control works correctly. because you set `MyControlTest` to be the startup project in the previous section, pressing F5 or clicking the Start button causes `MyControlTest` to run.

To start the test project, press F5; choose Debug, Start from the menu system; or click the Start button on the Toolbar. The form will load, and the topmost combo box in the NameText control will get the focus.

Figure 16.10
Set the startup project to be the test Windows Application project. The custom control project starts automatically.

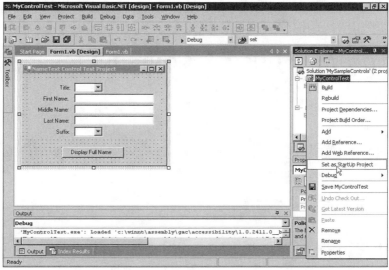

Fill out some or all the name component fields. When you click the Display Full Name button, a message box should appear to report the current value of the FullName property. Your custom NameText control is working properly! Figure 16.11 shows an example of the completed NameText control generating the FullName property.

Figure 16.11
The completed NameText control assembles a full name from component fields.

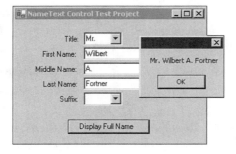

If you notice any problems; say, if you made a constituent control too small or left out a space in the concatenation of the name fields, simply stop the running program, open the Designer or Code window for the NameText control, and make any necessary changes. Run the test program again (which will cause the control to be rebuilt) to verify that your changes fixed the problems.

If you want to learn more about debugging a program, see Chapter 26, "Debugging and Performance Tuning." You can use the methods described there to step through the code in the FullName property procedure, examining the contents of the variables to verify that they are correct.

➔ For more information on dealing with unexpected errors in your programs, **see** "Working with Exceptions in Visual Studio," **p. 718**

ADDING YOUR CUSTOM CONTROLS TO OTHER PROJECTS

When you *built* your control during the development process, a Dynamic Link Library (DLL) file named `MySampleControls.dll` was created in the `bin` folder under the `MySampleControls` project folder. The DLL file contains all the instructions necessary for other projects to utilize the custom NameText control that you created (as well as any other custom controls that you may have added to the `MySampleControls` project).

If you have made any changes to the control project since the last time you built it, be sure to build it again so there is a fresh copy of the DLL file available.

ADDING CUSTOM CONTROLS TO THE TOOLBOX

You will probably want to use custom controls that you have already designed, tested, debugged, and built in other Visual Basic .NET projects. You could, of course, just add the Windows Control Library project(s) to each Visual Basic .NET solution you create. This is not good practice, however, as you will have multiple copies of the control's source spread around; if you fix an error or enhance the control in one copy, you must repeat the process in other copies or you will have mismatched versions of the same control floating around.

A better way to include the functionality of new controls and control libraries is to add a reference to the controls' DLLs to each project in which you want to use the controls. To demonstrate how to add custom control references to new projects, follow these steps (which assume that you have completed the NameText sample project earlier in this chapter):

1. Start a new Windows Application project. Give it any name you desire.

2. With the Designer window for your project's main form visible, click the Toolbox tab to display the Toolbox.

3. Right-click anywhere in the Windows Forms area of the Toolbox (right-clicking an existing control is fine), then choose Customize Toolbox from the pop-up menu. The Customize Toolbox dialog box appears, as shown in Figure 16.12.

4. In the Customize Toolbox dialog box, click the .NET Framework Components tab to display the components that are available through .NET.

5. Click the Browse button and browse to the filename and location of your compiled DLL file, then click the Open button. (For the purposes of the sample NameText control created earlier in this chapter, look for the file `MySampleControls.dll`, which is stored in the `bin` folder under your `MySampleControls` project folder.)

6. Your DLL and the individual custom control(s) contained in it are added to the .NET Framework Components tab of the Customize Toolbox dialog box, as illustrated in Figure 16.13.

Figure 16.12
The Customize
Toolbox dialog box
allows you to manage
the controls available
to your programs.

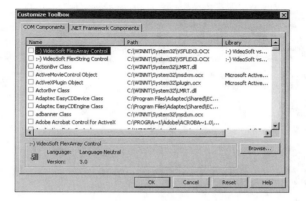

Figure 16.13
Custom-built controls
contained in DLL files
can be added to the
Toolbox via the
Customize Toolbox
dialog box.

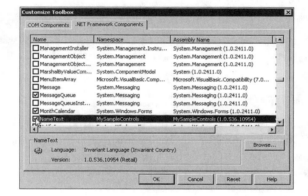

7. Make sure that the desired controls are checked, then click OK to close the Customize Toolbox dialog box.

8. Scroll the Toolbox until you see the custom control(s) you just added, as shown in Figure 16.14. You can now add a NameText control to this new Windows Application project.

After you have added a new custom control to your project, you may want to examine the References folder in the Solution Explorer to see that a reference to the custom control's library has been added to your project as well.

Tip

Once you have added your new custom controls to the Toolbox, they are available to all projects.

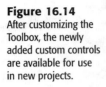

Figure 16.14
After customizing the Toolbox, the newly added custom controls are available for use in new projects.

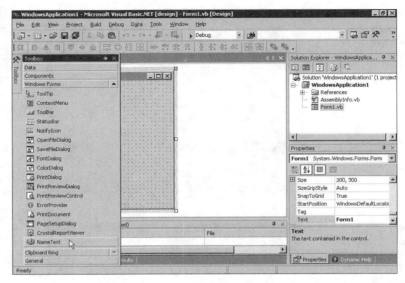

ENHANCING A WINDOWS CONTROL

The example you worked through earlier in this chapter introduced the concepts involved in creating a custom Windows control by combining existing controls into a single object. However, you can also create "new" controls simply by adding capabilities to an existing control. This means that you are working with a single base control but adding properties, methods, and events to provide additional capabilities to the user. For example, you might want to create a special scrollbar control that uses letters instead of numbers or a text box that accepts only certain characters.

Placing the code that performs these tasks into a separate Windows control makes it easier to use the code in future programs. For example, rather than add special code to every TextBox control in your program, you can simply use your "enhanced" control in place of the text box. To create these enhanced controls, you use many of the same techniques that you learned in the previous sections:

1. Start a new Windows Control Library project.
2. Add the base control to the UserControl window.
3. Add code for properties, methods, and events.

The following sections walk you through these steps, using a text box as the base control. Your "enhanced" text box will be known as a "Limited Character Text Box." It will have a user-defined property that allows the programmer to choose a set of acceptable characters that the user can enter. This additional property, `CharAccept`, will allow the user to restrict text entry to only letters, only numbers, or allow both.

The complete `EnhancedTextBox` sample project that you will create in this section, parts of which are excerpted in code listings, is available for download from www.quepublishing.com. Look for the file named `EnhTextBox.zip`.

SETTING UP THE BASE CONTROL

The steps for creating the enhanced TextBox control are similar to the steps you used to create the NameText control. For the enhanced TextBox control, the steps are as follows:

1. Start a new Windows Control Library project named **EnhancedTextBox**.
2. Change the control's FileName property from UserControl1.vb to EnhTextBox.vb.
3. Click the Designer window to display the design-time properties for the control. Change its Name property to **EnhTextBox**.
4. Add a TextBox control to the Designer window. Set its Location property to 0, 0 (the upper-left corner), and its Size property to 100, 20.
5. Set the TextBox control's AutoSize property to False. This will allow your code to dynamically resize both the height and width of the TextBox control as the user resizes the EnhTextBox control.
6. Name the text box txtCharSet, and clear its Text property.
7. Click a blank area of the Designer window to select the EnhTextBox control, then set its Size property to match the size of the txtCharSet text box it contains (100, 20).

   After you set up the user interface of the enhanced text control, it should look like the one in Figure 16.15.

Figure 16.15
The base control, pictured here, will be enhanced with additional capabilities.

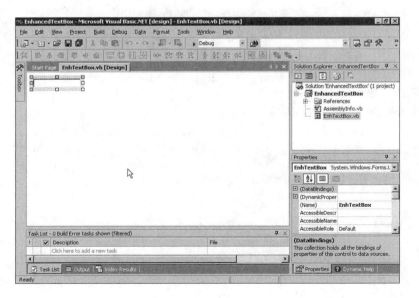

8. Right-click the Designer window, then choose View Code from the pop-up menu.

9. Choose (Base Class Events) in the Code window's Class Name box, then choose Resize in the Method Name box to display the control's Resize event handler.

10. Add the following lines of code to the procedure:

```
txtCharSet.Height = Me.Height
txtCharSet.Width = Me.Width
```

This simple two-line Resize event handler is all the code necessary for the user interface of the sample control. Its purpose is to keep the text box the same size as the UserControl object.

11. Save your project.

Before moving on, test the Resize event handler by performing the following steps:

1. Right-click the EnhancedTextBox project in the Solution Explorer window, then choose Build from the pop-up menu. This compiles the project's DLL.

2. Close the object's Code and Designer windows.

3. Choose File, Add Project, New Project; select the Windows Application template and give it any name you want.

4. Draw an instance of the EnhancedTextBox control on Form1.vb, and try resizing it. Notice that as you resize the EnhancedTextBox control, the constituent text box resizes itself.

> **Note**
>
> When you are developing a custom control, the code you write is used at design time in the host program. In other words, the client control's runtime is the host project's design time.

Now, it is time to work on enhancing the control. Close the test project's Form1.vb for now.

ENHANCING THE BASE CONTROL

The enhancement you are going to make to the txtCharSet TextBox control that comprises the EnhancedTextBox control is to tell it whether it should accept just letters, just numbers, or any characters as input. You can do so by adding your own property, called CharAccept, which can have one of the following three values:

- 0—Accepts any character
- 1—Accepts only numeric characters
- 2—Accepts only alpha characters

DECLARING THE CharAccept PROPERTY

To declare the CharAccept property, you need to add a private variable to store the property value internally. We will call this private variable mCharAccept (m- is often used as a naming convention prefix to denote *m*emory variables that are used internally in a class). The code that we write for the control will examine the value of this private variable and act according to its value.

To declare the private variable, open the Code window for EnhTextBox.vb and enter the following line of code below the "Windows Form Designer Generated Code" designator:

```
Private mCharAccept As Integer
```

DEFINING PROPERTY VALUES

As mentioned earlier, the CharAccept property will be designed to accept three possible values—0, 1, and 2. To make the control easier to use by developers, it would be nice to have mnemonic values predefined for the three values, giving the user (developer) an easy way of remembering the purpose of each value. To accomplish this, we first need to set up an *enumeration*, or a predefined list of values that together represent a custom type. For example, when you add a TextBox control to a form and select the TextAlign property in the Properties window, you can use a drop-down box to choose from three possible predefined property values—Left, Right, or Center.

We will create an enumeration to contain mnemonic representations of the three possible CharAccept values. The mnemonics that we will use for the three values will be AnyCharacter, NumericOnly, and AlphaOnly, representing the three values 0, 1, and 2, respectively.

To create the enumeration, enter the following code into the Code window for the EnhTextBox control. A good place would be just after the Private mCharAccept As Integer declaration you placed just below the "Windows Form Designer Generated Code" section:

```
Public Enum EnhTextBoxConstants
    AnyCharacter = 0
    NumericOnly = 1
    AlphaOnly = 2
End Enum
```

The name you gave to the enumeration, EnhTextBoxConstants, will be used when coding the property.

CODING THE CharAccept PROPERTY

Next, you need to write the code for the new CharAccept property and expose it to users of your control. You will do so by coding a Property procedure, as discussed earlier in this chapter. In this case, the Property procedure will need to be read/write; that is, your control's users should be able to both read (Get) and assign (Set) the value of the CharAccept property.

The code for the `CharAccept` property is fairly easy to understand. When the host application needs to read the value of the `CharAccept` property, the `Get` portion of the `Property` procedure simply passes what is stored in the `mCharAccept` private variable. When the value of the `CharAccept` property is modified by the host application, the `Let` portion of the `Property` procedure assigns one of the valid values to the private variable.

Begin coding the `Property` procedure by typing the procedure's declaration, `Property CharAccept() As EnhTextBoxConstants`, just above the `End Class` statement at the bottom of `EnhTextBox`'s Code window. When you press Enter after typing that line of code, the shell of the complete `Property` procedure is filled in for you. Note that we are using the enumeration we created as the declared type of the property. The user can set the property to one of the three values defined in the enumeration.

Listing 16.3 shows the code for the complete `Property CharAccept` procedure, including comments:

LISTING 16.3 ENHTEXTBOX.ZIP—CREATING THE `CharAccept` PROPERTY

```
Property CharAccept() As EnhTextBoxConstants
    Get
        'Set the property to the current value of
        ' the private mCharAccept variable.
        CharAccept = mCharAccept
    End Get
    Set(ByVal Value As EnhTextBoxConstants)
        Select Case Value
            Case 1, 2
                'If the user has set the property to 1 or 2,
                ' use that as the new value of the private
                ' mCharAccept variable.
                mCharAccept = Value
            Case Else
                'If the user has entered
                mCharAccept = 0
        End Select
    End Set
End Property
```

> **Note**
>
> If you ever worked with custom controls in previous versions of Visual Basic, you may recall having to write cumbersome code for the `PropertyBag` object and the `PropertyChanged`, `ReadProperties`, and `WriteProperties` events, allowing custom controls to retain the values of their properties between instances. Thankfully, properties for custom controls in Visual Basic .NET are inherently persistent; that is, they retain their values without any explicit work on the part of your program.

PREPARING TO RAISE AN EVENT

If the user enters an invalid character into the text box (based on the setting of the CharAccept property), you may want to let the host application know of this occurrence in addition to not accepting the character. You can do so by raising an event when invalid input is received; developers using your control can choose to react to the event or ignore it.

To have a control raise a custom event, you must first declare the event. This lets the control know that you may possibly be raising that event. You will see how to raise the event in the next section. To declare the event, add the following line of code below the section, near the mCharAccept declaration you added earlier:

```
Public Event BadKeyEntered()
```

To raise the event, you simply use the RaiseEvent statement at the appropriate place(s) in the control's code. When your control raises the event, it works just like any other event as far as the host application is concerned. Your control's user can write code in the host program's controlname_BadKeyEntered event handler to respond to the occurrence of a BadKeyEntered event.

WRITING CODE TO CHANGE THE TEXT BOX'S BEHAVIOR

Now that you have defined a custom property for the control and declared the existence of a potential event, the next step in this sample project is to create the code that utilizes the value of the CharAccept property to make the limited character text box do something different from a normal text box. In this case, you can use the text box's KeyPress event to scan each character as it is entered by the end user.

Each time the KeyPress event occurs (that is, each time the user presses a key while the txtCharSet control has the focus) Visual Basic .NET will invoke the KeyPress event handler, passing an argument named e, whose type is System.Windows.Forms.KeyPressEventArgs. Arguments of this type support a KeyChar property, which contains the keyboard character matching the key that the user has pressed.

The KeyPress event handler will determine the equivalent ASCII code value of the key that the user pressed, which will make it easier to determine whether the character is within the acceptable range (based on the CharAccept property). This ASCII code will be stored in a variable named KeyASCII (which VB6 users may recognize as the name of a similar argument passed to the KeyPress procedure in previous versions).

Because three possible values of the CharAccept property need to be handled, you can use a Select statement to handle the choices. If CharAccept is set to 0 (AnyCharacter), then the user's input is accepted and the procedure is exited. If, however, CharAccept is set to one of the other two possible values, the user's input is examined for validity. If he enters a valid

PART

III

CH

16

character, the procedure is exited and processing continues normally. When an invalid character is entered, the `Handled` property of the e argument is set to `True` (which instructs the program that the key press has been handled and can be ignored); the `BadKeyEntered` event is raised, and the `Beep` function is called to give the user audio feedback that the character he typed was rejected.

Here's one other item of note: You need to allow the use of the Backspace key (ASCII character 8) in any of the character sets that you use. Otherwise, the user cannot delete the previous character. The code for the complete `KeyPress` event handler is shown in Listing 16.4, with comments to help you follow the logic.

LISTING 16.4 ENHTEXTBOX.ZIP—CODING THE TEXT BOX'S ENHANCED BEHAVIOR

```
Private Sub txtCharSet_KeyPress(ByVal sender As Object, _
    ByVal e As System.Windows.Forms.KeyPressEventArgs) _
    Handles txtCharSet.KeyPress
    Dim KeyASCII As Short

    'Convert the KeyChar argument to an ASCII value
    KeyASCII = Asc(e.KeyChar)

    'If the user pressed Backspace, it's OK
    If KeyASCII = 8 Then Exit Sub

    'Decide what to do base on the CharAccept property
    Select Case mCharAccept
        Case 0 'Any character is acceptable
            Exit Sub
        Case 1 'Only numbers may be entered
            If KeyASCII >= 48 And KeyASCII <= 57 Then
                Exit Sub
            Else
                e.Handled = True
                RaiseEvent BadKeyEntered()
                Beep()
            End If
        Case 2 'Only letters may be entered
            If KeyASCII >= 65 And KeyASCII <= 90 Then
                Exit Sub
            ElseIf KeyASCII >= 97 And KeyASCII <= 122 Then
                Exit Sub
            Else
                e.Handled = True
                RaiseEvent BadKeyEntered()
                Beep()
            End If
    End Select
End Sub
```

TESTING THE ENHANCED TEXT BOX

After you enter all the code for the control, you can test the EnhTextBox control by following these steps:

1. Save your project.

2. You probably still have a test Windows Application project as part of the current solution; if not, add one.

3. Close the Designer and Code windows for the EnhTextBox control.

4. Rebuild the EnhTextBox control by right-clicking it in the Solution Explorer and choosing Build.

5. Open the Designer window for your test project. Delete any existing previous instances of the EnhTextBox control and add a new one.

6. Right-click the EnhTextBox control, then choose View Code. Notice that you can create a BadKeyEntered event handler for the control. Add the following line of code to the EnhTextBox1_BadKeyEntered event handler:

   ```
   MsgBox("You pressed a bad key!")
   ```

7. Run the test program and try out the control. Try setting the CharAccept property to different values to verify that it accepts only the keystrokes you want, and that the BadKeyEntered event is invoked when you enter an invalid character.

If you have problems with the control, you can use the same debugging techniques to find the problems in a control as you do to find problems in standard programs. You can set breakpoints and step through the code line by line, whether in the EnhTextBox control project or in the Windows Application project. (See Chapter 7, "Controlling the Flow of Your Program," for more information on debugging your code.)

→ For more information on locating errors in your programs, **see** "Debugging and Performance Tuning," **p. 717**

FROM HERE . . .

Now that you have learned to create your own Windows controls, you might want to examine the following topics:

- In Chapter 19, "Web Controls," you will learn how to design controls that can be utilized on the World Wide Web.

- Appendix A, "Packaging Your Applications," shows you how to package and deploy the projects you create, including custom controls.

WORKING WITH THE WEB

USING ACTIVE SERVER PAGES.NET

In this chapter

To the end user, the Web appears as a series of documents that contain all types of content. The Web is so easy to use, even the most novice computer user can search for information, go shopping, or participate in discussion groups by accessing Web pages. As an application developer, you may wonder what sort of intelligence exists on the other end to generate the resulting pages. For example, how does that online music store process orders submitted from its Web pages? How does the shipping company display the location of your package? The answer is that some type of program is running on the Web server, accepting input from the end user and dynamically generating Web pages. This chapter introduces you to Active Server Pages.NET, a component of the .NET framework that allows developers to create Web sites with dynamic, code-driven content.

In this chapter you will learn how to use ASP.NET to build Web sites. However, before we dive in to the many facets of ASP.NET development, some understanding of basic Web technology is required. To appreciate the full benefit of ASP.NET, you should first be familiar with the underlying architecture of the Web, as well as with its universal language, HTML. In addition, you will need to get a Web server machine prepared to test the samples discussed throughout this chapter. Therefore, the first section in this chapter is a quick primer on Web basics. To begin, we'll create a new directory on the Web server and set up some sample pages. You will learn how to create simple Web pages using a text editor or the Visual Studio HTML editor. In doing so we will lay the groundwork for your understanding of ASP.NET.

UNDERSTANDING WEB COMMUNICATION

Web browsing is a process of communication between clients and servers on a network. The clients are the users running browser software, such as Internet Explorer or Netscape. The servers are Web servers, such as Microsoft's Web server product, Internet Information Server (IIS). The network can be the worldwide Internet or a even an isolated corporate intranet. To use Active Server Pages.NET, you need access to a machine that is running the IIS software and has the .NET Framework installed. If you are not already running IIS, it can be installed on most of the recent Microsoft operating systems, including Windows 2000 Professional. For the purposes of this chapter, your Web server can be the same machine that you are using for Visual Studio development.

→ For more details on finding a Web server and installing IIS, **see** Chapter 3, "Creating your First Web Application," **p. 49**

CREATING WEB DIRECTORY STRUCTURES

After you have access to a Web server, making a Web page available to other users on the network is simply a matter of placing a file on the Web server. To access a given Web page, the end user simply enters the URL, as in the following example:

```
http://www.vbinsider.com/Family/Pictures/Reunion.htm
```

The previous example address indicates the Web server name, `www.vbinsider.com`, as well as the desired Web page, `/Family/Pictures/reunion.htm`. On a given Web server, the "root" directory is considered to be the top-level Web site. The `reunion.htm` page is two levels deep, inside the /Family/Pictures subdirectory. This works very much like the directory structure in the Windows operating system, with two important exceptions:

- Web servers have *virtual directories*, which allow the name and location of a Web folder to remain independent from the corresponding physical folder on the disk.

- Virtual directories (and the pages contained within them) on an IIS server are considered to be ASP.NET *applications*.

To further expound on the significance of virtual directories, consider the following sample Web sites, which might be set up on a typical corporate intranet:

```
http://myintranet/hr
http://myintranet/accounting
```

In this example, hr and accounting would probably be set up as separate virtual directories. Files related to hr would be placed in the hr folder, such as a corporate phone book search. As you will learn in the upcoming section, "Configuring Your ASP.NET Application," ASP.NET applications share common configuration properties and can exchange information between pages.

> **Note**
>
> IIS allows you to specify default document names for an application, usually default.htm, default.asp, or default.aspx. (The last extension, .aspx is new to ASP.NET). The default document (if it exists) is displayed when a Web surfer just requests the virtual directory name without specifying a file; that is http://server/ASPTest.

When creating a directory structure on your Web server, the names and organization seen by the Web do not necessarily have to match those on the Web server. For example, the /hr virtual directory might correspond to the subdirectory d:\hrfiles\productionwebsite\ on the hard drive.

> **Note**
>
> Any subdirectories created within a virtual directory (that are not virtual directories themselves) are part of the same ASP.NET application as their parent directory.

CREATING A VIRTUAL DIRECTORY IN IIS

The first step in setting up a new ASP.NET application on your Web server is creating the virtual directory. To demonstrate, we'll set up a directory for the samples in this chapter. When you download the sample files, you can copy them to the folder that corresponds to your virtual directory. To create the new Web site, perform the following steps:

1. Open Windows Explorer or My Computer and find the C:\Inetpub\wwwroot directory. This is the root directory of your Web server, which was created when IIS was installed.

2. Right-click an empty area in the wwwroot folder and choose New Folder. Create a new folder called ASPTest.

3. Return to your computer's desktop. Right-click the My Computer icon and choose Manage.

4. When the Computer Management screen appears, navigate to Services and Applications, Internet Information Services. This part of the management console, shown in Figure 17.1, is used to manage your Web server directories.

Figure 17.1
The Internet Services manager and other management utilities are integrated into the Microsoft Management Console.

5. Right-Click Default Web Site and choose New, Virtual Directory.

6. Click Next and you will be prompted for the directory Alias. This is the name that browsers will use to access pages in the virtual directory. To create the sample directory for this chapter, enter ASPTest and click Next.

7. The next screen prompts you for the path to the physical directory. Enter the path of the folder you just created with Windows Explorer, C:\Inetpub\wwwroot\ASPTest, and click Next.

> **Note**
>
> In the scenario presented here, the virtual directory name and physical directory name are the same. This arrangement is very typical of what happens in the real world. However, your Web pages do not have to be located in the existing C:\Inetpub\ wwwroot structure, nor does the virtual directory name have to match the Windows folder name.

8. On the Access Permissions screen, make sure the Read and Run Scripts options are selected. Click Next and then Finish to complete the operation.

When you have finished creating the new virtual directory, close the Computer Management screen. You are now ready to begin placing your Web site files in the ASPTest folder.

> **Tip**
>
> If you have not already done so, change the default Windows Explorer Folder Options to make working with files easier. By default, Windows hides file extensions and other information not required by the average user. However, as a programmer you will certainly require detailed access to operating system files. To change these settings, choose Folder Options from the Tools menu, and select the View tab. Next, uncheck the options to hide file extensions and system folders.

USING HTML WITH ASP.NET

To add new Web pages to the ASPTest application, all you need to do is place files in the ASPTest folder. When your browser requests a Web page from this folder, the IIS program is responsible for processing the correct file and responding to the request. The information returned to the browser from the IIS server consists of plain text plus HTML formatting codes, as shown in Listing 17.1.

LISTING 17.1   ASPTEST.ZIP—A SIMPLE HTML PAGE, WELCOME.HTM

```
<HTML>
<BODY>
<FONT SIZE="+2" COLOR="BLUE"> This is a sample web Page! </FONT> <BR>
<B> I hope you enjoy it! </B> <BR>
</BODY>
</HTML>
```

The HTML syntax is very simple to follow. Most but not all tags have a corresponding start and ending tag, which affects the text between them. Figure 17.2 shows how Internet Explorer interprets the HTML code from Listing 17.1

Figure 17.2
Web pages can be created by typing HTML in a text editor, saving an Office document in HTML format, or using a Web design tool such as Visual Studio .NET or FrontPage.

HTML documents are very easy to create. As a VB programmer, you should have no trouble picking up HTML basics. A complete HTML tutorial is available on the Web at www.cnet.com.

> **Tip**
>
> You can also learn more by viewing the HTML source code behind any of your favorite Web pages. To do this, choose View Source from the Internet Explorer View menu.

Because an HTML file is saved in a plain text format, a lot of developers use Notepad or another text editor to create Web pages. Although Notepad does not have a lot of advanced editing features, it is simple and quick.

> **Note**
>
> Both `.HTML` and `.HTM` are valid extensions for standard HTML files, although Windows Web sites seem to prefer the three-character version, which is probably a result of naming conventions inherited from DOS.

> **Tip**
>
> If you edit a lot of Web pages or other files with Notepad, add a Notepad shortcut to the `SendTo` directory for your windows profile. This shortcut will make editing easier, because you can right-click any file and send it to Notepad.

After you create the `welcome.htm` file in the `ASPTest` directory, you can view the Web page by entering its address in your browser: `http://servername/ASPTest/welcome.htm`, where *servername* is the name of your Web server. You should see the Web page as pictured in Figure 17.2. If your Web server is on a network, you should also be able to view the page from other computers.

EDITING HTML WITH VISUAL STUDIO

Although editing HTML with Notepad is somewhat primitive, it shows you just how simple creating a Web page can be. A lot of developers use a text editor to make quick edits to their Web pages, even if they were originally created using a more robust design tool. However, the latest version of Visual Studio includes a built-in HTML editor that promises to make HTML editing much friendlier than Notepad. To see how it works, open the `welcome.htm` page we just created:

1. Start Visual Studio .NET.
2. From the File menu, choose Open File.
3. Browse to the `C:\Inetpub\wwwroot\ASPTest` directory.
4. Double-click the `welcome.htm` file to open it.

After opening the HTML file, you will see the Web page displayed in graphical design mode, which looks like what you would see in the browser. Design mode allows you to create a Web page in a graphical manner so you do not have to think about HTML codes. For example, you can type text into the document, then highlight it and use buttons on the toolbar to change its size and color. This process works just like using a modern word processor and automatically generates the underlying HTML code. However, if you need to view or edit the HTML code for your document directly, click the HTML button at the bottom of the design screen. Figure 17.3 shows how the Visual Studio HTML editor uses indentation and color to produce a more readable HTML listing.

Figure 17.3
Use the buttons labeled Design and HTML to control the view of your Web page.

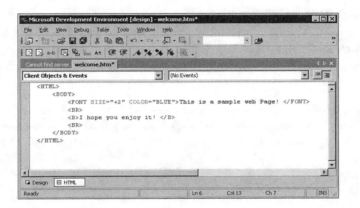

PART
IV
CH
17

The Visual Studio .NET HTML editor provides the best of both worlds for the Web page designer: While in HTML mode, you can enter HTML tags directly and switch back to Design mode to view the results. Also note that HTML pages can be added to a Visual Studio solution, but you can also edit them as stand-alone files, as we did in this example.

BRINGING DYNAMIC CONTENT TO THE WEB

In the early days of the Web, most pages were just static HTML documents. However, eventually more complex Web applications emerged, such as online stores and library catalogs. Other than the ability to exchange data with the server, HTML by itself does not have any real programming power. To make complex Web applications work, the Web server software has to do more than just relay the contents of an HTML file back to a browser; instead it actually has to generate HTML dynamically. One early way of creating dynamic content was to write a program in C or another language that was executed by the Web server. The server acted as a "gateway" between the Web and the program, which could perform activities such as connect to a database and return the desired information, formatted as HTML. In this case, there is no physical file corresponding to the requested Web page, only the HTML output of a program. From the browser's point of view, this arrangement works out quite well, because the client browser does not really know or care what happens on the Web server. As long as the returned stream of information contains HTML codes the browser understands how to display, the browser's request can be fulfilled.

> **Note**
>
> Arguably, the most powerful enhancements to Web technology have been made on the Web server. However, for completeness we should mention that modern Web browsers also support script code and DHTML (dynamic HTML) to create a more interactive Web experience.

INTRODUCING ACTIVE SERVER PAGES

Several years ago, Microsoft came out with a technology known as Active Server Pages (ASP), which allows you to mix Visual Basic code and HTML code in a single file on your Web server. When IIS processes an ASP file, it returns the HTML directly to the browser, but executes the Visual Basic code on the server.

> **Note**
>
> When a user requests a standard `.htm` file, the Web server simply reads the file from the disk drive and passes it back to the browser. However, when IIS processes an `.aspx` file, it executes code embedded within the file. This code can take different actions on the server, including generate the HTML that is returned to the browser.

ASP technology has become very popular and can be found on a significant number of Web sites. To see how it works, we will create a sample Active Server Page. To create your first ASP.NET page, perform the following steps:

1. Start the Notepad editor.
2. Open the HTML file we created earlier, `C:\inetpub\wwwroot\asptest\welcome.htm`.
3. Alter the contents of the file to match Listing 17.2.
4. Save your file in the same folder, with the new name and extension: `welcome.aspx`.

> **Note**
>
> Users familiar with previous versions of ASP should note that `.aspx` is the new extension used with Active Server Pages.NET. (The `.asp` extension is still supported for backwards compatibility, although you will not have access to ASP.NET features.)

LISTING 17.2   ASPTEST.ZIP—USING ASP.NET TO CREATE A DYNAMIC PAGE

```
<HTML>
<BODY>
<FONT SIZE="+2" COLOR="BLUE"> This is a sample Web Page! </FONT> <BR>
<%
Dim intCounter AS Integer

For intCounter = 1 to 10
   Response.Write ("<B> I hope you enjoy it! </B><BR>")
Next
```

LISTING 17.2   CONTINUED

```
Response.Write ("Page Created: " & DateTime.Now)

%>

</BODY>
</HTML>
```

Listing 17.2 resembles Listing 17.1, except for the addition of a few lines of VB code, including a For loop. To see how the page looks, open Internet Explorer and enter the address of your new ASP.NET page, which is `http://servername/ASPTest/welcome.aspx` where *servername* is the name of your Web server. You should see the Web page as pictured in Figure 17.4.

Figure 17.4
ASP.NET allows you to dynamically generate HTML from the Web server by adding Visual Basic code to an .aspx file.

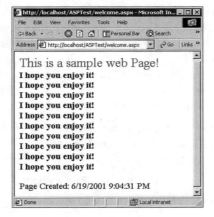

Click the Refresh button in your browser, and you should notice the time displayed on the page will change. This is because the server generated the line of HTML containing the time dynamically. Using Listing 17.2 as a guide, note the following properties of a typical ASP.NET page:

- The script tags <% and %> in an ASP.NET file mark Visual Basic code to be executed by the server. Any other text in the file, such as standard HTML, is sent directly back to the client browser.

- Several built-in objects are included in ASP.NET for manipulating Web content. In Listing 17.2, the `Response.Write` method is used to send a string of HTML back to the client browser.

- The client browser cannot view the server-side code. If you choose View Source, you will only see the HTML generated by the code, not the code itself.

Although this example seems trivial, it does open up some interesting possibilities. Because ASP.NET allows you to create pages "on the fly" with Visual Basic code, you can perform more complex actions such as connecting to a database and returning HTML containing field values.

KEY ENHANCEMENTS IN ASP.NET

Users of previous versions of ASP will notice the following major improvements:

- **Compiled Code**—The code in ASP.NET pages is compiled for faster execution. (Previous versions of ASP were interpreted.) When you make changes to an .aspx file, IIS recompiles the file the next time it is requested.

- **Robust Language**—The full power of the Visual Basic language (or any language in the Visual Studio family) is available for use with ASP.NET. (Previous versions of ASP used only the more limited VBScript and JScript languages on the server.)

- **Forms-based Programming**—A new programming model, *Webforms*, has been created that allows greater separation between the user interface and the code in an ASP page.

Of all those enhancements, the last one listed promises to make the most significant impact on the way you develop Web applications. ASP.NET is a core technology in Visual Studio .NET, used in both Web Applications and Web Service projects. Rather than thinking about sending data to and from the client browser, you can program against a control-and-event model you are already familiar with from standard VB applications. Programming with Web forms within Visual Studio, which was introduced in Chapter 3, "Creating Your First Web Application," is covered in more detail in the next two chapters.

→ For more details on Web Applications, **see** Chapter 18, "Web Applications and Services," **p. 475**

→ For more details on Web Controls, **see** Chapter 19, "Web Controls," **p. 501**

In the following sections, we will explore ASP.NET at the page level, introducing you to its built-in classes and fundamental concepts. If you are currently an ASP developer, read this chapter to get started quickly with ASP.NET.

CREATING ASP.NET PAGES

ASP.NET pages have an .aspx extension. To get started with ASP.NET you'll need an editor. As we mentioned earlier, Notepad is a good editor for simple Web pages and will suffice for the ASP.NET samples in this chapter. As you will see in later chapters, Visual Studio provides the means for working with ASP.NET pages as you would forms in a project. However, you can still use Visual Studio's HTML editor to edit .aspx files outside a project. To do this, start with an HTML file and then save it with an .aspx extension. While in the HTML editing mode, you can type Visual Basic code directly into the file.

UNDERSTANDING SCRIPT TAGS

To separate your VB code from HTML tags in an ASP.NET page, you use *script tags*. While processing the page, Internet Information server executes only the code within the special script tags, two forms of which are listed here:

- The HTML `<SCRIPT>` tag with the `RUNAT="SERVER"` attribute indicates declarative server-side code.

- The `<%` and `%>` tags mark the beginning and end of the server-side code to be executed.

The later syntax is shorter and is probably familiar to users of previous versions of ASP. However, ASP.NET has slightly different rules about the use of the different script tag forms. Starting with ASP.NET, you cannot use the short form if your code contains a custom function declaration. For example, the following code would work fine in ASP, but is no longer supported in ASP.NET:

```
'THIS WILL NOT WORK IN ASP.NET!
<%
    Sub Test()
        Response.Write("Hey")
    End Sub

    Call Test()
%>
```

Starting with ASP.NET, use the <SCRIPT> tag for function declarations and the <% and %> tags for statements to be executed during page processing. For example, you would have to rewrite the previous code to run in ASP.NET as follows:

```
<SCRIPT LANGUAGE="VB" RUNAT="SERVER">
    Sub Test()
        Response.Write("Hey")
    End Sub
</SCRIPT>

<%
    Call Test()
%>
```

PART
IV
CH
17

> **Note**
>
> Starting in ASP.NET, you must use the longer `<SCRIPT RUNAT="SERVER">` tag to define functions.

More information on migration from ASP to ASP.NET is available in the Quickstart Tutorials included with the .NET Framework SDK. You probably already have these samples installed on the machine on which you installed Visual Studio. To view this very useful ASP.NET information, open the following URL: `http://localhost/quickstart`.

IMPORTING NAMESPACES

In Chapter 5, "Visual Basic Building Blocks," we introduced the concept of a namespaces and described how to use the `Imports` statement in a Visual Basic application to specify namespaces used within your program. You can also import namespaces in ASP.NET page, although the syntax is a little different:

```
<% @Import Namespace = "System.IO" %>
```

The previous line of code imports the `System.IO` namespace for use in the current ASP.NET page. Note that this statement must precede any variable declarations.

→ For more details on Importing a Namespace, **see** Chapter 5, "Visual Basic Building Blocks," **p. 113**

Because ASP.NET includes the full power of the VB language, you can, of course, define your own namespaces and import them for use as an ASP application. By placing compiled DLLs in a bin subdirectory of an ASP.NET application, you can import a custom namespace. For more information, see the topic "Working with Business Objects" in the ASP.NET Quickstart tutorial.

CONFIGURING YOUR ASP.NET APPLICATION

One initiative of the .NET framework was ease of setup and deployment through the use of user-editable configuration files. Configuration files, which can control many different settings in an .NET applications, are text-based XML files, which mean they are readable and can be edited easily by humans. For example, remote administration of ASP.NET applications can be performed, even if you do not have the IIS management software installed. By placing a file called web.config in a directory on your Web server, you can override the default configuration settings.

> **Note**
>
> The default settings for an application are inherited from the most recent configuration settings in the parent directory path. The default master configuration files for the machine are located in the \windows\Microsoft.Net\Framework\version\ CONFIG directory, where windows is your Windows directory and version is the version of the .NET Framework installed on the machine.

A configuration file starts with a <configuration> tag and contains several sections, each related to a specific configuration area. One of the first things you'll probably want to do with a configuration file is alter ASP.NET's custom error handling. In previous versions of ASP, when an unhandled error occurs it is sent to the client. However, ASP.NET allows you to easily substitute it with your own error page:

```
<configuration>
    <system.web>
        <customErrors mode="On" defaultRedirect="errorpage.aspx"/>
    </system.web>
</configuration>
```

The third line of the previous configuration file sets the default error page to errorpage.aspx. This means if the code in the ASP.NET application throws an unhandled exception, the user will not see the error text. Instead, he will see the custom error page, which can be programmed to display a friendlier message:

```
Response.Write ("An error has occurred in the following page:")
Response.Write (Request.QueryString("aspxerrorpath"))
Response.Write ("<BR>Please call tech support if you dare!")
```

For troubleshooting and development purposes, you will probably want to set the custom error setting to Off. Another interesting use of a configuration is to store static, app-specific settings such as a connection string. To do so, simply add a section to your `config.web` file containing a key-value pair:

```
<appSettings>
  <add key="ConnectionString" value="server=BSSQL;database=ap;UID=apweb" />

</appSettings>
```

The previous sample configuration text creates an application setting called `ConnectionString`. The following code can be used from any page in the same ASP.NET application to retrieve its value:

```
Dim strConn As String  = ConfigurationSettings.AppSettings("ConnectionString")
```

To learn more about the different types of configuration settings, see the help topic "Configuring .NET Framework Applications."

USING ASP.NET's BUILT-IN CLASSES

Starting with ASP.NET, the full Visual Basic language is available to Active Server Page developers, so the language concepts in the rest of this book also apply to ASP.NET development. In addition, Microsoft has provided several Web-centric classes that are exposed as objects in any ASP.NET page. You have already seen an example use of one such object, the Response object, used to manage the server's response to a Web request. Many of these objects will be familiar to ASP developers, but with new features or subtle changes. In the remainder of this chapter, we'll look at some important objects provided by the ASP.NET architecture and how they can be used in your ASP.NET applications.

USING THE Session OBJECT

A *session* with an ASP.NET application can be compared to a session with a psychiatrist. It starts when you enter the psychiatrist's office, ends when you leave, and is over after a fixed period of time. During your visit, you might discuss a variety of topics; analogous to the various Web pages you visit on a Web site. One popular feature of Active Server Pages that is still available in ASP.NET is *session variables*. Session variables are user-specific and have a scope of the current ASP.NET session. They are stored on the Web server and are accessible from server-side code. To set a session variable, you simply give it a name and assign a value:

```
Session("UserId") = "bsiler"
Session("CurrentPurchases") = 19.95
Session("ShippingMethod")="Standard"
Session.Add("YearsWarranty",5)
```

The previous lines of code show how to set session variables. The last line uses the Add method, which is new to ASP.NET. After you have created a session variable, the Web server will maintain its value until the user's session ends. Some of the ways in which a session can end are as follows:

- A user closes the browser.
- The session *times out* after the number of minutes specified in the `Session.Timeout` property. (As long as the user continues to interact with the server, the session will remain active.)
- Your code calls the `Session.Abandon` method to purposely terminate the session.

Note There is nothing preventing a user from bouncing all over the Web; don't count on being able to precisely know who is logged in and when.

After a session ends, the contents of any session variables are destroyed. They are best suited for temporary information that you do not want to store on the client.

MANAGING SECURITY WITH SESSION VARIABLES

One frequent use of session variables is to control security across multiple pages. For example, suppose you have an intranet site with a login page. The login page could set a session variable containing the name of the current user, which would then be available to other pages. Suppose you have the following three pages on your intranet site:

- `usermenu.aspx`—Displays a list of links to other pages, based on the current user name.
- `hrsalary.aspx`—Displays payroll reports.
- `cafemenu.aspx`—Displays the offerings of the company lunchroom.

On our fictional intranet, the first page a user sees after signing in is `usermenu.aspx`, which would read a database and display a list of links to the other two pages, depending on whether the user had access. For example, everyone would probably be able to view the lunchroom offerings, but only selected users would see the menu option for payroll reports. It is easy enough to read a database and generate a page of links customized for a given user ID, but how do you prevent users from simply typing in the address of the page they want, bypassing the menu page entirely? One solution is to include a security check at the top of every page:

```
<%
If Not CheckValidUser("hr",Session("UserID")) Then
   Response.Write("Access denied!")
   Response.End
End If
%>
```

The previous lines of code pass the name of the application (hr) and the value of the `UserID` session variable to a custom function, `CheckValidUser`. If the `CheckValidUser` function returns `False`, any code or HTML beneath the security check is not processed. (A real-world application would probably redirect the user to a page requesting he sign in again, in case the session timed out.)

Creating a Custom Security Database

With all the talk about security and hackers, it is easy to get confused about the different types of security involved in running a Web site. Security can exist at the *network level* to prevent people from spying or altering the data being transmitted over a network connection. This type of security is usually implemented using firewalls or a secure sockets protocol, and by itself could be the topic of a whole book. (By the way, when you see `https` in a URL, you are using secure sockets.) The security discussion in this chapter is more closely related to *application security*, which falls closer to the realm of application design than network security. Security at the application level is concerned with making sure the application is aware of the end user's identity so it can display the appropriate information. For a recent project, my workgroup was able to design a SQL database and associated Visual Basic classes that we use to administer security company-wide across all our Web applications. In designing such a database, it is important to make it as flexible as possible. At a minimum you will need tables to represent application tasks, users, and user permissions for those tasks. In addition, you may want to consider the following when designing a security model:

- What information will you need to store about the user? For example, will users at the corporate office need to see a different home page and therefore need to be designated as special user types in the database?

- Does your security model need to assign access for individual users, groups of users, or both?

- Will your security model be date sensitive? If so, you will need start and end date fields on the user and/or permission records.

- How are the units of your company organized? This is a very important question, because it will determine the granularity of your security model. For example, suppose you manage multiple restaurants. Each restaurant will probably have some internal company ID number. In this case, you will probably want to include this ID number in your security database. This will permit you to assign each application task to specific users for specific restaurants.

In addition to designing a flexible security database, you will need to apply the same types of considerations when creating classes to access that database. By using classes rather than having the applications directly access the database; you can keep the security logic separated from the application logic. These classes should be generic to apply to multiple applications, but still support a useful level of security. For example, you may need to write some ASP code that displays a menu of reports. Continuing with the restaurant example, you should be able to ask a security business object a question like "return a list of restaurant ID's for task 123 for user jsmith" that the application could then process appropriately.

MAINTAINING A SESSION ACROSS SERVERS

Session variables are both useful and easy to use, but they can be a bad habit. If you have been to any ASP seminars in the past year, you have probably heard Microsoft preaching *against* their use. There are two main reasons for this: insufficient use of server resources and incompatibility with server farms. Each session variable takes up some amount of memory on the server. In an environment where the number of users may vary widely, this problem will compound itself the more session variables per user you have defined. Because a lot of sessions are terminated by timeouts, your Web site may not be very scalable due to wasted memory. Of course, it is not a big deal to store a one object in a session variable, such as a userid. Given a userid, you can probably easily retrieve anything else your page needs to function with a VB method call or database lookup.

However, if your Web site uses multiple servers, you may not even have the option of using session variables. A *server farm* is a group of servers that acts as a single Web site for load balancing purposes. With each request for a Web page, you may be directed to a different physical server. In this scenario, traditional session variables stored on the server just do not work. To get around this problem, you need to use another method such as a database. Hidden form fields and cookies, which we will explore in a later section, can be used to store the database key on the user's machine. Although the intricacies of a Web farm are beyond the scope of this book, it is worth mentioning that the latest version of ASP does take server farms into consideration. ASP.NET allows you to specify a SQL database in which to store session information. For more information, see the help file topic "Session State in ASP.NET."

CONTROLLING OUTPUT WITH THE Response OBJECT

Every time the client requests a page from the Web server, a response is sent. The `Response` object, which is an instance of the `HttpResponse` class, is used to manage the server response. We have already introduced to you one of its most common uses, sending the contents of a variable or other HTML codes back to the client with the `Write` method.

Table 17.2 lists some of the most useful properties and methods of the `Response` object.

TABLE 17.2   FREQUENTLY USED MEMBERS OF THE Response OBJECT

Member Name	Description
Write	Sends text to the browser.
End	Ends the current response.
Redirect	Sends the browser to another page.
IsClientConnected	Checks for user connection.
Cookies	Provides access to client cookies.
Cache	Controls caching of page content.

REDIRECTING THE USER TO ANOTHER PAGE

We have already seen examples of the `Response.Write` and `Response.End` methods. `Response.Redirect` tells the browser to request another page, as in the following example:

```
<%
If Not CheckValidUser("hr",Session("UserID")) Then
   Response.Redirect("/security/login.htm")
End If
%>
```

The previous code sample is a security example from the last section, rewritten to send the user back to the login page. Note that `Response.Redirect` can only be used if no other HTML has been sent back to the browser. If the file contained any HTML or a `Response.Write` prior to the `Redirect` statement, an error would occur.

Note

As an alternative to `Response.Redirect`, newer versions of IIS offer `Server.Transfer`. `Response.Redirect` involves an extra round trip to the client and back (the server tells the browser to request a new page) whereas the `Server.Transfer` function substitutes one page for another at the server level.

TERMINATING A LONG RESPONSE

The `IsClientConnected` property provides the capability to check whether a user is connected to the `Response` being generated. A typical request-response scenario takes only a few seconds, but for a lengthy response you might want to stop responding if the user has terminated the session:

```
<%

Call LongProcessNumberOne()
If Not Response.IsClientConnected Then
    Response.End
End If
Call LongProcessNumberTwo()
Response.Write("Done!")
%>
```

In the previous example, we assume the function calls each take a significant amount of time. By checking the `IsClientConnected` property, we can avoid extraneous processing if the user has given up waiting.

SENDING COOKIES TO THE CLIENT

Cookies are little pieces of data stored on the client. With each Web request the cookies are sent back to the server and accessible from ASP.NET code, which allows you to perform tasks such as site personalization. (IIS actually uses cookies to help manage sessions.) For example, the following lines of code send a `Zipcode` cookie back to the user:

```
Dim ckZip As New HttpCookie("Zipcode")
ckZip.Value = "38138"
ckZip.Expires = DateTime.Now.AddDays(30)
Response.Cookies.Add(ckZip)
```

When the user accesses the site again, the `Zipcode` cookie will be sent to the server, allowing it to display the weather or other ZIP Code-related information automatically. The `Expires` property of the cookie instructs the browser to throw it away after 30 days.

Note

> If you are curious how and where cookies are stored, look in the Temporary Internet Files folder. To view these files from Internet Explorer, choose Internet Options from the Tools menu and click View Files. Drag one of the cookie files (begins with the word `cookie`) to the desktop and then open it in a text editor.

In addition to storing scalar values, a single cookie object can store multiple related values, as in the following example:

```
Dim ckFavoriteStocks As New HttpCookie("Stocks")
ckFavoriteStocks.Values.Add("MSFT", "Microsoft")
ckFavoriteStocks.Values.Add("HLT", "Hilton")
ckFavoriteStocks.Values.Add("FDX", "FedEx")
Response.Cookies.Add(ckFavoriteStocks)
Dim MyCookie As New HttpCookie("LastVisit")
MyCookie.Value = CStr(DateTime.Now())
Response.Cookies.Add(MyCookie)
```

As you can see, cookies are good for small bits of machine or session-specific information. For the problem we mentioned earlier (managing session state), one solution is to store a cookie that acts as a database key. However, because cookies are stored as plain text, I would recommend the following precautions when using cookies to keep track of a user's identity:

- Use a random number (that is a GUID) rather than any actual key value from the database.
- If your Web site has a list of users, do not display their random number in URLs.

Without taking the previous precautions, a user could edit his cookie file and impersonate another user.

CONTROLLING RESPONSE CACHING

Another useful property of the Response object is the ability to set a *cache policy*. Your browser will store all the HTML and images associated with a response in its temporary directory for a certain length of time for speed purposes. By manipulating the `Cache` property of the `Response` object, you can send directives to the browser informing it of how long the page should live in the cache:

```
'SETS CACHE TIME TO 25 MINUTES
Dim ts As New TimeSpan(0, 25, 0)
Response.Cache.SetMaxAge(ts)
```

The previous lines of code set the maximum age of the current response to 25 minutes. For certain types of applications, such as an up-to-the-minute Webcam, you may want to set the cache expiration time to a very low value, or even use the `Response.Cache.SetNoStore` method to direct the browser to always retrieve the page from the server.

RETRIEVING DATA WITH THE Request OBJECT

The Request object allows ASP.NET code to access information about an incoming Web page request. The most common use of the object is to retrieve data from HTML form submissions or cookies for use in VB code. However, the Request object also provides a number of properties that you can use to obtain information about the files and directories associated with an incoming request.

RETRIEVING QUERYSTRING DATA

As you may have noticed, the URL of a Web page can contain parameters following the address. Consider the following example URL:

```
http://bshome/getreport.aspx?title=Payroll&dept=23&format=PDF
```

The previous address refers to the getreport.aspx page, and passes three parameters: title, dept, and format. Values for parameters can be accessed by name using the Request.QueryString collection. The following lines of code retrieve the values of parameters from the example URL and store them in variables:

```
Dim strTitle As String
Dim intDeptNumber As Integer
Dim strFormat AS String

strtitle = Request.QueryString("title")
intDeptNumber = Request.QueryString("dept")
strFormat = Request.QueryString("format")
```

As you will see in an upcoming exercise, you can use the Response.Write statement to dynamically create a hyperlink containing URL parameters.

Note

When using parameters in a URL, separate the address and first parameter with a question mark (?) and each subsequent parameter with an ampersand (&).

Be careful what information you expose to the user in the URL. Security is worthless if it can be overridden by a change in a URL. For example, I have seen poorly designed Web sites that store a SQL statement in the URL, giving the user free reign over the database!

RETRIEVING DATA FROM HTML FORMS

In order to transfer data to the server from the client, you can set up a form in HTML. Forms are enclosed by the <FORM> tag and contain <INPUT> fields. When a form is submitted to the Web server, the values of the fields are available via the Request.Form collection. To see how this might work in practice, create a new file in the ASPTest directory called default.htm and enter the code from Listing 17.3.

PART
IV
CH
17

LISTING 17.3   ASPTEST.ZIP—SUBMITTING FORM VARIABLES

```
<HTML>
<BODY>
<H1>Security Check</H1>
<HR>
<FORM ACTION="checkuser.aspx" METHOD="POST">
User ID: <INPUT TYPE="TEXT" NAME="txtUserID"><BR>
Password: <INPUT TYPE="PASSWORD" NAME="txtPassword"><BR>
<INPUT TYPE="SUBMIT" VALUE="LOGIN">
</FORM>
</BODY>
</HTML>
```

Listing 17.3 contains a simple HTML form with two form fields and a Submit button. The form appears as shown in Figure 17.5.

Figure 17.5
Form elements using the POST method are not visible in the URL, as with the QueryString.

To process the form, create a file in the ASPTest directory called checkuser.aspx. Enter the following lines in the new file:

```
<%
If Request.Form("txtPassword").ToLower = "password" Then
   Response.Write ("Congratulations, " & Request.Form("txtUserId"))
   Response.Write ("<BR>You entered the right password!")
Else
   Response.Write ("Sorry, " & Request.Form("txtUserId"))
   Response.Write ("<BR>Access denied!")
End If
%>
```

To test the sample page, open your browser to the address http://servername/ASPTest. You should see the page shown in Figure 17.5. Enter your user name and see what happens when you enter password for the password and when you enter something else.

Caution

> Unencrypted HTML form data sent back and forth across a network can be "sniffed" by someone on the same network who is analyzing data packets. If you are concerned about exposing passwords, you may want to investigate a secure connection for the login form using the `https` protocol.

Forms and URL parameters are a common way to pass simple values from page to page without using session variables, as long as you don't mind that value being seen by the client. One type of form field that is very useful in this regard is the HIDDEN type, which works like an invisible text box. However, the user can read even the data in a hidden form field if he chooses the View Source option.

DETERMINING COOKIE VALUES

As we saw earlier, the Response object contains methods for sending cookies to the client. Similarly, the Request object contains methods for retrieving those values. One way to do this is to use the same collection-based approach:

```
Dim strZipCode As String
If Not IsNothing(Request.Cookies("ZipCode")) then
    strZipCode = Request.Cookies("ZipCode").Value
End If
```

Note that unlike the other collections in the Request object, we have to explicitly specify the Value property to specify the value stored in the cookie object, rather than the cookie object itself. You can also declare an HttpCookie object, which may be an easier method of accessing multi-value cookies. The following code reads the stock cookie example from the last section:

```
Dim ckStocks AS HttpCookie
Dim i As Integer
Dim strSymbols() AS String

If Not IsNothing(Request.Cookies("Stocks")) then

   ckStocks = Request.Cookies("Stocks")

   'Get all the key names into an array
   strSymbols=ckStocks.Values.AllKeys

   'Use the key name to retrieve the description
   For i = LBound(strSymbols) To UBound(strSymbols)
         Response.Write ("Symbol=" & strSymbols(i) & "<BR>")
         Response.Write ("Description=" & _
            ckStocks.Values(strSymbols(i)) & "<BR>")
   Next

End If
```

Reading a multi-value cookie is a little more complicated. Of course, in this example the stock data is so simple you could easily store it all in a single comma-delimited string. It is left as an exercise to the reader to judge which method is easier.

RETRIEVING VALUES BY NAME

Throughout this section we have identified several collections of values stored in the Response object. One new collection to ASP.NET is the Params collection, which acts as a combination of cookies, QueryString values, server variables, and form fields. The following code shows how to access some of the values from previous examples using the Params collection:

```
strZipCode = Request.Params("ZipCode")
strPassword = Request.Params("txtPassword")
intDeptNumber = Request.Params("dept")
```

For accessing simple values by name, the preceding lines of code work just as well as any other method. However, from the point of view of good programming practice, you should know where your values are stored.

UNDERSTANDING THE SERVER AND APPLICATION OBJECTS

The Server object allows you to control perform actions on the Web server, such as creating objects and executing code. In previous versions of ASP, the Server object was the only means of accessing your external business objects (late bound), using the CreateObject method. However, in the .NET world you have access to all the power of VB, including early bound objects and importing namespaces as discussed earlier. The CreateObject method is still available for compatibility with existing COM objects:

```
<%
Dim cn As Object
cn = Server.CreateObject("MyComObj.MyComClass")
%>
```

Hopefully, you will need to use the CreateObject method sparingly if ever. Note that for some COM objects, you may need to add the directive <%@ Page aspcompat=true %> at the top of your page. For more information on compatibility with COM, see the help files.

As mentioned earlier, the Server object also provides a way to substitute one page for another at the server level. The Server.Transfer method accepts the new page address as a parameter:

```
Server.Transfer("default.aspx")
```

The preceding line of code transfers control of the current response to the default.aspx page. In some cases it may be more desirable than the Response.Redirect method because it avoids an extra round trip to the client. Another advantage is it can be called even after writing HTML back to the client. However, keep in mind when using Server.Transfer the URL the user sees for the page may not represent the actual page displayed.

Note

Server.Transfer cannot be used with .htm files, only .aspx files.

Another interesting object available in ASP.NET is the `Application` object. The `Application` object allows you to set variables that are available to all users of an application:

```
Application("CompanyStockPrice") = 64
```

These variables work similarly to session variables, and the value is preserved as long as the application is active (there is at least one active session).

EXERCISE: CREATING A WEB PHOTO ALBUM

Now that you have learned the basics of ASP.NET, it is time to test your knowledge by building a sample ASP.NET application. In this section, we'll create an ASP.NET application that allows users to upload and view pictures. One use of this type of application would be to collect and share digital camera photos. For this sample application, we will create four `.aspx` files:

- `category.aspx`—Allows users to pick a category of pictures to view, or create a new category.
- `pictures.aspx`—Displays all the pictures in a given category.
- `thumbnail.aspx`—Creates a smaller version of an image for faster downloading.
- `upload.aspx`—Allows users to upload a new picture.

In creating this application, we will use many of the ASP.NET concepts discussed earlier in the chapter, as well as some graphics and file manipulation techniques discussed in other chapters.

CREATING THE APPLICATION FOLDER

Our sample Web site will be located in its own virtual directory, `Photos`. To set up the application, do the following:

1. Create the directory `C:\inetpub\wwwroot\Photos` using Windows Explorer.
2. Open the IIS management console and find the Default Web site. Although we have not yet created the virtual directory, you will see the `Photos` folder located under the Default Web site.
3. Right-click the `Photos` folder and choose Properties.
4. Click the Create button to create a new application.
5. Make sure Write permission is selected, because users will need write access to upload photos. The properties window for the Photos directory should look similar to Figure 17.6.

Figure 17.6
The Properties window allows you to control security and other configuration details for an ASP.NET application.

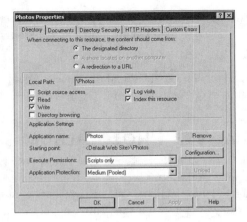

After you have completed making the appropriate settings, click OK to close the Properties window.

MANAGING PHOTO CATEGORIES

To allow for better organization of image files, we will allow the user to specify a category for each picture. The categories will be implemented as a separate subdirectory beneath the Photos application directory. We'll allow the user to name the categories and use VB code to create a subdirectory with the same name. Because these new subdirectories will be located beneath the Photos folder, IIS will consider them part of the same application. The code for the category.aspx page is shown in Listing 17.4.

LISTING 17.4   PHOTOS.ZIP—CREATING SUBDIRECTORIES WITH ASP.NET

```
<% @Import Namespace = "System.IO" %>
<SCRIPT LANGUAGE="VB" RUNAT="Server">

Private Sub DisplayCategorylist()
   Dim strAppRoot As String
   Dim strCatList() As String
   Dim strCatLink AS String
   Dim strShortName AS String
   Dim intPos AS Integer
   Dim i As Integer

   'Get an array of subdirectory names
   strAppRoot = Server.MapPath("/Photos")
   strCatList = Directory.GetDirectories(strAppRoot)

   For i = LBound(strCatList) to UBound(strCatList)

          'Extract the directory name from the full path

             intPos = strCatList(i).toUpper.IndexOf("PHOTOS") + 7
```

LISTING 17.4 CONTINUED

```
        strShortName = strCatList(i).SubString(intPos)

        'Build a hyperlink and send it to the browser
        strCatLink = "<A HREF=""pictures.aspx?category="
        strCatLink &= strShortName & """>" & strShortName
        strCatLink &= "</A><BR>"
        Response.Write(strCatLink)
    Next

End Sub

Private Sub CreateNewCategory(strName As String)
    Dim strAppRoot As String
    Dim strNewFolder As String

    strAppRoot = Server.MapPath("/Photos")
    strNewFolder = strAppRoot & "\" & strName
    Call Directory.CreateDirectory(strNewFolder)
End Sub

Private Sub Page_Load(ByVal sender As System.Object, _
ByVal e As System.EventArgs) Handles MyBase.Load
    If Not (Request.Form("txtNewCatName") Is Nothing) Then
        Call CreateNewCategory(Request.Form("txtNewCatName").ToString)
    End If
End Sub

</SCRIPT>

<HTML>
<BODY>
<H1>Web Photo Archive</H1>
<HR>
Click a category name below to view photos:<BR>
<%
Call DisplayCategoryList
%>
<HR>
<BR>
Enter a new category name to create:
<FORM ACTION="category.aspx" METHOD="POST" NAME="frmTest">
<INPUT TYPE="TEXT" NAME="txtNewCatName">
<INPUT TYPE="SUBMIT" VALUE="Create">
</FORM>
</BODY>
</HTML>
```

Listing 17.4 contains two custom functions: `DisplayCategoryList` and `CreateNewCategory`. `DisplayCategoryList` outputs a HTML hyperlink for each photo category. For example, if there were a category called `Vacation`, the `For` loop in Listing 17.4 would generate the following line of HTML for this category:

```
<A HREF="pictures.aspx?category=Vacation">Vacation</A>
```

The `CreateNewCategory` subroutine creates a new folder on the hard drive. It is called from the `Page_Load` event only if the user has passed a category name from the HTML input form. Because our code involves creating and listing directories on the file system, we make use of the `Directory` class, discussed in Chapter 22, "Using ADO.NET (ADO)."

→ For more details on the Directory class, **see** Chapter 24, "Working with Files," **p. 681**

To create the category page for the sample application, copy the code from Listing 17.4 into the `category.aspx` page on your own server, in the `C:\Inetpub\wwwroot\Photos` directory.

CREATING THE PICTURE VIEWER PAGE

Now that we have given users a means to create and select photo categories, we need a Web page that lets them browse the pictures in a given category. To allow for viewing of multiple pictures at once, we will present a page of small uniform preview images, also known as *thumbnails*. Each thumbnail will also be a link to the underlying full-size picture. In the world of HTML, the `<IMG>` tag is used to display an image in an HTML page, as in the following example:

```
<IMG SRC="/stuff/picture2.gif">
```

When the preceding HTML is delivered to the client browser, the browser asks the Web server to send it the picture file specified in the `SRC` attribute. Although there are `HEIGHT` and `WIDTH` attributes to control display size, the browser will still download the whole image. As you may be aware, photos from a digital camera can vary widely in dimension and size. If you try to put several megabytes of images on a single Web page, it will load very slowly! Fortunately, the .NET framework provides a built-in thumbnail generator in the `Image` class. As you may recall from Chapter 14, "Designing an Effective User Interface," the `Image` class can be used for a variety of graphics-related tasks.

→ For more details on the Image class, **see** Chapter 14, "Designing an Effective User Interface," **p. 357**

To create our page of thumbnail images, we will use ASP.NET to scan a folder of images and dynamically generate an `<IMG>` tag for each image. Listing 17.5 shows the page that generates the table of images. Listing 17.6 shows `thumbnail.aspx`, a page that accepts a filename and returns a 100 × 100 thumbnail.

LISTING 17.5   PHOTOS.ZIP—THE PICTURE PREVIEW PAGE

```
<% @Import Namespace = "System.IO" %>
<HTML>
<BODY>
<%

Dim strAppRoot As String
Dim strFileList() As String
Dim strCategory AS String
Dim strPhotoPath As String
Dim strShortName As String
Dim strCurrentPic As String
Dim intPos AS Integer
Dim i As Integer
```

LISTING 17.5   CONTINUED

```
'Get path to physical directory
strCategory = "/Photos/" & Request.Params("Category")
strPhotoPath = Server.MapPath(strCategory)

'Get List of files
strFileList = Directory.GetFiles(strPhotoPath)

'Create photo thumbnail page, 5 pictures per table row
Response.Write("<H1>" & Request.Params("Category") & "</H1>")
Response.Write("<HR><TABLE>")
Response.Write("<TR>")

intPos = strPhotoPath.Length + 1
For i = LBound(strFileList) to UBound(strFileList)

    strShortName = strFileList(i).SubString(intPos)
    strCurrentPic = strCategory & "/" & strShortName
    Response.Write("<TD><A HREF=""" & strCurrentPic & """>")
    Response.Write("<IMG SRC=""thumbnail.aspx?FileName=" & _
        strCurrentPic & """")
    Response.Write("</A><TD>")

    If (i+1) mod 5 = 0 Then
            Response.Write("</TR><TR>")
    End If
Next

%>
</TR>
</TABLE>
<BR>
<A HREF="category.aspx">Back to category list</A><BR>
<%
Response.Write("<A HREF=""upload.aspx?category=")
Response.Write(Request.Params("Category") & """>Upload new image</A>")
%>
</BODY>
</HTML>
```

As the table is generated, the browser is told to retrieve each image from `thumbnail.aspx`, shown in Listing 17.6. Note that Listing 17.6 does not actually generate a thumbnail file on the disk. Instead, it saves the thumbnail to a `MemoryStream` object and then delivers the bytes in the stream to the client using the `Response.BinaryWrite` method.

LISTING 17.6   `PHOTOS.ZIP`—THE THUMBNAIL GENERATOR

```
<% @Import Namespace = "System.IO" %>
<% @Import Namespace = "System.Drawing" %>
<%

'This ASPX page generates a thumbnail of an image
'It can be used in an <IMG> tag
```

LISTING 17.6   CONTINUED

```
Dim strWebPath As string
Dim strFileName As String
Dim intLastSlash As string
Dim BytesRead As Integer
Dim ByteValues() As Byte
Dim intFileLength As Integer
Dim imgFullSize As System.Drawing.Image
Dim imgThumbnail As System.Drawing.Image
Dim stmThumbnail As MemoryStream

'Figure out the physical file name
strWebPath = Request.Params("FileName")
intLastSlash = strWebPath.LastIndexof("/")
strFileName = Server.MapPath(strWebPath.SubString(0,intLastSlash))
strFileName &= "\" & strWebPath.SubString(intLastSlash + 1)

'Load the image into memory
imgFullSize = System.Drawing.Image.FromFile(strFileName)

'Get a Thumbnail image
imgThumbnail = imgFullSize.GetThumbnailImage(100, 100, Nothing, Nothing)

'Save the image as a Memory Stream
stmThumbnail = New MemoryStream()
imgThumbnail.Save(stmThumbnail, Imaging.ImageFormat.Jpeg)

'Send the image back to the client browser
intFileLength = stmThumbnail.Length
ReDim ByteValues(intFileLength)
stmThumbnail.position=0

BytesRead = stmThumbnail.Read(ByteValues, 0, intFileLength)
If BytesRead > 0 Then
        Response.BinaryWrite(ByteValues)
End If
stmThumbnail.Close()
%>
```

To continue with the sample exercise, copy the code from the previous listings into the pictures.aspx and thumbnail.aspx files in your C:\Inetpub\wwwroot\Photos directory.

CREATING THE UPLOAD PAGE

As a final step in our sample application, we will create the ASP.NET page necessary for the user to upload new photographs. To upload files from a Web browser, you have to add a special type of form field to your HTML file, and then write some VB code to save the submitted file to disk. ASP.NET's new programming model makes this easier by providing the HTMLInputFile control, an abstraction of the HTML upload process. When a file is posted to an ASP.NET page, you simply use the SaveAs method of this control to write it to disk, as shown in Listing 17.7.

LISTING 17.7 PHOTOS.ZIP—UPLOADING A FILE WITH ASP.NET

```
<HTML>
<SCRIPT LANGUAGE="VB" RUNAT="SERVER">

Sub btnUpload_Click(sender As Object, e As EventArgs)

    Dim strCatFolder As String
    Dim strUserFileName As String
    Dim strFileName As String
    Dim intLastBackslash As Integer

    'Get the file name without the user's local path
    strUserFileName = filePicture.PostedFile.FileName
    intLastBackslash = strUserFileName.LastIndexOf("\")
    strFileName = strUserFileName.SubString(intLastBackslash + 1)

    'Get the physical path to the category folder
    strCatFolder = Server.MapPath("/Photos") & "\" & txtCategory.Value

    'Save the file
    filePicture.PostedFile.SaveAs(strCatFolder & "\" & strFileName)

    'Display the pictures page again
    Server.Transfer("pictures.aspx?category=" & txtCategory.Value)

End Sub

Private Sub Page_Load(ByVal sender As System.Object, _
ByVal e As System.EventArgs) Handles MyBase.Load

    'Loads the category name into the hidden text field
    txtCategory.Value=Request.Params("Category")

End Sub

</SCRIPT>

<BODY>
<H1>Upload a new Image</H1>
<HR>

<FORM ENCTYPE="multipart/form-data" RUNAT="SERVER" ACTION="UPLOAD.ASPX">
Select image File:
<INPUT ID="filePicture" TYPE="FILE"    RUNAT="SERVER">
<INPUT ID="txtCategory" TYPE="HIDDEN" RUNAT="SERVER">
<INPUT ID="btnUpload"    TYPE="BUTTON" RUNAT="SERVER"
VALUE="Upload" OnServerClick="btnUpload_Click">
</FORM>
</BODY>
</HTML>
```

PART
IV

CH
17

The code in Listing 17.7 uses server-side Web controls, which will be discussed in more detail in subsequent chapters. When the user uploads a picture, it is written to the disk in the appropriate category folder.

TESTING THE SAMPLE APPLICATION

After you have created all the files for the sample application, test it by performing the following steps:

1. Open Internet Explorer and display the category page, `http://servername/photos/category.aspx`, where *servername* is the name of your Web server.

2. Enter a category name in the box and click the `Create` button. The page will then show your new category, as shown in Figure 17.7.

Figure 17.7
You can verify the correct function of the `category.aspx` page by checking to see whether a corresponding directory is created on your hard drive.

3. Click the category name to display the pictures in that category. The thumbnails of the pictures in that folder will be displayed, as pictured in Figure 17.8.

Figure 17.8
To test the thumbnail page, copy or upload some image files into the category folder. The VB should automatically generate a thumbnail for each image.

4. At the bottom of the picture page, click the link to upload a new picture.

5. Click the Browse button and select an image file on your hard drive.

6. Click the Upload button. The picture page should be displayed and contain the new thumbnail image.

FROM HERE...

As you can see from the example, with just four ASP.NET files you can create a very functional Web site. If you are interested in working more with a photo-sharing site, consider the following enhancement suggestions:

- The sample application accepts any type of file. However, in the real world you may want to place restrictions on the file type, file size, or number of images uploaded.

- Improve the thumbnail code to take into account the proportions and size of the original image.

- Make the photo pages database-driven, using an identity column for the server filename. This will have pictures in multiple categories, as well as make it easy to store comments and annotations.

PART
IV
CH
17

WEB APPLICATIONS AND SERVICES

In this chapter

In this chapter, we'll explore two new types of Web projects available in Visual Basic .NET: Web Applications and Web Services. Both types of projects are built on ASP.NET and contain code that executes on a Web server. ASP.NET Web Applications include a new programming model called Web Forms, which promises to make Web development much easier for the developer. Web Services, on the other hand, do not have a user interface, but can be used to expose business functionality to other programs and users via the Internet.

Technically speaking, an ASP.NET Web Application is just a collection of related files in a virtual directory. These files can be coded "by hand" using a text editor, or created in the Visual Studio development environment. Either way, when you create a Web page using ASP.NET you can use a powerful new programming model available, known as Web Forms. In this chapter, we will examine how Web Forms work, discuss some common coding techniques, and finally examine some issues involved with managing a Web Application project in Visual Studio .NET.

UNDERSTANDING THE WEB FORMS PROGRAMMING MODEL

The Web Forms programming model is Microsoft's attempt to do for Web development what earlier versions of Visual Basic did for Windows development. The traditional method of programming the World Wide Web has been to write code on a Web server that generates HTML for the client browser. This approach (which we covered in the last chapter) is perfectly functional, but not very elegant. Let's examine why, by looking at the code you would need to allow a user to update his address via a Web page. In a traditional Web application, you would have to write the following code:

- You need to access the database and generate the initial HTML form for the end user. First, you use ADO.NET to get the user's address and store it as a variable. (ADO.NET is a set of classes that allow your code to access a database.) Next, as the page is generated and sent to the browser, your code creates the HTML form on the fly by setting up the address field with a `Response.Write` statement:

```
Response.Write("<INPUT TYPE=""TEXT"" NAME=""txtAddress"" VALUE=""" & _
  strAddress & """">")
```

- After the user has updated the text field, he will submit the HTML form back to the server for processing. Your code will then retrieve the address from the HTML field and update the database. You will also need to handle validating the data for errors and drawing the page again if necessary.

→ For more on database access with ADO.NET, **see** Chapter 22, "Using ADO.NET," **p. 599**

There is no doubt about it, the method of writing Web applications that I have just described works. There have been many ASP success stories. However, the drawback is that the code structure is often a spaghetti mixture of user interface elements and business logic. You can alleviate this problem somewhat, through the use of compiled business objects accessed from the ASP code. However, to make a Web page act as useful as a Windows form, you still have to get involved in state management, and other request and response communication issues. In short, with a traditional ASP application there is no way of avoiding a lot of messy HTML and unstructured code. Web Forms, on the other hand, provide a clean separation between the user interface and application code, as well as a familiar control-based programming model. Here's how you would create a Web Form for the user to update his address:

- Instead of using a traditional INPUT field to represent the address field, Web Forms allow you to use a *server-side control*, in this case a text box:

  ```
  <asp:TextBox id="txtAddress" runat="server"></asp:TextBox>
  ```

  If you are already familiar with HTML tags, you might notice the HTML in the previous line of code looks a little different. That is because it is not really standard HTML; instead it represents a server-side control to the ASP.NET framework. However, if you use Visual Studio .NET to create your Web form, you do not have to learn any of the new server-side control syntax.

- When the page loads, you can populate the field by setting the Text property of the control:

  ```
  txtAddress.Text = strAddress
  ```

- Finally, when the user submits the form, you can retrieve the updated address from the control just as easily:

  ```
  strNewAddress = txtAddress.Text
  ```

If the previous steps sound familiar, they should. When you program using the Web Forms model, you work with events and properties of a Web page and its components just as you would with those of a Windows form. In Chapter 2, "Creating Your First Windows Application," and Chapter 3, "Creating Your First Web Application," we built a loan payment calculator using Windows Forms in the former chapter and Web Forms in the latter. In each case, we wrote code that executed in response to events. (If you have not already completed the Loan Calculator exercise, it might be a good idea to do so now, so the discussion of Web Forms and controls that follows will make more sense.)

→ For a step-by-step example of designing a Web Form, **see** Chapter 3, "Creating your First Web Application," **p. 49**

UNDERSTANDING SERVER CONTROLS

The Web Forms model makes extensive use of server-side controls. ASP.NET server-side controls are components that execute on the Web server and are designed to isolate the developer from the underlying HTML forms. Consider our earlier example of a text box:

```
<asp:TextBox id="txtAddress" runat="server"></asp:TextBox>
```

Note the <asp:> and </asp:> tags, which indicate an ASP.NET server control. It is important to realize that server controls are only understood by the server; standard HTML is still sent to the browser. Figure 18.1 shows two views of the HTML source for the Loan Calculator program. The file on top is the original .aspx file as generated by Visual Studio. The file on the bottom is what happens when the user chooses View Source in his browser.

Figure 18.1
ASP Server controls do not require any special client components, because they are translated into standard HTML by the ASP.NET page processor.

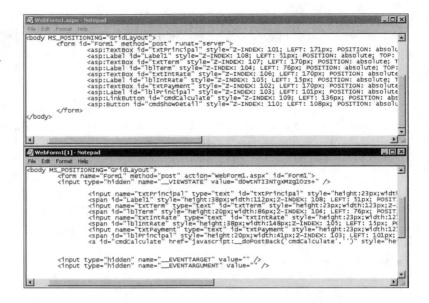

In the figure, you can see where the `<asp:TextBox>` tags were replaced with standard HTML `<INPUT>` fields. What this tells you is that the Web Forms programming model really does not do anything to change the way the Web works, it is strictly an aid to the developer. Each time a browser requests a Web page from a server, the server still has to generate an HTML page.

FORM POSTING AND ROUND TRIPS

Web applications are thought of as "thin client" applications, because all the processing logic typically resides on the server. Of course, this means that any updates to the page require a *round trip*; that is a request followed by a response. One particular type of request from the browser is a *post*, which means form field data is posted to the server with the Web page request. In a traditional ASP application, the developer has to write his or her own code to maintain form state across each round trip. For example, consider a Web page that requires data entry in thirty fields. Suppose the end user makes a mistake in one of the fields, which prevents the application from processing the form. In a Windows application, whatever the user had already typed in the other twenty-nine fields will still be there, because the form is only loaded once. In a browser-based application, however, the round trip will require the server to send a new page back to the client. A well-written application should of course not just send back a blank HTML form, but also include the data the user has already entered. In other words, maintaining a form's state over round trips means the user will only have to retype the incorrect value instead of all 30.

When you program using the Web Forms model, this problem goes away, thanks to something called *view state*. If you look at Figure 18.1 again, you will see that in addition to translating the ASP server controls into their equivalent HTML elements, the ASP.NET page processor also added some hidden form fields and other elements for its internal use. Notice the VIEWSTATE hidden field, which appears to be an unrecognizable string of characters. This field is generated automatically and used to maintain the values of your form fields across multiple round trips. Thanks to the view state feature, you do not have to code this yourself. Once the end user keys a value into a text box, the value will remain in the text box, regardless of how many round-trips the page makes, until your code changes it or he moves to another Web page.

Note

Maintaining field data over several round trips for a single Web form (view state) is a different issue from maintaining information across several Web pages (session state). For more information, see the upcoming section "Distinguishing Between View State and Session State."

WRITING CODE BEHIND A WEB FORM

In the Web Forms programming model, you have a choice of where to put the VB code; it can reside with the HTML in an .aspx file (as described in Chapter 17, "Using Active Server Pages.NET"), or in a separate .vb file that contains just code. Keeping the code and user interface separate is one of the great features of the Web Forms programming model, so Visual Studio .NET makes this choice for you by creating a *webformname*.aspx.vb file automatically when you add a new Web form to your project. This separate file is known as the *code-behind* file, because it contains the code "behind" the Web form interface.

Visual Studio makes the fact that there are two files transparent to the developer; choosing View Code in the Solution explorer displays the .vb file, whereas choosing View Source displays the .aspx file. Internally, the files are linked together thanks to the concept of inheritance. Your code-behind file contains a class for the Web form (for example, Webform1), which inherits the Page class from the System.Web.UI namespace. The .aspx file in turn inherits the Webform1 class. Thanks to inheritance, all the objects we discussed in Chapter 17 (Request, Response, Session) are available in your Web form class, with the added benefit of Intellisense and other editing features you don't get in Notepad!

→ For more on ASP.NET objects, **see** Chapter 17, "Using Active Server Pages.NET," **p. 443**

WRITING PAGE INITIALIZATION CODE

Most types of applications (Windows or Web) require some initialization code. For example, if your form includes drop-down lists for the user to select his state and country name, you need to populate this list when the form is initially loaded. In the Windows environment, your form is typically only created once per application session, so you can put the initialization code in the form's New method and be confident it will only execute once. However, in the Web environment, your form may be loaded in the browser many times, depending on the number of round trips it makes before the user is finished.

To accommodate program initialization, you can check the IsPostBack property in the Page Load event. Every time a Web page is loaded, the Page_Load event handler executes on the server before the page is returned to the client. When the page processor creates an instance of a Web form, it sets the IsPostBack property to True if the page has already made a round trip, or False if the page has not been previously loaded. You use this property to determine when to execute your page initialization code. Listing 18.1 shows an example of loading a drop-down list box containing state names when a Web form is initially loaded.

LISTING 18.1   WEBFORMTEST.ZIP—CODING THE Page_Load EVENT

```
Private Sub Page_Load(ByVal sender As System.Object, _
ByVal e As System.EventArgs) Handles MyBase.Load

    'Put user code to initialize the page here
    If Not Page.IsPostBack Then
        Call FillStateList()
    End If
    lblInfo.Text = "Company Stock: " & GetStockPrice()

End Sub

Private Sub FillStateList()
    Dim rdrPeople As SqlDataReader
    Dim cn As SqlConnection
    Dim cmd As SqlCommand
    Dim strState As String
    Dim strDesc As String

    lstStates.Items.Clear()
    cn = New SqlConnection("server=bserver\NetSDK;uid=sa;pwd=;database=Brian")
    cn.Open()
    cmd = New SqlCommand("Select state, description from statelist", cn)
    rdrPeople = cmd.ExecuteReader()

    While rdrPeople.Read()
        strState = rdrPeople.GetString(0)
        strDesc = strState & " - " & rdrPeople.GetString(1)
        lstStates.Items.Add(New ListItem(strDesc, strState))
    End While

    cn.Close()

End Sub
```

Listing 18.1 calls the GetStockPrice function every time the page is loaded, which means this function will execute on each round trip. The idea behind this function is that if the page happens to be making a round trip to the server anyway, why not update the stock price. The FillStateList function, on the other hand, will be executed only during the first page load. This will eliminate the overhead of connecting to the database and the list of states. During future page loads, the view state feature described in the previous section will maintain the state drop-down list and the user's selected state automatically. Figure 18.2 shows the sample page generated by the code in Listing 18.1.

Figure 18.2
The list box containing states and the stock price were populated in the `Page_Load` event.

➜ To learn more about retrieving information from a database, **see** Chapter 22, "Using ADO.NET," **p. 599**

Note

Pressing F5 or the clicking browser's Refresh button causes the `IsPostBack` property to be reset, as if you are loading the Web page for the first time.

DISTINGUISHING BETWEEN VIEW STATE AND SESSION STATE

It is important to distinguish the view state feature of ASP.NET Web Forms from the session state feature. The most important differences are

- View state information exists only during round-trips for the same Web form. Session state data, such as the name of the logged-in user, can be shared across all multiple forms.
- View state information is generally maintained automatically. The developer creates session state information explicitly through the use of session variables.
- Information about the current view state is carried along with each round trip and stored on the client. Session state information is stored on the server and linked to the user through an internal session ID.

As we mentioned in Chapter 17, you can maintain your own session variables by accessing the `Session` object. For example, if you had several Web Forms which needed to display a list of states and their abbreviations, you might retrieve them in a dataset and store the dataset in a session or application variable. In Chapter 3, we used session variables to pass parameters to the amortization form in the Loan Calculator application.

➜ For an example use of session variables with a Web form, **see** Chapter 3, "Creating Your First Web Application," **p. 49**

SECURITY AND WEB FORMS

It is worth noting that efficiency is not the only thing you should consider when thinking about state management. Remember, anything stored in HTML form fields (or cookies) is sent to the browser as plain text and available on the end user's machine.

> **Caution**
>
> As an example of poor use of HTML forms, I can recall an early online banking application that stored an account number in a hidden form field. This was extremely poor programming practice, because by simply choosing view source and editing the hidden form field, one could easily enter a new account number and gain access to someone else's information! Remember, just because your ASP code sends down the initial form to the end user doesn't mean he cannot send his own form back.

Although by no means a complete list, here are a few simple tips to remember:

- You don't need to be too concerned with information that the user has to key in anyway, such as a text box. In this case, using Web Form view state is perfectly acceptable.

- You can use view state for pick lists, drop-down lists, and hidden form fields, but keep in mind to be extra safe you need to include server-side validation to make sure the values being posted are valid.

- Some information you just shouldn't transmit to the client browser, such as an internal user number or password. In this case, you can use a session variable on the server, or generate a random key and store it in a cookie or hidden form field. The random key can then be used in a server-side database lookup.

These concerns do not indicate flaws in the Web architecture; people do business on the Web every day. Rather, they are intended to remind the developer to be careful when sending information over the Internet.

CONTROL EVENTS AND THE AutoPostBack PROPERTY

When working with ASP.NET server controls, you program event procedures just as you would in a Windows Application, but they execute on the Web server. However, not every event available in Windows control exists in the equivalent server control, and even if a particular event exists it may behave differently in the Web environment. For some events, such as the Mouse Move event, it is just not practical to raise an event on a remote server, due to the time it takes to make a round trip across the network and redraw a page. Therefore, the server controls do not have Mouse Move events.

Another example is the TextChanged event of a text box, which in a Windows application fires with every keystroke. However, the TextChanged event of an ASP TextBox control only fires during a round trip, and even then only if the text in the text box has changed since it was last sent to the browser. With some server controls, you can cause additional round trips by setting the AutoPostBack property to True. To demonstrate the effect of the AutoPostBack property, create the following example:

1. Start a new Web Application project. Add the following controls to the Web form, as shown in Figure 18.3: a text box, button, check box, and list box.

2. Add the following code to the Page_Load and TextChanged events:

```
Private Sub Page_Load(ByVal sender As System.Object, _
ByVal e As System.EventArgs) Handles MyBase.Load
```

```
        ListBox1.Items.Add("Page loaded " & Now.ToString)
        If CheckBox1.Checked Then
            TextBox1.AutoPostBack = True
        Else
            TextBox1.AutoPostBack = False
        End If
    End Sub
    Private Sub TextBox1_TextChanged(ByVal sender As System.Object, _
    ByVal e As System.EventArgs) Handles TextBox1.TextChanged
        ListBox1.Items.Add("Text change event: " & Now.ToString)
    End Sub
```

3. Run the sample program. Enter some text in the text box and click the button to force a round trip. The list box should report that the TextChanged event fired.

4. Click the check box and click the button. You have now set the AutoPostBack property to True.

5. Enter some new text and press the Tab key to exit the text box field. The TextChanged event should fire without your pressing the button.

Figure 18.3
If you set the AutoPostBack property to True, certain events may cause your Web form to be loaded again.

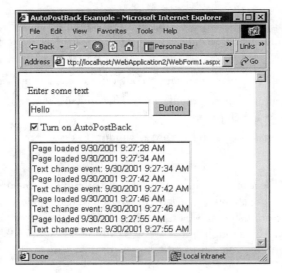

Based on the setting of the AutoPostBack property, the TextChanged event will fire either when the form is submitted or when the control loses focus. However, in either case, the event will only indicate changes made since the last round trip. In other words, suppose your text box initially contains the word Hello. If you repeatedly key in and delete one hundred different words, but change the text back to Hello before the next round trip, the TextChanged event will not fire at all.

Note

The setting of the AutoPostBack property on one server control can cause events to fire for other controls by forcing a round trip.

In Chapter 19, "Web Controls," we will explore other properties and events of the ASP.NET server controls in more detail.

WRITING CLIENT-SIDE SCRIPT CODE

The basic model for Web Forms as we have described thus far involves only server-side code execution. No processing logic exists within the page delivered to the client. This is actually one of the strengths of a Web application, because very little is required to make your application work on an end user's machine. However, most Internet browsers also support some type of *client scripting*, such as JavaScript or VBScript.

Note

On the Web, you will encounter JavaScript more often than VBScript, because JavaScript works in both the Netscape browser and Internet Explorer. However, relying too heavily on client scripting of any kind is unwise, because it may be disabled on some users' browsers and unsupported on others.

Although you don't really need client scripting in a Web application, Web designers often add script code on the client that executes within the user's browser, typically for one of the following reasons:

- Client script can capture events that server code cannot, such as mouse movement.
- Using client script allows you to provide a more dynamic user interface, by highlighting or animating parts of a Web page.
- Client script code can spawn a child browser window to display multiple Web pages at the same time.

In the remainder of this section, we will demonstrate an example of opening a secondary browser window using some client-side JavaScript code. We will enhance the Loan Calculator application from Chapter 3 by making the amortization screen appear in a smaller pop-up window. To accomplish this, we will call the JavaScript `window.open` function. To learn how to do this, you can follow along with the example. To create the example, follow these steps:

1. Load the working loan calculator project from Chapter 3.
2. Display the Web Forms designer for `WebForm1.aspx` and choose the HTML view.
3. Locate the `</HEAD>` tag, which indicates the end of the Web page header. Insert a new line at the end of the header by pressing Enter. This is where we will put a JavaScript function.
4. Right-click on the blank line and choose to Insert Script Block, Client from the pop-up menu. `<SCRIPT>` tags will be inserted for you.
5. Enter the following lines of code to create a JavaScript function called `openamortwindow`. Your screen should look similar to Figure 18.4.

```
function openamortwindow() {
window.open("frmamort.aspx","amortwindow",_
"fullscreen=no,toolbar=no, menubar=no")
}
```

Figure 18.4
The Visual Studio
.NET HTML editor
provides intelligent
editing features and
automatic event pro-
cedure stubs for client
objects.

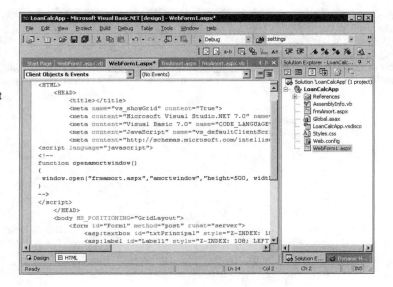

Now that we have a function to open the `frmAmort.aspx` in a new window, we just need to provide a way for the user to execute it at the appropriate time. In the original program, we used a server-side control to redirect the browser to a new page. However, because this function has to be called from the client, we will generate a standard HTML button that calls the `openamortwindow` function. To make this modification to the loan calculator, do the following:

1. Switch back to design view and delete the `cmdShowDetail` server control from the Web form.

2. Right-click `WebForm1.aspx` in the Solution Explorer and choose View code.

3. Delete the line `cmdShowDetail.Visible = True` from the end of the `cmdCalculate_Click` procedure.

4. Enter the following lines of code at the end of the `cmdCalculate_Click` procedure:
   ```
   Session.Add("Principal", txtPrincipal.Text)
   Session.Add("IntRate", txtIntRate.Text)
   Session.Add("Term", txtTerm.Text)
   Session.Add("Payment", txtPayment.Text)
   Dim strButton As String
   strButton = "<INPUT TYPE=""BUTTON"" VALUE=""Amort. Scheudle""
   ONCLICK=""javascript:openamortwindow()"">"
   Response.Write(strButton)
   ```

Finally, you are ready to run the program. Click the Start button to begin, and repeat the steps used to test the program in Chapter 3. When you display the amortization schedule, it should appear in a separate browser window, as shown in Figure 18.5.

Figure 18.5
JavaScript allows you to open additional browser windows and perform other client-side user interface enhancements.

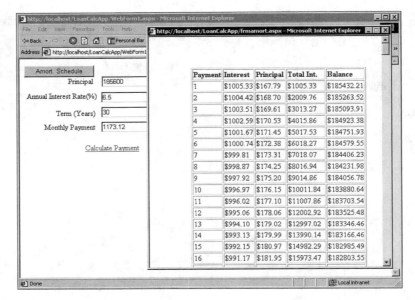

Although it works, this example is a very rudimentary demonstration. In a real application, you might want to use a placeholder or some additional HTML to make the button appear at the bottom of the screen instead of the top. In addition, session variables are probably a waste of resources in this case. It is left as an exercise to the reader to add additional JavaScript to post the field values directly to `frmAmort.aspx`.

MANAGING YOUR WEB APPLICATION PROJECT

So far we have shown that the process of developing a Web application is very similar to that that of a Windows application with some subtle but important differences. Similarly, there are some special considerations that you may have to deal with when managing your Web project and associated files. For the most part, Web projects work as you would expect, but there are a few tricks you need to know.

WORKING WITH AN OFFLINE PROJECT

When you create a new Web Application project, all the project files are stored on the Web server. As we discussed in Chapter 3, the Web server may or may not be running on the same physical computer on which Visual Studio is installed.

Note

Although the project code and compiled files are on the Web server, the solution file (`.sln` file) is stored locally.

Suppose however, that you need to work on your Web application when the Web server is not available, such as when you are working on a disconnected laptop computer. In this case, you can work with your Web project in *offline* mode. The option to take a Web Project offline appears under the Project, Web Project menu, as pictured in Figure 18.6.

Figure 18.6
When you take a Visual Studio Web Application Offline, you can work on a local copy, provided you have IIS installed.

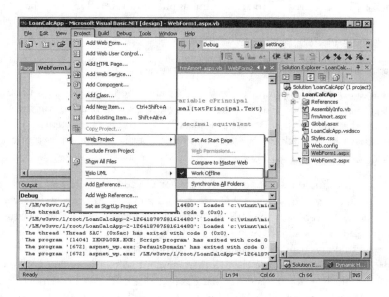

When you choose to take a project offline, Visual Studio works from the local VSWebCache directory, rather than the Web server's virtual directory for the project. As you work with the offline copy, you can add new pages. Until the pages are synchronized with the master copy on the Web server, they will appear with a flag icon next to them in the Solution Explorer, also shown in Figure 18.6.

When you are finished working offline, deselect the Work Offline menu option from the Project menu. Your local files will be synchronized with the Web server and you can work online again. If the online project was modified while you were working offline, you will be prompted whether to load the new version.

Note

If you want to synchronize your files or check for changes while remaining offline, you can use the Synchronize and Compare options, also located in the Web Project menu.

SETTING THE START PAGE AND DEFAULT DOCUMENT

Windows Applications with forms have a Startup form, which is displayed when the application starts. Similarly, Web applications have a Start page. You can set the Start page by using the Web Project menu described in the last section, or by right-clicking your form in the Solution Explorer and choosing Set as Start Page. When debugging in the Visual Studio environment, the Start Page is the page that opens the browser. From that point, links or controls on the Start Page can open other pages.

However, the start page for a Web application only works in Visual Studio. To demonstrate, suppose you have created an accounting application located in the /accounting virtual directory of your Web server. It has two forms, login.aspx and invoiceentry.aspx. The URLs for these forms would be the following:

```
http://servername/accounting/login.aspx
http://servername/accounting/invoiceentry.aspx
```

When you start your application in Visual Studio, the browser is automatically directed to the start page (presumably, login.aspx). However, users who need to run the application in production, that is, outside of Visual Studio, will have to type in the entire URL, including the aspx extension. A much easier address to remember is just the address of the virtual directory:

```
http://servername/accounting
```

Ideally, users should just be able to remember the address of the accounting application, not an individual page. To achieve this effect, your application needs a *default document*. A default document is a Web page that IIS automatically returns when just the virtual directory name is requested. The standard name for a default document is default, so in our example all you need to do is change the name of the startup Web form from login1.aspx to default.aspx. Alternatively, you could use the IIS management software to change the default for the directory, but it is much easier to change the name of the Web form without leaving Visual Studio. When you rename a Web form, Visual Studio automatically updates the name of the associated code behind file as well.

CONTROLLING PAGE NAVIGATION

Another concern with Web form addresses is that the end user can access them directly by simply remembering the name of the URL and typing it in the browser. In our example, you wouldn't want the end user to access the invoiceentry.aspx page without first visiting the login page. Not only would this be a security violation, but also the login page might perform database lookups or other information needed for the invoice entry page. To prevent this, you can use session variables. For example, the login page could set a session variable called LoggedIn to True, and then subsequent pages could check for this variable in their Page_Load event:

```
If Not Session.Item("LoggedIn") Then
        Response.Redirect("default.aspx")
End If
```

The previous If statement checks to see whether the user has logged in before visiting this page. Depending on your level of security, you may need to perform additional checks to see whether they are authorized to visit the requested page.

LAYING OUT YOUR PAGE

Another difference between designing forms for windows and the Web is the pageLayout property of a Web form. As you may recall from Chapter 3, whenever you create a new Web form, a curious message regarding this property appears in the middle of the designer until you draw your first control. The message indicates which layout mode you are in. There are two values for this property:

- GridLayout—Uses absolute positioning with x, y coordinates on a grid.
- FlowLayout—You place elements on the Web page one after the other, giving up some control over their position.

"Why," you might ask, "would I ever want to give up the additional control of the GridLayout mode?" The answer is that in some instances you may want the elements of your Web page to be responsive to the end user's browser resizing. Figure 18.7 shows an example of two rows of text boxes, which were drawn using different layout modes.

Figure 18.7
The top row of text boxes was positioned using grid layout mode, the bottom row of text boxes uses flow layout and adjusted automatically to fit the browser size.

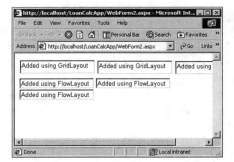

In the designer, the developer positioned the text boxes next to each other. However, only the text boxes positioned using FlowLayout mode responded to the resize of the browser. Making the objects on a Web form flow with the page may also become more advantageous in the future, as smaller mobile devices gain popularity.

Note

When you use FlowLayout mode, you cannot draw a control with the crosshairs. You must instead drag it from the toolbox to the designer.

SHARING FUNCTIONALITY WITH WEB SERVICES

Another type of Web project available in Visual Basic .NET is the Web Service. Web Services provide a standard framework for sharing functionality and data within different areas of your organization, or even the whole world via the Internet. Like Web Applications, Web Services are built on ASP.NET technology and run in IIS. However, they do not have a user interface component; people do not access Web services, programs do. Some other important characteristics of Web services are

- Clients and Web services communicate by passing text messages using standard communication protocols. This layer of abstraction makes it easier to use Web services across different operating systems, because most operating systems can easily handle text messages.

- The client of a Web service only knows how to send and receive messages; it is not concerned with implementation of the Web service.

- Because of their message-passing nature, Web services and their clients are said to be *loosely coupled*. They are designed to make different systems work together, rather than being a part of one tightly integrated system. (For another way to call remote methods that allows more tight coupling, see the section on Remoting in Chapter 9, "Creating Code Components.")

- Web services have *discovery* capabilities, which means you can browse the Web services available on a particular Web server and obtain details about the available methods and parameters. Visual Studio .NET uses the discovery feature to allow you to add a *Web reference* to your project. A Web reference lets you program against the Web service using Intellisense editing features.

In the remainder of this section, we will create a sample Web service and then show how to access it from a Visual Basic .NET application. Our sample Web service will provide the loan calculation logic from the Loan Calculator sample application introduced earlier.

CREATING A WEB SERVICE

To begin creating the new Web service, start Visual Studio and choose to create a new project. For the project type, select ASP.NET Web Service. For the project name, enter LoanCalcService. Visual Studio .NET will then create project files on the Web server. The structure of a Web Service project is very similar to that of a Web Application project. Each project contains one or more classes, although they are called Web services instead of Web Forms.

A Web service has both a visual representation and a code window, although the visual representation is just for the developer's benefit; Web services do not have a user interface. (The reason for a visual mode is so you can add components to the class from the Toolbox, such as the Timer control.) Much like Web applications, there are two files that make up a Web service class: an .asmx file that is the entry point for the service and a .vb file that contains the code. As usual, Visual Studio automatically assigns a generic name to a new Web

Service project, in this case `Service1.asmx`. Before we begin writing code for our sample service, let's change it to a more descriptive name. To change the name of the Web service, you have to change both the filename and the class name in code:

1. Right-click `Service1.asmx` in the Solution Explorer and choose Rename.

2. Change the name of the file to `LoanInfo.asmx`. Your Solution Explorer should look similar to the one in Figure 18.8.

Figure 18.8
A Web Service project consists of one or more Web service classes, represented by an `.asmx` file in the Solution Explorer.

3. Next, right-click `LoanInfo.asmx` and choose View Code.

4. In the code editor, change the name of the class from `Service1` to `LoanInfo`.

Now that you have set up a new Web Service project, you can start adding Web methods in the code editor.

UNDERSTANDING WEB METHODS

The class that contains the code for a Web service is just like any other class in a Visual Studio .NET project in that you add methods to it by simply entering them in the code editor. These methods can contain modifiers (`Public`, `Private`, and so forth) to indicate their accessibility level. However, for a method to be accessible via a Web service, it must be declared in the following manner:

1. Make sure the method is declared to be `Public`.

2. Add the special `<WebMethod()>` tag before the method name.

The following code defines two methods in a Web service class, but only one method is directly accessible to clients:

```
<WebMethod()> Public Function HelloYou(ByVal YourName As String) As String
    Return CreateHelloString(YourName)
End Function

Public Function CreateHelloString(ByVal Name As String) As String
    Return "Hello and welcome, " & Name
End Function
```

The previous code sample contains two public functions, `HelloYou` and `CreateHelloString`. However, only the `HelloYou` function will appear available to clients of the Web service.

Even though the CreateHelloString method is marked as Public, it will not be available through IIS, because there is no <WebMethod()> tag. (Of course, you can still register the class directly in another project and call the CreateHelloString method, but that's not really the point of a Web service.) This brings about an interesting question: How much code should you put in a Web service? Consider these options:

- You can code all your business logic in a single Web service class and simply mark the methods you want to expose through the Web service.

- You can create a separate business layer and use the Web service as one of many interfaces to it.

As a developer, you have an enormous amount of flexibility in where to put your code. In our loan calculator Web service, we will just put code in the Web service class itself. However, in more complex applications with a number of different interfaces, you should take the more flexible second approach. We will discuss the concept of breaking an application up into different layers further in Chapter 22.

→ For a description of multi-tier applications, **see** Chapter 22, "Using ADO.NET," **p. 599**

CREATING THE LOAN CALCULATOR METHODS

As you may recall from the example in Chapters 2 and 3, the loan calculator program had basically two functions: calculating a monthly payment and an amortization schedule. These two functions correspond nicely to two Web methods in a Web service. The code from the original loan calculator example will also have to be changed somewhat, so it can function as a service. In the original example, the business logic and user interface were mixed, so you could directly access the text boxes on the form. However, a Web service does not know or care about the user interface. Instead, it follows the request-and-response model of the World Wide Web. Therefore, we will need to create functions with all the necessary parameters to perform the calculation and return the result to the calling program. Listing 18.2 contains the code for the CalculatePayment and CalculateAmortization methods.

LISTING 18.2 LOANCALC.ZIP—CREATING WEB METHODS

```
<WebMethod()> Public Function CalculatePayment( _
 ByVal PrincipalAmount As Decimal, _
 ByVal InterestRate As Decimal, _
 ByVal TermInYears As Integer) As Decimal
    Dim TermInMonths As Integer

    'Convert interest rate to its decimal equivalent
    ' i.e. 12.75 becomes 0.1275
    InterestRate = InterestRate / 100

    'Convert annual interest rate to monthly
    ' by dividing by 12 (months in a year)
    InterestRate = InterestRate / 12
```

LISTING 18.2   CONTINUED

```
    'Convert number of years to number of months
    '  by multiplying by 12 (months in a year)
    TermInMonths = TermInYears * 12

    'Calculate and return the monthly payment.
    Return PrincipalAmount * (InterestRate / _
    (1 - (1 + InterestRate) ^ -TermInMonths))
End Function

<WebMethod()> Public Function CalculateAmortization( _
    ByVal PrincipalAmount As Decimal, _
    ByVal InterestRate As Decimal, _
    ByVal TermInYears As Integer, _
    ByVal MonthlyPayment As Decimal) As DataSet

    Dim MonthInterest As Decimal         'Interest part of monthly payment
    Dim TotalInterest As Decimal = 0     'Total interest paid
    Dim MonthPrincipal As Decimal        'Principal part of monthly payment
    Dim TotalPrincipal As Decimal = 0    'Remaining principal
    Dim Month As Integer                 'Current month
    Dim NumPayments As Integer           'Number of monthly payments
    Dim i As Integer                     'Temporary loop counter
    Dim ScheduleTable As DataTable       'DataTable to hold schedule
    Dim ResultSet As DataSet             'DataSet to return
    Dim rowTemp As DataRow               'Used to add rows to the table

    'Set up the data table object with the column names and data types
    ScheduleTable = New DataTable("AmortizationSchedule")
    ScheduleTable.Columns.Add("PaymentNumber", GetType(Integer))
    ScheduleTable.Columns.Add("Interest", GetType(Decimal))
    ScheduleTable.Columns.Add("Principal", GetType(Decimal))
    ScheduleTable.Columns.Add("TotalInterest", GetType(Decimal))
    ScheduleTable.Columns.Add("Balance", GetType(Decimal))

    'Calculate the Amortization Schedule
    NumPayments = TermInYears * 12
    TotalPrincipal = PrincipalAmount
    For Month = 1 To NumPayments
        'Determine Values for the Current Row
        MonthInterest = (InterestRate / 100) / 12 * TotalPrincipal
        TotalInterest = TotalInterest + MonthInterest
        MonthPrincipal = MonthlyPayment - MonthInterest
        If MonthPrincipal > PrincipalAmount Then
            MonthPrincipal = PrincipalAmount
        End If
        TotalPrincipal = TotalPrincipal - MonthPrincipal

        'Add the values to the datatable
        rowTemp = ScheduleTable.NewRow
        rowTemp.Item("PaymentNumber") = Month
        rowTemp.Item("Interest") = MonthInterest
        rowTemp.Item("Principal") = MonthPrincipal
        rowTemp.Item("TotalInterest") = TotalInterest
```

PART

IV

CH

18

LISTING 18.2   CONTINUED

```
        rowTemp.Item("Balance") = TotalPrincipal

    ScheduleTable.Rows.Add(rowTemp)
Next Month

    'Finally, return the data table to the caller
    ResultSet = New DataSet()
    ResultSet.Tables.Add(ScheduleTable)
    CalculateAmortization = ResultSet

End Function
```

Each function in Listing 18.2 accepts several numeric parameters used to perform loan payment calculations. The `CalculatePayment` function returns a value of type `Double`, whereas the `CalculateAmortization` function returns a more complex data type, a `DataSet`. We will discuss data and `DataSets` further in Chapter 22, but for now just consider a `DataSet` a structure that can accommodate the entire amortization schedule in tabular format. Web services can return almost any type of data structure to a client, provided that structure is *serializable*, or convertible to and from text.

→ For an example of `DataSets`, **see** "Understanding Datasets," **p. 613**

TESTING YOUR WEB SERVICE

Web Services can be tested by calling their methods from another application. However, the Web Service framework also provides a test page you can use to perform rudimentary testing of some of your Web methods. After entering the code from Listing 18.2, press F5 to start the Web service project in Visual Studio. You will see the default test page for a Web service, which lists all your public Web methods. Click the `CalculatePayment` link and an HTML form will be generated so you can test the method, as pictured in Figure 18.9.

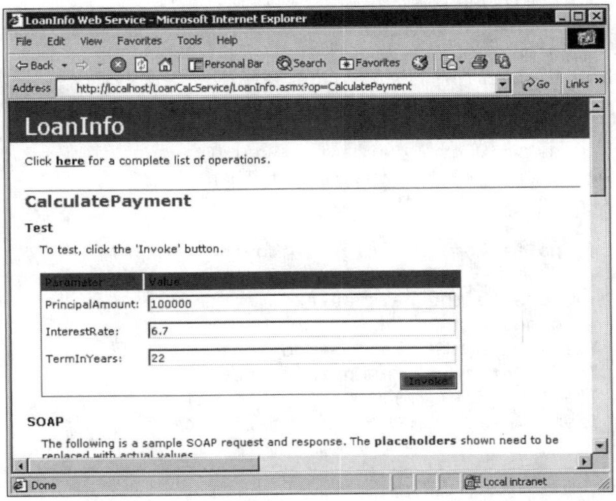

Figure 18.9
The .NET framework provides a test page for Web services that appears when you enter the Web service address in a browser.

Go ahead and enter the parameters for the `CalculatePayment` function and click the Invoke button. Your browser should display the response from the Web service, which is formatted as XML:

```
<?xml version="1.0" encoding="utf-8" ?>
<double xmlns="http://tempuri.org/">725.0596381989036</double>
```

Even if you don't know XML, the response from the Web service is simple enough that you can pick out the monthly payment value, $725.06. To see how a more complex data type is represented using XML, execute the `CalculateAmortization` method from the test page.

> **Note**
> You may have noticed the reference to the `tempuri.org` Web site in the XML response. Tempuri is not a way to cook shrimp, but rather a temporary Universal Resource Indicator for your Web service's namespace. For more information on creating your own namespace, see the help topic "XML Namespaces."

When executing a Web method from the test page, note that the parameters to the function call are visible in the URL query string, because the test page used a simple GET request to execute this function. Web methods can be called either by submitting http GET and POST requests, or by sending a SOAP (Simple Object Access Protocol) message to the server. The Web Services test page only supports simple parameter types that can be typed in directly; if your Web method had contained a data set or array as an input parameter, the test page would not be able to invoke it. However, as long as you are developing in Visual Studio, the communication process is transparent, as we will see in the next section.

> **Note**
> For developers still working with Visual Basic 6.0, Microsoft has developed a program that creates a type library so you can call Web Services from VB 6.0. For more information, search the `msdn.Microsoft.com` Web site for "Web Service Proxy Wizard."

ACCESSING A WEB SERVICE

Now that you have created a Web service, let's access it from an application. Assuming you ran the test successfully as described in the previous section, you can close the Web service project you have been working on. Go ahead and start a new Windows Application project. Set up the controls on the form as described in Table 18.1. Arrange the controls as shown in Figure 18.10.

TABLE 18.1   CONTROLS FOR THE LOAN CALCULATOR

Control Type	Control Name	Text Property
Label	lblPrincipal	Principal
Textbox	txtPrincipal	(blank)

PART

IV

CH

18

TABLE 18.1 CONTINUED

Control Type	Control Name	Text Property
Label	lblInterest	Interest (%)
Textbox	txtInterest	(blank)
Label	lblTerm	Terms in years
Textbox	txtTerm	(blank)
Label	lblPayment	Payment
TextBox	txtPayment	(blank)
Button	btnCalculate	Calculate
DataGrid	dgAmortization	(n/a)

Figure 18.10
In this version of the loan calculator we will use a DataGrid to display the amortization schedule, which we will calculate at the same time as the payment.

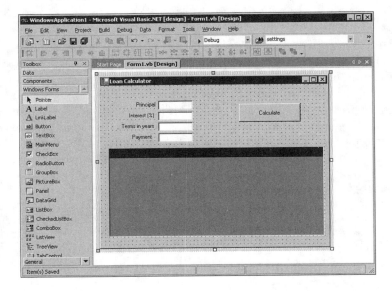

ADDING A WEB REFERENCE

To make the methods of a Web service available to your program, you have to add a Web reference. First, right-click the References folder in the Solution Explorer and choose Add Web Reference. The Add Web Reference dialog box will appear, where you can type in the address of a server and/or Web service. In the Address field, enter `http://computername`, where *computername* is the name of the Web server on which you created the LoanCalcService Web service. Press the Enter key and Visual Studio will then query the Web server and display a list of the available Web references on the server. Click the link for the LoanCalcService and the dialog box will display additional information about the service, as shown in Figure 18.11.

Note

You do not have to browse the available services if you enter the complete name of the desired Web service.

Figure 18.11
The Add Web Reference dialog box can be used to browse Web services and Web service documentation before adding a reference.

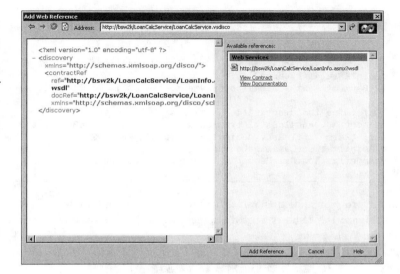

The page shown in Figure 18.11 contains links for the Web Service *description* and *contract*. The description link takes you to the test pages so you can try the Web service's methods. The contract link takes you to an XML page containing detailed information about the structure of the messages necessary to communicate with this Web service.

To complete adding the Web reference to your project, click Add reference to close the dialog box. The Solution Explorer should now show the name of your Web server under the Web references section.

USING THE WEB SERVICE OBJECTS

The classes exposed by the Web service can now be accessed in your program. Just type the server name followed by a dot and you will see the `CalculatePayment` and `CalculateAmortization` methods available. Enter the code from Listing 18.3 in the button's `Click` event to complete the sample application:

LISTING 18.3   LOANCALC.ZIP—ACCESSING A WEB SERVICE

```
Private Sub btnCalculate_Click(ByVal sender As System.Object, _
ByVal e As System.EventArgs) Handles btnCalculate.Click

    Dim LoanCalcService As localhost.LoanInfo
    Dim dsAmort As DataSet
    Dim decPayment, decIntRate, decPrincipal As Decimal
    Dim intYears As Integer
```

LISTING 18.3   CONTINUED

```
decIntRate = Convert.ToDecimal(txtInterest.Text)
decPrincipal = Convert.ToDecimal(txtPrincipal.Text)
intYears = Convert.ToInt32(txtTerm.Text)

'Create an instance of the Web service class
LoanCalcService = New localhost.LoanInfo()

'Determine the payment amount
decPayment = LoanCalcService.CalculatePayment(decPrincipal,_
decIntRate, intYears)
txtPayment.Text = Format(decPayment, "$0.00")

'Determine the amortization schedule
dsAmort = LoanCalcService.CalculateAmortization(decPrincipal, _
decIntRate, intYears, Decimal.Round(decPayment, 2))
dgAmortization.DataSource = dsAmort
dgAmortization.DataMember = "AmortizationSchedule"
End Sub
```

Run the program and enter values for the principal amount, interest rate, and number of years. Figure 18.12 shows what the screen will look like after it has retrieved information from the Web service.

Figure 18.12
The Loan Calculator Web service can be accessed from Windows or Web-based Applications.

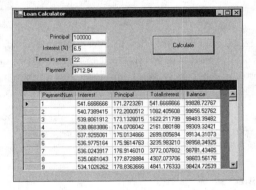

> **Note**
>
> Because the Web service and client are independent processing units, you may want to investigate asynchronous calls for longer requests. Microsoft includes a great example of some Visual Basic code to do this on the MSDN Web site; just visit http://msdn.microsoft.com/code and search for "Web Service."

CHANGING THE WEB SERVER

When you add a Web reference to your project, Visual Studio automatically associates the reference with the server where it found the discovery information about the Web service. However, sometimes you might want to dynamically change the location of the Web service in the client app; for example, if you want to switch between development and production Web servers running the same service. To override the default location, you can set the URL property of your Web service class, as in the following example:

```
Dim LoanCalcService As LoanCalc.LoanInfo
LoanCalcService = New LoanCalc.LoanInfo()
LoanCalcService.Url = "http://servername/LoanCalcService/LoanInfo.asmx"
```

Note that the URL setting includes the complete path to the .asmx file. In addition, notice the name of our Web reference is LoanCalc. By default, when adding a Web reference, the server name is used, for example localhost. However, you can rename the reference in the Solution Explorer if you want to use a more generic name in your code. By using a generic name and setting the URL property dynamically, you can avoid tying your client to one particular Web service host.

FROM HERE. . .

In this chapter, we have introduced you to two types of Web projects available in Visual Basic .NET: Web Applications and Web Services. Both of these topics are new and exciting areas of Web software development; the World Wide Web is where you will find the latest news and information about them. To learn more about other Visual Studio .NET technologies that you might use in these Web projects, please see the following chapters:

- To find out more about the DataSet class and data access with ADO.NET, please see Chapter 22, "Using ADO.NET."
- Explore the many ASP Server controls in Chapter 19, "Web Controls."
- Learn to debug your applications and make them perform better in Chapter 26, "Debugging and Performance Tuning."

PART
IV

CH

18

WEB CONTROLS

In this chapter

We begin our chapter on Web controls with an overview of some general guidelines for using controls in the Web forms environment. In the remainder of the chapter, the Web forms controls are broken into groups and described in detail. After reading this chapter, you will be familiar with some of the many useful Web components built into the ASP.NET framework.

USING ASP.NET SERVER CONTROLS

By now, the purpose of fundamental controls such as the Label, TextBox, and Button should be clear to you, regardless of whether you are working with Web forms or Windows forms. However, if you are familiar with the Windows versions of these controls, you may notice some big differences. For example, when you draw an ASP.NET Label control on a Web form, the first thing you should notice is several properties are missing! For example, there is no way to force text alignment to the left or right, as with a Windows control. (If you want to do this, you can use a Table cell, as described in the upcoming section "Displaying Information in a Table.") Although lack of support for identical features may seem like a big limitation at first, it is outweighed by the fact your application can run in almost any browser. Remember that a browser's display capabilities are limited to standard HTML. An ASP.NET server control mimics as much of the functionality of the corresponding Windows control as it can, but must function within the constraints of the Web platform. As you will see, in some areas Web controls even provide additional capabilities. In this section, we'll look at some general features of the way Web controls work and describe a few controls that are essential to Web page navigation and organization.

ALLOWING THE BROWSER TO ADJUST CONTROL SIZE

As we mentioned in Chapter 18, "Web Applications and Services," when you arrange controls on a Web form you may do so in Grid Layout mode or Flow Layout mode. If you choose Flow Layout mode, the end user's browser has more freedom to adjust control position. Similarly, when setting the Height and Width properties of a Web control, the programmer can choose to exercise varying degrees of control (pun intended) over an object's size. For example, the following statements show three different ways to set the Width property of a Label control:

```
Label1.Width = Unit.Pixel(300)
Label2.Width = Unit.Percentage(75)
Label3.Width = Unit.Empty
```

The first statement sets the width of a Label control to 300 pixels. The second statement specifies the label should be 75% of the browser window size. The final line of code lets the browser determine the label width, based on the length of the label text and the size of the browser window. Figure 19.1 shows the effect of executing these three code statements on identical labels.

Figure 19.1
Setting a relative width or no width allows a Web control to dynamically adjust to the size of the browser window; a width specified in pixels prohibits automatic resizing.

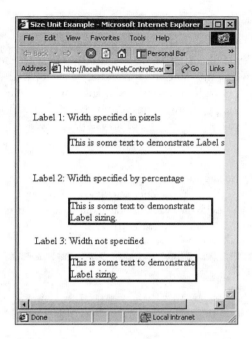

PART

IV

CH

19

Note

When entering a size number in the Properties window at design time, you can type **px** to indicate pixels or **%** to indicate a percent value.

As you can see from Figure 19.1, specifying an object's size in pixels provides the greatest degree of control but disables automatic resizing.

SETTING A RELATIVE FONT SIZE

In a Web application, fonts can also be specified in relative or absolute units, using the FontUnit structure:

```
Label1.Font.Size = FontUnit.Point(10)
Label2.Font.Size = FontUnit.Larger
Label3.Font.Size = FontUnit.XLarge
```

In some browsers, such as Internet Explorer, the user can choose whichever text size is easiest to read for her. Using relative font sizes allows your Web page to adjust to these changes, while a font size specified in points remains fixed.

USING A STYLE SHEET

You may notice that many of the Web controls have a property called CSSClass. A .css file, which stands for Cascading Style Sheet, allows you to specify visual attributes such as color, size, and font names. You can link the same style sheet file to one or more Web pages to ensure that all your pages look visually consistent. Not only can you define the style of standard Web page elements like hyperlinks, but you can also define custom style classes that can be associated with Web controls via the CSSClass property.

NAVIGATING THE STYLE SHEET

By default, Web application projects automatically include a style sheet called Styles.css. To view the contents of the style sheet, right-click the Styles.css file in the Solution Explorer and select Open. Two new windows will open: the style sheet itself and the CSS Outline window, both of which are pictured in Figure 19.2.

Figure 19.2
The CSS Outline Window provides a way to visually navigate a style sheet.

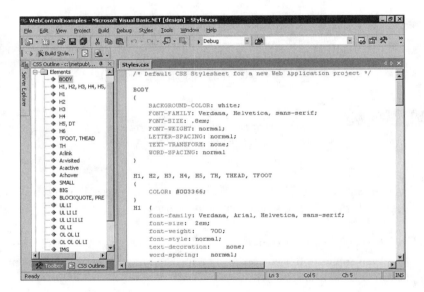

As you can see from Figure 19.2, the font names and sizes for various Web page elements are defined in the style sheet. To view the style attributes for body text, right-click the BODY element in the CSS Outline Window and select Style Builder. The Style Builder dialog box, shown in Figure 19.3, allows you to visually define the properties of a style.

Figure 19.3
The Style Builder allows you to manipulate the contents of a Cascading Style Sheet in a graphical manner.

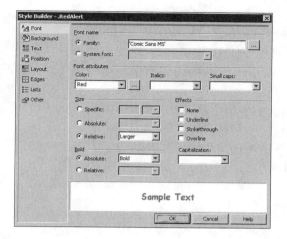

CREATING A CUSTOM CSS CLASS

In addition to setting styles for the various predefined elements of a Web page, style sheets can also be used to define custom style classes. To demonstrate, we'll create our own style class called RedAlert to draw attention or indicate a problem. To create a new style class, perform the following steps:

1. Right-click the Classes folder in the CSS Outline Window and select Add Style Rule.
2. Click the Class Name Option and enter RedAlert.
3. Click OK. The following skeleton style class is added to your style sheet:
   ```
   .RedAlert
   {
   }
   ```
4. Right-click the RedAlert class in the CSS Outline Window and select Build Style to display the Style Builder.
5. Set the Font color to Red and the Font size to X-Large.
6. Click OK to close the Style Builder. Note that your font attributes have been added to the style sheet.

Congratulations, you have just created a new style class.

USING YOUR CSS CLASS

To use your new CSS class, you will need to link the style sheet to a Web form and then set the CSSClass property of a control to RedAlert. Even though the Styles.css file is included in your project, you still need to add the following line of HTML to tell the Web form about it:

```
<LINK REL="stylesheet" Type="text/css" HREF="styles.css">
```

PART

IV

CH

19

The previous line of code links the styles in a particular HTML document to the style sheet file. It is typically placed in the header section of an HTML document. To add this link in your own project, do the following:

1. Open the designer for your Web form and click the HTML button to display the HTML view.
2. Find the <HEAD> tag in the HTML file. Add the LINK statement from the previous line of code on a new line after the <HEAD> tag.
3. Click the Design button to return to the design view.
4. Add a Label control.
5. Display the Properties window for the label and find the CSSClass property. Enter **RedAlert** for the CSSClass property value.

After performing these steps, the label control should be automatically updated to reflect the new style.

USING THE PANEL CONTROL TO ORGANIZE YOUR PAGE

One useful ASP.NET server control is Panel, which can contain other Web controls. Placing controls in a panel allows you to hide or show a group of controls at the same time, as well as have controls resize to fit panel rather than page boundaries. By adding borders to a panel, you can create visual boundaries, as shown in Figure 19.4.

Figure 19.4
Panels can be used to group controls.

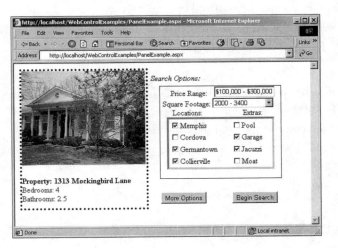

Using the Panel control at design time is a little tricky. To add controls to it, you have to drag them from the toolbox directly to the panel or copy and paste them from the Web form. The Panel is more suited to dynamically generating controls. Listing 19.1 shows how to generate an ImageButton control in a Panel at runtime.

LISTING 19.1   WEBCONTROLS.ZIP—ADDING CONTROLS TO A PANEL

```
'Create a new button
Dim MyButton As ImageButton
MyButton = New ImageButton()
MyButton.ImageUrl = "/Win2000.gif"
AddHandler MyButton.Click, AddressOf MyClickHandler

'Add it to the panel
Panel1.Controls.Add(MyButton)
Panel1.HorizontalAlign = HorizontalAlign.Center
Panel1.Visible = True
```

The code in Listing 19.1 creates an instance of the `ImageButton` class and then sets the image location and `Click` event handler. Next, it is added to a panel using the `Add` method. Finally, the `Panel`'s `HorizontalAlign` property is set to center the control, and the `Visible` property is set to `True`. The resulting form would not look any different than if you had simply drawn the button at design time. However, the flexibility of generating buttons and other controls at runtime may be useful when creating a Web form based on the results of a database query.

Note

When adding buttons to a panel dynamically, you need to execute the `AddHandler` statement in the `Page_Load` event. If you set up an event handler inside the `Click` event procedure of another button, for example, the event handler does not respond correctly. To work around this, you can have the first button set a variable that cause the dynamic button to be created in the next `Page_Load` event.

PART
IV

CH

19

MASTERING PAGE NAVIGATION

In a Windows application, you can show forms programmatically by creating an instance of the form class. In Web forms, you have to get the ASP.NET page processor to create the instance. One way to move from page to page in a Web application is to link the pages using hyperlinks. Another is to transfer the user to another page in response to a server-side event. Visual Studio .NET includes controls to accomplish both.

ADDING HYPERLINKS

If you have ever used the Web, you are familiar with the concept of a hyperlink. Hyperlinks allow you to navigate to a different Web page. Creating a hyperlink manually using HTML is easy:

```
<A HREF="http://www.vbinsider.com">Brian's Web Site</A>
```

The previous line of code would cause the text `Brian's Web Site` to be displayed in the user's browser. Clicking the text would transfer the user to the `http://www.vbinsider.com` Web site. In the world of Web forms, you can use a `HyperLink` control to add hyperlinks to your Web pages. Although the HTML for a hyperlink is trivial, using the server-side control version allows you to access it seamlessly using server-side code. For example, you could set the Visible property to hide or show the hyperlink depending on whether the user has completed a data entry form.

When you create a new instance of the HyperLink control, you typically set the following properties:

- Text—The clickable text shown to the user.
- NavigateURL—The address of the Web page to which you want the hyperlink to navigate.
- ImageURL—Setting this property to the address of an image will override the Text property and display a clickable image instead.
- Target—Allows you to open the new page in a specified frame or new browser window.

To aid in specifying URL addresses, you can display the Select URL dialog box when specifying the NavigateURL and ImageURL properties. The dialog box, shown in Figure 19.5, helps you locate a file by providing browse and preview capabilities.

Figure 19.5
When linking Web forms in the same application, relative URLs allow you to move the application from server to server without changing the URL path.

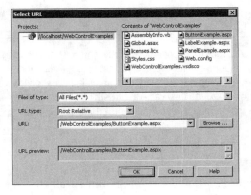

RAISING SERVER-SIDE EVENTS WITH BUTTONS

Button controls provide a way for a user of your Web application to initiate an action on the server. This is the main thing that sets a button apart from a hyperlink—the fact that a server-side event is raised. A hyperlink, on the other hand, causes the end user's browser to directly move to a new page without first talking to the server. There are three different types of button controls to choose from:

- Button—The standard button control that appears as a gray box.
- LinkButton—It looks like a HyperLink control but raises a server-side event.
- ImageButton—Allows you to put a clickable image on your Web page. (Set the ImageURL property to specify the image.)

Figure 19.6 shows an example of the different types of Web buttons.

Figure 19.6
The different types of `Button` controls in the Web forms model vary in appearance but are similar in functionality.

All the buttons work basically the same, in that the most important event is the `Click` event, which occurs when the user clicks the button with the mouse. However, the `ImageButton` also provides the x,y coordinate of the click, which can be useful in creating an image map. Listing 19.2 shows how to retrieve coordinates from an image map using the `Click` event.

LISTING 19.2   WEBCONTROLS.ZIP—CREATING AN IMAGE MAP

```
Private Sub ImageButton1_Click(ByVal sender As_
System.Object, ByVal e As_
System.Web.UI.ImageClickEventArgs) Handles ImageButton1.Click

    Dim sNewPage As String
    sNewPage = WhereDoIGo(e.X, e.Y)
    Response.Redirect(sNewPage)

End Sub

Private Function WhereDoIGo(ByVal X As Integer,_
ByVal Y As Integer) As String
    If X > 50 Then
        Return "http://www.microsoft.com"
    Else
        Return "http://www.yahoo.com"
    End If
End Function
```

The code in Listing 19.2 redirects the user's browser to a different Web page depending on where she clicked the image.

VALIDATING USER INPUT

In addition to accepting input, *validating* that input is an important function of a data entry program. A typical data entry form contains validation code that must execute successfully

PART

IV

CH

19

before the information can be committed to the database. If the validation tests do not pass, then the program displays a message requesting that the user correct the erroneous data. When you build a form, certain types of controls do not require much or any validation code. For example, in a drop-down list the user is restricted to selecting a fixed set of choices that you, the programmer, control. However, a text box control allows the end user to enter almost any type of numeric or character data. Therefore, more stringent validation logic must be used before committing a text box value to the database. To aid in the process of validating user input on the Web, the .NET Framework provides several `Validator` classes, which are available for use on a Web form as the following controls:

- `RequiredFieldValidator`—Checks whether a user has entered a value in a field
- `CompareValidator`—Performs an equal, a greater, or a less than between two fields or a field and a value
- `RangeValidator`—Determines whether a value falls within a specified range
- `RegularExpressionValidator`—Validates that a field value matches a regular expression
- `CustomValidator`—Allows you to add custom code to determine the validity of an input field
- `ValidationSummary`—Combines the error messages from multiple validation controls

The main purpose of validation controls is to simplify the process of checking for and informing the user of invalid data. When designing a Web form, validators appear as labels that contain the validation error message. They are typically placed near the field with which they are associated, as shown in Figure 19.7.

Figure 19.7
Validator controls are special labels, which automatically display error messages if an associated field does not pass a validation test.

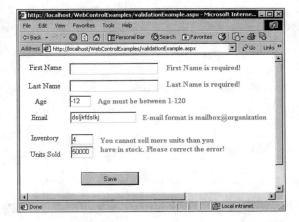

PERFORMING BASIC VALIDATION

To demonstrate the ease with which you can use Validator controls in a Web application, we will create a simple example with several text box fields. Ultimately, your example will look like Figure 19.7. To begin, create a new Web application and set up the Web form as follows:

1. Set up six `TextBox` controls with the following names: `txtFirstName`, `txtLastName`, `txtAge`, `txtEMail`, `txtInventory`, and `txtUnitsSold`.

2. Delete the default text in the `Text` properties of each text box so that the initial text in each of them is blank.

3. Place a `Label` control to the left of each text box to describe the text box.

4. Place a `Button` control at the bottom of the form. Set its `Text` property to `Save` and its `Name` property to **btnSave**.

Now that we have set up a basic data entry form, we will add validation controls to each field. As you will see, using the validator controls is very easy; simply set a few properties to control the error message text, associated field, and any other inputs needed for the validation test.

CHECKING FOR REQUIRED FIELDS

You may have seen examples of *required fields* when filling out forms in real life. For example, if you leave the dollar amount on a check blank, the bank will not know how much money to withdraw. Similarly, our sample Web form contains fields for last and first name that we do not want the user to leave blank. To add required field validation for the name fields, perform the following steps:

1. Add two `RequiredFieldValidator` controls to your form.

2. Position one validator control to the right of the `txtFirstName` and `txtLastName` text boxes.

3. Set their `Name` properties to `valLastName` and `valFirstName`.

4. Using the Properties window, set the `ErrorMessage` property of each control to *last/first*`Name Cannot be left blank`.

5. Also in the Properties window, find the `ControltoValidate` property, which will display a drop-down list of the validateable controls on the form. Set this property to the name of the text box to the immediate left of each validator control.

Now, run the program and click the Save button, without entering any text in the last name or first name field. The error message you specified earlier should automatically appear when the page is refreshed.

VALIDATING INPUT RANGES

In addition to determining whether there is any input in a given field, sometimes you also want to make sure the input falls within a specified range of values. The age field on our sample form is a good example. Although the back-end database would probably not allow character values in a numeric field, there still may be numeric values for age that the database would accept but are not valid; 1,000 for example. Setting up a `RangeValidator` control is almost as easy as using the `RequiredFieldValidator`; the only additional step is setting a few more properties to control the range value.

To set up a range validation for our sample form do the following:

1. Place a RangeValidator control on the form to the right of the txtAge text box.

2. Set its Name property to valAge.

3. Enter the following lines of code in the Page_Load event:
   ```
   valAge.ControlToValidate = "txtAge"
   valAge.ErrorMessage = "Age must be between 1-120"
   valAge.Type = ValidationDataType.Integer
   valAge.MinimumValue = 1
   valAge.MaximumValue = 120
   ```

Although you could have easily used the Properties window to configure the control, the previous code sample demonstrates how to configure the control programmatically by setting properties at runtime. To specify a range for the validation test, you need to set the MinimumValue, MaximumValue, and Type properties. The sample code causes the control to check the value of the txtAge field to determine if it falls between the range of 1 and 120.

> **Note**
>
> Setting the Type property to let the RangeValidator control know what data type you are using is very important because strings and integers are ordered differently. For example, in the domain of strings 2 is not in the range between 1 and 120 as is the case with integers.

COMPARING FIELD VALUES

Another useful validation control is the CompareValidator. A compare validator can perform a basic mathematical comparison between a text box value and a comparison value, such as determining whether the text box value is greater than or equal to the comparison value. It can also validate a field's data type.

As with the other validation controls, you need to set the associated text box name using the ControltoValidate property. To set up the type of comparison, set the Operator and Type properties. Next, you need to identify the comparison value according to the following rules.

- If you are comparing the values in two text boxes, set the ControltoCompare property to the name of the second text box. Do not set the ValuetoCompare property.

- If you are validating the value of a text box against a literal value, set the ValuetoCompare property to this value. Do not set the ControltoCompare property.

- If you are validating the text box data type, you do not need to set either of the preceding properties. It is only necessary to set the Type and ControltoValidate properties.

The comparison can be thought of like an expression in an If statement, with the ControltoValidate value on the left, followed by the operator, followed by the comparison value. If the expression evaluates to True, the validation succeeds. Using this knowledge, return to the sample program and set up a validation alert that checks to make sure the value of `txtUnitsSold` is less than or equal to the value of `txtInventory`.

> **Note**
>
> The `CompareValidator` control considers an empty text box control to be valid. You can of course use a `RequiredFieldValidator` control on the same text box to check for this condition.

VALIDATING AN ENTIRE PAGE

You already know that using validator controls enables you to alert the user of invalid data, but your code still has to make the final decision to commit the data from the form. Each validator control has an `IsValid` property, which is set to `True` if its validation test succeeded. The `IsValid` property of the `Page` object can be used to check all your validator controls in one fell swoop:

```
Private Sub btnSave_Click(ByVal sender As System.Object, _
       ByVal e As System.EventArgs) Handles btnSave.Click

       If Page.IsValid Then
           Call YourSaveDataFunction()
           Response.Redirect("http://www.vbinsider.com")
       End If
End Sub
```

The previous code sample calls the save function and moves to a new page only if the `Page.IsValid` property is set to `True`. By using validation controls, you can reduce the messy task of validating HTML form data to a few lines of code.

CONTROLLING VALIDATION MESSAGES

If you have followed the sample program, you have seen that validation controls can be located right next to the fields they are validating. This user interface style is typical of a Web application. However, where screen space is limited you may want to use a `ValidationSummary` control. A `ValidationSummary` control is not associated with a particular input field, but instead consolidates the error messages from any other validation controls present on the page having an `IsValid` property value of `False`.

Because the validation summary text is built automatically from other validation controls, you still need to set their `ErrorMessage` properties. However, you can add your own custom header to the validation summary by setting the `HeaderText` property, as in the following example

```
valSum.HeaderText = "Your request cannot be processed because:"
valSum.DisplayMode = ValidationSummaryDisplayMode.BulletList
```

Notice in the second line of code we set the `DisplayMode` property, which determines the format of the validation summary text. In addition to displaying the lists on the Web page, the `ValidationSummary` control can also generate a message box for browsers that support client scripting. Figure 19.8 shows a message box generated on the client side with the `ValidationSummary` control.

Figure 19.8
Many of the ASP.NET Server controls will generate client script if the browser supports it.

To use a message box, set the ShowMessageBox property to True. To hide the summary text inside the browser, set the ShowSummary property to False.

VALIDATING EXPRESSIONS AND OTHER VALUES

Most of the validation controls included in the ASP.NET framework perform simple validation tests. However, the programming model does accommodate more complex tests by providing a regular expression validation, as well as the ability to program your own validation function.

USING REGULAR EXPRESSIONS

You can validate that text in a text box matches complex string patterns using the RegularExpressionValidator control. *Regular expressions* are special characters that can be used to describe string patterns. For example, in our sample form, we have a field for the user to enter an e-mail address. E-mail addresses typically contain a mailbox name, followed by an at symbol (@), followed by the Internet domain name. If you are following along with the example, add a RegularExpressionValidator control to our sample Web form. Set its ControltoValidate property to txtEmail. Then, all you need to do is specify the appropriate regular expression for a valid e-mail address. Fortunately, Visual Studio already knows it. The Regular Expression Editor, shown in Figure 19.9, includes a lot of predefined expressions for addresses, phone numbers, and other common string fields.

Figure 19.9
Regular expressions are a powerful tool for searching and validating text data.

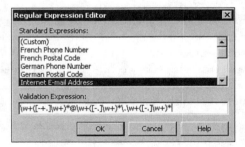

To display the Regular Expression Editor dialog box, click the ValidationExpression property in the Properties window. For the sample project, select Internet Email Address from the list and click OK. Finally, set the ErrorMessage property to Invalid e-mail address. Now, run the sample program. If you enter invalid e-mail addresses, you should see the error message displayed.

CREATING YOUR OWN VALIDATION FUNCTION

If none of the other validation controls meet your validation requirements, you may want to use a `CustomValidator` control. The `CustomValidator` control automatically calls your custom validation function when necessary, which in turn sets the value for the `IsValid` property. The validation function can perform whatever tasks you need, such as a database lookup. Listing 19.3 shows a custom subroutine to check whether a date entered in a text box is a weekday.

LISTING 19.3   WEBCONTROLS.ZIP—EXECUTING A CUSTOM VALIDATION FUNCTION

```
Private Sub CheckWeekDay(ByVal source As Object, _
        ByVal args As ServerValidateEventArgs)

    Dim UserInput As String = args.Value

    If IsDate(UserInput) Then
        Dim TheDate As Date = Convert.ToDateTime(UserInput)
        If TheDate.DayOfWeek = DayOfWeek.Saturday _
        Or TheDate.DayOfWeek = DayOfWeek.Sunday Then
            args.IsValid = False
        Else
            args.IsValid = True
        End If
    Else
        args.IsValid = False
    End If
End Sub
```

As you can see from Listing 19.3, the second parameter passed to a custom validation function contains two important properties. The first is the `Value` property, which contains the value to be validated. The second is the `IsValid` property, which your custom code can set depending on whether the value is valid. To make the function work, you have to add an event handler for the server-side event:

```
AddHandler valMeetingDate.ServerValidate, AddressOf CheckWeekDay
```

> **Note**
>
> You can also program a custom JavaScript validation function, which the `ValidatorControl` will execute on the client. For more details, see the help topic "CustomValidator class."

PART
IV
CH
19

WORKING WITH LISTS AND GRIDS

In addition to text input fields, a frequent method of accepting user input is to display a list and allow the user to select one or more items. Even if you do not require the user to select a list item, lists can be used to display information in an organized manner. The Web Forms model contains several controls suitable for displaying all types of lists, everything from a single column of string values to an editable, data-bound grid. In this section we will cover the ASP.NET Server controls that allow you to add lists and grids to your program.

CREATING SIMPLE LISTS

If you need to display a simple list of strings for the user of a Web forms application, you have a variety of controls to choose from:

- ListBox—A ListBox control displays multiple list items on the screen at the same time. Depending on property settings, you can allow the user to select one or multiple items by highlighting them with the mouse.

- DropDownList—The DropDownList control lets the user pick a single item from a list. It only takes up about as much room as a text box because the list of items is hidden when the user is finished browsing it.

- CheckListBox—A CheckListBox allows the user to select multiple list items. A check mark is displayed next to each selected item. Unlike the ListBox control, a CheckListBox can display items in multiple columns.

- RadioButtonList—The RadioButtonList control works similarly to the CheckListBox, except it allows the user to select only one value at a time. A dot appears next to the selected item.

Most of these controls behave similarly to their Windows versions, although the Web versions are generally more limited in their functionality. For example, the familiar ListBox control does not have automatic sorting on the Web, and it can store only simple values. This of course makes sense because the list items must be able to be rendered in a browser using standard HTML. Figure 19.10 shows what the simple list controls look like to an end user.

Figure 19.10
List controls are input fields that allow the user to select from a group of predefined items.

WORKING WITH ITEMS IN A ListControl

Each of the simple list controls pictured in Figure 19.10 derives from a common class called the ListControl. Therefore, once you know how to manipulate list items for one type of control, you can easily apply that knowledge to the others. Each type of list control has an Items collection that contains the list items. Each list item has a Text property, which is displayed for the user, and a Value property, which is associated with the displayed item but not displayed on the screen. Listing 19.4 shows a function that fills a list control with a list of the planets in the solar system.

LISTING 19.4   WEBCONTROLS.ZIP—USING LIST CONTROLS

```
Private Sub ListPlanets(ByVal MyList As ListControl)

    Dim PlanetNames() As String = {"Mercury", "Venus", "Earth",_
 "Mars",
                        "Jupiter", "Saturn", "Uranus",_
"Neptune", "Pluto"}
    Dim OrbitInYears() As Double = _
                        {0.2, 0.6, 1, 1.9, 11.9, 29.5,_
84, 164.8, 247.9}

    Dim i As Integer

    For i = 0 To 8
       MyList.Items.Add(New ListItem(PlanetNames(i),_
OrbitInYears(i)))
    Next

End Sub
```

The ListPlanets function in Listing 19.4 specifies the Value and Text properties for each item using the constructor function of the ListItem class. This function will work with any of the previously mentioned list controls on a Web form.

PART
IV
CH
19

Note

> You are not required to populate the Value property of a list item. It is intended to store another piece of information about the list item that is needed by your program, such as an ID number for a database retrieval.

All controls inherited from the ListControl class allow the user to select some range of items. The DropDownList and RadioButtonList controls are designed for situations where the user must pick one and only one item. The CheckListBox control allows the user to select one, several, or no items, entirely at his discretion. The ListBox control has two selection modes, which determine whether the user can highlight one or multiple items. In any case, each element in the Items collection has a Selected property that can be used to programmatically determine whether the user selected it:

```
Dim TempItem As ListItem
For Each TempItem In MyList.Items
   If TempItem.Selected Then
      lblInfo.Text &= "You selected " & TempItem.Text & vbCrLf
   End If
Next
```

The previous lines of code use a loop to check each member of the Items collection. However, if you are working with a single selection list, there is a much easier way to determine the selected item:

```
If Not IsNothing(MyList.SelectedItem) Then
    lblInfo.Text = "You selected " & MyList.SelectedItem.Text
Else
    lblInfo.Text = "No item selected!"
End If
```

As the example demonstrates, the SelectedItem property returns the currently selected list item. If you access the SelectedItem property for a multiple-selection list, you will get the item with the lowest list index.

> **Note**
>
> To create default selections, you can set the Selected property of the desired items to True when building the list.

You can also access items in a list by their numeric index numbers. Each ListItem has a numeric index, which can be used to retrieve or set item values:

```
MyList.Items(2).Text = "Hey you"
```

To find out the index number of the selected item, use the SelectedIndex property. If no item has been selected, this property contains the value -1. To determine the number of elements in the Items collection of a list, use the Count property.

> **Note**
>
> Index values are zero-based, so if the count of items in a list control is 20, their index values will range from 0 to 19.

The Items also contains other useful methods for managing a list, including search and delete functions:

```
TempItem = MyList.Items.FindByText("Pluto")
If Not IsNothing(TempItem) Then
    MyList.Items.Remove(TempItem)
End If
```

There are two find methods, FindByText and FindByValue. These functions perform an exact-match, case-sensitive search of the Items collection and return the first item matching the search string.

USING A ListBox

The ListBox control allows the user to view multiple items on the screen at the same time and provides a scrollbar if there are too many items to display at once. As with other controls, you can set the size of a list box when you draw it or set its Height and Width properties. However, the list box also allows you to control its height based on the number of items you want to display on the screen at once, by setting the Rows property. To use the Rows property, you must delete any value for the Height property. If you do set the Height property, the size of the list box is rounded to fit an exact number of rows; it will not display partial rows. Figure 19.11 shows two list boxes using different height settings.

Figure 19.11
The height of the left-most list box was set using the Rows property to display only two rows; the height of the list box on the right was set using the Height property.

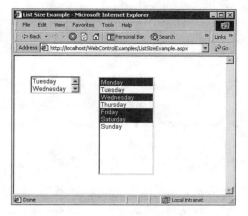

Notice that Figure 19.11 also demonstrates a list box that contains multiple selected items, indicated by their highlighted backgrounds. To allow the user to select multiple items in a list box, you must set the SelectionMode property to Multiple. To use a multiple-selection list box, single-click the desired items with the mouse while holding down the Ctrl key or use the Shift key to select ranges.

PART
IV
CH
19

Tip

Make sure your ListBox control is sized appropriately in relation to the number of items it contains. For example, it may be very difficult for the user to scroll through 100 items if the list is sized to show only three at a time. If you have a very large number of items, you may want to consider breaking your list into multiple parts and having the user narrow down her choices gradually.

Tip

The keyboard can be used to quickly move through a list. The PageUp, PageDown, Home, End, and arrow keys cause the list box to scroll. For sorted lists, typing the first letter of a word causes the list to jump to an item that begins with that letter.

Displaying Items in Multiple Columns

Items in the ListBox and DropDownList controls are always stacked vertically, but the RadioButtonList control and CheckBoxList controls allow you to arrange them in columnar format. By setting the RepeatColumns property, you can specify how many columns you want in your list. The RepeatDirection property determines how the list is filled, horizontally or vertically. Figure 19.12 illustrates the use of this property.

Figure 19.12
The RadioButtonList controls were filled in the same order, to show the effect of different RepeatDirection settings; the CheckBoxList controls demonstrate the use of the RepeatFlow property.

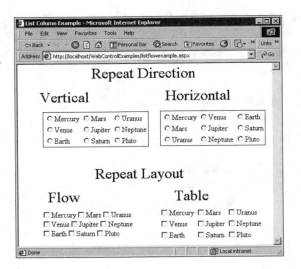

Also note the two CheckBoxList controls. By default when you use a multi-column list, the columns are arranged using an HTML table so they line up. However, you can turn off this property if desired.

> **Note**
>
> When filling a multi-column list dynamically, you may want to delete any setting for the Width property while in design mode. This will allow it to automatically expand as necessary.

DISPLAYING INFORMATION IN A TABLE

Although list controls can be used for displaying selecting items, their formatting capabilities are somewhat limited. HTML tables, on the other hand, have always been popular elements on a Web page for displaying lists. Not only can you use them to organize your Web page, but they are also very well suited to handling multiple columns of information. To work with tables in the Web Forms programming model, you use the Table control. Every table is made up of rows, which in turn are made up of cells. Table, TableRow, and TableCell are all classes in the .NET framework whose properties closely resemble their HTML counterparts. Figure 19.13 shows an example of a Table control that was filled with data from a database at runtime.

Figure 19.13
The Table control provides an easy way to display a read-only, multi-column list. Special formatting can easily be applied to the entire table, certain rows, or individual cells.

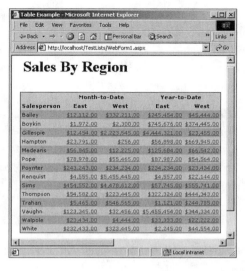

In Chapter 3, "Creating Your First Web Application," we demonstrated the code necessary to dynamically add rows and cells to a table by creating TableRow and TableCell objects.

→ For a step-by-step example of adding data to a Table control, **see** Chapter 3, "Creating Your First Web Application," **p. 49**

CONTROLLING TABLE APPEARANCE

As you learned, the Text property of a TableCell determines what text actually appears in the cell. However, there are also many other properties available to control the table's appearance. The sample table in Figure 19.13 has alternating light and dark rows for easy readability. To create this effect, simply change the BackColor property of the row depending on the contents of a variable:

```
bDark = Not bDark
If bDark Then
    CurRow.BackColor = Color.FromName("#AAAADD")
End If
```

Assuming the code sample is placed in the middle of a loop, the first statement will cause the variable bDark to alternate between values of True and False. In effect, the previous code sample sets the background color to dark for every other iteration of the loop, making the table rows resemble old-fashioned "greenbar" computer paper. Some of the other types of table elements you can customize are

- **Borders**—You can customize the width and style of the border surrounding each table cell by setting the GridLines, BorderStyle, and BorderWidth properties.

- **Alignment**—You can center or justify the text in a cell by setting the HorizontalAlign and VerticalAlign properties. In Figure 19.13, the cells containing currency values are aligned to the rightmost side of the cell so the decimal points line up.

PART
IV
CH
19

- **Size and Spacing**—You can control cell height, width, padding, as well as whether text in a cell wraps to multiple lines.
- **Fonts and Colors**—Fonts and colors for the foreground and background can be set for the entire table, each row, or even each cell. You can also place a background image behind the table by setting the `BackImageURL` property.

You customize the look of a table by setting properties at the table, row, or cell level. Some properties, such as colors and fonts, apply to lower levels unless overridden by other values. (That is why we didn't have to set a light background color explicitly in the previous code sample.) You can set table properties at runtime or at design time. If you set up a table at design time, you probably will need to access the Collection Editor dialog box, shown in Figure 19.14. This screen is used to set cell and row properties and can be displayed from the Properties window.

Figure 19.14
You can set up table headers and fonts within Visual Studio at design time.

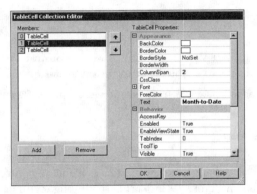

Although most of the time you will probably be adding the data in a table's cells dynamically with code, the Collection Editor provides an easy way to set up the table headings.

USING HTML IN THE Text PROPERTY

Part of the advantage of using the Web Forms programming model is the fact that as a developer you do not have to deal with HTML. However, HTML is what is sent to the end user's browser, so it makes sense that at certain times you might want to have precise control over it. For example, if you have ever coded a `<TABLE>` in HTML manually, you know that you can put almost anything in a table cell, such as a hyperlink or an input field. You can do this with the ASP.NET `Table` control by putting HTML codes in the `Text` property:

```
CurrCell.Text = "<A HREF=detail.asp?id=" & IDNumber_
& ">" & SalesAmount & "</A>"
```

The previous line of code builds a hyperlink in the `Text` property. When the table control appears in the user's browser, the cell will contain a link to the `detail.asp` page.

WORKING WITH DATA BOUND LISTS

In our examples thus far, we have populated lists by adding one item at a time. However, many of the ASP.NET server controls, such as `ListBox`, also support *data binding*. Data binding means the contents of a list are associated with a data source. Rather than explicitly setting up each list item, you simply tell the list a data source to provide it some data. In Chapter 22, "Using ADO.NET," we discuss data binding in the context of ADO.NET and describe how to use the `DataGrid` control. The `DataGrid` control allows the end user to edit the items stored in a list and update the underlying data source. In this case, the grid is a vehicle for data entry, rather than just a simple selection and display list. You'll learn more about binding database fields to controls in Chapter 22.

→ For more on data binding, **see** "Using a DataGrid Control," **p. 618**

However, for the purposes of this chapter, you need to know about data binding because two of the list-related controls, `Repeater` and `DataList`, *only* support data binding to set up the list. Although it is more common to use data binding with an ADO.NET `DataSet`, data binding also works with arrays, so do not worry if you have not yet read the ADO.NET chapter.

CREATING A CUSTOM HTML LIST

If you want total control over how your list is rendered in the end user's browser, you need to investigate using the `Repeater` control. The `Repeater` control makes it easy to create a custom HTML list through the use of *templates*. You simply define a template for how each item in your list should appear, and then the `Repeater` control takes care of merging the template with each list item. The easiest way to define a template is just to type it into the HTML view in the Web form designer. Listing 19.5 shows a Repeater item template that specifies an image hyperlink followed by some text.

LISTING 19.5   WEBCONTROLS.ZIP—CREATING A REPEATER TEMPLATE

```
<asp:Repeater id="Repeater1" runat="server">
    <ItemTemplate>
          <a href="displayreport.aspx?id=<%#_
Container.DataItem.ReportID %>">
          <img src="/print.gif"></a>
          <%# Container.DataItem.ReportName %> Report <br>
    </ItemTemplate>
</asp:Repeater>
```

When you draw a `Repeater` control, the `<asp:Repeater>` tag is automatically added to your Web form. To create the template for items in the Repeater list, enclose your HTML in an `<ItemTemplate>` tag.

Note

You can also specify templates for other parts of a Repeater list, such as the header and footer.

PART
IV
CH
19

BINDING A DATASOURCE TO THE REPEATER

To get the reader to display your list items, you need to reference them in the template. To accomplish this, access the `Container.DataItem` object with server-side script tags. In Listing 19.5, the `ReportID` and `ReportName` fields are used in each list item. Listing 19.6 shows the code necessary to provide this data to the `Repeater` control.

LISTING 19.6   WEBCONTROLS.ZIP—SETTING UP THE REPEATER

```
Private Class ReportInfo
    Public ReportName As String
    Public ReportID As Integer

    Public Sub New(ByVal Name As String, ByVal ID As Integer)
        Me.ReportName = Name
        Me.ReportID = ID
    End Sub
End Class

Private Sub Page_Load(ByVal sender As Object, _
    ByVal e As EventArgs) Handles MyBase.Load

    Dim ReportList As New ArrayList()

    ReportList.Add(New ReportInfo("Profit and Loss", 1))
    ReportList.Add(New ReportInfo("General Ledger", 2))
    ReportList.Add(New ReportInfo("Accounts Payable", 3))
    Repeater1.DataSource = ReportList
    Repeater1.DataBind()

End Sub
```

Figure 19.15 shows how the list looks when the template is merged with the data items in the `ReportList` array.

Figure 19.15
The Repeater allows you to generate custom HTML for each item in a data set.

SPECIAL-PURPOSE WEB CONTROLS

In this chapter we have covered several different categories of Web controls. Although the controls in this final section provide some useful and interesting features, they don't fit neatly into any one category. Therefore, we've lumped them together as special-purpose controls.

USING THE Calendar CONTROL

One very useful ASP Server control is the Calendar control. Like its Windows counterpart, the Web Calendar control provides an onscreen calendar, making it easier for the user to select a date. For example, you could include both a text box date field and a Calendar control on your form to allow the user the flexibility of typing the date quickly or browsing with the calendar. Some examples of the Calendar control are shown in Figure 19.16.

Figure 19.16
The Calendar control allows you to set individual styles and fonts for many of its different elements.

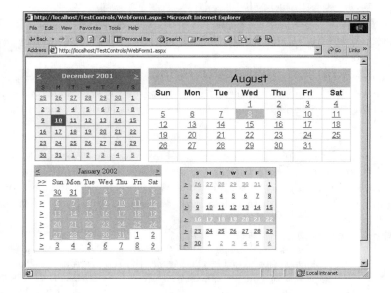

MAKING YOUR CALENDAR STYLISH

As you might imagine, properties are available to customize the appearance of the Calendar control. For example, the ShowGridLines property determines whether lines are displayed between the days of your calendar. Many of the properties you use to tailor the calendar's appearance are *style properties*, which means they have multiple parts; you set the font, color, alignment, and other aspects individually to create a desired style. You can also link the style to a predefined CSS class, as described earlier. The Calendar control contains the following style properties:

- DayHeaderStyle—Sets the headings for the days of the week labels. You can also choose what format to display these in (that is, M, Mon, Mo, Monday) by setting the DayNameFormat property.

- DayStyle—Sets the style for the days in the currently displayed month.

- NextPrevStyle—Sets the style for the navigation buttons that allow the user to select the next or previous month. Setting the ShowNextPrevMonth property to False hides these navigation buttons, although the user can still move from month to month by clicking a day in the next or previous month.

- OtherMonthDayStyle—Sets the style for days from adjacent months. To hide these days, set the ForeColor property to match the background color.

- SelectedDayStyle—Controls the style for the date or day selected by the user.

- SelectorStyle—To accommodate the selection of multiple days, a selector column can be added to the calendar; control the style by setting the SelectorStyle property.

- TitleStyle—Allows you to customize the style for the month name at the top of the calendar. You can also hide the calendar title by setting the ShowTitle property to False, or you can customize the text by setting the TitleFormat property.

- TodayDayStyle—You can apply special formatting to the current date by setting this style property.

- WeekendDayStyle—If you want to use the calendar to draw attention to workdays or weekends, you can use this property to make the weekend style different. You can also set the FirstDayofWeek property to move a particular day to the leftmost column of the calendar.

The previous settings provide a lot of control over the way a calendar looks. If you want it to look better than it does by default, but do not want to have to set a bunch of individual properties, you can use one of the Autoformat settings. Just display the Properties window for a calendar and click Autoformat to select a Classic, Simple, or Professional calendar.

Note

Many of the navigation and selection elements of the calendar appear as a greater-than symbol (>) or a less-than symbol (<). Because HTML uses these symbols to delimit tags, the special characters &gt and &lt are used in HTML to represent greater than and less than, respectively. You can customize these navigation elements by entering your own custom text.

SELECTING A DATE

Use the SelectedDate property of a Calendar control to set or retrieve the currently selected date. This property can be set using a variable of type DateTime or by using a literal date. The following code sample illustrates setting and retrieving this property:

```
'Retrieves the Selected Date
Dim dtSelDate AS DateTime
dtSelDate = calmain.SelectedDate

'Sets the Selected Date
calMain.SelectedDate = #8/16/1977#
'Displays August 1977 month
calMain.TodaysDate = #8/1/1977#
```

Notice the final line of the sample code also sets the TodaysDate property. This is one of the ways in which the Web Calendar control behaves differently from its Windows counterpart; it does not automatically update the calendar to display the month specified by the SelectedDate property.

Note

When you select a date in the `Calendar` control, the `SelectionChange` event is fired on the server. You can use this event to update a text box or other field associated with the calendar.

WORKING WITH MULTIPLE DATES

Another feature of the Web `Calendar` control is the selection of multiple days. Although this functionality is more limited than in the Windows version, the user can select a week or an entire month by clicking special selectors. However, the user cannot select arbitrary days in different weeks, or multiple weeks, using the user interface. To determine the way the `Calendar` control handles multiple date selection, set the `SelectionMode` property to one of the following values:

- `None`—No selection is allowed, the calendar dates do not contain hyperlinks, and the dates will not raise events.
- `Day`—Allows the user to select a single date. This is the default setting.
- `DayWeek`—Adds a week selector links for selecting a week. Selecting individual days is still possible by clicking them.
- `DayWeekMonth`—Adds hyperlinks for selecting weeks and the entire month. Selecting individual days is still possible by clicking them.

Note

Although the selection capability is somewhat limited through the Calendar interface, you can select any group of dates by setting the `SelectedDates` property.

When you are working with multiple dates, you use the `SelectedDates` property instead of the `SelectedDate` property to determine or set the selected days of the calendar:

```
Dim DesiredDates As SelectedDatesCollection
Dim i As Integer

DesiredDates = calMain.SelectedDates

For i = 0 To DesiredDates.Count - 1
    Call MarkScheduleBusy(DesiredDates(i))
Next
```

The `SelectedDates` property is a collection of type `SelectedDatesCollection` that can contain zero or more `DateTime` values.

SELLING OUT WITH THE AdRotator

Just a few years ago, if someone had suggested that Visual Basic programmers needed an easy way to display advertisements in their programs, I would have laughed. However, the ubiquitous banner ad has become such a part of Web culture that Microsoft has deemed it necessary to incorporate this task into an ASP.NET control: the `AdRotator`. When placed on a Web form, the `AdRotator` control will automatically pick and display advertisements for you. Each advertisement is defined by the following properties:

■ `ImageURL`—The URL of the advertisement image

■ `NavigateURL`—The address of the Web page that opens when the user clicks the advertisement

■ `Impression`—An integer which controls the likelihood of an ad being displayed

You can define an ad dynamically in code, but it is even easier to create an XML file containing the ad specifications. The following XML file defines an advertisement:

```
<Advertisements>
    <Ad>
        <ImageUrl>/images/vbbook.gif</ImageUrl>
        <NavigateUrl>http://www.vbinsider.com</NavigateUrl>
        <Impressions>50</Impressions>
    </Ad>
</Advertisements>
```

To make the sample ad work with an `AdRotator` control, all you need to do is create a file containing the XML code in the virtual directory for the project and set the `AdvertisementFile` property of the `AdRotator` control to the filename.

> **Note**
>
> To learn more about XML and its role in the .NET world, see the help topic "XML in Visual Studio."

> **Note**
>
> Because the `AdRotator` control shrinks or expands the ad images to meet its dimensions, be sure to use a consistent image size for your ad images. A common advertisement size used on the Web is 468 pixels wide by 60 pixels high.

When you have defined multiple advertisements, the `Impressions` property determines how the `AdRotator` picks the ad to display. A higher number can be used to make a particular ad appear more often. If this method of picking ads is too simplistic, the `AdRotator` also offers the ability to include your own ad-selection logic. Instead of setting the `AdvertisementFile` property, you can set the `ImageURL` and other ad properties dynamically by adding code to the `AdCreated` event.

USING THE `CrystalReportViewer` CONTROL

For better or worse, Crystal Reports remains married to VB as the default reporting tool. The `CrystalReportViewer` control provides an easy way to display a Crystal Report on a Web form. In Chapter 23, "Creating and Using Reports," you learn how to design a Crystal Report. For the purposes of this chapter, we will assume you have already created a report and concentrate on how to display it in your application. Figure 19.17 shows the `CrystalReportViewer` in action.

→ For more on designing Crystal Reports, **see** Chapter 23, "Creating and Using Reports," **p. 637**

Figure 19.17
Although severely crippled by lack of printing capability, the `Crystal ReportViewer` control makes it easy for Web application users to browse reports online.

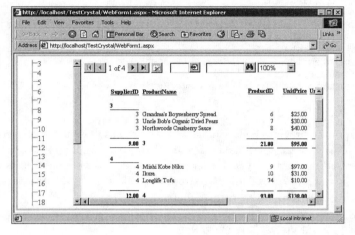

As you can see from Figure 19.17, the `CrystalReportViewer` control has a toolbar. One of the main purposes of this toolbar is navigation; as the user clicks buttons to display the next or previous page, the `CrystalReportViewer` control automatically handles drawing the appropriate page.

CONTROLLING REPORT VIEWER DIMENSIONS

When you draw a `CrystalReportViewer` control on a Web form, it appears as a simple gray square; the actual report viewer control is not rendered until you run the application. The default behavior for the `CrystalReportViewer` control is to take up the entire page. However, if you have other controls on your Web form, you will need to set the dimensions of the report viewer so it does not overlap them. To do this, you first need to set the `BestFitPage` property to `False`. Then, size the control to the desired dimensions. You can also display a border around the report viewer by setting the `BorderStyle`, `BorderWidth`, and `BorderColor` properties.

CHOOSING THE REPORT FILE

When you create a Crystal Report, the layout and data source information are stored in a file with an `.rpt` extension. To let the `CrystalReportViewer` control know which report file to use, you should set the `ReportSource` property to the name of the file in the `Page_Init` event, as in the following example:

```
Private Sub Page_Load(ByVal sender As System.Object, _
    ByVal e As System.EventArgs) Handles MyBase.Init
```

PART
IV
CH
19

```
            'CODEGEN: This method call is required by the Web Form Designer
            'Do not modify it using the code editor.
            InitializeComponent()

        MyCRViewer.ReportSource = "c:\inetpub\wwwroot\_
myapp\MonthlySales.rpt"

        Dim RegionParameter As CrystalDecisions.Shared.ParameterField
        Dim RegionValue As New CrystalDecisions.Shared._
ParameterDiscreteValue()
        RegionParameter = MyCRViewer.ParameterFieldInfo(0)
        RegionValue.Value = "EAST"
        RegionParameter.CurrentValues.Add(RegionValue)

    End Sub
```

Note that in the previous code sample we used the absolute path to the report file. At the time of this writing, a URL-based path or relative path would not work. Another common task when setting up the `CrystalReportViewer` control is assigning values to parameters required by the report. As demonstrated in the code sample, the `ParameterFieldInfo` property provides access to the report parameters.

CUSTOMIZING THE VIEWER'S APPEARANCE

The following properties allow you to customize the look of the report viewer by hiding or showing toolbar buttons and other elements:

- `DisplayGroupTree`—If your report includes groups, they will automatically be displayed to the left of the main report. Clicking a group name navigates to the appropriate page in the report. If your report does not have any groups or you do not want to display the group tree, set this property to `False`.

- `DisplayToolbar`—Determines whether the navigation toolbar is displayed.

- `HasGotoPageButton`—Determines whether the user can enter a page number directly in the toolbar.

- `HasSearchButton`—The search field and button on the toolbar allow the user to type in a search phrase. The `CrystalReportViewer` will search forward through the pages of the report and stop on a page containing the phrase.

- `HasPageNavigationButtons`—Controls whether the four buttons for page navigation are visible.

- `HasZoomFactorList`—Controls whether the Zoom button is visible, which allows the user to adjust report font size.

- `PagetoTreeRatio`—Determines how the screen space is split between the group tree and the report page.

As you may have noticed, one major difference in the Web version of the `CrystalReportViewer` control from its Windows counterpart is the lack of a Print button. The reason is that the Web `CrystalReportViewer` only delivers HTML to the client browser one page at a time. Printing requires some type of code on the client to be able to retrieve each page and send it to the printer. For certain types of reports, namely those without a lot of fields and records, you may be able to get around this limitation by using the browser's Print option. If you set the `SeparatePages` property to `False`, the `CrystalReportViewer` will return all the data rows on one screen. You can also hide the toolbar and other buttons, and the printout might actually look decent. However, if your report has multiple pages of data, you may have to install the .NET framework on the end user's PC and have her use the Windows version of Crystal Reports.

FROM HERE...

In this chapter we have covered a wide variety of Web controls. To learn more about Web-related topics, please see the following chapters:

- To learn to build a Web application step-by-step, see Chapter 3.
- For more information on building Crystal Reports, see Chapter 23.
- For an overview of the Web Forms programming model, see Chapter 18.
- Discover how to build Web pages dynamically in Chapter 17, "Using Active Server Pages.NET."

PART

IV

CH

19

PART V

VISUAL BASIC AND DATABASES

DATABASE BASICS

In this chapter

Most business-oriented applications work with data in one form or another. We're not talking about computer data like a loop counter variable, but actual business information, such as the number of units sold or customer name. For business data stored on a computer to be useful, you need a system that allows you to efficiently analyze and maintain it. A *database management system* (or database for short) is one way to store such data.

This is the first of four chapters in this book related to databases. As you will learn, Visual Basic .NET can create powerful data management programs with a little planning and effort. The most fundamental part of that planning is in how the database is structured. A poorly designed database can doom even the most well-intentioned program from the start. On the other hand, a well-designed database can make a programmer's life much easier.

Another key issue with managing data is using the database to answer queries. In the second half of this chapter, we will introduce the Structured Query Language (SQL). By learning a few SQL commands, you can retrieve information from a database and issue commands to manipulate the data contained within it.

UNDERSTANDING DATABASES

What is so special about a database, you might ask? There are other ways of storing data, such as a creating a file format of your own design. For example, you might just store information in a comma-delimited text file. However, a database management system provides a lot of advantages, such as the following:

- Databases allow you to forget about how data is physically stored on the hard drive and just concentrate on the information itself. If you store information in a custom file, any programs that use the file have to know not only what information they are looking for, but also how to get it from the file.

- Databases can handle multiple users accessing data at the same time, and process user requests as separate units of work. If you just store data in a text file, you need to write code to ensure that multiple programs can access the file at the same time, and that their manipulations of the data do not interfere with each other.

- Databases provide a way to query data through the use of a query language and application programming interfaces.

- Databases can be optimized for speed, through the use of indexes and internal tuning algorithms.

As you can see, you would have to write a lot of extra code to make a text file act like a database. Some examples of different types of database systems are Microsoft SQL Server, Oracle, Microsoft Access, Sybase, and the Microsoft Database Engine.

WHAT IS A RELATIONAL DATABASE?

This book discusses a type of database known as a *relational database*. Relational databases are probably the type of database most widely used in business applications and are very easy to understand. In a relational database, information is stored in *tables*, which have rows and columns like an Excel spreadsheet. A sample table is shown in Figure 20.1.

Note

Each table in the database has a name, which is specified when the table is created. The name of the table in the picture is MyCDs.

Figure 20.1
A sample table in a relational database stores information about your CD collection.

The column headers shown in Figure 20.1 are the *fields* in the table. A field represents one fact, or piece of information. For example, if you wanted to store information about your CD collection, you might want to include fields with names like title, artist, year published, genre, and so on. Fields have a data type and a value, just like variables. In our example, the year published field would be defined as a numeric type, so it could contain values such as 1999, 2000, and so on. The artist field would contain a string of characters that represent the artist's name.

Each row in the table, which represents a collection of field values, is known as a *record*. Each of your CDs would be represented by one record; each record would contain all of the field values relevant to that CD. One important point to note is that even if a particular field does not contain any information (for example, if you do not know the price you paid for a particular CD), that (empty) field is still contained in that CD's record. So, each record in a table has the same field names, but may have different values stored in those fields.

A database can hold multiple tables. For example, you may have a database called media that stores information about your CD and DVD collection. The database might contain a table for your CDs (which, in turn, has one record for each CD), another table for your DVDs, and so on. In this scenario, the records in the DVD table may contain different fields than the records in the CD table (for example, your DVD table may contain a field to store the screen aspect ratio, which is not relevant to a CD). This means that each table has its own structure, or definition of what fields comprise the table.

PART
V

CH
20

Note

Many database management systems, such as Microsoft SQL Server, can contain multiple databases.

QUERIES AND RELATIONSHIPS

One great feature of a database is its ability to execute *queries*. For example, you can query the database to retrieve the titles of CDs by artists whose names start with the letter *B* and were published in 1969. If you were to run this query on the database containing the table pictured in Figure 20.1, you would get the following result:

```
The Red Album
Flabby Road
```

As you can see, a query can be used to specify what fields you want (that is, just `title`) as well as what records you want (published in 1969 and artist names that start with *B*). Our example query is used to retrieve information from the database. This is the most common type of database query, although later in the chapter you will learn about other queries that can delete or update records as well.

> **Note**
> Queries can be developed externally and sent to the database for execution, or stored within the database. Queries stored within the database are sometimes known as *stored procedures*, and work like procedures in your VB programs.

Another powerful feature of the relational database model is the ability to establish *relationships* between tables and then *join* those tables in a query. Relationships are based on shared fields between tables. For example, suppose we added another table to our database called `RecordLabels`. It would contain just two fields: `artist` and `record label`. We would then be able to join the `RecordLabels` table to the `MyCDs` table based on the `artist` field and ask more complex queries. For example, suppose we wanted to know the titles of the CDs published by Siler records in 1972. To determine the answer to this query, we would have to use information from both tables. As you will see in a moment, joining tables and writing queries using SQL is very easy to do.

DESIGNING A DATABASE

As we mentioned in Chapter 1, "Introduction to Visual Basic .NET," the first step in creating any program is talking to the users to determine the program requirements, or *functional specifications*. In the case of a database application, you will also need to determine what data the program needs to maintain to organize it into a database. For example, knowing that you have to produce directories and mailing lists tells you that the database needs to contain addresses and phone numbers.

➜ For more Design Tips, **see** Chapter 1, "Introduction to Visual Basic .NET," **p. 11**

In this section, you examine many of the considerations involved in designing databases. You can apply these concepts to any type of relational database, not just those that you may be designing to use in your Visual Basic .NET applications.

Like most tasks, designing a database starts with a plan. After all, you wouldn't try to build a house without a blueprint, and most people wouldn't attempt to prepare a new dish without a recipe. Designing a database starts with identifying the information you need to store in it. You then create a model of the database on paper to organize it using tables, fields, and relationships. Finally, you implement your design by actually creating the database in a database management system.

The most important thing to keep in mind when designing your database is that it provides an accurate representation of the data, regardless of how you will access it with a program. A good database design does the following:

- Eliminates redundant data
- Provides minimum search times when locating specific records
- Stores data in the most efficient manner possible to keep the database from growing too large
- Makes data updates and maintenance as easy as possible
- Is flexible enough to allow inclusion of new functions and enhancements required of the program

In the case of a relational database, you will perform the following key activities when creating the database:

- Organizing the data into tables
- Setting index and validation requirements for the data
- Creating and storing any necessary queries for the application
- Reviewing the design

ORGANIZING DATA INTO TABLES

One of the key aspects of database design is determining how the data will be organized in the database. In a relational database, data is stored in tables, so database organization involves determining how many tables your database will have, and what fields will be stored in the tables. To have a good design, you should organize the data in a way that accurately represents the relationships between the different pieces of information. You should try to be as efficient as possible, eliminating wasted space and repeated information. In addition, use keys to enforce data integrity. In this section we will take a brief look at some important issues that will come up when designing tables.

TABLES AS TOPICS

A table is a collection of information related to a particular topic. By thinking of a key topic for the table, you can determine whether a particular piece of data fits into the table. For example, if a country club wants to track information about members and employees, you might be tempted to put both in the same table (because both groups refer to people).

However, consider the different data required for each group. The employee group requires information about payroll and tax status, whereas the membership group may require a membership expiration date. If these groups of information were combined, each record would contain a lot of wasted space, as shown in Figure 20.2.

Figure 20.2
If you have a lot of wasted space in your table, you may need to consider breaking it up into multiple tables.

SSN	LastName	FirstName	Age	Address	City	State	Zipcode	Dept	Salary	HireDate	DuesOwed
897-98-5726	Siler	Brian	28	123 Fourth Stre	Cordova	TN	38018	Front Desk	25,000.00	3/14/94	
586-89-8479	Kramer	Carrie	24	87 Wyndham F	Memphis	TN	38117				$190.00
797-78-5677	Boykin	Hamp	32	823 Hunters Ri	Dallas	TX	80987	Kitchen	12,000.00	1/23/86	
284-73-7769	Clifton	Tony	19	17 North Main S	Hollywood	CA	90078	Lounge	40,000.00	9/5/88	
797-88-9798	Siler	Ben	21	823 Rebel Roa	Tuscaloosa	AL	23435				$0.00
582-72-6578	Smith	John	35	2935 Penny La	Miami	FL	89206	Kitchen	13,000.00	1/23/79	
688-33-3330	Doe	Jane	55	1313 Mockingb	Calhoun	GA	38018				$123.45
111-22-3333	Thrasher	Marge	13	West Highland	Queens	NY	38018				$19.95

Looking at the data more closely, you can see that the two groups of people (employees and members) have some fields in common because they are both people. Figure 20.3 shows an improved design, in which separate tables are used to store member-specific and employee-specific information.

Figure 20.3
A more efficient design eliminates wasted space.

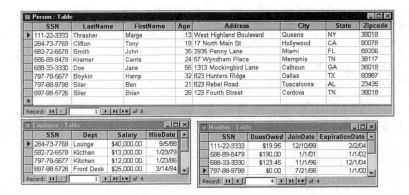

With the design in Figure 20.3, the shared information has been moved into a new `Person` table, which can be joined to the `Member` or `Employee` table using the `SSN` field.

This new design provides several advantages:

- Wasted space is eliminated. Because database records are physically smaller, queries will execute more rapidly.
- A person can be both an employee and a member.
- A mailing list can be created for all persons.

By thinking of a topic for each table, you can determine more easily whether a particular piece of information belongs in the table. If the information results in wasted space for many records, the data belongs in a different table.

DATA NORMALIZATION

Data normalization is the process of eliminating redundant data within a database. Taking data normalization to its fullest extent results in each piece of information in a database appearing only once, although that's not always practical.

Consider the example of order processing. For your program to process an order it will need to know the item being ordered, price, order number, and order date, as well as the customer's name, address, and phone number. If you place all this information in one table, the result looks like the table shown in Figure 20.4.

Figure 20.4
Non-normalized data produces a large data table with repeated information, which is inefficient.

OrderNo	OrderDate	ItemNo	ItemDesc	ItemPrice	CustLastName	CustFirstName	CustPhone	CustAddress
1001	5/1/2001	21891	Yankees Mug	$14.95	Smith	Martha	555-3344	123 Oak Blvd.
1002	5/1/2001	11692	Tigers Flag	$29.99	Cawein	Chris	555-2345	622 Jackie Ave
1002	5/1/2001	111262	Bama Shirt	$2.50	Cawein	Chris	555-2345	622 Jackie Ave
1002	5/1/2001	20984	Triple Bubble	$17.50	Cawein	Chris	555-2345	622 Jackie Ave
1003	5/2/2001	21891	Yankees Mug	$14.95	Smith	Martha	555-3344	123 Oak Blvd.
1003	5/2/2001	20984	Triple Bubble	$17.50	Smith	Martha	555-3344	123 Oak Blvd.
1004	5/2/2001	21891	Yankees Mug	$14.95	Morrison	Robert	555-6990	811 Redbird Plaza
1005	5/2/2001	11692	Tigers Flag	$29.99	Newsom	Steve	555-1109	701 Yankee Place
1006	5/2/2001	50202	Hogs Shirt	$19.77	James	Bob	555-1212	147 Cathy Lane
1007	5/2/2001	119465	DVD Rack	$48.51	Boland	Craig	555-9011	387 Ford Lane
1008	5/3/2001	87461	Britney Shirt	$25.00	Burton	Eric	555-8765	12 Music Place
1009	5/4/2001	21893	Yankees Flag	$37.17	Smith	Martha	555-3344	123 Oak Blvd.
1010	5/5/2001	21891	Yankees Mug	$14.95	Brown	Zondra	555-6234	489 Tatum Trail
1011	5/5/2001	117474	Nap Pillow	$14.00	Barnes	Lisa	555-1111	99 Edmaiston
1012	5/6/2001	21891	Yankees Mug	$14.95	Dacus	Tyler & Nan	555-9551	1 Popcorn Place
1012	5/6/2001	87461	Britney Shirt	$25.00	Dacus	Tyler & Nan	555-9551	1 Popcorn Place
1013	5/7/2001	20984	Triple Bubble	$17.50	Smith	Martha	555-0002	456 Elm St.

As you can see, much of the data in the table is repeated. Although the item information is unique, each record stores the customer's name and phone number. This repetition introduces two problems. The first problem is the same one we discussed in the last section: wasted space. The second problem is one of data accuracy or currency. If, for example, a customer changes his or her phone number, you have to change it for all the records that apply to that customer—with the possibility that you will miss one of the entries. In the table in Figure 20.4, notice that Martha Smith's address and phone number were changed in the latest entry but not in the earlier entries. If an employee looks up Martha Smith and uses an earlier entry, that employee would not find Martha's updated contact information.

A better solution for handling the data is to put the customer information in one table and the sales order information in another table. You can assign each customer a unique ID and include that ID in the sales order table to identify the customer. This arrangement yields two tables with the data structure shown in Figure 20.5.

With this type of arrangement, the customer information appears in only one place. Now, if a customer changes his or her phone number, you have to change only one record.

Note

It is important to realize that even with normalized tables, your program can still retrieve the customer and order information in a single record (similar to Figure 20.4) by using a query with appropriate joins. However, the advantage of the normalized design is that the information is not actually stored this way in the database.

Figure 20.5
Normalized customer and order tables eliminate data redundancy.

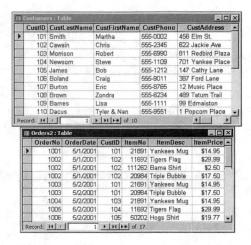

Carrying normalization a step further, you can redesign the items sold and order information. This leads to the development of four tables, but the organization of the tables is much more efficient. You can be sure that when information must be changed, it will change in only one place. This arrangement is shown in Figure 20.6. With the four-table arrangement, the Orders table and the Items Ordered table provide the links between the customers and the retail items they purchased. The Items Ordered table contains one record for each item of a given order. The Orders table relates the items to the date of purchase and the customer making the purchase.

Figure 20.6
Complete normalization of the tables provides the greatest efficiency.

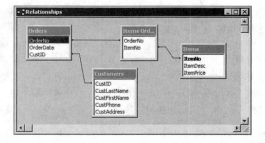

Figure 20.6 shows a diagram of the database's relationships. The fields in each table are listed, and the lines between the tables represent relationships.

CREATING PRIMARY KEYS

When you work with a table, you usually need some way to uniquely identify a record in the table. *Primary keys* provide a way for you to tell a database management system what field or fields in a record must be unique within the table. For example, look at the Person table in Figure 20.3. Because the SSN field is defined as the primary key for the Person table, no two records in the `Person` table can contain the same value in the `SSN` field. For example, if a program or user attempted to insert a record with an SSN value of 111-22-3333, the database would generate an error message and reject the new record because a record with this SSN already exists.

When you design a new table, it is important to set the primary key. Look at Figure 20.3 again. Notice the `Employee` table. You might also think that `SSN` would be a good key for this table, and it might. However, what happens if your database needs to accommodate an employee who works in two different departments? If the primary key was just SSN, the database design could not handle this. By making the `SSN` and `Dept` fields both part of the primary key, you can accommodate the requirement of an employee working in two different departments.

Figure 20.7 shows the SQL Server table design screen for the `Employee` table. A key icon to the left of the field indicates the primary key.

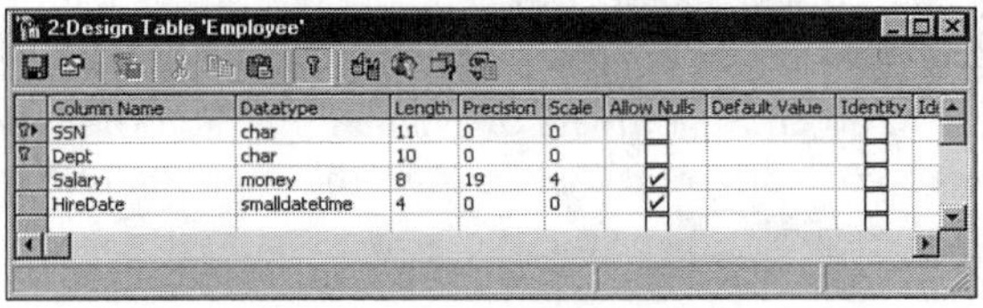

Figure 20.7
In SQL Server and Access, you can create a primary key by highlighting the desired fields and clicking the Key button on the toolbar.

USING LOOKUP TABLES

A *lookup table* is another way to store information to prevent data redundancy and to increase the accuracy of data entry functions. Typically, a lookup table is used to store valid data entries (for example, a state abbreviations table). When a person enters the state code in an application, the program looks in the abbreviations table to make sure that the code exists.

You also can use a lookup table in data normalization. If you have a large mailing list, many of the entries use the same city and state information. In this case, you can use a ZIP Code table as a related table to store the city and state by ZIP Code (remember that each ZIP Code corresponds to a single city and state combination). Using the ZIP Code table requires that the mailing list use only the ZIP Code of the address, and not the city and state. During data entry, you can have the program check an entered ZIP Code against the valid entries.

RULES FOR ORGANIZING TABLES

Although no absolute rules exist for defining what data goes into which tables, here are some general guidelines to follow for efficient database design:

- Determine a topic for each table, and make sure that all data in the table relates to the topic.
- If several of the records in a table have fields intentionally left blank, split the table into two similar tables. (Remember the example of the employee and member tables.)

- If information is repeated in a number of records, move that information to another table and set up a relationship between the tables.

- Repeated fields indicate your design might not be flexible enough. For example, if you have Item1, Item2, Item3, and so on in a table, you might want to move the items to another table that relates back to the parent table. This would make adding a fourth item easier.

- Use lookup tables to reduce data volume and to increase the accuracy of data entry.

- Do not store information in a table if it can be calculated from data in other tables.

As stated previously, these guidelines for defining tables are not hard-and-fast rules. Sometimes, deviating from the guidelines makes sense. One of the most frequent reasons for deviating from the guidelines just given is to improve performance. Believe it or not, there is a process called *denormalization* in which tables are combined for speed purposes! If obtaining a total sales figure for a given salesperson requires summing several thousand records, for example, you might find it worthwhile to include a Total Sales field in the salesperson table that is updated each time a sale is made. This way, when reports are generated, the application doesn't have to do large numbers of calculations, and the report process is dramatically faster. However, your program must ensure that the Total Sales field is consistently and accurately updated.

Deviating from the guidelines results in two major consequences. The first is increasing the size of the database because of redundant data. The second is the possibility of having incorrect data in some of the records because a piece of data was changed and not all the affected records were updated. There are trade-offs between application performance and data storage efficiency. For each design, you must look at the trade-offs and decide on the optimum design.

USING INDEXES

When you create a table, you can tell the database management system to maintain one or more indexes on the table. Indexes are used to improve query performance. For example, suppose you want to query the Person table pictured in Figure 20.3 for all persons having last names between A and F. In effect, you are asking the database to return records where the LastName field is within a certain range.

Without an index, however, the only way the database can determine the records within this range is to perform a *table scan*. A table scan means the database management system will look at *every* record in the table to determine whether it should be included in the results.

The reason each record needs to be examined is that records in a table are usually stored in the order in which they are added. This order is the *physical order* or *natural order* of the data. An *index* is a special structure that contains a key value (derived from the values of one or more table fields) for each record in the table. The index itself is stored in a specific *logical order*, such as alphabetically. For example, an index on the LastName field would contain all the last names in the table and a pointer to the actual records with that last name, as pictured in Figure 20.8.

Figure 20.8
The database can search the ordered index and then retrieve the associated records quickly.

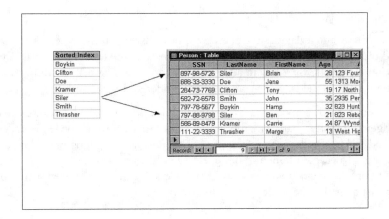

Database indexes work similarly to the index in the back of this book. By using the book's index, you easily can look up key words or topics, because the index is alphabetical and contains pointers (page numbers) to tell you where to find the information. To get an idea of the value of such an index, imagine a phone book that lists the customer names in the order in which they signed up for phone service. If you live in a large city, finding a person's number could take forever, because you have to look at each line until you find the one you want.

DIFFERENT TYPES OF INDEXES

When you create an index, you specify the type of index and the fields to be indexed, and the database management system does the rest. We have already discussed one type of index, the primary key. Primary keys are known as *unique* indexes because the keys in the index must be not be duplicated. The index pictured in Figure 20.8 is not unique, because the index may contain multiple keys (last names) with the same value. Some database systems also provide *clustered* and *non-clustered* indexes. *Clustered* means the data in the table is physically stored in the order of the index. As you might expect, each table can only have one clustered index, while any other indexes are non-clustered.

An index can also be classified as a *single-key index* or a *multiple-key index*. A single-key index is based on the value of a single field in a table. Examples of this type of index are Social Security number, ZIP Code, employee ID, and last name. Although single-key expressions are valuable in presenting data in a specific order, imposing an even more detailed order on the table is often necessary. You can do so by using multiple-key indexes. As you can infer from the name, a *multiple-key index* is based on the values of two or more fields in a table. As an example, suppose your program is trying to look up the name John Smith in a table with millions of records. If you created an index only on the LastName field, the database could quickly find the Smiths, but it would it still have to perform a table scan on all the Smith records (which could be a lot) to find John Smith. In this case, a multiple-key index on LastName and FirstName would be useful.

DETERMINING WHEN TO USE INDEXES

When you design a database, you create indexes based on the types of queries that will be asked of the database. Often, additional indexes are added to the database during testing of the application. If you know in advance that you are going to be running a lot of queries on a certain field or fields, you may want to consider adding an index.

However, it is not a good idea to create an index on every field, because the database management system has to maintain the index every time a recorded is added, deleted, or updated. A lot of indexes may help if your table is used for mostly reading and very little updating. However, a bunch of unnecessary indexes on a table that is frequently updated or joined only on one or two key fields may adversely affect query performance. Once again, you must consider the trade-offs in the database design.

INTRODUCING THE STRUCTURED QUERY LANGUAGE

Structured Query Language (SQL) is a specialized set of database programming commands that enable the developer or other database users to perform tasks in a database management system. Some examples of the types of tasks you can perform with SQL are

- Retrieve data from one or more tables in one or more databases.
- Change data in tables by inserting, deleting, and updating records.
- Obtain summary information about the data in tables such as total and average values.
- Create, modify, or delete database objects such as tables, indexes, and queries.

A SQL statement contains one or more lines of text, much like a code statement in Visual Basic. As you can see from the preceding list, SQL statements fall into two basic categories: The first three items in the list are examples of how SQL is used to manipulate data in the database, the last item demonstrates how SQL can be used to define the database itself. In this chapter we will be mostly concerned with data manipulation statements. Specifically, we will be covering the data manipulation statements listed in Table 20.1.

TABLE 20.1   DATA MANIPULATION STATEMENTS

Statement	Function
SELECT	Retrieves a set of records from the database.
INSERT INTO	Inserts a set of records into a table.
UPDATE	Assigns new field values for a set of records.
DELETE	Removes a set of records from a table.

Note

Data-manipulation language (DML), and data-definition language (DDL) are terms used to categorize SQL statements.

> **Note**
>
> SQL, the language, is different from SQL Server, the database management system created by Microsoft. The Structured Query Language is an ANSI standard that can be used on a variety of database management systems.

> **Note**
>
> The abbreviation SQL is pronounced like "sequel" in conversations, as in movie sequel. However, don't forget SQL is an acronym. Nothing screams beginner quite like someone who types "sequel server" in e-mail!

FOLLOWING ALONG WITH THE EXAMPLES

In later chapters, you will learn how to send SQL statements to a database and retrieve the results using a Visual Basic program. However, regardless of what interface you use to process a SQL statement, you still will need to learn to write SQL statements correctly. In addition, a working knowledge of SQL will be necessary to maintain and manage most databases. If you want to follow along with the SQL examples in this chapter, we suggest you use the interactive query tool provided by your database management system.

To run the sample SQL statements presented in this section, you'll need to create some database tables and populate them with data. The file SAMPLEDB.ZIP, available for download from the Web site for this book, contains both a sample Access database and the scripts necessary to create the sample tables in a SQL server database.

There are many different ways you can execute the sample queries. In this section we will review three of them:

- SQL Query Analyzer, the interactive query tool shipped with Microsoft SQL Server.
- Microsoft Access' SQL Query View
- Visual Studio .NET's Database Project

All the previous tools allow you to type a SQL statement on the keyboard, click a button, and view the results in a window. This is very helpful for those who are learning SQL. Visual Studio .NET even includes a graphical view of your queries, which is updated when you change your SQL statement.

PART
V
Сн
20

> **Note**
>
> The examples in this section are compatible with Microsoft SQL Server 2000 and Microsoft Access. (Access is based on the Jet database engine, so there may be some small differences in the SQL syntax as noted in the chapter.) If you use a different database system, the supported features and syntax of some of the statements may vary.

USING THE SQL SERVER QUERY ANALYZER

SQL Server is Microsoft's enterprise-wide database management system. It generally is installed on a server machine and clients connect to it over a network. The Microsoft Database Engine is a stripped-down version of SQL Server. It does not ship with any client tools, but can be accessed using the SQL Server Client tools. MSDE can be used to distribute the SQL database engine with your application.

Note

The Microsoft Database Engine represents an exciting step forward for Visual Basic developers, because it provides the advanced features of SQL Server at no cost. At the time of this writing, you can download MSDE from Microsoft's Web site for free. (It is also included on the Office 2000 CD and with the .NET framework.) Microsoft's Web site has many articles that explain how to automatically install and configure the database engine with your applications.

Note

Microsoft's Web site recommends developing your application with SQL Server Personal Edition (included with some editions of Visual Studio) and then using MSDE to distribute it.

You can connect to Microsoft SQL Server or the Microsoft Database Engine using the SQL Server Client tools installed on your PC. You will, of course, need a login and password with sufficient access. To enter SQL statements using SQL Server, perform the following steps:

1. Find the Microsoft SQL Server program group in your Start menu.
2. Open the SQL Query Analyzer program.
3. Enter your server name, user name, and password.
4. A screen should appear that looks similar to Figure 20.9.

Note

If you receive an error message attempting to connect to SQL Server, verify that you have entered the password correctly. If you are still having difficulties, read the troubleshooting section at the end of this chapter.

5. Using the database drop-down box, select the correct database if it is not already selected.
6. To execute a SQL statement, just type it in the query window and click the Execute button (or press the Alt+X shortcut keys). The results will be displayed in the results window.
7. You can enter multiple SQL statements in the query window and highlight the one you want to execute with the mouse. If you do not highlight anything, SQL Server will attempt to execute all statements present in the query window.

Selected database

Query window   Execute button

Figure 20.9
The SQL Query
Analyzer provides a
way to interactively
execute SQL
statements.

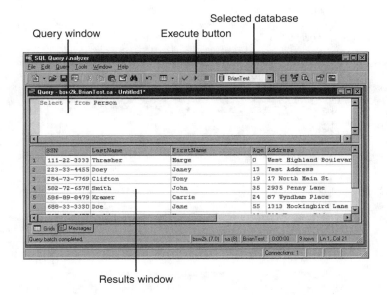

Results window

EXECUTING SQL QUERIES IN ACCESS

Microsoft Access was not designed to be an enterprise-wide database management system like SQL Server, but it is still a very widely used database and quite capable of executing SQL queries. To use Microsoft Access with the samples in this chapter, follow these steps:

1. Start Access and open the MDB file included with this chapter.

2. From the database window, select Queries.

3. Double-click Create query in design view.

4. By default, Microsoft Access will display the graphical design view for the new query, which includes the Show Table dialog box. Click Close to hide the Show Table dialog box.

5. From the View button on the toolbar, select SQL view. The query window will change to a blank white box where you can enter SQL statements.

6. After entering your query, click the Run button on the toolbar, which appears as an exclamation mark.

7. After your query is executed, you will need to use the View button again to return to the SQL statement.

Note

You also can link to a SQL Server database using Access. However, in the author's opinion, the interface provided by Visual Studio .NET is superior.

Figure 20.10 shows a SQL statement entered using Microsoft Access.

PART

V

CH

20

Figure 20.10
To enter SQL in
Microsoft Access,
you need to switch
to the SQL view
using the toolbar
or View menu.

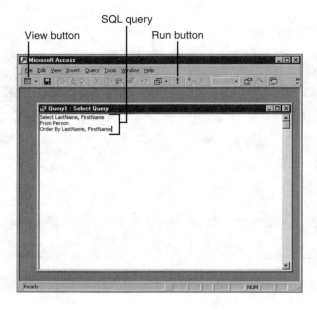

USING VISUAL STUDIO .NET

Visual Studio .NET includes a new project type called Database Project, which is similar to the Database Tools program included with earlier versions. It allows you to manage your database queries and scripts within the Solution Explorer. You'll find the Database Project option under Other Projects in the New Project dialog box, shown in Figure 20.11.

Figure 20.11
A Database Project
allows you to create
and test database
queries from within
the Visual Studio
environment.

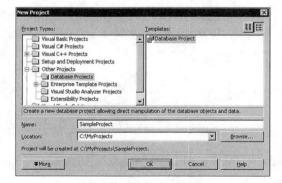

Follow the steps provided in the next few sections to learn how to use Visual Studio .NET to execute SQL queries.

CONNECTING TO YOUR DATABASE

To simplify the process of maintaining database connections, Visual Studio .NET introduces the concept of a *Database Reference*. A database reference is just connection information for a particular database that can be stored with a Visual Studio project. If you have not yet created any Database References in Visual Studio, the dialog box, shown in Figure 20.12, will automatically be displayed.

Note

If you have already created previous database connections in Visual Studio, another dialog box will appear. This dialog box allows you to reuse one of the previous database connections or add a new one using the screen shown in Figure 20.12.

Figure 20.12
The Data Link window is where you specify the server name, database type, user name, and password.

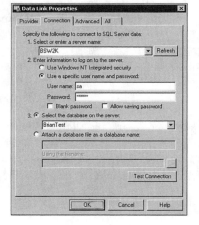

Notice the four tabs pictured in Figure 20.12. These tabs allow you to specify various types of connection information:

- **Provider**—Used to specify what type of database (for example, Jet or SQL Server). SQL Server is the default setting.

- **Connection**—This is the most important part of the Data Link dialog box. Here you specify the password and user name to gain access to your database.

- **Advanced**—This area controls advanced connection settings, such as network timeouts.

- **All**—Lists all the configuration settings in a tabular format.

PART

V

CH

20

By default, the Connection tab is activated. Under normal circumstances, this screen is all you will need to fill out in order to connect to a SQL Server or MSDE database. To test your connection, perform the following steps:

1. Enter the name of the SQL server containing the sample database.
2. Enter your user name and password.
3. Select the database name where you created the sample database.
4. Click the Test Connection button.

If everything goes smoothly, you will see a message indicating the connection test was successful. If you receive an error message, skip ahead to the troubleshooting section at the end of this chapter and return after resolving your connection problem.

Click OK to close the Data Link Properties dialog box. If you get an error message, please see the troubleshooting section at the end of this chapter before continuing.

> **Note**
>
> If you have problems connecting to a SQL server, please see "Troubleshooting Hints" at the end of this chapter.

When you create a database project you may notice it looks slightly different than other Visual Studio projects. The Server Explorer window, pictured in Figure 20.13, allows you to explore the database objects on your server in a tree-like fashion. For example, you can see a list all of the tables in a particular database and view or even edit the data contained within them.

Figure 20.13
One of the many features of the Server Explorer window is its ability to view objects in a database.

If you will be following along with the sample SQL statements in this chapter, verify that you have Employee and Person in the table list.

ADDING A NEW QUERY TO THE PROJECT

Another difference in the look of the Database Project is the Solution Explorer; instead of forms and classes it contains database-related items, as pictured in Figure 20.14.

Figure 20.14
The Solution Explorer can be used to organize database connections and objects together in a Visual Studio project.

Right-click the project name in the Solution Explorer and choose Add Query. This will display the Add New Item dialog box, shown in Figure 20.15.

Figure 20.15
The process of adding a new item to a Database Project is very similar to adding a form to a Windows Application.

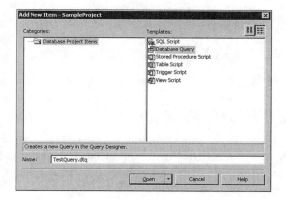

Enter a query name and click OK. Like Access, Visual Studio assumes you want to design queries graphically and displays a dialog box to select the tables in your query. However, this step is optional. Close the dialog box and you will see the Query Designer appear, as shown in Figure 20.16. The Query Designer is divided into several sections, or *panes*, each of which can be hidden or shown with the toolbar buttons. The following steps can be used to execute a SQL query:

1. Type your query into the SQL pane.

2. (Optional) Click the Verify SQL Syntax button to make sure the statement does not contain errors.

3. Click the Run button. The results of the query are displayed in the results pane.

Verify SQL Syntax button

Run button   Query toolbar

Figure 20.16
Each pane in the
Query Designer can
be shown or hidden
as desired; modifica-
tions to any of the
design panes affect
the underlying query.

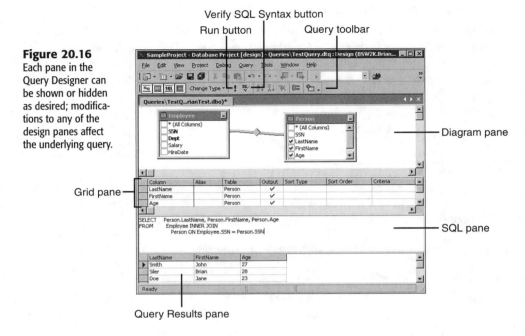

Diagram pane

Grid pane

SQL pane

Query Results pane

USING THE SELECT STATEMENT

The SELECT statement is perhaps the most frequently used SQL command. It retrieves
records (or specified fields from records) from one or more tables in the database. In
this section, we will cover some simple SELECT statements, which take the following
general form:

```
SELECT fieldlist FROM tablename [WHERE where clause]
```

Note

In this chapter, statement formats are listed with the SQL keywords in all capital letters.
The italicized words indicate terms that a programmer would replace in an actual statement, and phrases inside square brackets ([ ]) are optional parts of the statement.

The simplest, most common example of a SELECT statement is selecting all fields from a single
table. To display all of the data in the person table, execute the following SELECT statement:

```
SELECT * FROM Person
```

The statement would list every field of every record in the Person table.

Note

SQL keywords such as SELECT are not case sensitive. However, table and field
names may be case sensitive depending on the configuration of your database
management system.

CHOOSING THE FIELD LIST

In the *fieldlist* portion of a SELECT statement, you can specify the asterisk (*) or a list of specific field names. The asterisk indicates that you want to display all fields in the table. If you want to display only certain fields, you need to include a comma-separated list of fields, as in the following example:

```
SELECT SSN, LastName, FirstName FROM Person
```

Figure 20.17 shows the output from the preceding SQL statement.

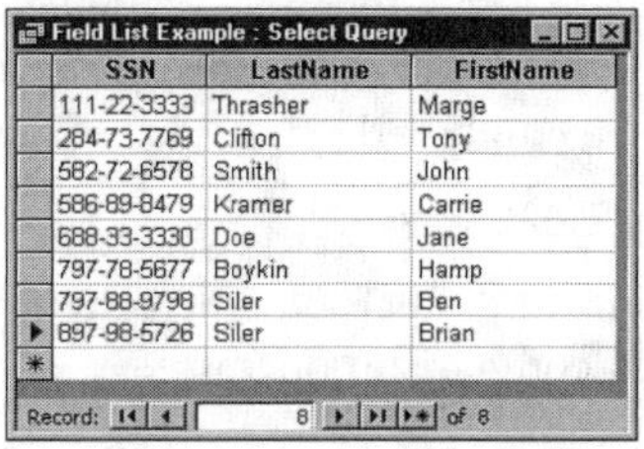

Figure 20.17
A field list allows you to return only the desired fields for each record.

SSN	LastName	FirstName
111-22-3333	Thrasher	Marge
284-73-7769	Clifton	Tony
582-72-6578	Smith	John
586-89-8479	Kramer	Carrie
688-33-3330	Doe	Jane
797-78-5677	Boykin	Hamp
797-88-9798	Siler	Ben
897-98-5726	Siler	Brian

In general, it is good programming practice to specify a field list whenever possible, rather than just using asterisk, for the following reasons:

- Field lists return only the desired fields, minimizing network traffic.
- Field lists control the order in which fields are returned to the calling program. For example, you might decide to change the field order of the Person by adding a new field before the FirstName field, such as MiddleInitial. However, the order of fields returned by the SELECT statement would be unaffected by these changes.

Although I do not recommend it, modern database systems allow you to include spaces in your field and table names. If you decide to do this, your SQL statements must include square brackets ([ ]) around each name with a space:

```
SELECT SSN, [Last Name], [First Name] FROM Person
```

In this example, the brackets indicate to the query processor that the words Last and Name together represent a single field name. Again, the authors recommend for simplicity's sake that you do not use spaces in database field names.

PART
V
CH
20

FILTERING THE RECORDS

One of the most powerful features of SELECT (and other SQL commands) is the ability to control the records affected using a WHERE clause. A WHERE clause includes the keyword WHERE followed by a logical expression used to identify the desired records. For example, to return only the names of the Smiths in the Person table, you could execute the following SELECT statement:

```
SELECT LastName, FirstName FROM Person WHERE LastName = 'Smith'
```

This statement would return the `LastName` and `FirstName` fields only for those records that matched the `WHERE` expression; in this case, only records where the `LastName` field value is `Smith`.

Also note that the fields in the field list are independent from those in the `WHERE` clause. A `WHERE` clause can use any field from the tables specified in the `FROM` clause:

```
SELECT LastName, FirstName FROM Person WHERE ZipCode='38117'
```

In the previous example, we are using the `ZipCode` field to filter records, but only displaying the name fields.

In the SQL examples thus far, we have included only one field name, and asked for an exact match using the equals (=) operator. However, the logical expressions `WHERE` clause can contain a number of conditions which can be combined using `AND`, `OR`, and `NOT`:

```
SELECT * FROM Person WHERE Age >= 30 AND Age < 50
```

The preceding SQL query returns records from the `Person` table where the person's age is between 30 and 49. Table 20.2 lists the field comparison operators:

TABLE 20.2 COMPARISON OPERATORS USED IN THE WHERE CLAUSE

Operator	Definition
<	Less than
<=	Less than or equal to
=	Equal to
>=	Greater than or equal to
>	Greater than
<>	Not equal to

For all comparisons, both expressions must be of the same type (for example, both must be numbers or both must be strings). You can compare field values or a field value to a literal value of the same type. The comparison values for strings and dates require special formats. Strings must be enclosed in quotes. Dates can be enclosed between pound signs (for example #5/15/94#), and on some databases single quotes.

Note

In a `WHERE` clause, literal string expressions are enclosed in quotes (') and numbers are not. Some database management systems allow you to use double quotes ("), while others do not. If your string value contains a quote, you need to double the single quote, as in the following example:

```
SELECT * from Person Where Name = 'O''Connor'
```

The query tool included with SQL Server 2000 expects single quotes (double-quotes are used to identify field names, unless you execute the [SET QUOTED_IDENTIFIER OFF] statement.)

In addition to comparisons, you can use other types of logical statements in a WHERE clause. For example, at the beginning of this chapter we mentioned a query that would return records where someone's name started with a certain letter. The following SQL statement uses the LIKE keyword to perform pattern matching in the WHERE clause:

```
SELECT * FROM Person WHERE Age >= 30 AND LastName LIKE 'S%'
```

Notice the percent sign in the string expression. This is a wildcard indicator that means any characters match the pattern. The preceding statement would return any records where the age was 30 or greater and the last name begins with the letter S.

Table 20.3 lists some other keywords used with the WHERE clause:

TABLE 20.3   KEYWORDS USED IN THE WHERE CLAUSE

Keyword	Action
LIKE	Compares field to pattern
IN	Compares field to list of valid values
BETWEEN	Compares field to value range

The following SQL statements illustrate the use of the above keywords:

```
SELECT * From Person Where State IN ('TN', 'AL', 'GA')
SELECT * From Person Where Age NOT BETWEEN 30 And 49
SELECT * From Person Where FirstName BETWEEN 'B' AND 'D'
```

It should be noted that the range specified in BETWEEN is an *inclusive search*, meaning that if the value is equal to one of the endpoints of the range it is included. The preceding sample statements also indicate using a NOT operator to return records outside the range.

Note

Some flavors of SQL, such as Microsoft Access, use the asterisk (*) as a wild card indicator. However, most databases (*even Microsoft Access when connecting via ADO*) use the percent symbol (%). This is very confusing, because you can actually create stored queries in Access that don't work when run from within Access but do work when executed by ADO! To avoid confusion, we suggest you look up LIKE in your database's help files to familiarize yourself with the syntax.

Note

An entirely separate SQL query, known as a *sub-select*, can be used with the IN clause to provide a list of valid values from another table:

```
SELECT * from Person WHERE State IN (SELECT State FROM_
MyFavoriteStates)
```

PART

V

CH

20

UNDERSTANDING THE NULL VALUE

As we mentioned earlier, each record in a table has the same set of fields, even if it does not have a value in each field. A special value, *null*, is used to indicate an empty field. When you create a table, you can determine whether the database will allow users to place a null value in the field. (Primary keys cannot be null). The expression IS NULL can be used in a WHERE clause to check for an empty field:

```
Select * from Employee Where HireDate IS NOT NULL
```

CONTROLLING THE ORDER OF RETURNED RECORDS

One additional feature of the SELECT statement is the ability to return records in a desired order. For example, you might want to print a class roster ordered by name, or mailing labels ordered by ZIP Code for a discounted postage rate. To control the order of records returned from a SELECT query, you add an ORDER BY clause to your SQL statements. The general format and position of an ORDER BY clause is shown next:

```
SELECT fieldlist FROM tablename [WHERE where clause] [ORDER BY fieldlist [DESC]]
```

You can order records by one or more fields, as in the following examples:

```
SELECT LastName, FirstName, Age FROM Person ORDER BY LastName, FirstName
SELECT LastName, FirstName, Age FROM Person ORDER BY Age DESC
```

The default sort order for all fields is ascending (that is, A-Z, 0-9). You can place the DESC keyword after a field name to indicate you want to sort the field in descending order. (The DESC keyword affects only the field immediately preceding it.)

Figure 20.18 shows the order of some records returned with the previous two ORDER BY clauses.

Figure 20.18
The ORDER BY clause specifies the order of the records returned from a SELECT query.

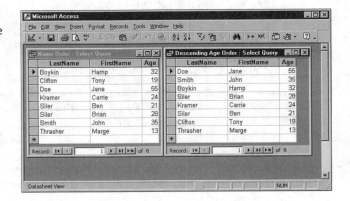

JOINING TABLES WITH SELECT

When you design database tables, you use key fields so that you can relate the tables to each other. In our earlier example, the SSN field relates the records in the Person table to the records in the Employees table. You can use these same key fields in a SELECT statement to set the table relationships so that you can display the related data. There are two types of clauses you can use to specify the relationships between tables:

- **JOIN**—The JOIN clause is located near the FROM keyword and can be used to combine two tables on their related fields. The syntax of the JOIN clause is:

```
SELECT fieldlist FROM table1name jointype JOIN table2name ON join expression
```

- **WHERE**—Although we have already discussed how the WHERE clause can be used to filter records, it can also be used to join tables, because the join is itself a type of filter. This type of join syntax is older than the JOIN clause but still widely used. The only difference between this and the SQL statements we have already discussed is the multiple tables listed in the FROM clause:

```
SELECT fieldlist FROM table1name, table2name WHERE join expression
```

As an example, the following two queries join the Person table to the Employee table, returning the joined records. Figure 20.19 shows the records returned when either of the following statements is executed:

```
SELECT * from Person INNER JOIN Employee ON Person.SSN = Employee.SSN
SELECT * from Person, Employee WHERE Person.SSN = Employee.SSN
```

When you join tables, you specify the join expression using the key field or fields to link the two tables together. If more than one field makes up the key, simply continue the join expression using the AND keyword to join the additional fields. In our example, the key field is named SSN in both tables, but the fields' names do not necessarily have to match. (Note that if they do match, the table name has to be specified so that the query processor can identify the correct field, as in the previous example.)

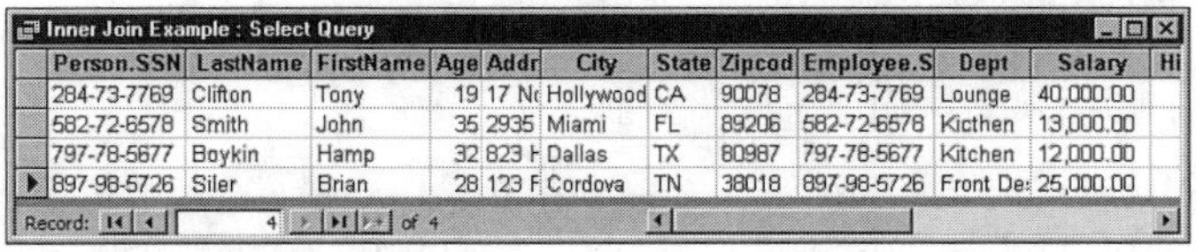

Figure 20.19
With the default join type (inner join), only records that appear in both tables are included in the result.

Person.SSN	LastName	FirstName	Age	Addr	City	State	Zipcod	Employee.S	Dept	Salary	Hi
284-73-7769	Clifton	Tony	19	17 Nc	Hollywood	CA	90078	284-73-7769	Lounge	40,000.00	
582-72-6578	Smith	John	35	2935	Miami	FL	89206	582-72-6578	Kitchen	13,000.00	
797-78-5677	Boykin	Hamp	32	823 H	Dallas	TX	80987	797-78-5677	Kitchen	12,000.00	
897-98-5726	Siler	Brian	28	123 F	Cordova	TN	38018	897-98-5726	Front De:	25,000.00	

PART
V
CH
20

> **Note**
>
> Some programmers prefer the JOIN clause syntax, because table joins usually do not change and tend to clutter up the filter conditions in the WHERE clause. Others programmers like the WHERE clause syntax, because it can be easier to read when joining a lot of tables. Still others do their joins graphically in Access and let the program write the SQL statement for them!

USING ALIASES FOR TABLE NAMES

As you can see in Figure 20.19, the asterisk returns all of the fields from *both* tables in the join. If you want to specify a field list to limit the fields returned, you must specify the table name for any fields that exist in both tables:

```
SELECT Person.SSN, LastName, FirstName, Salary FROM Person_
INNER JOIN Employee ON Person.SSN = Employee.SSN
```

Because the SSN field exists in both tables, we have to specify the table name when we list it in the field list, join expression, or WHERE clause. LastName, FirstName, and Salary only exist in one table, so the query processor automatically knows which field you are talking about.

> **Note**
>
> To specify all the fields from just one of the tables in the join, use the table name followed by a period and then an asterisk.

The preceding SQL statement works, but in the author's opinion it could be written more clearly. First, readability will become a problem if you add more fields, because the full table name will appear repeatedly. Second, well-written SQL statements consistently identify the table name for every field or do not identify it at all; the previous statement is not consistent. Using *aliases* for the table names in your SQL queries solves both of these problems. You create an alias by simply typing a space after the table name then the desired alias name. Typically, aliases are only one or two letters:

```
SELECT P.SSN, P.LastName, P.FirstName, E.Salary FROM Person P_
INNER JOIN Employee E ON P.SSN = E.SSN
```

The preceding SELECT statement assigns the alias P to the Person table and the alias E to the Employee table. The shorter alias takes up less space than the table name and can be used in all parts of the SQL statement.

UNDERSTANDING JOIN TYPES

When you join tables together, you link them by one or more key fields. If a record from one table does not match any keys in the other table, that record falls out of the join and is not returned in the results. For example, notice that Figure 20.3 shows that a record exists in the Person table for Marge Thrasher (whose SSN is 111-22-3333). However, in Figure 20.19, Marge is missing from the query results. This is because no record existed in the employee table with her SSN.

The join shown in Figure 20.19 is the default type of join, known as an *inner join*. In an inner join, records have to exist in all of the joined tables to be included in the result.

Note

Microsoft Access requires the word INNER to be placed in the SQL statement before the word JOIN, but SQL Server allows you to just use the word JOIN by itself to indicate an inner join. Joining fields in a WHERE clause using the equality operator is also an inner join.

SQL also supports another type of join, the *outer join*. If you join two tables using an outer join, records from one table will always appear in the results, even if no corresponding record exists in the other table. For example, if we wanted to get a list of all persons and include salaries if possible, the following query would suffice:

```
SELECT P.SSN, P.LastName, P.FirstName, E.Salary FROM Person P_
LEFT OUTER JOIN Employee E ON P.SSN = E.SSN
```

The results of the previous query would include our missing person, Marge, even though she is not an employee. Normally, her record from the Person table would fall out of the results, because there is no corresponding record in the Employee table. However, the LEFT OUTER JOIN statement forces the query to always include records from the leftmost table (Person). Table 20.4 summarizes the differences between the types of SQL joins.

TABLE 20.4   RECORDS RETURNED BASED ON THE TYPE OF JOIN USED

Join Type	Records from Left Table	Records from Right Table
INNER	Only records with corresponding record in the right table	Only records with corresponding record in the left table
LEFT OUTER	All records	Only records with corresponding record in the left table
RIGHT OUTER	Only records with corresponding record in the right table	All records

PART

V

CH

20

Note

The word OUTER is usually optional and you can just specify LEFT or RIGHT. If you use the WHERE join syntax, place an asterisk on the left or right side of the equals to indicate the type of outer join, as in the following left join example:

```
SELECT * from Person, Employee WHERE Person.SSN *= Employee.SSN
```

→ For more on join types, **see** the Microsoft Access Help topic "Join types and how they affect query results" or the SQL server books online topic "Join Fundamentals."

WORKING WITH MORE COMPLEX JOINS

Simple joins between two tables are fairly easy to understand. However, you will often be joining more than two tables using a number of fields and a mixture of join types. When using the WHERE join syntax, you just list the tables in the FROM clause, making sure to join all the appropriate fields in the WHERE clause. However, with the join syntax, you may want (or need, depending on the DBMS) to add parentheses to separate multiple joins, as in the following example:

```
SELECT
    S.Description,
    P.LastName,
    P.FirstName
FROM
    (StateList S INNER JOIN Person P ON S.State = P.State)
    INNER JOIN Employee E ON E.SSN = P.SSN
ORDER BY
    S.Description,
    P.LastName,
    P.FirstName
```

The previous query uses a lookup table, StateList, to provide the state names. The easiest way to visualize the way the joins work in the preceding statement is to use the parentheses as a guide; the first join combines the StateList and Person tables, and the second part joins the result of the first to the Employee table.

Note

You can join across to another database on the same SQL server (provided you have permission) by using the dot notation, as in the following example:

```
select * from master..sysprocesses
```

The table mentioned previously is a system table used to track current processes and connections on the server.

Other join expressions you might run into are the WHERE EXISTS and WHERE NOT EXISTS clauses:

```
SELECT * FROM StateList S
WHERE NOT EXISTS (Select * FROM Person P Where P.State=S.State)
```

The previous statement displays all the states for which there is no entry in the Person table; that is, you have no employees or members in the states returned by this query. Although it may not look like it, the query is a join. The outermost SELECT statement is joined to the sub-select statement by the State field.

EXISTS and NOT EXISTS are both features that can be replaced by joins. For example, you may recall that an outer join returns a record containing fields from both tables, even if a record does not exist. By checking for the Null value, the previous NOT EXISTS example could be rewritten as follows:

```
SELECT S.* FROM
StateList S
LEFT OUTER JOIN Person P ON P.State=S.State
WHERE P.State IS NULL
```

CALCULATED VALUES AND AGGREGATE FUNCTIONS

In addition to retrieving data from one or more tables, SQL SELECT statements can be used to create calculated values. These values can be entirely made up or based on existing fields values combined with mathematical operations. In addition, built-in aggregation functions can perform calculations on field values from multiple records. The results of these calculations are not stored in the database, but instead calculated during the execution of your SELECT query.

CALCULATING VALUES

Using mathematical operators and aliases, you can create fields that are calculated on the fly by your SELECT statement. For example, the following SQL statement calculates total cost based on quantity and unit price:

```
Select itemno, unitprice, quantity, unitprice * quantity AS TotalCost From orders
```

Notice when using aliases with field names, you have to supply the keyword AS. (If you do not supply an alias, some DBMSs like Access will assign a default name such as Expr1001 to your calculated field.) You also can perform manipulation on string fields, such as concatenation:

```
Select LastName, FirstName, RTrim(LastName) + ', '_
+ FirstName AS CompleteName From Person
```

The preceding statement uses string concatenation and the RTRIM function to create a combined names field. For example, the CompleteName field in the record for Jane Doe would contain the following value:

```
Doe, Jane
```

When the results of the query are returned to your program, the fake complete name field will look just like any other field to the program.

AGGREGATION AND GROUP BY

In addition to the operations we just described that work on individual records, SQL provides several built-in functions that *aggregate* or group records. For example, the COUNT function can be used to count records in a table:

```
SELECT Count(*) FROM Person WHERE State = 'FL'
```

The preceding statement returns the total number of people in the Person table whose address is in Florida. Similar functions exist for other types of aggregations, including the following:

Function	Purpose
SUM	Adds values together
MAX	Finds the largest value
MIN	Finds the minimum value
AVG	Finds the average
COUNT	Returns record count

Note   To find out about all of the built-in functions of your database management system, consult its help file.

Each of the functions listed earlier can be used on the table as a whole or on just one set of records by adding a WHERE clause. However, these aggregation functions become even more powerful when combined with the GROUP BY clause. GROUP BY allows you to aggregate multiple groups of records in a single query. Consider our earlier example, where we counted the number of people in Florida. Suppose we wanted to count all of the records in the Person table by state. You could run a query for each state, but a more efficient method would be to use GROUP BY:

```
SELECT State, COUNT(*) As PersonCount FROM Person_
GROUP BY State ORDER BY PersonCount DESC
```

The previous statement lists each state and the number of records associated with it, in descending order. Note that when you use GROUP BY, any other field not being aggregated must appear in the GROUP BY clause.

USING SQL ACTION STATEMENTS

As you have seen, the SELECT statement is used for returning records from a database. However, there are several other types of SQL statements, known as *action queries*, that do not return records. These queries, listed next, just manipulate data in the database:

- **DELETE FROM**—An action query that removes records from a table
- **INSERT INTO**—An action query that adds records to a table
- **UPDATE**—An action query that sets the values of fields in a table

As you will see in the following sections, action queries work very similarly to SELECT statements in that you can join tables and specify a WHERE clause.

USING THE DELETE STATEMENT

The DELETE statement's purpose is to delete specific records from a table. You specify the records using a WHERE clause. The format of the DELETE statement is as follows:

```
DELETE FROM tablename [WHERE where clause]
```

The WHERE clause is an optional parameter. If you omit the WHERE clause, then all records in the table are deleted. The following is an example of a DELETE statement:

```
DELETE FROM Votes WHERE State='FL'
```

As you can see, the syntax of a simple DELETE statement is straightforward. However, you can also join to other tables to help filter the records to delete:

```
DELETE Employee FROM Employee E JOIN Person P ON E.SSN = P.SSN WHERE
P.LastName='Thrasher' and P.FirstName='Marge'
```

The previous SQL statement (which works on SQL Server but not Access) only deletes a record from the Employee table. Although the Person table is used to look up the record to delete by name, its contents are unchanged by the statement.

> **Note**
>
> If you are manually cleaning up a database by deleting records, it is a good idea to SELECT what you are about to delete first, or use transactions, as described later in this section.

USING THE INSERT STATEMENT

Like the DELETE statement, the INSERT statement is another action query. There are two basic forms of the INSERT statement:

```
INSERT INTO tablename SELECT rest-of-select statement
INSERT INTO tablename (fieldlist) VALUES (valuelist)
```

The first form is generally used to copy records from one table to another, but can also be used to insert literal values. The second form is used to insert literal values provided by the user or parameters of a stored procedure.

COPYING RECORDS FROM ANOTHER TABLE

In the form of INSERT that uses a SELECT, you build the SELECT portion of the statement exactly as you would any other SELECT statement. Let's suppose a rival corporation, who happens to use the same database, buys our country club. In order to merge the employee tables, we could copy the records from one table to another using INSERT:

```
INSERT INTO Employee SELECT SSN, Department, Salary FROM OldEmployees
```

When an INSERT INTO is used in this manner, you have to make sure to include a value for each field in the new table, as well as make sure the order of the field list is correct. (This example also assumes there are no duplicates in the two tables. In reality, you might need to make the query more robust by adding a WHERE NOT EXISTS clause to avoid SSN key violations.)

INSERTING NEW RECORDS

You do not have to use records from another table with INSERT INTO statement. Consider the following examples, which add new records to the Employee table:

```
INSERT INTO Employee SELECT '000-11-2222', 'Housekeeping',12000
INSERT INTO Employee (SSN,Department,Salary) VALUES ('111-22-3333','Valet',10000)
```

As with the previous example, when using the form of INSERT with SELECT, you have to be sure the order and number of fields matches the destination table. The second example, which uses an explicit field list with a VALUES clause, is a safer method when you are adding new records. Suppose, for example, a new field was added to the table or the field order was changed. As long as the data types and field count matched, the INSERT INTO ... SELECT will not fail and might actually put the wrong data in a field. The second form of the INSERT

PART
V

CH
20

(with the VALUES clause) provides a more definite order. The first item in the values list is put in the first field in the field list, and so on. The designer of the table can actually add new fields and, as long as they are not required, the INSERT query will continue to work without changes.

> **Note**
>
> In general, when using an INSERT you have to supply a value for every field that does not accept a Null value or define a default value. However, special fields known as *identity* fields are an exception to this rule. Identity columns (also known as Autonumber fields in Access) contain a numeric value that is supplied by the database and automatically incremented with each inserted record.

USING THE UPDATE STATEMENT

The UPDATE statement is used to change the values of specific fields in a table. The syntax of the UPDATE statement is as follows:

```
UPDATE tablename SET fieldname=newvalue[,fieldname=newvalue][WHERE where clause]
```

If one of the ladies in your Person table gets married, you need to update her LastName field. The following UPDATE statement would change her record:

```
UPDATE Person SET LastName = 'Smith' WHERE SSN = '111-22-3333'
```

If you're wondering why we used the SSN rather than the old last name in the WHERE clause, the answer is because we only want to update a specific employee's record, and there is no guarantee other employees do not have the same last name.

In addition to using literal values, UPDATE also allows you to use field values and calculations. For example, suppose a hacker gains access to your Employee table and decides to double everyone's salary:

```
UPDATE Employee SET Salary = Salary * 2
```

The sample statement takes the existing salary, multiplies it by two, and assigns the result back to the Salary field. Because there is no WHERE clause, all records in the Employee table are affected.

TRANSACTIONS AND DATA INTEGRITY

A *transaction* is a unit of work that involves multiple sub-parts, but must succeed or fail as a whole. A real-life example is a bank account transfer of money. There are two parts: subtracting money from one account and adding it to another account. However, the transaction must succeed or fail as a whole, because only performing half of it would leave an account out of balance.

In the database world, transactions provide *data integrity* if a SQL statement fails to execute properly. As an extreme example, suppose you have to execute 20 INSERT statements just to add an order to your database. If the twelfth INSERT statement fails, (for key violation or other reason) what do you do? Leaving the database in an inconsistent state is a bad idea, because future joins might not work properly. However, by defining all of your inserts as a single transaction, you can have the database automatically roll back any changes in the event of an error.

Although transactions are important and we are about to tell you some SQL statements to control them, we don't recommend the SQL commands! An even easier way to manage transactions is from within Visual Basic objects. You can actually create transactions across one or more Visual Basic classes. Methods within these classes can execute SQL queries and determine whether to roll back or commit the transaction from within your Visual Basic code.

In the context of this chapter, transactions come in handy when testing SQL statements. For example, if you accidentally update or delete the wrong records, you can roll back your transaction. The following statements are used to define a transaction in SQL:

- **BEGIN TRANSACTION**—Start a new transaction.
- **COMMIT**—Tell the database the transaction is complete.
- **ROLLBACK**—Cancel a transaction in progress.

Note

These SQL statements do not apply to Microsoft Access.

As an example of undoing an accidental delete, execute the following statements:

```
BEGIN TRANS
DELETE FROM Person Where FirstName='Marge'
```

Now, verify that Marge's record is gone with the following query:

```
SELECT * FROM Person Where FirstName='Marge'
```

Finally, execute the ROLLBACK command to undo your delete. Execute the SELECT command and notice Marge has reappeared! If you had executed the COMMIT statement instead of the ROLLBACK, the record would be permanently deleted.

USING DDL STATEMENTS

Data-definition-language statements (DDL) are a subset of SQL that let you create, modify, and delete database objects. Although most modern databases allow you to do this through a graphical interface, there are times when you might have to do it programmatically, such as within a stored procedure or script. Although a comprehensive discussion of DDL is beyond the scope of this book, we will introduce some of the more-frequently used statements.

Note

The DDL syntax presented in this section does *not* work with Microsoft Access but has been tested successfully on SQL Server.

DEFINING TABLES WITH DDL STATEMENTS

Three DDL statements are available to define database tables:

- **CREATE TABLE**—Defines a new table in a database
- **ALTER TABLE**—Changes a table's structure
- **DROP TABLE**—Deletes a table from the database

CREATING A NEW TABLE

The CREATE TABLE statement creates a new SQL table in the current database. The following example shows the CREATE TABLE statement for the Person table:

```
CREATE TABLE Person (
    SSN char (11) PRIMARY KEY,
    LastName char (20) NOT NULL ,
    FirstName char (20) NOT NULL ,
    Age int NOT NULL,
    Address char(30) NULL,
    City char(30) NULL,
    State char(2) NULL,
    Zipcode char (10) NULL
)
```

Notice that each field is listed along with an option to indicate whether Null values are allowed. The entire field list is enclosed in parentheses. The PRIMARY KEY keywords indicate that the SSN field is the primary key for the Person table.

> **Note**
>
> If you create a table using a SQL command interface, you may need to refresh the table list for it to appear in any already-connected graphical database tools, such as the Server Explorer.

> **Note**
>
> The SELECT statement can be used to create a new table from records in an existing table using the INTO keyword, as in the following example:
>
>   SELECT * INTO BackupPerson FROM Person
>
> If your database options are set to allow SELECT INTO use, the preceding statement creates a new table called BackupPerson containing the same data and fields as Person.

MODIFYING A TABLE

By using the ALTER TABLE statement, you can add or drop columns from an existing table, change field sizes, and add constraints to your table. Under certain circumstances this may be easier than recreating the entire table and restoring the data. (You can, of course, select the data into a backup table, create the new table, and insert the data back into it.)

The following examples show a few typical uses of the ALTER TABLE statement:

```
ALTER TABLE Person ADD Sex Char(1)
ALTER TABLE Person ALTER COLUMN LastName char(100)
ALTER TABLE Employee ADD CONSTRAINT EmployeePrimaryKey PRIMARY KEY (SSN, Dept)
```

The first example statement adds a new field to the Person table to store a person's sex. The second statement expands the LastName field to 100 characters, leaving the existing data intact. The last line of code creates the primary key for the Employee table. For more uses of the ALTER TABLE statement, see the help file included with your database.

DELETING A TABLE

You can delete a table from the database using the DROP TABLE statement. The following SQL statement removes the StateList table from the database:

```
DROP TABLE StateList
```

Note

Temporary tables can be created in SQL Server which will be automatically dropped when you disconnect. To create a temporary table, use the pound symbol (#) in front of the table name in a CREATE TABLE or SELECT INTO statement.

Note

SQL Server 2000 includes the table variable type, which allows you to create variables that act like tables. Memory used by these variables is automatically freed after the execution of your query or stored procedure.

STORING SQL STATEMENTS IN THE DATABASE

Throughout this chapter, we have discussed how to write SQL queries. One way to use SQL is to create a query in a string variable and then pass it to the database using ADO or some other data access technology. However, an even better method is to store the SQL queries in the database itself, and just call the stored query using ADO. Queries stored on a SQL server are called *stored procedures* and can be executed like any other SQL query. (In Microsoft Access, all queries are stored queries, because you have to create a new query object to even key in a SQL statement.) Stored queries act similarly to functions or subroutines in Visual Basic, and can include input and output parameters. Using stored queries presents several advantages over creating SQL from within your program:

PART
V

CH
20

- You can use the SQL statement more easily in multiple locations in your program or in multiple programs.

- Making changes to the SQL statement in a single location is easier, and does not require recompilation of the program.

- Because stored queries can be optimized and cached by the database management system, they run faster than those that are handled by parsing the statement from code every time.

- Creating multiple interfaces (Web, client/server, and so on) to the same data is easier because less database code has to be written.

In the later chapters on ADO, we will show you how to execute stored procedures from within Visual Basic. In this section, we will explain how to create them in your database management system.

→ For more on executing stored procedures, **see** Chapter 22, "Using ADO .NET," **p. 599**

CREATING A SIMPLE STORED PROCEDURE

To create a stored procedure, you use the CREATE PROCEDURE statement in the following general format:

```
CREATE PROCEDURE procedurename [parameterlist] AS SQL Query
```

The following SQL statement creates a stored procedure in the database called spGetEmployeeBySSN:

```
CREATE PROCEDURE spGetEmployeeBySSN

@strSSN char(11)

AS

SELECT
    P.SSN, P.LastName, P.FirstName,
    E.Salary, E.Dept

FROM     Person P INNER JOIN Employee E ON P.SSN = E.SSN

WHERE E.SSN = @strSSN
```

As with variables and other functions, it is customary to follow a naming convention. The preceding sample stored procedure uses sp as a prefix to indicate it is a stored procedure, and the data type prefix str for the input parameter strSSN. The heart of the stored procedure is a SQL query, which is written just like any other SQL query. However, notice that the input parameters to the stored procedure can be used in the WHERE or SELECT clauses.

TESTING YOUR STORED PROCEDURE

To execute a stored procedure, you can simply type its name followed by values for all of its parameters, as in the following example:

```
spGetEmployeeBySSN '111-22-3333'
```

Notice the parameter is enclosed in quotes, because it is a character data type. Numeric parameters do not need to be enclosed in quotes.

Note

> To execute multiple stored procedures within the same SQL session, or execute one stored procedure from within another, include the keyword `exec` before the stored procedure name.

Note

> SQL Server itself includes some built-in stored procedures, such as `sp_help` and `sp_helptext`, which display information about a specified table or stored procedure, respectively.

Note

> You can execute stored procedures on other SQL servers on the network, provided you have linked the servers together. This can be a quick way to import data from another server's table into your own, as in the following example:
>
> ```
> INSERT INTO MyTable EXEC YourServer.YourDB..spGetEmployee_
> '111-22-3333'
> ```
>
> For more information, see the SQL Server Help topic "Linked Servers."

If you need to delete a stored procedure from the database, use the DROP PROCEDURE statement, which accepts the procedure name as a parameter.

TROUBLESHOOTING HINTS

SQL Server is a complex and versatile program, and it would be foolish to think we could explain all of its intricacies in one chapter. However, the authors have noticed some common issues people run into when getting started. In this section we will attempt to give you some hints if you are having trouble connecting to or using your SQL server.

UNDERSTANDING LOGIN OPTIONS

As you may recall from Figure 20.12, when you connect to a database, you have the option of using *integrated security* or entering a user name and password defined in the database. Integrated security means that your Windows login account has the authority defined on the database server. For example, my Windows user id is `bsiler` so I could allow access to this account on the SQL server.

Another method of establishing access, the one recommended by the author, is to define a database login within SQL Server itself. These logins are independent of Windows user accounts. For example, I could create an employee user login within SQL Enterprise Manager, and anyone could use this login to access the employee database, independent of how he or she is logged in to his or her PC. The advantage of using the database login method is most of the applications you will be developing probably will not require the user to connect to the database directly, so there is no reason to maintain individual user accounts. For example, when your Web server connects to the SQL server to retrieve information, the Web server is making the connection to the database, not the user browsing the Web site. (Of course, this does not mean you have to drop Windows authentication entirely, the Web page could be secured using it.)

By default, SQL Server includes the sa login, which stands for system administrator. This login has full access to all databases and SQL Server operations. For the purposes of development on your own PC on an internal network, you can use this login to avoid security restrictions. However, when you move to a production environment, be sure to create a new login with security restricted to only the necessary database objects.

Note

A lot of people have left their sa passwords blank! This is a sure recipe for disaster—don't do it!

NETWORK CONNECTION PROBLEMS

In addition to a login and password, there are several different *protocols* available that you can use to connect to a SQL server. A protocol is just a set of rules for two computers to exchange information. Whoever installs the SQL Server software has the option of enabling or disabling these protocols. The most common protocols are the following:

- **Named Pipes**—This protocol works very similarly to mapping a drive in Windows NT, in that it uses your Windows NT login and password to establish a connection with the server.

- **TCP/IP**—This protocol works like browsing a Web site. You connect via an IP address and port number.

One of the most frequent causes of connection problems is attempting to connect with Named Pipes without sufficient authority. Even if you have the sa login to SQL Server, if you do not have NT access to the communication pipe, you may receive messages such as "access denied" or "Connection Open:createfile( )."

The fastest and most trouble-free protocol is TCP/IP. To make sure you are connecting via TCP/IP, open the SQL Client Network Utility, which should be located in your Microsoft SQL Server program group. Within this utility, you can set the protocol, IP, and Port information for individual SQL servers.

SPECIFYING SQL SERVER INSTANCES

When referring to a particular database server with which they want to interact, developers often refer to the server by computer name alone. However, SQL Server 2000 allows you to run multiple copies (or *instances*) of the SQL Server service on the same physical computer. Each instance contains its own set of databases and is generally independent from other instances on the computer. (From a TCP/IP point of view, each instance runs on a separate port.) If you configured the .NET SDK samples included with Visual Studio, the installation process created an instance of SQL Server called `NetSDK` on your machine.

To specify an instance name when connecting to a SQL server you use a backslash, as in the following example:

```
MyServer\NetSDK
```

The machine name in the example is `MyServer` and the instance name is `NetSDK`. When the database administrator sets up a new instance, he specifies the instance name and port, which must be unique on the machine. Each computer running SQL Server can also have one *default instance*, which works just like previous versions of SQL Server; you do not need to specify an instance name when connecting to the default instance.

ACTIVEX DATA OBJECTS (ADO)

In this chapter

In the last chapter, we looked at the basics of accessing a database and creating SQL statements. This chapter is the first of two that explore the ActiveX Data Objects, or ADO. ADO is a means by which you can access all sorts of databases from Visual Basic code. In the latest version of Visual Basic, ADO has been replaced with ADO.NET. However, ADO is an established technology and there are many existing programs that use it. In addition, many of the concepts described in this chapter are a good way to learn about interacting with a database, regardless of the technology used. This chapter provides an introduction to ADO, which may be useful if you are maintaining existing applications. If you are building a new application, please read Chapter 22, "Using ADO.NET."

USING THE ADO OBJECTS

ADO was introduced before the .NET initiative and has since become an essential part of many Web sites and Visual Basic applications. As with any external object, before you can use ADO you must add a reference to it, as shown in Figure 21.1.

Figure 21.1
ADO is located under the "COM" tab of the Add Reference dialog box.

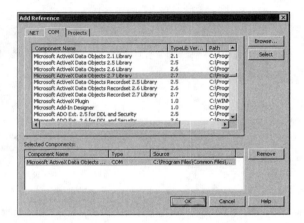

> **Note**
>
> If you are developing a new application, ADO.NET (discussed in the next chapter) is the preferred method of data access in Visual Studio .NET.

Once you have added a reference to ADO, the objects that make up the ADO object model are available to use in your program. These objects are listed in Table 21.1.

TABLE 21.1   ACTIVEX DATA OBJECTS

Object	Description
Recordset	Contains the records that make up the results of a query
Connection	Allows control over the connection to the data source

Object	Description
Command	Executes database commands and queries
Error	Retrieves errors from ADO
Field	Represents a piece of data in a recordset
Parameter	Works with the Command object to set up a parameter in a query or stored procedure
Property	Allows you access to ADO object properties

Note

The reference Microsoft ActiveX Data Objects 2.x Library contains all the objects listed in Table 21.1. The reference Microsoft ActiveX Data Objects Recordset 2.x Library contains just the Recordset object, which we will discuss later in this chapter.

When creating the objects in Table 21.1, you can use the ADODB prefix, as in the following example:

```
Dim cn AS ADODB.Connection
```

In the following sections, you'll explore some of the properties, methods, and events of the ADO objects. Comprehensive documentation for ADO, as well as updates and examples, is available on the Web at www.microsoft.com/data/ado.

USING THE CONNECTION OBJECT

Before you can manipulate data in a database, you have to establish a connection to the database. The Connection object provides a means to connect and disconnect from a database. The first step in opening a connection is to create a new instance of the ADODB.Connection object, as follows:

```
Dim cn As ADODB.Connection
Set cn = New ADODB.Connection
```

After the object instance is created, all you have to do to establish a connection is provide the connection string and call the Open method. You can set the connection string in two ways, the first being to assign it to the ConnectionString property:

```
Dim strInfo As String
strInfo = "User ID=sa;Password=elvis;Database=pubs;Server=bsw2k\NetSDK;_
        Provider=SQLOLEDB"
cn.ConnectionString = strInfo
cn.Open
```

Note

Please remember when using the code samples from this book that you might need to adjust the computer name, database, and password contained in the sample connection strings to match your own configuration.

The code sample first assigns the connection string to a string variable and then sets the ConnectionString property to the value of that variable. However, you can also pass the variable or literal string to the Connection object when calling the Open method as follows:

```
cn.Open "UID=joe;PWD=;DATABASE=pubs;SERVER=bsw2k;DRIVER={SQL Server}"
```

Note

> Some of the other ADO objects (such as the Command object) have a Connection property, which will accept either a connection string or a Connection object.

After you finish using a connection, call the Close method to disconnect from the database.

```
cn.Close
```

In the remainder of this section, we'll discuss connection strings in more detail and show how to use the Connection object to retrieve data and execute database commands.

UNDERSTANDING CONNECTION STRINGS

As you can see from the preceding example, a connection string can contain many different types of information, including user ID, password, and default database name. Notice that elements of the connection string are listed in name-value pairs separated by semicolons. When creating a connection string, you will generally specify the following types of information:

- The type of database you are connecting to; that is, SQL Server, Access, or Oracle. When making connections with ADO, you can specify the name of an ODBC driver by entering a Driver value, or the name of an OLE DB Provider by entering a value for Provider.

- Your sign-in information for the database (if necessary) specified by the User ID and Password values. (Note that UID and PWD also work as an alternative spelling.)

- The location of the database. This might include a Server and Database value for SQL Server, or just a filename for Microsoft Access.

Note

> ADO.NET provides classes specifically designed to connect to a Microsoft SQL Server. When using ADO.NET SQL classes, you do not have to specify a Provider.

The following lines of code show some examples of ADO connection strings:

```
'Microsoft Access using OLEDB Provider for Jet
"Provider=Microsoft.Jet.OLEDB.3.51;Data Source=d:\temp\biblio.mdb"

'Access using ODBC Driver for Access
"Driver=Microsoft Access Driver (*.mdb);DBQ=D:\temp\biblio.mdb"

'SQL Server Using OLEDB Provider for SQL
"Provider=SQLOLEDB;Password=groovy;User ID=apowers;Server=SQLSRV1; _
Database=employee"
```

```
'SQL Server Using SQL ODBC Driver
User ID=eisuser;PWD=jan96;DATABASE=devstats;SERVER=eisdb2;DRIVER={SQL Server}
```

> **Note**
>
> Your driver or provider may have additional connection string options. For example, the SQL Server driver can accept values to determine the type of network connection (TCP versus named pipes). To determine available connection options, see your database system help files.

One key issue when creating your connect string is whether to use an ODBC Driver or an OLE DB Provider. You determine this in the connect string by specifying a Driver value or a Provider value, but not both. ODBC stands for Open Database Connectivity, a standard for database drivers that has existed for several years. OLE DB is a newer, lower-level driver and for this reason the authors' recommendation is to use an OLE DB Provider whenever possible.

> **Tip**
>
> You can store your connection string in the registry and access it using the techniques described in Chapter 24, "Working with Files."

USING A DATA SOURCE NAME

Although less popular now than it used to be, a Data Source Name (DSN) can be used in a connection string to specify an ODBC Data Source, as follows:

```
cn.Open "DSN=LocalServer;UID=apowers;PWD=groovy"
```

The connection string in the preceding line of code is extremely simple; it just lists the DSN, user ID, and password. All the other database information is stored in the ODBC Data Source as defined on the computer. To set up an ODBC Data Source, click the Data Sources icon in the Administrative Tools section of the Windows Control panel. Figure 21.2 shows the Data Source Administrator, which is used to enter connection information.

Figure 21.2
System DSNs are available to everyone on the computer, whereas User DSNs are user-specific.

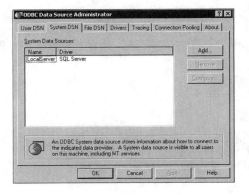

Although the connection string for an ODBC data source looks a lot simpler, the disadvantage of using it is that an extra step is required to get your program to run on a particular PC. By putting all the required connection information in the connection string, your application is more portable. However, for some database drivers with lots of required options but little documentation, creating a connection string that works may be easier said than done. In such cases, setting up an ODBC Data Source in the Control Panel is an easier way to get connected.

USING THE Execute METHOD

In addition to controlling database connections, the ADO Connection object's Execute method allows you to run a SQL statement against a data source. If the SQL statement returns records, you can access them simply by assigning the return value of the Execute method to an ADO Recordset object.

Note

In ADO, you can accomplish the same goal in many different ways. Retrieving information is a perfect example. You can take your pick from the Recordset, Command, or Connection objects; they all have a method used to pull data from a database.

If you installed the sample SQL database included with Visual Studio .NET, you can test the Execute method with the following simple example:

1. Start a new Windows Application project, and add a reference to ADO as described earlier.

2. Add a list box control to the form, and name it lstAuthors.

3. Add a button to the form, and name it btnLoadList.

4. Place the following lines of code in the button's Click event (modifying the connection string where appropriate):

```
Dim strConnect As String
Dim sSSN, sName As String
Dim cn As ADODB.Connection
Dim rs As ADODB._Recordset

'Replace "bsw2k" with your PC name in the connection string
strConnect = "UID=sa;PWD=;DATABASE=pubs;SERVER=bsw2k\NetSDK;Provider=SQLOLEDB"

cn = New ADODB.Connection()
cn.Open(strConnect)

rs = cn.Execute("Select * from Authors")

While Not rs.EOF
    sSSN = rs.Fields("au_id").Value.ToString
    sName = rs.Fields("au_lname").Value.ToString.Trim & ", " &
rs.Fields("au_fname").Value.ToString
```

```
        lstAuthors.Items.Add(sSSN & vbTab & sName)
        rs.MoveNext()
    End While

    rs.Close()
    cn.Close()
```

5. Run the program and click the button. You should see results similar to those pictured in Figure 21.3

Figure 21.3
The results of a simple SELECT query were created by using the Execute method of the Connection object.

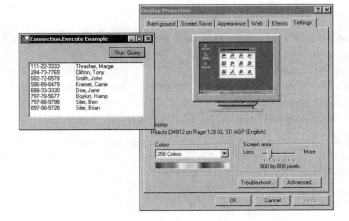

The Execute method of the Connection object returns a Recordset object, which is stored in the variable rs. Next, a While loop is used to move through the recordset, adding each person's name and social security number to the list box.

You can also use the Execute method to run SQL statements that do not return a recordset, as in the following examples:

```
cn.Execute "Delete from Person where LastName = 'Doe' and FirstName = 'John'"
cn.Execute "exec spTimeLogAdd 'Brian',123456,'Test'"
```

The first statement deletes a record from the Person table, and the second executes a stored procedure called spTimeLogAdd. You can also use the Execute method to insert records or perform other database commands.

BASIC RECORDSET OPERATIONS

In the last section, you saw how to pull data into an ADO Recordset object. A recordset represents rows of data from one or more tables in a database, and is usually created by executing a query. Even though the query may involve multiple tables, the resulting recordset always looks like a single table to your Visual Basic program; it has fields (such as Name and Phone Number) and values for those fields (such as Robert Allen and 555-1212). Each set of field values that go together makes up a single record, and all these records together make up a recordset.

→ For more on tables and records, **see** Chapter 20, "Database Basics" **p. 535**

PART
V
CH
21

> **Note**
>
> In the next chapter, we'll discuss the `Datatable` object, which is the .NET version of a set of records, as well as the more advanced `Dataset` object, which can store multiple table results and relationships.

In this section we will describe how to create a recordset and browse the records it contains using Visual Basic code.

CREATING A RECORDSET FROM A DATABASE QUERY

You have already learned how to create and populate a `Recordset` object by using the `Execute` method of the `Connection` object. However, a `Recordset` object has its own methods and properties that can be used to retrieve data. As with all objects, to use these properties, you need to create a new instance of the `Recordset` object first:

```
Dim rsPerson As ADODB.Recordset
rsPerson = New ADODB.Recordset
```

Next, you can use properties of the object to specify the connection, record source, and recordset type. To specify a data source for a `Recordset` object, set the `ActiveConnection` property equal to an ADO `Connection` object or connection string:

```
rsPerson.ActiveConnection = cn
rsPerson.ActiveConnection = "DSN=BIBLIO"
```

The first line of code assumes that `cn` represents an open connection that points to a data source, as discussed earlier. The second line demonstrates the use of a connection string, in which case a connection object will be implicitly created.

A recordset's `Open` method causes the recordset to be populated with data. The code in Listing 21.1 creates a new `Recordset` object and then prints the data it contains in the Output window.

LISTING 21.1   ADOTEST.ZIP—CREATING AN ADO RECORDSET

```
Dim rsPerson As ADODB.Recordset
Dim cn As ADODB.Connection
Dim strConnect As String
Dim sSQL As String

strConnect = "UID=sa;PWD=;DATABASE=BrianTest;SERVER=localhost;Provider=SQLOLEDB"
SSQL = "Select LastName,FirstName from Person Where LastName like 'S%'"

cn = New ADODB.Connection()
cn.Open(strConnect)
rsPerson = New ADODB.Recordset()
rsPerson.ActiveConnection = cn
rsPerson.Open(sSQL)

While Not rsPerson.EOF
    Debug.Write(rsPerson.Fields(0).Value.ToString)
    Debug.WriteLine(rsPerson.Fields(1).Value.ToString)
```

```
        rsPerson.MoveNext()
End While

rsPerson.Close()
cn.Close()
```

The code in Listing 21.1 runs a SQL query that selects the last and first names of all persons having last names that begin with the letter *S*.

→ To learn how to set up the sample database, **see** Chapter 20, "Database Basics," **p. 535**

DISPLAYING FIELD VALUES

Listing 21.1 uses a numeric index to retrieve field values from the `Recordset` object's `Fields` collection. The SQL `SELECT` query retrieves two fields (`LastName` and `FirstName`), which correspond to indexes 0 and 1 in the fields collection, respectively. However, as we saw in the earlier discussion of the ADO `Connection` object, you can also reference fields by name. The following statements show an example of both types of field access:

```
rsPerson.Fields("LastName")
rsPerson.Fields(0)
```

> **Note**
>
> The method of referring to field names using the exclamation mark, as in *recordset!field name*, is no longer supported.

Another interesting thing to note about the earlier lines of code is that they return `Field` objects. In previous versions of Visual Basic, this was enough to retrieve the field values, because `Value` was the default property. However, Visual Studio .NET's strong typing requires that you specify the `Value` property explicitly. The following lines of code use `For` loops to print both the field names and values of the fields in any given recordset:

```
'PRINT THE FIELD NAMES
For i = 0 To rsPerson.Fields.Count - 1
  Debug.Write(rsPerson.Fields(i).Name & vbTab)
Next i
Debug.WriteLine("")

'PRINT VALUES OF ALL FIELDS FOR EACH RECORD
rsPerson.MoveFirst()

While Not rsPerson.EOF
  For i = 0 To rsPerson.Fields.Count - 1
    Debug.Write(rsPerson.Fields(i).Value.ToString.Trim & vbTab)
  Next i
  Debug.WriteLine("")
  rsPerson.MoveNext()
End While
```

As you can see from the sample code, field indexes start at zero and end at one less than the number of fields in the recordset. The number of fields in a recordset is available through the `Count` property of the `Fields` collection.

Note

> When accessing fields using a numeric index, keep in mind that any changes to the SQL statement (or tables themselves if you are using SELECT * will make the indexes change). For this reason, we suggest using stored procedures and field lists whenever possible, as described in the previous chapter.

RECORDSET NAVIGATION

After data has been retrieved into a Recordset object, you can access and update the values of fields in the *current record*. Think of the recordset as a long sequential file. At any given time, the current record is a pointer to a location within that file. To work with different records, you can use the following navigation methods to change the current record:

- MoveFirst—Moves to the first record, just after the beginning-of-file marker (BOF)
- MoveLast—Moves to the last record, just before the end-of-file marker (EOF)
- MoveNext—Moves to the next record after the current record (toward EOF)
- MovePrevious—Moves back to the record before the current record (toward BOF)
- Move—Moves forward or backward a specified number of records

BOF and EOF are properties that indicate the beginning and ending points of a recordset, respectively.

NAVIGATION AND THE CursorType PROPERTY

In the examples up to this point, you have seen only two methods used to navigate within a recordset: the MoveFirst and MoveNext methods. In Listing 21.1, you used a While loop to move forward through the records in an open recordset until the EOF property was True.

Note

> Looping through recordsets in a forward-only manner is typical for certain types of operations, such as creating a Web page. In Chapter 22 we will discuss ADO.NET's DataReader class, which can be used to create quick, forward-only result sets.

As a matter of fact, attempting to use MovePrevious or MoveLast with Listing 21.1 would cause an error, because it is invalid for the selected *cursor type*. A cursor in a recordset is like a cursor on a computer screen; it is a pointer to a current position.

Because you did not specify a value for the Recordset object's CursorType property, it was set to the default value of adOpenForwardOnly. The ramifications of the CursorType property are discussed shortly; but for now just remember that a "forward only" cursor does not support MovePrevious and MoveLast navigation methods.

USING NAVIGATION METHODS

As an example of recordset navigation, you will create a project that uses the navigation methods. To get started, create a new Standard EXE project with a list box named lstData, three command buttons (btnPrevious, btnNext, and btnJump), and a text box named txtJump.

The sample program runs a query against the membership database from Chapter 20 and then allows the user to execute the navigation methods to browse the recordset. The code for the sample project is shown in Listing 21.2.

LISTING 21.2   ADONAV.ZIP—USING RECORDSET NAVIGATION METHODS

```
Private rs As ADODB.Recordset
Public Sub New()
    MyBase.New()

    'This call is required by the Windows Form Designer.
    InitializeComponent()

    'Add any initialization after the InitializeComponent() call
    rs = New ADODB.Recordset()
    rs.CursorType = ADODB.CursorTypeEnum.adOpenStatic
    rs.Open("Select * from Person", _
    "Server=mypc\NetSDK;UID=sa;pwd=;Database=pubs;Provider=SQLOLEDB")
    DisplayCurrentRecord()
End Sub

Private Sub DisplayCurrentRecord()
    Dim i As Integer
    Dim s As String

    If rs.BOF Then rs.MoveFirst()
    If rs.EOF Then rs.MoveLast()

    lstData.Items.Clear()
    For i = 0 To rs.Fields.Count - 1
        s = rs.Fields(i).Name & ": " & rs.Fields(i).Value.ToString
        lstData.Items.Add(s)
    Next i
    Me.Text = "Current Position:" & rs.AbsolutePosition
End Sub

Private Sub btnNext_Click(ByVal sender As System.Object, _
        ByVal e As System.EventArgs) Handles btnNext.Click
    rs.MoveNext()
    DisplayCurrentRecord()
End Sub

Private Sub btnPrevious_Click(ByVal sender As System.Object, _
        ByVal e As System.EventArgs) Handles btnPrevious.Click
    rs.MovePrevious()
    DisplayCurrentRecord()
End Sub
```

PART

V

CH

21

LISTING 21.2   CONTINUED

```
Private Sub btnJump_Click(ByVal sender As System.Object, _
        ByVal e As System.EventArgs) Handles btnJump.Click
    rs.Move(convert.ToInt32(txtJump().Text))
    DisplayCurrentRecord()
End Sub
```

The sample code creates a recordset using a static cursor, which, unlike the forward-only cursor, allows navigation in both directions. The use of the navigation methods in the sample project is straightforward. The only part that merits further explanation is the DisplayCurrentRecord function. Notice that it checks for BOF or EOF conditions before displaying the field names and values for the current record. This step is necessary because attempting to access the Field object without a current record would cause an error. The working project is pictured in Figure 21.4.

Figure 21.4
A sample program demonstrates the Move methods of the Recordset object.

USING THE RecordCount PROPERTY

Another useful property used with recordset navigation is the RecordCount property, which determines the number of records returned in a recordset. While it is easy to check the EOF property during navigation, using the RecordCount property may allow you to avoid even more extra processing:

```
rsInvoices.Open("spGetInvoicestoProcess")
If rsInvoices.RecordCount = 0 Then
    MessageBox.Show("No invoices to process")
Else
    PreparePrinter()
    ProcessInvoices(rsInvoices)
End If
```

In this sample code, the PreparePrinter function is called only if rsInvoices contains records. Another use of the RecordCount property might be to display a progress bar indicating the number of records remaining until all are processed.

Note

Depending on the CursorType and CursorLocation property settings, an accurate record count may not be available. For example, a forward-only server-side cursor will contain –1 if records are available. If you do not get the accurate record count you need, try changing the cursor type or executing the MoveLast method before accessing the RecordCount property.

SORTING AND FILTERING A RECORDSET

As you may recall from our discussion of SQL statements in the previous chapter, a WHERE clause can be used to filter records returned from a SQL query, and the ORDER BY clause can be used to control their order. The Recordset object contains Filter and Sort properties that can alter these same attributes without executing an additional SQL query. To sort a recordset, simply set the Sort property to a comma-separated field list, as in the following examples:

```
rs.Sort = "State, City, LastName, FirstName"
rs.Sort = "Age DESC, LastName, FirstName"
```

As with the ORDER BY clause, you can specify whether the records are sorted in ascending order (the default) or descending order. The Filter property works just like a WHERE clause:

```
rs.Filter = "Age > 15 AND LastName Like 'S%'"
rs.Filter = "State = 'AL' OR State = 'NY'"
```

Keep in mind that while these properties act similarly to their SQL counterparts, they are not as versatile. For example, the second line of code uses an OR to specify multiple states because the Filter property does not support an IN clause.

> **Note**
>
> When you set the Filter or Sort properties, the contents of the recordset are updated immediately to reflect the changes.

CHANGING DATA IN A RECORDSET

Now that you know how to get information into a Recordset object and display it, you can take the next step and change (or update) the information in the database. If your recordset has been set up appropriately, you can change the underlying database information easily. Simply navigate to the appropriate record, assign a new value to each field you want to change, and finally call the Update method, as follows:

```
rs.Fields("FirstName").Value = "Dweezil"
rs.Update()
```

Adding new records to a Recordset object is similar to changing the content of existing records, but with one extra step:

1. Call the AddNew method.
2. Assign values to the fields.
3. Call the Update method.

The code in Listing 21.3 adds a new record to the Person table.

LISTING 21.3   ADOTEST.ZIP—ADDING A NEW RECORD TO AN ADO RECORDSET

```
Dim rs As ADODB.Recordset


'OPEN A RECORDSET
rs = New ADODB.Recordset()
rs.CursorType = ADODB.CursorTypeEnum.adOpenStatic
rs.LockType = ADODB.LockTypeEnum.adLockOptimistic
rs.Open("Select * from Person",_
    "Server=localhost;UID=sa;pwd=;Database=BrianTest;Provider=SQLOLEDB")


'ADD A NEW RECORD
rs.AddNew()
rs.Fields("SSN").Value = "000000007"
rs.Fields("LastName").Value = "Bond"
rs.Fields("FirstName").Value = "Jimmy"
rs.Fields("Address").Value = "MI-6 Headquarters"
rs.Fields("City").Value = "London"
rs.Fields("Age").Value = 39
rs.Update()

rs.Close
```

As with a SQL INSERT statement, you must provide values for fields that do not accept nulls; otherwise, an exception will be thrown.

Note

If you do not call the Update statement when adding records, changes will not be written to the database and the new record will be lost when you perform a navigation method.

To delete the current record from a recordset, use the Delete method:

```
rs.Delete()
```

Note that after calling the Delete method, the current record will be invalid, so you will have to use a navigation method before attempting to access field values.

UNDERSTANDING RECORD LOCKING

By default, ADO recordsets are read only. Attempting to change a field value in a read-only recordset causes an error. To add, change, or delete records in an ADO recordset, you must set the LockType property to a different value than the read-only default, as shown in the following line of code from Listing 21.3:

```
rs.LockType = ADODB.LockTypeEnum.adLockOptimistic
```

You might wonder why the LockType property is important. The answer is that if you are editing records in a multiuser database, you have to be concerned with *record locking*. Record locking means preventing other users from trying to edit the same database record at the same time. Record locking is controlled with the `LockType` property, which has the following values:

- `adLockReadOnly`—Sets data in the recordset as read only
- `adLockPessimistic`—Provides pessimistic record locking, which means the record is locked while you are editing it
- `adLockOptimisitc`—Provides optimistic record locking, which means records are locked only when you call the `Update` method
- `adLockBatchOptimisitc`—Updates multiple records at a time with the `UpdateBatch` method

Why are the parameters named after attitudes (optimistic and pessimistic)? Because attempting to update a locked record causes an error in your program. You can be optimistic that a record will be available when you need to update it, or pessimistic and lock it for as long as you need it.

VIEWING OTHERS' CHANGES

Another concern with multiuser databases is making sure the data in your recordset is as accurate as it needs to be. If you recall an earlier section, you know that the `CursorType` property can restrict recordset navigation. However, the main point of the different cursor types, listed in Table 21.2, is to control how your recordset is linked to the underlying data.

TABLE 21.2   THE `CursorType` PROPERTY

Constant	Description
adOpenForwardOnly	Provides for fast retrieval of data, but allows only forward movement.
adOpenKeySet	Your program can see some of the data changes made by other users.
adOpenDynamic	Your program can see all the data changes made by other users.
adOpenStatic	This property provides a static picture of the database; you cannot see others' changes.

As you will find out from using ADO, not all cursor types are supported by all databases. For Access databases, the default `adOpenForwardOnly` cursor is intended for a quick read-only pass through the database, whereas the `adOpenKeySet` cursor is better suited for updates and more complex operations. As we will see in a moment, another important property when dealing with recordsets is the `CursorLocation` property. This property determines whether the recordset is linked to the database or disconnected from the database.

THE `Command` OBJECT

When you are working with a set of data, most of the time you are working with properties and methods of the `Recordset` object. However, to retrieve that data, you will find that the ADO `Command` object is indispensable. It allows you to encapsulate a query or SQL stored procedure into a reusable object, which is especially ideal if you need to perform the operation multiple times. You can even store the parameters from your query or stored procedure in the object's Parameters collection, which means you don't have to worry about building an appropriate SQL string with associated quotation marks. After you set up a Command object, you can change the parameters of the object and call it repeatedly.

For example, recall the SQL statement from Listing 21.1, which was used to select persons whose last names begin with the letter *S*. Suppose we created a stored procedure, spSearch that contained a parameter:

```
CREATE PROCEDURE spSearch

@strSearchLetter char(1)

AS

SELECT *
FROM Person
WHERE LastName Like @strSearchLetter + '%'
```

→ For more on stored procedures, **see** Chapter 20, "Database Basics," **p. 535**

To create a Command object for this stored procedure, you need to tell it the name of the stored procedure and parameter information, as shown in Listing 21.4.

LISTING 21.4 ADOTEST.ZIP—USING A COMMAND OBJECT

```
Dim rs AS ADODB.RecordSet
Dim cmd As New ADODB.Command()
Dim prm As ADODB._Parameter
Dim cn As New ADODB.Connection()

'Open a connection to the database_
cn.Open("Server=localhost;uid=sa;pwd=;Database=BrianTest;Provider=SQLOLEDB")

'Set up the command object
cmd.CommandType = ADODB.CommandTypeEnum.adCmdStoredProc
cmd.CommandText = "spSearch"
cmd.ActiveConnection = cn

'Set up the parameter object
prm = cmd.CreateParameter("@strSearchLetter", _
      ADODB.DataTypeEnum.adChar, _
      ADODB.ParameterDirectionEnum.adParamInput, _
      1, _
      "S")
cmd.Parameters.Append(prm)

'Set up the recordset object
rs = New ADODB.Recordset()
rs.CursorType = ADODB.CursorTypeEnum.adOpenStatic
rs.LockType = ADODB.LockTypeEnum.adLockOptimistic

'Execute the command
rs.Open(cmd)
```

The code in Listing 21.4 makes use of every ADO object we have discussed in this chapter. The Command object contains a collection of Parameter objects, each of which represents a parameter in the underlying stored procedure. After a Command object has been created, you can manipulate its parameters and call it again with just a few lines of code:

```
cmd.Parameters("@strSearchLetter").Value = "T"
rs.Close()
rs.Open(cmd)
```

The preceding lines of code would re-open a recordset after changing the command parameters. If these lines of code were executed subsequently to those in Listing 21.4, the recordset would contain those people whose last names began with *T*.

Note

The Command object also has an Execute method that works similarly to the Connection.Execute method.

USING DISCONNECTED RECORDSETS

If you have worked with older VB data access technologies, you will find that ADO has features that allow you to manipulate data in ways that were never before possible. For example, in most traditional applications a recordset in your program is always linked to the underlying database. As long as the recordset is loaded into memory, you are maintaining an active connection to the database. However, the rise of the Internet and "loosely connected" applications have brought about the concept of a *disconnected* recordset. This term means that you can have a recordset in memory that is not attached to a database. Disconnected recordsets can be manipulated independently of the database, saved to disk, and synchronized to the database later if necessary. This works great in heavily used Internet applications. Consider a Web server that has 100,000 users trying to display product lists at the same time. By creating a business object that returns a disconnected recordset from the database server to the Web server, you can minimize the connection time and resource drain on the database.

DISCONNECTING A RECORDSET FROM THE DATABASE

The key to creating a disconnected recordset is setting the CursorLocation property. This property determines whether a cursor in the database will be associated with the data in the recordset. To create a disconnected recordset (or "client-side cursor"), perform the following steps:

1. Create the new Recordset object.
2. Set the CursorLocation property to adUseClient.
3. Populate the Recordset object with data.
4. Set the ActiveConnection property to Nothing.

PART
V

CH
21

Recall the example from Listing 21.2, which displayed information in a list box. By modifying the code in the New subroutine, you can easily change it to use a disconnected recordset:

```
Dim cn As New ADODB.Connection()
rs = New ADODB.Recordset()
rs.CursorType = ADODB.CursorTypeEnum.adOpenStatic
rs.CursorLocation = ADODB.CursorLocationEnum.adUseClient
rs.Open("Select * from Person",_
  "Server=localhost;UID=sa;pwd=;Database=BrianTest;Provider=SQLOLEDB")
rs.ActiveConnection = Nothing
DisplayCurrentRecord()
```

The only changes from Listing 21.2 were to add two lines of code. You set the CursorLocation property so that records are stored on the client, and you disconnect the recordset by destroying its ActiveConnection object. If skeptics in the audience need even more evidence that the recordset is indeed disconnected from the database, run the sample program then stop the SQL database server. You will find that the program still functions normally. However, you cannot start the program a second time unless the database is accessible.

CREATING A RECORDSET WITH CODE

A disconnected recordset is a useful structure for passing data around in an application, especially because it contains built-in methods for filtering and sorting. As you just saw, it is easy to populate a recordset from an existing database. However, you can also create a recordset "from scratch" using just a few lines of VB code. In order to do this, you simply create a new Recordset object, create a Fields collection, and finally add records using the methods described earlier. Listing 21.5 shows how to create a Recordset object that contains fields for names and phone numbers.

LISTING 21.5   ADOTEST.ZIP—CREATING AN ADO RECORDSET WITH CODE

```
Dim rs As New ADODB.Recordset()

'Create the structure
rs.Fields.Append("Name", ADODB.DataTypeEnum.adVarChar, 30)
rs.Fields.Append("Phone", ADODB.DataTypeEnum.adVarChar, 18,_
    ADODB.FieldAttributeEnum.adFldIsNullable)


'Add a record
rs.Open()
rs.AddNew()
rs.Fields("Name").Value = "George Kaplan"
rs.Fields("Phone").Value = "901-555-1212"
rs.Update()
```

Recordsets can also be saved to disk with a single line of code:

```
rs.Save("c:\temp.xml", ADODB.PersistFormatEnum.adPersistXML)
```

The previous line of code saves the recordset structure in data in XML format. Disconnected recordsets can be loaded from a saved file just as easily:

```
Dim rs As New ADODB.Recordset()
rs.Open("C:\temp.xml")
```

Notice that you use the Open method, but instead of specifying a SQL query or Command object, you supply the desired file path.

UPDATING THE DATABASE

Earlier, you learned how records are locked to prevent multiple users from fighting over the same record. Record locking takes on a different meaning when you use disconnected recordsets. If you are not connected to a database, then you are, in a sense, checking out the records, like you would check out books from a library. If you edit or change the data in the recordset, the changes are not reflected until you check in the records. For some types of recordsets, such as read-only data, you may never want or need to apply changes back to the database. However, if you do need to update the database you have two options: Let ADO perform a *batch update*, or manually process each record in the disconnected recordset by calling a stored procedure to update the associated database record.

UPDATING A BATCH OF RECORDS

Batch updates allow you to make multiple changes to a recordset and apply them to the underlying database at once with the UpdateBatch method. You can even make a change to a disconnected recordset, reestablish the connection, and update the database.

First, to use UpdateBatch, you must change the Recordset object's LockType property to use the adLockBatchOptimistic record-locking method:

```
rs.LockType = adLockBatchOptimistic
```

After you retrieve a disconnected recordset, as described in the preceding section, change one or more of the records:

```
rs.Fields("zipcode").Value = "00000"
rs.Update()
rs.MoveNext()
rs.Delete()
```

Next, re-establish the connection to the database by setting the recordset's ActiveConnection property to an open Connection object, as shown here:

```
rs.ActiveConnection = cn
```

Finally, execute the code that actually performs the database update:

```
rs.MarshalOptions = adMarshalModifiedOnly
rs.UpdateBatch
```

I hope you were watching closely because I just introduced a new property, MarshalOptions. This property determines whether the whole recordset is returned for updating or just the changed records, for the most efficient use of resources over a slow network connection. The second line of code actually performs the update with the UpdateBatch method. In the preceding sample, the UpdateBatch would change the ZipCode field for one record and delete another record.

UPDATING RECORDS MANUALLY

In some cases, you might want more control than the default handling of UpdateBatch can provide. In this case, you can use the Status property of a Recordset object to determine what type of update was done to a particular record:

```
While Not rs.EOF

  Select Case rs.Status
    Case ADODB.RecordStatusEnum.adRecNew
         'THIS IS A NEW RECORD, EXECUTE INSERT STATEMENT
    Case ADODB.RecordStatusEnum.adRecModified
         'THIS IS A CHANGED RECORD, EXECUTE UPDATE STATEMENT
  End Select
  rs.MoveNext

End While
```

If you set the MarshalOptions property to return all records, you will also get back the original records, which will have a status of adRecUnModified.

USING REMOTE DATA SERVICES (RDS)

Remote Data Services (RDS) is a part of ADO, which acts as a link between Internet Information Server and your custom classes. It is often used to pass disconnected recordsets across the Internet using ADO. If you need to create a COM object remotely over the Internet, RDS provides an easy way to do it. However, keep in mind that the DLLs you create with Visual Studio .NET are *not* COM DLLs, so the information in this section is only applicable if you are calling a Visual Basic 6.0 DLL from a .NET program. Remotely creating objects in the .NET world was discussed in Chapter 9, "Creating Code Components."

Note

In Visual Basic .NET, RDS has been replaced by the concept of *remoting*, as described in Chapter 9.

The key to using RDS is its DataSpace object. You can create an instance of the RDS Data Space on the Internet client, as follows:

```
Set objRDS = CreateObject("RDS.DataSpace")
```

You can then use the RDS Data Space to create remote objects on a Web server:

```
Set objTest = objRDS.CreateObject("MyDLL.MyClass", _
"http://server.somewhere.com")
```

Notice the difference in the two calls to CreateObject. The first line of code creates a local object. The second line of code creates a remote object, objTest. This process is somewhat similar (but not exactly like) using DCOM to create an instance of an object on a remote machine, but then using the features of that object on a local machine.

The sample object objTest is an instance of a DLL that runs on the Web server. After you create this instance, you can make method calls and pass data to and from it. The ADOR object library mentioned earlier is a minimal implementation of an ADOR Recordset (the *R* stands for remote) designed for this type of use. You can create functions in your ActiveX DLL to pass ADOR recordsets to the Internet client, which can then return the changed records to the server.

Note

To set RDS up on the server side, registry entries (ADCLaunch) and IIS permissions may need to be modified. For more details, search the Microsoft On-Line Knowledge Base for RDS.

EXERCISE: DISPLAYING A RECORDSET IN A DATAGRID

In most of the examples in this chapter, we have used print statements or some other simplistic method to display data. However, Visual Basic has always allowed some type of automatic *data binding*, or associating a set of records with controls on a form. The controls in Visual Basic .NET (such as the DataGrid) are designed for use with ADO.NET. Fortunately, you can take advantage of the fact that XML is a shared format between the older ADO Recordset and ADO.NET DataSet. In this section, we will perform a simple exercise used to display an ADO Recordset in a DataGrid control.

To begin, you'll need to have the Membership database created in a database and be able to successfully connect to it as described throughout this chapter. Next, start a new Windows Application and begin following the steps.

1. Using the procedure described earlier, add a reference to Microsoft ActiveX Data Objects 2.7 to your project.
2. Add three Button controls to the form. Set their Name properties to btnLoadRecordset, btnWriteDataSet, and btnLoadDataSet. Set their Text properties to Load Recordset, Write DataSet, and Load DataSet.
3. Add a DataGrid control to the form. Set its Name property to grdPersonList.
4. Add the code from Listing 21.6 to the form.

PART

V

CH

21

LISTING 21.6   `ADOGRID.ZIP`—CONVERTING A RECORDSET TO A DATASET

```
Private dsPerson As DataSet

Private Sub btnLoadRecordset_Click(ByVal sender As System.Object, ByVal e As
System.EventArgs) Handles btnLoadRecordset.Click

  Dim rs As ADODB.Recordset
  rs = New ADODB.Recordset()
  rs.CursorType = ADODB.CursorTypeEnum.adOpenStatic
  rs.Open("Select * from Person",_
  "Server=localhost;UID=sa;pwd=;Database=BrianTest;Provider=SQLOLEDB")
  If System.IO.File.Exists("c:\temprs.xml") Then
    System.IO.File.Delete("c:\temprs.xml")
  End If
  rs.Save("c:\temprs.xml", ADODB.PersistFormatEnum.adPersistXML)
  dsPerson = New DataSet()
  dsPerson.ReadXml("c:\temprs.xml", XmlReadMode.InferSchema)
  grdPersonList().DataSource = dsPerson
  grdPersonList().DataMember = "row"
  messagebox.Show("The grid has been loaded from the database using ADO.")

End Sub

Private Sub btnWriteDataSet_Click(ByVal sender As System.Object,_
    ByVal e As System.EventArgs) Handles btnWriteDataSet.Click

  If System.IO.File.Exists("c:\tempds.xml") Then
    system.IO.File.Delete("c:\tempds.xml")
  End If
  dsPerson.WriteXml("C:\tempds.xml")
  messagebox.Show("The contents of the dataset bound to the_
    grid have been written to c:\tempds.xml")

End Sub

Private Sub btnLoadDataSet_Click(ByVal sender As System.Object,_
    ByVal e As System.EventArgs) Handles btnLoadDataSet.Click

  If System.IO.File.Exists("c:\tempds.xml") Then
    dsPerson = New DataSet()
    dsPerson.ReadXml("c:\tempds.xml", XmlReadMode.InferSchema)
    grdPersonList().DataSource = dsPerson
    grdPersonList().DataMember = "row"
    messagebox.Show("The grid has been loaded from the XML file c:\tempds.xml.")
  Else
    messagebox.Show("Click write first.")
  End If

End Sub
```

5. Run the program and click the `btnLoadRecordset` button. You should see results similar to those in Figure 21.5.

Figure 21.5
Visual Basic .NET's
`DataGrid` control
allows you to edit and
sort a DataSet that is
bound to it.

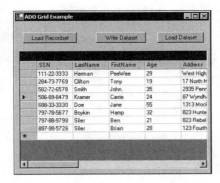

When you click the button, data is retrieved from the database into a recordset and then saved as an XML file. The XML file is then loaded into a `DataSet` object, which is bound to the `DataGrid` control.

Notice that the `DataGrid` control allows to you add, edit, and delete rows.

6. Alter the data by typing in the grid, that is, change someone's last name.

7. Click the `btnWriteDataSet` button. This will write the dataset object in memory to an XML file.

8. Stop the program and restart it. Click the `btnLoadDataSet` button and you should see the record, including the change that was made using the data grid.

As you can see, by using XML we can easily create a `DataSet` object from a `Recordset` object. In the next chapter we'll explore datasets and other ADO.NET concepts in more detail.

CHAPTER 22

USING ADO.NET (ADO)

In this chapter

ActiveX Data Objects.NET is the cornerstone data access technology behind Visual Studio .NET and the .NET framework. In this chapter, we introduce fundamental ADO.NET concepts as well as describe how to build a data access layer that can be used in your multi-tier Visual Basic applications.

DATA AND YOUR APPLICATION

As we mentioned in the first chapter of this book, a good design is the foundation of a successful database project. ADO.NET, Microsoft's latest entry into the data access arena, represents a shift in thinking from previous data access technologies and is clearly geared toward Internet applications. In this section, we will provide a brief overview of the motivation behind ADO.NET and introduce the major ADO.NET classes. In the sections that follow, we will explore ADO.NET in more detail.

UNDERSTANDING DISCONNECTED DATA ACCESS

One important component of ADO.NET is the ability to provide *disconnected* data access to an application. To understand why this is important, we need to first describe some application design strategies. Consider the traditional client-server architecture, an example of which is pictured in Figure 22.1.

Figure 22.1
The client-server model, which has passed the peak of its popularity, requires a database connection for each active user.

APPLICATION

In the client-server model, each client connects to a database server and maintains the connection as long as needed. The client application, usually a Visual Basic executable installed on the user's desktop, contains all the application logic. Database operations are performed from the application directly against the connected database server.

The client-server model works well, but the advance of the World Wide Web brought about another model, known as the multi-tier (or n-tier) architecture. Figure 22.2 shows a type of multi-tier architecture.

Figure 22.2
A multi-tier application is divided into layers that clearly separate the user interface, business, and database logic.

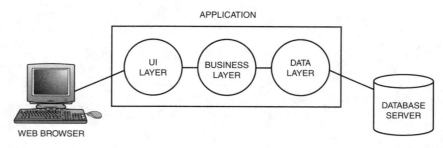

WEB BROWSER

With an application that has been segmented in this manner, maintaining a database connection for every user is not practical or even desired. Instead, data is passed around from tier-to-tier while disconnected from the database. Connections are made from the data layer to the database server for only the brief moment when data needs to be retrieved or updated, then the connection is immediately dropped.

Consider some important advantages provided by this new architecture:

- **Flexibility**. Because the application is in logical parts, layers can be interchanged with minimal effort. For example, a database layer that communicates with Sybase can be replaced with another database layer that communicates with a Microsoft SQL Server without changing the business layer.

- **Reusability**. Multiple user interfaces, such as a telephone system and a Web site, can use the same business layer. Because the layers are usually implemented as classes, they can be easily used in new applications or shared as Web services.

- **Scalability**. This often-thrown-around buzzword is precisely the reason why the n-tier model fits a Web site much better than the client-server model. If something "scales" well, it handles an increase in simultaneous users without severe performance loss. Because the user is not continuously connected to the database, the database server can handle more users. In addition, the layers of an n-tier application are usually written to be *stateless*, which means you do not need to access the same object instance when communicating with a particular layer. The layers of such an application can be easily split across multiple physical computers, creating a "server farm" to further increase scalability. Contrast this approach to the older client-server model, where the only thing you can do to increase scalability is buy a more powerful database server and add additional connection licenses.

In short, Microsoft has designed ADO.NET to make it the ideal choice for an n-tier application.

UNDERSTANDING THE ADO.NET CLASSES

At the core of any data access technology are the classes you use to actually perform operations on the database. One change in the .NET environment from previous ADO versions is the addition of SQL Server–specific data access classes. In previous ADO versions, when you wanted to execute a command, you used a Command object whether you were connecting to SQL Server, Oracle, Access, and so on. ADO.NET, however, includes both a SQLCommand object and an OleDbCommand object. The SQLCommand object talks to SQL Server using API routines specifically optimized for SQL Server, whereas the OleDbCommand object accesses a database through an OLEDB provider. Understandably, the SQL-specific classes will provide better performance than the OLEDB provider classes when accessing SQL server databases.

Note

When accessing a Microsoft SQL Server database, use the ADO.NET classes with the SQL prefix. For other types of databases, use the OLEDB-prefixed classes.

Table 22.1 provides a list of the most important ADO.NET classes that we will be covering in this chapter and lists the classes that have multiple SQL and OLE-DB versions.

TABLE 22.1   IMPORTANT ADO.NET CLASSES

Class Name	Purpose
SQLConnection, OLEDBConnection	Used for establishing a connection to a data source.
SQLDataReader, OLEDBDataReader	Used for read-only, forward-only processing of records while connected to a database.
DataSet	Disconnected store for data. Can contain multiple tables and relationships.
SQLCommand, OLEDBCommand	Represents a database command, such as a stored procedure or other SQL statement.
SQLParameter, OLEDBParameter	A parameter used in a database command.
SQLDataAdapter, OleDbDataAdapter	Used for synchronizing records in a data source to those in a DataSet.
DataTable	Represents a single table of data, containing columns and rows of data.

The classes listed in Table 22.1 are available in the System.Data.SQLClient and System.Data.OleDb namespaces. To use ADO.NET, make sure you have a reference to System.Data.DLL (usually included automatically) and add an Imports statement for the appropriate namespace.

→ For more on namespaces and Imports, **see** Chapter 5, "Visual Basic Building Blocks," **p. 113**

Our discussion of ADO.NET will apply to both the SQL and OLEDB data access classes, with differences noted where applicable. In addition, several ADO.NET classes (such as the DataSet) are the same, no matter what type of database you are using on the back end.

EXECUTING DATABASE COMMANDS

If you read Chapter 20, "Database Basics," you already know that a SQL statement is a type of database command. By using SQL you can query a database, update records, and perform other activities.

→ For more on SQL, **see** Chapter 20, "Database Basics," **p. 535**

In this section, we'll describe how to execute SQL commands using ADO.NET's connection and command classes.

CONNECTING TO THE DATABASE

To get or update data in a database, you have to first *connect* to the database. Connecting to a database is similar to logging in to your favorite Web site. In ADO.NET, you establish connections using the appropriate connection class. The Open method establishes the connection, and the `Close` method terminates the connection. While the connection is in the open state, you use other ADO.NET objects to do something to the database such as execute a query. The following lines of code show how to connect to a Microsoft SQL server with the `SQLConnection` object:

```
Dim strInfo As String
Dim cn As SqlConnection

strInfo = "server=bsw2k;uid=hruser;pwd=elvis;database=BrianTest"
cn = New SqlConnection()
cn.ConnectionString = strInfo
cn.Open()

'   PERFORM OPERATIONS ON DATABASE HERE

cn.Close()
```

Even more important than the `Open` and `Close` methods is the *connection string*, shown in the third line of the previous code. The connection string contains whatever information is necessary to successfully establish a connection to your database, such as a user name and password. In the last chapter, we discussed connection strings in detail and provided several examples.

> **Note**
>
> Different types of databases require different connection strings. For example, when using the `OleDbConnection` object, you'll need to supply the name of an OLE DB provider or ODBC driver. However, because a `SQLConnection` only connects to one type of database, you just specify the name of the desired SQL server. One easy way to determine a valid connection string for the `OleDbConnection` object is to create the connection in the Server Explorer, then copy the connection string into your code.

➔ For more on connection strings, **see** Chapter 21, "ActiveX Data Objects," **p. 575**

As you can see, opening and closing a database connection is very simple. One important point is to make sure you close a database connection as soon as you are through with it. Each connection to a database represents a certain amount of system and network resources, which are limited. It is easy enough to remember to call the `Close` method in your code, but what happens if an exception occurs? As you may recall from Chapter 5, "Visual Basic Building Blocks," when an exception is thrown the normal flow of code is interrupted. In the previous code example, an exception during a database query operation might cause the call to the `Close` method to be skipped.

➔ For more on exceptions, **see** Chapter 5, "Visual Basic Building Blocks," **p. 113**

> **Note**
>
> Closed connections are placed in a "pool" of available connections for a period of time. If another connection request is made using the same connection string, ADO.NET can use the pooled connection, which is quicker than establishing a new one. For more information on connection pooling, see the help topic "Connection Pooling for the SQL Client .NET Provider."

Fortunately, Visual Basic's structured error handling makes it easy to ensure a connection is always closed:

```
Dim strInfo As String
Dim cn As SqlConnection

strInfo = "server=bsw2k;uid=hruser;pwd=elvis;database=BrianTest"

Try
    cn = New SqlConnection()
    cn.ConnectionString = strInfo
    cn.Open()

    '   PERFORM OPERATIONS ON DATABASE HERE

Catch exc As SqlException

    '   HANDLE EXCEPTION HERE

Finally
    If cn.State = ConnectionState.Open Then
        cn.Close()
    End If
End Try
```

In the preceding code, there are basically two operations during which an exception may occur: when establishing the connection or when performing operations on the database. As these statements are all enclosed in the same `Try` block, the connection might be open or closed after an exception occurs. Because attempting to close a connection that is already closed would throw another exception, we first need to check the `State` property and only call the `Close` method if necessary.

SETTING UP A COMMAND OBJECT

Now that you know how to establish a connection, you can execute database commands over it. The `SQLCommand` and `OleDbCommand` command classes encapsulate the functionality of a SQL statement in ADO.NET. By setting properties of a command object, you determine the SQL statement you want to execute. Then, you simply associate it with a valid connection object and call a method to execute the command.

DETERMINING THE COMMAND TEXT

The SQL statement itself is stored in the `CommandText` property, as shown in the following lines of code:

```
Dim cmd AS SqlCommand
cmd = New SqlCommand()
cmd.CommandText = "SELECT LastName, FirstName FROM Person"
```

Setting up the `SQLCommand` object in the previous example is very straightforward—just set the `CommandText` property to the actual SQL statement. However, as you may recall from Chapter 20, SQL statements can also be compiled in the database as stored procedures for greater efficiency. Executing a stored procedure not only requires setting the `CommandText` property to the stored procedure name, but also setting the `CommandType` property appropriately:

```
Dim cmd AS SqlCommand
cmd = New SqlCommand()
cmd.CommandType = CommandType.StoredProcedure
cmd.CommandText = "spGetEmployeeBySSN"
```

`CommandType` has three possible values, each of which influences ADO.NET's interpretation of the `CommandText` property:

- `Text`—The default setting, used for any type of SQL statement other than a stored procedure, such as a `SELECT` or `INSERT` statement.
- `StoredProcedure`—If you choose this option, ADO.NET expects the `CommandText` property to contain the name of the stored procedure you want to execute.
- `TableDirect`—Equivalent to executing the SQL query `SELECT * FROM` *tablename* where the `CommandText` property contains the name of the table. This option is only available for the `OleDbCommand` object and, in the author's opinion, should be used rarely if at all.

SETTING THE Connection PROPERTY

Before you can execute a command, you also need to assign the `Connection` property of the command to an active connection object, as in the following example:

```
Dim cmd As New SqlCommand("SELECT * From Employee")
Dim cn As New SqlConnection("server=bsw2k;uid=hruser;pwd=elvis;database=Testdb")
cn.Open()
cmd.Connection = cn
```

Although the previous code example opens the connection before assigning `cn` to the `cmd.Connection` property, it is only necessary that the connection be open before the command is executed.

CREATING COMMAND PARAMETERS

Most stored procedures (and even some SQL statements) have one or more *parameters*. A parameter is just a value that is substituted for a token in the SQL statement before it is executed. Parameters are especially useful in stored procedures, because the stored procedure works just like a VB function. For example, in Chapter 20, we define a stored procedure that requires an SSN parameter, `spGetEmployeeBySSN`. All the calling program needs to know is the name of the stored procedure and the parameter; the actual SQL query is stored in the database (and can easily be modified without recompiling your VB program). In ADO.NET, each stored procedure parameter is represented in the `Parameters` collection of a command object. Table 22.2 lists the important properties of a parameter object:

TABLE 22.2   SETTING UP A COMMAND PARAMETER

Property	Description	Example
Name	Parameter name in procedure	@strSSN
Type	The parameter's data type	String
Length	Size of the data type	11
Direction	Use of the parameter	Input
Value	Value to use in the query	111-22-3456

You add parameters by using the `Add` method of the `Parameters` collection in a command object, as shown in the following example:

```
cmd.CommandType = CommandType.StoredProcedure
cmd.CommandText = "spGetEmployeeBySSN"

Dim pmTemp AS SqlParameter
pmTemp = cmd.Parameters.Add(New SqlParameter("@strSSN", SqlDbType.Char, 11))
pmTemp.Direction = ParameterDirection.Input
pmTemp.Value = "284-73-7769"
```

In the code example, the `Name`, `Type`, and `Length` properties of `pmTemp` were set using an object constructor. The `Direction` property indicates the parameter is used for input to the stored procedure. The `Value` property contains the SSN value for which we want to search. Although we set a lot of properties in the previous code example, ADO.NET is actually smart enough to interpret most parameters with only the `Name` and `Value` properties. For example, the last four lines in the previous code example could be replaced with the following single line of code:

```
cmd.Parameters.Add(New SqlParameter("@strSSN", "284-73-7769"))
```

Each parameter object you set up in VB must match the name and data type of a corresponding parameter in the stored procedure. If you have a different number of parameters or an incorrect data type, an exception may occur.

Note

SQL Server stored procedures can have *optional parameters*, which are indicated by providing a default value for the parameter in the CREATE PROCEDURE statement. When setting up a SQLCommand object's Parameters collection, you can omit default parameters if desired.

The majority of stored procedure parameters are input parameters, but a parameter can also be used to return data to the calling program. These types of parameters are called *output parameters*, and are useful when you only want to return one or two pieces of data, rather than an entire record. The following stored procedure shows an example use of an output parameter:

```
CREATE PROCEDURE spGetMaxAgeByState

@strState char(2),
```

```
@intResult int OUTPUT

AS

SELECT @intResult = Max(Age) FROM Person
WHERE State = @strState
```

The example stored procedure, spGetMaxAgeByState, uses an output parameter called @intResult to store the maximum age. Note the keyword OUTPUT, which indicates an output parameter. An alternative approach would be to just let the results of the SELECT query be returned as a record. However, returning an integer value requires less overhead than returning a record. The following two lines of code set up a Parameter object for the @intResult parameter:

```
pmTemp = cmd.Parameters.Add(New SqlParameter("@intResult", sqldbtype.Int))
pmTemp.Direction = ParameterDirection.Output
```

As you can see from the example, to specify an output parameter in an ADO.NET command, you set the Direction property to ParameterDirection.Output. After executing the command (described in the next section), simply examine the Value property of an output parameter to determine the resulting value:

```
Dim intMaxAge As Integer
intMaxAge = Convert.ToInt32(cmd.Parameters("@intResult").Value)
Messagebox.Show("The maximum age in " & strStateAbbreviation & " is " & intMaxAge)
```

Because the Value property stores a value of type Object, the sample code converts the parameter value into an integer so it can be stored in a variable of type Integer.

> **Note**
>
> One of the settings for a parameter's Direction property is ReturnValue, which can be used to retrieve the result of a RETURN statement from a stored procedure.

CHOOSING AN EXECUTE METHOD

After you have set the properties of a SQLCommand or OleDbCommand, including any necessary parameters, you can execute the command by calling one of the command's execute methods, as listed here:

- ExecuteNonQuery—Executes a SQL statement that does not return records; that is, a DELETE, UPDATE, or INSERT statement. Also can be used if your stored procedure only returns output via parameters.

- ExecuteReader—Executes a SQL statement and returns a SqlDataReader object that contains any resulting records.

- ExecuteScalar—Used when you need to return only a single value (column) of data from a SQL SELECT statement.

- ExecuteXMLReader—*Available only for the SQLCommand*—Similar to ExecuteReader, but returns an XMLReader.

The reason there are so many different types of execute methods is that each one is optimized for a particular type of SQL statement. Although the selection of an execute method is somewhat flexible, for efficiency's sake you should try to pick the method that most closely matches the data returned by the SQL statement.

Note
The CommandTimeout property can be used to specify a maximum time to execute in seconds, after which a timeout exception will be thrown.

EXECUTING NON-QUERY SQL STATEMENTS

Because a DELETE statement does not actually return rows of data, it would be wasteful to declare a variable to contain a result set. Instead, a more appropriate choice would be the ExecuteNonQuery method, shown in Listing 22.1.

LISTING 22.1 COMMANDEXAMPLES.ZIP—USING THE ExecuteNonQuery METHOD

```
Private Function DeleteEmployee(ByVal strSSN As String,_
        ByVal strDept As String) As Integer
    Dim intRowsDeleted As Integer
    Dim strDeleteSQL As String
    Dim cmd As New SqlCommand()
    Dim cn As New SqlConnection()

    'BUILD THE SQL STRING
    strDeleteSQL = "DELETE FROM Employee WHERE SSN='" & strSSN & "'"
    strDeleteSQL &= " AND Dept = '" & strDept & "'"

    'SET UP COMMAND AND CONNECTION
    cn.ConnectionString = "server=CSQL1;uid=hruser;pwd=elvis;database=DevHR"
    cn.Open()
    cmd.Connection = cn
    cmd.CommandText = strDeleteSQL

    'EXECUTE COMMAND
    intRowsDeleted = cmd.ExecuteNonQuery()

    'CLOSE CONNECTION, RETURN NUMBER OF ROWS
    cn.Close()
    Return intRowsDeleted

End Function
```

Listing 22.1 uses the ExecuteNonQueryMethod to delete a record from the Employee table. The return value of the ExecuteNonQuery method is the number of rows affected by the command. In the case of a DELETE statement, this value contains the number of rows deleted. Another example would be the spGetMaxAgeByState procedure defined in the last section. Because this procedure does not return records, but instead uses an output parameter, ExecuteNonQuery would be an appropriate choice to execute it.

USING A DATA READER

When you execute a SELECT query or stored procedure that returns records, you need to use an execute method that allows you to access those records. We'll start with an easy one: the ExecuteReader method. The ExecuteReader method returns a DataReader object, which can be loosely compared to the read-only, forward-only Recordset object in previous ADO versions. (One important difference, however, is that a DataReader cannot be used in a disconnected fashion.) The SQLDataReader and OleDbDataReader classes are designed to get records out of a database as quickly as possible to be processed sequentially. Therefore, navigation capability is limited to moving forward through the records. Listing 22.2 shows a typical use of a data reader with a while loop:

LISTING 22.2   COMMANDEXAMPLES.ZIP—USING THE SQLDataReader

```
Dim rdrPeople As SqlDataReader
Dim cn As New SqlConnection("server=CSQL1;uid=hruser;pwd=elvis;database=DevHR")
Dim cmd As New SqlCommand("Select LastName, FirstName, Age From Person", cn)
Dim strName As String

cn.Open()

rdrPeople = cmd.ExecuteReader()

While rdrPeople.Read()

    'BUILD STRING CONTAINING LAST AND FIRST NAME
    strName = rdrPeople.GetString(1).Trim & " " & rdrPeople.GetString(0).Trim

    'DISPLAY NAME AND AGE IN A MESSAGE BOX
    Messagebox.Show("Hello, " & strName & ". You are " &_
        rdrPeople.Item("Age").ToString & " years old!")

End While

cn.Close()
```

The code in Listing 22.2 queries the Person table and returns a SQLDataReader object. Each call to the rdrPeople.Read method positions a pointer in the data reader to the next record. Therefore, if your query returns five records, the loop will execute five times. The Read method returns False after all records have been processed, exiting the While loop.

The code in Listing 22.2 demonstrates a couple of ways to access column values in the current row of a data reader. One method is to use the Item property and supply the name or index of the column. Another is to use one of the SQLDataReader's many Get methods to return a column of information in a particular data type. In the example, we know that the LastName and FirstName fields contain string data, so we used the GetString method.

Note

> The purpose of the `Trim` method in Listing 22.2 is to remove trailing spaces from the data field. When working with string comparisons to data fields, remember the length of a `Char` will field always be constant, while a `VarChar` field can have a varying number of characters.

Some other useful methods and properties of the data reader object are listed next:

- `GetName` method—Returns the name of a data column. In the example in Listing 22.2, `GetName(0)` returns `LastName`.

- `FieldCount` property—Returns the number of data columns. The example in Listing 22.2 has three columns.

- `IsDBNull` method—Used to check for a null value in a database column.

In addition to working with multiple records in a set, the `DataReader` can also be used to retrieve multiple result sets in a sequential manner. One example of this would be a stored procedure that contains several `SELECT` queries. To access additional result sets in a `DataReader`, use the `NextResult` method.

RETRIEVING SINGLE VALUES

Sometimes, you may want to just return a single value from a stored procedure, rather than rows of data. We have already covered how to do this using an output parameter. However, you can also retrieve a value that results from a `SELECT` query. One typical example is when you are using an *identity column*. An identity column is like an autonumber field in Microsoft Access—it is a number generated automatically by the database. To understand when you need an identity column, consider our sample `Person` table, which uses the social security number as the primary key. If you were not able to obtain a person's SSN or another identifying number, you could create a primary key using the identity column. One example might be logins and passwords for a Web site. The following `CREATE TABLE` statement defines a table called `WebUsers` with an identity column:

```
CREATE TABLE WebUsers (
   UserNumber int IDENTITY (1, 1) NOT NULL PRIMARY KEY,
   UserID char(10) NOT NULL,
   Password char (10) NOT NULL,
   UserDescription varchar (50) NULL,
   AccessLevel tinyint NOT NULL
)

ALTER TABLE WebUsers ADD CONSTRAINT UniqueUserID UNIQUE NONCLUSTERED (UserID)
```

The `UserNumber` field in the `WebUsers` table is both a primary key and an identity column. When records are inserted into the table, the database assigns this field an integer starting at the number 1 and increments with each new record. You can then use this identity column as a foreign key in other tables. The advantage of having the database create the identity column rather than attempting to generate a unique number yourself is that the database handles concurrent user requests while keeping the number unique.

Note

Identity columns are great for numbers that are keys throughout your database. However, if you need just a temporary string that is unique, you can also store a global-unique identifier (GUID) in the database.

If you need to update several tables at the same time that you insert a record in the `WebUsers` table, you need to know what `UserNumber` was assigned. The following stored procedure, `spWebUserInsert`, adds a record to the table and then returns the value of the `UserNumber` field for that record:

```
CREATE PROCEDURE spWebUserInsert
@strUserID char(10),
@strPassword char(10),
@strDescription varchar(50),
@intAccessLevel tinyint

As

INSERT INTO WebUsers
VALUES (@strUserId, @strPassword,@strDescription,@intAccessLevel)
SELECT @@IDENTITY
```

The `spWebUserInsert` procedure first executes an `INSERT` statement using the parameter values, then selects the system variable `@@IDENTITY`, which contains the identity value most recently inserted.

The `spWebUserInsert` stored procedure returns a record with one column containing the identity value. This, of course, could be retrieved using the `ExecuteReader` method. However, in order to avoid declaring a `SQLDataReader` object, you can use the `SQLCommand` object's `ExecuteScalar` method, which returns a single object variable. Listing 22.3 shows an example of using `ExecuteScalar`:

LISTING 22.3   COMMANDEXAMPLES.ZIP—USING `ExecuteScalar`

```
Private Function InsertWebUser(ByVal strUserId As String,_
    ByVal strPassword As String, ByVal strName As String,_
    ByVal intAccessLevel As Short) As Integer

Dim cn As New SqlConnection("server=corpwww;uid=admin;pwd=xyz;database=security")
Dim cmd As SqlCommand
Dim intNewUserNumber As Integer

cn.Open()
cmd = New SqlCommand()
cmd.Connection = cn
cmd.CommandType = CommandType.StoredProcedure
cmd.CommandText = "spWebUserInsert"
cmd.Parameters.Add(New SqlParameter("@strUserID", strUserId))
cmd.Parameters.Add(New SqlParameter("@strPassword", strPassword))
cmd.Parameters.Add(New SqlParameter("@strDescription", strName))
cmd.Parameters.Add(New SqlParameter("@intAccessLevel", intAccessLevel))
intNewUserNumber = Convert.ToInt32(cmd.ExecuteScalar())
```

LISTING 22.3 CONTINUED

```
cn.Close()
Return intNewUserNumber

End Function
```

The `InsertWebUser` function in Listing 22.3 uses the `ExecuteScalar` method in conjunction with the stored procedure to retrieve the user number. The following lines of code show how this function might be called:

```
intUserNumber = InsertWebUser("bsiler", "secret", "Brian Siler", 5)
Call SetupUserColors(intUserNumber, "Default")
Call SetupUserWeatherInfo(intUserNumber, strZipcode)
```

This example includes additional function calls that make use of the new user number returned by the `InsertWebUser` function. Presumably in addition to the `WebUsers` table, the database contains tables for Web site preferences that use `UserNumber` as a key.

RETRIEVING XML FROM SQL SERVER

As part of Microsoft's ubiquitous XML initiative, support for XML processing is built into SQL Server 2000. By adding special clauses to your SQL statement, you can cause SQL Server to format the results of a query as XML:

```
Select * from Person FOR XML AUTO, XMLDATA
```

Notice the `FOR XML AUTO` clause in the previous SQL query, which tells SQL Server to return records in XML format. The `XMLDATA` argument lets SQL Server know you want to include field definitions in XML as well. If you use these options when executing the previous SQL query interactively, the output records are represented in XML and may look similar to this:

```
<PERSON SSN="684-99-0012" LastName="Vandelay" FirstName="Art" Age="47"
Address="123 Fourth Street" City="Paramus" State="NJ" Zipcode="12345"/>
```

In order to make processing XML results easier, the `SQLCommand` class contains a method called `ExecuteXMLReader`, which can parse the XML as it is returned to your program. The `XMLReader` class returned by this method contains several methods that allow you to read XML attributes and values:

```
cmd = New SqlCommand("Select * from Person FOR XML AUTO, XMLDATA", cn)
Employees = cmd.ExecuteXmlReader()
While Employees.Read()
    If Employees.NodeType = Xml.XmlNodeType.Element Then
        Employees.MoveToAttribute("LastName")
        If Employees.HasValue Then
            Debug.WriteLine("Current Employee=" & Employees.Value)
        End If
    End If
End While
```

The previous code sample writes all of the last names in the Person table in the output window. The `XMLReader` class is designed for forward-only processing of XML data. In a later chapter, we'll introduce the XMLDocument class, which can be used to represent an entire XML document in memory.

→ For more on XML, **see** Chapter 24, "Working with Files," **p. 667**

To learn other means of accessing data as XML, see the help topic "Reading XML Data Using XMLReader."

UNDERSTANDING DataSets

One of the big advances in ADO.NET is the introduction of a new class called the *DataSet*. In a multi-tier application, data can extracted from a source database, stored in a DataSet, and passed among the tiers. A DataSet is more powerful than an ADO Recordset because it can contain multiple tables and be aware of the relationships between them. It is *never* connected to an underlying database, making it ideal for disconnected data applications. In a sense, the DataSet is almost like a portable database unto itself. With all this power comes added complexity, so if you are used to previous data structures (such as the ADO Recordset) you may have to learn a few new things. In this section, we will show you how to get records from a database into a DataSet object, modify them, and finally send changes from a DataSet to a database.

INTRODUCING THE DATA ADAPTER

As we just mentioned, a DataSet does not have an underlying database associated with it. In order to transfer records to and from a DataSet, you use one of the Data Adapter classes. A data adapter is like a bridge or conduit between a data source and a DataSet object. (This is different from the command classes we discussed in the last section, which behaved like functions that returned records.) A DataAdapter has several properties that represent individual command objects: SelectCommand, UpdateCommand, InsertCommand, and so on. When you pass data through a data adapter, it uses these commands to transfer records to and from the source database. The primary concern of a data adapter is how data is mapped to and from a source database. As we cover the DataSet class in the sections that follow, we will also describe the SqlDataAdapter in more detail.

FILLING A DataSet

To retrieve records from a database and populate a DataSet, you use the Fill method of a data adapter object. The following lines of code show a simple transfer of some fields from the Person table to a DataSet object:

```
Dim cn As SqlConnection
Dim cmdGetPeople As SqlCommand
Dim strSQL As String
Dim adPerson As SqlDataAdapter
Dim dsResults As DataSet

'INITIALIZE OBJECTS
cn = New SqlConnection("server=BrianPC;uid=test;pwd=xyz;database=Test")
```

```
adPerson = New SqlDataAdapter()
dsResults = New DataSet()

'SET UP COMMAND
strSQL = "SELECT SSN, LastName, FirstName, Age FROM Person"
cmdGetPeople = New SqlCommand(strSQL, cn)
adPerson.SelectCommand = cmdGetPeople

'FILL DATASET
cn.Open()
adPerson.Fill(dsResults)
cn.Close()
```

The previous code invokes the `Fill` method of the data adapter, passing a `DataSet` object, dsResults, as a parameter. The `Fill` method uses the `SelectCommand` (which is an ordinary SQL command, discussed earlier) to retrieve records from a database.

ACCESSING FIELD VALUES

Accessing individual records in populated `DataSet` is different than in a `DataReader`, because there is no current record or associated movement method. Instead, collections are used to organize tables, rows, and field values. The following line of code would display the contents of the first field in the first record of the first table:

```
Messagebox.Show(dsResults.Tables(0).Rows(0).Item(0).ToString)
```

As with any collection hierarchy, you can make navigating easier by using named identifiers, loops, and the `With` statement:

```
With dsResults.Tables(0)
    For i = 0 To .Rows.Count - 1
      Debug.WriteLine(.Rows(i).Item("LastName"))
    Next
End With
```

The sample code prints the `LastName` field for each row to the Output window.

LOADING MULTIPLE TABLES

Filling a `DataSet` object with a single table is relatively easy. (As we will see in a moment, the `DataTable` object can also be created independently of a `DataSet` if you need it.) However, to really take advantage of the power of a `DataSet`, you can put data from two or more tables in the same `DataSet` and establish relationships between the tables. To accomplish this, you could take one of the following approaches:

1. Call the `Fill` method on multiple data adapter objects using the same `DataSet` as an argument.

2. Execute a stored procedure with more than one `SELECT` statement. In this case, only a single `SQLDataAdapter` object is necessary.

By using either of these techniques, you can cause data from different databases or tables to be included in the same `DataSet`.

USING MULTIPLE COMMANDS The code shown in Listing 22.4 puts records from both the Employee and Person tables into the dsResult DataSet.

LISTING 22.4   COMMANDEXAMPLES.ZIP—FILLING A DataSet

```
Dim cn As SqlConnection
Dim cmdGetPeople As SqlCommand
Dim cmdGetEmployee As SqlCommand
Dim strSQL As String
Dim adPerson As SqlDataAdapter
Dim adEmployee As SqlDataAdapter
Dim dsResults As DataSet

'INITIALIZE OBJECTS
cn = New SqlConnection("server=bsw2k;uid=sa;pwd=;database=BrianTest")
adPerson = New SqlDataAdapter()
adEmployee = New SqlDataAdapter()
dsResults = New DataSet()

'SET UP COMMANDS
strSQL = "SELECT SSN, LastName, FirstName, Age FROM Person"
cmdGetPeople = New SqlCommand(strSQL, cn)
strSQL = "SELECT SSN, Dept, Salary, HireDate FROM Employee"
cmdGetEmployee = New SqlCommand(strSQL, cn)

adPerson.SelectCommand = cmdGetPeople
adPerson.TableMappings.Add("Table", "Person")
adEmployee.SelectCommand = cmdGetEmployee
adEmployee.TableMappings.Add("Table", "Employee")

'FILL DATASET
cn.Open()
adPerson.Fill(dsResults)
adEmployee.Fill(dsResults)
cn.Close()
```

Listing 22.4 also introduces the concept of *mappings*. A mapping tells the data adapter which DataSet fields and tables to use when filling the DataSet. In other words, you can use a mapping to name a field differently in your DataSet than in the original source database. The mapping in Listing 22.4 is a very high-level mapping; it just lets the data adapter know the name of the destination tables in the DataSet.

Note

To learn more about detailed table and column mappings, see the help file topic "DataTableMapping Class."

Note

Adding a table mapping allows you to access a table by its name within the DataSet.

The Add method of the data adapter's TableMappings collection accepts a source and destination table name. From the data adapter's point of view, every result set generated by a command is a table. By default, the source tables in a data adapter are named Table, Table1, and so on.

USING A STORED PROCEDURE Using multiple data adapters allows you to populate a DataSet with tables from completely independent database servers. However, if your tables reside on the same SQL server, you might want to consider using a stored procedure to return the tables at the same time:

```
CREATE PROCEDURE spGetAllEmployeeInfo
AS
SELECT SSN, LastName, FirstName, Age FROM Person
SELECT SSN, Dept, Salary, HireDate FROM Employee
```

The stored procedure declaration for spGetAllEmployeeInfo includes two SELECT queries. The following code, slightly modified from Listing 22.4, retrieves both tables using a single SQLDataAdapter object:

```
Dim cn As SqlConnection
Dim cmdGetAll As SqlCommand
Dim adAllInfo As SqlDataAdapter
Dim dsResults As DataSet

'INITIALIZE OBJECTS
cn = New SqlConnection("server=bsw2k;uid=sa;pwd=;database=BrianTest")
adAllInfo = New SqlDataAdapter()
dsResults = New DataSet()

'SET UP COMMAND
cmdGetAll = New SqlCommand("spGetAllEmployeeInfo", cn)
cmdGetAll.CommandType = CommandType.StoredProcedure
adAllInfo.SelectCommand = cmdGetAll

'SET UP MAPPINGS
adAllInfo.TableMappings.Add("Table", "Person")
adAllInfo.TableMappings.Add("Table1", "Employee")

'FILL DATASET
cn.Open()
adAllInfo.Fill(dsResults)
cn.Close()
```

The two sets of records returned by the stored procedure are assigned the generic names Table and Table1 in the data adapter, so mappings were added to give them more meaningful names in the DataSet. When thinking of the tables in a data adapter keep in mind the number of "tables" is based on the number of sets of records returned, not the number of tables in the SQL statement itself. In other words, the following SQL statement would look like a single table (called Table) to the data adapter:

```
SELECT * FROM Person P, Employee E WHERE P.SSN = E.SSN
```

If multiple fields with the same name are returned in the same source table (SSN in the preceding example), the data adapter follows the same naming convention as it does with tables (SSN, SSN1, and so on).

ADDING CONSTRAINTS AND RELATIONSHIPS

In addition to storing tables, a DataSet object has the capability to store relationships and constraints, just like a regular database. Because a DataSet can be modified while disconnected from the database, the database management system is not present to enforce constraints such as unique fields and primary keys. Recall our last example, in which we created a DataSet containing the Person and Employee tables we created in Chapter 20. When these tables were created in the DataSet, key and constraint information was not automatically transferred. Fortunately, this information can be added with a few lines of code, as shown in Listing 22.5.

LISTING 22.5   DATAGRIDEXAMPLE.ZIP—ADDING KEY CONSTRAINTS

```
'SET UP COLUMN OBJECTS FOR EASY ACCESS
Dim colSSNP, colSSNE As DataColumn
colSSNP = m_dsMain.Tables("Person").Columns("SSN")
colSSNE = m_dsMain.Tables("Employee").Columns("SSN")

'CREATE PRIMARY KEYS
Dim arPersKey(1) As DataColumn
Dim arEmplKey(2) As DataColumn
arPersKey(0) = colSSNP
arEmplKey(0) = colSSNE
arEmplKey(1) = m_dsMain.Tables("Employee").Columns("Dept")
m_dsMain.Tables("Person").PrimaryKey = arPersKey
m_dsMain.Tables("Employee").PrimaryKey = arEmplKey

'CREATE FOREIGN KEY FOR CASCADING DELETE
Dim fkSSN As ForeignKeyConstraint
fkSSN = New ForeignKeyConstraint("SSNForKey", colSSNP, colSSNE)
fkSSN.DeleteRule = Rule.Cascade
m_dsMain.Tables("Employee").Constraints.Add(fkSSN)
```

The code in Listing 22.5 introduces a new object, the DataColumn, which represents a field in a data table. The PrimaryKey property of each table in a DataSet can be set to an array of these columns to define the primary key. The SSN column is the primary key for the Person table. The SSN and Dept columns together are the primary key for the Employee table. SSN is also a foreign key in the Employee table, so in order to maintain database integrity, we should delete a record from the Employee table if the corresponding person was deleted from the Person table. By creating a ForeignKeyConstraint object, we can ensure that this happens automatically.

DISPLAYING A DataSet'S CONTENTS

Sometimes visual aids can help a presentation. As we continue to discuss the many aspects of the DataSet class, you may want to display the actual records to get a feel for what is happening behind the scenes. In our discussion this far, we have only mentioned using a message box or a Debug.Writeline statement to display field values. However, with only a few lines of code you can display this data on the screen in a tabular format. This is accomplished through the magic of *data binding*.

UNDERSTANDING DATA BINDING

The concept of data binding means associating a control on a form with a field or data table. The control handles navigation, updates, and deletes so you do not have to write code to update the records in the DataSet bound to it. In previous versions of Visual Basic, data binding meant foregoing a lot of control over the communication between your application and the database. As a result, data binding received a bad reputation in the VB community. Many developers think that data binding is for novice programmers only. However, in a disconnected environment, data-bound controls do not talk to the database directly, but rather to a local data store. In this case, data binding may once again become acceptable in the user interface tier.

USING A DATAGRID CONTROL

If you have created the sample database from Chapter 20 and are following along with the code samples, the following exercise will allow you to display contents of a DataSet containing the Person and Employee tables.

1. Start a new Windows Application project.
2. Add a Button control to the form. Set its Name property to btnLoad and its Text property to Load Data.
3. Add two DataGrid controls to the form. Set their Name properties to grdPerson and grdEmployee.
4. Add the code from Listing 22.6 to the form class.

LISTING 22.6   DATAGRIDEXAMPLE.ZIP—DISPLAYING DATA IN A DATAGRID CONTROL

```
Imports System.Data.SqlClient
Public Class frmMain
    Inherits System.Windows.Forms.Form
    Private m_dsWork As DataSet
    Private Sub btnLoad_Click(ByVal sender As System.Object,_
    ByVal e As System.EventArgs)_
        Handles btnLoad.Click
        Dim cn As SqlConnection
        Dim cmdGetAll As SqlCommand
        Dim adAllInfo As SqlDataAdapter

        'INITIALIZE OBJECTS
        cn = New SqlConnection("server=localhost;uid=sa;pwd=;database=BrianTest")
        adAllInfo = New SqlDataAdapter()
        m_dsWork = New DataSet()

        'SET UP COMMAND
        cmdGetAll = New SqlCommand("spGetAllEmployeeInfo", cn)
        cmdGetAll.CommandType = CommandType.StoredProcedure
        adAllInfo.SelectCommand = cmdGetAll

        'SET UP MAPPINGS
        adAllInfo.TableMappings.Add("Table", "Person")
        adAllInfo.TableMappings.Add("Table1", "Employee")
```

LISTING 22.6 CONTINUED

```
            'FILL DATASET
            cn.Open()
            adAllInfo.Fill(m_dsWork)
            cn.Close()

            'SET UP COLUMN OBJECTS FOR EASY ACCESS
            Dim colSSNP, colSSNE As DataColumn
            colSSNP = m_dsWork.Tables("Person").Columns("SSN")
            colSSNE = m_dsWork.Tables("Employee").Columns("SSN")

            'CREATE PRIMARY KEYS
            Dim arPersKey(1) As DataColumn
            Dim arEmplKey(2) As DataColumn
            arPersKey(0) = colSSNP
            arEmplKey(0) = colSSNE
            arEmplKey(1) = m_dsWork.Tables("Employee").Columns("Dept")
            m_dsWork.Tables("Person").PrimaryKey = arPersKey
            m_dsWork.Tables("Employee").PrimaryKey = arEmplKey

            'CREATE FOREIGN KEY FOR CASCADING DELETE
            Dim fkSSN As ForeignKeyConstraint
            fkSSN = New ForeignKeyConstraint("SSNForKey", colSSNP, colSSNE)
            fkSSN.DeleteRule = Rule.Cascade
            m_dsWork.Tables("Employee").Constraints.Add(fkSSN)

            'BIND TABLES TO GRIDS
            grdPerson.DataSource = m_dsWork
            grdPerson.DataMember = "Person"
            grdPerson.CaptionText = "Person"

            grdEmployee.DataSource = m_dsWork
            grdEmployee.DataMember = "Employee"
            grdEmployee.CaptionText = "Employee"
        End Sub
End Class
```

The code in Listing 22.6 is a combination of the code from previous sections, with two important differences. First, the DataSet variable has been moved to the class level, so it will not fall out of scope as long as the form is loaded. Second, four lines of code were added to bind the DataSet to the two DataGrid controls. Each grid has a DataSource property, which is assigned to the DataSet m_dsWork. The tables are specified using the DataMember property. Run the sample application and your form should look similar to Figure 22.3.

Figure 22.3
Changes made to the data grids will be reflected in the DataSet.

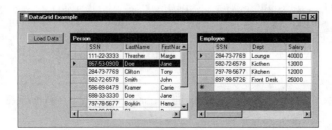

You should be able to enter new records, edit values, or even delete a record (by using record selector column and pressing the Delete key). Note that if you delete a record from the Person table, the corresponding record or records in the Employee table will disappear due to our foreign key constraint.

USING A FILTER TO DETERMINE DISPLAY ROWS

In Listing 22.6, we assigned the DataTable object to the DataMember property of the grid, and it dutifully displayed every field in the table with full editing capabilities. However, there may be times when you only want to display certain rows, or prohibit users from editing their contents. You determine the records within a table that are visible using a *filter*. A filter is like a WHERE clause in SQL—it limits the records returned based on criteria. Continuing with the example from the last section, perform the following steps to create a filtered view of the Person table:

1. Add another Button control to your form. Set its Name property to btnFilter and its Text property to Filter.

2. Add a text box to the form. Set its Name property to txtFilter and its Text property to a blank string.

3. Add the following code to the Click event for btnFilter:

```
'CLEAR CURRENT BINDING
grdPerson.DataMember = ""
grdPerson.DataSource = Nothing

'MODIFY AND BIND DEFAULT TABLE VIEW
With m_dsWork.Tables("Person")
    .DefaultView.RowFilter = "LastName Like '" & txtFilter.Text & "%'"
    .DefaultView.AllowDelete = False
    .DefaultView.AllowEdit = False
    .DefaultView.AllowNew = False
    grdPerson.DataSource = .DefaultView
End With

grdPerson.CaptionText = "Filtered on Last Name"
```

4. Start the sample program and click the Load Data button.

5. Enter the first few characters of a last name into the text box and click the Filter button. You should see the data grid change to reflect the filter.

The code in Step 3 introduces the concept of a view, which is very similar to a table but can be filtered and sorted as desired. A view does not contain its own data, but rather points to the data in the underlying data table. In addition to modifying the default view, you can create your own DataView objects and bind them to various controls.

Note

DataView objects can be used to control table access and filter records, but not columns like a SQL view.

VERIFYING MODIFIED RECORDS

A `DataTable` object contains multiple `DataRow` objects, each of which represents a record in the table. You can modify the contents of your `DataSet` either by changing the values of a particular `DataRow` object, or using a bound control like the data grid as described in the previous section. One interesting feature of the `DataSet` class is the ability to tell which rows have been modified. This is important because your `DataSet` is disconnected from a database; you need some way to know if rows were added, deleted, or updated so changes can be sent to a database. For example, suppose your table contains 1,000 rows of data and the end user modifies only a single row. Depending on the design of your application, it may be more efficient to pass only the changed row back to the business layer. The following properties and methods can be used to manage changes in a `DataSet`:

- `RowState`—Determines what change has been made to a row, if any.
- `GetChanges`—Returns a new `DataSet` object containing only the changed rows.
- `AcceptChanges`—Commits all outstanding changes to the current `DataSet`, resetting the `RowState` property.
- `RejectChanges`—Rolls back `DataSet` changes to the original version, or the version since the last call to `AcceptChanges`.

To test these methods, again return to the sample project. Perform the following steps:

1. Add three new button controls, `btnAccept`, `btnReject`, and `btnView`. Set their `Text` properties to `Accept Changes`, `Reject Changes`, and `View Changes`.

2. Add the code from Listing 22.7 to your form:

LISTING 22.7 DATAGRIDEXAMPLE.ZIP—VIEWING CHANGED RECORDS

```
Private Sub btnAccept_Click(ByVal sender As System.Object,_
    ByVal e As System.EventArgs) Handles btnAccept.Click
  m_dsWork.AcceptChanges()
  grdPerson.DataSource = m_dsWork
  grdEmployee.DataSource = m_dsWork
End Sub

Private Sub btnReject_Click(ByVal sender As System.Object,_
    ByVal e As System.EventArgs) Handles btnReject.Click
  m_dsWork.RejectChanges()
  grdPerson.DataSource = m_dsWork
  grdEmployee.DataSource = m_dsWork
End Sub

Private Sub btnView_Click(ByVal sender As System.Object,_
    ByVal e As System.EventArgs) Handles btnView.Click
  Dim dsTemp As DataSet
  dsTemp = m_dsWork.GetChanges()
  dsTemp.Tables("Person").DefaultView.RowStateFilter = _
  Dataviewrowstate.ModifiedCurrent Or dataviewrowstate.New
  dsTemp.Tables("Employee").DefaultView.RowStateFilter = _
```

LISTING 22.7   CONTINUED

```
    Dataviewrowstate.ModifiedCurrent Or dataviewrowstate.New
    grdPerson().DataSource = dsTemp
    grdEmployee().DataSource = dsTemp
End Sub
```

---

3. Run the sample program and click `Load Data`. Pick one of the rows of data and modify the person's name. Delete another row. Finally, move to the bottom of the grid and enter a new row for the `Person` table.

4. Click the `View Changes` button. The grids should show the records you added and modified. (The grid does not display deleted rows, although they can be accessed via code.)

5. Click the `Reject Changes` button and the grids should return to their original state, erasing any changes you made.

6. Repeat Step 3 and then click the `Accept Changes` button.

7. Click `View Changes`. This time the grids should be blank, because you accepted outstanding changes.

The code in Listing 22.7 again makes use of a view, although instead of filtering records we filter the row state. You can use an `Or` expression to filter multiple row states, although deleted records will not be displayed in a bound data grid.

UPDATING THE SOURCE DATABASE

You already have enough knowledge to update a database from a `DataSet`. For example, you could loop through the changed rows in a `DataSet` and call the appropriate stored procedure depending on the value of the `RowState` property. However, Microsoft has attempted to do some of the work for you by providing the `Update` method of the data adapter. You can set up additional command objects in the data adapter and then call the `Update` method to process changes in the `DataSet`. The process is similar to filling a `DataSet`, in that you set up a command and provide mappings.

SETTING UP THE COMMANDS

In the example `DataSet` used throughout this chapter, we selected a few columns from the `Person` table. The following stored procedure processes an update to the `Person` table for all those fields:

```
CREATE PROCEDURE spPersonUpdate
  @strOriginalSSN char(11),
  @strNewSSN char(11),
  @strLastName char(20),
  @strFirstName char(20),
  @intAge  int
AS
  UPDATE Person
  SET SSN=@strNewSSN,
      LastName=@strLastName,
```

```
        FirstName=@strFirstName,
        Age=@intAge
    WHERE SSN = @strOriginalSSN
```

As you may recall from previous sections, a `SQLCommand` object for the previous stored procedure will require several `Parameter` objects. However, instead of setting the `Value` property to define the value passed to the stored procedure, we will use two new properties: `SourceColumn` and `SourceVersion`. The following lines of code show how these properties are used to map the stored procedure parameters to `DataSet` columns:

```
Dim cmdUpdate As SqlCommand
Dim parmTemp As SqlParameter

cmdUpdate = New SqlCommand()
cmdUpdate.CommandText = "spPersonUpdate"
cmdUpdate.CommandType = CommandType.StoredProcedure
cmdUpdate.Connection = cn

parmTemp = cmdUpdate.Parameters.Add("@strOriginalSSN", SqlDbType.Char)
parmTemp.SourceColumn = "SSN"
parmTemp.SourceVersion = DataRowVersion.Original

parmTemp = cmdUpdate.Parameters.Add("@strNewSSN", SqlDbType.Char)
parmTemp.SourceColumn = "SSN"
parmTemp.SourceVersion = DataRowVersion.Current

parmTemp = cmdUpdate.Parameters.Add("@strLastName", SqlDbType.Char)
parmTemp.SourceColumn = "LastName"
parmTemp.SourceVersion = DataRowVersion.Current

parmTemp = cmdUpdate.Parameters.Add("@strFirstName", SqlDbType.Char)
parmTemp.SourceColumn = "FirstName"
parmTemp.SourceVersion = DataRowVersion.Current

parmTemp = cmdUpdate.Parameters.Add("@intAge", SqlDbType.Int)
parmTemp.SourceColumn = "Age"
parmTemp.SourceVersion = DataRowVersion.Current
```

In the preceding sample code, the `SourceColumn` property is the name of the data table column that will be sent for each row to be updated. The `SourceVersion` property is usually set to `Current` to provide the most current version of the column value. However, when updating a primary key field, you need both the current and original version to update the correct record. Therefore, we pass two versions of the `SSN` column to the stored procedure.

CALLING THE Update METHOD

After creating the commands for each type of database change, you need to assign the `SQLCommand` objects to the `InsertCommand`, `UpdateCommand`, and `DeleteCommand` properties of a `SQLDataAdapter` object:

```
Dim adPerson As SqlDataAdapter
adPerson = New SqlDataAdapter()
adPerson.UpdateCommand = cmdUpdate
adPerson.DeleteCommand = cmdDelete
adPerson.InsertCommand = cmdInsert
```

Finally, execute the Update method, specifying the name of the DataSet and data table to be updated:

```
cn.Open()
adPerson.Update(m_dsWork, "Person")
cn.Close()
```

The Update method will execute the appropriate SQLCommand object, depending on how a given row in the data table has been modified. After executing the previous lines of code, any changes made in the DataSet should be reflected in the Person table.

Note

If you call the Update method using a DataSet in which records have been deleted, inserted, or updated, you must have valid command objects associated with these actions or an exception will occur. (If you only want to process a particular type of update, use the GetChanges function described earlier to create a new DataSet with the desired row states.)

LIMITING NETWORK TRAFFIC

In our previous examples, we populated the DataSet object from a database. This is perfectly acceptable for most applications, especially if the user needs to edit existing information. However, if your application just needs to add new records, you may want to create a blank DataSet with code to avoid an unnecessary database query. This way, your application does not incur the overhead of talking to the database until it is actually ready to insert new records. To create a DataSet object from code, create DataTable objects and then append them to a DataSet object, as in the following example:

```
Dim tblStates As DataTable
tblStates = New DataTable()
tblStates.Columns.Add(New DataColumn("State", GetType(String)))
tblStates.Columns.Add(New DataColumn("Population", GetType(Long)))

Dim dsStateInfo As DataSet
dsStateInfo = New DataSet()
dsStateInfo.Tables.Add(tblStates)
```

The data table in the previous example only contains two columns and no constraints, so the code to create new data set is minimal. However, if your DataSet requires a lot of tables with very complex relations, writing code to create an empty DataSet could be a daunting task. The performance gain is not always worth the effort of duplicating a table definition that already exists in a database. If you are on a fast network and have to connect for other reasons, you may want to consider using the Fill Schema method, shown here:

```
adAllInfo.FillSchema(m_dsWork, SchemaType.Mapped)
```

The previous code sample creates a new DataSet containing the *schema* of any tables. A table schema is the definition of a table's column names and data types. If the previous line of code were used in place of the Fill method from Listing 22.6, the DataSet m_dsWork would contain blank Person and Employee tables. Although it required a connection to the database, no actual rows were transferred back to the client. You can, of course, still add new rows on the client with code:

```
Dim rowTemp As DataRow
Dim tblPerson As DataTable

tblPerson = m_dsWork.Tables("Person")

'CREATE THE NEW ROW
rowTemp = tblPerson.NewRow
rowTemp.Item("SSN") = "123-45-6789"
rowTemp.Item("LastName") = "Simpson"
rowTemp.Item("FirstName") = "Homer"

'ADD THE NEW ROW
tblPerson.Rows.Add(rowTemp)
```

These lines of code add a new row to the Person table. Notice that we used the NewRow method to initialize rowTemp with the correct schema.

> **Note**
>
> New rows added to a DataSet will have a RowState of New until you call the AcceptChanges method as described earlier.

It should also be mentioned that the DataTable can be created and used independently of the DataSet, and is a valid parameter to both the Fill and FillSchema methods of a DataAdapter:

```
tblTemp = New DataTable()
adPerson.Fill(tblTemp)
grdEmployee.DataSource = tblTemp
```

If your data requirements are simple enough, you may want to use the DataTable object instead of the more complex DataSet.

USING TYPED DataSets

Another interesting feature of the .NET framework is the ability to represent DataSet objects as typed entities within your program. Consider the following two lines of code:

```
LastName = dsResults.Tables(0).Rows(5).Item("LastName")
FirstName = dsResultsTyped.Person(5).FirstName
```

The first line of code accesses the LastName field of the Person table using the traditional, collection-based approach. The second line of code uses typed data access, identifying the table and field names directly in Visual Basic code. Typed DataSets allow you to access their members using full Intellisense capability, just as you would any other object in your program.

Because data generally comes from a database and is generated dynamically at runtime, you must define the custom DataSet class at design time in order to access it in a typed manner. The .NET framework uses XML to represent DataSets, and Visual Studio includes an XML designer that lets you easily create a custom DataSet class. You can set up the tables and field definitions manually, or connect to a database and import them. In an upcoming chapter, you will see how to create a typed DataSet definition from an existing DataSet object.

→ To learn about creating a schema from a DataSet, **see** Chapter 23, "Creating and Using Reports," **p. 637**

To add a new DataSet to your program, right-click the project name in the Solution Explorer and choose to Add a New Item, then DataSet from the menu. A new file with an xsd extension will be added to your product. (XSD stands for XML Schema Definition. The schema stores information about the DataSet, not data itself.) The easiest way to build your DataSet is to use the Server Explorer. As you learned in Chapter 20, the Server Explorer allows you to browse the contents of a database visually. To add table definitions to your DataSet, drag the table name from the Server Explorer to the XML designer. Figure 22.4 shows the XML designer after dragging adding Employee and Person tables to the designer.

→ To find out how to connect to a database with the Server Explorer, **see** Chapter 20, "Database Basics," **p. 535**

Figure 22.4
A custom data class can be built using Visual Studio .NET's XML designer.

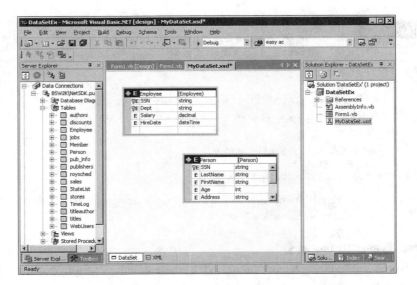

Once you have completed designing the DataSet, you can create an instance of it in your project just as you would any other object:

```
Dim dsInfo as New MyDataSet()
```

Because the MyDataSet class is inherited from the DataSet class, you can fill the DataSet from a database using the same methods described earlier.

Note

To change the type name for your custom DataSet, set the dataSetName property in the XML designer.

BUILDING A REUSABLE DATA ACCESS LAYER

The layers of a multi-tier application are usually specific to the application's domain. The data layer, for example, contains code to execute only the stored procedures used by that particular application. Layers can be reusable in other applications if the functions they perform are needed elsewhere. For example, the business tier in an Accounts Payable application could talk to the business tier in Personnel to validate employee names on expense reports. This type of reusability is one of the main advantages of object-oriented programming. However, across all your applications there will likely be some common data-layer functions. For example, you need code to connect to a database, execute a stored procedure by name, and so on, no matter what the application domain. Rather than duplicating these functions with each new data layer, you can build a data access module that will be used in each project. Some advantages of using a shared data access module are as follows:

- Developers can quickly access database functions.

- Connection strings are easy to maintain and change.

- Monitoring and tuning database activity can be performed in one place.

- Data access techniques are consistent across multiple projects.

In this section, we'll walk through developing a module that performs several common data access functions. You may want to use this code (or some version of it) in your own projects.

> **Note**
>
> The sample Data Access layer described here is designed for SQL Server, although it would not be hard to adapt it to create an OLEDB version. To do this, you will need to replace the SQL-prefixed classes with their OLEDB equivalents and modify the connection string appropriately.

DESIGNING THE DATA ACCESS MODULE

Any application that uses a database has several basic data operations: queries, inserts, updates, and deletes. Each of these activities can be characterized as either returning rows or not returning rows. In addition, these tasks may be performed using dynamic SQL generated by your program or, more ideally, using stored procedures. Therefore, in designing a generic data access module, we need functions that perform at least the following operations:

- Execute a stored procedure, with or without returning data.

- Perform a dynamic SQL query, with or without returning data.

To meet these requirements, we will need to define several custom functions in our data layer, as described in the following sections.

Managing Database Connections

One benefit of a shared data access module is making connection management easier for the application developer. To achieve this goal in our data module, we will store connection strings in a common area, the Windows registry. Each data access function will have an AppID parameter, which stands for "Application ID." The data access module will use this application ID to find the appropriate connection string. The code in Listing 22.8 defines a function called GetConnectionString that retrieves connection information from the registry using a key based on the application ID.

Listing 22.8 DATALAYER.ZIP—Managing Connections

```
Private Function GetConnectionString(ByVal strAppID As String) As String

    Const CompanyRegistryArea As String = "SOFTWARE\MyCompany\"
    Dim strRegPath As String = CompanyRegistryArea & strAppID
    Dim RegTemp As RegistryKey

    RegTemp = Registry.LocalMachine.OpenSubKey(strRegPath, False)
    Return RegTemp.GetValue("ConnectionString", "").ToString

End Function
```

The code in Listing 22.8 uses the Registry class (discussed in Chapter 24) to retrieve information from a common area of the registry.

→ For more on accessing the registry from VB.NET, **see** Chapter 24, "Working with Files" **p. 667**

Each application setting is stored in a key under a common area for the entire company. For example, connection information for the WEBSTORE application would be located under the following registry key:

HKEY_LOCAL_MACHINE\SOFTWARE\MyCompany\WEBSTORE

Storing connection information in the registry makes it easy to connect to different databases without recompiling your application. Simply set the ConnectionString value to a valid connection string using the REGEDIT utility. In addition, when the developer writes code, he only needs to be concerned with setting the correct application ID.

Note

Accessing the registry every time you make a database connection does require some overhead, but in the author's opinion, the overhead is outweighed by increased flexibility.

Managing Parameters

As we mentioned earlier, one common function of every data access layer is the ability to execute stored procedures. Stored procedures usually have parameters. Although the names and data types of any given stored procedure's parameters are application-specific, the process of executing a parameterized stored procedure is not. Therefore, we should be able to include a generic function in our data access module to set up a SQLCommand object for any given stored procedure. In order to accomplish this, we need a way for the calling function to pass in a set of parameters, as well as a method of returning output parameters. This brings about an interesting dilemma. In order to write a function that accepts an arbitrary number of parameters, we'll need to make use of an array or collection. The Parameters collection would be ideal, but it is part of a command object and cannot be created independently. Therefore, we'll need to accept parameters in a variable array and then add them to the SQLCommand using the Add method. The code in Listing 22.9 defines the necessary functions so the data access module can covert the parameter arrays to and from the SQLCommand object.

LISTING 22.9 DATALAYER.ZIP—MANAGING PARAMETERS

```
Private Sub PopulateCommandParms(ByVal arParms() As SqlParameter,_
     ByRef cmd As SqlCommand)

   'Adds each parameter in the array to the command object
   Dim i As Integer
   For i = LBound(arParms) To UBound(arParms)
      cmd.Parameters.Add(arParms(i))
   Next

End Sub

Private Sub PopulateOutputParms(ByVal cmd As SqlCommand,_
     ByRef arParms() As SqlParameter)

   'Copies output parameter values back into the array
   'Assumes parameter array is already populated
   Dim i As Integer
   For i = LBound(arParms) To UBound(arParms)
      If arParms(i).Direction = ParameterDirection.Output Then
            arParms(i).Value = cmd.Parameters(arParms(i).ParameterName).Value
      End If
   Next

End Sub
```

At first glance, the code in Listing 22.9 may seem like an unnecessary step, because adding parameters to a command is very easy. However, the benefit is that the calling function does not have to get involved with setting up the SQLCommand object at all.

CREATING THE PUBLIC FUNCTIONS

Now that we have created all the necessary support functions for our data access module, we will define the Public functions available to the data layer. The functions in Listing 22.10 can execute arbitrary stored procedures and SQL statements.

LISTING 22.10 DATALAYER.ZIP—CREATING THE ExecSP AND ExecSQL SUBROUTINES

```
Public Sub ExecSP(ByVal strAppID As String, _
               ByVal strProcName As String, _
               ByRef intReturnVal As Integer, _
```

LISTING 22.10   CONTINUED

```
                        Optional ByRef ParmArray() As SqlParameter = Nothing, _
                        Optional ByRef dsResults As DataSet = Nothing)

    Dim cn As SqlConnection
    Dim cmd As SqlCommand
    Dim adt As SqlDataAdapter

    'ESTABLISH THE CONNECTION
    cn = New SqlConnection()
    cn.ConnectionString = GetConnectionString(strAppID)
    cn.Open()

    'SET UP THE SQLCOMMAND OBJECT
    cmd = New SqlCommand()
    cmd.CommandText = strProcName
    cmd.CommandType = CommandType.StoredProcedure
    cmd.Connection = cn

    'SET UP PARAMETERS
    If Not (ParmArray Is Nothing) Then
        Call PopulateCommandParms(ParmArray, cmd)
    End If

    'EXECUTE THE COMMAND
    If dsResults Is Nothing Then
        intReturnVal = cmd.ExecuteNonQuery()
    Else
        dsResults = New DataSet()
        adt = New SqlDataAdapter()
        adt.SelectCommand = cmd
        intReturnVal = adt.Fill(dsResults)
    End If

    'CLOSE CONNECTION
    cn.Close()

    'POPULATE OUTPUT PARAMETERS
    If Not (ParmArray Is Nothing) Then
        Call PopulateOutputParms(cmd, ParmArray)
    End If

End Sub

Public Sub ExecSQL(ByVal strAppID As String, _
                   ByVal strSQLCmd As String, _
                   ByRef intReturnVal As Integer, _
                   Optional ByRef dsResults As DataSet = Nothing)

    Dim cn As SqlConnection
    Dim cmd As SqlCommand
    Dim adt As SqlDataAdapter

    'FIRST, ESTABLISH THE CONNECTION
    cn = New SqlConnection()
```

LISTING 22.10   CONTINUED

```
cn.ConnectionString = GetConnectionString(strAppID)
cn.Open()

'SET UP THE SQLCOMMAND OBJECT
cmd = New SqlCommand(strSQLCmd, cn)

'EXECUTE THE COMMAND
If dsResults Is Nothing Then
    intReturnVal = cmd.ExecuteNonQuery()
Else
    dsResults = New DataSet()
    adt = New SqlDataAdapter()
    adt.SelectCommand = cmd
    intReturnVal = adt.Fill(dsResults)
End If

'CLOSE CONNECTION
cn.Close()
```

```
End Sub
```

The key to the versatility of the code in Listing 22.10 is the parameter list. By using optional parameters and the `ByRef` keyword, the `ExecSP` and `ExecSQL` subroutines are able to handle a variety of different SQL statements.

→ For more on function parameters, **see** Chapter 8, "Managing Program Tasks with Procedures." **p. 201**

For example, if the calling function does not pass a `DataSet` object, the `ExecSP` procedure uses the `ExecuteNonQuery` method and returns the number of rows affected. In addition, the `PopulateCommandParms` function is only called if necessary, allowing the execution of parameter-less stored procedures.

EXERCISE: USING THE DATA ACCESS MODULE

Now that we have created a set of generic database functions, we'll put them to use in a sample project. To begin, create a new Windows Application project, called `TestApp`. Perform the following steps to set up all the necessary components of this project:

1. Rename the form to `frmUILayer`.
2. Add two new classes to the project, named `clsBusinessLayer` and `clsDataLayer`.
3. Add a new module to the project, named `DataFuncs.vb`.
4. Copy the code from Listings 22.8, 22.9, and 22.10 into the `DataFuncs.vb` module.

When you have completed these steps, open the Solution Explorer window and verify that it looks like the one in Figure 22.5.

Now that you have set up the framework for the application, we can begin programming the individual layers. For the sake of expediency, we will continue to use the existing `Person` table.

Figure 22.5
The sample project is a simple multi-tier application.

PLANNING THE REQUIREMENTS

The motivation for any program starts with the requirements. For our sample project, let's assume the requirement is to determine the maximum age of a person in a particular state. (As you may recall from earlier in the chapter, we have already defined a stored procedure that will accomplish this task). From this basic requirement, we can determine the shell of some functions in the business layer:

- GetMaxAgeByState—This function accepts a state parameter (as a String) and returns an integer containing the maximum age.

- GetStateList—This subroutine simply returns a list of valid states.

The user interface layer will call the preceding two functions in the business layer. To get started with the sample application, open the Code editor for the clsBusinessLayer class. Enter the following lines of code:

```
Public Sub GetMaxAgeByState(ByVal strState As String, ByRef intMaxAge As Integer)

End Sub
Public Sub GetStateList(ByRef dsStates As DataSet)

End Sub
```

In a multi-tier environment, the user-interface layer only talks to the business layer. Although the code in our business layer does not actually do anything yet, defining the skeleton functions allows us to work on the business layer or the user interface independently.

BUILDING THE USER INTERFACE

To design the user interface for our sample application, open the designer window for the frmUILayer form. Perform the following steps to create the UI code that interacts with the clsBusinessLayer class.

1. Add a Button control to the form. Set its Name property to btnGetAge and its Text property to Find Max Age.

2. Add a ComboBox control to the form. Set its Name property to cmbStateList and its DropDownStyle property to DropDownList.

3. Add the following lines of code to the end of the form's New subroutine.

```
Dim BusObj As clsBusinessLayer
Dim dsStates As DataSet
DsStates = New DataSet()
BusObj = New clsBusinessLayer()
Call BusObj.GetStateList(dsStates)
cmbStateList.DataSource = dsStates.Tables(0).DefaultView
cmbStateList.DisplayMember = "State"
```

4. Add the following lines of code to the Click event for btnGetAge.

```
If cmbStateList.SelectedIndex = -1 Then
    messagebox.Show("Please select a state!")
Else
    Dim BusObj As clsBusinessLayer
    Dim intMaxAge As Integer
    Dim strStateCode As String

    BusObj = New clsBusinessLayer()
    strStateCode = cmbStateList().Text
    Call BusObj.GetMaxAgeByState(strStateCode, intMaxAge)
    Messagebox.Show("Maximum age is " & intMaxAge.ToString)

End If
```

After completing the previous steps, you have completed the user interface layer of the sample application. The next step is to complete the data layer.

CODING THE DATA LAYER

The data layer of an application is based on a database, so you need to make sure the database contains the necessary stored procedures. If you have been following the examples throughout the chapter, you should have already created the spGetMaxAgeByState stored procedure. If you have not already done so, create the stored procedure now. In addition, you need to edit the registry using REGEDIT and add the connection string for your database, as described earlier. Finally, enter the following code in the clsDataLayer class to create the data layer:

```
Public Sub GetStates(ByRef dsStates As DataSet)
    Dim strSQL As String
    Dim intRetval As Integer
    strSQL = "SELECT DISTINCT State FROM Person ORDER BY State"
    Call ExecSQL("MYAPP", strSQL, intRetval, dsStates)

End Sub

Public Sub GetMaxAgeByState(ByVal strState As String, ByRef intAge As Integer)

    Dim intRetVal As Integer
    Dim parmArray(1) As SqlParameter

    parmArray(0) = New SqlParameter("@strState", SqlDbType.Char)
    parmArray(0).Value = strState

    parmArray(1) = New SqlParameter("@intResult", SqlDbType.Int)
    parmArray(1).Direction = ParameterDirection.Output
```

```
    Call ExecSP("MYAPP", "spGetMaxAgeByState", intRetVal, parmArray)

    intAge = Convert.ToInt32(parmArray(1).Value)

End Sub
```

The GetStates and GetMaxAgeByState routines make use of our data access module defined earlier to execute a stored procedure and a dynamic SQL query.

COMPLETING THE BUSINESS OBJECT

The final step in the sample application is to complete the business tier by finishing the two functions entered earlier. To accomplish this, open the clsBusinessLayer class and complete the functions as follows:

```
Public Sub GetStateList(ByRef dsStates As DataSet)
    Dim objData As clsDataLayer
    objData = New clsDataLayer()
    Call objData.GetStates(dsStates)
End Sub
Public Sub GetMaxAgeByState(ByVal strState As String, ByRef intMaxAge As Integer)
    Dim objData As clsDataLayer
    objData = New clsDataLayer()
    Call objData.GetMaxAgeByState(strState, intMaxAge)
End Sub
```

The previous business layer functions don't do a lot other than pass parameters to the data layer. Although you might be tempted just to call the data layer directly from the UI, don't! Remember, the business layer knows about *business* logic, and in a real application some changes to the data or creation of other structures might be required.

EXECUTING THE PROGRAM

Finally the sample application is complete. To test the application, execute the program. The combo box will be populated with a list of state abbreviations. Select one and click the button to display the maximum age in the state.

It may seem like a lot of work to create all the various classes and modules for a relatively simple task. However, look at all the advantages:

- By using the DataFuncs.vb module, you were able to execute database queries with fewer lines of code.
- The application was segmented so that only the data layer had to be concerned with connecting to the database.
- You can easily point the application to another SQL server by editing the registry.
- You can use an entirely different type of database by replacing the data layer, without having to rewrite the entire application.

Congratulations on successfully implementing a multi-tier data access application! Although this chapter focused on the data aspects of such an application, there is a lot more to learn about this application architecture. For more information on related topics, please see the following sections:

- Chapter 9, "Creating Code Components" contains information about remoting, which enables you to access business objects across a network.

- Chapter 18, "Web Applications and Services" shows you how to expose a business object's functionality as a Web service.

- Chapter 26, "Debugging and Performance Tuning" describes a way to add error handling and performance monitoring to your database applications.

CREATING AND USING REPORTS

In this chapter

Despite the high availability of electronic and online information, the "paperless office" remains a fantasy. Printed reports are still an important part of most software systems. In this chapter, we will discuss two different techniques you can use to add report-printing capability to your Visual Basic applications. First, we will look at the Windows forms `Printing` namespace, which allows you to precisely control low-level printer operations using Visual Basic code. The second half of the chapter covers Crystal Reports, a professional reporting tool included with Visual Studio .NET that allows you to quickly design complex data-driven reports. To demonstrate these techniques, we will create sales reports for a fictitious company that produces toys and food for cats.

PRINTING WITH WINDOWS FORMS

The .NET framework includes several classes you can use to interact with your printer. You can print text and graphics, as well as control printer settings such as margins and resolution. In addition, several classes create dialog boxes that make it easy for the end user to select printers or view a report onscreen before sending it to the printer. Printing in Windows Forms is graphics-based. Even if you want to print only lines of text, you still lay out your printed pages using graphics methods. These methods are the same methods that you use to draw on a Windows form and are located in the `System.Drawing.Graphics` namespace.

→ For more on graphics methods, **see** Chapter 14, "Designing an Effective User Interface," **p. 357**.

The classes that provide the additional functionality necessary to send graphics to the printer are located in the `System.Drawing.Printing` namespace. In this section, we will introduce some of the many classes in the .NET framework used to facilitate the printing process. In doing so, we will create a sales report for a cat food company.

PLANNING A REPORT

Relative to computer operations, a *report* is a very high-level concept, such as a report listing sales figures by employee. To implement a report with Windows Forms, you must translate the reporting requirements into lower-level method calls that tell the printer what it needs to do. Often, it is helpful to separate the report requirements into two basic areas:

- **Report data**—Most reports are based on database data. Before you write a line of Visual Basic code, you should know what fields you want on the report, as well as have the SQL query created. In the case of our sample report, we'll need to display the salesperson's name, number of orders, and total amount of the orders.

- **Report layout**—Designing a report is similar to designing a form. However, when you create a report entirely with code, you don't have the advantage of immediate visual feedback. For the sample report, we will have a simple three-column layout with the data fields previously mentioned. In addition, our report will have a header on each page containing the report title and company logo.

To begin following along with the example, perform the following steps:

1. Start a new Windows application project in Visual Studio .NET.

2. Add a `Button` control to the form. Set its `Name` property to `btnPrint` and its `Text` property to `Print Report`.

3. Open the code window for the form and add the following `Imports` statements to the top of the form class:

```
Imports System.Drawing.Printing
Imports System.Data.SqlClient
```

4. For the sample report, we will use data from the Northwind database, which is included with the .NET Framework SDK. To install this sample database, click the Start button, and then find the Microsoft .NET Framework SDK program group. Select Samples and QuickStart Tutorials.

5. From the Samples and QuickStart tutorials page, follow the steps to install and configure the samples. This process will install an instance of the Microsoft Database Engine containing the Northwind database.

In the remainder of this section, we will describe the code necessary to connect to the database and produce the sample sales report.

CREATING A `PrintDocument` OBJECT

If you have used previous editions of Visual Basic, such as version 6.0, you might recall using the `Printer` object. Although Windows Forms is the .NET equivalent to this type of printing, there is a big change in that printing is now event driven. Instead of continuously directing the printer operation from the start to finish of your printed document, you write code for several event procedures and associate them with a print job. The .NET Framework calls these event procedures when needed. Although this is a different way of thinking in relation to controlling the printer, it gives you the freedom to concentrate more on formatting your report, as well as provides some great new features such as print preview. In the sample project, you will create the following custom procedures in the form class:

- `PrintSalesReport`—Initiates the printing process

- `PrintSalesPage`—Event procedure that handles printing a single page

- `PrepareReportData`—Establishes the database connection and retrieves data

- `ReportProcessed`—Event procedure that is called when the report is finished

The `PrintDocument` class represents a print job to your application. To create a new print job, you simply create an instance of this class and add the appropriate event handlers. To get started on the sample project, add the following function to the form class:

```
Private Sub PrintSalesReport()
    Dim SalesReport As PrintDocument

    SalesReport = New PrintDocument()
    AddHandler SalesReport.PrintPage, AddressOf PrintSalesPage
```

```
        AddHandler SalesReport.BeginPrint, AddressOf PrepareReportData
        AddHandler SalesReport.EndPrint, AddressOf ReportProcessed
        SalesReport.Print()
End Sub
```

The `PrintSalesReport` subroutine demonstrates the typical technique for using the `PrintDocument` class. First, the `SalesReport` object is instantiated. Next, the `PrintPage` event is connected to an event handler. Finally, the `Print` method is called, which actually initiates the printing process.

Note

> Although entirely optional, you can also set the `DocumentName` property to a name that will be displayed in the Windows Print Manager and other dialog boxes.

After you have entered the `PrintSalesReport` function, add the following line of code to the `Click` event for `btnPrint`:

```
Call PrintSalesReport()
```

Now that you have created the code to start the print job, you need to add code to process the job's events.

UNDERSTANDING THE `PrintPage` EVENT

When you create a print job in Windows Forms, you have to write code that generates one page at a time, in response to the firing of the `PrintPage` event. To handle this event in our sample project, enter the code in Listing 23.1, which handles one page of the sales report.

LISTING 23.1   PRINTINGEXAMPLE.ZIP—CODING THE `PrintPage` EVENT

```
Sub PrintSalesPage(ByVal sender As Object, ByVal e As PrintPageEventArgs)

    Const NameX As Integer = 100
    Const OrderX As Integer = 300
    Const SalesX As Integer = 500

    Dim CompleteName As String
    Dim RecordsPerPage As Integer = 20
    Dim CurrentRecord As Integer = 0
    Dim CurrentY As Integer = 300
    Dim ReportFont As New Font("Arial", 12, FontStyle.Regular)
    Dim ReportFontHeight As Integer = ReportFont.GetHeight(e.Graphics)


    While CurrentRecord < RecordsPerPage

        'Place information from data reader current record on the page
        CompleteName = rdrSalesInfo.GetString(1).Trim & _
        ", " & rdrSalesInfo.GetString(0).Trim
        e.Graphics.DrawString(CompleteName, ReportFont, _
                        Brushes.Black, NameX, CurrentY)
        e.Graphics.DrawString(rdrSalesInfo.GetInt32(2).ToString, _
                        ReportFont, Brushes.Black, OrderX, CurrentY)
```

```
        e.Graphics.DrawString(Format(rdrSalesInfo.GetValue(3), _
                "$##.00"), ReportFont, Brushes.Black, SalesX, CurrentY)

        CurrentY = CurrentY + ReportFontHeight

        'Move to the next record
        If Not rdrSalesInfo.Read() Then
            Exit While
        End If

        CurrentRecord += 1

    End While

    If CurrentRecord < RecordsPerPage Then
        e.HasMorePages = False
    Else
        e.HasMorePages = True
    End If


End Sub
```

The subroutine in Listing 23.1 is an event-handling routine for the PrintPage event. The PrintDocument object will keep firing the event until the HasMorePages property of the second event parameter, e, is set to False. Not only does this event parameter control when printing is complete, but it also provides the Graphics object that your code uses to render the page. Notice that each time you draw a line of text with methods of the e.Graphics object, you have to specify the location of the text using the x,y coordinate. Therefore, when placing text fields on the page, the sample code uses a counter variable called CurrentY to determine how far down on the page to start drawing text. (The GetHeight method of the Font class returns the height of a line of text in that font.)

Note that when programming the PagePrint event, it is up to the programmer to know what data needs to be printed. Our sample code uses a SQLDataReader, which has a method to advance to the next record. However, if you were using an array, you might use a variable to indicate the current array index. If you only need to print a single page report, you can just set the HasMorePages property to False at the end of your event handler.

USING OTHER PrintDocument EVENTS

At a minimum, you need to write code for the PrintPage event to provide the contents of each page to the PrintDocument object. However, two additional events are available that make it easy to perform initialization and cleanup tasks when printing a report. The BeginPrint and EndPrint events are raised before and after printing document pages, respectively. Because the code in Listing 23.1 assumes that you have an open SQLDataReader object, the BeginPrint event is a great place to connect to the database and initialize this object. Similarly, the EndPrint event procedure can be used to terminate the database connection. To continue with the sample project, enter the code in Listing 23.2, which demonstrates how these events can be used to set up a SQLDataReader object and inform the user when the print job is complete.

LISTING 23.2   PRINTINGEXAMPLE.ZIP—USING THE BeginPrint AND EndPrint EVENTS

```
Dim rdrSalesInfo As SqlDataReader
Dim cn As SqlConnection
Private Sub PrepareReportData(ByVal sender As Object,
  ByVal e As PrintEventArgs)

    Dim sSQL As String
    Dim sConnectString As String
    Dim cmd As SqlCommand

    'Open SQLDataReader and position to first record
    sConnectString = "server=localhost\NetSDK;uid=sa;pwd=;database=NorthWind"
    cn = New SqlConnection(sConnectString)
    sSQL = "SELECT E.FirstName, E.LastName,
    ➥Count(*) As TotalOrders, Sum(O.SubTotal) AS TotalSales"
    sSQL &= " FROM Employees E INNER JOIN "
    sSQL &= " (Orders INNER JOIN [Order Subtotals]
    ➥O ON Orders.OrderID = O.OrderID)"
    sSQL &= " ON E.EmployeeID = Orders.EmployeeID"
    sSQL &= " GROUP by E.LastName, E.FirstName"
    cmd = New SqlCommand(sSQL, cn)
    cn.Open()
    rdrSalesInfo = cmd.ExecuteReader()
    rdrSalesInfo.Read()

End Sub
Private Sub ReportProcessed(ByVal sender As Object, ByVal e As PrintEventArgs)
    cn.Close()
    MessageBox.Show("You report has been sent to the printer!")
End Sub
```

The PrepareReportData function in Listing 23.2 creates a SQLDataReader object and positions it to the first record. Note that the rdrSalesInfo object is declared at the class level because it needs to be accessible from the PrintPage event handler, shown earlier in Listing 23.1.

→ To learn more about using a SQL data reader, **see** Chapter 22, "Using ADO.NET," **p. 599**.

The ReportProcessed function closes the SQL connection, as well as displays a message indicating report processing is complete. In order for these two functions to be called at the appropriate times, they need to be connected to events of a PrintDocument object with AddHandler statements. As you may recall, the PrintSalesReport function defined previously contains these statements.

The second parameter of the BeginPrint and EndPrint event delegates is of type PrintEventArgs, which is different from the PrintPage event's PrintPageEventArgs parameter. One useful property of this parameter type is the CancelPrint property, which can be used to cancel printing the report—for example, if no data exists in the database. In addition, you also should add exception handling logic so that your program terminates the print job in case of an error.

→ To learn more about handling exceptions, **see** Chapter 5, "Visual Basic Building Blocks," **p. 113**.

TESTING THE SAMPLE REPORT

If you have been following along with the example and have a printer attached to your computer, you can go ahead and test the sample program by starting the project and clicking the Print button on the form. If all goes well, you should see the message displayed informing you that the report has been sent to the printer. Note that, because Windows buffers the output sent to your printer, you probably will see the message indicating the print job is complete well before your printer has finished processing it. When the print job has been submitted to Windows, you can close your Visual Basic application and printing will continue.

PRINTING RELATIVE TO MARGINS

If you followed the example and printed a sales report, you know that creating your report layout is as simple as specifying the desired x,y coordinate of each report element. The code in Listing 23.1 used the graphics method DrawString to render text on the graphics object at specific x,y coordinates. Although the y coordinate was determined dynamically using a counter, we hard-coded the x coordinate for each column of text using constant values:

```
Const NameX As Integer = 100
Const OrderX As Integer = 300
Const SalesX As Integer = 500
```

The values listed previously are in the default graphics unit of Display, which is 1/75 of an inch. Hard-coding positions like this may work for specific reports and printers, but it is not a very flexible approach.

> **Note**
>
> To learn about the different types of measurement units available for use with graphics methods, search for "GraphicsUnit" in the help files.

To aid in locating objects relative to margins and page boundaries, the second event argument to the PrintPage event includes some useful properties:

- MarginBounds—Used to determine the margins of the current page.
- PageBounds—Used to determine the boundaries of the current page; useful for centering objects or creating footers. As noted in the help files, many printers cannot print all the way to the edge of the page.

Both of these properties return a Rectangle object, which itself contains properties you can use to determine its size and location. The code in Listing 23.3 shows how we can replace our hard-coded column positions from Listing 23.1 with columns that respect the margins and are based on a percentage of the page width.

LISTING 23.3   PRINTINGEXAMPLE.ZIP—DETERMINING COLUMN WIDTHS

```
Private Function GetColX(ByVal ColNum As Integer, ByVal Boundary As Rectangle)
   As Single

   Dim colWidthPct() As Integer = {70, 20, 10}

   If ColNum = 0 Then

       'The first column is placed at the page margin
       Return Boundary.X

   Else

       'X is at the end of the previous column
       Dim CurrentX As Single
       Dim i As Integer
       For i = 0 To ColNum - 1
           CurrentX = CurrentX + (colWidthPct(i) / 100) * Boundary.Width
       Next
       Return CurrentX

   End If

End Function
```

The column widths are defined by percentages in the `colWidthPct` array. Listing 23.3 uses the percentages to determine how many display units each column should take up. To call the `GetColX` function, you simply pass the zero-based column index and `MarginBounds` properties as arguments:

```
NameX = GetColX(0, e.MarginBounds)
```

Although this function helps you determine the x coordinate, it does not return the width of the column or prevent text from escaping column boundaries. However, compared to the previous method of locating objects on the report (hard-coded values), it provides an additional level of flexibility for the programmer. If you are interested in learning about other graphics methods that can help you with report layout code, see the help topic "System.Drawing Namespace."

ENHANCING THE PRINTING EXPERIENCE

Although we have shown the techniques necessary to send information to the printer, most users expect some control over the print job, or at least the opportunity to cancel the print request. In other words, printing immediately in response to a button click is not a very professional way to handle printing. In order to meet user expectations, you may also want to add some of the following features, which are common printing enhancements in Windows programs:

■ **Print Preview**—Lets the user view the pages of the document on the screen before sending them to the printer

- **Printer Selection**—Allows the user to select from the various printers installed on his system
- **Page Setup**—Provides the ability to change margins or other print quality settings

With each of the preceding features, you can determine how much control you want to give the end user over the printed output by using the included dialog box classes or setting properties manually with code. Some applications, such as Microsoft Word, allow the user to control detailed settings through the Print menu, while still including a toolbar button for quick printing. In the following sections, we'll explore how to implement these features in our sample report.

ADDING PRINT PREVIEW

The .NET framework provides two classes that enable you to add print preview capability to your application:

- `PrintPreviewDialog`—Provides a preview of your report on a separate form that contains a toolbar with buttons for zooming, printing, and selecting pages
- `PrintPreviewControl`—Provides a preview of your report that can be placed on an existing form to customize the print preview process

Each of these classes is also available as a control in your toolbox, although in the case of the `PrintPreviewDialog` class it is just about as easy to create the class entirely with code. Thinking back to our sales report from Listing 23.1, Listing 23.4 shows how to create a print preview dialog box for the report.

LISTING 23.4   `PRINTINGEXAMPLE.ZIP`—IMPLEMENTING BASIC PRINT PREVIEW

```
Dim SalesReport As PrintDocument
Dim dlgPreview As PrintPreviewDialog

SalesReport = New PrintDocument()
dlgPreview = New PrintPreviewDialog()
AddHandler SalesReport.PrintPage, AddressOf PrintSalesPage

dlgPreview.Document = SalesReport
dlgPreview.ShowDialog()
```

To try the code in Listing 23.4, perform the following steps:

1. Add a `Button` control to your form. Set its `Name` property to `btnPreview` and its `Text` property to `Print Preview`.
2. Enter the code from Listing 23.4 to the `Click` event procedure for the button.
3. Run the sample project and click the button to preview the report. The preview window should look similar to the one pictured in Figure 23.1.

Notice that nowhere in Listing 23.4 do we invoke the `Print` method of the `PrintDocument` class. Instead, the `dlgPreview` object handles sending the report to the printer.

Figure 23.1
It takes only a few extra lines of code to add a print preview form to your printed reports.

The toolbar on the preview dialog box includes many useful features, such as zoom and the ability to switch pages. It appears as an independent form in your Windows application. This is one way to implement print preview capability. However, some applications present the preview screens embedded within an existing window instead of opening a new one. If you want to embed print preview capability in one of your existing forms, you need to use the PrintPreviewControl class instead of the PrintPreviewDialog class. Figure 23.2 shows an example of a form containing a PrintPreviewControl control.

Figure 23.2
A Print Preview control provides the ability to include the print preview window on an existing form.

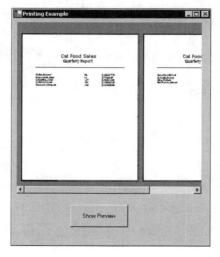

As with the PrintDialogControl, you follow the same basic steps to use the PrintPreviewControl:

1. Assign a print document object to the PrintPreviewControl.
2. Call the Show method to initiate the print preview.

Because the `PrintPreviewControl` class only provides the actual document view (and not the toolbar), you will have to write your own code to control page display, zooming, and other operations. In addition, you may use the following properties of the `PrintPreviewControl` to customize its appearance:

- `Columns` and `Rows`—These properties determine how many pages will be displayed in the preview window at the same time.
- `Startpage`—Sets the page being displayed in the preview window, or, if multiple pages are displayed, the page in the upper-left corner.
- `Zoom` and `AutoZoom`—Controls the size of the report in the preview window.

Although the `PrintPreviewControl` class does not have a print method built in, you can use the `Print` method of the `PrintDocument` object to send the report to the printer:

```
PrintPreviewControl1.Document.Print()
```

The previous line of code demonstrates that you can use the `Document` property of a `PrintPreviewControl` control to print the associated document. You could have just as easily used a reference to the `PrintDocumentObject` itself.

CONTROLLING PAGE SETTINGS

As we mentioned earlier, you can write printing code that is aware of margins and page boundaries. Sometimes you might want to give control over these boundaries to the user of your program. The .NET Framework provides classes that allow you to set margins programmatically or through a user dialog box. The code in Listing 23.5 shows how to do both; it first sets default page orientation and margins, but then it displays a Page Setup dialog box, which the user can use to change the defaults. The Page Setup dialog box is pictured in Figure 23.3.

LISTING 23.5   PRINTINGEXAMPLE.ZIP—SETTING PAGE MARGINS

```
Dim MySettings As PageSettings
Dim UserSetup As PageSetupDialog

'Set up your default settings
MySettings = New PageSettings()
MySettings.Landscape = True
MySettings.Margins = New Margins(150, 150, 150, 150)

'Display a dialog so the user can set their own
UserSetup = New PageSetupDialog()
UserSetup.PageSettings = MySettings
UserSetup.ShowDialog()

'Now associate the settings with the document
SalesReport.DefaultPageSettings = MySettings
```

Notice that you must set the PageSettings property of the PageSetupDialog object to retrieve the settings from it. Listing 23.5 also introduces the Margins class. Margins are specified in hundredths of an inch. The sample code sets the page margins to one and one-half inches on all sides.

Note

As with other dialog box forms, you can check the result of the ShowDialog method to determine if the user clicked the Cancel button.

→ To learn more about the ShowDialog method, **see** Chapter 13, "Using Dialog Boxes," **p. 335**.

Note

If you set the DefaultPageSettings property, it will control page settings for the entire document. However, you can programmatically override these settings on a per-page basis by handling the QueryPageSettings event of the PrintDocument object.

Figure 23.3
The PageSetup Dialog class can be used to display a standard Windows Page Setup dialog box.

The Page Setup dialog box is divided into several sections: margins, orientation, paper, and so on. You can limit the user from changing these by setting properties of a PageSetupDialog object:

```
UserSetup.AllowOrientation = False
```

The preceding line of code disables the orientation section of the Page Setup dialog box, although you can still set it in program code.

DETERMINING PRINTER SETTINGS

Not all printers are created equal. There is a wide variation in features and print qualities. Not to mention you may have several printers attached to your computer. To make your Windows forms printing more successful, Microsoft has provided the PrinterSettings class. This class allows you to list the printers on your system and determine their capabilities, as well as control printer settings. The code in Listing 23.6 enumerates all the printers on the system, displaying a message regarding their color printing capabilities.

LISTING 23.6   PRINTINGEXAMPLE.ZIP—QUERYING PRINTER INFORMATION

```
Dim MySettings As New PrinterSettings()
Dim PrinterNameList As PrinterSettings.StringCollection
Dim CurrentPrinterName As String
Dim i As Integer
Dim s As String

PrinterNameList = PrinterSettings.InstalledPrinters
For Each CurrentPrinterName In PrinterNameList

    MySettings.PrinterName = CurrentPrinterName
    If MySettings.SupportsColor Then

        s = CurrentPrinterName & " is a color printer, "
        s &= " supporting the following resolutions:" & vbCrLf
        For i = 0 To MySettings.PrinterResolutions.Count - 1
            s &= MySettings.PrinterResolutions(i).ToString & vbCrLf
        Next

    Else

        s = CurrentPrinterName & " is not a color printer."

    End If

    MessageBox.Show(s)

Next
```

The `PrinterSettings` class has one static property, `InstalledPrinters`, which can be used to retrieve a list of printers by name. To determine the features and settings of an individual printer, you have to first assign the printer to an instance of the `PrinterSettings` class by setting the `PrinterName` property.

Note

> In production applications, remember to add exception-handling code to handle printing errors.

→ To learn more about exception handling, **see** Chapter 5, "Visual Basic Building Blocks," **p. 113**

DISPLAYING A PRINT DIALOG BOX

As an alternative to setting individual properties of a `PrinterSettings` object, you can allow the user to control printer settings interactively by displaying a Print dialog box. A Print dialog box, shown in Figure 23.4, allows the user to select a printer as well as control the number of copies and other printer-specific settings.

Figure 23.4
Printer selection and page setup can be accomplished through the Print dialog box.

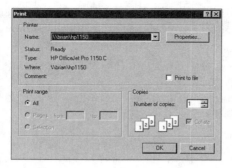

To create a Print dialog box, you first instantiate the `PrintDialog` class, then connect it to a report via its `Document` property, and finally invoke the `ShowDialog` method. Listing 23.7 shows how to display a Print dialog box.

LISTING 23.7 PRINTINGEXAMPLE.ZIP—**USING THE** `PrintDialog` **OBJECT**

```
Dim SalesReport As PrintDocument
Dim PrinterSetupScreen As PrintDialog
Dim ButtonPressed As DialogResult

'Set up the report
SalesReport = New PrintDocument()

AddHandler SalesReport.PrintPage, AddressOf PrintSalesPage
AddHandler SalesReport.BeginPrint, AddressOf PrepareReportData
AddHandler SalesReport.EndPrint, AddressOf ReportProcessed

'Display printer dialog
PrinterSetupScreen = New PrintDialog()
PrinterSetupScreen.Document = SalesReport
ButtonPressed = PrinterSetupScreen.ShowDialog()

'Print, if user clicked OK
If ButtonPressed = DialogResult.OK Then
    SalesReport.Print()
End If
```

As with the `PageSettingsDialog` class, there are several properties of the `PrintDialog` class you can use to customize the dialog box. For example, you can optionally display options that allow the user to select a range of pages for printing. However, because you have to provide the maximum and minimum pages, you have to know in advance how many pages are in the final document.

USING CRYSTAL REPORTS

Crystal Reports is the professional reporting tool that is bundled with Visual Studio .NET. This tool automatically handles low-level printing operations, such as paging and print preview, allowing the developer to concentrate on designing the content of the report. You design Crystal Reports graphically, by arranging report fields in the integrated Crystal Report Designer. The Crystal Reports engine merges your report layout with a data source to come up with the finished report. In this section, we demonstrate how to design a Crystal Report and display it in your program.

SETTING UP A DATA SOURCE

Crystal Reports are data-driven. Even before you begin designing a report, you need to have a good idea of where the data is coming from. Some examples of data sources suitable for Crystal Reports are SQL Server databases or ADO.NET datasets. Reporting on an ADO.NET dataset (which we discuss later in this chapter) is a little more complicated, since it is disconnected from any data source. For the example in this section, we use data from a stored procedure in the Northwind database, which is included with Visual Studio .NET. If you installed the .NET Framework SDK samples, you already installed an instance of SQL Server called NetSDK with the Northwind database. If you have not installed these samples, please see instructions in the earlier section called "Planning a Report." Before continuing, please verify that you can connect to the database and execute the `Employee Sales By Country` stored procedure. The sample stored procedure accepts two parameters (starting and ending dates) and returns information about each order shipped within the date range. To run the stored procedure and look at the data, execute the following SQL statement:

```
exec [Employee Sales by Country] '1/1/1990','12/31/2000'
```

> **Note**
>
> As we mentioned in Chapter 20, "Database Basics," database object names with spaces have to be enclosed in brackets. (We also mentioned that is probably not a good idea to use spaces in database object names due to this extra complication, but Microsoft wrote this procedure, not us!)

→ To learn how to execute SQL statements and stored procedures, **see** Chapter 20, "Database Basics," **p. 535**

As you will see in a moment, when you design a Crystal Report you specify the stored procedure name, and Crystal will retrieve information about that stored procedure's parameters and database fields. However, one peculiarity of Crystal Reports is that sometimes it is confused by the presence of date parameters in a SQL Server stored procedure. In other words, the Crystal Reports program might incorrectly think that the `Employee Sales By Country` stored procedure has no data fields because it has two date parameter fields. Fortunately, SQL Server is flexible enough to accept string parameters and automatically convert them to dates. To ensure your success with this example, make a minor modification to the stored procedure by performing the following steps:

1. Using the Server Explorer as described in Chapter 20, establish a connection to the Northwind database.
2. Navigate to the Stored Procedures list.
3. Right-click the `Employee Sales By Country` stored procedure and select Edit Stored Procedure.

4. Change the data type for the two parameters from `DateTime` to `char(10)`, as follows:
   `@Beginning_Date char(10)`, `@Ending_Date char(10)`

5. Click the Save button on the toolbar to update the stored procedure.

The authors are not sure if this is a bug in the Crystal Reports program, but at the time of this writing, the previous steps were necessary to get Crystal Reports to work successfully with date parameters.

DESIGNING A NEW REPORT

Now that we have identified the data source and prepared the stored procedure, we can proceed with designing a report. If you are following along with the sales report example from the Web site, `CrystalExample.zip`, add a new Crystal Report to your project by performing the following steps:

1. Right-click the project name in the Solution Explorer and select Add New Item.

2. From the list of item templates, select Crystal Report.

3. Enter a name for the report. For our example, use the name `SalesReport.rpt`. (Crystal's proprietary file format uses the `rpt` extension.)

4. Click Open. You will see the Crystal Report Gallery dialog box appear, as shown in Figure 23.5.

Figure 23.5
When creating a new Crystal Report, you can choose from several canned templates, create a blank report, or copy an existing report.

If you choose one of the Report Expert options (Standard, Cross-Tab, and so forth), you will be asked a series of questions and Crystal will automatically create a report layout for you. However, in the interest of learning as much as possible about how the report design process works, let's create a report entirely from scratch.

5. Select As a Blank Report and click OK to close the Crystal Report Gallery dialog box.

UNDERSTANDING REPORT SECTIONS

When you add a new Crystal Report to you project, the designer window for the new report is opened. As shown in Figure 23.6, the report designer is divided into several areas, or *sections*.

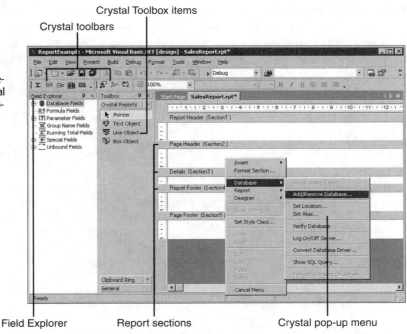

Figure 23.6
The Crystal Report Designer is fully integrated into the Visual Studio .NET development environment.

Crystal Toolbox items

Crystal toolbars

Field Explorer   Report sections   Crystal pop-up menu

As you design the report, you will use the Toolbox and Field Explorer to add items to the appropriate sections of your report. Each section takes on a different behavior when an end user views or prints the report, as summarized here:

- **Report Header**—This section appears once, at the very beginning of the report. You might want to use it to add a company logo or separator page.

- **Page Header**—Appears at the top of every page of the report. This section usually contains column headings for database fields in the Details section.

- **Details**—The contents of the Details section are repeated for every record in the data source.

- **Report Footer**—This section appears once at the very end of the report. One use for it would be a grand total or other summary information.

- **Page Footer**—This section appears at the bottom of every page of the report. This is a good place to add fields for page number and print date.

As you will see in a moment, you can also add additional sections to group records according to your specific reporting needs.

ENABLING STORED PROCEDURES

To retrieve data from a database, you have to come up with a query, whether it is a SQL statement or stored procedure. The Crystal Reports designer provides a graphical interface by which you can pick and join multiple tables from a database, and it will automatically generate a SQL query. However, I picked a stored procedure as the data source for our sample report to demonstrate an extra step that is required if you want to work with stored procedures. For some reason, each version of Crystal Reports in recent memory has made it unnecessarily difficult to use stored procedures by hiding a menu option somewhere that must be activated first. To enable reporting on stored procedures, you must perform the following steps:

1. Right-click anywhere in the white area of the report to display the pop-up menu.
2. From the Database submenu, select Log On/Off Server. The Data Explorer dialog box will appear.
3. Click the Options button. You should see the Default Settings dialog box, shown in Figure 23.7.

Figure 23.7
If you want to use a database stored procedure in a Crystal Report, don't forget to select the option to show them.

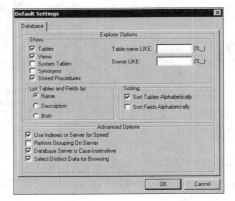

4. Select the check box labeled Stored Procedures and click OK.
5. Click Close to close the Data Explorer window.

CONNECTING TO A DATABASE

To make the database fields from your stored procedure available in the report, you need to connect the Crystal Report to the data source. To connect to the Northwind database, perform the following steps:

1. Right-click anywhere in the white area of the report to display the pop-up menu.
2. From the Database submenu, select Add/Remove Database. You will see the Database Expert dialog box, pictured in Figure 23.8.

Figure 23.8
Crystal can connect to
a wide variety of data
sources, including
databases and local
project items.

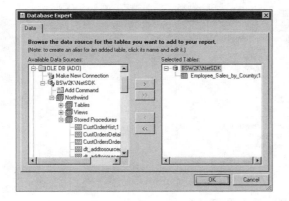

3. In the Available Data Sources panel, expand the OLE DB (ADO) folder. A dialog box will appear that allows you to specify a new connection to an OLE DB Provider.

4. From the list of OLE DB providers, select the Microsoft OLE DB Provider for SQL Server and click Next.

5. Fill in the Server name, User ID, and password fields appropriately. From the Database drop-down list, select Northwind.

6. Click Finish. Your database should be added to the list of Available Data Sources in the OLE DB connections folder.

7. Expand the connection list to navigate to the list of stored procedures in the Northwind database.

8. From the list of stored procedures, select the stored procedure named `Employee Sales By Country`.

9. Click the > button to move the stored procedure to the Selected Tables list.

10. Click OK to close the Database Expert dialog box.

Note

When using tables or views in a report, the Database Expert dialog box also contains a Link tab used to specify table joins.

Now that we have connected the Crystal Report to a data source, we can begin positioning fields from the data source on the report.

USING THE FIELD EXPLORER

To add fields to your report, you first need to make sure the Field Explorer window is visible. The Field Explorer window is pictured in Figure 23.9.

Figure 23.9
To display the Field Explorer, select View, Other Windows, Document Outline.

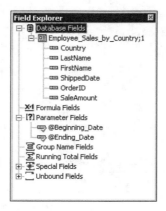

As you can see, the Field Explorer shows several different types of fields you can add to your report:

- **Database Fields**—The list of database fields contains the fields provided by the data sources in the report.
- **Formula Fields**—The value of a formula field is the result of a user-defined formula, which may or may not use other fields in the calculation.
- **Parameter Fields**—Parameter fields are passed to the report by program code or the end user and may be used in formulas or displayed on the report.
- **Group Name Fields**—Used to place section group names in your report; user-defined sections work similarly to the GROUP BY statement in SQL.
- **Running Total Fields**—Allows you to place calculated total fields (sum, maximum, recordcounts, and so on) on the report.
- **Special Fields**—Special report information generated by the Crystal Reports engine, such as the print date and time or current page number.
- **Unbound Fields**—Special-purpose formula fields.

> **Note**
>
> The items in the Field Explorer involve some calculation or relationship to the data; the items in the Crystal section of the Toolbox are static items designed to enhance the appearance of your report.

Let's add some fields to the report.

1. If you expand the Database fields section, you'll see the fields returned by the stored procedure.
2. Using the mouse, drag each of these fields from the Field Explorer window to the Details section of your report.
3. Arrange them so your report looks similar to the one shown in Figure 23.10.

> **Note**
>
> You can modify the size of each report section by sliding the section bars up and down with the mouse. You might want to do this to accommodate extra fields in a section or add whitespace to your report.

Figure 23.10
When you add a database field to the Details section, a text object label for the field is automatically added to the page header section.

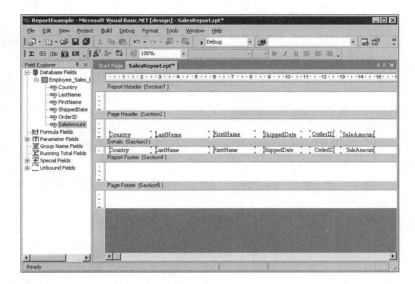

Congratulations, you have designed a very plain but functional Crystal Report. In a moment, we will return to the report designer and add more fields to enhance the usefulness and appearance of the report. However, first, we will demonstrate how to display and print the report in your program.

DISPLAYING THE REPORT

Visual Studio .NET includes two viewer controls for Crystal Reports: a Windows viewer for use in Windows applications and a Web viewer for use in Web applications. In this section we demonstrate using the Windows viewer. To learn more about the Web viewer, see Chapter 19, "Web Controls."

> **Note**
>
> Users of previous versions of Crystal Reports will note the conspicuous absence of the lightning bolt icon, which was used to preview the report while in design mode. Fortunately, because Crystal is completely integrated into the Visual Studio environment, it is very easy to preview a report using a Windows form.

→ For more on using a Crystal Report in a Web application, **see** Chapter 19, "Web Controls," **p. 501**

SETTING UP A `CrystalReportViewer` CONTROL

The Crystal Report viewer for Windows applications is called the `CrystalReportViewer` control and is located in the Windows Forms section of the toolbox. To display your new report using this control, you need to add the control to a Windows form and then let the control know the location of the report file. You can do this at design time by performing the following steps:

1. If you are already working with the sample report in a Windows application project, display the startup form. Otherwise, start a new Windows application project.

2. Add a `CrystalReportViewer` control to your form. Set its name property to `crViewer`. Size it so that it takes up most of the form area.

3. Open the Properties window for the `crViewer` control, and find the `ReportSource` property.

4. Using the Browse option in the `ReportSource` property, browse to the report file you just created, `SalesReport.rpt`.

5. Run the Windows application. The viewer will display dialog boxes requesting the start and end date parameters for the stored procedure.

6. After entering the report parameters, your report will be displayed in the viewer, as pictured in Figure 23.11.

Figure 23.11
The versatile `CrystalReportVie wer` control allows the end user to print, zoom, and export the displayed report.

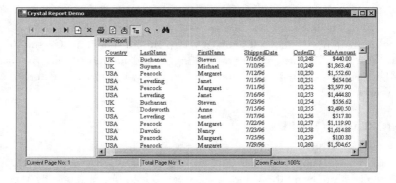

When your report is loaded in the viewer, you can use the toolbar to navigate and print the report.

DEALING WITH PARAMETERS

Although Crystal Reports will automatically provide a dialog box for the user to enter report parameters, you may not always want this to happen. For example, the parameters may be database keys or other numbers that the user is not required to know. Or, you may want to restrict the parameters the user can enter to a subset of values based on the user's identity. In either case, you can send parameters to a `CrystalReportViewer` control programmatically to avoid the appearance of parameter dialog boxes. To demonstrate with our sample report, return to the Properties window and set the `ReportSource` property to `None`. To set up the viewer at runtime, perform the following steps:

1. Expand your form so there is room for a `Button` control.

2. Add a `Button` control to your form. Set its `Text` property to `Display Report`. Set its `Name` property to `btnDisplayReport`.

3. Add the following line of code to the top of the code window for your form:

   `Imports CrystalDecisions.Shared`

4. Enter the code from Listing 23.8 in the `Click` event handler for `btnDisplayReport`.

LISTING 23.8   CRYSTALEXAMPLE.ZIP—SETTING REPORT PARAMETERS

```
'Clear previous report source
crViewer.ReportSource = Nothing

'Create the parameter value objects
Dim paramStartDate As New ParameterDiscreteValue()
Dim paramEndDate As New ParameterDiscreteValue()
paramStartDate.Value = "8/1/1996"
paramEndDate.Value = "8/31/1996"

'Create the parameters collection
Dim paramList As New ParameterFields()

'Create the parameter objects and add them to the collection
Dim paramTemp As ParameterField

paramTemp = New ParameterField()
paramTemp.ParameterFieldName = "@Beginning_Date"
paramTemp.CurrentValues.Add(paramStartDate)
paramList.Add(paramTemp)

paramTemp = New ParameterField()
paramTemp.ParameterFieldName = "@Ending_Date"
paramTemp.CurrentValues.Add(paramEndDate)
paramList.Add(paramTemp)

'Assign parameters collection to the report viewer
crViewer.ParameterFieldInfo = paramList

'Load the report
crViewer.ReportSource = Application.StartupPath & "\..\SalesReport.rpt"
```

The code in Listing 23.8 limits the date range of the records displayed to fixed values.

ENHANCING THE REPORT

Now that you have successfully created and displayed a Crystal Report, you can refine and enhance the report layout as necessary by returning to the report designer. For example, the appearance of our sample report is rather mundane. Figure 23.12 shows how elements from the Toolbox can make it more visually appealing.

Figure 23.12
Text boxes, lines, and images can make your report more professional looking.

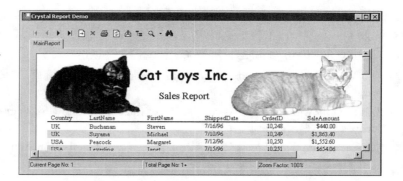

In addition to adding these static elements from the Toolbox, you can also format the dynamic elements, such as database fields, by using the Format Editor dialog box, shown in Figure 23.13.

Figure 23.13
To display the Format Editor, right-click a database field and select Format from the pop-up menu.

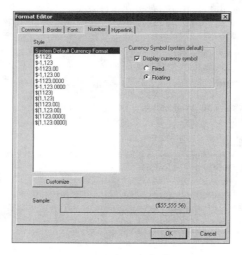

The Format Editor allows you to control field alignment, numeric and date formatting, font size, borders, and other formatting-related tasks.

CREATING A FORMULA FIELD

In addition to making a report more visually appealing, you can also make it more functional by adding a formula field. A formula field contains the result of a calculation, usually performed on one or more database fields. For example, the sales report has separate fields for last and first name, but we might want a complete name field on the report. Because the data source only returns the names separately, we can create a new formula field called CompleteName that combines them inside the report. To add this formula field, perform the following steps:

1. In the Field Explorer window, right-click the Formula Fields and select New.

2. For the formula name, type **CompleteName** and click OK. The Formula Editor should appear. The Formula Editor, shown in Figure 23.14, allows you to edit the formula that will be used to determine the formula field value.

3. At the bottom of the Formula Editor dialog box, type the following line of text:
   ```
   Trim ({spBriantest;1.LastName}) + ', ' + Trim ({spBriantest;1.FirstName})
   ```

4. Click the Save and Exit button to close the dialog box.

Figure 23.14
You can type your formula manually in the lower pane of the Formula Editor or double-click the objects in the upper pane to add text automatically.

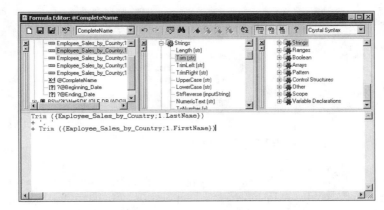

Now that you have created a new formula field, it will appear in the Field Explorer window. You can then drag it to the Details section just as you would any other database field.

ADDING A NEW REPORT SECTION

Another useful feature of Crystal Reports is the ability to add report groupings, also known as *breaks*. When you add a grouping, a new header and footer section are added to the designer. Each time the field you are grouping by changes, the header and footer are repeated on the report and can be used to display summary information for the group. For example, our sales report includes the country of each sale. With just a few mouse clicks, you can group the records by the Country field and have Crystal Reports display subtotals for each country:

1. First, you need to add a new group to the report. To do this, simply right-click Group Name in the Field Explorer and select Insert Group.

2. A dialog box will appear asking you for the group field and sort order. Select Country and click OK. New sections for the group header and footer will be added to the Design window.

3. Once you have added a new report group, you can add summary fields by right-clicking the desired field in the Details section and selecting Insert Summary.

There are several summary types to choose from, including count, summary, maximum, and minimum. Figure 23.15 shows the sales report as seen by the end user after we added summary fields for Country and Sales amount, as well as some text objects to label them.

Figure 23.15
Group names are displayed in the Group tree pane of the Crystal Report Viewer for easy navigation.

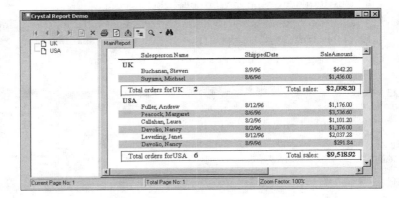

REPORTING FROM AN ADO.NET DATASET

As you have seen throughout this section, Crystal Reports is capable of retrieving information directly from a database server using an OLE DB provider. However, when working with disconnected data in a distributed application, it may not be desirable or even possible to have the Crystal Viewer make a direct connection to the database. Fortunately, you can use an ADO.NET Dataset object as the data source for a Crystal Report.

→ To learn more about datasets, **see** Chapter 22, "Using ADO.NET," **p. 599**

Because a dataset is not associated with any particular database, you have to go through the extra step of building a description of it, so that Crystal will understand the field definitions. Once you design a report based on a dataset, you can substitute any Dataset object with the same field definitions at runtime.

BUILDING THE DATASET SCHEMA

A description of database tables, including their field names and data types, is known as a *schema*. Schemas in ADO.NET are typically represented using XML. The Visual Studio .NET help files have a nice walk-through that shows you how to build a schema interactively by selecting an OLEDB provider, and then picking field names. However, to keep things interesting, we will demonstrate a quicker way to create a schema, by using an existing dataset. By simply filling a dataset and calling its WriteXMLSchema method, you can create a schema that is usable as a Crystal Report data source. To make this process even more painless, we will build on earlier knowledge by reusing our ADO.NET function library from Chapter 22. Assuming you have the ExecSP and associated functions available, you can generate a schema for the data returned by the Employee Sales By Country stored procedure with just a few lines of code. Listing 23.9 shows how to generate an XML schema.

LISTING 23.9 CRYSTALEXAMPLE.ZIP—REPORTING FROM A DATASET

```
Dim intRetVal As Integer
Dim parmArray(1) As SqlParameter

'Set up parameters
parmArray(0) = New SqlParameter("@Beginning_Date", SqlDbType.Char)
parmArray(0).Value = "1/1/1996"
parmArray(1) = New SqlParameter("@Ending_Date", SqlDbType.Char)
parmArray(1).Value = "12/31/1996"

'Fill dataset
Dim dsInfo As New DataSet()
Call ExecSP("MySample", "[Employee Sales By Country]", intRetVal,
    parmArray, dsInfo)

'Save Schema
dsInfo.WriteXmlSchema("c:\SalesInfo.xsd")
```

After executing the code in Listing 23.9, you should have a file called C:\SalesInfo.xsd located on your hard drive. If you open the file in Notepad, you can see your field definitions described in XML.

DESIGNING A REPORT FROM AN XML SCHEMA

If you have created the XML schema successfully, you can easily use it as a data source for the Crystal Report. Let's re-create the sales report example from earlier, except this time using a dataset as the data source. Perform the following steps to create the new report:

1. Add a new blank Crystal Report to your project, named SalesReport2.rpt.

2. Right-click in the white area of the report designer and select Add/Remove Database from the Database menu. The Database Expert dialog box will appear (refer to Figure 23.8).

3. In the Available Data Sources list, expand the More Data Sources folder, and then the ADO.NET (XML) folder.

4. When the dialog box appears, browse to the C:\SalesInfo.xsd file and click Finish. The new data source appears as a table called Table.

5. Select the Table table and click the > button to add it to the Selected tables list.

6. Click OK to close the Database Expert dialog box.

From this point, we can add fields and design the report just as we did in the previous sections, when using the SQL Server as a data source.

Note

> You can also add the .XSD file we created to your project and edit it using Visual Studio .NET. Datasets associated with a project appear in the Project Data folder of the Database Expert dialog box.

DISPLAYING THE FINISHED REPORT

With dataset-based reports, the report itself is only aware of the schema; it does not know how to connect to the underlying database. Therefore, you have to write code that creates an appropriate `Dataset` object and pass it to the report, as shown in Listing 23.10.

LISTING 23.10   CRYSTALEXAMPLE.ZIP—REPORTING ON A DATASET

```
Dim intRetVal As Integer
Dim parmArray(1) As SqlParameter

'Set up parameters
parmArray(0) = New SqlParameter("@Beginning_Date", SqlDbType.Char)
parmArray(0).Value = "1/1/1996"
parmArray(1) = New SqlParameter("@Ending_Date", SqlDbType.Char)
parmArray(1).Value = "12/31/1996"

'Fill dataset
Dim dsInfo As New DataSet()
Call ExecSP("MySample", "spBrianTest", intRetVal, parmArray, dsInfo)

'Set up report object
Dim MyReport As New SalesReport2()
MyReport.SetDataSource(dsInfo)

'Display Report
crViewer.ReportSource = MyReport
```

Listing 23.10 also takes a different approach to displaying the report, that is, setting the `ReportSource` property of the `CrystalReportViewer` control to an instance of the report class rather than the filename. This is necessary so that the report will have data associated with it before the viewer tries to display it.

FROM HERE...

This chapter covered two different ways of implementing reporting in your Visual Basic applications. To learn more about related topics, please read the following chapters:

- For a primer on writing SQL queries and stored procedures, see Chapter 20.
- To learn more about retrieving data with ADO.NET, see Chapter 22.
- For information on using the Web viewer for Crystal Reports, see Chapter 19.

ADVANCED PROGRAMMING TOPICS

CHAPTER 24

WORKING WITH FILES

In this chapter

No matter what development language and platform you use, at some point you will probably need to write code that interacts with underlying operating system files. For example, you might need to copy files or launch another program. You can do all this interactively by using Windows Explorer or a Command Prompt window. As you will see in this chapter, you can accomplish these same file operations easily by using Visual Basic code.

Another use for files is the storage and retrieval of information. In other chapters, you learned how to use databases to store information. However, sometimes the power of a database engine may not be necessary or even appropriate. For example, you may want to create a simple activity log or process a comma-delimited text file. In this chapter, you will examine a couple of options that allow you to store and access information in plain text files with minimal or no structure. We also will look at file streams, which can be used to work with many different types of data. In addition, we will discuss accessing the Windows Registry, where application settings and other information can be stored.

MANIPULATING THE FILE SYSTEM USING VB

Windows Explorer represents the contents of your hard drive graphically using file and folder icons. Many of the actions that you perform in Explorer (such as copying or renaming files) also can be accomplished in Visual Basic .NET via the `System.IO` namespace. The System assembly should be automatically referenced in your project, so you just need to add the following `Imports` statement at the top of your form or module:

```
Imports System.IO
```

The most useful classes for performing file operations are

- **FileSystemInfo**—The `FileSystemInfo` class represents an entry in the file system, whether it is a file or a folder. You cannot create an instance of a `FileSystemInfo` object with the `New` keyword but, as you will see in a moment, it is useful when processing both files and folders at the same time.

- **FileInfo**—You use the `FileInfo` class to manipulate operating system files. Each `FileInfo` object you create represents a file on the disk. This class is inherited from the `FileSystemInfo` class and contains additional, file-specific members.

- **DirectoryInfo**—The `DirectoryInfo` class allows you to control the folders of your file system. Like the `FileInfo` class, the `DirectoryInfo` class is inherited from the `FileSystemInfo` class and contains additional, directory-specific members.

- **File**—The `File` class contains static methods for performing operations on operating system files.

- **Directory**—The `Directory` class contains static methods for performing operations on operating system folders.

Astute readers may have already noticed there is some duplication in the previous list of classes. For example, both the `File` and `FileInfo` classes contain methods for determining whether a file exists, deleting a file, and so on. The reason is that the `Directory` and `File` classes contain all the *static* methods, while the `DirectoryInfo` and `FileInfo` classes contain all the *instance* methods. As you may recall from Chapter 9, a static method is a method of a class that can be called without first creating an object from the class.

→ For more on methods, **see** "Object-Oriented Programming," **p. 225**

When dealing with files, static methods can be more efficient if you do not need to perform multiple operations on the same file or directory, or access its properties. By avoiding the overhead of declaring a variable and storing an object instance, you use fewer of your system resources.

The terms *folder*, *directory*, and *subdirectory* are often used interchangeably in the PC environment. When DOS was king, subdirectories were created in the root directory (that is, `C:\WINDOWS` is a subdirectory of `C:\`). A lot of the DOS commands include directory in their names, such as `md`, which stands for `make directory`. Many of these DOS commands are still available in Windows today in the Command Prompt window. However, inside the Windows environment you create and manipulate folders using the Windows explorer. With the introduction of VBScript Microsoft provided a Folder object, so it is interesting to find a Directory object in the `System.IO` namespace. Perhaps this is a nod to other operating systems such as UNIX, which uses the term *directory*.

CHECKING TO SEE WHETHER A FILE OR DIRECTORY EXISTS

If you try to open a database or access a file that does not exist, an error occurs. However, you can use the `Exists` method of the `File` class before opening it to check whether it is really there, as in the following example:

```
Dim sFileToCheck As String = "C:\data\importantstuff.dat"

If Not File.Exists(sFileToCheck) Then
    MessageBox.Show("Cannot find the file. Please try again!")
    Application.Exit()
End If
```

The `Exists` method accepts a file path as a parameter and returns `True` if the file exists. (The `Exists` function is also available in the `Directory` class to check for the existence of a folder.) Some notes regarding the behavior of the `Exists` function are

- The `Exists` function is not case sensitive.
- The `PATH` environment setting on your PC has no effect on the `Exists` method; you must provide a path to the file in the method call.
- `Exists` accepts either a full path or one relative to the current directory. (Keep reading for more on paths and the current directory.)
- Wildcard expressions (that is, `*` and `?`) cannot be used with `Exists`.
- UNC paths (that is, `\\server\share\directory\filename`) can be used with `Exists`, although if you do not have permission to access the remote file, `False` will be returned.

Note

The `FileInfo` and `DirectoryInfo` classes also contain an `Exists` property, which can be used if you have an object reference declared.

→ For more information about providing ways for users to select files, **see** "Using Input Boxes to Get Information from the User," **p. 342**

LISTING THE FILES AND FOLDERS IN A DIRECTORY

Another frequently needed file system operation is the ability to get a list of filenames. After you have this list, you can present it to the user onscreen, store it in a database, or perform any number of other tasks. For example, the following lines of code use the `GetFiles` method of the `Directory` class to populate a listbox with the names of the executable files in the `C:\WINNT` folder:

```
Dim sFileList() As String
sFileList = Directory.GetFiles("C:\Winnt", "*.exe ")
ListBox1.Items.AddRange(sFileList)
```

The `GetFiles` method searches a directory for files and returns an array of strings containing the full path to each file. In order to specify the directory to be searched, you must supply at least one parameter, the directory name. If you supply an invalid directory name, an exception will be thrown. The search pattern, which is entirely optional, allows you to filter the filenames returned using wildcard expressions.

In addition to the `GetFiles` method, the `Directory` class also contains similar methods, called `GetDirectories` and `GetFileSystemEntries`, which can be used to retrieve an array of subdirectories or files and subdirectories, respectively. These static methods are easy to use and relatively efficient; however, they are not suited for more complex operations. For example, you may want to process each file as an object, using its properties such as size or extension to determine your program's course of action. The code in Listing 24.1 uses the `GetFileSystemInfos` method of the Directory class to retrieve a collection representing the file and directory objects file and directory in the root folder of the C drive.

LISTING 24.1   ListFiles.ZIP—ENUMERATING THE CONTENTS OF A FOLDER

```
Dim dirTemp As DirectoryInfo
Dim fsiTemp As FileSystemInfo

dirTemp = New DirectoryInfo("C:\")
lstFiles.Items.Clear()
lstFiles.DisplayMember = "Name"
For Each fsiTemp In dirTemp.GetFileSystemInfos()
    lstFiles.Items.Add(fsiTemp)
Next
```

In Listing 24.1, we first create an instance of the `DirectoryInfo` class, which represents the `c:\` directory. Next, we call the `GetFileSystemInfos` method, which returns a collection of objects corresponding to each item contained in the C:\ folder. Finally, each FileSystemInfo object is added to the Items collection of a list box. This process is a little more involved than the static methods described earlier, because we are processing files as objects rather than string values. However, the code in Listing 24.1 could easily be expanded to perform additional tasks using object members.

Note

> If you want to work with only files or directories, but not both, use the GetFiles or GetDirectories method instead of the more generic GetFileSystemInfos method presented here. All of the previous methods also contain an optional search pattern parameter, as described earlier in this section.

For example, Listing 24.2 shows how to retrieve object properties from the list box when the user double-clicks a filename.

LISTING 24.2 ListFiles.ZIP—EXPLORING FILE AND DIRECTORY PROPERTIES

```
Private Sub lstFiles_DoubleClick(ByVal sender As Object,_
ByVal e As System.EventArgs) Handles lstFiles.DoubleClick

Dim fsiTemp As FileSystemInfo
Dim strMessage As String

fsiTemp = CType(lstFiles.SelectedItem, FileSystemInfo)
If lstFiles.SelectedItem.GetType Is GetType(DirectoryInfo) Then
    Dim dirTemp As DirectoryInfo
    dirTemp = CType(fsiTemp, DirectoryInfo)
    strMessage = "You just clicked on a directory."
    strMessage &= "The directory's parent is " & dirTemp.Parent.ToString

ElseIf lstFiles.SelectedItem.GetType Is GetType(FileInfo) Then
    Dim filTemp As FileInfo
    filTemp = CType(fsiTemp, FileInfo)
    strMessage = "You just clicked on a file."
    strMessage &= "The size of the file is " & filTemp.Length.ToString
    strMessage &= "The complete path to it is " & filTemp.FullName

End If

MessageBox.Show(strMessage)


End Sub
```

The code in Listing 24.2 demonstrates accessing properties specific to both the DirectoryInfo and FileInfo classes, as well as the more generic FileSystemInfo class. Keep in mind that if you do not need to access the entire object, it is more efficient just to store the filenames in the list box as strings. The program in Listing 24.3 scans the C:\Program

Files directory and all of its subdirectories, adding the filenames of all the JPEG picture files (those with a JPG extension) that it finds. The user can then click a picture in the list box and it will be displayed on the form, as pictured in Figure 24.1.

LISTING 24.3 FindPics.ZIP—**JPEG FILE VIEWER**

```
Private Sub btnSearch_Click(ByVal sender As System.Object,_
ByVal e As System.EventArgs) Handles btnSearch.Click
    Dim dirTemp As New DirectoryInfo("C:\Program Files")

    lstFiles.Items.Clear()
    Call FindPictures(dirTemp)
    Me.Text = "Click the picture name to display it."
    MessageBox.Show("Click the picture name to display it.")

End Sub


Private Sub FindPictures(ByVal fsiTemp As FileSystemInfo)
    'The object passed to this function is either a file or directory.
    'If it is a JPG picture file, we will add it to the list box.
    'If it is a directory, we use recursion to continue the search.

    If fsiTemp.GetType Is GetType(FileInfo) Then
        If fsiTemp.Extension.ToUpper = ".JPG" Then
            lstFiles.Items.Add(fsiTemp.FullName)
        End If
    Else
        Dim dirTemp As New DirectoryInfo(fsiTemp.FullName)
        Dim fsiNew As FileSystemInfo
        Me.Text = "Searching " & dirTemp.Name
        For Each fsiNew In dirTemp.GetFileSystemInfos
            Call FindPictures(fsiNew)
        Next
    End If

End Sub


Private Sub lstFiles_SelectedIndexChanged(ByVal sender As System.Object,_
ByVal e As System.EventArgs) Handles lstFiles.SelectedIndexChanged
    If Not (lstFiles.SelectedItem Is Nothing) Then
        Me.BackgroundImage = Image.FromFile(lstFiles.SelectedItem.ToString)
    End If

End Sub
```

The heart of the code behind Listing 24.3 is the FindPictures subroutine, which employs a technique called *recursion*. A recursive function calls itself. In our example, the function will call itself in order to process any directories contained within the directory it is working on. By placing a breakpoint in the FindPictures function, you can watch the levels of recursion build using the Call Stack window.

Figure 24.1
The file viewer sample program allows you to browse all the pictures on your hard drive.

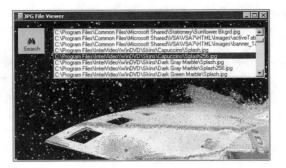

→ For more on debugging and the Call Stack window, **see** Chapter 26, "Debugging and Performance Tuning" **p. 717**

CHANGING THE ATTRIBUTES OF A FILE OR DIRECTORY

By accessing properties and methods of a `FileSystemInfo` object associated with a file or directory, you can read or change information about the file or directory. For example, if you right-click a file or folder in Windows Explorer and choose Properties, you will see a dialog box similar to the one pictured in Figure 24.2.

Figure 24.2
You can change many file attributes by setting properties of the `FileInfo` class or calling methods of the `File` class.

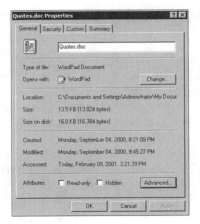

The following code sample will change the Read-Only attribute of a file, which will be reflected in the Windows Explorer Properties dialog box.

```
Dim MyFile As FileInfo

MyFile = New FileInfo("c:\temp\myfile.txt")

If MyFile.Attributes And IO.FileAttributes.ReadOnly Then
    MessageBox.Show("Your file is already set to read-only mode!")
Else
```

```
        MessageBox.Show("The read-only flag has been set!")
        MyFile.Attributes = MyFile.Attributes Or IO.FileAttributes.ReadOnly
End If
```

There are many different attributes of files and directories, such as ReadOnly, Hidden, and Archive. These attributes are stored as individual bits in the Attributes property. Therefore, you have to use bitwise boolean operations to extract or set their values, as demonstrated in the sample code. In addition to changing a file's attributes, you can also determine or set several dates associated with a file, such as when it was created or last modified.

COPYING, RENAMING, AND DELETING

The File class provides methods to copy, delete, and rename files. For example, File.Copy can be used to create a backup copy of a file:

```
File.Copy("c:\temp\quotes.doc", "C:\temp\quotesbackup.doc", True)
```

The parameters of the File.Copy method are

- **Source File**—The source file you want to copy. If the file does not exist, an exception will be thrown.
- **Destination File**—The path to the destination file you want to create.
- **Overwrite Existing File**—This parameter is optional and indicates whether you want to overwrite an existing destination file. If this parameter is omitted or set to False and the destination file already exists, the method will throw an exception.

As with many of the shared methods, there is a corresponding method for use with an object instance. If you have already created a FileInfo object, you can use the CopyTo method and simply provide the destination and overwrite parameters:

```
Dim filTemp As New File("C:\temp\quotes.doc")
filTemp.CopyTo("C:\temp\newquotes.doc", False)
```

Note

The Copy and CopyTo methods will throw an exception if you attempt to overwrite an existing read-only file, even if you have the overwrite parameter set to True. To overwrite an existing read-only file, you first need to turn off its read-only attribute.

The DirectoryInfo class does not have a Copy or CopyTo method. However, you can create a new directory using the Create method and then copy the files within it. As an exercise, adapt the recursive function from Listing 24.3 to copy all the files and subdirectories contained within a given directory.

The rename and delete methods are identical for files and directories:

- **Move**—Static method to rename a file or directory. Its parameters are a *source* and a *destination*.
- **MoveTo**—Instance method to rename a file or directory.
- **Delete**—Deletes the specified file or directory. Wildcards are not allowed. If the read-only attribute of the file you want to delete is set, the method call will throw an exception.

WORKING WITH PATHS

To manipulate a file in Visual Basic, you have to know the file path. The terms *filename* and *pathname* are often used interchangeably when referring to files. However, use of the term *path* usually means that some directory information is included with the filename. Consider the following examples, each of which represents a valid file path that can be used with most of the file functions in this chapter:

```
C:\MyApplication\Sounds\ding.wav
Sounds\ding.wav
ding.wav
```

Suppose your application is installed in the directory C:\MyApplication and needs to access some sound files in the C:\MyApplication\Sounds directory. Each of the previous three examples refers to a sound file named ding.wav. The first line is an example of an *absolute path*—there is absolutely no doubt as to the file's location. However, the other two examples are *relative paths*. Although the absolute path leaves no room for doubt, hard-coding a drive or folder name within your program is never a good idea. A commercial application such as Microsoft Office lets you change the default installation directory to anything you want. Even if you install the application in an off-the-wall location like D:\JUNK123\, it still can find all its other files (such as document templates and clip art) and function normally.

LOCATING FILES USING RELATIVE PATHS

Relative paths are based on a *current directory*. Think of the current directory as the folder you currently have open in Windows Explorer or the directory in a command prompt window. When your application needs to find other files using relative paths, there are two very useful members available, shown in Table 24.1:

TABLE 24.1 DETERMINING THE RIGHT PATH

Property Name	Namespace	Description
Directory.GetCurrentDirectory	System.IO	Sets or retrieves the current directory.
Application.StartupPath	System.Windows.Forms	Retrieves the directory from which the application was started.

When you start a Windows application, the `GetCurrentDirectory` function and `StartupPath` property to return the same directory as the application executable. The current directory can be changed as needed but the startup path cannot. Continuing our previous example, suppose your application will be doing a lot of work within its `Sounds` subdirectory. The following line of code allows any subsequent file functions to access the sound files using only their filename:

```
Directory.SetCurrentDirectory(Application.StartupPath & "\Sounds"
```

> **Note**
> You also may use a configuration file or registry settings to store the location of other files required by your application.

As you may have noticed, the backslash character (\) is used to separate directory names in a file path, so in the previous line of code we had to add a backslash before the new subdirectory name. Starting in Visual Basic .NET, a `Path` class has been provided to make parsing file paths easier for the programmer. For example, you can use the `Combine` method of the `Path` class, which automatically adds a slash if necessary:

```
strPath = Directory.Combine("C:\","Program Files")
strPath = Directory.Combine(strPath,"Netmeeting")
strPath = Directory.Combine(strPath,"blip.wav")
```

After the three lines of code had executed, `strPath` would contain the string `C:\Program Files\Netmeeting\blip.wav`. Keep in mind that the `Combine` method is only a string helper; it does not check whether the path is valid.

> **Note**
> In addition to combining paths, the `Path` class contains other useful path manipulation functions. For example, you can use methods in this class to extract the file extension or parse a file path in a platform-independent manner.

FINDING SPECIAL FOLDERS

Among the many folders on your hard drive are some that are used by the operating system for a variety of special purposes. For example, the `My Documents` folder allows users to consolidate all their documents in a single area. Other examples are the `Temp` directory, used for storing temporary files, and the Windows directory itself. These folders may have very different paths depending on the operating system. For example, Windows 95 users usually have Windows installed in the `C:\Windows` directory, and Windows 2000/NT users have a Windows directory called `C:\WINNT`. In addition, certain folders may be specific to the user who is logged in to the machine. Windows 2000 creates a separate `My Documents` and `Temp` directory for each user under the `Documents And Settings` folder.

If you want to find these special folders, you can use the operating system's *environment variables*. To see the environment variables, open a command prompt window and enter the command `SET`. You should see a screen similar to Figure 24.3.

Figure 24.3
Environment variables and command-line arguments can be determined by using methods in the `Environment` class.

In order to access these variables from code, you use the `Environment` class, which includes several useful members for dealing with environment variables, as shown in Table 24.2:

TABLE 24.2 WATCHING OUT FOR THE ENVIRONMENT

Member Name	Description
`GetEnvironmentVariable` method	Returns the value of a specified environment variable
`SystemDirectory` property	Returns the path of the Windows System directory
`OSVersion` property	Can be used to determine the operating system version and service pack level

The following sample code returns the path for a Windows 2000 user's `My Documents` directory:

```
strPath = Environment.GetEnvironmentVariable("USERPROFILE")
strPath = Path.Combine(strPath, "My Documents")
```

As an exercise, you could expand the previous code into a generic class that would find special folders on any operating system. To learn the names of all the special folders, see the help file topic "Special Folders."

WATCHING FOR FILE SYSTEM CHANGES

Often programmers need to work with files that are delivered by another person or program. For example, a user may want to have an Excel spreadsheet file published on the Web every time he updates it. Another example might be when someone sends you a data file via e-mail or FTP that you must import into a database on a periodic basis. Both of these activities involve waiting for a file to arrive and could be handled by repeatedly calling the `File.Exists` function. However, the .NET framework provides a class known as the `FileSystemWatcher` that can notify your application of many different types of file-related changes.

In this section we will build a program that watches a directory for the addition of new files and changes to existing files (see Listing 24.4). When these changes occur, they are noted in a listbox. The program in action is shown in Figure 24.4. Apart from the functions used to accept user input, there are really just three functions that are critical to the program's operation. The SetupWatcher function initiates the monitoring process; the FileChanged and FileRenamed functions receive file change notifications.

LISTING 24.4   FILEWATCH.ZIP—FILE WATCHER EXAMPLE

```
Private WithEvents fsWatchObj As FileSystemWatcher

Private Sub SetupWatcher(ByVal PathToWatch As String)

    fsWatchObj = New FileSystemWatcher(PathToWatch)
    fsWatchObj.IncludeSubdirectories = False
    fsWatchObj.EnableRaisingEvents = True

    AddHandler fsWatchObj.Created, AddressOf FileChanged
    AddHandler fsWatchObj.Changed, AddressOf FileChanged
    AddHandler fsWatchObj.Deleted, AddressOf FileChanged
    AddHandler fsWatchObj.Renamed, AddressOf FileRenamed

End Sub

Private Sub FileChanged(ByVal s As System.Object,_
ByVal EventInfo As FileSystemEventArgs)
    Dim DisplayMessage As String
    DisplayMessage = "File " & EventInfo.Name & " was "
    DisplayMessage &= EventInfo.ChangeType.ToString &_
 " at " & DateTime.Now.ToString
    lstFiles.Items.Add(DisplayMessage)
End Sub

Private Sub FileRenamed(ByVal s As System.Object,_
ByVal EventInfo As RenamedEventArgs)
    Dim DisplayMessage As String
    DisplayMessage = "File " & EventInfo.OldName
    DisplayMessage &= " was renamed " & EventInfo.Name &_
 " at " & DateTime.Now.ToString
    lstFiles.Items.Add(DisplayMessage)
End Sub
```

The following steps describe how to test the sample program. Doing so will give you a good idea of how the FileSystemWatcher class works.

1. Start a new Windows Application project.

2. Add the code from Listing 24.4 to the form class.

3. Add a ListBox control to the form. Set its name to lstFiles.

4. Add a Button control to the project, named btnStart.

5. In the Click event for btnStart, enter the following code:
   ```
   Call SetupWatcher("C:\temp")
   ```

6. Open Windows Explorer. If there is not already a folder called C:\TEMP, create it.

7. Start the sample program and click the button.

8. Arrange your desktop so you can watch the sample program and use Windows Explorer at the same time.

9. Copy, rename, and delete files in the C:\TEMP directory and note the changes in the listbox.

Figure 24.4
The FileSystemWatcher class contains functions to monitor file change events either synchronously or asynchronously.

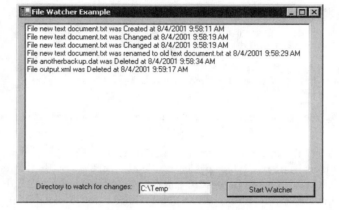

As you perform file operations in the C:\TEMP folder, the fsWatchObj object raises events, which write information received in the event parameters to the list box. This is a great example of asynchronous processing, because your program does not need to wait in a loop and the user can continue to perform other tasks. The FileSystemWatcher events are fairly straightforward, but note the following special circumstances:

- The arguments for the Renamed event delegate are different from the other FileSystemWatcher events. This is because it provides both the old and new filenames to the event.

- By setting the Filter property, you can control which files within the directory are monitored. For example, setting the filter to *.DOC would just raise events for Word documents.

- The Changed event may be fired several times in a row, because several aspects of a file (size, last write time, and so on) are changed at once during certain operations. This effect can be eliminated to some extent by using the NotifyFilter property, which offers additional control over change notification.

WORKING WITH OTHER PROCESSES

From time to time, you may need to launch another Windows program using Visual Basic code. For example, you could place a button on your form that runs calc.exe to provide users with easy access to Windows' built-in calculator. You might also want to find out the names about the programs that are currently running on a computer, or even terminate a misbehaving program. All these tasks can be accomplished by using the Process class. The Process class, which is part of the System.Diagnostics namespace, provides functionality that required complex API calls in previous versions of Visual Basic.

LAUNCHING ANOTHER WINDOWS PROGRAM

One frequently asked question has always been "How can I run an application from VB and wait for it to finish?" The following code segment shows how easy this is to do in .NET:

```
Dim procNotepad As Process

procNotepad = Process.Start("notepad.exe ")
procNotepad.WaitForExit(5000)

If procNotepad.HasExited Then
    MessageBox.Show("Notepad has been closed.")
Else
    procNotepad.Kill()
    MessageBox.Show("Notepad was still running, so I killed it!")
End If
```

The line following the Dim statement starts the Notepad executable and associates it with the procNotepad object. The parameter passed to the WaitForExit method indicates the number of milliseconds to wait for the process to end. In our example, the If statement will not be executed until the user closes Notepad or 5000 milliseconds (5 seconds) passes, whichever comes first.

Note   Omit the milliseconds parameter completely to specify an infinite wait time.

The previous code sample demonstrates launching another program and waiting for it to finish in a synchronous manner. However, if you want your program to continue executing and be notified when the process exits, you can install an event handler for the Exited event of the Process class:

```
Dim procNotepad As Process
procNotepad = Process.Start("notepad.exe ")
procNotepad.EnableRaisingEvents = True
AddHandler procNotepad.Exited, AddressOf NotepadExitEvent

Private Sub NotepadExitEvent(ByVal sender As Object, ByVal e As EventArgs)
    MessageBox.Show("Notepad has just exited!")
End Sub
```

The previous lines of code allow the user to continue working with your program after the notepad.exe process starts. When the Exited event fires, the NotepadExitEvent subroutine will be executed. In order to get a Process object to fire the Exited event, you must set its WatchForExit property to True.

ATTACHING TO AN EXISTING PROCESS

You can do a lot of neat things using the `Process` class. We have already demonstrated killing a process. You also can change its priority or determine CPU and memory usage statistics. Each of these features is easy to use and listed in the help files. However, before you can change process properties, you have to get the process associated with a `Process` object. As we have demonstrated, this is easy when you start the process from VB, but what about processes that are already running? The `Process` class provides several useful methods:

- `GetCurrentProcess`—Returns a `Process` object for the current process.
- `GetProcessByID`—Returns a `Process` object for the specified process id (the PID column listed in the Windows Task Manager).
- `GetProcesses`—Returns a collection of `Process` objects; each object represents a process on the system.
- `GetProcessesByName`—Returns a collection of `Process` objects that have a specified process name.

Note

> Even after a process has ended, the process resources are kept in place for a time, so these methods may return more than just running processes. The `HasExited` property can be checked to see whether the process has ended.

The following lines of code add the names of system processes to a listbox:

```
Dim procTemp As Process
For Each procTemp In Process.GetProcesses()
        lstProcesses.Items.Add(procTemp.ProcessName)
Next
```

You also can manipulate processes on remote machines by using the machine name as an optional parameter in the `GetProcesses` function.

WORKING WITH FILE STREAMS

Every file on your hard drive is just a sequence of characters. Text-based files are usually human readable and the characters can be edited in a text editor, such as Notepad. Binary files, on the other hand, contain data used by a program. If you try to open a binary file (such as an EXE file) in Notepad, the displayed text will not make any sense. This is because each character represents a byte of data in a format known only to the user of the file. In the case of an EXE file, the bytes are used by the operating system to run a compiled program. (As we will soon see, XML provides a good way to store structured data in readable text format.)

→ For more on the Byte and other data types, **see** in Chapter 6, "Understanding Data Types," **p. 143**

The Microsoft .NET framework introduces some new classes designed to work with *streams*. Files on the disk drive can be thought of as streams of character data, but streams also can reside in memory or be accessed over a network. As we will see, it is very easy to use the .NET framework classes to read and write data to a stream sequentially. You can also seek to a specific point in the stream, if the particular stream supports seeking.

READING AND WRITING SEQUENTIAL TEXT FILES

Although text files may seem really simple, sometimes you may not need the power of a database (not to mention the extra coding, configuration, and support files that go along with it). The `StreamReader` and `StreamWriter` classes are designed for dealing with text files in a sequential fashion. *Sequential* means that the file is accessed one byte after the other in sequence, rather than jumping to a specific location.

> **Tip**
>
> You can create batch files, FTP scripts, and many other simple file formats on the fly by using sequential text files.

You can process data in a sequential file a line at a time or by reading a specified number of characters. The following few lines of code read each line of a text file and print it in the Output window.

```
Dim TestFile As StreamReader
Dim LineofText As String

TestFile = File.OpenText(Directory.GetCurrentDirectory() & "\quotes.txt")
Do
    LineofText = TestFile.ReadLine()
    Debug.WriteLine(LineofText)
Loop Until LineofText Is Nothing
TestFile.Close()
```

The code for processing a text file line by line is very simple: Simply open the file and repeatedly call the `Readline` method of the `StreamReader` class. Another method, `Writeline`, allows you to write a line of text to a file. The following example reads each line in a file and then writes the uppercase version to another file:

```
Dim TestFile As StreamReader
Dim OutputFile As StreamWriter
Dim LineofText As String


TestFile = File.OpenText(Directory.GetCurrentDirectory() & "\quotes.txt")
OutputFile = File.AppendText(Directory.GetCurrentDirectory() &_
"\output.txt")

While TestFile.Peek() <> -1
    LineOfText = testfile.ReadLine()
    OutputFile.WriteLine(LineOfText.ToUpper)
```

```
    End While

    TestFile.Close()
    OutputFile.Close()
```

There are a couple of differences in the code examples for reading and writing a text file. First, notice we opened the file with the `File.AppendText` method, rather than the `File.OpenText` method. *Appending* means adding to a file, so the `AppendText` method will either add to an existing file or create the file if it does not exist. Repeatedly calling this function will cause the `output.txt` file to grow in size. On the other hand, if you want to erase the `output.txt` file before writing, you can open the file with the `CreateText` method:

```
    TestFile = File.CreateText("c:\temp\output.txt")
```

Appending to a file is useful for creating a log file, as you will see later in this chapter. In the second code example, we changed the `While` loop to use the `Peek` function. The `Peek` function returns the character code for the next character in the file, without reading it. Normally, each call to the `ReadLine` method advances to the next line in the stream. By peeking at the next character, you can determine whether the read will actually return anything. `Peek` returns –1 once you have reached the end of the file you are reading.

READING BINARY DATA TYPES

At the operating system level, a file is a series of bytes. The `StreamReader` and `StreamWriter` classes are designed to deal with these bytes as string data. However, the bytes in your file may not always represent characters of text, but instead be numbers. The .NET framework provides the `BinaryReader` and `BinaryWriter` classes to allow you to access this information in a file directly in the correct numerical format. Table 24.3 lists some of the available methods and their associated data types.

TABLE 24.3   USING THE `BinaryReader` AND `BinaryWriter` CLASSES

Method Names	Data Types
Read	Bytes or Characters
ReadBoolean	Boolean values
ReadByte	One Byte value
ReadBytes	Array of Bytes
ReadChar	One character
ReadChars	Array of characters
ReadString	String
ReadDecimal	Decimal
ReadInt16	Short
ReadInt32	Integer
ReadInt64	Long

To demonstrate the `BinaryReader` class, we'll read a text file, but this time using the `Byte` data type. You can process a file either a single byte at a time or by blocks in a size of your choosing. The code in Listing 24.5 reads a text file in blocks of 100 bytes. The bytes are converted to their ASCII character values and displayed in a text box.

LISTING 24.5   `FILESTREAM.ZIP`—READ BYTES AND CONVERT TO STRING

```
Const BLOCK_SIZE As Integer = 100

Dim TestFile As BinaryReader
Dim BytesRead As Integer
Dim ByteValues(BLOCK_SIZE) As Byte
Dim StringValue As String
Dim ASCIIConverter As System.Text.ASCIIEncoding

'Open a File for Reading
TestFile = New BinaryReader(File.Open("quotes.txt",_
IO.FileMode.Open, IO.FileAccess.Read))

'Read the file in byte blocks, converting bytes to ASCII
BytesRead = TestFile.Read(ByteValues, 0, BLOCK_SIZE)
ASCIIConverter = New System.Text.ASCIIEncoding()
While BytesRead > 0
    StringValue = ASCIIConverter.GetString(ByteValues, 0, BytesRead)
    txtMessage.text &= StringValue
    Array.Clear(ByteValues, 0, BLOCK_SIZE)
    BytesRead = TestFile.Read(ByteValues, 0, BLOCK_SIZE)
End While

TestFile.Close()
```

Using the `BinaryReader` class is more involved than the `StreamReader` class, but it offers more flexibility if you are working with `Byte` data. Listing 24.5 also demonstrates the relationship between text files and bytes; characters are stored in a text file using an *encoding* standard. The ASCII encoding stores a character per byte, whereas the Unicode encoding requires two bytes (and contains more characters). For more information, see the help topic entitled "Encoding."

PARSING XML FILES

XML, which stands for eXtensible Markup Language, is a core technology in Visual Basic .NET. For example, the XML format is used in VB Project files and Web services. As we learned in Chapter 22, XML is also a fundamental technology behind ADO.NET datasets. Although XML is capable of storing structured data, it also can be used in just about any other circumstance where you need to store data in a text format. The advantage of using XML over another format (such as comma-delimited) is that there are several classes included with the .NET framework that allow you to parse XML files. Because XML is an industry-standard technology, XML files should be easy to exchange with other companies or individuals. In this section we will discuss basic parsing of an XML file. To learn more about how data is stored in an XML file, see Chapter 22, "Using ADO .NET."

➜ For more on the XML in ADO .NET, **see** Chapter 22, "Using ADO .NET," **p. 599**

One example use of the XML file format is maintaining session variables on a Web farm. All the session variables can be condensed into a single string using XML and saved in a database file or files.

SAVING DATA IN XML FORMAT

As an example, let's suppose we are storing information about customers using the following classes:

```
Private Class OrderItem
    Public ItemName As String
    Public UnitPrice As Decimal
    Public Quantity As Integer
End Class

Private Class Customer
    Public Name As String
    Public ID As Integer
    Public OrderItems As ArrayList
    Sub New()
        OrderItems = New ArrayList()
    End Sub
End Class
```

The Customer class describes each customer as having a name, customer id, and arraylist of order items. Each order item has a name, price, and quantity. Assume we have an array of customer objects in memory and want to create an XML file to store the information. Listing 24.6 shows how we can accomplish this with two classes: the XMLDocument class, which manipulates XML in memory, and the XMLWriter, which writes XML to disk. Figure 24.5. shows what the resulting XML file looks like.

PART
VI
CH
24

LISTING 24.6 BasicXML.ZIP—USING THE XMLDocument CLASS

```
Dim cusTemp As Customer
Dim xmlDoc As New XmlDocument()
Dim RootNode As XmlNode
Dim TempCustomer, TempCustomerNode As XmlNode
Dim TempOrder, TempOrderNode As XmlNode
Dim ItemListNode As XmlNode
Dim i, j As Integer

'Create an empty customer node for use later
TempCustomer = xmlDoc.CreateNode(XmlNodeType.Element, "Customer", "")
TempCustomer.Attributes.Append(xmlDoc.CreateAttribute("ID"))

'Create an empty order item node for use later
TempOrder = xmlDoc.CreateNode(XmlNodeType.Element, "OrderItem", "")
TempOrder.Attributes.Append(xmlDoc.CreateAttribute("UnitPrice"))
TempOrder.Attributes.Append(xmlDoc.CreateAttribute("Quantity"))
TempOrder.Attributes.Append(xmlDoc.CreateAttribute("ItemName"))

'Create the root node of the XML document
RootNode = xmlDoc.CreateNode(XmlNodeType.Element, "Customers", "")
```

LISTING 24.6   CONTINUED

```
xmlDoc.AppendChild(RootNode)

For i = 0 To 39
    cusTemp = Customers(i)

    'Create a customer node, set ID and name
    TempCustomerNode = TempCustomer.Clone()
    TempCustomerNode.InnerText = cusTemp.Name
    TempCustomerNode.Attributes("ID").Value = cusTemp.ID.ToString

    'Add order items to customer node, if any
    If cusTemp.OrderItems.Count > 0 Then
        ItemListNode = xmlDoc.CreateNode(XmlNodeType.Element, "OrderItems", "")
        For j = 0 To cusTemp.OrderItems.Count - 1
            TempOrderNode = TempOrder.Clone()
            TempOrderNode.Attributes("Quantity").Value =_
             CType(cusTemp.OrderItems(j), OrderItem).Quantity.ToString
            TempOrderNode.Attributes("UnitPrice").Value =_
             CType(cusTemp.OrderItems(j), OrderItem).UnitPrice.ToString
            TempOrderNode.Attributes("ItemName").Value =_
             CType(cusTemp.OrderItems(j), OrderItem).ItemName
            ItemListNode.AppendChild(TempOrderNode)
        Next j
        TempCustomerNode.AppendChild(ItemListNode)
    End If

    'Add customer node to XML Document
    xmlDoc.DocumentElement.AppendChild(TempCustomerNode)
Next

'Write XML document object to file
Dim writer As New XmlTextWriter("output.xml", System.Text.ASCIIEncoding.ASCII)
writer.Formatting = Formatting.Indented
xmlDoc.WriteContentTo(writer)
writer.Close()
MessageBox.Show("XML File has been created. ")
```

As you can see from the code, each XML document is made up of nodes, each of which has a parent and a child. We called the root node of our XML document Customers to represent the highest level of data, the array of customers. Within the Customers node, a new node was added with each customer's information.

READING AN XML DOCUMENT

From Figure 24.5 you can see that each XML node object is represented as a tagged element in the resulting file. In creating our XML document we used both *attributes*, which are contained within a tag element, and the InnerText property that specifies what is contained within a tag. The tags used to delimit XML data are very similar to the tags used to describe HTML formatting. Notice that if no text is present (for example the orders use only attributes) the tag is ended with /> rather than the element name.

Figure 24.5
Although XML files can be displayed in Notepad or Visual Studio .NET, Internet Explorer provides a colorful and collapsible view.

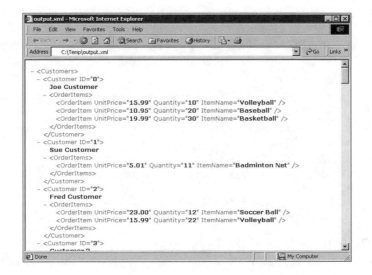

The XMLDocument class provides built-in functions to enumerate and manipulate XML nodes, so it is very easy to read our document back into memory:

```
Dim xmlDoc As New XmlDocument()
Dim tempnode As XmlNode
xmldoc.Load("c:\temp\output.xml")
For Each tempnode In xmlDoc.DocumentElement.ChildNodes
  Debug.WriteLine("Customer " & tempnode.InnerText &_
  " has " & TempNode.LastChild.ChildNodes.Count & " orders.")
Next
```

The previous For Each loop visits every child node of the root node (represented by the DocumentElement property), printing the number of order items and the customer name.

ACCESSING THE REGISTRY

The Windows registry is a hierarchical database used by the operating system to maintain a variety of system settings. For example, Internet Explorer stores option settings and recent URLs you have typed in the registry. The information for ODBC data sources you create also is stored in the registry. Figure 24.6 shows the Windows Registry Editor, which can be used to view and update registry information.

You can access the registry by running the regedit.exe program, as shown in Figure 24.6.

PART
VI
CH
24

DWORD data item

Figure 24.6
You can use the
registry to store
information related
to your application,
such as a recent file
list or database
connection string.

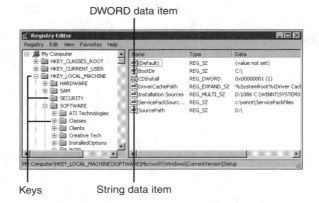

Keys   String data item

UNDERSTANDING THE REGISTRY'S STRUCTURE

As you can see from the figure, the registry is displayed visually as a tree of folders, much
like subdirectories on your hard drive in Windows Explorer. Each folder in the registry tree
is referred to as a *registry key*. If you run the regedit.exe program, you will notice there are
several top-level keys that begin with the prefix HKEY such as HKEY_CURRENT_USER, which provides an information store for the currently logged-in user.

A registry keys can contain additional keys (subkeys) as well as name-value pairs. The name-
value pairs may be binary, hex, decimal, or strings, depending on the needs of your application.

UPDATING AND READING REGISTRY VALUES

If you want to store or retrieve registry data, the Registry class in the Microsoft.Win32
namespace provides the necessary methods. You can associate a key in the registry with an
instance of the Registry class and then call methods to set or read values.

Note

Use caution when editing unknown values in the registry. Messing around with
Windows' internal settings could leave your system in an inoperable state!

Registry keys have a path, which like file paths is delimited by the slash character. To identify a key, you have to provide both a top-level key and a subkey path. Each top-level key is
associated with a static field in the Registry class, as described in Table 24.4:

TABLE 24.4 STATIC FIELDS FOR REGISTRY KEYS

Registry Class Field	Corresponding Registry Key
ClassesRoot	HKEY_CLASSES_ROOT
CurrentConfig	HKEY_CURRENT_CONFIG
CurrentUser	HKEY_CURRENT_USER

Registry Class Field	Corresponding Registry Key
DynData	HKEY_DYN_DATA
LocalMachine	HKEY_LOCAL_MACHINE
PerformanceData	HKEY_PERFORMANCE_DATA
Users	HKEY_USERS

To access a key in the registry, use the OpenSubKey method of the appropriate top-level field. The remaining subkey path is provided as a parameter to the OpenSubKey method, as in the following example:

```
Const WinLogonPath As String =_
"SOFTWARE\Microsoft\Windows NT\CurrentVersion\WinLogon"
Dim LogonKey As RegistryKey
LogonKey = Registry.LocalMachine.OpenSubKey(WinLogonPath, True)
```

In the third line of code, the LocalMachine field is used to identify the KEY_LOCAL_MACHINE top-level key, which stores information about the local PC. The OpenSubKey function accepts the remaining subkey path, followed by a Boolean variable that determines whether the key is updateable. If you just want to read information from the registry, set this parameter to False. If you plan on updating the registry, set this parameter to True.

With an instance of a RegistryKey object, you can manipulate values in the registry key by calling the GetValue and SetValue functions. The following example sets registry values in the Winlogon subkey that will cause a Windows 2000 or NT machine to automatically log on at startup:

```
LogonKey.SetValue("AutoAdminLogon", "1")
LogonKey.SetValue("DefaultUserName", "Administrator")
LogonKey.SetValue("DefaultPassword", "topsecret")
```

If a value does not already exist, then SetValue will create it. Reading a value from the registry is easy as well—simply use the GetValue method:

```
Dim strValue As String
strValue = LogonKey.GetValue("AutoAdminLogon", "?").ToString
```

The GetValue method returns an object that can be converted to a string or numeric value. A second optional parameter allows you to specify a default return value. In the previous example, if no AutoAdminLogon value exists, a question mark (?) will be returned. If the default value is not passed to the GetValue method and the value does not exist, Null will be returned.

TRADITIONAL VISUAL BASIC FILE FUNCTIONS

Up to this point we have shown how to access the file system using classes provided by the .NET framework. However, there is another group of file-related functions that have been around since early versions of Visual Basic (and in some cases, the original BASIC language).

If you work with a lot of existing Visual Basic code, you may run into these traditional file I/O functions. These functions are still supported via a compatibility namespace, although there are some changes to their syntax in Visual Basic .NET. We recommend you use the newer object-oriented classes whenever possible, but if you need to work with existing code you may find this section helpful.

Before using any of these functions, add the following Imports statement to your code:

```
Imports Microsoft.VisualBasic.FileSystem
```

USING Dir TO FIND FILES

One useful file function is the Dir function. This function works just like the dir command at an MS-DOS command prompt. You can use it to retrieve a list of one or more operating system files that match a path and file specification. For example, C:*.BAT is the path to all the files in the root directory of drive C having a BAT extension. The syntax of the Dir function is as follows:

```
stringvar = Dir(path[,attributes])
```

One common use of Dir is to determine whether a file exists. The function returns the filename without the full path if the specified file is found, or it returns an empty string if no files were found. The following code example uses Dir to check for the existence of a file:

```
Public Function bFileExists(sFile As String) As Boolean
        If Dir(sFile) <> "" Then bFileExists = True Else bFileExists = False
End Function
```

This function could then be used to check any filenames passed to the program by the user, as in the following example:

```
Dim sUserFile As String

sUserFile = InputBox("Enter the file name:")

If Not bFileExists(sUserFile) Then
        MessageBox.Show("The file does not exist. Please try again.")
        Application.Exit()

End If
```

Another use of the Dir function is to return a list of multiple files in the specified path. If you use the dir command at an MS-DOS prompt, each matching file is listed on the screen. However, because the Dir function is designed to return only a single string variable, you have to use a loop and retrieve one filename at a time.

Suppose that your C:\DATA directory contains several picture files with a BMP (bitmap) extension. The path used to retrieve these files with the Dir function would be C:\DATA*.BMP. You can use the following lines of code to retrieve the filenames and add them to a listbox:

```
Dim sNextFile As String

sNextFile = Dir("C:\Data\*.BMP")
```

```
While sNextFile <> ""
    lstPictureList.Items.Add(sNextFile)
    sNextFile = Dir()
End While
```

In the preceding example, notice that only the file path to `Dir` is supplied on the first call. Each subsequent call to `Dir` has no arguments, indicating that you want to use the previous file path and move to the next filename in the list. When no more files match, `Dir` returns an empty string and the `While` loop terminates.

The second, optional parameter of the `Dir` function is used to provide additional conditions (beyond the specified path) with which to select files. You add together constants defined in `FileAttributes` to control the types of files returned. For example, the following statement causes subdirectories and files that start with the letter S to be returned:

```
sNextFile = Dir("C:\Data\S*",FileAttribute.Directory)
```

The available constants and their purposes are listed under the help file topic "FileAttributes Enumeration."

FILE MANIPULATION FUNCTIONS

As with the `Dir` function, most of the file-manipulation commands in Visual Basic are as straightforward as their MS-DOS equivalents, although with a few limitations. These commands are summarized in Table 24.5.

TABLE 24.5 SUMMARY OF FILE FUNCTIONS

Action	Syntax
Copy a file	`FileCopy source, dest`
Delete one or more files	`Kill path`
Create a new folder	`MkDir pathname`
Remove an empty folder	`RmDir pathname`
Change current directory	`ChDir pathname`
Change current drive	`ChDrive drive`

The `FileCopy` command has the limitation that you cannot use wildcards to specify multiple files. `FileCopy` can copy files locally or over a network, as shown in the following examples:

```
'The following line copies a file while changing its name:
FileCopy ("D:\My Documents\Hey Now.txt",  "C:\DATA\TEST.TXT")

'The following lines of code use a network path for the source file:
Dim sDest As String = "\\myserver\deptfiles\budget98.XLS"
Dim sSource As String = "C:\DATA\BUDGET.XLS"
FileCopy sSource, sDest
```

The `FileCopy` statement automatically overwrites an existing file, unless the file is read-only or locked open by another application.

> **Note**
>
> The older `Name` and `App.Path` functions have been replaced by the newer `File.Move` and `Application.StartupPath` methods.

SEQUENTIAL TEXT FILES

Visual Basic's file input and output routines allow you to read and write sequential text data. Before you read or write information, you must open the file with the `FileOpen` function. The `FileOpen` statement associates the actual filename (that is, `C:\DATA\PEOPLE.TXT`) with a *file number*. A file number is an integer value used to identify the file in subsequent lines of code:

```
FileOpen(1, "C:\Data\People.txt", OpenMode.Input)
```

> **Note**
>
> In the preceding example, 1 is the file number. However, if you open and close multiple files throughout your program, using this number might not be a good idea. In that case, you should use the `FreeFile` function, which returns the next available file number, as in the following example:
>
> ```
> Dim FileNum As Integer
> FileNum = FreeFile()
> FileOpen(FileNum, "C:\Temp\quotes.txt", OpenMode.Input)
> ```

In addition to providing the filename and number association, the `FileOpen` statement tells Visual Basic how you intend to use the specified file. (Many different options are available with `FileOpen`, as discussed in the Help file.) The `Mode` parameter is set to `OpenMode.Input` to indicate that the file will be opened for sequential input. The following code uses a `LineInput` statement in a `While` loop to read the file one line at a time. A line in a file is delimited by an end of line marker, which in Windows is the carriage return character followed by the line feed character. The first `LineInput` statement reads the first line, the second `LineInput` reads the second line, and so on.

```
Dim FileNum As Integer
Dim TempString As String

FileNum = FreeFile()
FileOpen(FileNum, "C:\temp\output.xml", OpenMode.Input)
While Not EOF(FileNum)
    TempString = LineInput(FileNum)
    lstFiles.Items.Add(TempString)
End While
FileClose(FileNum)
```

If you try to read more lines of text than are in the file, an error occurs. Therefore, the sample code uses the `EOF` (end-of-file) function before attempting to read.

> **Note**
>
> VB6 users will notice the old-style file commands have been altered slightly in VB .NET. For example, the `Line Input` statement is now the `LineInput` function. Also, the following type of `Open` syntax is no longer supported:
>
> ```
> Open "C:\File.txt" for Input as #1_
> 'THIS WILL NOT WORK ANYMORE!
> ```

After you open the file, you can choose from several methods of reading information from it. In the example, each line was considered one piece of information, so no further processing on the string variable was done. However, sometimes you may want to read less than a whole line or store more than one piece of information on a single line. In these cases, you can use the `Input` function.

> **Note**
>
> Visual Basic provides a lot of nice string-manipulation functions. Again, the authors would like to suggest that for new projects, you use the object-oriented file functions.

The `Input` function is designed to read information stored in a delimited fashion. For example, the following line of a text file contains three distinct pieces of information: a string, a number, and a date. Commas, quotation marks, and the # symbol are used to delimit the information.

```
"Test",100,#1998-01-01#
```

The following lines of code read each item into an appropriately typed variable:

```
Dim TempString As String
Dim TempDate As DateTime
Dim TempInt As Integer

FileNum = FreeFile()
FileOpen(FileNum, "C:\Temp\test.txt", OpenMode.Input)

Input(FileNum, TempString)
Input(FileNum, TempInt)
Input(FileNum, TempDate)

FileClose(FileNum)
```

Remember that the `Input` function looks for delimiters, so exceptions will be thrown if your `Input` statements do not match the format of the file.

After you finish using a file, you should always close it with the `FileClose` function. This way, you can free up the file number for use with other files. If you do not specify a file number, `Close` closes all open file handles.

One good use of a sequential text file is a log file. For example, I have a scheduler application that runs programs and database updates. I rarely work at the machine on which the scheduler application is running, but I can connect over the network and view the log file to see whether the updates have completed.

As with the newer object-oriented file functions, the `FileOpen` method supports both append and output modes. Compare the following two lines of code, each of which opens a file for output:

```
'Append mode - adds to an existing file or creates a new one
FileOpen(FileNum, Application.StartupPath & "\errorlog.txt", OpenMode.Append)

'Output Mode - always creates a new file, erases any existing information
FileOpen(FileNum, Application.StartupPath & "\errorlog.txt", OpenMode.Output)
```

Append mode means data written to the file is added to the end of any existing data. This is perfect for the log file application because you want to keep adding to the log file. Opening a file for `Output` means that any existing data will be erased. In either case, the `Open` statement automatically creates the file if it does not exist. After a file has been opened for `Output`, you can use the `Print` or `PrintLine` statements to write string information to it. The `PrintLine` method inserts a new line character after the text.

Two other functions, `Write` and `WriteLine`, automatically add separators and delimiters. They are intended for use with the `Input` function described earlier. An example of the use of the `WriteLine` function is:

```
WriteLine(FileNum, "This is a Write Example", #12/10/1972#, 100 * 2)
```

The line that would be written to the file looks like this:

```
"This is a Write Example",#1972-12-10#,200
```

As you can see, the `Print` functions give you more control over output format, whereas the `Write` functions add delimiters for easy retrieval of information.

UNDERSTANDING INI FILES

INI files (pronounced *any files* by us southerners) are useful for storing program information and user settings. An INI file is basically a text file with a simple structure that allows you to save and retrieve specific pieces of information; its filename extension is INI, short for *initialization*. By storing information in an INI file, you can avoid hard-coding values in your program. This way, you can easily change values without recompiling the program. The structure of INI files is simple. INI files can be viewed and edited with Notepad, or any other text editor. A sample INI file is shown in Figure 24.7.

The three elements to an INI file are *sections*, *keys*, and *values*. (Microsoft calls a section an *application*; the reason for this involves the history of INI files when an application stored its own settings in WIN.INI.) The descriptions of these parts are summarized in Table 24.6.

Figure 24.7
Although Microsoft's direction seems to be using XML for everything, an INI file provides a portable and easy-to-understand configuration file format.

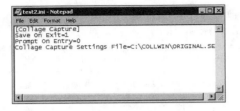

TABLE 24.6 PARTS OF AN INI FILE

Element	Description
Section	A name enclosed in brackets ([ ]} that groups a set of values and keys together.
Key	A unique string. The key will be followed by an equal sign (=) and a value. A key needs to be unique only within a specific section.
Value	The actual information from a particular key in the INI file. A section and key together are used to read or write a value.

The order of sections and keys within the file is not important because the section and key names (should) point to only one value. One final note on the structure of an INI file: A semicolon (;) is used to indicate a comment; any keys or values following a semicolon are ignored. For example, look at this INI section:

```
[Settings]
DBLocation=P:\USERINFO.MDB
;DBLocation=D:\CODE\TEST.MDB
```

In the preceding section, switching from a local development database to a production database is easy. You can simply comment out the line you don't want.

USING INI FILES IN VISUAL BASIC

One reason INI files are easy to use is that you do not have to worry about creating the file, opening the file, or finding the correct line; one function call is all it takes to save or read a value. Before you can use INI files, however, you have to declare two Windows API functions and write a couple of wrapper functions around them. We have already done this for you. Simply add the code in Listing 24.7 to the top of your form class.

Tip

Create your own DLL file and namespace that contains these functions, then you can reference them from any project. For more on how to do this read Chapter 9, "Creating Code Components."

LISTING 24.7 `INIFunctions.ZIP`—USING INI FILES IN YOUR PROGRAM

```
Declare Function GetPrivateProfileString Lib "kernel32" Alias _
                 "GetPrivateProfileStringA" (ByVal lpApplicationName _
                 As String, ByVal lpKeyName As String, ByVal lpDefault _
                 As String, ByVal lpReturnedString As String, ByVal _
                 nSize As Integer, ByVal lpFileName As String) As Integer
Declare Function WritePrivateProfileString Lib "kernel32" Alias _
                 "WritePrivateProfileStringA" (ByVal lpApplicationName _
                 As String, ByVal lpKeyName As String, ByVal lpString As String, _
                 ByVal lpFileName As String) As Integer

Public Shared Function sGetINI(ByVal sINIFile As String,_
ByVal sSection As String, ByVal sKey As String,_
ByVal sDefault As String) As String

        Dim sTemp As String = Space(255)
        Dim nLength As Integer


        nLength = GetPrivateProfileString(sSection, sKey, sDefault, sTemp, _
        255, sINIFile)
        Return sTemp.Substring(0, nLength)

End Function

Public Shared Sub writeINI(ByVal sINIFile As String,_
ByVal sSection As String, ByVal sKey As String,_
ByVal sValue As String)

        'Remove CR/LF characters
        sValue = sValue.Replace(vbCr, vbNullChar)
        sValue = sValue.Replace(vbLf, vbNullChar)

        'Write information to INI file
        WritePrivateProfileString(sSection, sKey, sValue, sINIFile)

End Sub
```

After the code in Listing 24.7 has been entered, you can use the function sGetINI and the subroutine writeINI to easily read and write to an INI file. Listing 24.8 shows how you can retrieve settings from an INI file for use at program startup.

LISTING 24.8 `INIFunctions.ZIP`—USING AN INI FILE FOR PROGRAM SETTINGS

```
Private Sub InitProgram()

    Dim sINIFile As String
    Dim sUserName As String
    Dim nCount As Integer
    Dim i As Integer

    'Store the location of the INI file
    sINIFile = Application.StartupPath & "\..\SETTINGS.INI"

    'Read the user name from the INI file
```

LISTING 24.8   CONTINUED

```
    sUserName = sGetINI(sINIFile, "Settings", "UserName", "?")

    If sUsername = "?" Then
        'No user name was present - ask for it and save for next time
        sUserName = InputBox("Enter your name please:")
        writeini(sINIFile, "Settings", "UserName", sUserName)
    Else
        Me.Text = "Welcome back " & sUserName
    End If



    'Fill up combo box list from INI file
    cmbRegion.Items.Clear()
    nCount = Convert.ToInt32(sGetINI(sINIFile, "Regions", "Count", "0"))

    If nCount > 0 Then
        For i = 0 To nCount
            cmbRegion.Items.Add(sGetINI(sINIFile, "Regions", "Region" & i, "?"))
        Next i

        'select the user's last chosen item
        cmbRegion.SelectedIndex = Convert.ToInt32(sGetINI(sINIFile,_
    "Regions", "LastRegion", "0"))
    End If
End Sub
```

PART
VI

CH
24

The code in Listing 24.8 first checks the INI file for a username. By providing the default value ?, you can determine whether the username already exists in the INI file. If it doesn't exist, you can prompt for it. The default value is a great feature because it does not matter whether the INI file even exists, which makes your program less likely to throw an exception. However, if the file is important enough that you don't want your program to run without it, you display an appropriate message for the user and exit.

The next part of the code example reads the number of regions from the INI file and uses that value to place each region in a combo box. The final statement sets the Text property of the combo box to a value from the INI file, using the first item in the list as a default.

Driving your program from INI files, as demonstrated in Listing 24.8, allows you to make minor changes to the program quickly and easily without even recompiling it.

QUESTIONS: USING FILES

1. I need to store configuration data with an application on the end-user's PC. Of all the different methods, which one should I use? The answer depends on what type of data you want to store. The following list contains some examples:

   - *Simple variable/value pairs*, such as default color scheme, file locations, or database connection string—If just you or your program needs to access these values, put them in the registry. If an end user needs to edit these outside of your program or copy them to another computer, consider an INI file.

- *Free-Form Text Message*, such as the license agreement for your software—Use a text file.

- *Structured data*, such as a list of states and their abbreviations for importing on program startup—Create an XML file containing the information and distribute it with your application. Use the XML parser to read it in.

  Keep in mind these are general suggestions and may be adjusted to fit your needs. If you have an application that is continuously communicating with a database, you may want to store the extra information there as well.

2. What issues will I run into with accessing files over the network? If permissions are a problem, investigate the security functions in the `FileIOPermission` class. You may also need to use the `Refresh` method of a `FileSystemInfo` object that is open for a long time, if another network user changes the file.

3. A user is sending me a large data file, but my file watcher program tries to upload it before he finishes sending the file and causes an error. How can I fix this? A professional scheduling package I looked at had an option to check whether a file size was stable over a period of time. You could write this functionality in VB pretty easily. However, an even easier fix is to get the user to send an empty file called `done.txt` after the data file is uploaded. Your program should then know when to start processing.

4. Can I save database information to a file and reload it without reconnecting to the database? Yes; please see the ADO chapters, 21 and 22, for more information.

CHAPTER 25

INTERACTING WITH OTHER APPLICATIONS

In This Chapter

With a little bit of programming, a Visual Basic .NET program can be made to control other applications that are installed on your computer, such as members of the Microsoft Office suite. This method of working "outside the box" lets you use Visual Basic to create incredibly useful tools that harness the existing power provided by these other programs. For example, if you would like to include Microsoft Excel functionality in a VB program, you can have your program automatically start Excel itself, acting as a remote control to drive the Excel application.

In this chapter, we will demonstrate how to create Visual Basic .NET applications that interact with both Microsoft Excel and Microsoft Word. As an added bonus, you will see how to use Visual Basic .NET's SmtpMail class to have your applications automatically send e-mail messages.

> **Note**
>
> In order for a Visual Basic .NET application to be able to control another program, that other program must be installed on the user's computer. It would be a good idea to include some error handling code to ensure that the target application does not fail to start up.

REMOTE-CONTROLLING MICROSOFT EXCEL

The Microsoft Excel object library, which is installed on a PC whenever Excel is installed, includes a group of objects that let applications control the Excel application behind the scenes. By leveraging this background process, you can create a Visual Basic program that begins an Excel session and works with an Excel workbook just as if a user were sitting at the keyboard and using Excel normally.

As you can see, the Excel object functionality is exposed as a Component Object Model (COM) component; however, Visual Basic .NET will be able to create a .NET platform bridge to Excel's COM functionality.

> **Note**
>
> In order to use these techniques to interact with Microsoft Excel, you must have Excel 2000 or later installed on your system.

ADDING A REFERENCE TO THE EXCEL OBJECT LIBRARY

To create an application that will interact with Microsoft Excel, you must first add a reference to the Excel object library to your application. Because the Office applications are exposed as COM components, a .NET "wrapper" will need to be created in order to utilize them within the .NET framework. You can begin creating the sample application, as well as creating the .NET wrapper for Excel, by following these steps:

1. Start a new Windows Application project. Name the project **ControlOfficeDemo**.

2. In the Solution Explorer window, right-click References (under the ControlOfficeDemo project); then select Add Reference from the Context menu.

3. In the Add Reference dialog box, click the COM tab to indicate that you want to add a COM reference.

4. Select Microsoft Excel 9.0 Object Library under Component Name, and then click the Select button to place this library in the Selected Components box, as depicted in Figure 25.1.

Figure 25.1
Use the Add Reference dialog box to add a COM component to your application.

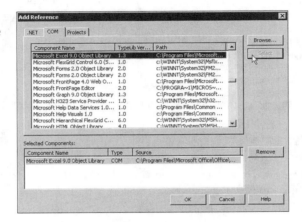

5. If you are presented with a primary interop assembly message asking if you would like to have a wrapper generated, as shown in Figure 25.2, click Yes. This action will cause a .NET wrapper for the Excel COM component to be generated, allowing the COM-based Excel component to be used in the .NET environment.

Figure 25.2
A .NET wrapper can be created to include COM components in your application.

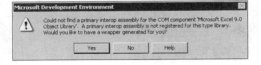

6. Notice in the Solution Explorer window that references for both Excel and Office have been added to the project.

At this point, you have added a reference to the Excel object library to your project. This will enable you to use Excel's built-in version of Visual Basic for Applications (VBA) to control it. In the remainder of this example, we will use simple VBA commands to interact with the Excel objects to control Excel programmatically.

Tip

If you want to learn more about Excel's implementation of VBA, including the objects that are exposed through the Excel COM component, you can utilize Excel's Help system. To get there, open Excel's Visual Basic editor by selecting Tools, Macro, Visual Basic Editor from the Excel menu system. If you do not see the Office Assistant, press F1 to display it. You can then ask the Office Assistant about the VBA commands.

SETTING UP THE SAMPLE EXCEL APPLICATION

We will now continue building the application by preparing the main form. Let's say that we want to create an application in which the user can type projected amounts for sales and expenses; then the program will set up an Excel worksheet containing his projected figures along with a formula to calculate net profit. The user can then manipulate the figures inside Excel however he desires. When he is done, the Visual Basic application will retrieve the final calculation from the Excel worksheet and then display it in a message box.

Of course, this is a very simple example of using Excel from within a VB application, but it demonstrates the power of the concept of remote application control.

Continue building the application by following these steps:

1. View Form1's Designer window. Set its Text property to **Office Remote Control Example**.

2. Add two TextBox controls to Form1; name them txtSales and txtExpenses. Clear their Text properties.

3. Add two Label controls to the left of the two TextBox controls on Form1; set their Text properties to **Sales:** and **Expenses:**.

4. Add a Button control to Form1. Name it **btnExcel** and set its Text property to **Launch Excel**.

Once you have completed building the sample application's interface, it should resemble Figure 25.3.

Figure 25.3
The sample application will allow the user to enter sales and expenses data and launch an Excel session to manipulate these entries.

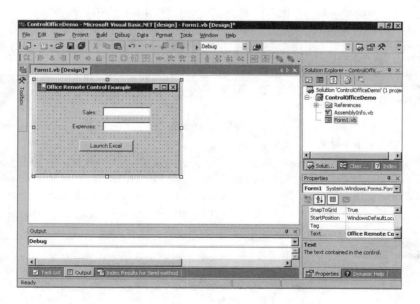

LAUNCHING THE EXCEL APPLICATION

Now it's time to write the code that will launch and control Excel. You will do this by creating an `Excel.Application` object in your program; this type of object is available through the referenced Excel object library. In turn, you will use objects, methods, and properties contained in the Excel object library to control the application instance you create.

Your code must first allow the `Form1` class to access the Excel functionality provided via the program's reference to the Excel object library; this will be accomplished by adding a reference to the Excel namespace that is available through the Excel object reference. Then, you will declare a variable named `ExcelApp`, which is of type `Excel.Application`; this object variable will act as the gateway to the Excel object library. Next, you will populate the `ExcelApp` object variable to create a new instance of the Excel application. After doing so, Excel will be running; however, it will not be visible to the user. You can remedy this by setting `ExcelApp`'s `Visible` property to `True`.

The following steps will get the application going:

1. View the Code window for `Form1`. Add a reference to the Excel namespace by typing **Imports Excel** at the very top of the Code window (even above the `Public Class Form1` line).

2. Display the `Click` event handler for the `btnExcel` Button control by selecting `btnExcel` from the Class Name drop-down and then choosing `Click` from the Method Name drop-down. (Alternatively, you can double-click `btnExcel` in the Designer window to display its `Click` event handler.)

3. We will need to declare a form-level variable of type **Excel.Application**. Enter the following variable declaration in the Code window, just below the Windows Form Designer generated code area:

```
Dim ExcelApp As Excel.Application
```

4. To invoke the new instance of Excel and make it visible, enter the following code into the `btnExcel_Click` event handler:

```
ExcelApp = New Excel.Application()
ExcelApp.Visible = True
```

Save and run the application at this point, then click the Launch Excel button. An instance of Excel starts up and becomes visible to the user. Your program has interacted with another application!

Note

The complete code for this application is presented as a listing later in this chapter. You can download the entire sample project at www.vbinsider.com. Look for the file named `ControlOfficeDemo.zip`.

Notice that the Excel application window does not contain any workbooks. When you start Excel "manually" through the Start menu, an empty workbook containing three worksheets is automatically created for your use. Because we are driving the instance of Excel, nothing is automatically created. If we want Excel to contain a workbook, we must arrange for it to be created. This will be handled in the next section.

For now, go ahead and manually close Excel. Stop your test application as well.

ADDING A BLANK WORKBOOK

As we mentioned, you probably want Excel to contain a blank workbook when it starts. You will accomplish this by creating a `Workbook` object, which will be added to the Excel Application object's `Workbooks` collection. To do so, add the following variable declaration just below the declaration of the `ExcelApp` variable:

```
Dim MyWB As Workbook
```

Then add the following line of code to the end of the `btnExcel_Click` event handler:

```
ExcelApp.Workbooks.Add(XlWBATemplate.xlWBATWorksheet)
```

Note the parameter passed to the `Add` method of the Excel Application object's `Workbooks` collection. This parameter specifies the template to be used to create the new workbook. The value `xlWBATWorksheet`, provided via the `XlWBATemplate` enumeration, indicates that the new workbook is to consist of a normal worksheet.

Save and run the application again. When you click the Launch Excel button, an instance of Excel starts again. This time, however, you will see a workbook containing a single blank worksheet. Close Excel manually again and end your application.

ADDING MORE WORKSHEETS

If you want to add more worksheets to the workbook contained in the Excel application, you can invoke the `Add` method of the `Worksheets` collection of the `Workbook` object. The `Add` method supports several parameters, the first two of which allow you to specify an existing member of the `Worksheets` collection before or after which the new worksheets are to be added. Members of the `Worksheets` collection are identified by a 1-based numbering scheme; therefore, the first (and only, so far) member of the `Worksheets` collection is `MyWB.Worksheets(1)` (or, alternatively, `ExcelApp.Workbooks.Worksheets(1)`, if we want to bypass the `Workbook` object `MyWB`). To add a single worksheet after `MyWB.Worksheets(1)`, add the following line of code to the `btnExcel_Click` event handler:

```
MyWB.Worksheets.Add(, MyWB.Worksheets(1))
```

If you save and run the application at this point, you will see that a second worksheet has been added to the open workbook. However, you may also notice that this second worksheet is now the active sheet, when you might reasonably expect the first worksheet to be active. We will remedy this situation in the next section.

CREATING A Worksheet OBJECT VARIABLE

The work of populating cells will be done at the worksheet level; therefore, it will be advantageous to us to create a Worksheet object variable representing the first worksheet in the open workbook. This is a simple matter. First, add the following code just below the other two form-level variable declarations you have already entered:

```
Dim MyWS As Worksheet
```

Then, add the following line of code to the end of the Click event handler that you have been working on:

```
MyWS = MyWB.Worksheets(1)
```

This code declares a worksheet-type variable named MyWS; then it sets it to the first member of the Worksheets collection of our Workbook object variable MyWB. We will be using the MyWS Worksheet variable in the next section to populate cells contained in that worksheet.

Now that we have created a Worksheet variable representing the first worksheet in the open workbook, we can use the Worksheet object's Activate method to bring that worksheet to the front of the workbook, fixing the problem we noted at the end of the last section. To do so, add the following line of code to the Click event handler:

```
MyWS.Activate()
```

POPULATING CELLS

Next, we want to populate some cells in the worksheet. Specifically, we want the following information contained in the respective cells:

Cell	Contents
A1	The label Sales
A2	The label Expenses
A4	The label Net Profit
B1	The contents of txtSales
B2	The contents of txtExpenses
B4	The formula =A1-A2, which will calculate net profit and display the result

To populate the cells, we will utilize the Range property of the MyWS Worksheet object variable, which exposes a Range object representing a range of cells in the worksheet. For simplicity's sake, we will work with single-cell ranges. Setting a Range object's Value property sets the contents of a cell; setting its Formula property lets you program a formula into the cell. Add the following code to btnExcel's Click event handler to populate the six cells specified previously:

```
MyWS.Range("A1").Value = "Sales"
MyWS.Range("A2").Value = "Expenses"
```

```
MyWS.Range("A4").Value = "Net Profit"
MyWS.Range("B1").Value = txtSales.Text
MyWS.Range("B2").Value = txtExpenses.Text
MyWS.Range("B4").Formula = "=B1-B2"
```

Save and run the application again. This time, before clicking the Launch Excel button, enter some numbers into the two text boxes. You will see a copy of Excel appear, a new sheet will be added, the original Sheet1 will be brought to the front of the workbook, and six of its cells will be populated by your program! The result is depicted in Figure 25.4.

Figure 25.4
This Excel worksheet was created and populated by a Visual Basic program.

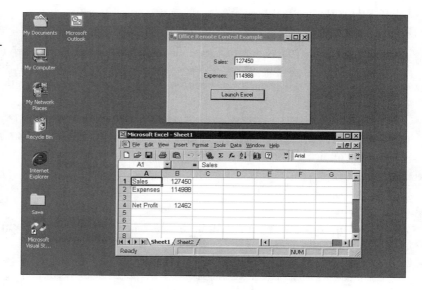

The complete btnExcel Click event procedure is shown in Listing 25.1.

LISTING 25.1 ControlOfficeDemo.ZIP—THE FORM-LEVEL CODE FOR THE EXCEL SPREADSHEET GENERATED BY YOUR VB APPLICATION

```
Private Sub btnExcel_Click(ByVal sender As Object, _
    ByVal e As System.EventArgs) Handles btnExcel.Click
    ExcelApp = New Excel.Application()
    ExcelApp.Visible = True
    MyWB = ExcelApp.Workbooks.Add(XlWBATemplate.xlWBATWorksheet)
    MyWB.Worksheets.Add(, MyWB.Worksheets(1))
    MyWS = MyWB.Worksheets(1)
    MyWS.Activate()
    MyWS.Range("A1").Value = "Sales"
    MyWS.Range("A2").Value = "Expenses"
    MyWS.Range("A4").Value = "Net Profit"
    MyWS.Range("B1").Value = txtSales.Text
    MyWS.Range("B2").Value = txtExpenses.Text
    MyWS.Range("B4").Formula = "=B1-B2"
End Sub
```

RETRIEVING INFORMATION FROM CELLS

Now that we have harnessed the power of Excel to perform data manipulation and calculations, we will demonstrate how to retrieve data from Excel. Specifically, we want to retrieve the Sales and Expenses figures from the worksheet, just in case the user modified them while Excel was active; we also want to retrieve the result of the calculation that is stored in cell B4. We will accomplish this by adding a second Button control to our application's main form and coding that button's Click event handler to perform the retrieval.

Perform the following steps to code the retrieval part of the sample application:

1. Add a Button control named **btnRetrieve** to the application's main form. Set its Text property to **Retrieve**, and place it next to the Launch Excel button.

2. Enter the following code as btnRetrieve's Click event handler:

```
Private Sub btnRetrieve_Click(ByVal sender As System.Object, _
    ByVal e As System.EventArgs) Handles btnRetrieve.Click
    Dim sTemp As String
    txtSales.Text = MyWS.Range("B1").Value
    txtExpenses.Text = MyWS.Range("B2").Value
    sTemp = "The calculated Net Profit is "
    sTemp += FormatCurrency(MyWS.Range("B4").Value) & "."
    MessageBox.Show(sTemp)
End Sub
```

The preceding code uses the Range property of MyWS to retrieve the current contents of cells B1 and B2, placing the retrieved values into txtSales and txtExpenses, respectively. It then retrieves the contents of cell B4, which contains the calculated Net Profit figure; formats it as Currency; and then creates a string to display the result using a message box.

Save and run the program (after shutting down any running copies of Excel that may be left over from previous trial runs). Enter sample data into the two text boxes; then click the Launch Excel button. This time, change the figures in the worksheet to different values and notice how the Net Profit changes. Finally, click the Retrieve button on the VB form to put the new values into the text boxes and display the calculated Net Profit. Figure 25.5 shows an example of the program after it has retrieved the new values from the worksheet.

PART

VI

CH

25

Figure 25.5
The application has retrieved modified data from the Excel worksheet.

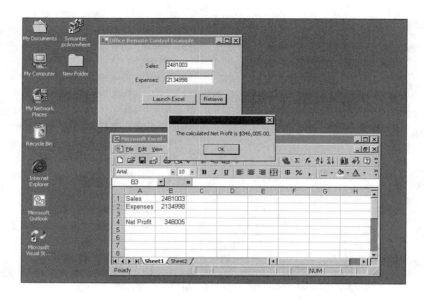

SHUTTING DOWN THE EXCEL APPLICATION

Depending on your program's purpose, you may want to close Excel automatically or leave it running for further interaction. In this example, let's assume that it has done its job and we want to close it automatically. Further, we will assume that we do not want to save the workbook that we created.

To accomplish this, add the following three lines of code to the end of the btnRetrieve Click event handler:

```
MyWB.Saved = True
MyWB.Close()
ExcelApp.Quit()
```

The first line of code "lies" to Excel and tells it that the current workbook (represented by MyWB) has been saved. This is to keep it from asking the user if he wants to save the workbook, which it will do if it detects that an unsaved workbook is about to be closed. The second line closes the MyWB workbook, and the last line shuts down the Excel application itself. If the user had other Excel workbooks open that had nothing to do with our VB application, they will remain open. Excel 2000 now treats open workbooks as independently running applications.

The complete btnExcel Click and btnRetrieve Click event handlers, along with the form-level variable declarations from Listing 25.1, are presented in Listing 25.2.

LISTING 25.2   ControlOfficeDemo.ZIP—CODE TO ADD EXCEL FUNCTIONALITY

```
Dim ExcelApp As Excel.Application
Dim MyWB As Workbook
Dim MyWS As Worksheet
```

```
Private Sub btnExcel_Click(ByVal sender As Object, _
    ByVal e As System.EventArgs) Handles btnExcel.Click
    ExcelApp = New Excel.Application()
    ExcelApp.Visible = True
    MyWB = ExcelApp.Workbooks.Add(XlWBATemplate.xlWBATWorksheet)
    MyWB.Worksheets.Add(, MyWB.Worksheets(1))
    MyWS = MyWB.Worksheets(1)
    MyWS.Activate()
    MyWS.Range("A1").Value = "Sales"
    MyWS.Range("A2").Value = "Expenses"
    MyWS.Range("A4").Value = "Net Profit"
    MyWS.Range("B1").Value = txtSales.Text
    MyWS.Range("B2").Value = txtExpenses.Text
    MyWS.Range("B4").Formula = "=B1-B2"
End Sub

Private Sub btnRetrieve_Click(ByVal sender As System.Object, _
    ByVal e As System.EventArgs) Handles btnRetrieve.Click
    Dim sTemp As String
    txtSales.Text = MyWS.Range("B1").Value
    txtExpenses.Text = MyWS.Range("B2").Value
    sTemp = "The calculated Net Profit is "
    sTemp += FormatCurrency(MyWS.Range("B4").Value) & "."
    MessageBox.Show(sTemp)
    MyWB.Saved = True
    MyWB.Close()
    ExcelApp.Quit()
End Sub
```

PART

VI

CH

25

REMOTE CONTROLLING MICROSOFT WORD

Just like Excel, Microsoft Word exposes a set of COM objects that can be utilized by other programs to drive a session of Word. Again, this object library, which will be accessed via a .NET wrapper around the COM component, will allow a program to control Word just like a user sitting at a keyboard.

ADDING A REFERENCE TO THE WORD OBJECT LIBRARY

As with Excel, in order for an application to be able to interact with Microsoft Word, you must first add a reference to the Word object library to your application. Again, you will do so by creating a .NET wrapper around the Word COM component. Follow these steps to begin enhancing the sample application for Word interactivity:

1. Begin with the ControlOfficeDemo sample application that you created in the previous section.

2. In the Solution Explorer window, right-click References under the ControlOfficeDemo project; then select Add Reference from the Context menu.

3. In the Add Reference dialog box, click the COM tab to indicate that you want to add a COM reference.

4. This time, select Microsoft Word 9.0 Object Library under Component Name, and then click the Select button to place this library in the Selected Components box.

5. Again, if you are presented with a `primary interop assembly` message asking if you would like to have a wrapper generated, click Yes. This will cause a .NET wrapper for the Word COM component to be generated, allowing the COM-based Word component to be used in the .NET environment.

6. Notice that the Solution Explorer window now shows a reference for Word in addition to the Excel and Office references that were added earlier.

Now that a reference to the Word object library has been added to the application, you can add code to remote control Word in much the same manner as you controlled Excel in the first part of the example.

ADDING WORD FUNCTIONALITY

We will now enhance the sample application to allow it to control Word. Just as we added the `Imports Excel` statement to the `Form1` class to bring in the Excel namespace, we will include the Word namespace with an `Imports Word` statement.

Next, we will declare a `Word.Application` variable named `WordApp` that will act as our representation of an instance of Word. Follow these steps to set up the namespace reference, create an object variable representing the Word application, invoke an instance of Word, and cause the Word instance to be visible to the user:

1. Add a Button control named **btnWord** to `Form1`'s interface. Set the button's `Text` property to **Launch Word**.

2. At the top of the code window for the `Form1` class, add the statement **Imports Word** just below the `Imports Excel` statement that you added earlier. This will make the Word namespace available to `Form1`.

3. Add the following code to the `Click` event handler for `btnWord`:
```
Dim WordApp As Word.Application
WordApp = New Word.Application()
WordApp.Visible = True
```

> **Note**
> The variables for this part of the example are being declared at procedure level because they will not be used in any other procedures.

Save and run the application at this point, and then click the Launch Word button. An instance of Microsoft Word will start; however, there will not be a document open inside the Word window. Stop the sample program; then manually close the Word window.

CREATING A WORD DOCUMENT

Just as you had to write code to open a blank workbook inside the copy of Excel that your program invoked, you must write code to have Word create a new blank document. Add the following code to the Click event handler for btnWord to accomplish this:

```
Dim MyDoc As Word.Document
MyDoc = WordApp.Documents.Add
```

Now, when you save and run the application, a new blank Word document is created and opened inside the copy of the Word application that was started. Be sure to manually close the instance of Word when you close the program.

ADDING TEXT TO THE WORD DOCUMENT

The Word document is represented by the variable MyDoc, which was created as a result of invoking the Add method of the Documents collection of WordApp, which is our variable that represents the running instance of Word. To add text to the document, which of course is the goal of using Word, we will work with the Range property of the Word document. The Range property exposes a Range object, which represents a range of characters in the document. The Range property is expressed by specifying the beginning and ending character positions that define the desired range; for example, MyDoc.Range(0,5) would represent the first five characters of the document (the counting is zero-based). The ending value, 5, is not included in the range. If you leave out the starting and ending character values, the Range property refers to the entire document.

Use Listing 25.3 to complete the Click event handler for btnWord. This will create a simple Executive Summary report using the sales figures entered by the user into the text boxes.

LISTING 25.3   REMOTE CONTROLLING MICROSOFT WORD

```
MyDoc.Range(0, 0).InsertAfter("Executive Profit Summary")
MyDoc.Range(0, 24).Font.Name = "Arial"
MyDoc.Range(0, 24).Font.Size = 18
MyDoc.Range(0, 24).Font.Color = Word.WdColor.wdColorBlue
MyDoc.Range.InsertParagraphAfter()
MyDoc.Range(0, 24).ParagraphFormat.Alignment = _
   Word.WdParagraphAlignment.wdAlignParagraphCenter
MyDoc.Range.InsertParagraphAfter()
Dim sTemp As String
sTemp = "In the current reporting period, we had total expenses of "
sTemp += FormatCurrency(txtExpenses.Text)
sTemp += " against sales of " & FormatCurrency(txtSales.Text)
sTemp += ", for a Net Profit of "
sTemp += FormatCurrency(txtSales.Text - txtExpenses.Text) & "."
MyDoc.Range.InsertAfter(sTemp)
```

Listing 25.3 uses the InsertAfter method of the Range object, which causes text to be inserted after the specified range. The Range object's Font property is used to format the font appropriately. The InsertParagraphAfter method, which is equivalent to pressing Enter in the Word document, is used to start a new paragraph. The Alignment subproperty of the `ParagraphFormat` property sets the paragraph alignment of the range to be centered (using the `wdAlignParagraphCenter` member of the `Word.WdParagraphAlignment` enumeration). Finally, a temporary `String` variable is used to construct the actual text of the report, using information from the two text boxes, and then to add the information to the Word document.

Save and run the application again. You will see a completed Word document, which has been constructed from the figures that the user typed into the text boxes, as illustrated in Figure 25.6. Again, close the Word document manually.

Figure 25.6
This Word document was created by a VB program.

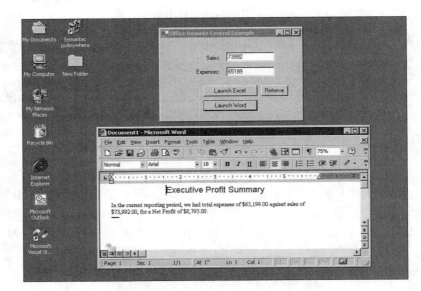

PRINTING AND CLOSING THE DOCUMENT

The last bit of code we will add to the sample application will print the customized report and then close the Word application. Of course, depending on your plans for the program, you may want to leave it open for the user to edit, add more text, and so on.

Add the following two lines of code to the end of the `btnWord Click` event handler:

```
MyDoc.PrintOut()
WordApp.Quit(False)
```

The first line uses the `PrintOut` method of the Word document object to print a single copy of the report on the user's default printer. (A number of parameters are available to customize the `PrintOut` method with options such as number of copies, which page(s) to print, and so on.) The second line uses the `Quit` method of the Word application object to shut down the instance of Word, specifying `False` as the value of the `Save` parameter, which tells Word not to try to save the (unsaved) open document.

This last time, when you run the application, the report will be printed after it is constructed; then the Word application will automatically shut down.

Tip

If you want your application to create and print a Word document without the user seeing Word appear, simply remove the line that sets the `Visible` property of the Word application object to `True`.

Listing 25.4 contains the complete `btnWord` `Click` event handler.

LISTING 25.4   ControlOfficeDemo.ZIP—CODE TO ADD WORD FUNCTIONALITY

```
Private Sub btnWord_Click(ByVal sender As System.Object, _
    ByVal e As System.EventArgs) Handles btnWord.Click
    Dim WordApp As Word.Application
    WordApp = New Word.Application()
    WordApp.Visible = True
    Dim MyDoc As Word.Document
    MyDoc = WordApp.Documents.Add
    MyDoc.Range(0, 0).InsertAfter("Executive Profit Summary")
    MyDoc.Range(0, 24).Font.Name = "Arial"
    MyDoc.Range(0, 24).Font.Size = 18
    MyDoc.Range(0, 24).Font.Color = Word.WdColor.wdColorBlue
    MyDoc.Range.InsertParagraphAfter()
    MyDoc.Range(0, 24).ParagraphFormat.Alignment = _
        Word.WdParagraphAlignment.wdAlignParagraphCenter
    MyDoc.Range.InsertParagraphAfter()
    Dim sTemp As String
    sTemp = "In the current reporting period, we had total expenses of "
    sTemp += FormatCurrency(txtExpenses.Text)
    sTemp += " against sales of " & FormatCurrency(txtSales.Text)
    sTemp += ", for a Net Profit of "
    sTemp += FormatCurrency(txtSales.Text - txtExpenses.Text) & "."
    MyDoc.Range.InsertAfter(sTemp)
    MyDoc.PrintOut()
    WordApp.Quit(False)
End Sub
```

PART
VI
CH
25

USING THE SmtpMail CLASS TO ADD E-MAIL FUNCTIONALITY TO AN APPLICATION

Visual Basic .NET's `SmtpMail` class is provided to allow your applications to send e-mail messages. It utilizes the Simple Mail Transfer Protocol (SMTP), which is the Internet standard for sending e-mail messages. The `SmtpMail` class uses the SMTP service built into Windows 2000 (and later versions) to pass a `MailMessage` object to an SMTP server, which in turn forwards the message to the intended recipient.

SENDING MAIL MESSAGES WITH THE MailMessage CLASS

The workhorse of the `SmtpMail` class is the `MailMessage` class, which provides the methods and properties necessary to send an e-mail message. To send an e-mail message, you create an instance of the `MailMessage` class, set various properties, and then use the `Send` method of the `SmtpMail` class to send the message.

Table 25.1 summarizes some of the properties of the `MailMessage` class that you will use most often.

TABLE 25.1   COMMON `MailMessage` PROPERTIES

Property	Purpose
Attachments	A list of attachments to be included with the e-mail message.
Bcc	A list of e-mail addresses to be "blind" carbon-copied on the message. Multiple e-mail addresses separated by semicolons can be included.
Body	The actual text of the message.
BodyFormat	Set to one of the `MailFormat` enumeration members, `Html` or `Text`, to specify whether the format of the message's body is HTML or plain text.
Cc	A list of e-mail addresses to be carbon-copied on the message. Multiple e-mail addresses separated by semicolons can be included.
From	The e-mail address of the sender.
Subject	The subject line of the e-mail message.
To	The e-mail address of the main recipient of the message. Multiple e-mail addresses separated by semicolons can be included.

CREATING A SAMPLE APPLICATION

Let's demonstrate the use of the `SmtpMail` class by creating a simple application to send an e-mail message. You must add a reference to the `SmtpMail` class, which is provided via the `System.Web.Mail` namespace, to your project's references before using the `SmtpMail` class. Follow these steps:

1. Start a new Windows Application project. Name it **SendSmtpMailDemo**. Set the `Text` property of `Form1` to **SmtpMail Demo**.
2. Add two TextBox controls to `Form1`. Name them **txtTo** and **txtSubject**, and clear their `Text` properties.
3. Add a third TextBox control to `Form1`. Name it **txtBody**, clear its `Text` property, and set its `MultiLine` property to `True`.
4. Add a Button control named **btnGo**. Set its `Text` property to **Send Mail**.
5. Add three Label controls to identify the TextBox controls. Set their `Text` properties to **To:**, **Subject:**, and **Body:**. Arrange the controls in a manner similar to Figure 25.7.

Figure 25.7
This sample application will allow you to send an e-mail message.

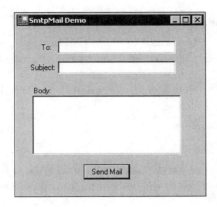

6. Right-click the References folder under the name of your project in the Solution Explorer window; then select Add Reference from the Context menu. In the Add Reference dialog box, make sure the .NET tab is selected. Select System.Web.dll under Component Name, click Select to move it to the Selected Components box, and then click OK. Note that a reference to System.Web now appears in your project's References folder.

This process is similar to adding a reference to Microsoft Excel or Word through the Add Reference dialog box shown in Figure 25.1. Just click the .NET tab instead.

7. Open the Code window for Form1. At the top of the window, even above Class Form1, enter the line **Imports System.Web.Mail**. This namespace contains the SmtpMail class.

8. Enter the following code as the Click event handler for btnGo:

```
Dim MyMessage As New MailMessage()
MyMessage.To = txtTo.Text
MyMessage.From = "yourname@yourdomain.com"
MyMessage.Subject = txtSubject.Text
MyMessage.Body = txtBody.Text
MyMessage.BodyFormat = MailFormat.Text
SmtpMail.SmtpServer = "your-smtp-server.yourdomain.com"
SmtpMail.Send(MyMessage)
MessageBox.Show("The message has been sent.")
```

Note

Enter your real return e-mail address as MyMessage's From property in the third line of the code, and enter the real name of your SMTP server as the SmtpServer property. You may need to contact your ISP or network administrator to get this information.

When you run this application, enter information for the To e-mail address, subject, and message body. When you click the Send Message button, an e-mail message will be generated and sent using this information.

PART
VI
CH
25

USING HTML FOR THE BODY FORMAT

One enhancement that you may want to make is to use HTML as the message body format, assuming your intended recipient's e-mail program supports HTML messages. To do so, simply change the sixth line of the code to `MyMessage.BodyFormat = MailFormat.Html`, and include HTML tags in the body of the message. For example, when entering the body of the message, you might include the following:

```
Don't forget that the <b>final exam</b> is_
<font size="+1"> this Friday!</font>
```

When the `BodyFormat` property is set to `MailFormat.Html`, the HTML tags will cause appropriate formatting to be applied to the text in the body of the e-mail message.

FROM HERE...

In this chapter, you have learned how to control other programs from your Visual Basic .NET applications. You can use these techniques to harness the functionality provided by the Microsoft Office suite of products. You also learned how to have your programs use the `SmtpMail` class to send mail messages. You may want to enhance the skills you have been exposed to in this chapter by consulting some of these resources:

- Que and other publishers provide a number of good books on Visual Basic for Applications. A solid reference book would allow you to use the techniques you learned in this chapter to greater benefit.

- Microsoft's Visual Basic for Applications Home Page, located at `http://msdn.microsoft.com/vba/`, has a wealth of information about using VBA, including reference materials, news, and code samples.

- Check the authors' Web site, `www.vbinsider.com`, for more sample applications that utilize the techniques described in this chapter.

CHAPTER **26**

DEBUGGING AND PERFORMANCE TUNING

In this chapter

In Chapter 5, "Visual Basic Building Blocks," we introduced the concept of debugging, or getting the mistakes out of your program. In this chapter we will explore the subject further by describing some debugging techniques, such as handling exceptions and logging errors. We will also explore the concept of performance monitoring, which can be used to increase the efficiency of your program.

WORKING WITH EXCEPTIONS IN VISUAL STUDIO

As you may recall from our earlier discussion in Chapter 5, exceptions are errors that occur during program execution. Exceptions are thrown by functions within your program and can be caught and handled by Try . . . Catch statements. Writing code to handle exceptions is important so your program can gracefully handle program errors at runtime.

→ For an introduction to exceptions in Visual Basic, **see** Chapter 5, "Visual Basic Building Blocks," **p. 113**

However, during the normal course of application development, exceptions are likely to occur before you have written code to handle them. In addition, you may want to disable your own exception handling code to troubleshoot program problems. In this section, we'll take a look at working with exceptions in the Visual Studio environment.

BREAKING FOR UNHANDLED EXCEPTIONS

To simplify our discussion, let's pick an exception that is easy to understand: an invalid database password. If you try to establish a connection to a database and do not provide a correct password, the database driver may throw an exception. The following three lines of code attempt to connect to a SQL server database using an ADO.NET SQLConnection object:

```
Dim cn As New SqlConnection()
cn.ConnectionString = "Server=MyServer;UID=sa;pwd=WRONG;Database=pubs"
cn.Open()
```

The first line of code creates a new SQLConnection object and the second line sets its ConnectionString property. These two lines of code should execute without error. However, if the password is incorrect, the call to the Open method in the last line of code would throw an exception. If you are debugging in Visual Studio and have not written code to handle this exception, you will see a message similar to the one in Figure 26.1.

Figure 26.1
Visual Studio displays a dialog box when unhandled exceptions occur during debugging.

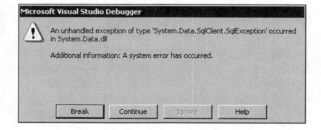

As you can see, the dialog box indicates that an unhandled SQL exception has occurred and gives the programmer a few choices:

- `Break`—Pauses execution, leaving Visual Studio in break mode. While in break mode, you can examine variable values, enter commands in the Immediate window, and even press F5 to attempt to continue. In our example, you could change the value of the `ConnectionString` property to contain the correct password and successfully continue execution.

- `Continue`—Continues execution, passing control to the exception handler. In our example, we have not written an exception handler, so Visual Studio just dumps detailed information to the Output window and ends the program.

- `Ignore`—Continues execution, skipping over the exception handler. Visual Studio purposely disables this option in some cases, and most of the time, choosing it is probably not a good idea. In our example we cannot connect to our SQL database, so ignoring this fact certainly won't allow us to retrieve data from it!

BREAKING FOR HANDLED EXCEPTIONS

By default, when an unhandled exception is thrown within the Visual Studio environment, several options are provided, such as entering break mode to troubleshoot the error. However, if you have written exception-handling code, Visual Studio will execute it when an exception occurs. For example, suppose we add a `Try . . . Catch` statement to our sample code:

```
Try
    cn.Open
Catch ex As Exception
    MessageBox.Show("Error occurred: " & ex.ToString)
    Application.Exit
End Try
```

This code simply displays a message and ends the program when any exception occurs, essentially duplicating the effect of clicking the Continue button in Figure 26.1. As a developer you may not always want to automatically execute the exception handler, because it will end the program before you have the opportunity to troubleshoot the problem. Fortunately, Visual Studio allows you to customize its behavior using the Exceptions dialog box, pictured in Figure 26.2.

The Exceptions dialog box allows you to determine whether Visual Studio will break or continue based on the exception type. By default, Visual Studio will continue if you have written exception-handling code, or break if you have not. In our example, the type of exception being thrown is a `SqlException`. By using the Exceptions dialog box, we could tell Visual Studio to break on the exception even though we have written code to handle it, thus changing the default behavior. To cause Visual Studio to break on SQL exceptions regardless of whether they are handled in code, click the Add button and add `SQLException` to the exception list. Then, select the Break into the Debugger option, as shown in Figure 26.2.

PART

VI

CH

26

Figure 26.2
The Exceptions dialog box can be displayed from the Debug menu or by pressing Ctrl+Alt+E.

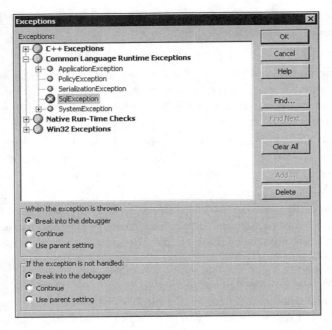

Note

As you can see from Figure 26.2, the exception list is organized in a tree structure. Therefore, changing the break settings at the `Common Language Runtime` level would break on not only our exception but all other `Common Language Runtime` exceptions as well.

FOLLOWING THE CALL STACK

Another useful troubleshooting tool is the Call Stack window. The Call Stack window, pictured in Figure 26.3, provides you the ability to follow the sequence of procedure calls in your program. This is especially important where procedures call other procedures that in turn call other procedures, and so on. The Call Stack window can be displayed from the Windows submenu of the Debug menu.

Figure 26.3
The Call Stack window provides a trail of procedure calls so you can determine how you arrived at the statement that caused an error.

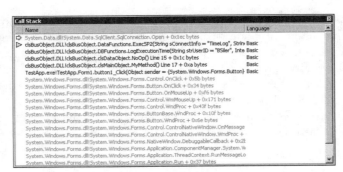

Each time a method is called, an entry with the method name and parameter values is added to the call stack. Note that you do not need to be troubleshooting an error to use the call stack; it can be displayed any time you are in break mode, such as when you are using breakpoints.

→ For more on breakpoints, **see** "Stopping Program Execution with a Breakpoint" in Chapter 5, "Visual Basic Building Blocks," **p. 129**

WRITING CODE TO HANDLE EXCEPTIONS

Users of your program are not likely to be developers or Visual Studio users. Therefore, to make your application more robust, you'll want to add exception-handling code to control its behavior after an exception is thrown. Good exception-handling code should do the following:

■ Make sure the error is logged accurately, so you know which method call actually caused the exception.

■ Depending on the severity of the exception, you may want to display a message for the end user. This message should be written so that the user can understand it, and if necessary it should provide instructions on how to resolve the problem.

In a complex application, you may have objects that call other objects in a nested manner. It is not uncommon to have 10 procedures on the call stack when an exception occurs. A typical error-handling strategy for an application with lots of nested calls is to keep throwing the exception back to the calling function until finally it reaches the user interface. However, depending on the severity of the exception, you may or may not always want the user to see it. Microsoft also suggests rather than just "bubbling up" the same exception, that you throw a new exception that adds some information from the current subroutine. In this section, we'll describe how to pass exceptions around, keep track of them in the Windows Event log, and create custom exception types.

PART
VI

CH
26

UNDERSTANDING FINALLY BLOCKS

Your code and the associated exception handling code can be thought of as existing in *blocks*, or sections of code bounded by Try and End Try statements. As you learned in Chapter 5, a typical section of code using exception handling has a Try block and a one or more Catch blocks:

```
Try

    'CODE YOU WANT TO EXECUTE

Catch ex As Exception

    'CODE TO HANDLE EXCEPTION

End Try
```

The previous code sample is a minimal implementation of exception handling. During a normal errorless execution of the program, code in the Catch block does not execute. However, when an exception is thrown, execution jumps to the `Catch` block, then proceeds at the first statement following the `End Try` statement. Therefore, when an exception occurs, lines of code in the `Try` block may not be executed. In certain situations, you may need to perform cleanup activities whether or not an exception occurs. For example, suppose you need to copy one hundred files, perform some action, and then delete the files. If you place the code for all of these activities in the `Try` block, it is possible some files could be copied but never deleted. Fortunately, VB .NET provides the `Finally` block, which will always execute regardless of exceptions:

```
Try

    For i = 1 to 100
        CreateTemporaryFile(i)
    Next
    ProcessTemporaryFiles()

Catch ex As Exception

    Messagebox.Show("Error occurred!")

Finally

    DeleteTemporaryFiles()


End Try
```

In the previous code sample, the `DeleteTemporaryFiles` function will always be executed. Although you could also add code to delete the files in both the `Try` and `Catch` blocks, using a `Finally` block makes your code easier to read and avoids duplication.

THROWING EXCEPTIONS TO THE CALLING FUNCTION

You throw exceptions in a program by executing the `Throw` method. You can throw an existing exception object, or create a new one and set its properties. It is also very common to declare and throw a new exception using a single line of code, as in the following example:

```
Throw New Exception("Error Opening File!")
```

The text in parentheses represents the message sent back to the calling program, which will receive a generic `Exception` object containing the message text. Of course, there are more specific types of exceptions (all inherited from the base class `Exception`), and you can also create your own custom exception types.

TAKING ADVANTAGE OF EXCEPTION TYPES

The advantage of catching a specific exception type is that they will often contain special properties that can be used to provide more detailed information about the exception. For example, the `SQLException` class has a `Server` property, which indicates the name of the server involved in the SQL-related exception:

```
Try
    cn.Open()
Catch sqlexc As SqlException
```

```
    Throw New Exception("Error connecting to " & sqlexc.Server)
Catch otherexc As Exception
    Throw New Exception("Error opening connection")
End Try
```

In the previous sample code, we have written code to catch both a SQLException and a regular exception. If a SQLException occurs, we create an error message that contains the server name. Otherwise, we use a generic message indicating that something went wrong. In either case, a new exception is thrown back to the calling function.

Note

Catch statements are evaluated in order, so make sure to place specific exception types before more general ones.

PROVIDING MORE DETAILED INFORMATION TO THE CALLER

In our previous example, the caller does not know that the password was invalid, only that an error occurred while connecting to a server. All the detailed information from the original SQLException was lost, because we declared a new Exception object with just a text message. An even better strategy is to send the original SQLException to the caller via the InnerException property of the new exception object:

```
Try
    cn.Open()
Catch sqlexc As SqlException
    Throw New Exception("Error connecting to " & sqlexc.Server, sqlexc)
Catch otherexc As Exception
    Throw New Exception("Error opening connection", otherexc)
End Try
```

Each exception has an InnerException property, which can be specified as a second parameter to the New constructor. In the preceding sample code, we send custom information back from the current function call, as well as the original exception that caused the problem. By following this strategy throughout your program, the exception at the top level will have detailed exception information that leads back through the nested calls to the actual problem:

```
System.Exception: Error calling ExecSP ---> System.Exception: Error
Connecting to bserver ---> System.Data.SqlClient.SqlException: Login
failed for user 'sa'.
   at System.Data.SqlClient.SqlConnection.Open()
```

Using the ToString property of the exception caught two levels up from our sample code retrieved the previous text. As you can see, arrows are automatically added by Visual Studio to separate each function call. The detailed information is not lost when moving up the chain, because the original exception was passed using the InnerException property.

PART

VI

CH

26

USING CUSTOM EXCEPTIONS

The example of a connection error is a severe exception caused by something external to your program. However, you may also want to throw exceptions when errors occur that are related to the business logic of your application.

> **Note**
>
> When creating custom exceptions, it is important to understand the difference between an exception (something that shouldn't normally occur) and data validation (something that normally occurs when processing user input). For example, if you need to check something every time data is entered, a function call might be more appropriate than an exception.

Suppose you are processing invoices for payment using a multi-tier application. The user interface could be a Web page or Windows application. The heart of the application would be a business object that actually processes the invoices, residing on a server somewhere. Figure 26.4 shows an example of our fictitious user interface.

> **Note**
>
> A business object is just a Visual Basic class of your own creation that contains rules to support a business application.

Figure 26.4
You can use exceptions to enforce business rules, such as a rule that detail amounts must add up to a total.

Notice that in Figure 26.4 the user interface has a total amount field as well as line-item amount fields that provide a detailed breakdown of the total. Therefore, it would make sense that this application includes code to make sure the detailed amounts added together must match the total. This is known as a *business rule*. Although it's generally a good idea to keep all the business logic together in one place, a typical application would also include basic data validation logic within the UI for speed purposes. So, in theory, the business object should never receive an "out of balance" invoice from the user interface.

However, should the business object just assume that any invoice it receives is valid? Probably not, because another programmer may want to use the same business object in the future and leave out the validation from his UI. To prevent erroneous invoices from being processed, you could throw an exception in the business object. By creating a custom exception class, you could add specific properties that apply to the task at hand.

CREATING A CUSTOM EXCEPTION CLASS

Listing 26.1 shows the code for creating and throwing a custom exception.

LISTING 26.1 Exception.ZIP—USING A CUSTOM EXCEPTION CLASS

```
Public Class BusLogicException
    Inherits Exception
    Public UserMessage As String
    Public TechnicalMessage As String
End Class

Public Class InvoiceProcessor
    Public Sub ProcessInvoice(ByVal TotalAmount As Single,_
ByVal DetailAmounts() As Single)

        Dim i As Integer
        Dim sngDetailTotal As Single = 0

        For i = 0 To UBound(DetailAmounts)
            sngDetailTotal += DetailAmounts(i)
        Next

        'THROW A CUSTOM EXCEPTION IF NECESSARY
        If sngDetailTotal <> TotalAmount Then
            Dim BalanceEx As New BusLogicException()
            BalanceEx.UserMessage = "Detail amounts do not balance with the total!"
            BalanceEx.TechnicalMessage = " Total=" & TotalAmount & _
            " InvalidTotal=" & sngDetailTotal
            Throw BalanceEx
        End If

        Try

            'PROCESS INVOICE HERE.

        Catch exc As Exception

            Throw New Exception("Error Processing Invoice.", exc)

        End Try


    End Sub
End Class
```

PART

VI

CH

26

As you can see from the listing, InvoiceProcessor is the name of our sample business object class, and BusLogicException is the name of a custom exception class. BusLogicException inherits from the Exception class and adds two new properties: TechnicalMessage and UserMessage. The UserMessage property might contain information that would make sense to the user, whereas the TechnicalMessage property could contain a more detailed description used to assist help desk personnel. Users don't know what a SQL server is (and shouldn't have to), but they will understand a message like "network connection problems." Note that the code in Listing 26.1 also includes a Try . . . Catch block for handling other exceptions besides the custom one, should they occur.

> **Note**
>
> For standard exceptions, the `Message` property of an exception contains just the error message. The output of the `ToString` method adds more detail, including a stack dump.

> **Note**
>
> Because our custom exception class inherits from the `Exception` base class, you can pass it as the `InnerException` when throwing a generic exception.

CATCHING A CUSTOM EXCEPTION

Catching a custom exception is no different from any other exception. You can use a generic `Exception` object, or specify the custom type to access the exception's special properties:

```
Dim objProcessor As New clsBusObject.InvoiceProcessor()

Try
    Call objProcessor.ProcessInvoice(sngTotalAmount, sngDetailArray)
    Messagebox.Show("Invoice Processed Successfully")

Catch blExc As clsBusObject.BusLogicException
    Messagebox.Show(blExc.UserMessage)

Catch exc As Exception
    Messagebox.Show("Unknown error: " & exc.Message)


End Try
```

In this example, the exception-handling code displays the `UserMessage` property for the custom exception, or the `Message` property of any other exception.

USING THE WINDOWS EVENT LOG

Within the Visual Studio environment, the call stack can help you locate the root cause of an exception. However, at runtime you may want to log errors for later analysis. Although errors can be logged to a text file or other custom location, the Windows Event log provides several advantages:

- The Windows Event log provides a central area you can use to determine the health of a server in general.
- Network administrators and other operational personnel may already be familiar with Microsoft's built-in Event Viewer utility, pictured in Figure 26.5.
- The Event Viewer allows you to check an event log remotely.
- You can use Visual Basic code to access an event log programmatically and alert others if certain types of events occur.

Figure 26.5
The Windows 2000 Event Viewer allows you to manage both standard and custom event logs.

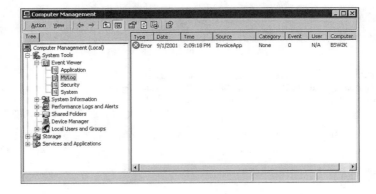

Before we begin discussing the technical details of using an event log, we need to clarify a couple of terms in more detail:

- An *event entry* is an event that happens on a computer and is entered in a log. Events are not always errors. For example, when your computer boots, several events are logged just for informational purposes. The Event Viewer provides icons that indicate the different types of events.

- An *event log* contains a record of related events. For example, the Security Event log contains events related to system security. Windows ships with three built-in logs (Application, System, and Security), plus you can add additional logs as desired. All these logs can be managed using the Event Viewer.

- An *event source* identifies the creator of the event log entry, such as the name of your application.

The `System.Diagnostics` namespace contains the classes necessary for manipulating Windows Event logs. In this section we will describe how to write and read these logs.

WRITING ERRORS TO THE EVENT LOG

In order to write errors to an event log, you have to specify an event source name. An event source is just a string value, which is usually just the name of your application or business object, such as `InvoiceProcessor`. For every event source, Windows keeps track of the associated event log, which is by default the Application log. However, you can also put your events in a custom event log. To associate an event source with a custom event log, you have to use the `CreateEventSource` method—but you only have to do it once. The computer remembers the log from that point forward. Actually writing the event information to the log is accomplished with the `WriteEntry` method, as shown in Listing 26.2.

PART
VI
CH
26

LISTING 26.2 EVENTLOG.ZIP—WRITING TO AN EVENT LOG

```
Public Sub LogException(ByVal FunctionName As String,_
                        ByVal NewException As Exception)

Dim evtLog As New System.Diagnostics.EventLog()
If Not evtLog.SourceExists(FunctionName) Then
    evtLog.CreateEventSource(FunctionName, "MyLog")
End If

evtLog.WriteEntry(FunctionName, NewException.ToString, EventLogEntryType.Error)
evtLog.Close()

End Sub
```

The LogException function accepts a function name and exception object as arguments, and writes the exception to a custom event log called "MyLog." Notice the third parameter of the WriteEntry function, which determines the type of event. By adding the LogException function to your application, you can write errors to the event log when they occur with just a single line of code.

Note

Certain types of errors (such as an out-of-balance invoice that is easily corrected at data entry) you should not write to the log. However, ADO and SQL exceptions, or any other unknown errors should be logged, because you weren't expecting them.

A typical use of the LogException function would be to log an error during exception handling, as in the following example:

```
Try

    Call ProcessInvoice(sngAmount,arDetails)

Catch ex As Exception

    Dim NewEx As New Exception("Error in ProcessInvoice", ex)
    LogException("InvoiceApp", MyEX)
    Throw MyEX

End Try
```

Figure 26.6 shows what a custom exception looks like when written to the event log.

Note

Many functions in the EventLog class also accept an optional parameter for a computer name, allowing you to write or read from remote logs. For more information, see the help files.

Figure 26.6
To display the event viewer in Windows 2000, right-click the My Computer icon and choose Manage.

MONITORING AN EVENT LOG

In addition to writing events to a log, you can also read an event log with Visual Basic code. For example, you could have a program automatically check your logs for errors from a certain source application (that is, "Nightly Data Update Process") and e-mail an administrator to notify him of an error. All the event entries are stored in the Entries collection of an EventLog object, which you can navigate with a For loop. However, an even more useful hook into the event system is the EntryWritten event, which can notify your program when an event occurs. Listing 26.3 shows an example of an event handler that checks for the string PROBLEM in an event message.

LISTING 26.3   EVENTLOG.ZIP—EVENT LOG NOTIFICATION

```
Dim evtTemp As System.Diagnostics.EventLog

Private Sub btnStart_Click(ByVal sender As System.Object,_
ByVal e As System.EventArgs) Handles btnStart.Click
    evtTemp = New System.Diagnostics.EventLog("MyLog")
    evtTemp.EnableRaisingEvents = True
    AddHandler evtTemp.EntryWritten, AddressOf CheckEvent
    btnStart.Enabled = False
End Sub

Private Sub CheckEvent(ByVal sender As Object,_
ByVal args As System.Diagnostics.EntryWrittenEventArgs)
    If InStr(args.Entry.Message.ToUpper, "PROBLEM") <> 0 Then
        Messagebox.Show("Houston, we have a problem!")
    End If
End Sub
```

PART

VI

CH

26

The preceding code starts the notification process by setting the `EnableRaisingEvents` property to `True` and then passing the address of the `CheckEvent` function using the `AddHandler` method. From that point forward, the `evtTemp` object will call your function any time a new event is added. The event entry is passed to the function, allowing you to determine that the message or other properties meet the criteria necessary to alert an end user.

MONITORING APPLICATION PERFORMANCE

Even if a program runs correctly, speed may be a factor in its success. Users do not like to wait on computers any longer than necessary. The process of *performance tuning* is modifying your program to make it faster. Some examples of performance tuning are changing database queries so they execute faster, eliminating unnecessary procedure calls, or caching data. Performance tuning can be especially important in a multi-tier Internet application, because each Web page request may create a Visual Basic object, which in turn can create other objects or update a database. In a complex architecture such as this one, there are several components to each user request (network data transfer, Visual Basic code execution, database stored procedures) that could potentially cause a performance bottleneck. How do you know which part of your application to attempt to optimize? In the remainder of this chapter, we'll show you a simple way to add a time log that will identify the average speed of your procedure calls. We'll also introduce *performance counters*, which can be used to determine which parts of your application undergo the heaviest use. As a programmer, having some basic tools to monitor performance will help you determine which areas to focus your performance optimization efforts.

MEASURING EXECUTION TIME

The `System.Environment` namespace has a `TickCount` property, which returns the number of milliseconds relative to an internal system timer. (This value is slightly different from the `Ticks` value discussed in Chapter 6, "Storing Information in Variables," because it represents milliseconds rather than nanoseconds and is stored in a variable of type `Integer`.) However, it is a great tool for measuring execution time, because we are not interested in the actual time value itself, but rather duration.

→ For more on dates and time spans, **see** Chapter 6, "Storing Information in Variables," **p. 139**

Listing 26.4 shows how you can subtract tick counts to determine the time it takes to execute a method:

LISTING 26.4   PERFORMANCE.ZIP—TICK COUNT EXAMPLE

```
Public Sub MyMethod()
        Dim intStartTime As Integer
        Dim intEndTime As Integer
        Dim intTimeToExecute As Integer
        intStartTime = System.Environment.TickCount
```

```
'MAIN CODE FOR
'THIS PROCEDURE
'GOES HERE

        intEndTime = System.Environment.TickCount
        intTimeToExecute = intEndTime - intStartTime
    Debug.WriteLine("Execution time: " &  intTimeToExecute)
End Sub
```

Listing 26.4 stores the value of the System.Environment.TickCount property before and after the procedure code executes. By subtracting these values, the execution time in milliseconds can be determined. The last statement in the subroutine prints the execution time in the Output window.

The code necessary to measure the execution time of any single method call is very easy to write. However, printing tick counts on the screen is not practical for a large application with hundreds of methods and hundreds of simultaneous users. In the remainder of this section, we will show you how to create a more useful time logging system. The goals of our time logging system include the following:

- Time logging should be able to be activated and deactivated at will, without recompiling the program. This is important because the act of logging time may actually decrease performance.

- To identify slow code, we should be able to easily filter the time log data by a specific method call name.

- We should be able to determine average execution times for a specific method call or user, because execution time may vary with the data used or system resources.

To accurately measure the time, you will have to add some code to every one of your method calls. However, as you will see in the next few sections, we have put most of the code in a separate, generic module to make the process as painless as possible. If the benefits of a time logging module are not yet obvious, keep reading.

UNDERSTANDING THE DATABASE REQUIREMENTS

To identify trouble spots and trends in our time logging data, we need to be able to run queries against it. Data queries and filtering can be easily accomplished through the use of the Structured Query Language (SQL). Therefore, our sample time logging system uses a SQL database to store its information.

→ For more on SQL, **see** Chapter 20, "Database Basics," **p. 535**

Of course, executing the code necessary to store the performance data in a SQL database will itself adversely affect performance! However, in most cases it should not slow your application too terribly. Typically, you will want to capture these statistics for only a few minutes or hours at a time, after which you will turn time logging off and analyze the data.

SETTING UP THE DATABASE OBJECTS

The performance data will be stored in a table called TimeLog. A stored procedure, spTimeLogAdd, provides insert capabilities for this table to the calling application. Listing 26.5 shows the statements necessary to create these database objects.

LISTING 26.5   PERFORMANCE.ZIP—CREATING THE TIMELOG DATABASE

```
CREATE TABLE TimeLog
(   UserID char(10) NOT NULL,
    TimeStamp smalldatetime NOT NULL,
    TickCount int NOT NULL,
    MethodName char(35) NOT NULL
)
GO
create procedure spTimeLogAdd

@charUserID                char(10),
@intTickCount              int,
@charMethod                char(35)

AS

Insert
Into  TimeLog
  (
  UserID,
  TimeStamp,
  TickCount,
  MethodName
  )
Values
  (
  @charUserID,
  getdate(),
  @intTickCount,
  @charMethod
  )
```

Following is a brief explanation of each field's purpose:

- UserID—Allows you to determine the execution time for all the method calls associated with a particular user. By comparing with other users' response times, you can determine whether performance problems are application-wide or isolated to a particular user's data set.

- TimeStamp—Allows you to monitor performance for a specific period of time; for example, just between 8:00 and 9:00 A.M.

- TickCount—Stores the execution time for an individual method call.

- MethodName—Lists the name of the method called.

As you can see, the database requirements for this project are very simple. To test the stored procedure, you can execute it from your interactive query tool by providing values for the three input parameters:

```
exec spTimeLogAdd 'John Doe', 123456,'TestFunction'
```

In an upcoming section, we will describe how to execute the spTimeLogAdd procedure from within your Visual Basic code.

WORKING WITH CAPTURED DATA

After you have captured some time logging data, you can run SQL queries to determine some interesting information about your application. For example, the following SQL query lists the average execution time of each method:

```
Select MethodName, Avg(TickCount) From TimeLog Group By MethodName Order BY
Avg(TickCount) DESC
```

If you have only a single user who complains about performance but everyone else is fine, you can compare his execution times to others by filtering on the UserID field.

One important note about this time logging system is that it is not intended to be left on all the time, but rather only when the developer or database administrator is actively participating in performance tuning. Because the TimeLog table has no primary key or indexes, leaving time logging on would adversely affect performance in short order. The general steps for using this system are as follows:

1. Clear the TimeLog table with a DELETE or TRUNCATE TABLE statement.
2. Turn on time logging in your VB application (as described in the next section).
3. After a period of time, turn off time logging and analyze the resulting data with SQL queries.
4. Improve your code with optimizations and repeat the process.

UNDERSTANDING THE TimeLog CODE

As you learned at the beginning of this section, the code for determining the elapsed time in ticks is very simple. Listing 26.6 shows the LogExecutionTime subroutine, which executes the spTimeLogAdd stored procedure:

LISTING 26.6 PERFORMANCE.ZIP—THE TimeLog CLASS

```
Public Sub LogExecutionTime(ByVal strUserID As String,_
                            ByVal intStartTickCount As Integer,_
                            ByVal intEndTickCount As Integer,_
                            ByVal strMethodName As String)
    Dim parms(2) As SqlParameter


    parms(0) = New SqlParameter("@charUserID", SqlDbType.Char)
    parms(0).Size = 10
    parms(0).Value = strUserID
```

LISTING 26.6   CONTINUED

```
        parms(0).Direction = ParameterDirection.Input

        parms(1) = New SqlParameter("@intTickCount", SqlDbType.Int)
        parms(1).Value = intEndTickCount - intStartTickCount
        parms(1).Direction = ParameterDirection.Input

        parms(2) = New SqlParameter("@charMethod", SqlDbType.Char)
        parms(2).Size = 35
        parms(2).Value = strMethodName
        parms(2).Direction = ParameterDirection.Input

            Dim intRetVal As Integer
    Call ExecSP("TimeLog", "spTimeLogAdd", intRetVal, parms)

End Sub
```

Note that the code uses the ExecSP function, which was defined in Chapter 22, "Using ADO.NET." Now that we have a means to execute the stored procedure, all we need to do is call this subroutine from within the application. Listing 26.7 shows a typical method call that executes the LogExecutionTime subroutine.

LISTING 26.7   PERFORMANCE.ZIP—TYPICAL USE OF EXECUTION TIME LOGGING

```
Public Sub TestMethod()
        Dim intStartTime As Integer
        Dim intEndTime As Integer

        If m_bLoggingEnabled Then
            intStartTime = System.Environment.TickCount
        End If

        'PERFORM WORK HERE

        If m_bLoggingEnabled Then
            IntEndTime = System.Environment.TickCount
            Call LogExecutionTime("TestUser", intStartTime,_
            intEndTime, "TestMethod")
        End If

End Sub
```

Notice that the LogExecutionTime function is not called unless the value of the Boolean variable m_bLoggingEnabled is True. A great way to set this variable is to have the component read a registry value at startup and set it to True if necessary. Accessing the Registry is described in Chapter 21, "ActiveX Data Objects."

→ For more on reading values from the registry, **see** "Managing Database Connections," **p. 628**

ENHANCING THE SYSTEM

The time logging system described here is a simplified version of one I have actually used in a multi-tier Web application. As with any program, there is always room for improvement.

For example, you might also want to add the ability to log method call execution time and stored procedure execution time separately. If all you care about optimizing is the database (and not VB code), the time logging could be taken care of entirely on the database end within a stored procedure. The good thing about logging time from Visual Basic code is that it more closely represents the time the user is experiencing.

EXERCISE: USING PERFORMANCE COUNTERS

In the last section, we discussed a way to measure the execution time of program functions. However, when optimizing the program there may be other factors that determine your optimization steps. For example, it is also helpful to know which functions are executed most frequently. Suppose you have an application used for data entry. If it takes 10 seconds to initially load the application and sign on, but another 10 seconds every time you press the Save button—you definitely should place a higher priority on optimizing the code behind the Save button. Another factor that may impact application performance is the computer on which your program is running. Extra high memory usage or a network bottleneck can wreak havoc on even the most well-written code. To troubleshoot these problems, you first have to know they exist. The Windows operating system provides *performance counters*, which can be used to examine what is happening on your system. You can keep track of how many times a particular piece of code is executed, as well as track certain system resources such as disk i/o requests. A counter in Windows works just like the speedometer on your car, in that it contains a value that changes in response to some condition of the system. Windows includes a tool called Performance Monitor, pictured in Figure 26.7, which allows you to view system counters in a graphical manner.

Figure 26.7
Visual Studio .NET provides classes to read the built-in performance counters or add your own.

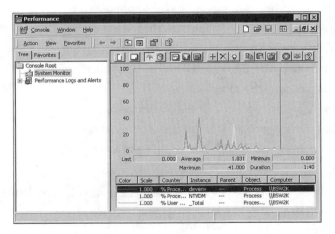

Note

On Windows 2000, the Performance Monitor is located in the Administrative Tools section of the Control panel.

In this section, we'll conclude our discussion of performance and optimization with an exercise that demonstrates how to access Windows Performance information from Visual Basic. We will show how you can add a performance counter to the system, as well as read the values of existing performance counters.

READING FROM A PERFORMANCE COUNTER

The easiest way to start working with performance counters in your program is to use the PerformanceCounter control, as shown in Figure 26.8.

Figure 26.8
The PerformanceCounter control is located in the Components section of the Toolbox.

To get started with the sample application, perform the following steps:

1. Start a new Windows Application in Visual Studio .NET.
2. Drag a PerformanceCounter control to the form.
3. Drag a Timer and a TextBox control to the form.
4. Using the Properties window, set the Interval property of the Timer to 1500.
5. Set the Enabled property of the Timer to True.
6. Set the CategoryName property of the performance counter to TCP.
7. Set the CounterName property of the performance counter to Connections Established.
8. Enter the code for the Timer's Tick event from Listing 26.8.

LISTING 26.8   PERFCOUNTER.ZIP—READING PERFORMANCE COUNTER VALUES

```
Private Sub timer1_Tick(ByVal sender As System.Object,_
ByVal e As System.EventArgs) Handles timer1.Tick

        TextBox1.Text = PerformanceCounter1.RawValue.ToString


End Sub
```

9. Press F5 to run the sample program. The text box will display the current number of TCP network connections to your computer.

10. Establish another connection by opening a Web browser or SQL query tool. The text box value should be updated to reflect the new number of network connections.

As you can see, the PerformanceCounter control is an easy way to find out a lot of information about your system related to the processor, memory, and other statistics. In order to select a counter, you have to set three properties:

- CategoryName—A group of related performance counters. For example, the Memory category has counters related to the memory on your machine.

- CounterName—A specific performance measure, such as the number of bytes of available memory.

- InstanceName—An instance of a performance counter. For example, if you are using a machine with four processors, each processor represents a separate instance of processor-related counters. (This property is optional for some counters.)

After you have set up a PerformanceCounter control, you can access the value of the associated counter using the RawValue property. For example, you might want to monitor the available memory or disk space and send an alert to an administrator if the value reaches a certain level.

WRITING TO A PERFORMANCE COUNTER

In addition to accessing performance counters that already exist on your system, you can add a custom performance counter with just a few lines of code. Once added, this custom performance counter is available in the Windows Performance Monitor for yourself and others to view. The exercise described in the section shows how to create a new category called VBAppCounters, which contains two counters: TestCounter1 and TestCounter2.

CREATING THE SAMPLE PROGRAM

The System.Diagnostics namespace contains all the classes for working with performance counters. To create a sample performance counter, perform the following steps:

1. Start a new Visual Basic Windows application.

2. Drag three Button controls to the form. Set their Name properties to btnAdd, btnSubtract, and btnClear. Set their Text properties to Add, Subtract, and Clear.

3. Add the code from Listing 26.9 to your form class.

4. Run the program and click the Add button once. This will create the custom performance category and associated counters.

5. Open the Windows Control panel. Select Administrative Tools, and then click the Performance icon.

PART
VI
CH
26

6. Click the plus (+) icon on the Performance Monitor toolbar, and you should see a screen similar to Figure 26.9.

7. From the Category List select VBAppCounters. You should see TestCounter1 and TestCounter2 appear as available counters.

8. Choose the All Counters option.

9. Click the Add button and then the Close button to close the dialog box. You should see a red vertical line slowly moving across your screen as the performance monitor samples the test counter values.

10. Arrange the Visual Basic form and the Performance Counter window so you can see both on the screen at the same time.

11. Rapidly click the Add button. Notice the change in the performance counter. (You can also click Subtract to decrease the performance counter or Clear to set its value to 0.)

LISTING 26.9   PERFCOUNTER.ZIP—USING A CUSTOM PERFORMANCE COUNTER

```
Private TestCtr1 As PerformanceCounter
Private TestCtr2 As PerformanceCounter

Private Sub InitCustomCounters()

    Dim CCD As CounterCreationDataCollection
    Dim CNT As CounterCreationData

    If Not PerformanceCounterCategory.Exists("VBAppCounters") Then
       CCD = New CounterCreationDataCollection()
       CNT = New CounterCreationData("TestCounter1", "test.",_
                    PerformanceCounterType.NumberOfItems32)
       CCD.Add(CNT)
       CNT = New CounterCreationData("TestCounter2", "test2.",_
                    PerformanceCounterType.RateOfCountsPerSecond32)
       CCD.Add(CNT)

       PerformanceCounterCategory.Create("VBAppCounters", "Test Category", CCD)
    End If

    TestCtr1 = New PerformanceCounter("VBAppCounters", "TestCounter1", False)
    TestCtr2 = New PerformanceCounter("VBAppCounters", "TestCounter2", False)

End Sub

Private Sub btnAdd_Click(ByVal sender As System.Object,_
ByVal e As System.EventArgs) Handles btnAdd.Click
    InitCustomCounters()
    TestCtr1.Increment()
    TestCtr2.Increment()

End Sub
Private Sub btnSubtract_Click(ByVal sender As System.Object,_
ByVal e As System.EventArgs) Handles btnSubtract.Click
```

```
        InitCustomCounters()
        TestCtr1.Decrement()
        TestCtr2.Decrement()

End Sub
Private Sub btnClear_Click(ByVal sender As System.Object,_
ByVal e As System.EventArgs) Handles btnClear.Click

        InitCustomCounters()
        TestCtr1.RawValue = 0
        TestCtr2.RawValue = 0

End Sub
```

Figure 26.9
You can add your own custom categories to the Windows performance counter.

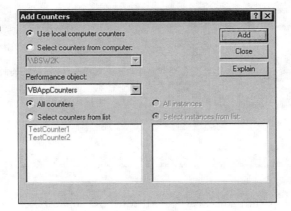

In this exercise we have demonstrated how to create a performance counter and change its value. A performance counter object works just like any other object, in that it can be manipulated through methods and properties. However, keep the following key points in mind when using performance counters:

- When creating a custom performance counter, you have to create the category and any counters in the category *at the same time*. The code in Listing 26.9 builds a collection of counters and then creates all the custom counters and their category using the `Create` method.

- Different types of counters are available. For example, as you clicked the Add button, you may have noticed the graphs of the two lines were slightly different. The constant `RateOfCountsPerSecond32` caused `TestCounter2` to measure on a per-second basis. For a complete list of constants and their description, see the help files.

- When declaring an instance of a `PerformanceCounter` object whose value you want to change, set the `ReadOnly` property during initialization of the object. At the time of this writing, setting the `ReadOnly` property after creating the object instance had no effect.

Another point we did not make in the previous exercise is performance counters can be created, accessed, and deleted from within Visual Studio by using the Server Explorer. The list of performance counters as shown in the Server Explorer window is shown in Figure 26.10.

Figure 26.10
To delete or create a performance counter, right-click in the Server Explorer window.

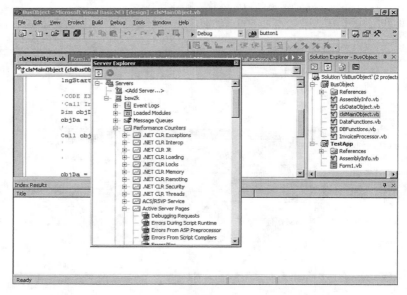

Monitoring application performance, particularly for those applications that are heavily used, enables you to tune and optimize critical areas so your users can enjoy increased processing speed. As we have demonstrated, using a custom performance counter is an easy way to take advantage of the Performance Monitor utility provided by Windows 2000.

CHAPTER **27**

WRITING A POCKET PC APPLICATION

In this chapter

As computer technology continues to advance at a breathtaking pace, a variety of small handheld computers are starting to appear on the market. These computers, sometimes called PDAs (personal digital assistants) perform a variety of tasks, such as organizing contacts and using e-mail. One particular type of device, the Pocket PC, is of particular interest to the Visual Basic developer. Figure 27.1 shows a typical Pocket PC, which is tiny in comparison to traditional personal computers.

Figure 27.1
Visual Basic developers can easily create applications for Pocket PCs such as this Compaq H3600 series.

A Pocket PC runs a slimmed down version of the Windows operating system known as *Windows CE*. Windows CE is very similar in function to the standard Windows operating system, so users will find the transition easy. In addition, Microsoft has created a special tool for VB programmers, *eMbedded Visual Basic*, to develop applications for Windows CE devices. In this chapter, we will demonstrate how to develop an application using eMbedded Visual Basic that runs on a Pocket PC.

INSTALLING EMBEDDED VISUAL BASIC

eMbedded Visual Basic is a separate, stand-alone edition of Visual Basic. You must install it separately from Visual Studio .NET. At the time of this writing, the latest version of eMbedded Visual Basic (3.0) was available absolutely free for download from Microsoft's Web site. Figure 27.2 shows the eMbedded Visual Basic development environment.

Note   To download eMbedded Visual Basic, visit www.microsoft.com/mobile and click the Developer link.

Figure 27.2
eMbedded Visual
Basic's development
environment should
be familiar to Visual
Basic programmers.

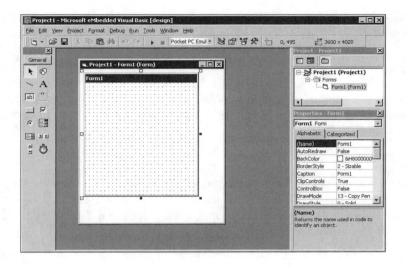

The eMbedded Visual Basic IDE contains a Project Explorer, Forms Designer, and Toolbox, just like other editions of Visual Basic. Although there are some differences and limitations, you should be able to use the VB development concepts you already know (that is, coding event procedures) to quickly get started using this tool.

USING POCKET PC EMULATION

You might think that you need to run out and buy hardware to start developing applications for a Pocket PC, but you do not. When you install eMbedded Visual Basic, you can also install the Pocket PC Software Development Kit (SDK). This SDK includes an *emulator*, which simulates a Pocket PC on your desktop screen. To try the emulator, find the program group called Microsoft Platform SDK for Pocket PC and click Desktop Pocket PC Emulation. You should see a screen similar to that in Figure 27.3.

Figure 27.3
The Pocket PC emula-
tor can be "turned
off" by clicking the
power button at the
bottom of the screen.

Power button

Note
At the time of this writing, Microsoft's Pocket PC emulator would not run under Windows 95/98, but would run under Windows 2000.

When you run an application in eMbedded Visual Basic, your forms appear on the emulator screen (or the Pocket PC itself, depending on your settings) rather than on your Windows desktop.

LOCATING HELP

In the following sections, we will introduce the basics of creating a Pocket PC application. However, if you decide to pursue serious Pocket PC development, you may find you need more detailed help in a particular subject. Keep in mind the following resources when searching for information:

- *Help Files*—Select Contents from the Help menu and you will find extensive help files installed on your hard drive.

- *API Text Viewer*—Open the Tools program group and you will find the API Text Viewer, which provides a list of Windows CE operating system functions you can call from your programs.

- *Internet Discussion Groups*—Set your Internet newsreader to a news server such as msnews.microsoft.com, where you will find several Pocket PC-related newsgroups.

- *Web Sites*—In addition to Microsoft's mobile area mentioned earlier and the official www.pocketpc.com site, you can find lots of great Web sites with sample code and tips. Some examples are www.pocketpcpassion.com and www.purece.com.

CREATING THE SAMPLE APPLICATION

This section demonstrates building a user interface using eMbedded Visual Basic forms. In creating the application, you will create a program that will run on the Pocket PC, which works like a Windows Application project running on a desktop PC. Our sample application is an inventory-tracking program for a warehouse. As truck drivers load and unload products, the warehouse manager enters the data on a Pocket PC he carries at the loading dock. Later, when the manager returns to his office, the information he gathered can be automatically loaded to a central database via his desktop PC. To begin building the sample application, you'll need to start eMbedded Visual Basic and choose to create a New Windows CE for the Pocket PC Project. In this section, we'll write the code that actually runs on the Pocket PC. In the following sections, we will explore how to transfer data from the Pocket PC to a PC database.

DESIGNING THE USER INTERFACE

A Pocket PC has a much smaller screen than a standard PC, so the available space for controls on a form is very limited. The Pocket PC pictured in Figure 27.1 has a total screen area of 240 × 320 pixels, which is much smaller than a typical desktop PC. In addition, a Pocket PC does not usually have a keyboard attached, so a "virtual" keyboard appears on the screen for text input. When the keyboard is displayed on the screen, parts of your form may be obscured. For these reasons, you need to put extra thought into user interface design for the Pocket PC. As we will see, the controls provided with eMbedded Visual Basic provide a good number of options for designing user interfaces.

ADDING THE BASIC CONTROLS

For our sample inventory tracking application, we will design the user interface so that typed data entry is kept to a minimum. To set up the form, perform the following steps:

1. Set the Name property of the form to frmMain and the Caption property to Inventory Maintenance.
2. Set the Name property of the project to prjInventory.
3. Add the controls to the form as specified in Table 27.1, setting their Name and Caption properties appropriately.

TABLE 27.1   SETTING UP CONTROLS FOR THE SAMPLE APPLICATION

Control Type	Name	Caption
Label	lblDriver	Driver Name
Label	lblProduct	Product
Label	lblQuantity	Quantity
ComboBox	cmbDriver	
ComboBox	cmbProduct	
Timer	tmrQuantity	
TextBox	txtQuantity	0
OptionButton	optShipped	Shipped
OptionButton	optReceived	Received
CommandButton	cmdPlus	+
CommandButton	cmdMinus	-
CommandButton	cmdConfirm	Confirm

PART

VI

CH

27

4. Set the `Value` property for `optReceived` to `True`.

5. Set the `Enabled` property for `tmrQuantity` to `False`.

6. Set the `Text` property of `cmbDriver` and `cmbProduct` to a blank string.

ADDING ADDITIONAL CONTROLS

All the controls listed in Table 27.1 are included in the Toolbox by default. However, several other controls are available by selecting Components from the Project menu. In our sample project, we will be using two of these controls, the ListView control and the FileSystem control. To set up these controls, perform the following steps:

1. From the Project menu, choose Components. Select the Microsoft CE ListView Control and the Microsoft CE File System Control. Press OK to close the dialog box.

2. Add a ListView control to your form. Set its `Name` property to `lvData`.

3. Add a FileSystem control to your form. Set its `Name` property to `fsMain`.

4. From the Project Explorer, right-click `frmMain` and choose View Code. Add the following lines of code to the form's `Load` event:

```
lvData.View = lvwReport
lvData.ColumnHeaders.Add , , "Entered", 750
lvData.ColumnHeaders.Add , , "Driver", 1000
lvData.ColumnHeaders.Add , , "Qty.", 500
lvData.ColumnHeaders.Add , , "Product", 900
```

5. Arrange all the controls on the form so that your form appears similar to Figure 27.4.

Figure 27.4
You can arrange controls and set their properties in eMbedded Visual Basic using the same techniques that you use in Visual Basic .NET.

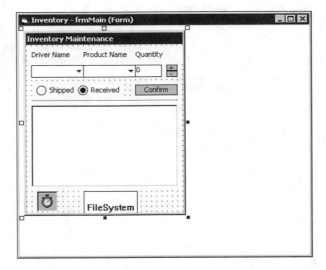

As we continue coding the project, we will see how to use the FileSystem control to check the Pocket PC file system, and the ListView to display data in a tabular fashion.

DYNAMICALLY RESIZING THE FORM

Now that you have added all the controls to your form, you need to write some code so the user interface behaves appropriately in the Pocket PC environment. When browsing through the form's event procedures you may have noticed a couple of CE-specific events:

- OKClick—Notice that the OKClick event procedure is already filled in for you with an App.End statement. Pocket PC applications generally have an OK button at the top of the form, which closes the current screen.

- SIPChange—You can add code to this event to move controls or resize the form when the Pocket PC's onscreen keyboard is displayed.

The keyboard and handwriting recognition capabilities of a Pocket PC are known as the *soft input panel*, or SIP. Other than the size, this is probably the most obvious difference between using a Pocket PC and a desktop PC. By handling the SIPChange event in your code, you can automatically alter the appearance of the form when the SIP is present. To add this capability to the sample application, perform the following steps:

1. Make sure the form's FormResize property is set to vbFormFullSIPResize. This will cause the form to be displayed full-screen, with borders that automatically resize when the SIP is displayed.
2. Add the following line of code to the SIPChange event:
   ```
   lvData.Height = frmMain.Height - 1500
   ```

This line of code causes the height of the list view to be set to 1,500 pixels less than the form's height whenever the SIPChange event fires.

> **Note**
> Although the user is ultimately in control of the SIP, setting the SIPBehavior property of a form gives the programmer control over whether the SIP is displayed at startup. You can also turn on an automatic mode so that the keyboard will appear when certain types of controls receive focus.

AIDING THE USER WITH TEXT INPUT

In our sample application, the user will need to update the quantity text box with the number of products being shipped or received at the warehouse. The SIP can be used with any text box to enter text. However, trying to type on a miniature keyboard at a busy loading dock may not always be convenient. Therefore, our user interface includes two small command buttons to increment or decrement the quantity in the text box. The simplest way to code the function of these buttons would be to add a line of code to their Click events. However, making large changes to the quantity would require repeated clicks, which is also inconvenient.

If you have set a digital clock or timer, you may have noticed that by holding the button down you can vary the speed with which the number changes. By adding a few extra lines of code and a timer control, we can add similar functionality to the UI of our sample application. To accomplish this, add the code from Listing 27.1 to your form:

LISTING 27.1   PPCDEMO.ZIP—CHANGING THE QUANTITY QUICKLY

```
Dim m_nIncrement  As Integer

Private Sub cmdMinus_MouseDown(ByVal Button As Integer, ByVal Shift As Integer,_
    ByVal X As Single, ByVal Y As Single)
    m_nIncrement = -1
    tmrQuantity.Interval = 300
    tmrQuantity.Enabled = True
End Sub
Private Sub cmdMinus_MouseUp(ByVal Button As Integer, ByVal Shift As Integer,_
    ByVal X As Single, ByVal Y As Single)
    tmrQuantity.Enabled = False
End Sub

Private Sub cmdPlus_MouseDown(ByVal Button As Integer, ByVal Shift As Integer,_
    ByVal X As Single, ByVal Y As Single)
    m_nIncrement = 1
    tmrQuantity.Interval = 300
    tmrQuantity.Enabled = True
End Sub
Private Sub cmdPlus_MouseUp(ByVal Button As Integer, ByVal Shift As Integer,_
    ByVal X As Single, ByVal Y As Single)
  tmrQuantity.Enabled = False
End Sub

Private Sub tmrQuantity_Timer()
    txtQuantity.Text = CLng(txtQuantity.Text) + m_nIncrement
    If CLng(txtQuantity.Text) < 0 Then txtQuantity.Text = 0
    tmrQuantity.Interval = tmrQuantity.Interval - 50
    If tmrQuantity.Interval < 50 Then
        m_nIncrement = m_nIncrement * 5
        tmrQuantity.Interval = 400
    End If
End Sub
```

Listing 27.1 employs a Timer control that is enabled as long as the mouse (or in the case of a Pocket PC, the finger or stylus) is depressed. By decreasing the value of the timer's Interval property and changing the quantity increment variable, the value in the text box changesmore rapidly as the user continues to hold down the button.

TESTING THE USER INTERFACE

Before continuingwith coding, you should test the basics of your user interface. This will mean running your eMbedded Visual Basic program for the first time. To do so, we will need to set the remote project name and target. This can be accomplished by using the Project Properties dialog box, shown in Figure 27.5. Display the dialog box by selecting Properties from the Project menu. Next, make sure "Pocket PC Emulation" is selected in the Run on Target combo box. Finally, change the Remote Path to \Windows\Start Menu\Inventory.vb.

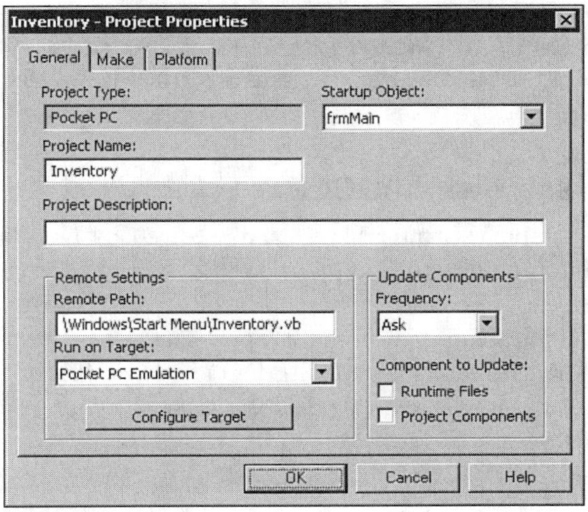

Figure 27.5
You can also change the target directly from the eMbedded Visual Basic toolbar.

After you have changed the settings to match Figure 27.5, press the Start button and your application should appear on the emulator screen, as shown in Figure 27.6.

Figure 27.6
When you run an application in embedded VB, you can choose to run it on the emulator or an actual Pocket PC.

Test the UI features we just implemented by clicking on the keyboard icon to display the SIP, as well as clicking and holding the plus and minus buttons to change the quantity value. To end your debugging session, press the OK button on the emulator, or the Stop button in eMbedded Visual Basic.

PART

VI

CH

27

Note

Each time you run a Pocket PC project on the device or emulator, the files are copied to the target, so you can execute the project directly from the Start menu of the target device.

ADDING DATABASE CAPABILITY WITH ADOCE

Now that we have the sample user interface created, we need a way to transfer database information to and from the Pocket PC application. (Keep in mind we're assuming that the Pocket PC does not have a live continuous network connection; if that was the case your application could communicate directly with a Web or database server.) The Windows CE operating system supports a minimal version of ADO known as ADOCE. In this section, you will learn how to use ADOCE to create database tables on your Pocket PC, as well as update information in an ADOCE recordset.

→ For more on ADO, **see** Chapter 21, "ActiveX Data Objects," **p. 575**

To begin using ADOCE, add a reference to it by selecting References from the Project menu. From the references dialog box, shown in Figure 27.7, select Microsoft CE ADO Control.

Figure 27.7
Before you can use ADOCE in your eMbedded Visual Basic project, you must add a reference.

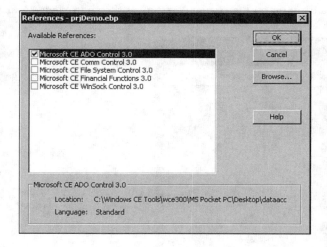

The process of installing ADO or other controls on the emulator is handled automatically when you start a debugging session with eMbedded Visual Basic.

CREATING A DATABASE ON THE POCKET PC

Because our sample database is designed for data gathering and subsequent upload to a central database, the data structure on the Pocket PC will be very simple: just a single table containing a record of each inventory transaction. For ease of installation, we'll add code to automatically create the database on the Pocket PC if it does not exist. After creating the database table, we will store references to the database in form-level variables. All these tasks are accomplished by the InitDatabase custom function, shown in Listing 27.2.

LISTING 27.2   PPCDEMO.ZIP—DDL STATEMENTS USING ADOCE

```
Private Sub InitDatabase()
    'This function prepares the database and is called at program startup
    Dim rsTemp As ADOCE.Recordset
    Const sDBPath = "\My Documents\InventoryDB.cdb"
    'If database file does not exist then create it
    If fsMain.Dir(sDBPath) = "" Then
        Set rsTemp = CreateObject("adoce.recordset.3.0")
        rsTemp.Open "CREATE DATABASE '" & sDBPath & "'"
    End If

    'Connect to the database file
    Set m_cnLocal = CreateObject("ADOCE.Connection.3.0")
    m_cnLocal.Open (sDBPath)

    'If database table does not exist then create it
    Set rsTemp = m_cnLocal.Execute_
    ("Select * from MSysTables Where TableName = ➥'InventoryInfo'")
    If rsTemp.RecordCount = 0 Then
        Call m_cnLocal.Execute("CREATE table InventoryInfo (DateEntered DateTime,
➥DriverName varchar(30), Quantity Integer, Product varchar(15))")
    End If
    Set rsTemp = Nothing

    'Open module-level recordset
    Set m_rsData = CreateObject("ADOCE.Recordset.3.0")
    Set m_rsData.ActiveConnection = m_cnLocal
    m_rsData.Open "Select * from InventoryInfo", , adOpenKeyset, adLockOptimistic

    'Call function to load data in listview
    Call DisplayEnteredData

End Sub

Private Sub Form_OKClick()
    Set m_rsData = Nothing
    m_cnLocal.Close
    Set m_cnLocal = Nothing
    App.End
End Sub
```

The `InitDatabase` subroutine in Listing 27.2 uses the `Dir` method of the FileSystem control to check whether a database file named `InventoryDB.cdb` exists in the current directory. If the file does not exist, then the database and table are created. Also note that the `OKClick` event procedure has been modified to close the data connection and recordset before the program ends.

→ For more on `Dir` and other file system functions, **see** Chapter 24, "Working with Files," **p. 667**

ADOCE's native database file format uses the `cdb` extension. A Windows CE database is a limited version of the Microsoft Access Database (`mdb`) format. ADOCE supports the familiar `Recordset` and `Connection` objects from ADO, which are used in the example to execute several SQL statements. As you may recall from the Database Basics chapter, you can use SQL statements to create database objects as well as query and update data.

→ For more on SQL statements, **see** Chapter 20, "Database Basics," **p. 535**

The code in Listing 27.2 uses a CREATE DATABASE statement to create the database file. Next, it executes a query on the MSysTables table to determine whether the InventoryInfo table exists. If the table does not exist, it is created with a CREATE TABLE statement. Finally, a SELECT query is executed to open a module-level Recordset object, m_rsData. By manipulating the m_rsData object, we can read or write to the database table.

> **Note**
>
> The data types available in ADOCE are slightly different from those in Access or SQL server. For more details, see the eMbedded Visual Basic help topic "Converting Data to a Device."

> **Note**
>
> ADOCE can also be used to connect to ODBC or OLEDB data sources on a connected network. There is even a version of SQL Server designed to run on the PocketPC. Visit www.pocketpc.com for more information.

ADDING DATA TO THE RECORDSET

The call to the Open method in Listing 27.2 specifies the cursor and lock types so that the returned recordset is updateable. To write the code that adds a new record, simply add the following statements to the Click event of cmdConfirm.

```
Private Sub cmdConfirm_Click()
    'Add a new record to the recordset
    m_rsData.AddNew
    m_rsData.Fields("DateEntered") = Now
    m_rsData.Fields("DriverName") = cmbDriver.Text
    m_rsData.Fields("Quantity") = txtQuantity.Text
    m_rsData.Fields("Product") = cmbProduct.Text
    m_rsData.Update

    'Call function to load data in listview
    Call DisplayEnteredData

End Sub
```

The preceding code starts the process of adding a new record by calling the AddNew method. Next, it assigns values to the fields. Finally, the Update method is invoked to commit the data to the database. As you can see, ADOCE recordsets work very much like ADO recordsets.

> **Note**
>
> You can also use SQL statements to update data by executing an INSERT command.

DISPLAYING DATA IN THE LISTVIEW

Now that we have a means to enter data on the Pocket PC, we need to add code to populate the list view with data from the InventoryInfo table. This will give the user a running list of the data as he enters it. To keep the list current, we will update it at program startup and every time a new record is added. A custom subroutine, DisplayEnteredData, will populate the list view by browsing through the recordset. Listing 27.3 shows this function.

LISTING 27.3   PPCDEMO.ZIP—USING A LISTVIEW

```
Private Sub DisplayEnteredData()
    Dim itm As ListItem

    lvData.ListItems.Clear
    If m_rsData.RecordCount <> 0 Then
        m_rsData.MoveFirst

        'Load recordset data in the list view
        While Not m_rsData.EOF
            Set itm = lvData.ListItems.Add(, ,_
            FormatDateTime("" & m_rsData.Fields("DateEntered"), vbShortTime))
            itm.SubItems(1) = m_rsData.Fields("DriverName")
            itm.SubItems(2) = m_rsData.Fields("Quantity")
            itm.SubItems(3) = m_rsData.Fields("Product")
            m_rsData.MoveNext
        Wend

        'Display list of entered drivers, products
        Call UpdateComboBox(1, cmbDriver)
        Call UpdateComboBox(3, cmbProduct)

        'Sort data by entry time
        lvData.SortKey = 0
        lvData.SortOrder = lvwDescending
    End If

End Sub

Private Sub UpdateComboBox(nSortKey As Integer, cmbX As ComboBox)
    'Fill up a combo box with distinct listview items
    '(because we cannot use SELECT DISTINCT with a CDB file)
    Dim i As Integer
    Dim sLastItem As String
    Dim sCurrItem As String
    lvData.SortKey = nSortKey
    lvData.SortOrder = lvwAscending
    lvData.Sorted = True
    cmbX.Clear
    For i = 1 To lvData.ListItems.Count
        sCurrItem = lvData.ListItems(i).SubItems(nSortKey)
        If sCurrItem <> sLastItem Then
            cmbX.AddItem sCurrItem
```

LISTING 27.3   CONTINUED

```
                sLastItem = sCurrItem
        End If
    Next
End Sub

Private Sub lvData_ColumnClick(ByVal Index As Long)
    'Sorts the list view when a column is clicked
    Dim nTemp As Integer
    nTemp = Index - 1
    If nTemp < 0 Then nTemp = 0
    If nTemp >= 0 And nTemp < lvData.ColumnHeaders.Count Then
        If lvData.SortOrder = lvwAscending Then
            lvData.SortOrder = lvwDescending
        Else
            lvData.SortOrder = lvwAscending
        End If
        lvData.SortKey = nTemp
        lvData.Sorted = True
    End If
End Sub
```

The UpdateComboBox subroutine in Listing 27.3 updates the combo boxes with the list of drivers and products already entered, so the user will not have to retype them. In addition, the ColumnClick event procedure contains code to sort the list view when the user clicks on a column header.

TESTING THE SAMPLE APPLICATION

Because the data access code is more complicated than the user interface code, you may run into errors when executing your program. eMbedded Visual Basic contains the same types of debugging tools as regular Visual Basic, with some notable limitations:

- You can set breakpoints and step through code in eMbedded Visual Basic, but you cannot change the code "on the fly."

- The Set Next Statement function is not available when debugging in eMbedded Visual Basic.

- Only limited error handling is available (non-structured with On Error Resume Next and checking the Error variable).

- Breakpoints must be initiated from the desktop PC. In other words, you cannot press Ctrl+Break on the Pocket PC and then return to Visual Basic.

Although these restrictions may seem very limiting at first, keep in mind you are actually running your program on a separate operating system, optimized for pocket computing. If you do encounter errors, set up breakpoints at the beginning of suspected functions and then step through the code to find them.

After your sample application is working, run it on the emulator and perform a test of the data entry capabilities:

1. Click in the Driver combo box and use the keyboard to enter a driver's name.
2. Click in the Product combo box and use the keyboard to enter a product name.
3. Click and hold the Plus button to select a quantity.
4. Select Received to specify a positive quantity.
5. Click Confirm and your information should show up in the list.
6. Click the arrow next to the Driver combo box and pick the driver's name you previously entered.
7. Click in the Product combo box and use the keyboard to enter a product name.
8. Click in the Quantity box and use the keyboard to enter a quantity number.
9. Click Confirm and the list should now contain two rows of information.
10. Click the Product and Quantity column headers to sort the list.

If the program is working correctly, you should be able to enter data and see it displayed on the screen, as shown in Figure 27.8.

Figure 27.8
The sample application updates the grid each time a new record is added.

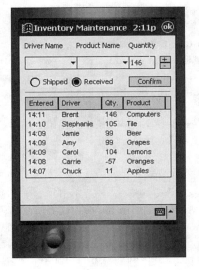

After you have finished testing your application, close the emulator and connect your real Pocket PC. Change the target device setting to Pocket PC (Default Device) and test the application on the Pocket PC by repeating the preceding steps. The process of running the application on your Pocket PC will create a Start Menu item for the inventory project. The remainder of this chapter assumes you have closed eMbedded Visual Basic and the emulator and are running the finished sample application directly from your Pocket PC Start menu.

PART

VI

CH

27

SYNCHRONIZING APPLICATION DATA

Although some Pocket PCs are equipped with wireless network cards, most of them can only exchange data with another PC when connected in their docking station. This process is known as *synchronizing* your PC with your Pocket PC. Microsoft includes a program called ActiveSync, pictured in Figure 27.9, which performs this process.

Figure 27.9
Microsoft ActiveSync, available for free download, updates databases, e-mail, and offline Web pages on your Pocket PC.

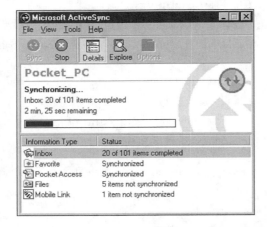

If you have the ActiveSync program installed, it will automatically appear and begin exchanging information with your Pocket PC each time you dock it. For our sample application, we'll need to move the inventory data we gathered to the desktop PC for processing. As you might imagine, you can manage this process manually by allowing ActiveSync to transfer the information to an Access database. However, in order to make the process as easy as possible for the end user, we will show how to use API calls to control it from within a VB .NET application.

UNDERSTANDING THE API CALLS

When you transfer information between the Pocket PC and another PC using ActiveSync, you are essentially just transferring files. ActiveSync has *filters* that convert a specific file type on the Pocket PC to its Desktop PC counterpart. In the case of an ADOCE database, a filter is provided that converts a cdb file to the mdb (Access) file format. To transfer the inventory database, we will make use of this filter via API calls. To begin, start Visual Studio .NET and create a new Windows Application project. Enter the following API declarations at the top of your form class:

```
Private Declare Function DEVICETODESKTOP Lib_
"c:\program files\Microsoft ActiveSync\adofiltr.dll" _
(ByVal desktoplocn As String, _
        ByVal tablelist As String, _
        ByVal sync As Boolean, _
```

```
         ByVal overwrite As Integer, _
         ByVal devicelocn As String) As Long

Private Declare Function DESKTOPTODEVICE Lib_
"c:\program files\Microsoft ActiveSync\adofiltr.dll" _
(ByVal desktoplocn As String, _
         ByVal tablelist As String, _
         ByVal sync As Boolean, _
         ByVal overwrite As Integer, _
         ByVal devicelocn As String) As Long
```

The purpose of these two API calls is self-explanatory. You simply call the appropriate function depending on the desired direction of data transfer.

Note

As with any API declaration, a reference to an external DLL is required. If you installed ActiveSync in a directory other than the default, you will need to search your hard drive for `adofiltr.dll` and modify the path appropriately.

Keep in mind the following notes regarding use of the parameters:

- The `desktoplocn` and `devicelocn` parameters describe the paths to the `mdb` and `cdb` files, respectively. Note that the `devicelocn` parameter will never contain a drive letter.
- By specifying the `tablelist` parameter, you can choose to copy only certain tables within a database. Sending an empty string will copy all tables.
- Setting the `sync` parameter to `True` will register the process with the ActiveSync program under the `Pocket Access` Sync Options tab.
- To overwrite an existing database file, set the `overwrite` parameter to `1`.

More information on the `DESKTOPTODEVICE` and `DEVICETODESKTOP` API calls is available in the eMbedded Visual Basic help files.

CODING THE DATA TRANSFER

Synchronizing our inventory database will be a three-step process. First, we will copy the data from the Pocket PC to a folder on the PC hard drive. Next we will process the data and delete old records. Finally, we will send the updated database back to the Pocket PC. To set up the data transfer application, perform the following steps.

1. Open Windows Explorer and create a new folder on your hard drive called `C:\InventoryInfo`. This folder will store the Access `mdb` file.
2. Add a Button control to your form. Set its `Name` property to `btnSyncData` and its `Text` property to `Transfer Inventory Database`.
3. Add the code in Listing 27.4 to your form.

LISTING 27.4   PPCDEMO.ZIP—DATABASE TRANSFER WITH THE POCKET PC

```
Private Sub UpdateInventoryDatabase()
    Const sMDBPath As String = "C:\InventoryInfo\Inventory.mdb"
    Const sCDBPath As String = "\My Documents\InventoryDB.cdb"
    Dim result As Long
    Dim Answer As DialogResult

    'Show a message box to confirm that they really want to do this
    Answer = Messagebox.Show("Transfer Inventory data from Pocket PC?",_
    "Are you sure?", MessageBoxButtons.OKCancel, MessageBoxIcon.Question)

    If Answer = DialogResult.OK Then
        Me.Text = "Copying Data from device..."
        result = DEVICETODESKTOP(sMDBPath, "", False, 1, sCDBPath)

        Me.Text = "Processing Data..."
        Call ProcessNewInventory()

        Me.Text = "Copying data to device..."
        result = DESKTOPTODEVICE(sMDBPath, "", False, 1, sCDBPath)

        Me.Text = "Done!"
    End If

End Sub

Private Sub ProcessNewInventory()
    Dim cn As OleDbConnection
    Dim cmd As OleDbCommand
    Dim dtPurgeDate As Date = Today.Now.AddHours(-1)
    Const sMDBPath As String = "C:\InventoryInfo\Inventory.mdb"

    cn = New OleDbConnection(_
    "Provider=Microsoft.Jet.OLEDB.4.0;Data Source=" & sMDBPath)
    cn.Open()
    cmd = cn.CreateCommand()
    cmd.CommandType = CommandType.Text

    'This command deletes records more than an hour old
    cmd.CommandText =_
    "Delete from InventoryInfo Where DateEntered < #" &_dtPurgeDate.ToString & "#"

    cmd.ExecuteNonQuery()
    cn.Close()
End Sub

Private Sub btnSyncData_Click(ByVal sender As System.Object,_
    ByVal e As System.EventArgs) Handles btnSyncData.Click
    Call UpdateInventoryDatabase()
End Sub
```

The UpdateInventoryDataBase function uses the two ADOCE API calls to transfer data to and from the Pocket PC. During this process, the form caption is updated with status information so the user knows what is happening. When the data has been loaded to the PC, the code calls the `ProcessNewInventory` function. In our sample application, this function uses ADO .NET to delete records from the table that are more than an hour old. However, you could also upload data to a central SQL database, print reports, or any other desired tasks.

TESTING THE DATA TRANSFER

If you have not already entered some inventory items on your Pocket PC, do so now. After you have finished, click the OK button to close the application on the Pocket PC. Finally, dock your Pocket PC and perform the following steps:

1. Press the Start button in Visual Basic .NET to start your data transfer application.
2. When the form appears, click the Transfer button.
3. Answer OK to the confirmation message.
4. The data will be transferred to your PC and back.

After completing the transfer process, connect to the file `C:\InventoryInfo\Inventory.mdb` using Access or the Visual Studio .NET Server Explorer. Open the `InventoryInfo` table and you should see the data you entered on the Pocket PC. If you had any data that was an hour old, it should be deleted from both the Pocket PC and the PC database table.

AUTOMATICALLY RUNNING THE TRANSFER PROGRAM

As a final enhancement to the transfer program, you can automatically start it each time the Pocket PC is docked. This is easily accomplished by performing the following steps:

1. Remove the button control from your form and add the following lines of code to the end of the form's `New` method:

```
Call UpdateInventoryDatabase
Messagebox.Show("Done")
Application.Quit
```

2. Compile your program by choosing `Build` from the Build menu.
3. Copy your program's executable to the `C:\InventoryInfo` folder.
4. From the Windows Start menu, choose Run and type `Regedit` to display the Registry Editor.
5. Using the Registry Editor, navigate to the following key:

```
HKEY_LOCAL_MACHINE\SOFTWARE\Microsoft\Windows CE Services\AutoStartOnConnect
```

6. Right-click the key and choose to add a new string value.
7. Name the string `MySync` program and for the value enter the path to your executable, `C:\InventoryInfo\PocketSync.exe`, as shown in Figure 27.10.

By adding additional registry entries, you can cause any number of programs to be executed when a Pocket PC is connected or disconnected.

Figure 27.10
You can automatically launch programs when a PC is docked or undocked by simply adding a registry value.

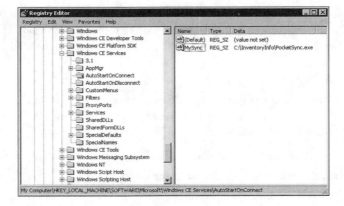

FROM HERE . . .

Congratulations on creating your first Pocket PC application! Although this technology is relatively new, it promises to be an exciting area of application development in the future. If the introduction has gotten you interested, here are some other areas to explore:

- The method of synchronizing data described in this section is just one of many. You can also use Outlook to send mail or save your data to a text file and let ActiveSync copy it to the Pocket_PC My Documents folder.

- As we mentioned earlier in the chapter, there is a version of SQL Server, SQLCE, that runs on the Pocket PC. This product will allow you to perform more advanced database operations.

- Peruse the API reference included with eMbedded Visual Basic to learn more about network and graphics functions.

PACKAGING YOUR APPLICATIONS

In this appendix

Once you have created, tested, and debugged your Visual Basic .NET application, you will most likely want to create a way to deploy it for use on computers other than your own. Whether you have created a utility for your workgroup, a system for your company's customers, or a shareware package for distribution via the Internet, creating an installer for your application ensures that it is properly installed on the user's computer.

The proper way to deploy a Windows Application project is to create an *installer*. An installer is a special type of application that utilizes the Microsoft Windows Installer built into Windows 2000, Windows Me, and Windows XP, and which is also available for earlier versions of Windows. The process of deploying Visual Basic .NET applications is based on Windows Installer technology. Simply put, an installer is a setup package that a user can run to install an application on his computer, just as he might do after purchasing a commercial software package.

The output of a setup project is an .MSI (Microsoft Installer) file, which recent versions of Windows recognize as an installer package. Double-clicking an MSI file will invoke the Windows Installer to install and configure your application for use on the user's PC. Setup packages that utilize the installer technology built into Windows in this manner are more robust than traditional setup.exe installations, as use of the Windows installer ensures that program components are properly installed and registered. In addition a setup package that you distribute does not have to "reinvent the wheel" by including the underlying code that actually performs the installation, as this functionality is already contained in the Windows Installer.

CREATING AN INSTALLER

The easiest way to create an installer for an application is to add a setup project to the solution containing the application. You can manually add a setup project to an open solution by selecting File, Add Project, New Project from Visual Basic .NET's menu system, selecting Setup and Deployment Projects as the project type, and then selecting setup project as the template for the new project. You will then have an empty setup project included in your open solution.

To make things even easier, Visual Basic .NET provides the Setup Project Wizard, which not only adds a setup project to an application, but also populates the important parts of the project with the information needed to create a standard setup package from the application. You can then customize the setup project as needed, but the bulk of the work will have been done for you by the wizard.

In this appendix, we will show you how to use the Setup Project Wizard to create installers for Windows Application projects and Web Application projects. Due to the potential complexity and many options available, an exhaustive discussion of creating setup projects from scratch is beyond the scope of this appendix; however, the Visual Basic .NET Help system contains step-by-step walkthroughs of manually creating installers. Look for the help topic Installers, walkthrough.

Note

The Windows-compliant installer package that will be created as part of a setup project will automatically include uninstall functionality. After the user installs an application using the Windows Installer and the .MSI file created by the setup project, he will be able to uninstall the software by using the Add/Remove Programs applet in Control Panel.

USING THE SETUP PROJECT WIZARD TO CREATE A SETUP PROJECT FOR A WINDOWS APPLICATION

As discussed previously, the Setup Project Wizard offers an easy-to-use interface encompassing the most commonly used setup project options. You can use the Setup Project Wizard to create an installer in four simple steps. If you need to include more functionality in an installer than the wizard supports, you can manually enhance the installer that the wizard creates.

To illustrate the process of creating an installer for a Windows Application project, start with an existing project or create a test project for deployment. Any Windows Application project will do; our goal here is to create an installer package that will allow you to deploy the application on a user's computer. Even if the user does not have Visual Studio .NET installed on his system, the installer package will ensure that the components required by the application are installed and registered on the client PC.

For the purposes of this demonstration, I will be working with the Loan Calculator application that we created in Chapter 2, "Creating Your First Windows Application." You can follow along by using that project. If you do not have the code for that project, you can download it from www.vbinsider.com. Look for the file named LoanCalc.zip.

To see the Setup Project Wizard in action, follow these steps:

1. Begin by opening the Loan Calculator project.
2. Once the Loan Calculator project is open, select File, Add Project, New Project in Visual Basic .NET's menu system. You will see the Add New Project dialog box, illustrated in Figure A.1.

Figure A.1
The Add New Project dialog box lets you select among a number of Setup and Deployment type projects.

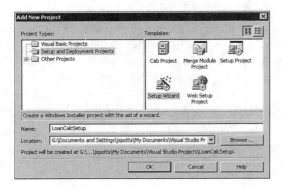

3. In the Project Type (left) pane of this dialog box, select Setup and Deployment Projects.

4. In the Templates (right) pane, select Setup Wizard.

5. Type **LoanCalcSetup** as the name of the project. Note that since there is already a solution open in the Visual Basic .NET IDE, you can choose to have the setup project added to the current solution or to close the current solution before continuing.

6. Click OK to close the New Project dialog box. You will see Step 1 of the Setup Project Wizard, as shown in Figure A.2.

Figure A.2
The Setup Project Wizard consists of five steps.

7. Click Next to continue to Step 2 of the wizard.

Step 2 of the Setup Project Wizard, shown in Figure A.3, allows you to choose the project type for the installer you are creating. You have these four options:

- Create a Setup for a Windows Application
- Create a Setup for a Web Application
- Create a Merge Module for Windows Installer
- Create a Downloadable CAB File

For a simple Windows Application project, you will select the first option; Web Applications require the second option. Either of the first two options leads to the creation of a setup program that the user will run to install the application on his PC. The third and fourth options will create a redistributable package, which can be combined with other packages to form a complete, customizable setup solution in which individual components can be updated easily without affecting the overall package.

Figure A.3

In Step 2 of the Setup Project Wizard, you specify the type of project for which your setup package is to be created.

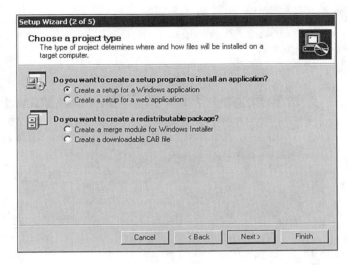

8. For this example, select the first option (Create a Setup for a Windows Application) and click Next. You will see the third step of the Setup Project Wizard, depicted in Figure A.4.

Figure A.4

Step 3 of the Setup Project Wizard lets you specify the components to include in your setup package.

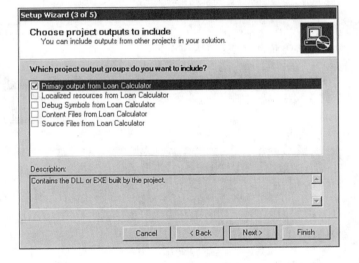

9. Step 3 of the Setup Project Wizard is where you specify what is to be included in your setup package. Typically, you will want to include at least the primary output of your project, which consists of the EXE (or DLL) file that is created when the application is built. You may also choose to include other things such as the actual source files that were used to create the project. Select any of the other available options to see a description of that option. Check Primary Output, and then click Next.

APP

A

10. In Step 4 of the Setup Project Wizard, shown in Figure A.5, you can include any additional files that you want to be distributed to your end user. Examples of these additional files include Read Me files, documentation, help files, initial databases, and so on. Click the Add button to designate files to include; when you are done, click Next.

Figure A.5
The wizard lets you add extra files that you want to be distributed to your user. This would be a good place to include an End-User License Agreement (EULA), for example.

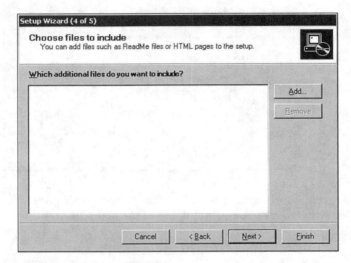

11. Step 5 of the Setup Project Wizard, which summarizes the actions that the wizard will perform, is shown in Figure A.6. Click Next.

Figure A.6
The wizard is ready to complete its task.

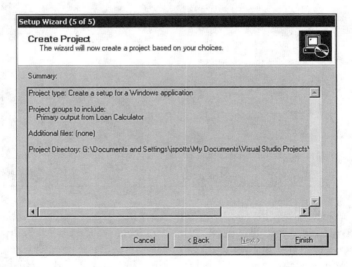

After the wizard has completed, a new setup project is created and added to the current solution. The Solution Explorer window, shown in Figure A.7 undocked from its usual position, now includes this new setup project. You can see that the setup project includes a merge module file, which has a .msm extension. merge modules are used by the Windows Installer to deliver the components that will be installed during the setup process. Typically, each application that is part of a setup package will be represented by its own merge module file. Merge modules also contain version information for each component so that the Windows Installer can ensure that it is not replacing components with earlier versions.

Figure A.7
The solution now includes the new setup project.

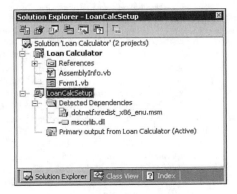

As mentioned earlier, the Setup Project Wizard creates a setup project with many of the commonly used options already populated. Before building the setup project and creating the setup package, however, you will probably want to modify at least some of the options. The following sections introduce you to some of the options that you may want to modify.

SETTING OPTIONS FOR THE SETUP PACKAGE

Like any other type of project, a setup project has a set of options that govern its behavior. When the wizard created the setup project, it set many of the options; however, some of them may need tweaking. To alter or customize the setup project's options, start by selecting the project in the Solution Explorer window. The Properties window will then allow you to manage the properties that apply to the setup project. Table A.1 summarizes some of the options that you will want to be concerned with.

TABLE A.1   CUSTOMIZABLE PROPERTIES FOR THE SETUP PACKAGE

Property	Usage
AddRemoveProgramsIcon	You can set this property to the name of a file containing an icon that will be displayed in the Add/Remove Programs dialog box in the Control Panel on the user's computer.
Author	The name of the author of the program.
Description	A free-text field in which you can type a description of the project.

APP

A

TABLE A.1   CONTINUED

Property	Usage
DetectNewerInstalledVersion	When set to True (the default), if the installer detects that a version of the program with a higher version number already exists on the target PC, the installation will not continue.
Manufacturer	Specifies the name (typically a company name) of the manufacturer of the application.
ProductName	The name of the application being installed. The default value is the setup project's name; you will typically want to set it to something user-friendly that describes what is being installed. For this example, I changed the ProductName property to **Loan Calculator**, which describes what is being installed. When the user runs the setup package, the value you set for the ProductName property will be used as the title bar of the setup wizard's screens, as well as in messages to the user. For example, if you set the ProductName property to **Bob's Cool Program**, the setup package will display messages like **Welcome to the Bob's Cool Program Setup Wizard** and **The installer will install Bob's Cool Program to the following folder**.
RemovePreviousVersions	When set to True, the installer will remove previous versions of the application that it detects during installation. The default value is False.
Title	Specifies the title of the installer package. As with the ProductName, the Title property defaults to the project name, but you can change it to something more user-friendly.

As you will see, two of the most important properties that you will want to ensure are set correctly are the Manufacturer and ProductName properties.

CUSTOMIZING THE USER'S FILE SYSTEM

Of course, the main function performed by a setup package is to modify the file system of the user's computer. To manage the modifications that the setup package will make to the target PC's file system, double-click the Primary Output item under the setup project in Solution Explorer. This will open the File System pane for the project in the Visual Basic .NET IDE, as shown in Figure A.8.

By default, a Windows Application setup package created by the Setup Project Wizard will install the application's primary output (typically an EXE or a DLL file) into the user's Program Files folder. There will be no Start menu or other shortcuts generated unless you customize the setup package. This section discusses how to modify the location into which the application's primary output is placed, as well as how to control the creation of program shortcuts on the user's computer.

Figure A.8
The File System pane lets you control how the setup package modifies the user's file system.

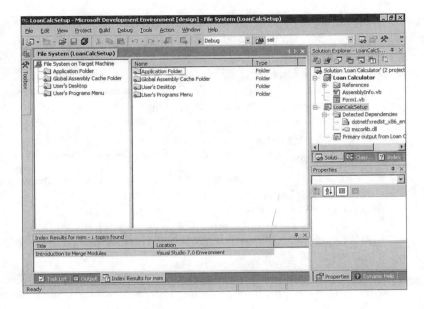

THE APPLICATION FOLDER

As mentioned, the only file system modification automatically generated by the wizard is to place the program's primary output in an application folder on the user's PC. The exact location is determined by the Application folder's `DefaultLocation` property. To access the `DefaultLocation` property, click Application Folder in the File System pane (after you have double-clicked the project's Primary Output in the Solution Explorer, as directed previously). The Properties window now shows properties for the Application folder.

As you can see in the Properties window, the default value of the `DefaultLocation` property is `[ProgramFilesFolder][Manufacturer]\[ProductName]`. This causes the application's output to be placed in a folder named for the `ProductName` property, which is created in a folder named for the `Manufacturer` property, which is in turn created under the user's Program Files folder. Therefore, if the manufacturer's name (stored in the `Manufacturer` property) is `Pyramid Custom Systems`, and the `ProductName` property has been set to `Loan Calculator`, the default installation location will be `C:\Program Files\Pyramid Custom Systems\Loan Calculator` (assuming that the user's Program Files location is the standard `C:\Program Files`).

Of course, the user has the option of modifying the installation location when he runs the setup package.

If you want to include files in the Application folder other than those that are already included, right-click the Application Folder icon; then select Add, File from the Context menu. You can browse to files that you want to include.

APP

A

ADDING A SHORTCUT TO THE USER'S START MENU

Typically, you will want to create one or more Start menu shortcuts that your users can use to start your application. By default, the Setup Project Wizard does not automatically set up such shortcuts. The User's Programs Menu folder, which represents your end user's Start/Programs folder, is provided in the File System pane for you to manage the creation of shortcuts for your program. Normally, you should not place your program's shortcut(s) in the top level of the user's Start/Programs folder; you should create a folder for your program's shortcuts. To create a folder for your program's shortcuts on the user's PC, and to create the actual Start menu shortcuts, follow theses steps:

1. Right-click the User's Programs Menu folder in the File System pane; then select Add, Folder from the Context menu. A new folder is created under the User's Programs folder; you can rename this new folder to be the container for your application's shortcut(s). (You can use a similar process if you want your application's Start Menu folder to have subfolders.)

2. Under the Application folder, right-click the Primary Output from (*projectname*) icon that represents your project's compiled EXE or DLL file. Select Create Shortcut to Primary Output in the Context menu. This process is depicted in Figure A.9.

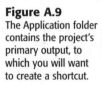

Figure A.9
The Application folder contains the project's primary output, to which you will want to create a shortcut.

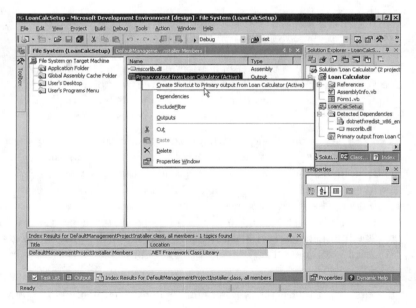

3. A shortcut to the primary output will be created and placed in the Application folder. You may want to rename the shortcut to something that may be meaningful to the user, such as the name of the program (without "Shortcut to").

4. Drag the shortcut from the Application folder to the appropriate subfolder that you created under the User's Programs Menu folder.

Now, when the user runs the setup package, his Start menu will be updated to include a shortcut to your application according to the specifications that you laid out previously.

If you want to include other shortcuts to other items in the user's Start menu, such as system utilities or documentation, you can add them using the User's Programs Menu folder as described previously. You can right-click the appropriate folder and select Add, or you can even drag-and-drop items such as shortcuts or other files directly into this window.

THE USER'S DESKTOP FOLDER

If you want to have items installed directly onto your user's desktop, you can do so by manipulating the user's Desktop folder in the File System pane using the techniques described previously. Be judicious in doing so, however, as users are often irritated when programs litter their desktops against their wishes.

BUILDING THE SETUP PROJECT

Once you have configured the setup project, you will need to build it in order to create its primary output, a Windows Installer package. Building the project is a simple matter. Follow these steps:

1. Right-click the setup project in the Solution Explorer window; then select Properties from the Context menu. In the (projectname) Property Pages window, select the target configuration. If you are still testing, leave the configuration set to Active (Debug). Once you are through testing and ready to create your production setup package, change the configuration to Release. You can also change the output filename here if you like. Click OK to close the Property Pages window when you are happy with the configuration.

2. Again, right-click the setup project in the Solution Explorer window, and then select Build from the context menu. The setup project will be compiled and built, and the output .MSI file will be generated. This process may take several minutes.

Tip

If the main project has changed since the last time it was built, be sure to rebuild it before building the setup package so that the most recent version of your application is deployed.

3. After the build process is complete, the final output—the MSI installer package—is created and stored in either the Debug or Release folder under the Setup Project's folder, depending on whether you selected Debug or Release as the project's configuration in step 1 previously.

DEPLOYING THE MSI INSTALLER PACKAGE

Your setup project is now complete, and you can distribute the resulting MSI file to your users. When the user executes the self-contained installer package, he is taken through a typical software installation, and your application is installed on his system.

TIPS ON CONVERSION FROM VB6

In this appendix

If you have used Visual Basic 6.0 (or any previous versions of Visual Basic), you have probably already discovered that Visual Basic .NET represents a complete and total overhaul of the Visual Basic development environment that you have grown to love. You may be concerned that the VB development skills you have spent years honing will no longer be of benefit to you. As you get your feet wet with Visual Basic .NET, however, you will discover that although the underlying infrastructure has indeed changed dramatically, the fundamental concept of Rapid Application Development (RAD) using Visual Basic is essentially the same. You will quickly learn that your existing VB skills will help you ramp up in the Visual Basic .NET development environment very quickly.

In this appendix, we will discuss changes that have occurred to the development environment as well as to the Visual Basic language itself. In addition, we will show you how to import your VB6 projects into Visual Basic .NET and present you with several miscellaneous tips about other things that have changed from the VB you grew up with.

WHY THE VISUAL BASIC LANGUAGE HAS CHANGED

Before Visual Basic .NET appeared, earlier versions of Visual Basic created applications and components targeted for Windows client applications. Of course, Visual Basic .NET is designed to create applications and components for the Windows platform as well. However, Visual Basic .NET now includes a framework for creating Web services and Web applications, greatly increasing the target platforms that you can work with. Because of this new increase in target platforms for which applications and services can be created, Visual Basic .NET supports the new *Common Language Specification (CLS)*. The CLS identifies a set of features of a programming language that is supported by a wide array of development tools. Components that adhere to the CLS standard are guaranteed to work with other CLS-compliant components. Underlying the CLS is the new *common language runtime*, which is the foundation of the .NET framework.

What does all this have to do with the Visual Basic language? Simply put, because Visual Basic .NET applications are CLS-compliant, they must generate code for the common language runtime, which in turn means that some fundamental changes to the Visual Basic language were in order as Visual Basic .NET was in development. In addition, because a major overhaul of the Visual Basic language was required for the creation of Visual Basic .NET, Microsoft took the opportunity to "clean up" some inconsistencies and outdated features that had developed in the Visual Basic language over the course of its evolution through six previous versions. Therefore, you will note a number of changes that have been made to provide interoperability with other programming languages, all for the good of the CLS.

CHANGES TO THE LANGUAGE

The following sections detail a number of changes that have occurred to the Visual Basic language since version 6.0. For a more complete reference to the Visual Basic language changes, look for the topic "Language Changes in Visual Basic" in the Visual Basic .NET Help system, which can be found in the Help index under "Visual Basic/changes to."

ARRAY BOUNDS

When you declared an array in VB6, the default behavior was for the lowest-numbered element of the array to be element 0. In other words, declaring an array with the line `Dim MyArray(3) As Integer` created an array containing four elements: `MyArray(0)`, `MyArray(1)`, `MyArray(2)`, and `MyArray(3)`. However, you could use the statement `Option Base` to cause arrays to begin with element 1 instead of element 0; if `Option Base 1` were used, `Dim MyArray(3) As Integer` would lead to three elements, not four. In Visual Basic .NET, the `Option Base` statement is no longer supported; all arrays begin with element 0.

CHANGING THE SIZE OF AN ARRAY

In VB6, you could specify the upper and lower limits of an array with a statement like `Dim Sales(0 to 4) As Single`; the size of such a fixed array could not be changed later with the `ReDim` statement. Visual Basic .NET does not support fixed-size arrays. Any array can be resized with the `ReDim` statement. For example, if you have declared an array named `Sales` that can contain four elements, and it needs to be expanded to allow for up to ten elements, the following line of code will increase its upper bound:

```
ReDim Sales(10)
```

USE OF THE ReDim STATEMENT

Unlike VB6, Visual Basic .NET does not allow you to use `ReDim` in the initial declaration of an array. A variable array must be declared with a `Dim` statement (or equivalent, such as a `Public` statement) before using `ReDim` on that array.

FIXED-LENGTH STRINGS

Visual Basic .NET no longer supports fixed-length strings. Declaring a VB6-style fixed-length string with a statement like `Dim sLastName As String * 20` is no longer allowed. All strings are now declared as variable-length strings (`Dim sLastName As String`). In this case, the `sLastName` variable can contain a string of any length.

CHANGES TO INTEGER DATA TYPES

Visual Basic .NET has modified the Integer data types to more closely match the data types supported by the CLS. The following mini-table summarizes the old and new Integer types:

VB6 Type	VB .NET Type	Range of Values
Integer	Short	–32,768 to 32,768
Long	Integer	–2,147,483,648 to 2,147,483,647
(None)	Long	–9,223,372,036,854,775,808 to 9,223,372,036,854,775,807

VARIANT DATA TYPE

In VB6, the universal data type (which could store data of any type) was Variant. In Visual Basic .NET, Object is now the universal data type.

CURRENCY DATA TYPE

Visual Basic .NET no longer supports the Currency data type. The new Decimal data type, which is part of the CLS, is recommended for storage of money amounts. The Decimal data type provides greater precision on both sides of the decimal point than the old Currency data type; in fact, up to 28 total places of precision are possible.

DATE DATA TYPE

In VB6, the Date data type stored a date using a Double (four-byte) type. Visual Basic .NET supports the CLS DateTime data type, which stores dates as an eight-byte Integer.

Property PROCEDURES

When declaring PROPERTY procedures for user-defined classes in VB6, you created separate Property Get, Property Let, and Property Set procedures. Visual Basic .NET introduces a more streamlined single Property procedure, which contains Get and Set portions that do the same job as their respective VB6 counterparts. See Chapter 16, "Creating Your Own Windows Controls," for more information.

Type STATEMENTS REPLACED BY THE Structure CONSTRUCT

In VB6, you could create a user-defined type with a Type...End Type construct. This construct is no longer supported. Instead, in Visual Basic .NET, you use the Structure...End Structure construct to define structures and user-defined types.

DECLARING MULTIPLE VARIABLES

In VB6, if you declared multiple variables on the same line, you had to declare a type for each variable; otherwise, untyped variables defaulted to Variant type. In other words, the statement Dim a, b, c As Integer would create two Variants named a and b and a single Integer named c. In Visual Basic .NET, you can have multiple declarations on the same line without repeating the type. That is, Dim a, b, c As Integer will create three Integer variables named a, b, and c. You can still declare variables of two different types on the same line. Dim a, b As Integer, c as String would give you two Integer variables named a and b and a single String variable named c.

BLOCK-LEVEL VARIABLE SCOPE

Visual Basic .NET introduces a new block-level variable scope. That is, if you want to have a variable available only within a block-type construct, such as a For...Next loop or an If...End If block, you can declare that variable inside the block, and the variable will exist only within that block. For example, the variable sMsg declared inside the following If...End If block would only be available within the block:

```
If x > 120 Then
    Dim sMsg As String
    sMsg = "Please enter a smaller value."
    MessageBox.Show(sMsg)
End If
```

However, the following code is invalid, as it tries to utilize the sMsg variable outside the If...End If block:

```
If x > 120 Then
    Dim sMsg As String
    sMsg = "Please enter a smaller value."
End If
MessageBox.Show(sMsg)
```

INITIALIZING VARIABLES WHEN DECLARED

In Visual Basic .NET, you can now set initial values for variables as you declare them. For example, the following variable declaration will create a variable named sLastName and set its initial value to Fortner, which had to be done on a separate line in VB6:

```
Dim sLastName As String = "Fortner"
```

CHANGES TO While...Wend

The VB6 While…Wend construct, which loops through code statements as long as the test condition is true, still exists in Visual Basic .NET, but the Wend keyword has been replaced by End While. Wend is no longer supported.

PASSING ARGUMENTS TO Sub PROCEDURES

In VB6, you could pass arguments to a Sub procedure without parentheses if you did not use the Call keyword, as in ProcessEmployee "Eric Burton", 99, although parentheses were always required when calling a Function. Visual Basic .NET always requires the use of parentheses, as in ProcessEmployee("Eric Burton", 99).

RETURNING VALUES FROM Function PROCEDURES

In VB6, you returned values from a Function procedure by setting the name of the procedure equal to the return value, as in the following example:

```
Function AddNums(ByVal a As Single, ByVal b As Single)
    Dim x As Single
    x = a + b
    AddNums = x
End Function
```

While this technique still works, the preferred method in Visual Basic .NET is to use the Return statement to set the return value of the function, simultaneously returning control to the calling code:

```
Function AddNums(ByVal a As Single, ByVal b As Single)
    Dim x As Single
    x = a + b
    Return x
End Function
```

PARAMETER PASSING IS NOW ByVal

Previously, when passing parameters to procedures, they were assumed to be passed by reference (ByRef) unless you included the ByVal keyword. In Visual Basic .NET, parameters are now passed by value (ByVal) by default. This helps protect the parameters from being changed by the called procedures. Of course, if you want a procedure to be able to change the value of a passed parameter, you can use the ByRef keyword to explicitly pass parameters by reference.

CHANGES TO PROJECT FILES

When you saved a project in VB6, each form was stored in a file with a .frm extension, classes were stored in .cls files, the overall project was stored as a .vbp file, and groups (multiple projects) were stored in .grp files. In Visual Basic .NET, forms (as well as other classes) are stored in files with an extension of .vb. The filename extension for project files is .vbproj. Solutions (containers for related projects) are stored in .sln files.

In addition to these basic project components, Visual Studio .NET works with several other file types as well. See the Help system topic "File Types and File Extensions in Visual Studio. NET" for a more thorough listing of supported file types.

CHANGES TO CONTROLS

The way some controls work has been changed since VB6. This section lists some of these controls and the things about them that have changed.

DEFAULT PROPERTIES

In VB6, most controlsand other objects supported the use of default properties. For example, the default property of a TextBox control was the Text property; therefore, you could set a TextBox control's Text property with the code txtLastName = "Hajek" instead of the longer (but equivalent) txtLastName.Text = "Hajek". Visual Basic .NET no longer supports the use of default properties; you must explicitly specify the name of the property you want to set or retrieve in code.

Tip

There is one exception to this guideline. Objects that take arguments do support the use of a default property. For instance, a Recordset object (in ADO) supports the default property of Fields; therefore, rsSales.Fields("qtr1") and rsSales("qtr1") are equivalent.

Text PROPERTY REPLACES Caption PROPERTY

In VB6, the Caption property defined the text that appeared in a Label control, in the title bar of a form, and on the face of a button, among other objects. In Visual Basic .NET, the Caption property of Label controls, Button controls, Forms, and several other objects has been replaced by the Text property.

BUTTON CONTROL REPLACES COMMANDBUTTON CONTROL

The CommandButton control from previous versions of Visual Basic is now called the Button control. Its functionality is the same; however, as mentioned previously, its Text property replaces the CommandButton control's Caption property.

GROUPBOX CONTROL AND PANEL CONTROL REPLACE FRAME CONTROL

In previous versions of Visual Basic, the Frame control was used as a container to create logical groupings of controls (such as option buttons). In Visual Basic .NET, this functionality is provided by the new GroupBox and Panel controls. The main difference between the two is that the GroupBox control has a visible border and may include a caption (by setting its Text property). The Panel control is invisible to the user at runtime and cannot have a caption, but it provides grouping functionality nonetheless.

THE TIMER CONTROL

In VB6, the event that the Timer control fired at regular intervals was called the Timer event. In Visual Basic .NET, the Timer control's Timer event has been replaced by the Tick event, which is also fired at regular intervals as defined by the Timer control's Interval property.

THE MAINMENU CONTROL

In previous versions of Visual Basic, you used the Menu Editor to create Menu controls, which provided menus for your forms. Visual Basic .NET provides the MainMenu control, which you can add to a form from the Toolbox just like any other controls. You can then manipulate the control at design time to add menu and submenu items to the form. The MainMenu control is discussed in detail in Chapter 10, "Understanding Windows Forms."

ANCHORING AND DOCKING CONTROLS

Two new properties, Anchor and Dock, allow you to position controls on forms in a way that remains consistent even as the forms are resized. The Anchor and Dock properties are discussed in Chapter 12, "Advanced Controls."

> **Note**
>
> There are a number of Visual Basic programming elements that are no longer supported in Visual Basic .NET. The Help topic "Visual Basic 6.0 Programming Elements Not in Visual Basic .NET" contains a very handy alphabetical list of VB6 elements that you may be used to using that have been removed from Visual Basic .NET.

CONVERTING AN EXISTING VB6 PROJECT TO VISUAL BASIC .NET

Visual Basic .NET provides the Visual Basic Upgrade Wizard to streamline the process of converting existing VB6 projects to Visual Basic .NET. You invoke the wizard simply by opening a VB6 project in the Visual Basic .NET IDE. It should be noted that the Upgrade Wizard does not change your existing VB6 project; instead, it creates a new Visual Basic .NET project from the VB6 project, leaving the original project untouched.

The following steps walk you through the use of the Visual Basic Upgrade Wizard to convert a VB6 project to the Visual Basic .NET architecture. You may want to open one of your own existing VB6 projects or simply create a sample VB6 project to see how it works:

1. If Visual Basic .NET is not already running, start it; then click Open Project on the Start page. If Visual Basic .NET is already running, select File, Open, Project from the menu system.

2. In the Open Project dialog box, browse to the .vbp file from the VB6 project you want to convert; then click Open. The Visual Basic Upgrade Wizard starts, as shown in Figure B.1.

Figure B.1
The Visual Basic Upgrade Wizard lets you convert your VB6 projects to the Visual Basic .NET environment.

3. Click Next to display Page 2 of the wizard. Depending on the type of project that your VB6 project is, you will need to specify the target platform for the Visual Basic .NET project. In Figure B.2, the wizard has detected that the VB6 is a Windows Application project, so we can open it as an .EXE project.

Figure B.2
In Step 2 of the Visual
Basic Upgrade Wizard,
you specify the type of
project that you are
converting.

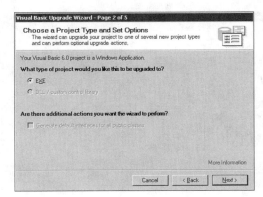

4. Click Next to display Page 3 of the wizard, where you can specify the location into which you want the converted project saved. By default, the wizard offers to create a folder named *projectname*.NET, where *projectname* represents the name of the VB6 .vbp file that you are opening. Figure B.3 illustrates this step.

Figure B.3
Step 3 of the wizard
allows you to specify
a location for your
converted Visual Basic
.NET project.

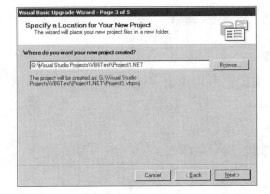

5. Click Next, and you will be asked to verify that you want to create the new folder into which the project will be converted (if the folder does not exist already). Click Yes to create the folder.

6. Figure B.4 shows Page 4 of the wizard, which simply reports that it now has enough information to begin the conversion process.

Figure B.4
The wizard is ready to begin converting the project.

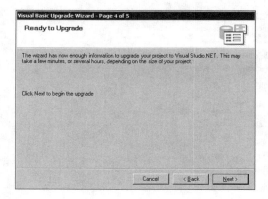

7. Click Next to start the conversion. Page 5 of the wizard shows how the conversion is progressing.

8. Once the conversion is complete, the new (converted) project is open and shown in the Solution Explorer, as shown in Figure B.5.

Figure B.5
The converted project is now ready for development in Visual Basic .NET.

The Visual Basic Upgrade Wizard will take care of things such as simple syntax changes, converting from the use of a control's Caption property to the new Text property, and so on. However, if there are issues that it can't resolve, these issues will be presented in the Upgrade Report, which is an HTML page named _UpgradeReport.htm shown in the Solution Explorer. This page reports the results of the conversion process. If there are any issues that you need to deal with, which might keep your program from running as intended, you can click the plus sign next to either Global Issues or one of the forms or other classes for a list of suggested remedies. Figure B.6 shows a sample upgrade report that contains issues that the programmer must resolve before the program will run correctly.

Figure B.6
The Upgrade Report lists any issues that may have arisen during the conversion.

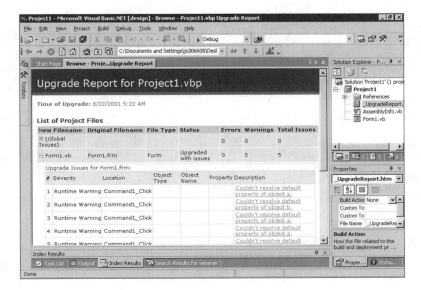

INDEX

C